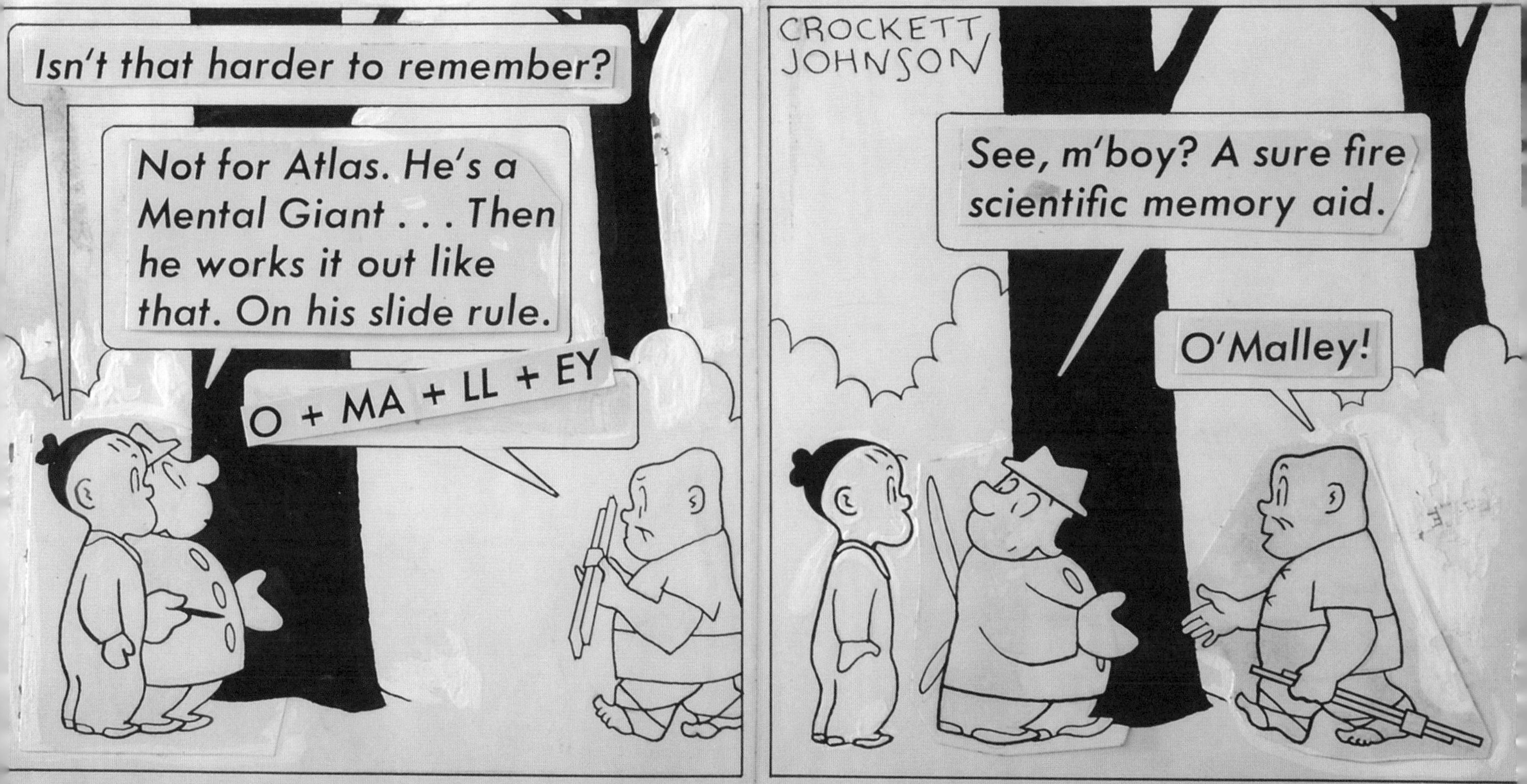
Isn't that harder to remember?
Not for Atlas. He's a Mental Giant . . . Then he works it out like that. On his slide rule.
O + MA + LL + EY
CROCKETT JOHNSON
See, m'boy? A sure fire scientific memory aid.
O'Malley!

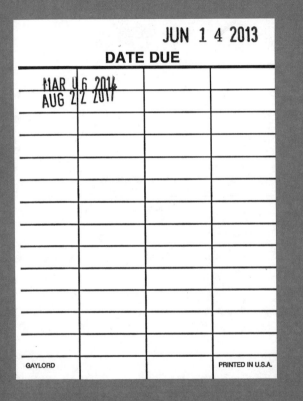

Barnaby

BAR

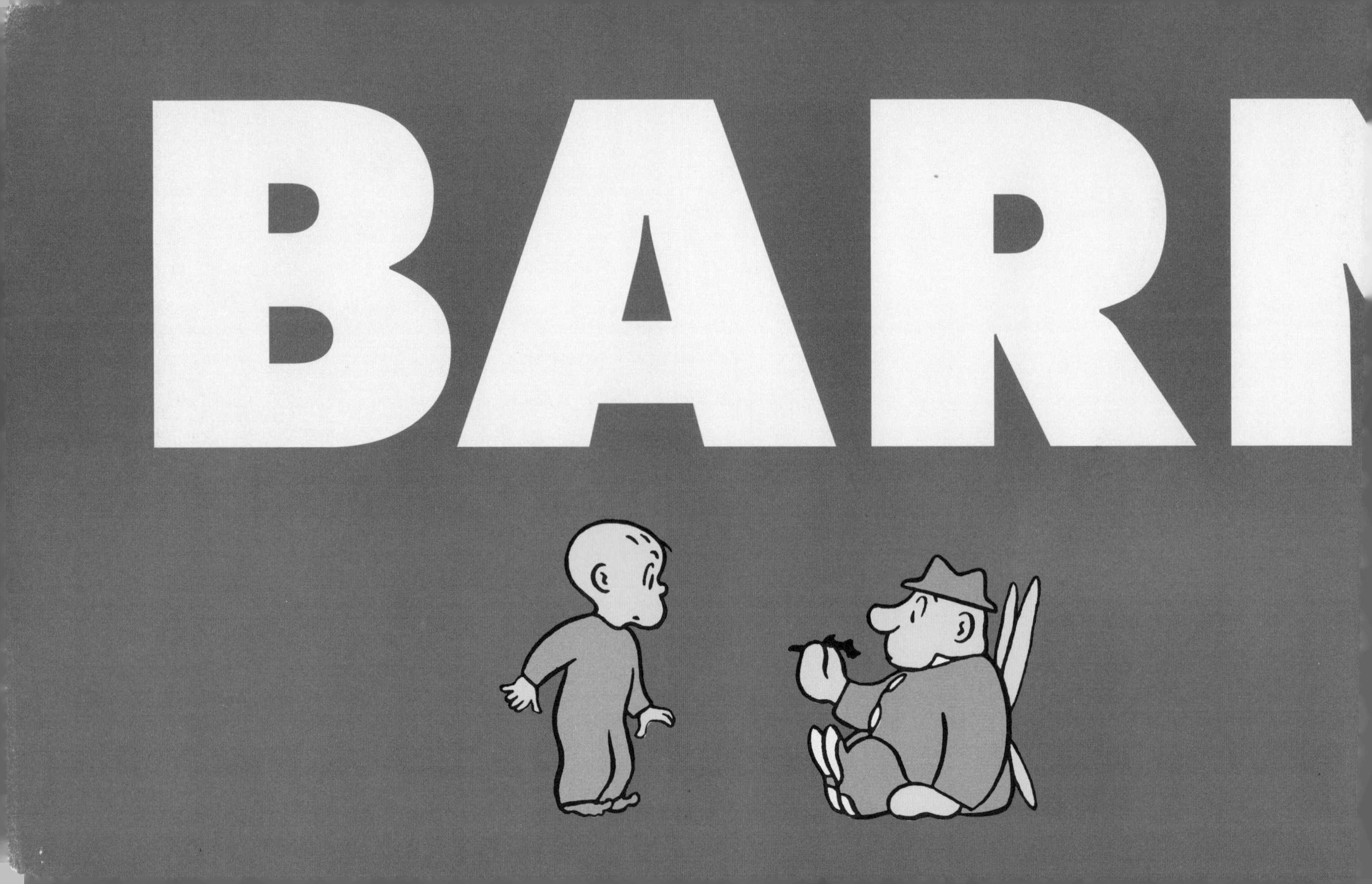

ARNABY

By CROCKETT JOHNSON

VOLUME ONE: 1942-1943

FANTAGRAPHICS BOOKS · SEATTLE, WA.

Editors: Philip Nel & Eric Reynolds
Book Design: Daniel Clowes
Production: Tony Ong and Paul Baresh
Art Restoration: John Ohannesian
Associate Publisher: Eric Reynolds
Publishers: Gary Groth & Kim Thompson

FANTAGRAPHICS BOOKS, INC.
Seattle, Washington, USA

For a full-color catalog of comics, including reprints of such other classic comic strips as *Peanuts, Pogo, Popeye, Prince
Valiant, Nancy* and *Krazy Kat,* call 1-800-657-1100 in North America, email us at fbicomix@fantagraphics.com, or
write Fantagraphics Books, 7563 Lake City Way NE, Seattle, WA 98115, USA.

ISBN 978-1-60699-522-8

First Printing: March, 2013
Printed in China

CONTENTS

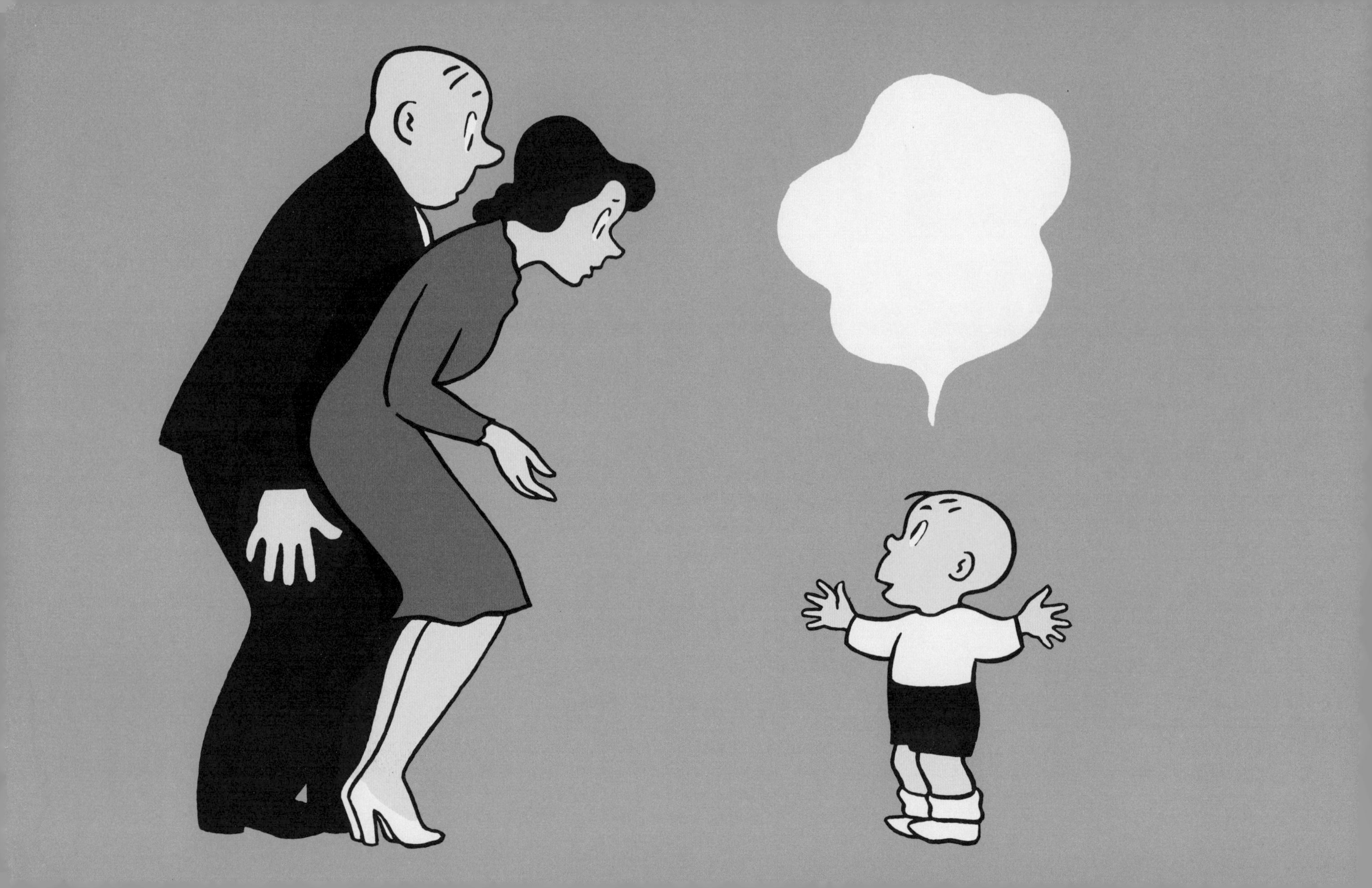

FOREWORD *by* CHRIS WARE

WHEN I WAS A KID, Crockett Johnson's work scared the heck out of me. Like many children, long before I found *Barnaby,* I read *Harold and the Purple* Crayon. For those who aren't familiar with *Harold,* the book turns on the single simple idea of a small, flatly-drawn boy in footie pajamas who both explores and makes his world solely with the marks of a thick purple crayon. From page to page Harold stays exactly the same size while his drawings — mountains, seas, flowers, pie — enlarge, dwarf and very nearly swallow him. Shallowly-read, it seems a perfect librarian-pleasing homily to the value of imagination and creativity, but the very impulses which amuse Harold also finish him: at the end of the book, weary of his exploring, he goes home and goes to sleep. Or, more precisely, he outlines his own bedroom and bed, and "draws himself" up into its covers.

The metaphysical implications of this hugely isolating ending still upset me. But presented with Johnson's characteristically gentle whimsy, the page-turning impetus that gets you there feels just timed enough with the momentum of thought that it all goes down more or less painlessly. In short, the conclusion is terrible, but still tolerable for its very inevitability. And thankfully, once you reach it, you can put the book down and get on with your own life.

Also, Harold was black. At least he looked like it to me. Not that this should be unusual or weird, but for a protagonist in a 1950s children's book, it was. To me, there seemed to be some strange, mysterious relationship between his purple crayon and his tawny skin (the only tint in the entire series). Since the books seemed to exist entirely out of the realm of color and light, the pointedly purple-qua-purpleness of its creator's crayon standing for Everything Except Harold, you almost felt (rather than saw) your way through his story, and Harold's tinted skin seemed as much a shell to be inhabited by the reader as Harold himself inhabited his purple creations.

Fast forward a few years to my college discovery of *Barnaby* in the pages of Bill Blackbeard and Martin Williams' Bible of my cartooning life, *The Smithsonian Collection of Newspaper Comics.* I instantly recognized Barnaby as the black kid from those creepy children's books I'd been afraid of as a child. But what was he doing in a comic strip? Had he started as a comic strip, or become one? Had the artist been a cartoonist? Or the cartoonist an artist? The satisfying continuity of Blackbeard and Sheridan's excerpt had the same airy timelessness, the same eternal frozenness that I'd remembered chilling the pages of *Harold.* And as Harold had seemed to move page to page, here Harold (rechristened as "Barnaby") seemed to move between black and white panel to panel, often between panels behind which a continuous background stretched. The effect was genuinely odd, highlighting comics' capacity for seeing characters in both the past and the future simultaneously.

And now Harold could talk! But Barnaby/Harold "spoke" in a what must be one of the strangest and most brilliant decisions ever made by a cartoonist — to typeset, rather than hand-letter, all of the strip's dialogue. To say that it gave the strip a "modern" look is to entirely miss the point; what it did was to imbue all of the dialogue with a sort of internal, literary transcendentalism, if not the very taint of the imaginary. It also allowed the cartoonist, David Johnson Leisk (rechristened as "Crockett Johnson") to cram a whole lot into a small space while leaving areas of white and black that felt very, very vast. Johnson's stories had a compact, almost Thurberish middle-of-the-night humor to them, and they played on puns, accents and the peculiarity of the characters' voices bouncing between each other in a sort of dreamy unreality, all crystallizing into a feverish, antagonizing unease.

I won't spoil the story by simplifying it here. As Art Spiegelman has said of *Nancy*, it's easier to read than it is to not read, and *Barnaby*'s energetically plain panels crackle with the same ecstatic sort of cling. *Barnaby*'s consistently-sized characters live on the page in their proscenium boxes better than in almost any other strip, the whole lifting off as easily as a kite let go on a Saturday afternoon. The basic twist of its story, an imaginary fairy godfather (or is he imaginary?) sets the reader to instant page-turning. I'll risk insulting that same reader by noting that the so-called first modern novel, *Don Quixote,* and one of the most popular recent modern comic strips, *Calvin and Hobbes,* pivot on similar points of self-doubt and imagination. (And *Ellen's Lion*, a series of Johnson's other children's books about a little girl's talking stuffed lion, begs a certain familiarity with the latter, as well.)

As a cartoonist, I'm professionally eager to cast my ballot as to Johnson's antecedents and influences. Though I can't say for sure (and Jeet Heer elaborates more on this topic in his fantastic introduction) I think he was greatly enamored of Gluyas Williams. Williams (1888 – 1982) was the original "clear line" artist, inspired by H. M. Bateman's and Caran D'Ache's work, and to whom everyone from Hergé to Otto Soglow to Joost Swarte could file a paternity claim, his spidery-thin lines and solid black shapes popularly punctuating *Collier's* and most famously *The New Yorker* in the 1920s through the 1940s. Admittedly, Johnson's drawings are more intentionally diagrammatic than Williams', but the basic feel and set are there — Johnson even appears to have lifted Williams' blank, bland signature. Johnson's earliest surviving cartoon (1921 — "An Off Day," above) almost

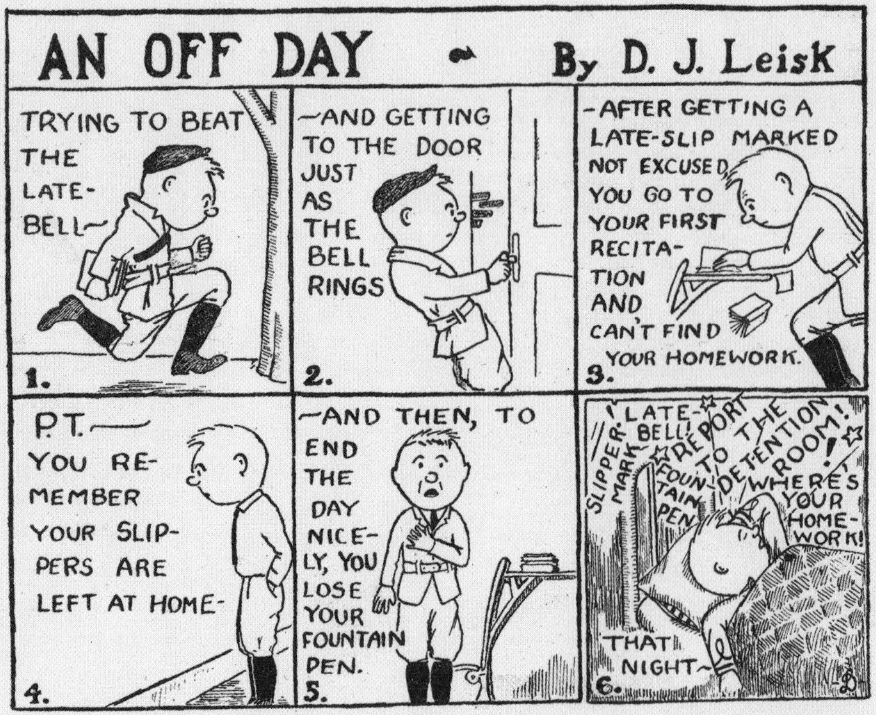

AN OFF DAY
By D. J. Leisk
TRYING TO BEAT THE LATE-BELL~
1.
~AND GETTING TO THE DOOR JUST AS THE BELL RINGS
2.
-AFTER GETTING A LATE-SLIP MARKED NOT EXCUSED, YOU GO TO YOUR FIRST RECITA-TION AND CAN'T FIND YOUR HOMEWORK.
3.
P.T.— YOU RE-MEMBER YOUR SLIP-PERS ARE LEFT AT HOME-
4.
~AND THEN, TO END THE DAY NICE-LY, YOU LOSE YOUR FOUNTAIN PEN.
5.
LATE-BELL!
REPORT TO THE DETENTION ROOM!
WHERE'S YOUR HOME-WORK!
SLIPPER MARK
FOUN-TAIN PEN
THAT NIGHT~
6.

completely imitates Williams' quotidian tone, layout and Briggsian "thwarted by life" conceit. There's something of George McManus in Johnson's flat-on views and austere penmanship, too, but where McManus seemed to always be going for tremendous mass and solidity, Johnson's world feels as weightless as the ink on page that makes it.

The world of newspaper comic strips has enjoyed an amazing revival over the past decade, and the best strips of all – *Gasoline Alley, Krazy Kat, Little Nemo, Peanuts* – have seen a total or near-total reprinting by the scholars, artists and writers who love them. I never thought I'd see this day, but the book you hold is, well, the last in that line. It's the *last great comic strip*. Yes, there are dozens of other strips worth rereading, and even some sort of worth reprinting, but none are this Great; this is great like Beethoven, or Steinbeck, or Picasso. This is so great it lives in its own timeless bubble of oddness and truth, surviving its Roosevelt/Truman-era origins, its gridiron club gags, and my own misunderstood chronology of the author's work and his characters' apparent ethnicity. Barnaby (or Harold or Ellen) all exist frozen in some ur-zone of idealized child-identity, where anything is possible, and when images and words could still make magic, and make up – rather than simply recount – the world.

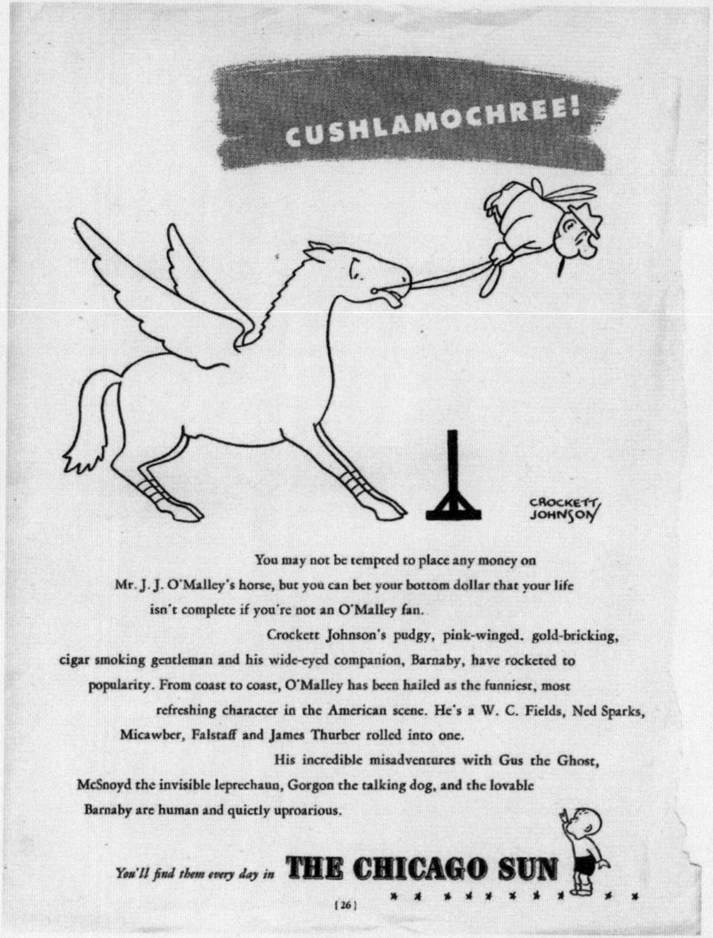
CUSHLAMOCHREE!
CROCKETT JOHNSON
You may not be tempted to place any money on Mr. J. J. O'Malley's horse, but you can bet your bottom dollar that your life isn't complete if you're not an O'Malley fan.
Crockett Johnson's pudgy, pink-winged, gold-bricking, cigar smoking gentleman and his wide-eyed companion, Barnaby, have rocketed to popularity. From coast to coast, O'Malley has been hailed as the funniest, most refreshing character in the American scene. He's a W. C. Fields, Ned Sparks, Micawber, Falstaff and James Thurber rolled into one.
His incredible misadventures with Gus the Ghost, McSnoyd the invisible leprechaun, Gorgon the talking dog, and the lovable Barnaby are human and quietly uproarious.
You'll find them every day in THE CHICAGO SUN
[26]

Chicago Sun *advertisement for* Barnaby. *Image courtesy of the Smithsonian Institution.*

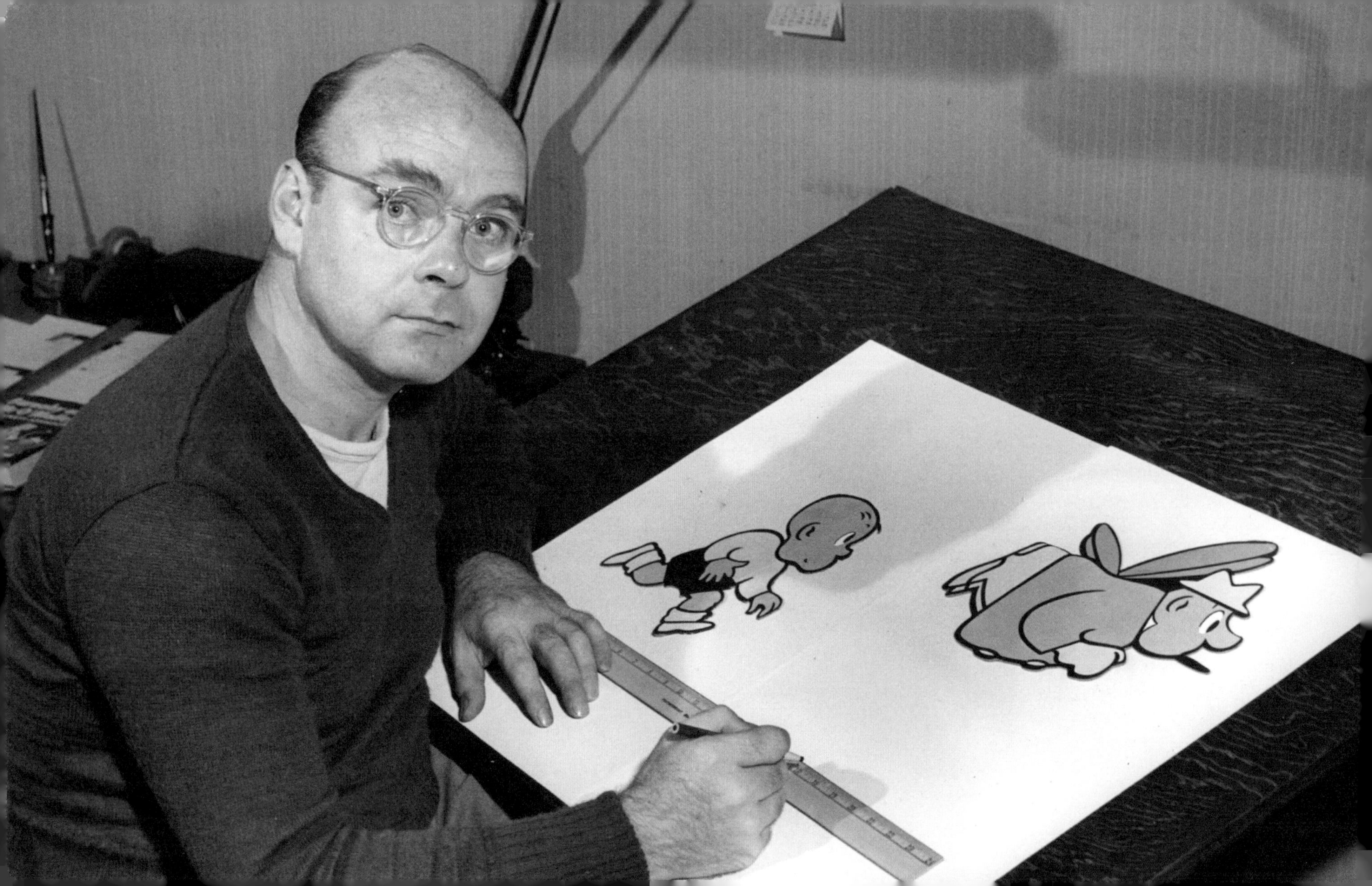

BARNABY AND AMERICAN CLEAR LINE CARTOONING

by JEET HEER

It's hard to talk about Crockett Johnson's *Barnaby* without raving. Although only a middling success in terms of newspaper circulation during its initial run in the 1940s, this beguiling comic strip has long been championed by a loyal cadre of admirers. Even the notoriously cynical and jaded Dorothy Parker was reduced to writing a gushy love letter when she reviewed the first *Barnaby* book in 1943.

Deceptively low-key and modest, the strip wins you over through the sheer quirky charm of cast members, particularly the stars of the show, Barnaby Baxter, an alert and clear-eyed, five-year-old boy and his Fairy Godfather Jackeen J. O'Malley. Mr. O'Malley, as Barnaby invariably calls him, is an especially endearing creation, half-pixie and half-grifter, an otherworldly being most at home in low-life dives and gambling dens, a raider of other people's fridges and cigar boxes, an inept wizard whose magic only works intermittently and often with unintended consequences, a self-mythologizer whose account of his own past glories is an improbable farrago of tall tales, a rhetorician quick to smooth over any difficultly with rococo eloquence and irrelevant digressions.

Readers first met Barnaby in 1942. As a preschooler in that year he would have been a child of Depression and War, very much in need of a protector, particularly since the adults in his life, including his well-meaning parents John and Ellen Baxter, are so preoccupied by pressing concerns that they can't give the little boy much mind. It's both a piece of subtle irony and quiet pathos that Mr. O'Malley, although supposedly a guardian angel, is often as obtusely inattentive to Barnaby as the other adults in the strip. Aside from "gosh," Barnaby's most frequently uttered word is surely "But–," which he often futilely interjects as he tries to dissuade his Fairy Godfather from some ill-conceived scheme. Yet as irritatingly oblivious as Mr. O'Malley so often is, as ineffectual as his sorcery too often proves to be, as embarrassing as the jams and misadventures he invariably leads his ward into are, Barnaby never loses faith in his Fairy Godfather and indeed loves him. Although unspoken, Barnaby's trusting affection for Mr. O'Malley pervades the strip, giving it an understated but genuine emotional heft.

We need to exercise some historical imagination to appreciate how radical it was in 1942 to start a strip about a kid that reflected the realities of World War II on the homefront (the rationing, the victory gardens, the air raid wardens and so forth). Most strips with kids at the time were nostalgic in orientation, looking back to either an idealized rural life or the rowdy physical comedy of the late 19th century.

Barnaby by contrast dealt with what at the time must have seemed like a very modern suburb, a setting well-mirrored by Johnson's sleek art. The fantastic elements in *Barnaby* are grounded by the countless small touches of verisimilitude that pepper the strip, which serve to make the fairytale elements of the stories more piquant.

In the history of comics, *Barnaby* belongs in the elite tradition of literate and psychologically acute strips that runs from George Herriman's *Krazy Kat* to Charles Schulz's *Peanuts*. Like *Krazy Kat*, the dialogue is rich in the interplay of clashing idioms and rhetorical styles. Crockett Johnson was reticent about his artistic influences, so we don't know if Herriman was a direct precursor. What is evident, though, is that both Herriman and Johnson brought into the comics the sparkling verbal humor that was brought to early 20th century popular literature and film by creators like Damon Runyon and W.C. Fields. *Barnaby* is a dialogue-rich strip in part because Johnson was very conscious of the fact that he was living in a time where witty wisecracking banter was flourishing in all sorts of venues ranging from *The New Yorker* to the classic screwball comedies of Hollywood. It's telling that Dorothy Parker, who rode the wave of this comedic efflorescence, was a *Barnaby* fan. Equally telling is the offhand allusion Mr. O'Malley makes to the 1928 Ben Hecht and Charles MacArthur play *The Front Page*, a prime example of the spitfire verbal comedy that shaped Johnson's sensibility. Schulz greatly admired *Barnaby* and it's hard not to see *Peanuts* owing a strong debt to Crockett Johnson's elegantly streamlined art and attention to the neuroses of childhood.

Even before you start reading one word of *Barnaby*, the strip makes a strong impression through sheer stylistic

TONIGHT
5 to 7 P. M., at Norlyst Art Gallery, 59 W. 56 St., CROCKETT JOHNSON, creator of *Barnaby* (and his Fairy Godfather, Mr. O'Malley), opens a showing of his original drawings, and will autograph copies of *Barnaby* itself.

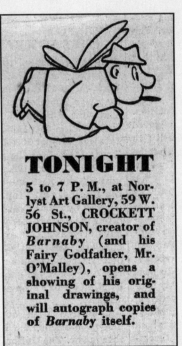

Advertisement for opening of Crockett Johnson's Norlyst Gallery show, 9 Nov. 1943. Image courtesy of the Smithsonian Institution.

distinctiveness. In the early 21st century, simplicity in comic strip art is often synonymous with stick-figure crudeness, as evidenced in the utterly grubby art found in *Dilbert* or many other newspaper features. Any panel of *Barnaby* is a reminder that simplicity, far from being invariably proof of a lack of skill, can be a tool of sophistication. The figures in *Barnaby* are drawn in blunt outlines.

Very rarely, in a night scene, Johnson will allow himself some shading in the form of Ben-Day dots, but otherwise the strip is almost entirely a display of decisive linework, with perhaps one or two small islands of black ink in a typical panel to highlight some object (Barnaby's short pants, the hair of Barnaby's mother, the stark trees that are often set against a barren background, or the odd overcoat). The interplay between black ink and the white page is one of Johnson's major artistic concerns in *Barnaby*, a fact most obvious in the night scenes and also in the sound effects, which often involve creatively mixing up black letters on a white background with white letters on a black background (and on occasion having these two styles flow together).

The clarity of Johnson's artwork is wonderfully evocative of childhood. Like all of us, kids live in a visual world that is a buzzing, blooming confusion of shapes, colors and shadings, but it seems that children, even more than adults, find comfort in art that reduces that visual chaos to sharply delineated objects which can be named and understood. In his celebrated series of kids' books devoted to Harold and his purple crayon, Johnson captured one of the central pleasures of childhood, the use of crisply demarcated drawings as a way of understanding and classifying the world. Johnson created *Barnaby* more than a decade before developing the *Harold* series, but the style of the comic strip shows his longstanding preoccupation with the link between childhood and art.

The comics historian Ron Goulart has shrewdly suggested that Johnson's art was influenced by *The New Yorker* cartoonist Gluyas Williams, who was a master at drawing comics that combined minimal penwork with maximum graphic impact. Again, Johnson's disinclination to talk about his artistic roots makes it impossible to be certain about this, yet it is hard to look at *Barnaby* and not see it as an offspring of Williams' work. Williams was a giant in the field of magazine illustration and graphic design, a world that Johnson himself joined in the late 1920s, so it is highly unlikely that Johnson was unaware of Williams' work. It is particularly useful to compare the figure of the body language of children that Williams drew in pages like "Portrait of a Boy Reading" and *Barnaby*. In both Williams and Johnson, there is an exquisite awareness of the natural nonchalance of young kids, the way they throw their legs in the air while lounging on the sofa or walk around holding their hands behind their backs.

In bringing to comics a minimalist aesthetic, Gluyas Williams was the spearhead of a major revolution in the world of cartooning that had an enormous impact in both North America and Europe. The cartoonist Chris Ware has suggested the preeminent European master Hergé attended to the lessons of Williams while forging the famous "clear line" style. Hergé's roundfaced Tintin could be seen as a distant cousin to Johnson's Barnaby (with his peanut-shaped profile) and Schulz's Charlie Brown (who takes the ideal of a spherical visage to the extreme).

Hergé once described Tintin as resembling "the degree zero of typeage." This description might just as aptly be applied to Barnaby, who is often unflappably noncommittal even amid all the wonders he experiences, which makes it easier for readers to pour their emotions into him.

To talk about type, of course, brings to mind the other distinctive visual feature of *Barnaby*, the fact that all the dialogue is done in the font italicized Futura medium. The use of type in comics dialogue is relatively rare. George Herriman had briefly experimented with typewritten dialogue in 1910 and subsequent to *Barnaby* other artists would dabble with printed dialogue, but it's fair to say that Johnson is the only cartoonist who has used typed dialogue successfully, so that it seems perfectly suited to the art. Part of the reason Johnson pulled it off is that he brought the sensibility of a typographer and designer to comics. During his aborted education at Cooper Union, Johnson studied typography, and he would make a name for himself in the early 1930s as a graphic designer. But more centrally, the cast of *Barnaby* were characters in several senses of the word, including in the fact that they resembled typed letters, having the definitive outlines we associate with the alphabet.

To say that Johnson's characters were types is not to deny that they had personalities. Quite the reverse: precisely because they are so crisply marked out, Johnson is able to imbue his people with a surprising amount of depth. We've already discussed the amazing paradoxes of Mr. O'Malley, who remains lovable despite all his foibles. Yet O'Malley is merely the head of a much larger parade that includes Gorgon the talking dog (whose ability to speak is mitigated by the fact that he's a bit of a bore); the derisive, low-brow leprechaun Launcelot McSnoyd (who accuses O'Malley of "woiking the Fairy Godfather racket"); Gus the nerdy, nervous nelly ghost; and Barnaby's skeptical neighbor, Jane Schultz. Because Mr. O'Malley is quite real, Jane comes to acknowledge him but still remains properly dubious about his claims. One nice touch in the strip is the quiet way that Jane and O'Malley constantly disdain each other, with the Fairy Godfather not bothering to learn her name but calling her "little girl."

Although many of these characters are as pint-sized as Barnaby, they all have their pride. A recurring motif in the strip is how they take offense at some slight, usually an obnoxious remark by O'Malley, or the disinclination of the adult world to believe in their existence.

The major theme of *Barnaby* is the interaction between reality and imagination. Because they never see Mr. O'Malley themselves, Barnaby's parents fear that he has a "wild imagination" and even seek psychological counseling. Yet we know that Mr. O'Malley is real because not only does Barnaby see him but so do a few other select souls, including other kids like Jean but also the odd drunk, eccentric or criminal. But if *Barnaby* is well-grounded and reality-based, Mr. O'Malley is not entirely to be trusted, and not just because of his implausible yarns. Ironically, on occasion Mr. O'Malley is himself as hardnosed a skeptic as Barnaby's parents, such as when he launches a congressional investigation into Santa Claus.

Barnaby's father asserts that "seeing is believing." Mr. O'Malley reverses the adage and argues that "Believing is Seeing is the way I put it ... Same idea of course." Despite this confident claim, the two ideas are far from being the same: in the world of *Barnaby* there is a constant tension between the narrow-minded philosophy that only believes what it sees and the equally dangerous tendency of letting belief guide sight. The first philosophy leads to a soul-crushing empiricism that denies the imagination any freedom, while the second philosophy leads to flights of unreality (of the type that Mr. O'Malley specializes in). Barnaby has to walk a tightrope between these two philosophies, making sure that he balances his imagination with his sense of reality.

To talk about philosophy in a comic strip about a five-year-old boy and his Fairy Godfather is to risk sounding like an over-enthusiastic egghead. Yet the wonder of *Barnaby* is that it can be read on many different levels. It's a wonderful kids strip that can be enjoyed by very young readers, but it also delves deeper into many other topics, including politics and psychology, as well as the perennial philosophic questions about the nature of reality. *Barnaby* has many claims on our attention because Crockett Johnson crafted a strip that nourishes both the heart and the mind, with lively characters that both amuse us and make us think.

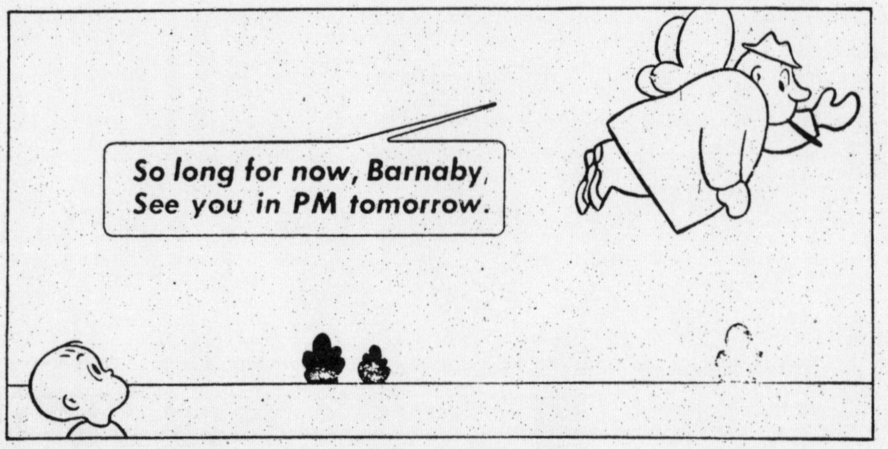
So long for now, Barnaby, See you in PM tomorrow.

Crockett Johnson, advertisement for Barnaby, *19 April 1942*

Barnaby

20 APRIL 1942 – 31 DECEMBER 1943

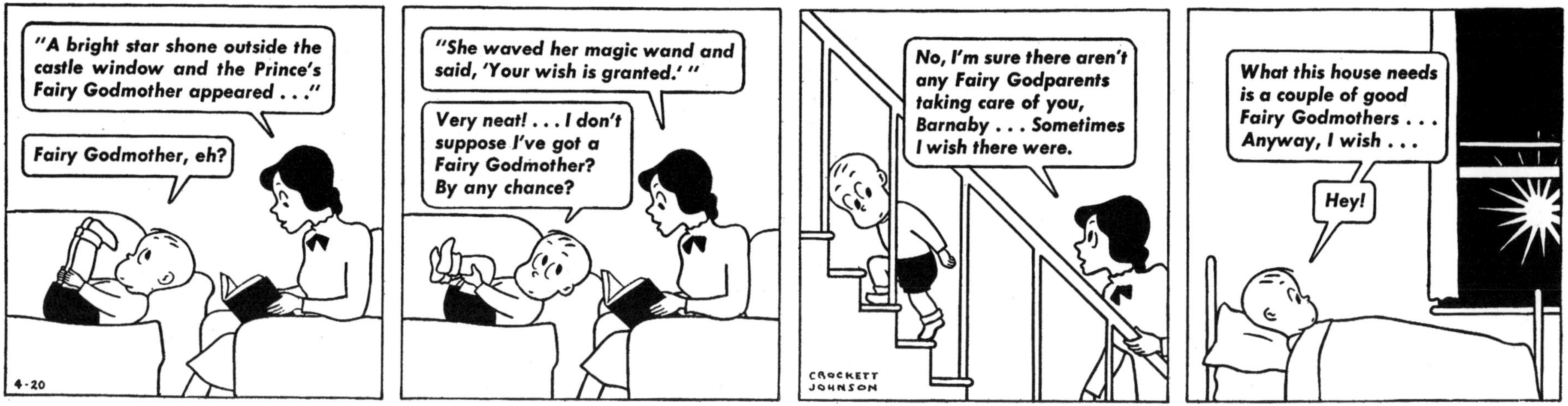
"A bright star shone outside the castle window and the Prince's Fairy Godmother appeared . . ."
Fairy Godmother, eh?
4-20
"She waved her magic wand and said, 'Your wish is granted.' "
Very neat! . . . I don't suppose I've got a Fairy Godmother? By any chance?
CROCKETT JOHNSON
No, I'm sure there aren't any Fairy Godparents taking care of you, Barnaby . . . Sometimes I wish there were.
What this house needs is a couple of good Fairy Godmothers . . . Anyway, I wish . . .
Hey!

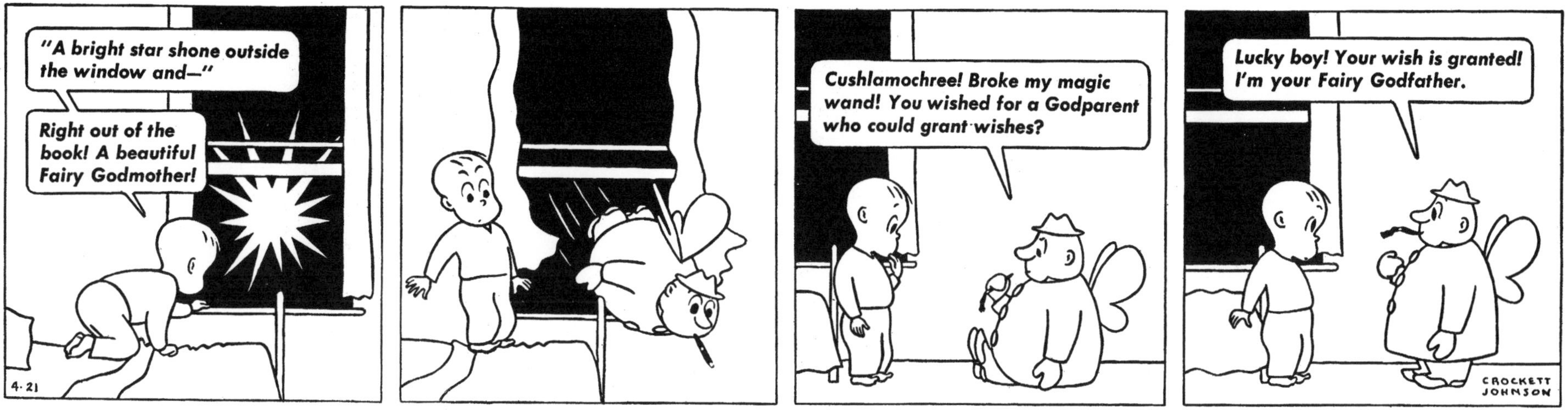
"A bright star shone outside the window and—"
Right out of the book! A beautiful Fairy Godmother!
4-21
Cushlamochree! Broke my magic wand! You wished for a Godparent who could grant wishes?
Lucky boy! Your wish is granted! I'm your Fairy Godfather.
CROCKETT JOHNSON

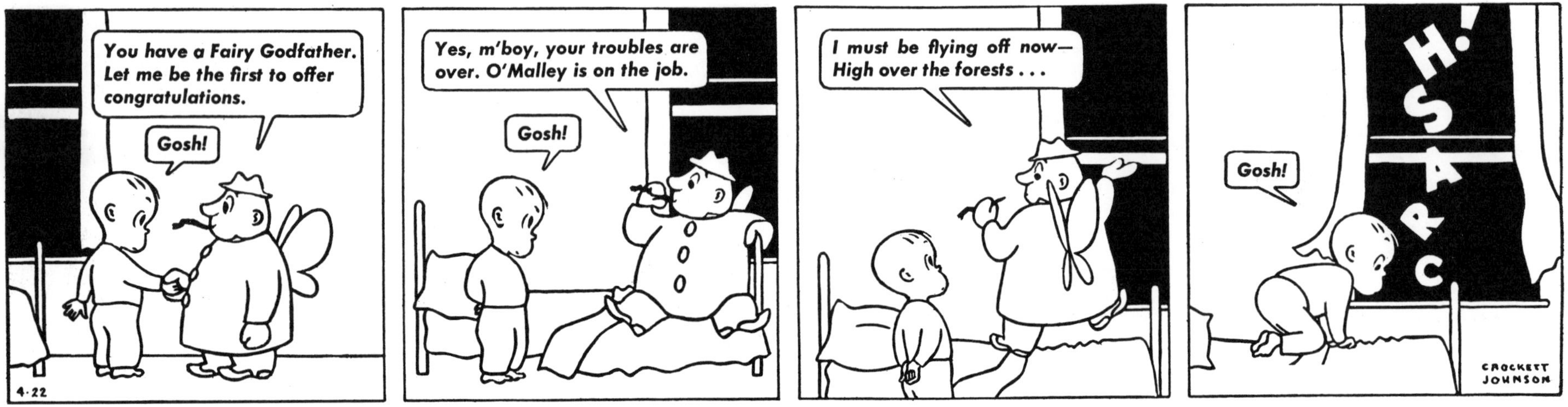
You have a Fairy Godfather. Let me be the first to offer congratulations.
Gosh!
4·22
Yes, m'boy, your troubles are over. O'Malley is on the job.
Gosh!
I must be flying off now— High over the forests . . .
CRASH!
Gosh!
CROCKETT JOHNSON

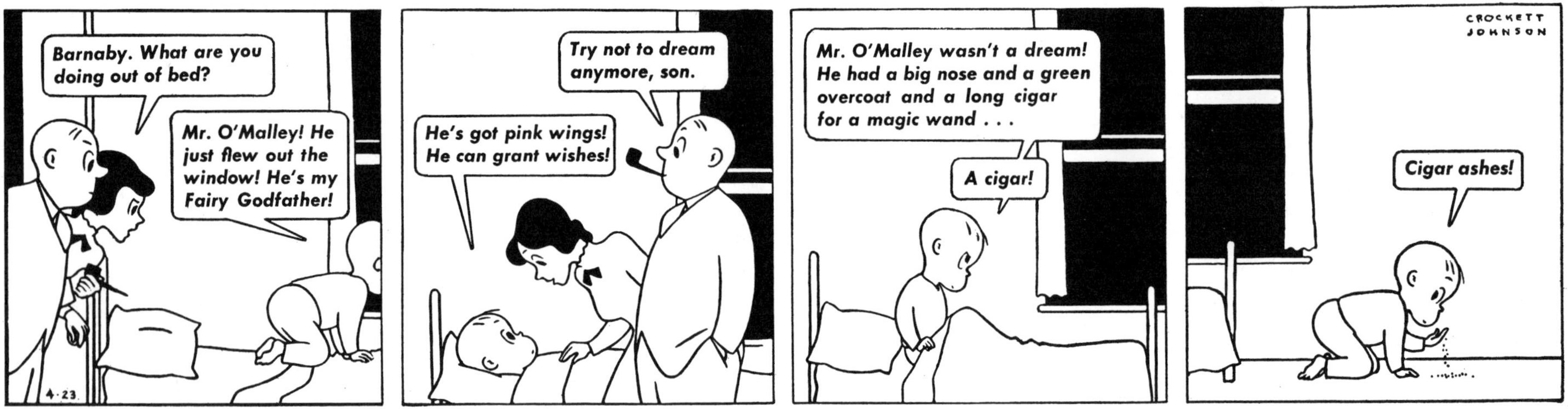
Barnaby. What are you doing out of bed?
Mr. O'Malley! He just flew out the window! He's my Fairy Godfather!
4·23
Try not to dream anymore, son.
He's got pink wings! He can grant wishes!
Mr. O'Malley wasn't a dream! He had a big nose and a green overcoat and a long cigar for a magic wand . . .
A cigar!
CROCKETT JOHNSON
Cigar ashes!

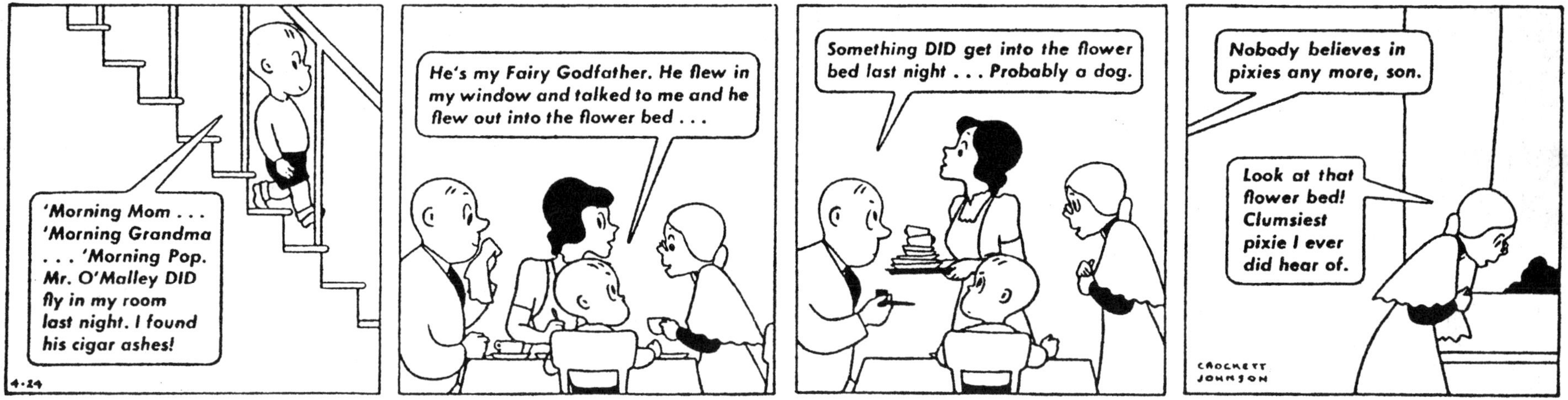
'Morning Mom . . . 'Morning Grandma . . . 'Morning Pop. Mr. O'Malley DID fly in my room last night. I found his cigar ashes!
4-24
He's my Fairy Godfather. He flew in my window and talked to me and he flew out into the flower bed . . .
Something DID get into the flower bed last night . . . Probably a dog.
Nobody believes in pixies any more, son.
Look at that flower bed! Clumsiest pixie I ever did hear of.
CROCKETT JOHNSON

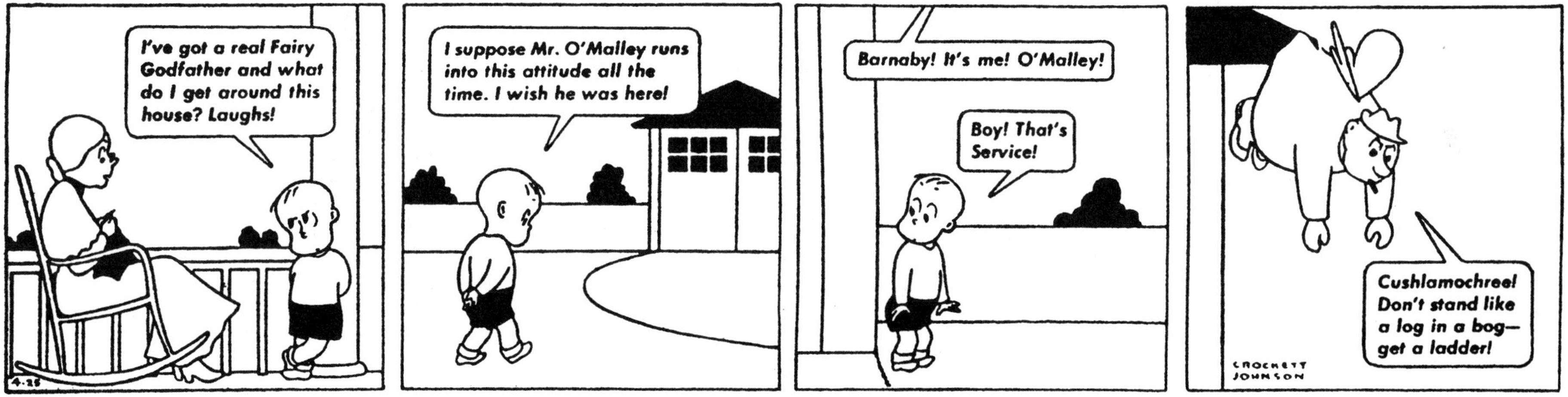
I've got a real Fairy Godfather and what do I get around this house? Laughs!
4-25
I suppose Mr. O'Malley runs into this attitude all the time. I wish he was here!
Barnaby! It's me! O'Malley!
Boy! That's Service!
Cushlamochree! Don't stand like a log in a bog—get a ladder!
CROCKETT JOHNSON

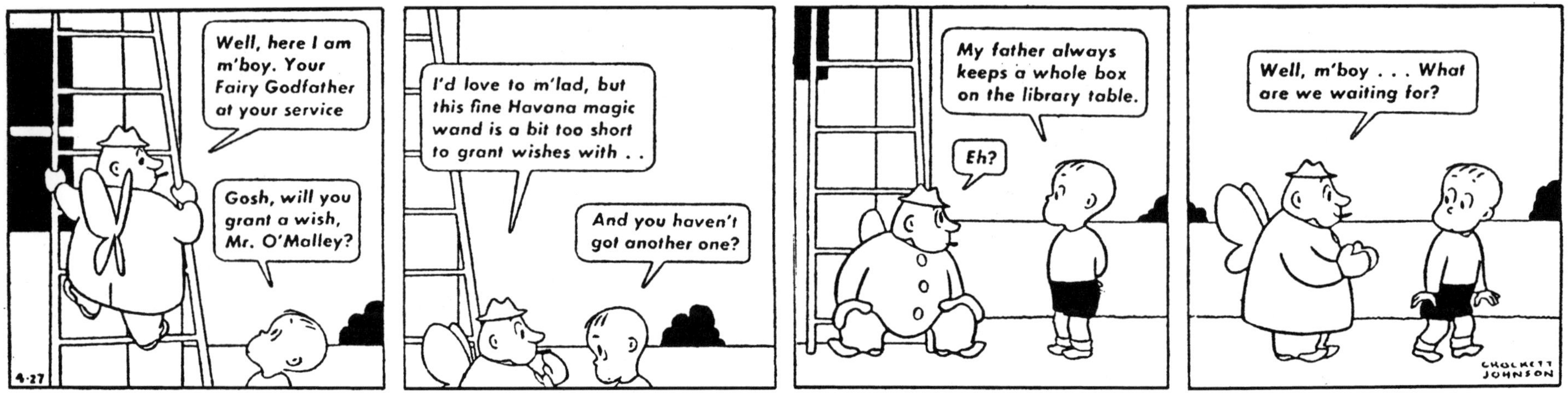
4-27
Well, here I am m'boy. Your Fairy Godfather at your service
Gosh, will you grant a wish, Mr. O'Malley?
I'd love to m'lad, but this fine Havana magic wand is a bit too short to grant wishes with . .
And you haven't got another one?
My father always keeps a whole box on the library table.
Eh?
Well, m'boy . . . What are we waiting for?
CROCKETT JOHNSON

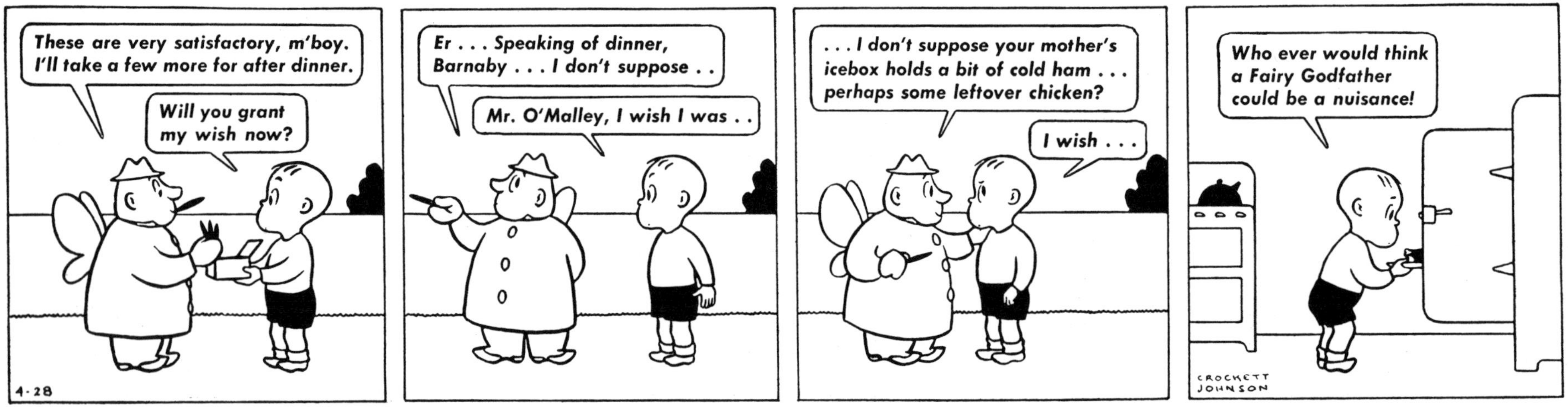
4-28
These are very satisfactory, m'boy. I'll take a few more for after dinner.
Will you grant my wish now?
Er . . . Speaking of dinner, Barnaby . . . I don't suppose . .
Mr. O'Malley, I wish I was . .
. . . I don't suppose your mother's icebox holds a bit of cold ham . . . perhaps some leftover chicken?
I wish . . .
Who ever would think a Fairy Godfather could be a nuisance!
CROCKETT JOHNSON

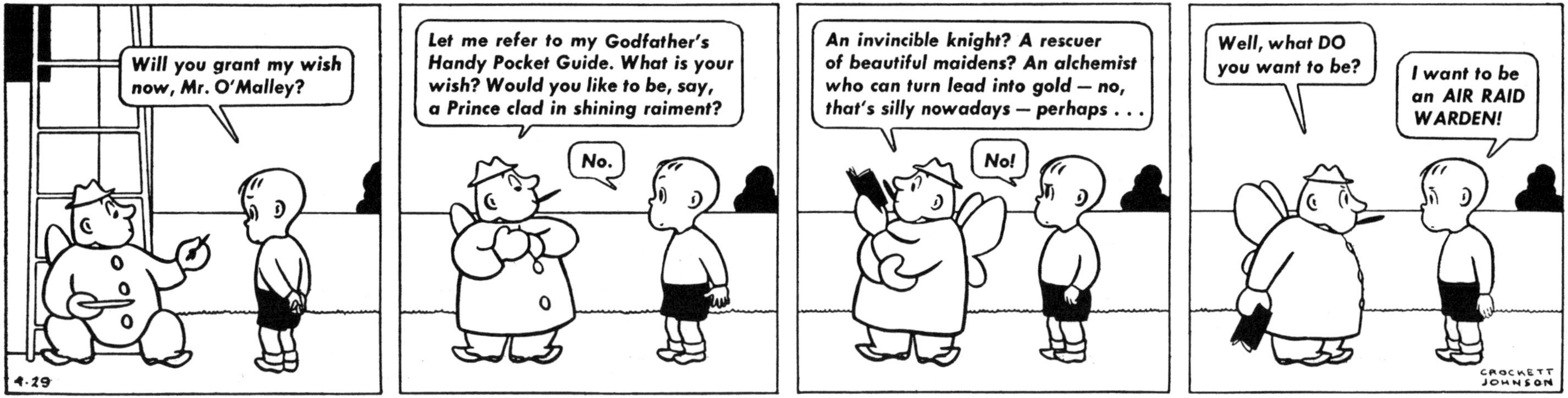
Will you grant my wish now, Mr. O'Malley?
4·29
Let me refer to my Godfather's Handy Pocket Guide. What is your wish? Would you like to be, say, a Prince clad in shining raiment?
No.
An invincible knight? A rescuer of beautiful maidens? An alchemist who can turn lead into gold — no, that's silly nowadays — perhaps . . .
No!
Well, what DO you want to be?
I want to be an AIR RAID WARDEN!
CROCKETT JOHNSON

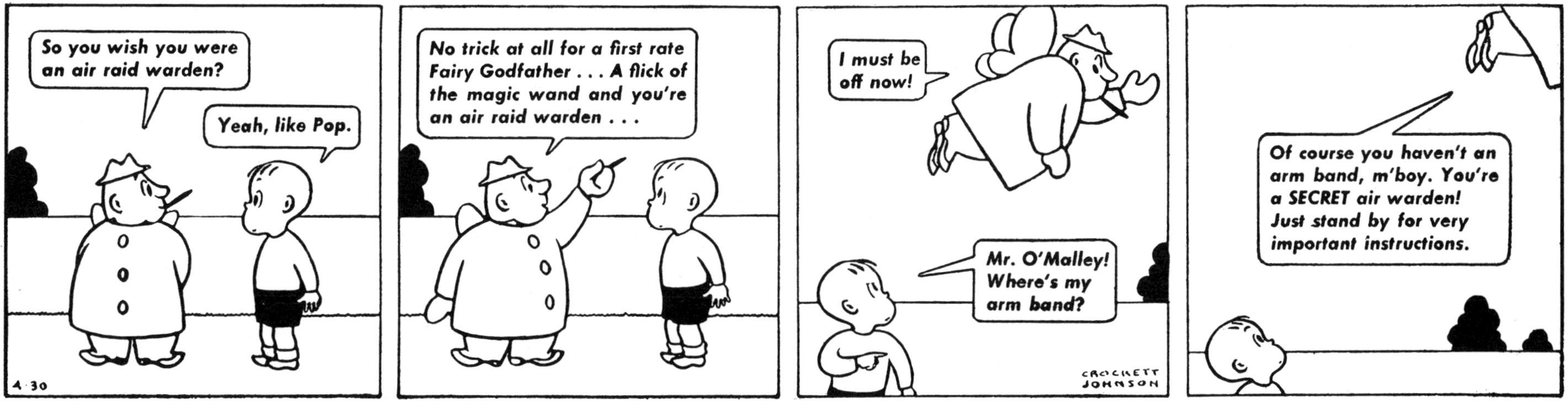
So you wish you were an air raid warden?
Yeah, like Pop.
4·30
No trick at all for a first rate Fairy Godfather . . . A flick of the magic wand and you're an air raid warden . . .
I must be off now!
Mr. O'Malley! Where's my arm band?
CROCKETT JOHNSON
Of course you haven't an arm band, m'boy. You're a SECRET air warden! Just stand by for very important instructions.

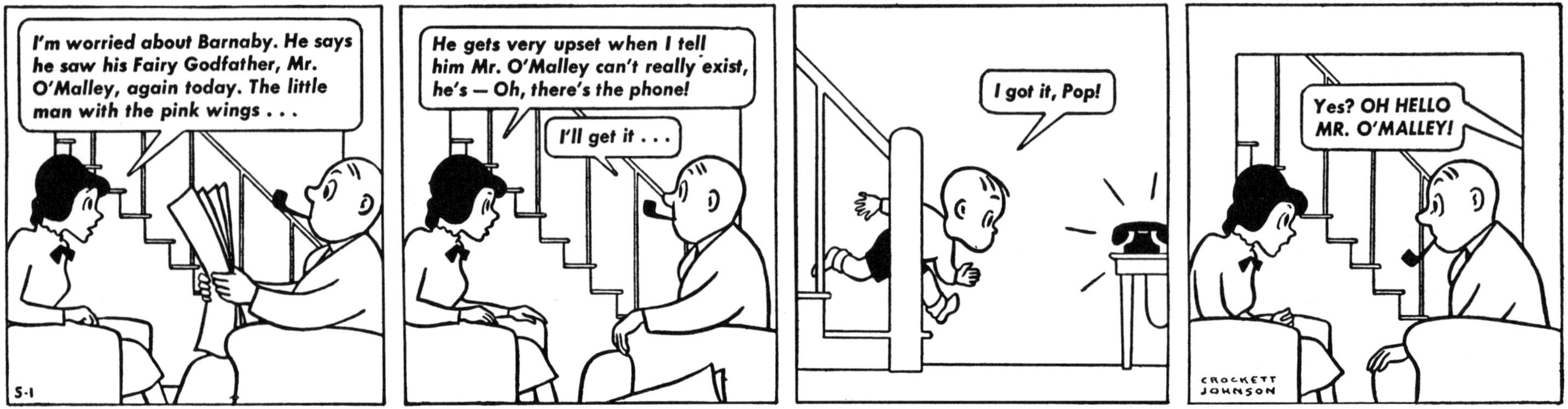

5-1
I'm worried about Barnaby. He says he saw his Fairy Godfather, Mr. O'Malley, again today. The little man with the pink wings . . .
He gets very upset when I tell him Mr. O'Malley can't really exist, he's — Oh, there's the phone!
I'll get it . . .
I got it, Pop!
Yes? OH HELLO MR. O'MALLEY!
CROCKETT JOHNSON

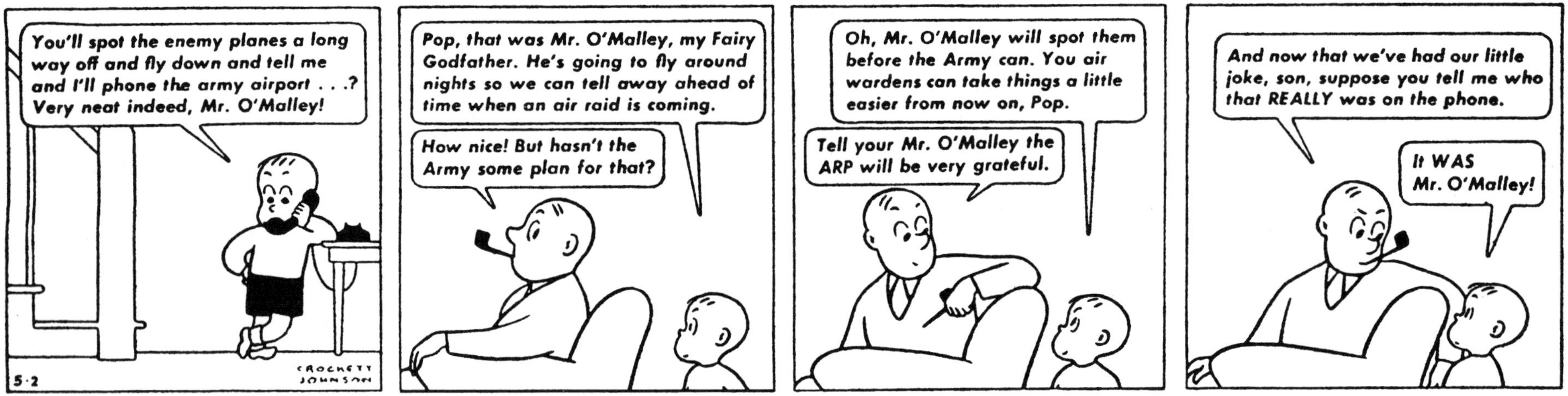

5-2
You'll spot the enemy planes a long way off and fly down and tell me and I'll phone the army airport . . .? Very neat indeed, Mr. O'Malley!
CROCKETT JOHNSON
Pop, that was Mr. O'Malley, my Fairy Godfather. He's going to fly around nights so we can tell away ahead of time when an air raid is coming.
How nice! But hasn't the Army some plan for that?
Oh, Mr. O'Malley will spot them before the Army can. You air wardens can take things a little easier from now on, Pop.
Tell your Mr. O'Malley the ARP will be very grateful.
And now that we've had our little joke, son, suppose you tell me who that REALLY was on the phone.
It WAS Mr. O'Malley!

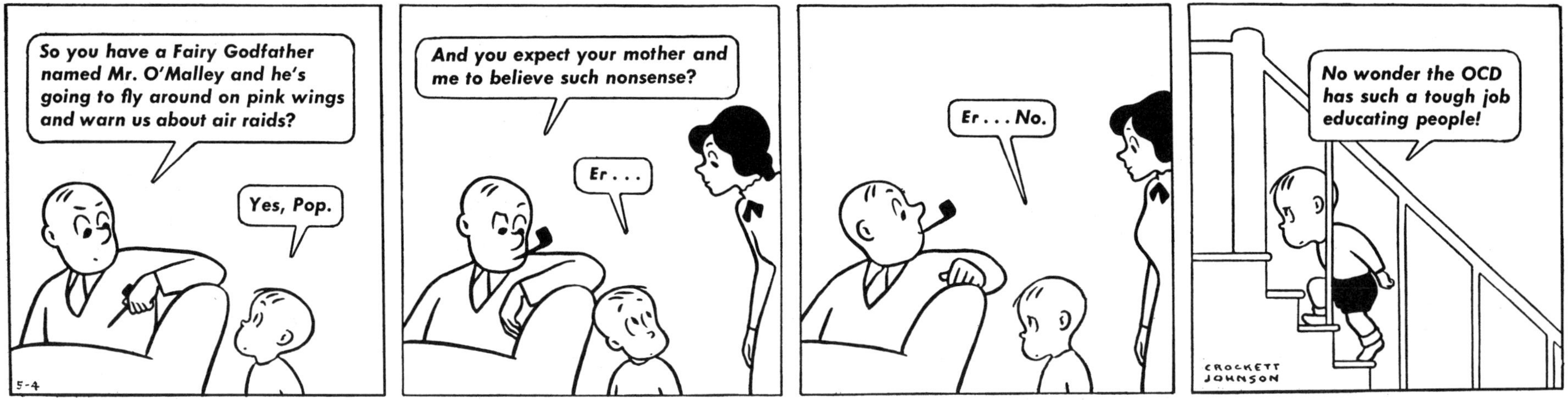
So you have a Fairy Godfather named Mr. O'Malley and he's going to fly around on pink wings and warn us about air raids?
Yes, Pop.
5-4
And you expect your mother and me to believe such nonsense?
Er . . .
Er . . . No.
No wonder the OCD has such a tough job educating people!
CROCKETT JOHNSON

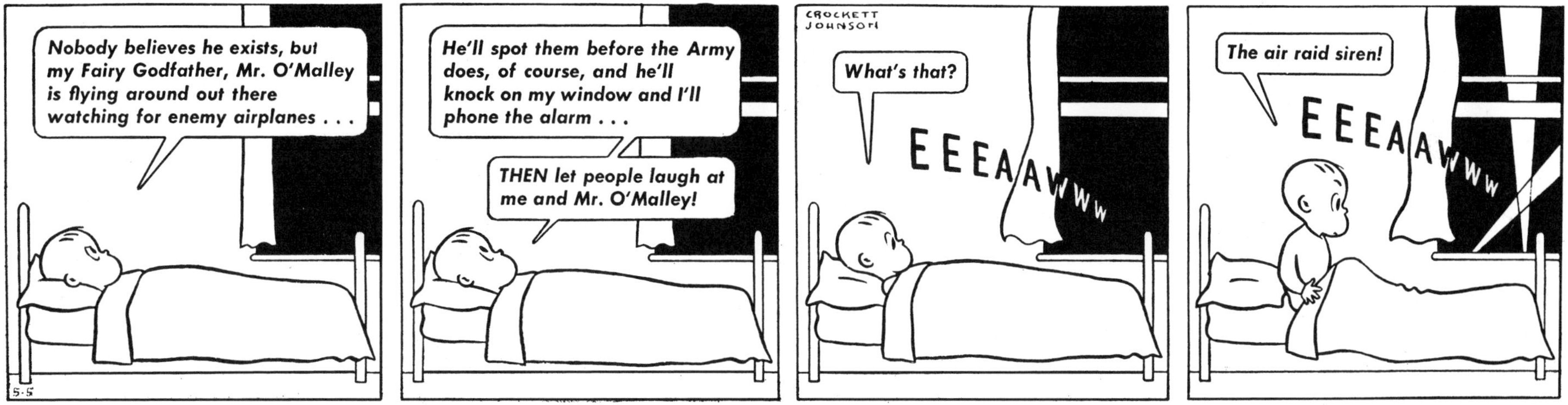
Nobody believes he exists, but my Fairy Godfather, Mr. O'Malley is flying around out there watching for enemy airplanes . . .
5-5
He'll spot them before the Army does, of course, and he'll knock on my window and I'll phone the alarm . . .
THEN let people laugh at me and Mr. O'Malley!
CROCKETT JOHNSON
What's that?
EEEAAWWWW
The air raid siren!
EEEAAWWWW

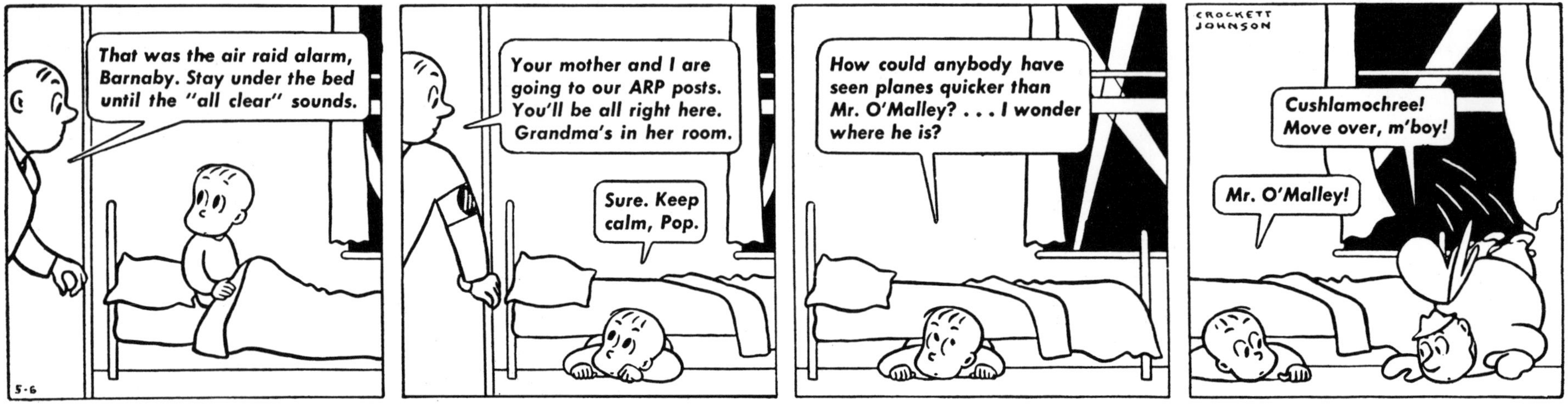
That was the air raid alarm, Barnaby. Stay under the bed until the "all clear" sounds.
5-6
Your mother and I are going to our ARP posts. You'll be all right here. Grandma's in her room.
Sure. Keep calm, Pop.
How could anybody have seen planes quicker than Mr. O'Malley? . . . I wonder where he is?
CROCKETT JOHNSON
Cushlamochree! Move over, m'boy!
Mr. O'Malley!

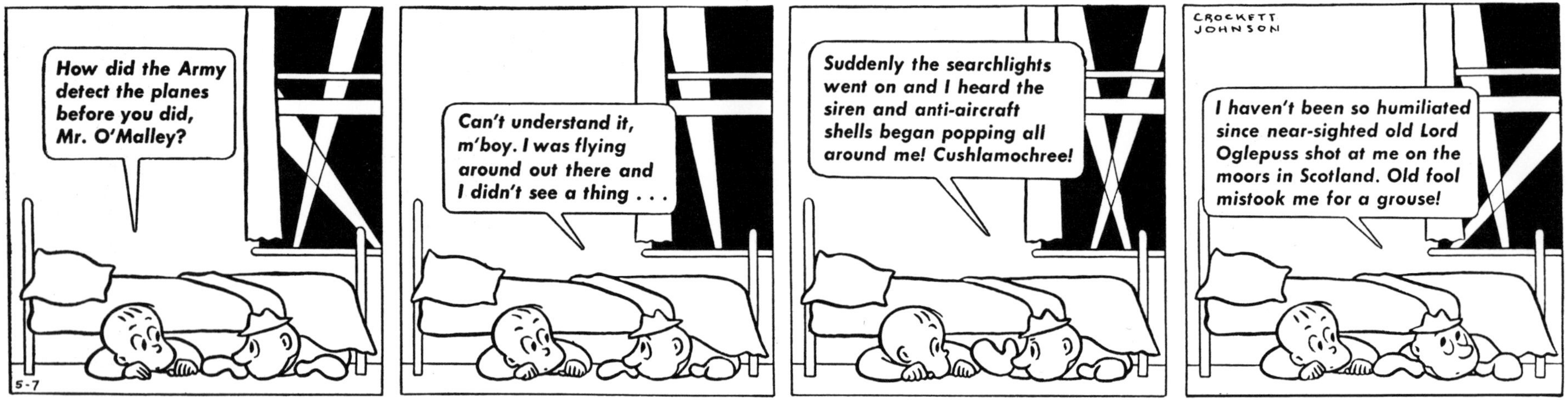
How did the Army detect the planes before you did, Mr. O'Malley?
5-7
Can't understand it, m'boy. I was flying around out there and I didn't see a thing . . .
Suddenly the searchlights went on and I heard the siren and anti-aircraft shells began popping all around me! Cushlamochree!
CROCKETT JOHNSON
I haven't been so humiliated since near-sighted old Lord Oglepuss shot at me on the moors in Scotland. Old fool mistook me for a grouse!

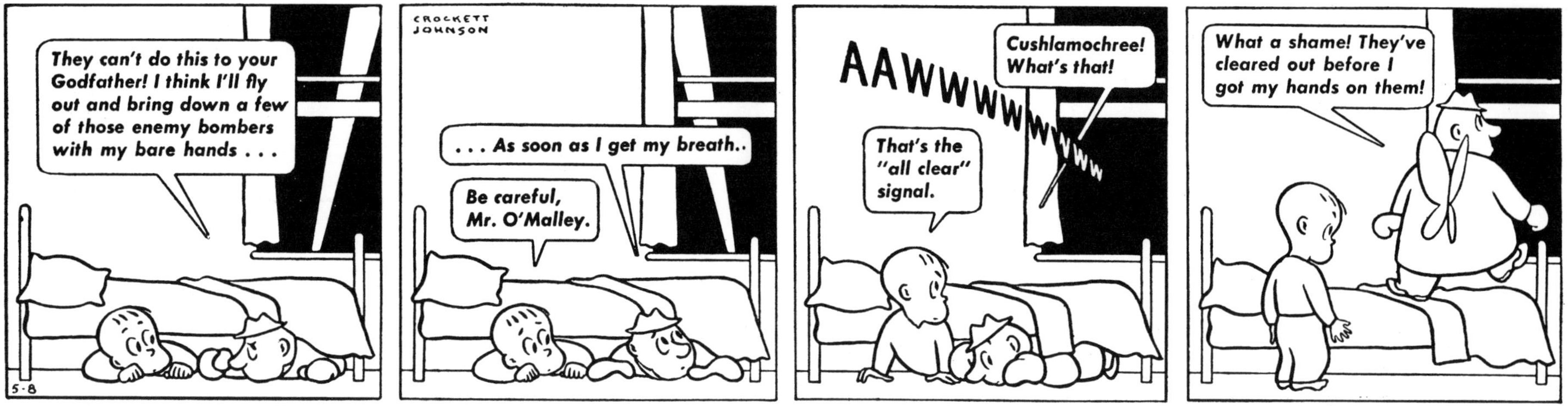
They can't do this to your Godfather! I think I'll fly out and bring down a few of those enemy bombers with my bare hands . . .
5-8
CROCKETT JOHNSON
. . . As soon as I get my breath..
Be careful, Mr. O'Malley.
AAWWWWWWWWWW
Cushlamochree! What's that!
That's the "all clear" signal.
What a shame! They've cleared out before I got my hands on them!

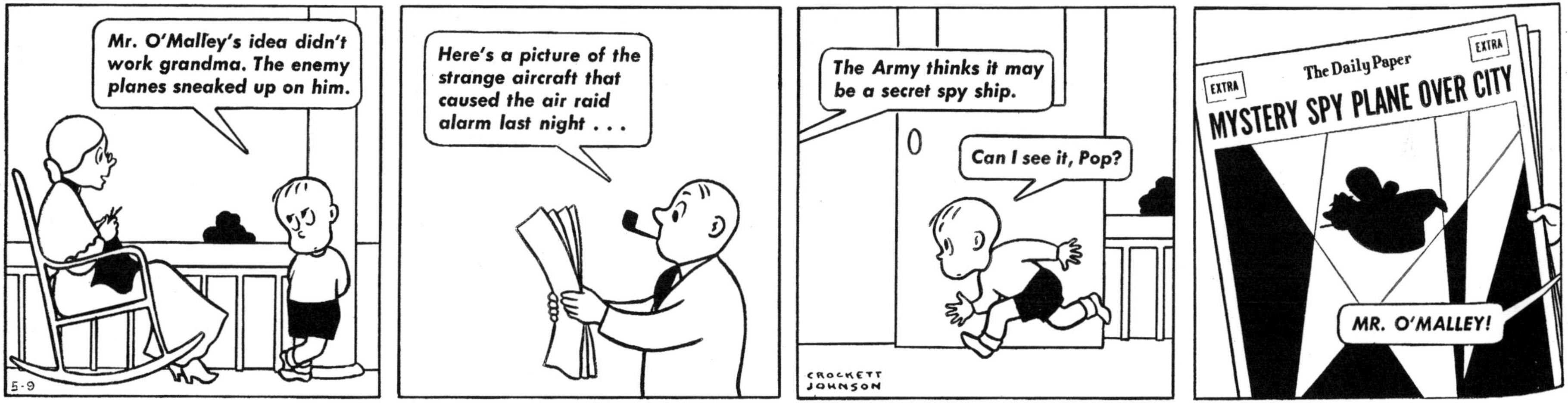
Mr. O'Malley's idea didn't work grandma. The enemy planes sneaked up on him.
5-9
Here's a picture of the strange aircraft that caused the air raid alarm last night . . .
The Army thinks it may be a secret spy ship.
Can I see it, Pop?
CROCKETT JOHNSON
EXTRA
The Daily Paper
EXTRA
MYSTERY SPY PLANE OVER CITY
MR. O'MALLEY!

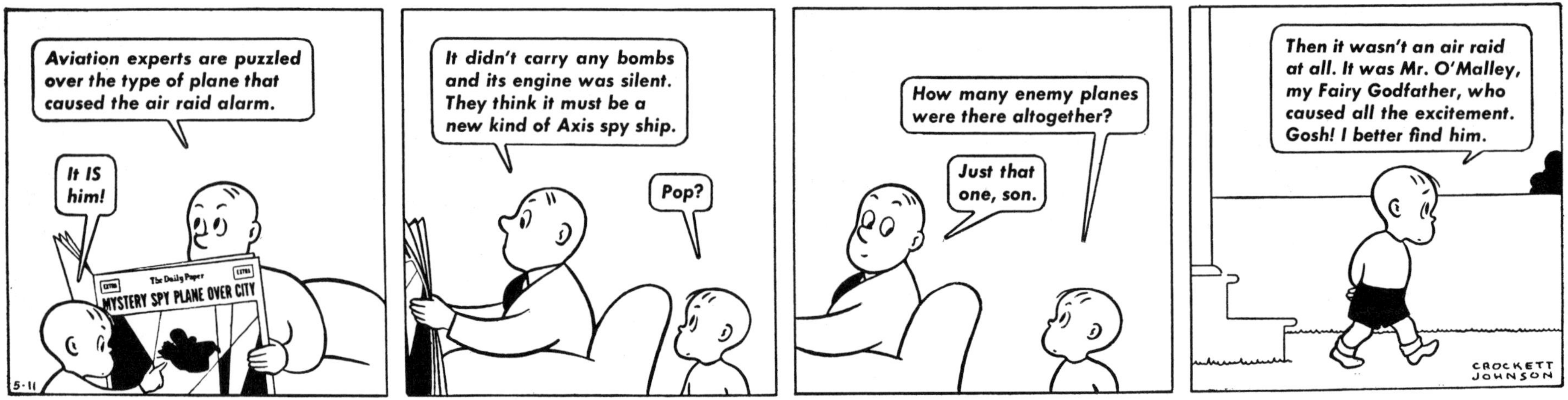
Aviation experts are puzzled over the type of plane that caused the air raid alarm.
It IS him!
The Daily Paper
MYSTERY SPY PLANE OVER CITY
5-11
It didn't carry any bombs and its engine was silent. They think it must be a new kind of Axis spy ship.
Pop?
How many enemy planes were there altogether?
Just that one, son.
Then it wasn't an air raid at all. It was Mr. O'Malley, my Fairy Godfather, who caused all the excitement. Gosh! I better find him.
CROCKETT JOHNSON

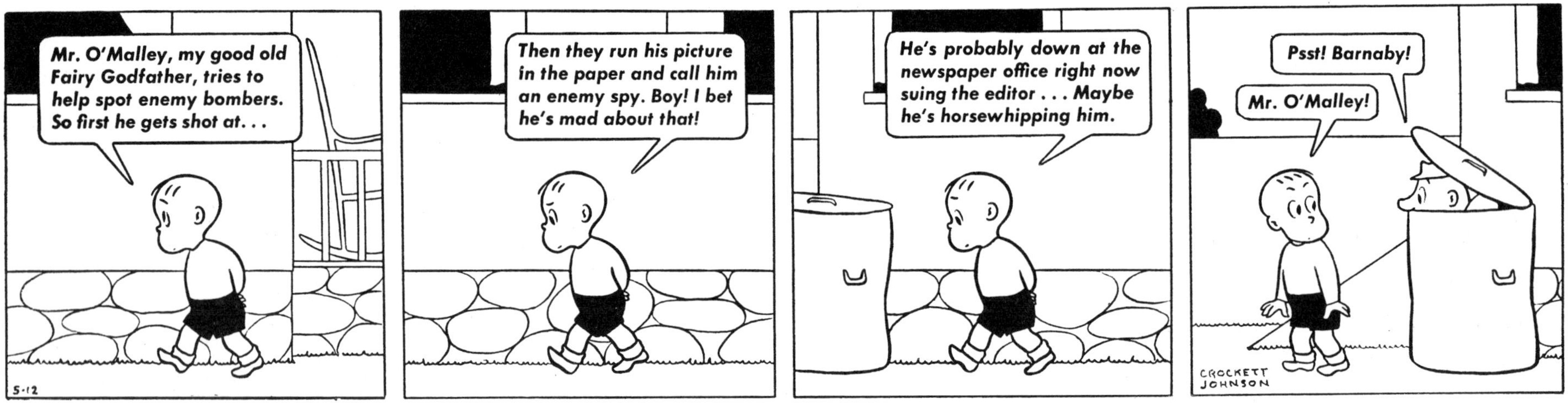
Mr. O'Malley, my good old Fairy Godfather, tries to help spot enemy bombers. So first he gets shot at...
5-12
Then they run his picture in the paper and call him an enemy spy. Boy! I bet he's mad about that!
He's probably down at the newspaper office right now suing the editor . . . Maybe he's horsewhipping him.
Mr. O'Malley!
Psst! Barnaby!
CROCKETT JOHNSON

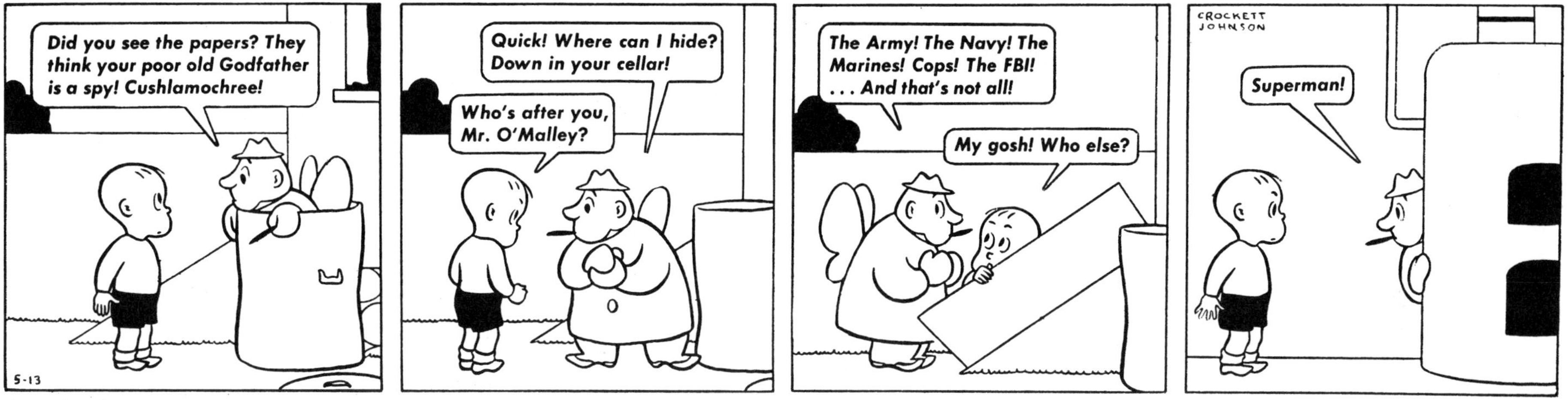

CROCKETT JOHNSON
5-13
Did you see the papers? They think your poor old Godfather is a spy! Cushlamochree!
Quick! Where can I hide? Down in your cellar!
Who's after you, Mr. O'Malley?
The Army! The Navy! The Marines! Cops! The FBI! . . . And that's not all!
My gosh! Who else?
Superman!

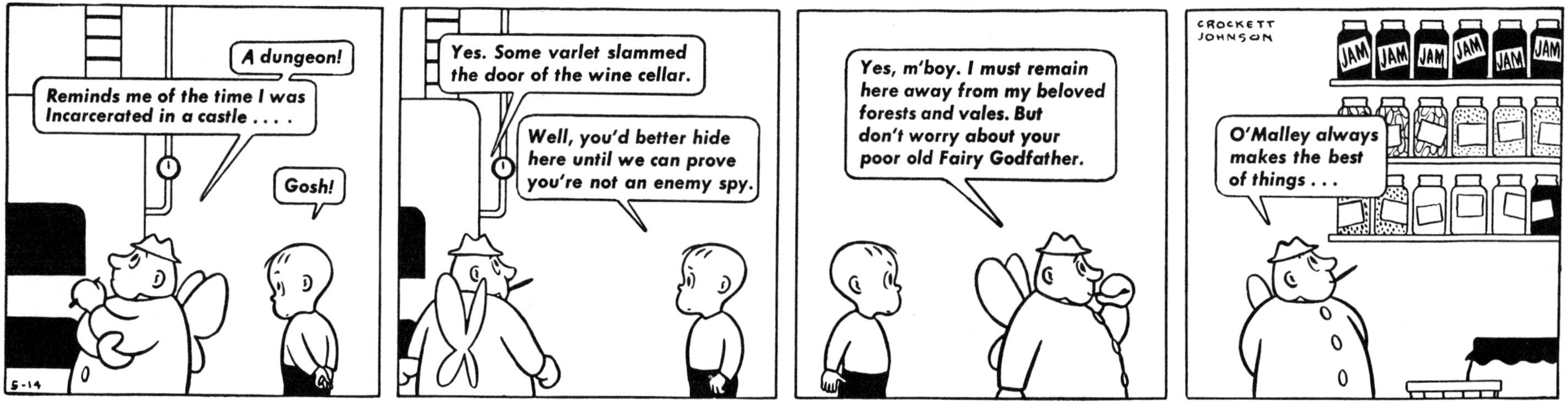

CROCKETT JOHNSON
5-14
A dungeon!
Reminds me of the time I was Incarcerated in a castle . . . .
Gosh!
Yes. Some varlet slammed the door of the wine cellar.
Well, you'd better hide here until we can prove you're not an enemy spy.
Yes, m'boy. I must remain here away from my beloved forests and vales. But don't worry about your poor old Fairy Godfather.
JAM
JAM
JAM
JAM
JAM
JAM
O'Malley always makes the best of things . . .

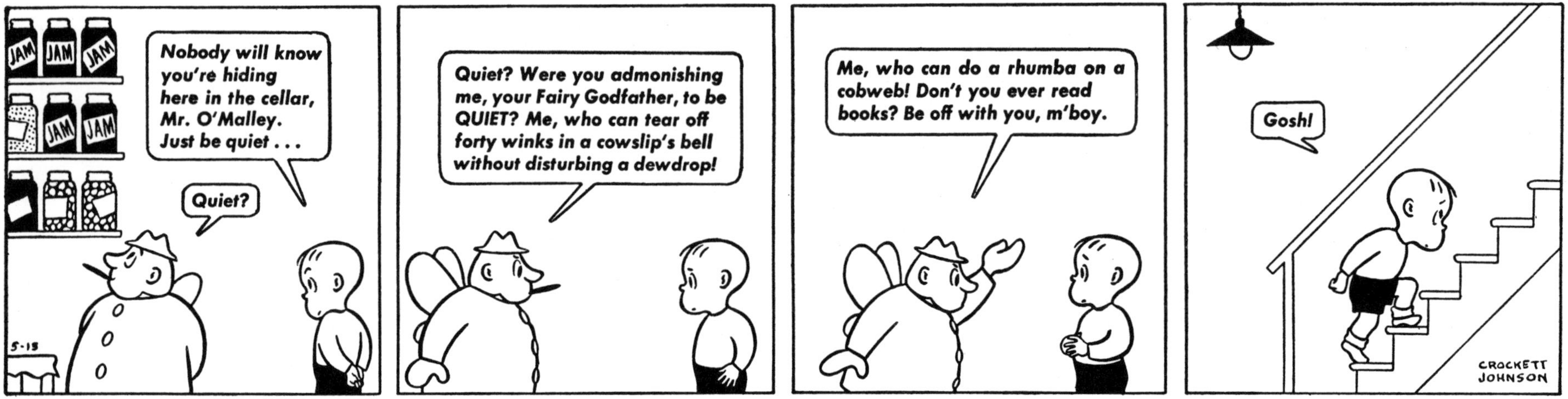
JAM JAM JAM
JAM JAM
Nobody will know you're hiding here in the cellar, Mr. O'Malley. Just be quiet . . .
Quiet?
5-15
Quiet? Were you admonishing me, your Fairy Godfather, to be QUIET? Me, who can tear off forty winks in a cowslip's bell without disturbing a dewdrop!
Me, who can do a rhumba on a cobweb! Don't you ever read books? Be off with you, m'boy.
Gosh!
CROCKETT JOHNSON

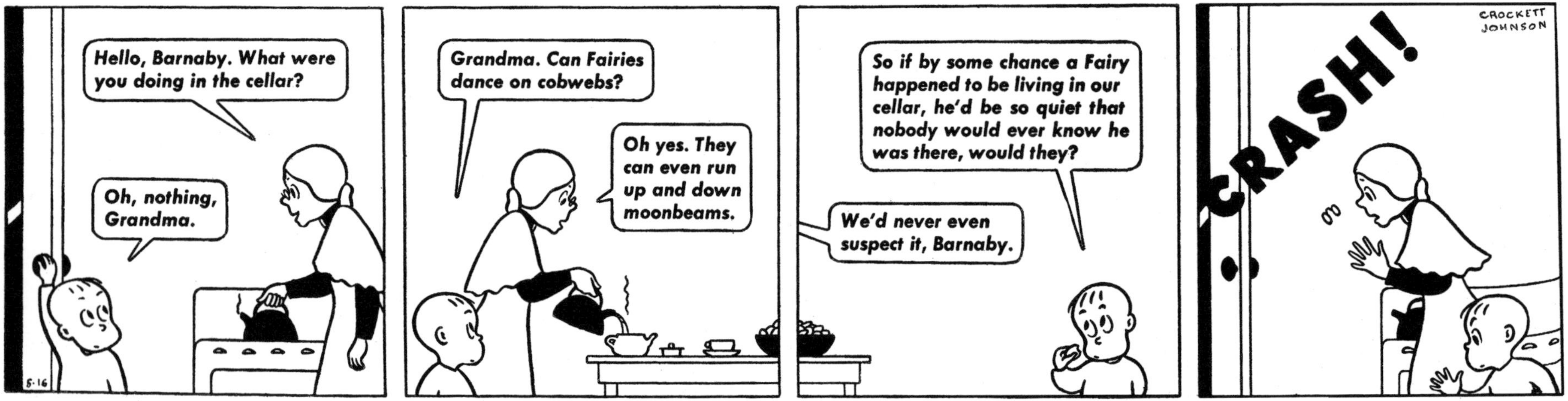
Hello, Barnaby. What were you doing in the cellar?
Oh, nothing, Grandma.
5-16
Grandma. Can Fairies dance on cobwebs?
Oh yes. They can even run up and down moonbeams.
So if by some chance a Fairy happened to be living in our cellar, he'd be so quiet that nobody would ever know he was there, would they?
We'd never even suspect it, Barnaby.
CROCKETT JOHNSON
CRASH!

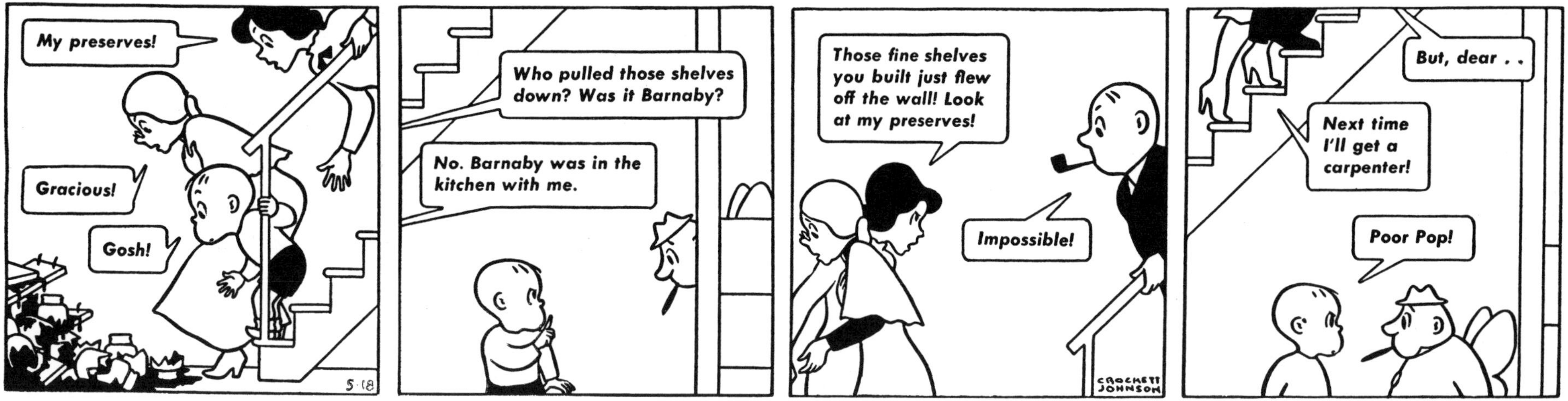
My preserves!
Gracious!
Gosh!
5·18
Who pulled those shelves down? Was it Barnaby?
No. Barnaby was in the kitchen with me.
Those fine shelves you built just flew off the wall! Look at my preserves!
Impossible!
CROCKETT JOHNSON
But, dear . .
Next time I'll get a carpenter!
Poor Pop!

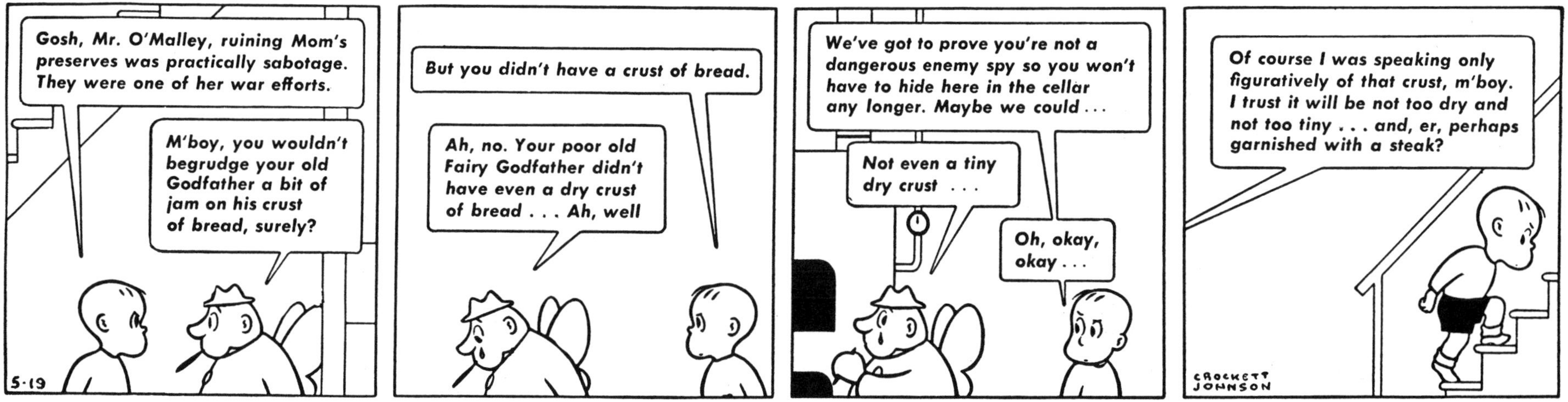
Gosh, Mr. O'Malley, ruining Mom's preserves was practically sabotage. They were one of her war efforts.
M'boy, you wouldn't begrudge your old Godfather a bit of jam on his crust of bread, surely?
5·19
But you didn't have a crust of bread.
Ah, no. Your poor old Fairy Godfather didn't have even a dry crust of bread . . . Ah, well
We've got to prove you're not a dangerous enemy spy so you won't have to hide here in the cellar any longer. Maybe we could . . .
Not even a tiny dry crust . . .
Oh, okay, okay . . .
Of course I was speaking only figuratively of that crust, m'boy. I trust it will be not too dry and not too tiny . . . and, er, perhaps garnished with a steak?
CROCKETT JOHNSON

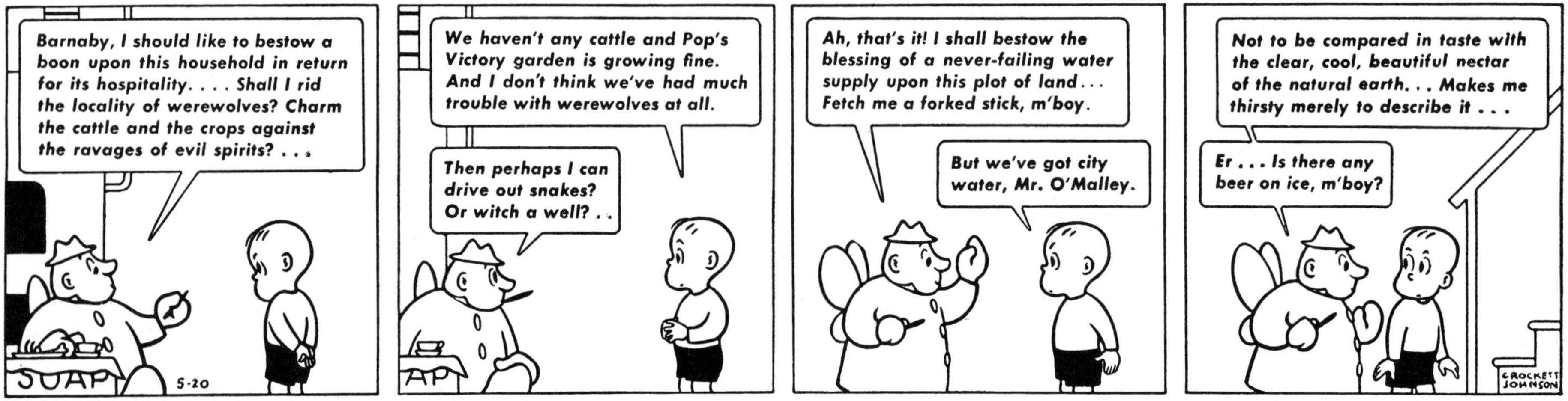
Barnaby, I should like to bestow a boon upon this household in return for its hospitality. . . . Shall I rid the locality of werewolves? Charm the cattle and the crops against the ravages of evil spirits? . . .
5-20
We haven't any cattle and Pop's Victory garden is growing fine. And I don't think we've had much trouble with werewolves at all.
Then perhaps I can drive out snakes? Or witch a well? . .
Ah, that's it! I shall bestow the blessing of a never-failing water supply upon this plot of land . . . Fetch me a forked stick, m'boy.
But we've got city water, Mr. O'Malley.
Not to be compared in taste with the clear, cool, beautiful nectar of the natural earth. . . Makes me thirsty merely to describe it . . .
Er . . . Is there any beer on ice, m'boy?
CROCKETT JOHNSON

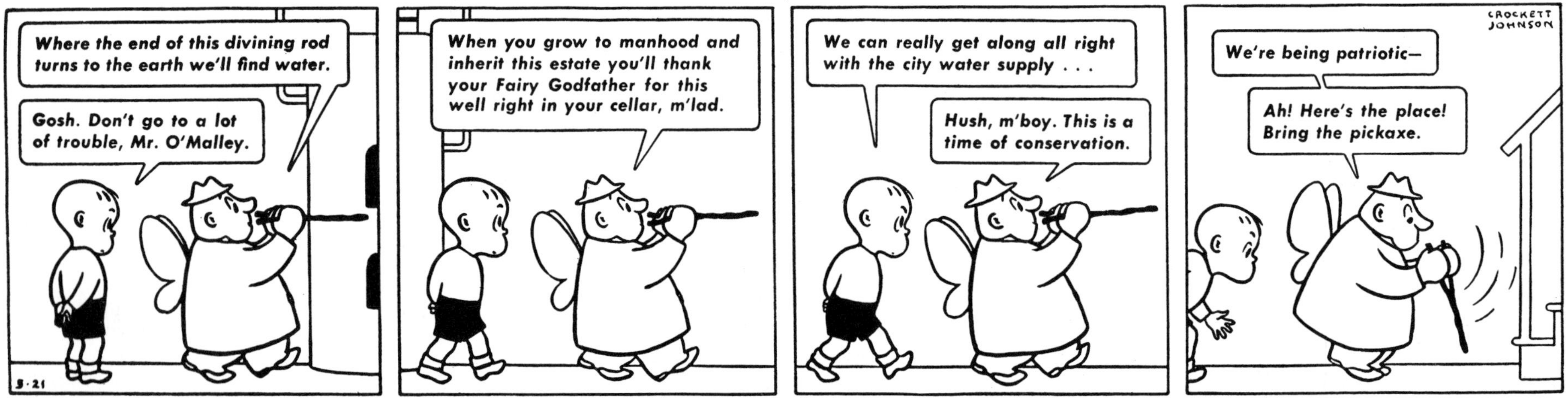
Where the end of this divining rod turns to the earth we'll find water.
Gosh. Don't go to a lot of trouble, Mr. O'Malley.
5-21
When you grow to manhood and inherit this estate you'll thank your Fairy Godfather for this well right in your cellar, m'lad.
We can really get along all right with the city water supply . . .
Hush, m'boy. This is a time of conservation.
CROCKETT JOHNSON
We're being patriotic—
Ah! Here's the place! Bring the pickaxe.

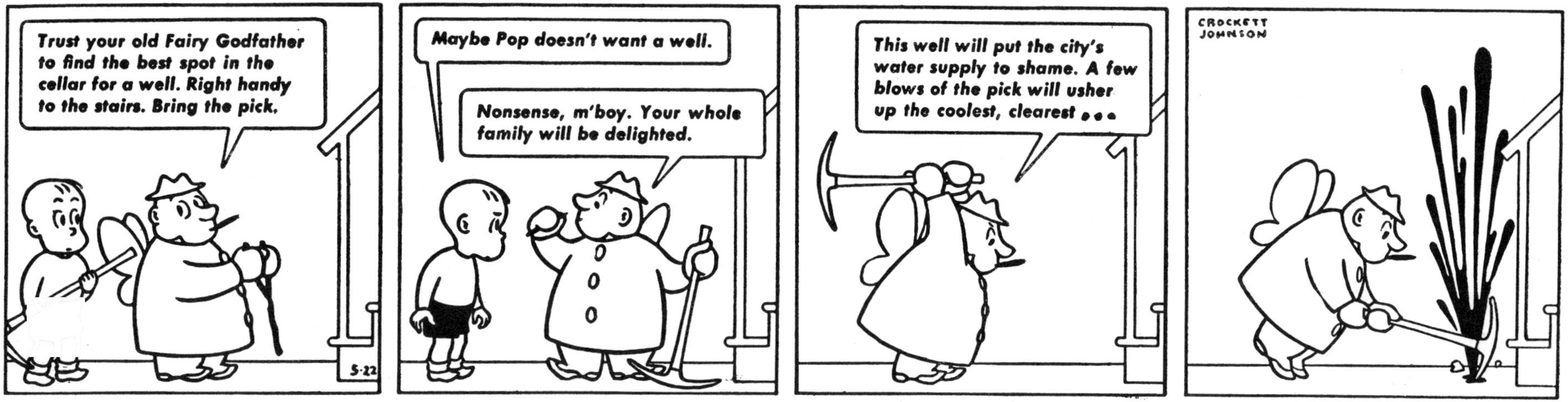

Trust your old Fairy Godfather to find the best spot in the cellar for a well. Right handy to the stairs. Bring the pick.
5·22
Maybe Pop doesn't want a well.
Nonsense, m'boy. Your whole family will be delighted.
This well will put the city's water supply to shame. A few blows of the pick will usher up the coolest, clearest . . .
CROCKETT JOHNSON

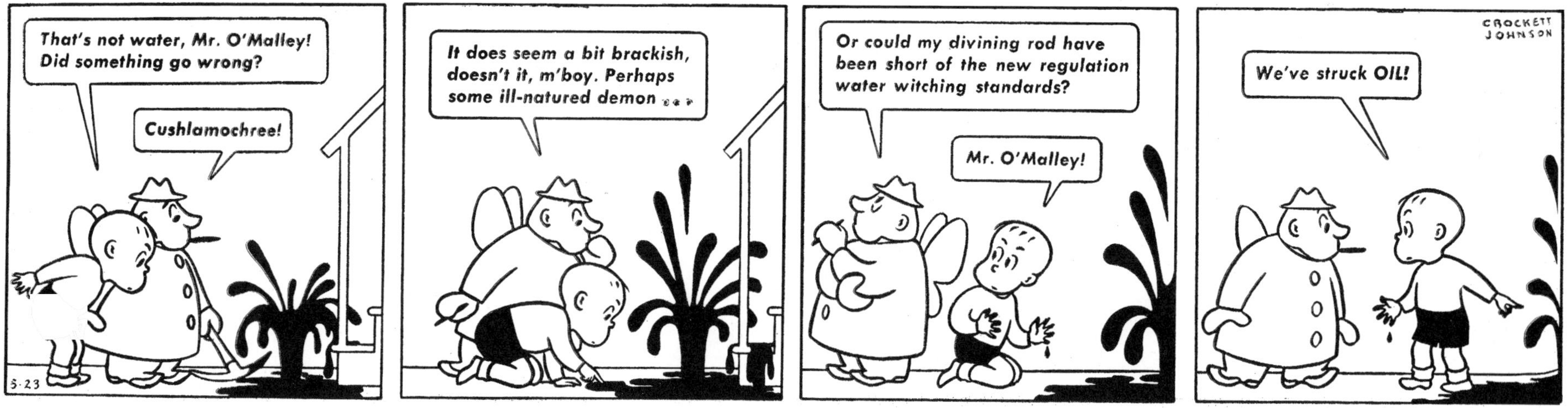

That's not water, Mr. O'Malley! Did something go wrong?
Cushlamochree!
5·23
It does seem a bit brackish, doesn't it, m'boy. Perhaps some ill-natured demon . . .
Or could my divining rod have been short of the new regulation water witching standards?
Mr. O'Malley!
CROCKETT JOHNSON
We've struck OIL!

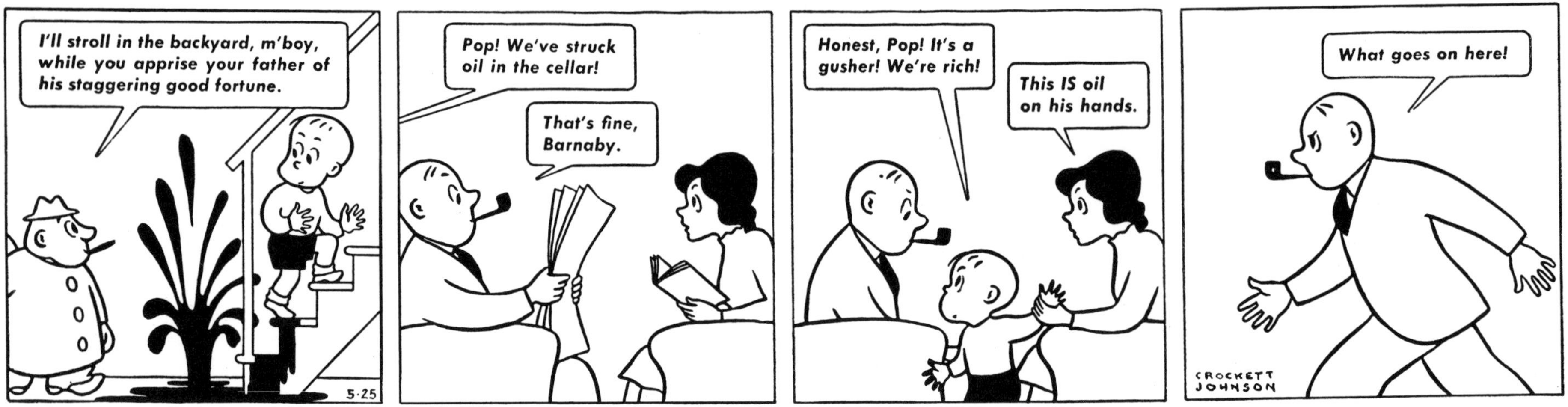
I'll stroll in the backyard, m'boy, while you apprise your father of his staggering good fortune.
5·25
Pop! We've struck oil in the cellar!
That's fine, Barnaby.
Honest, Pop! It's a gusher! We're rich!
This IS oil on his hands.
What goes on here!
CROCKETT JOHNSON

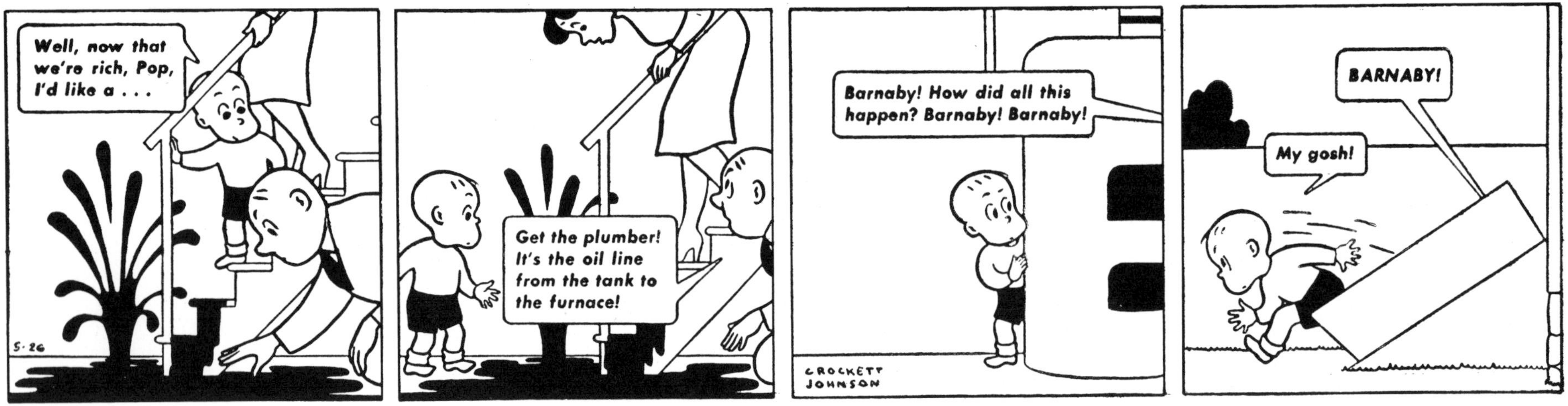
Well, now that we're rich, Pop, I'd like a . . .
5·26
Get the plumber! It's the oil line from the tank to the furnace!
Barnaby! How did all this happen? Barnaby! Barnaby!
CROCKETT JOHNSON
BARNABY!
My gosh!

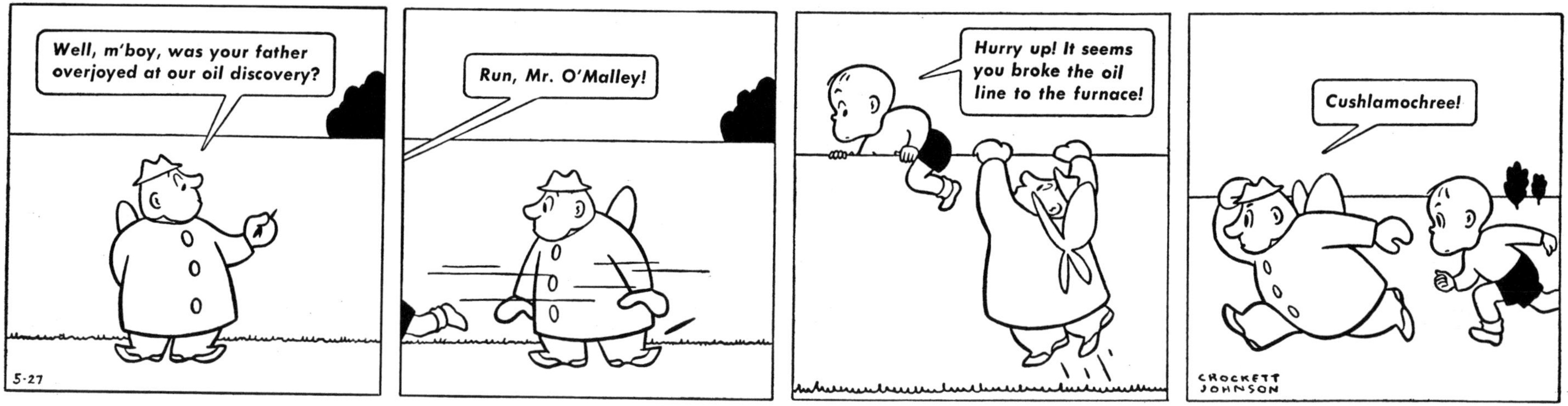
Well, m'boy, was your father overjoyed at our oil discovery?
5-27
Run, Mr. O'Malley!
Hurry up! It seems you broke the oil line to the furnace!
Cushlamochree!
CROCKETT JOHNSON

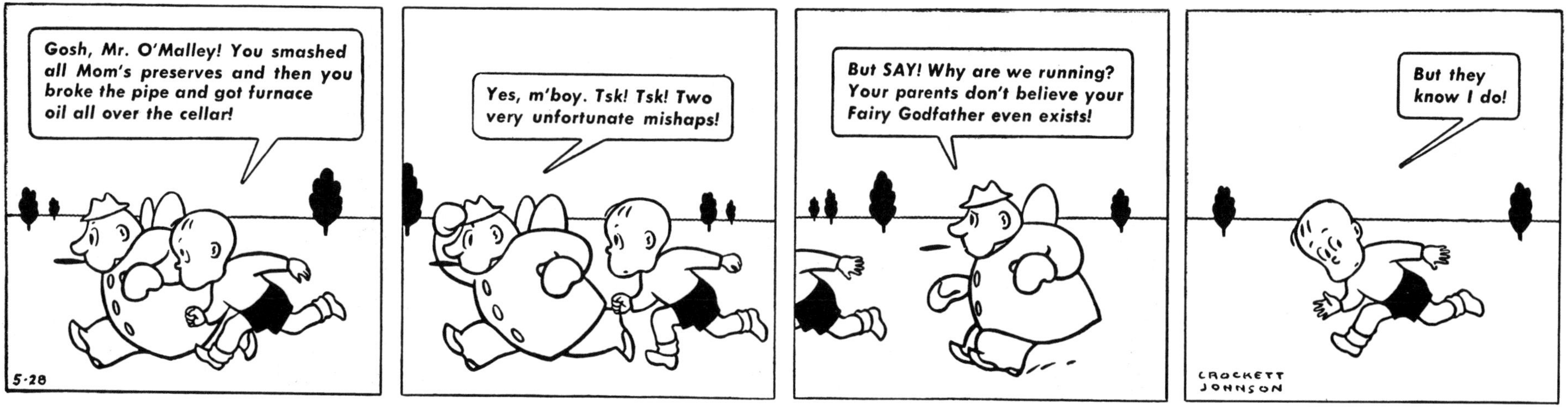
Gosh, Mr. O'Malley! You smashed all Mom's preserves and then you broke the pipe and got furnace oil all over the cellar!
5-28
Yes, m'boy. Tsk! Tsk! Two very unfortunate mishaps!
But SAY! Why are we running? Your parents don't believe your Fairy Godfather even exists!
But they know I do!
CROCKETT JOHNSON

May 27 – 28

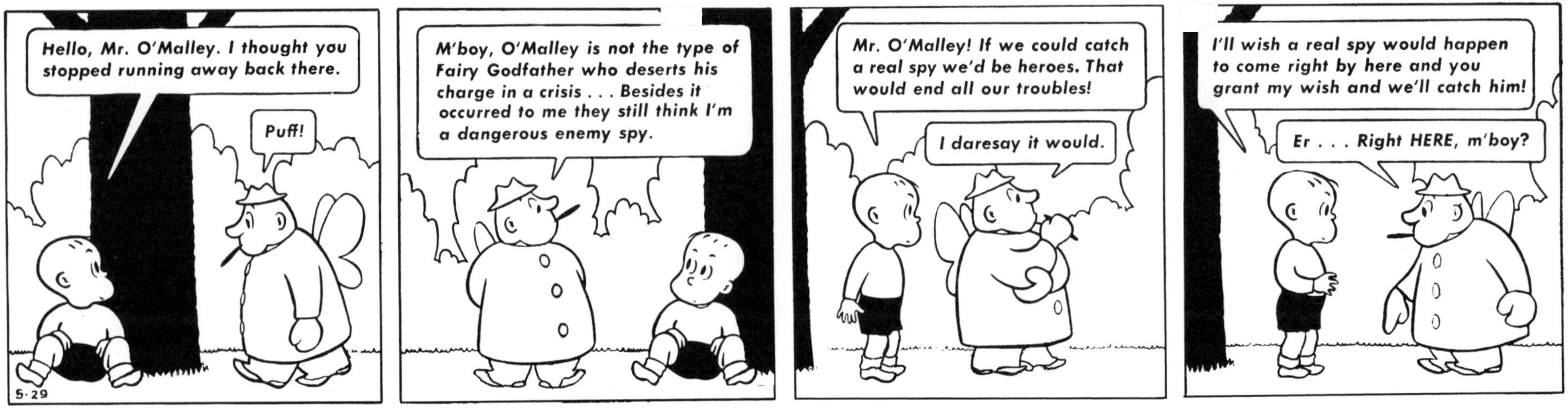
Hello, Mr. O'Malley. I thought you stopped running away back there.
Puff!
M'boy, O'Malley is not the type of Fairy Godfather who deserts his charge in a crisis . . . Besides it occurred to me they still think I'm a dangerous enemy spy.
Mr. O'Malley! If we could catch a real spy we'd be heroes. That would end all our troubles!
I daresay it would.
I'll wish a real spy would happen to come right by here and you grant my wish and we'll catch him!
Er . . . Right HERE, m'boy?
5-29

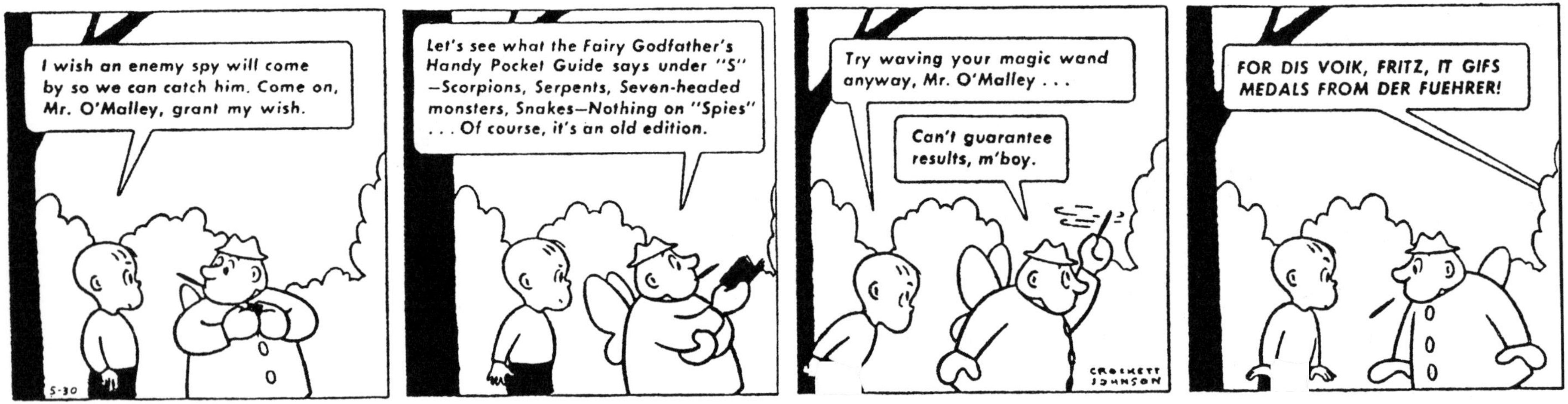
I wish an enemy spy will come by so we can catch him. Come on, Mr. O'Malley, grant my wish.
Let's see what the Fairy Godfather's Handy Pocket Guide says under "S" —Scorpions, Serpents, Seven-headed monsters, Snakes—Nothing on "Spies" . . . Of course, it's an old edition.
Try waving your magic wand anyway, Mr. O'Malley . . .
Can't guarantee results, m'boy.
FOR DIS VOIK, FRITZ, IT GIFS MEDALS FROM DER FUEHRER!
5-30
CROCKETT JOHNSON

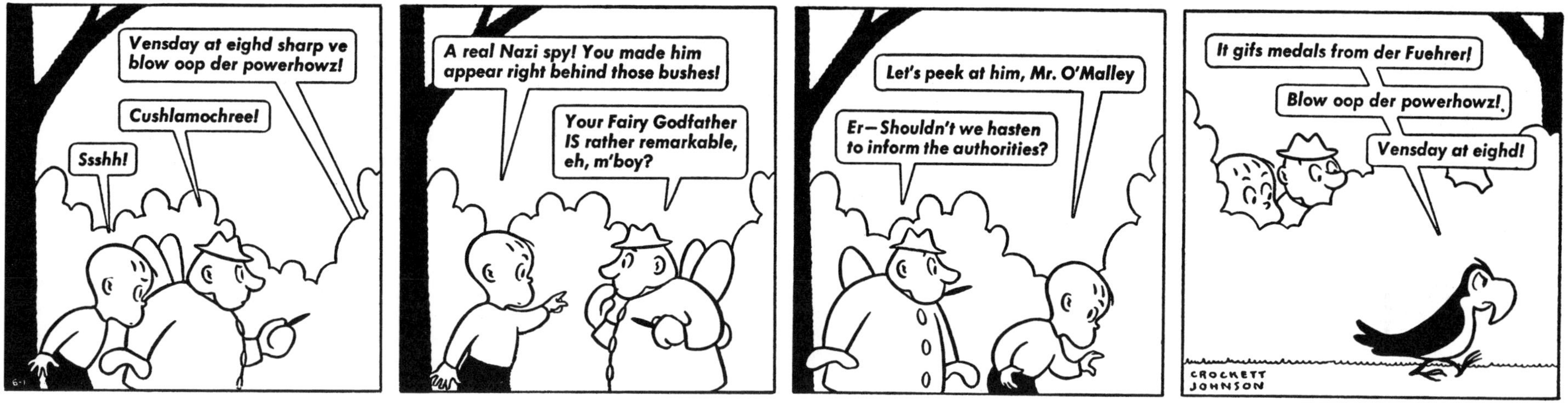
Vensday at eighd sharp ve blow oop der powerhowz!
Cushlamochree!
Ssshh!
6-1
A real Nazi spy! You made him appear right behind those bushes!
Your Fairy Godfather IS rather remarkable, eh, m'boy?
Let's peek at him, Mr. O'Malley
Er—Shouldn't we hasten to inform the authorities?
It gifs medals from der Fuehrer!
Blow oop der powerhowz!
Vensday at eighd!
CROCKETT JOHNSON

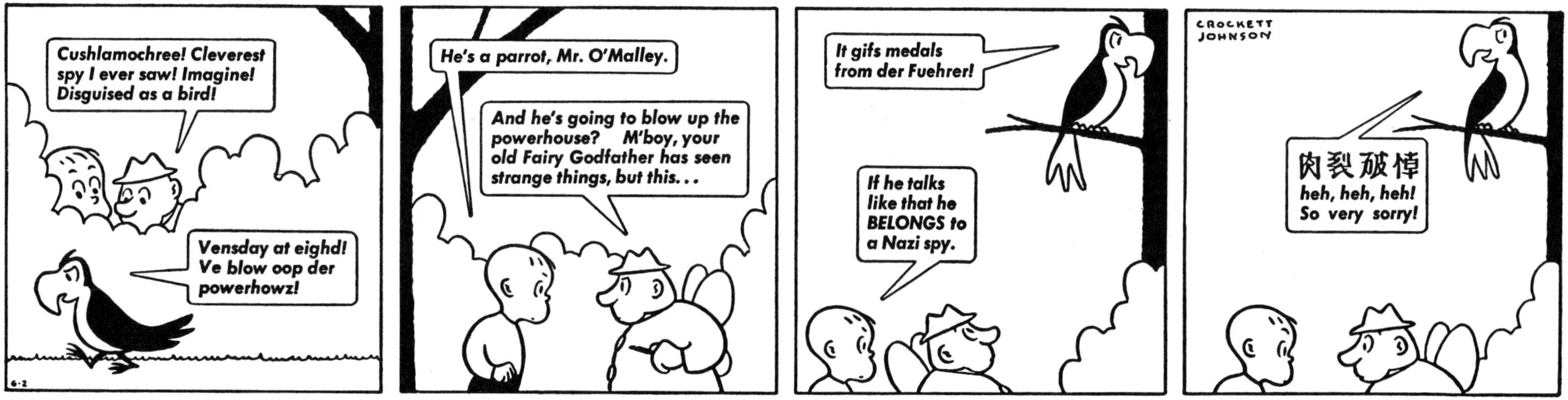
Cushlamochree! Cleverest spy I ever saw! Imagine! Disguised as a bird!
Vensday at eighd! Ve blow oop der powerhowz!
6-2
He's a parrot, Mr. O'Malley.
And he's going to blow up the powerhouse? M'boy, your old Fairy Godfather has seen strange things, but this...
It gifs medals from der Fuehrer!
If he talks like that he BELONGS to a Nazi spy.
CROCKETT JOHNSON
肉裂破悼 heh, heh, heh! So very sorry!

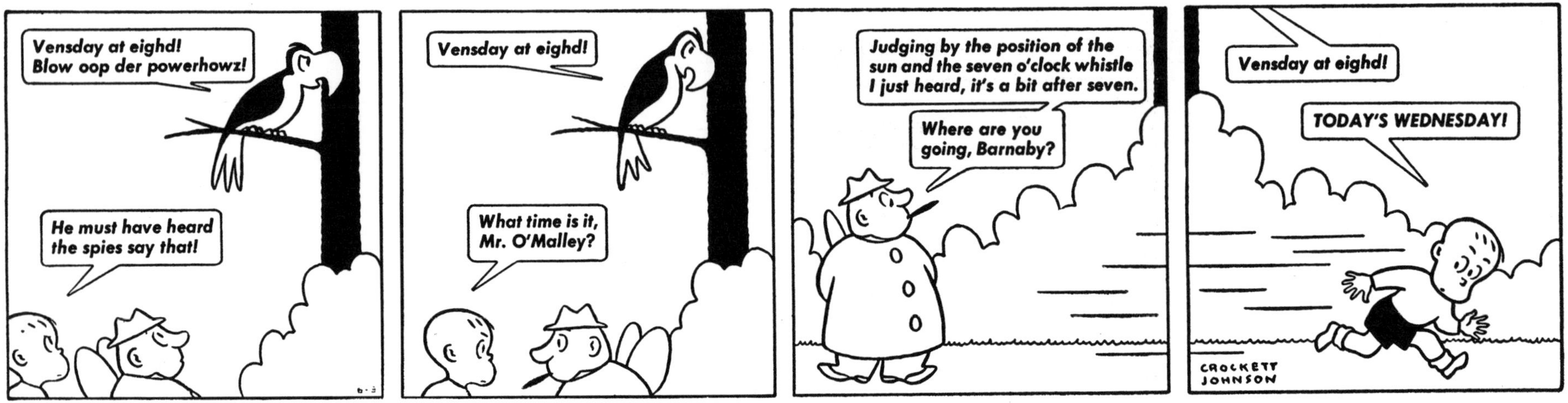
Vensday at eighd!
Blow oop der powerhowz!
He must have heard the spies say that!
Vensday at eighd!
What time is it, Mr. O'Malley?
Judging by the position of the sun and the seven o'clock whistle I just heard, it's a bit after seven.
Where are you going, Barnaby?
Vensday at eighd!
TODAY'S WEDNESDAY!
CROCKETT JOHNSON

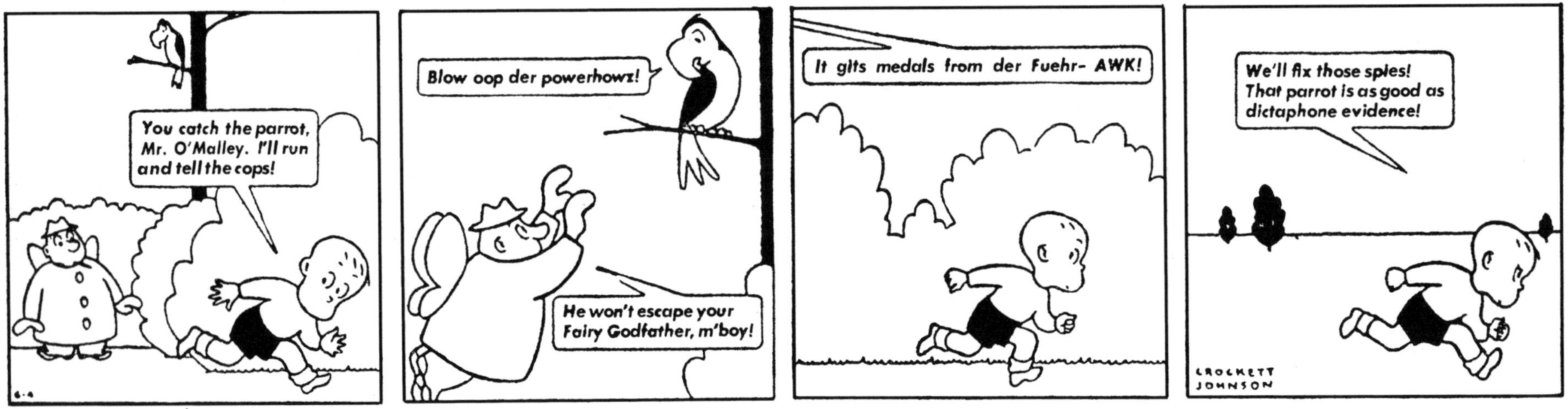
You catch the parrot, Mr. O'Malley. I'll run and tell the cops!
Blow oop der powerhowz!
He won't escape your Fairy Godfather, m'boy!
It gits medals from der Fuehr- AWK!
We'll fix those spies! That parrot is as good as dictaphone evidence!
CROCKETT JOHNSON

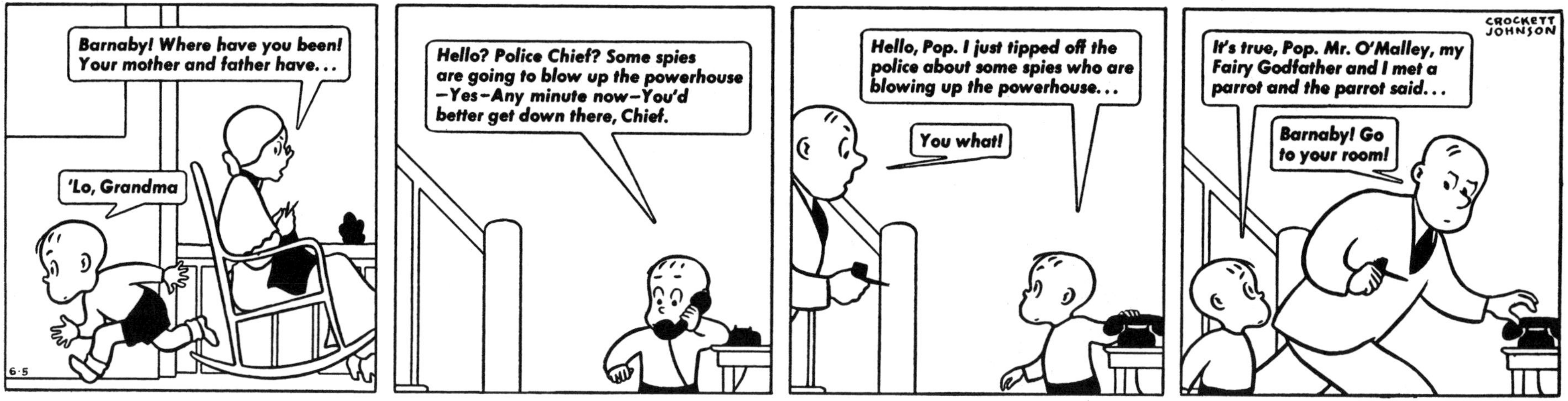
6·5
Barnaby! Where have you been! Your mother and father have...
'Lo, Grandma
Hello? Police Chief? Some spies are going to blow up the powerhouse —Yes—Any minute now—You'd better get down there, Chief.
Hello, Pop. I just tipped off the police about some spies who are blowing up the powerhouse...
You what!
It's true, Pop. Mr. O'Malley, my Fairy Godfather and I met a parrot and the parrot said...
Barnaby! Go to your room!
CROCKETT JOHNSON

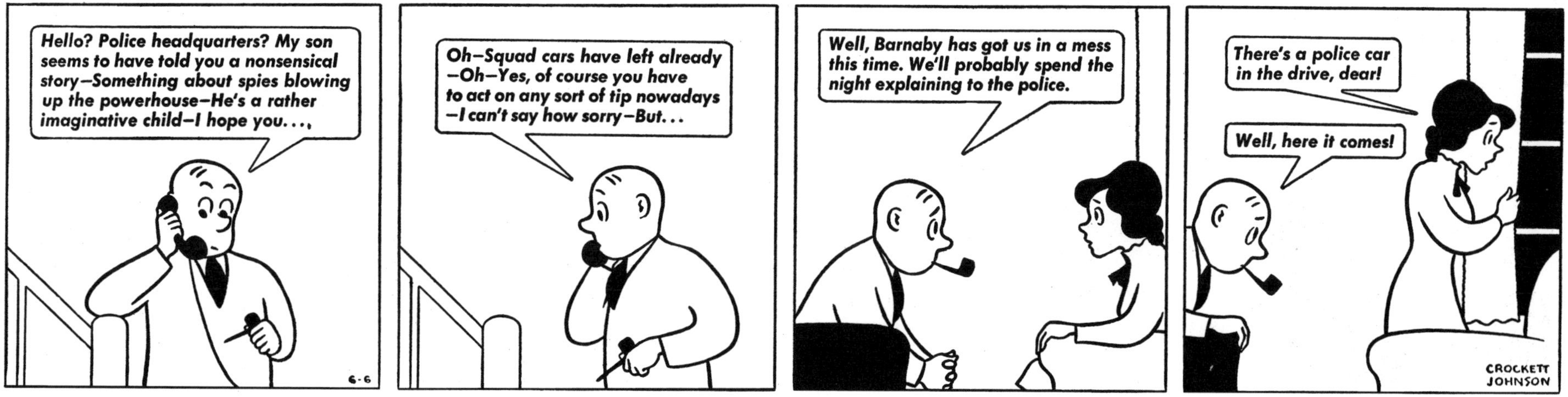
Hello? Police headquarters? My son seems to have told you a nonsensical story—Something about spies blowing up the powerhouse—He's a rather imaginative child—I hope you...,
6·6
Oh—Squad cars have left already —Oh—Yes, of course you have to act on any sort of tip nowadays —I can't say how sorry—But...
Well, Barnaby has got us in a mess this time. We'll probably spend the night explaining to the police.
There's a police car in the drive, dear!
Well, here it comes!
CROCKETT JOHNSON

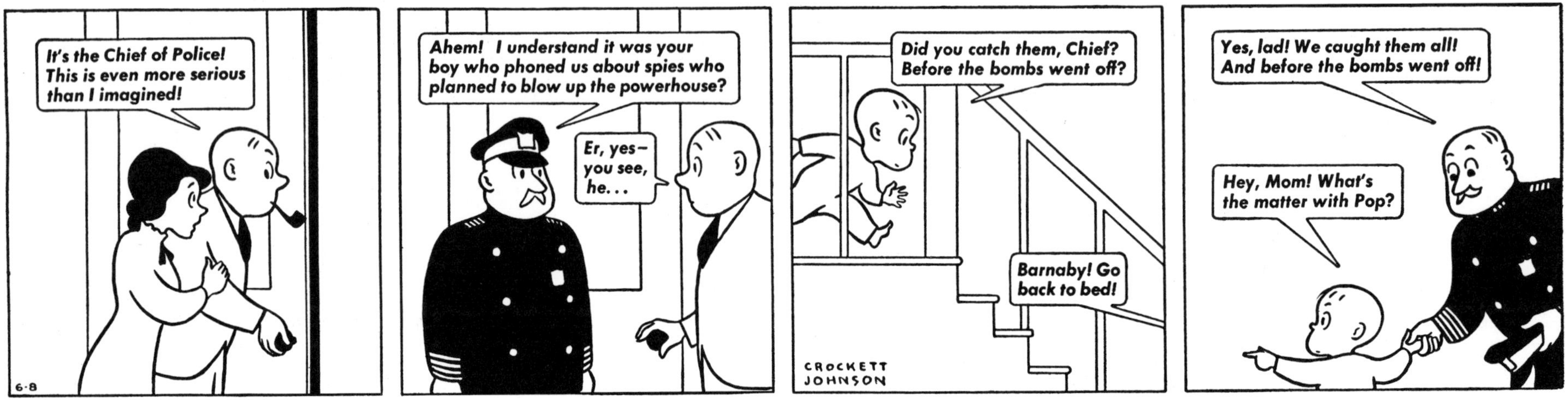
It's the Chief of Police! This is even more serious than I imagined!
6-8
Ahem! I understand it was your boy who phoned us about spies who planned to blow up the powerhouse?
Er, yes– you see, he...
Did you catch them, Chief? Before the bombs went off?
Barnaby! Go back to bed!
CROCKETT JOHNSON
Yes, lad! We caught them all! And before the bombs went off!
Hey, Mom! What's the matter with Pop?

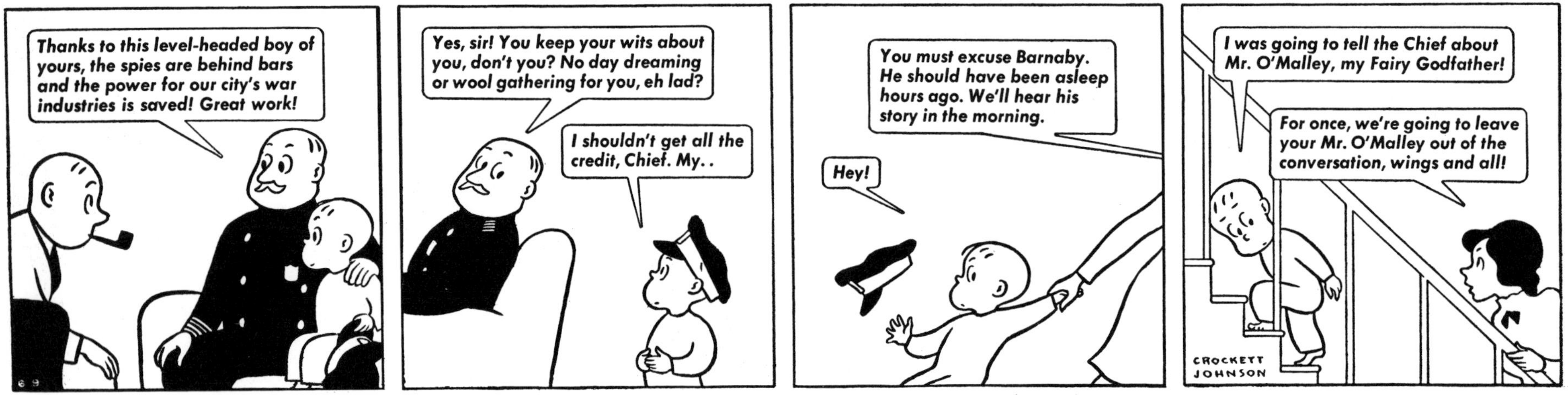
Thanks to this level-headed boy of yours, the spies are behind bars and the power for our city's war industries is saved! Great work!
6-9
Yes, sir! You keep your wits about you, don't you? No day dreaming or wool gathering for you, eh lad?
I shouldn't get all the credit, Chief. My..
You must excuse Barnaby. He should have been asleep hours ago. We'll hear his story in the morning.
Hey!
I was going to tell the Chief about Mr. O'Malley, my Fairy Godfather!
For once, we're going to leave your Mr. O'Malley out of the conversation, wings and all!
CROCKETT JOHNSON

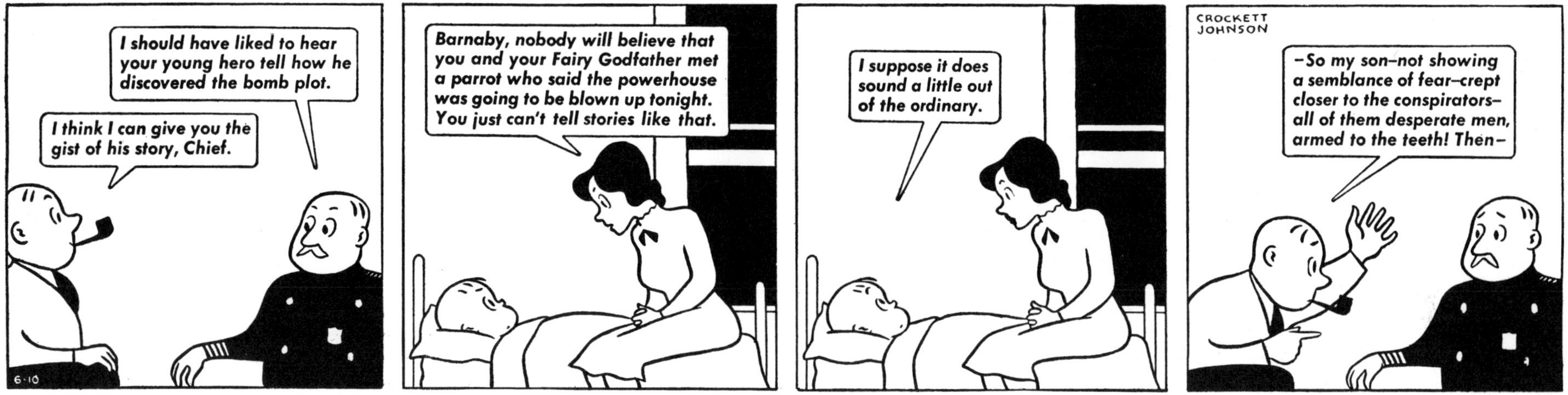
I think I can give you the gist of his story, Chief.
I should have liked to hear your young hero tell how he discovered the bomb plot.
Barnaby, nobody will believe that you and your Fairy Godfather met a parrot who said the powerhouse was going to be blown up tonight. You just can't tell stories like that.
I suppose it does sound a little out of the ordinary.
CROCKETT JOHNSON
–So my son–not showing a semblance of fear–crept closer to the conspirators–all of them desperate men, armed to the teeth! Then–

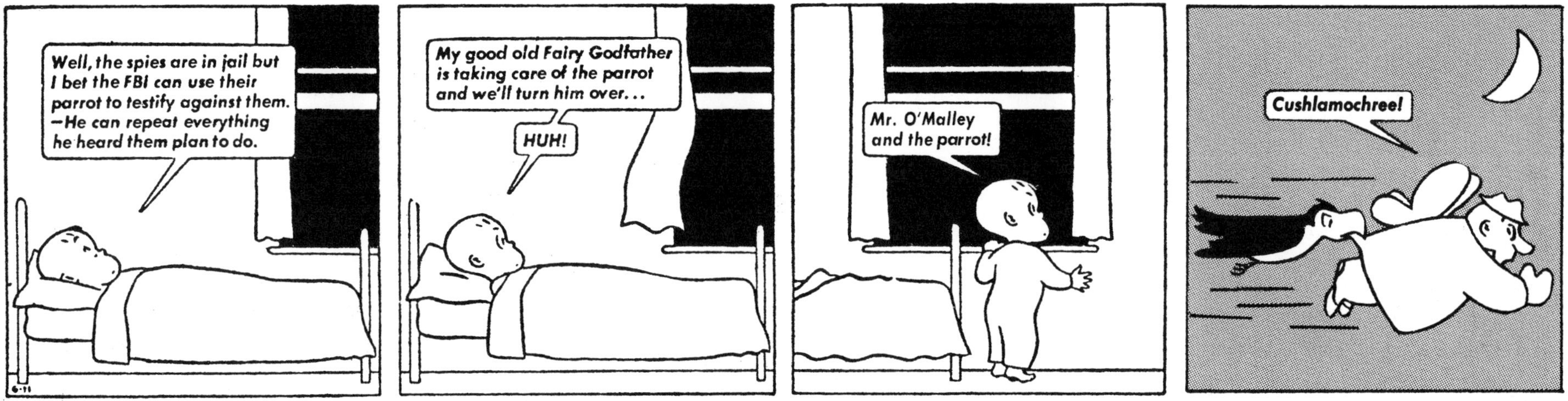
Well, the spies are in jail but I bet the FBI can use their parrot to testify against them. –He can repeat everything he heard them plan to do.
My good old Fairy Godfather is taking care of the parrot and we'll turn him over...
HUH!
Mr. O'Malley and the parrot!
Cushlamochree!

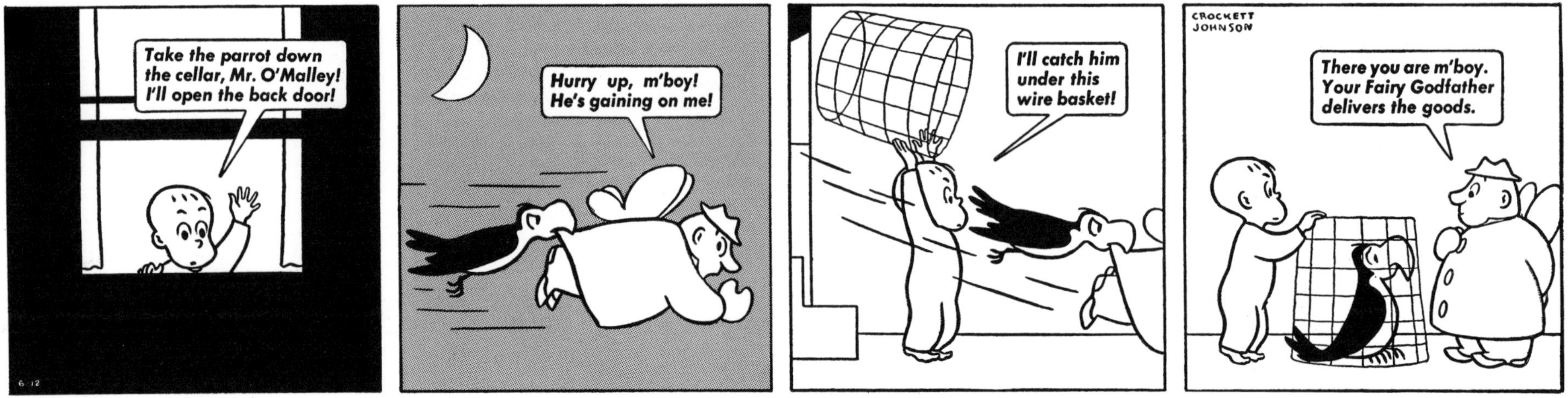
CROCKETT JOHNSON
Take the parrot down the cellar, Mr. O'Malley! I'll open the back door!
Hurry up, m'boy! He's gaining on me!
I'll catch him under this wire basket!
There you are m'boy. Your Fairy Godfather delivers the goods.
6-12

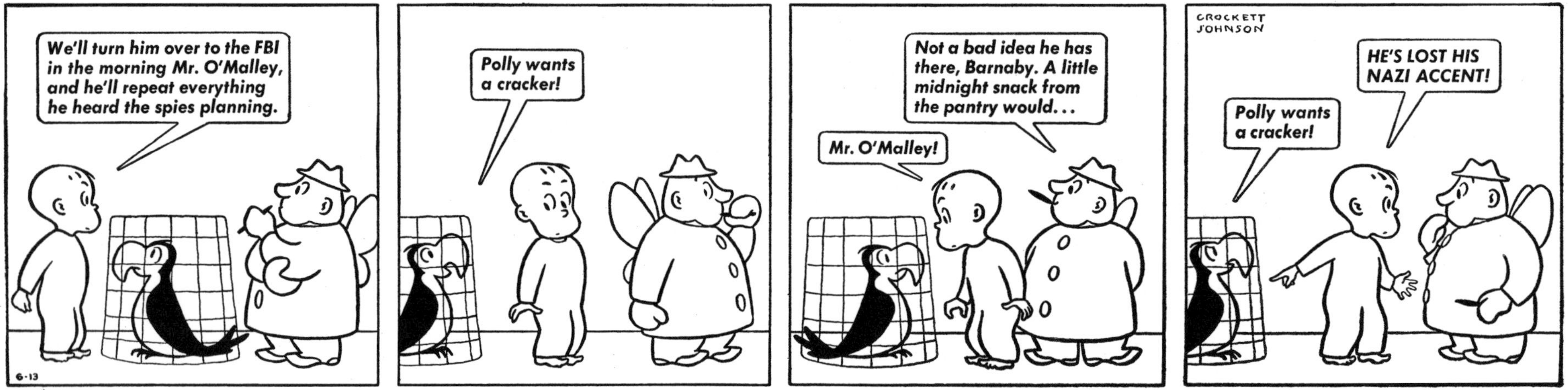
CROCKETT JOHNSON
We'll turn him over to the FBI in the morning Mr. O'Malley, and he'll repeat everything he heard the spies planning.
Polly wants a cracker!
Not a bad idea he has there, Barnaby. A little midnight snack from the pantry would...
Mr. O'Malley!
HE'S LOST HIS NAZI ACCENT!
Polly wants a cracker!
6-13

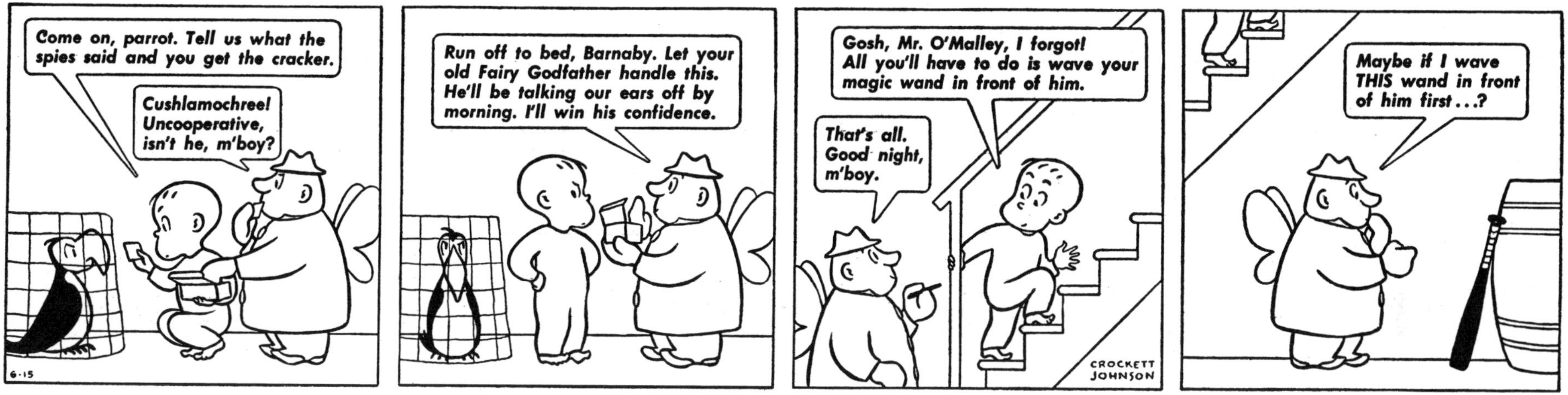
Come on, parrot. Tell us what the spies said and you get the cracker.
Cushlamochree! Uncooperative, isn't he, m'boy?
6·15
Run off to bed, Barnaby. Let your old Fairy Godfather handle this. He'll be talking our ears off by morning. I'll win his confidence.
Gosh, Mr. O'Malley, I forgot! All you'll have to do is wave your magic wand in front of him.
That's all. Good night, m'boy.
CROCKETT JOHNSON
Maybe if I wave THIS wand in front of him first...?

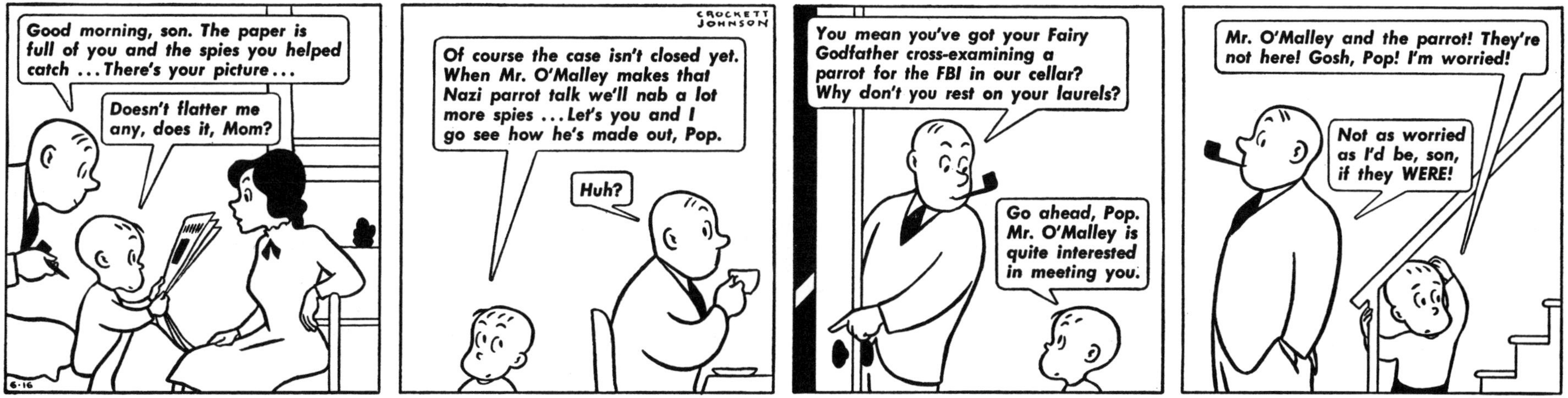
Good morning, son. The paper is full of you and the spies you helped catch ... There's your picture ...
Doesn't flatter me any, does it, Mom?
6·16
CROCKETT JOHNSON
Of course the case isn't closed yet. When Mr. O'Malley makes that Nazi parrot talk we'll nab a lot more spies ... Let's you and I go see how he's made out, Pop.
Huh?
You mean you've got your Fairy Godfather cross-examining a parrot for the FBI in our cellar? Why don't you rest on your laurels?
Go ahead, Pop. Mr. O'Malley is quite interested in meeting you.
Mr. O'Malley and the parrot! They're not here! Gosh, Pop! I'm worried!
Not as worried as I'd be, son, if they WERE!

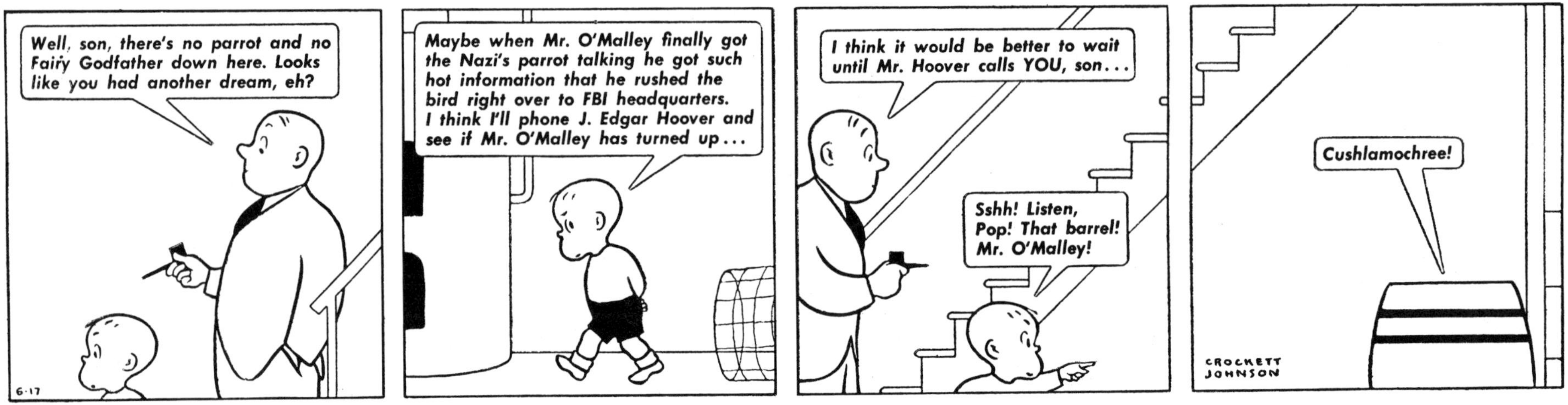
Well, son, there's no parrot and no Fairy Godfather down here. Looks like you had another dream, eh?
6·17
Maybe when Mr. O'Malley finally got the Nazi's parrot talking he got such hot information that he rushed the bird right over to FBI headquarters. I think I'll phone J. Edgar Hoover and see if Mr. O'Malley has turned up...
I think it would be better to wait until Mr. Hoover calls YOU, son...
Sshh! Listen, Pop! That barrel! Mr. O'Malley!
Cushlamochree!
CROCKETT JOHNSON

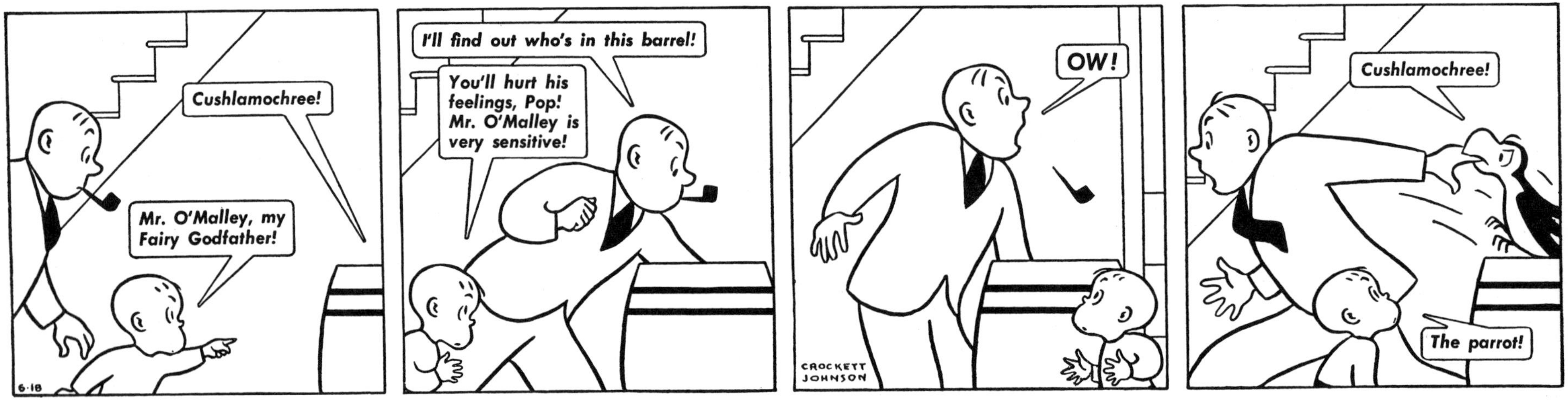
Cushlamochree!
Mr. O'Malley, my Fairy Godfather!
6·18
I'll find out who's in this barrel!
You'll hurt his feelings, Pop! Mr. O'Malley is very sensitive!
OW!
CROCKETT JOHNSON
Cushlamochree!
The parrot!

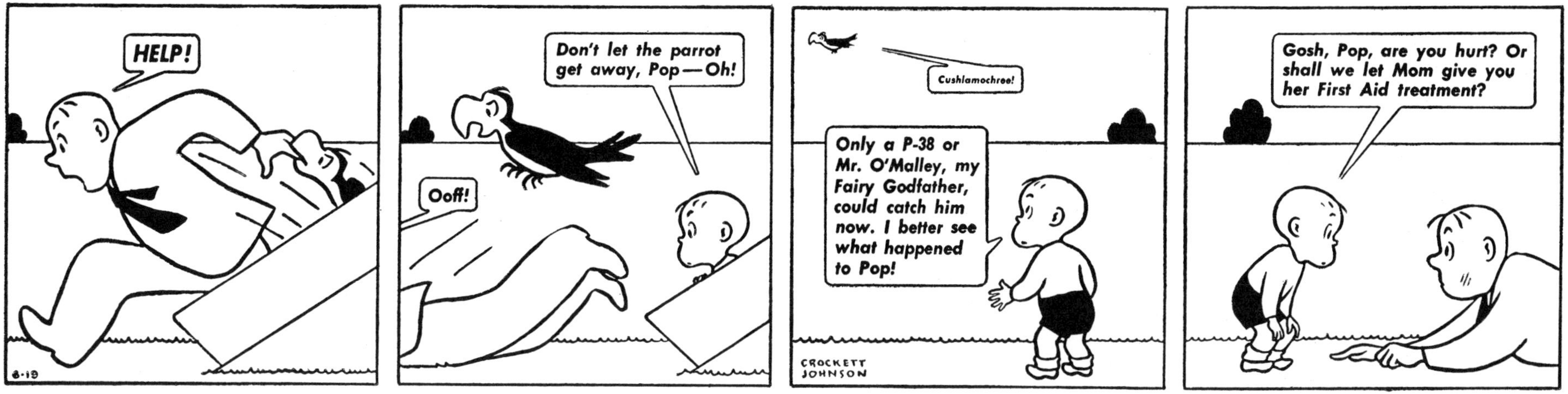
6-19
HELP!
Don't let the parrot get away, Pop—Oh!
Ooff!
Cushlamochree!
Only a P-38 or Mr. O'Malley, my Fairy Godfather, could catch him now. I better see what happened to Pop!
CROCKETT JOHNSON
Gosh, Pop, are you hurt? Or shall we let Mom give you her First Aid treatment?

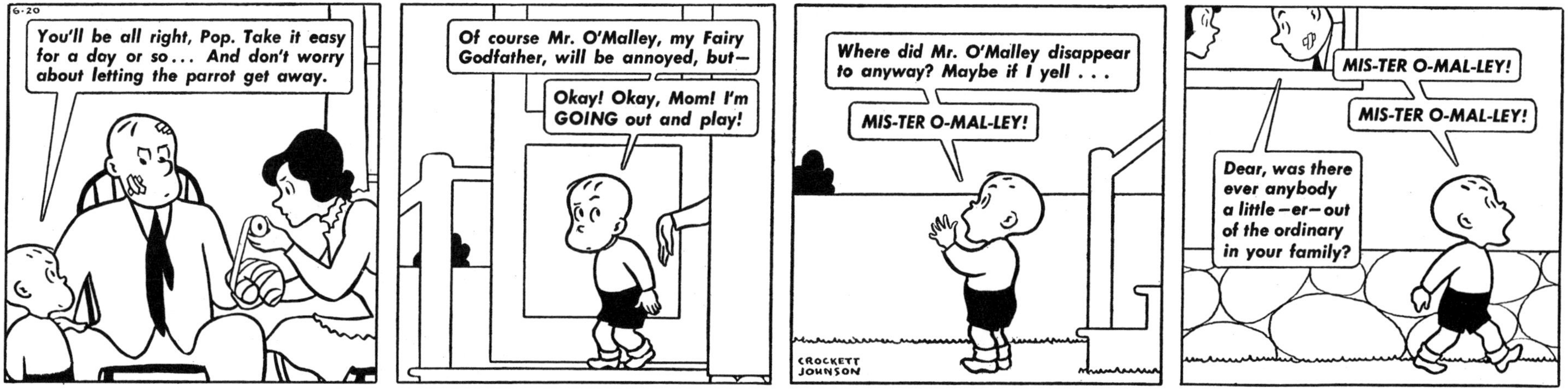
6-20
You'll be all right, Pop. Take it easy for a day or so... And don't worry about letting the parrot get away.
Of course Mr. O'Malley, my Fairy Godfather, will be annoyed, but—
Okay! Okay, Mom! I'm GOING out and play!
Where did Mr. O'Malley disappear to anyway? Maybe if I yell . . .
MIS-TER O-MAL-LEY!
CROCKETT JOHNSON
MIS-TER O-MAL-LEY!
MIS-TER O-MAL-LEY!
Dear, was there ever anybody a little—er—out of the ordinary in your family?

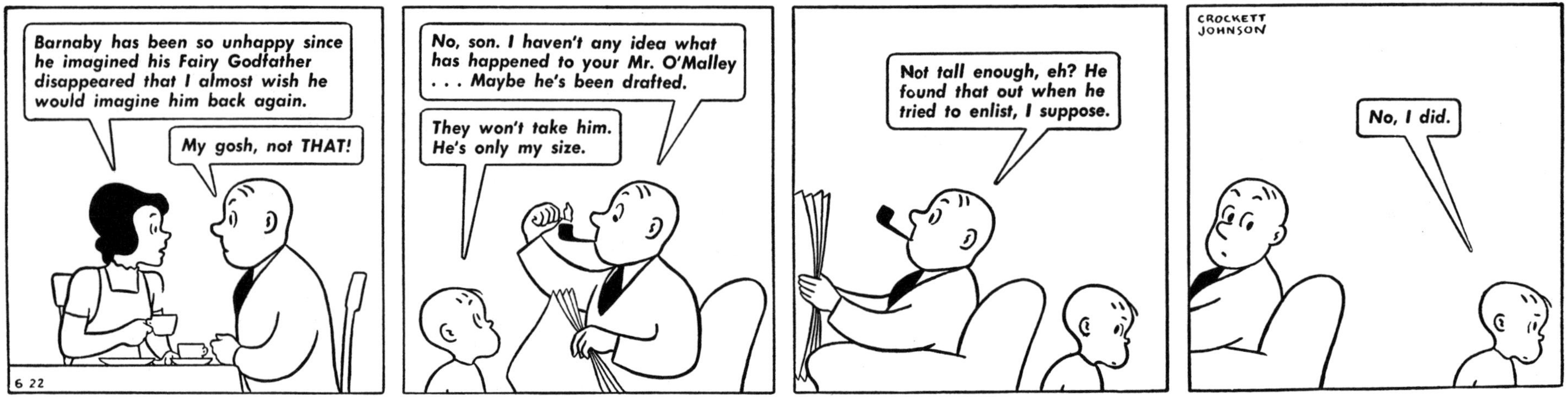

Barnaby has been so unhappy since he imagined his Fairy Godfather disappeared that I almost wish he would imagine him back again.
My gosh, not THAT!
6 22
No, son. I haven't any idea what has happened to your Mr. O'Malley . . . Maybe he's been drafted.
They won't take him. He's only my size.
Not tall enough, eh? He found that out when he tried to enlist, I suppose.
CROCKETT JOHNSON
No, I did.

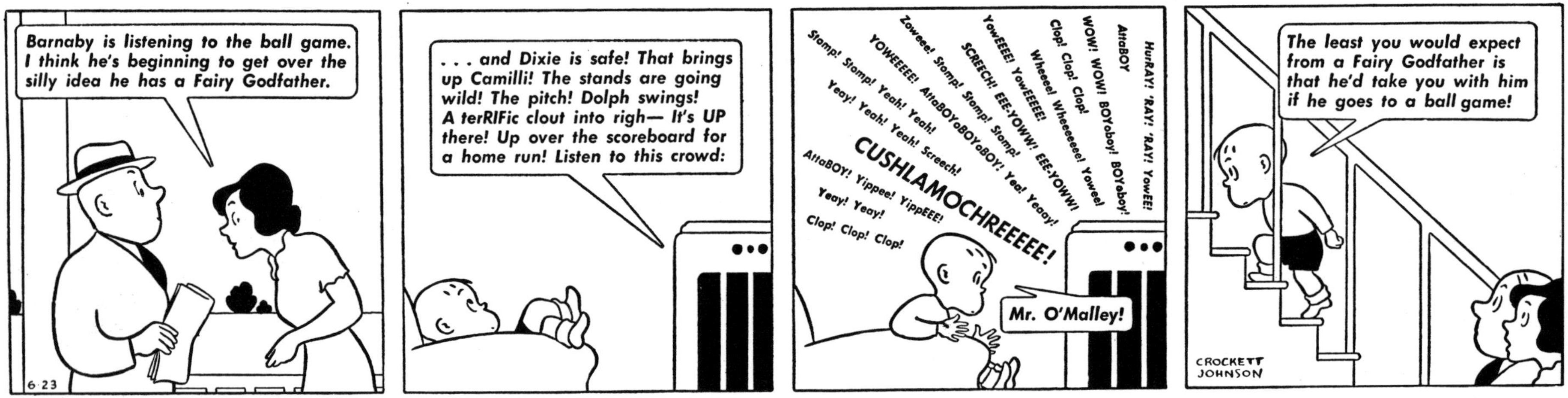

Barnaby is listening to the ball game. I think he's beginning to get over the silly idea he has a Fairy Godfather.
6·23
. . . and Dixie is safe! That brings up Camilli! The stands are going wild! The pitch! Dolph swings! A terRIFic clout into righ— It's UP there! Up over the scoreboard for a home run! Listen to this crowd:
HurRAY! 'RAY! 'RAY! YowEE!
AttaBOY
WOW! WOW! BOYoboy! BOYoboy!
Clop! Clop! Clop!
Wheeee! Wheeeeeee! Yowee!
YowEEEE! YowEEEEE!
SCREECH! EEE-YOWW! EEE-YOWW!
Zoweee! Stomp! Stomp! Stomp!
YOWEEEEE! AttaBOYoBOYoBOY! Yea! Yeaay!
Stomp! Stomp! Yeah! Yeah!
Yeay! Yeah! Yeah! Screech!
CUSHLAMOCHREEEEEE!
AttaBOY! Yippee! YippEEE!
Yeay! Yeay!
Clop! Clop! Clop!
Mr. O'Malley!
The least you would expect from a Fairy Godfather is that he'd take you with him if he goes to a ball game!
CROCKETT JOHNSON

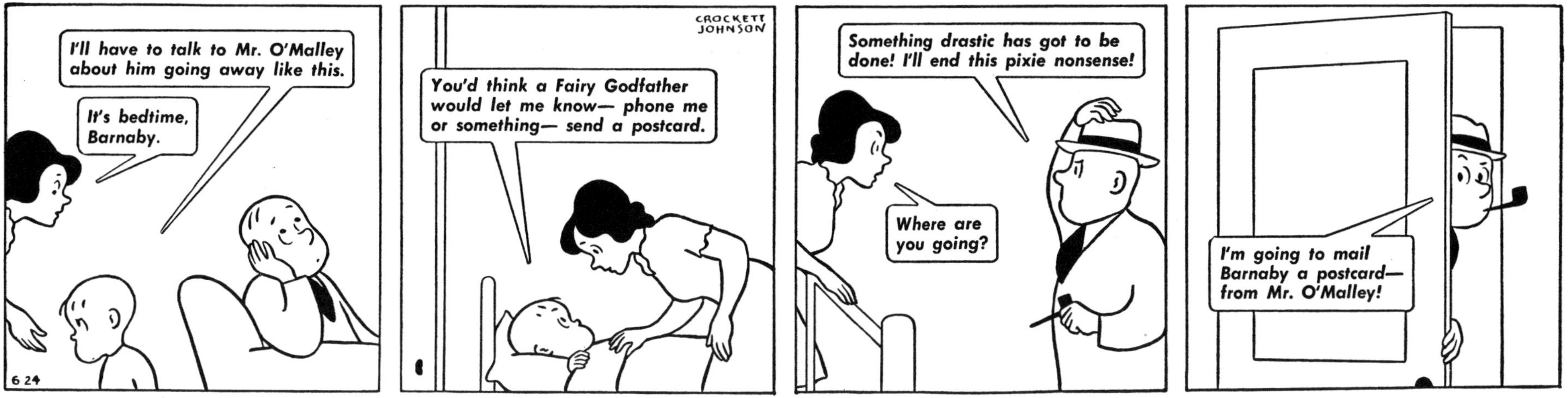

I'll have to talk to Mr. O'Malley about him going away like this.
It's bedtime, Barnaby.
6 24
CROCKETT JOHNSON
You'd think a Fairy Godfather would let me know— phone me or something— send a postcard.
Something drastic has got to be done! I'll end this pixie nonsense!
Where are you going?
I'm going to mail Barnaby a postcard— from Mr. O'Malley!

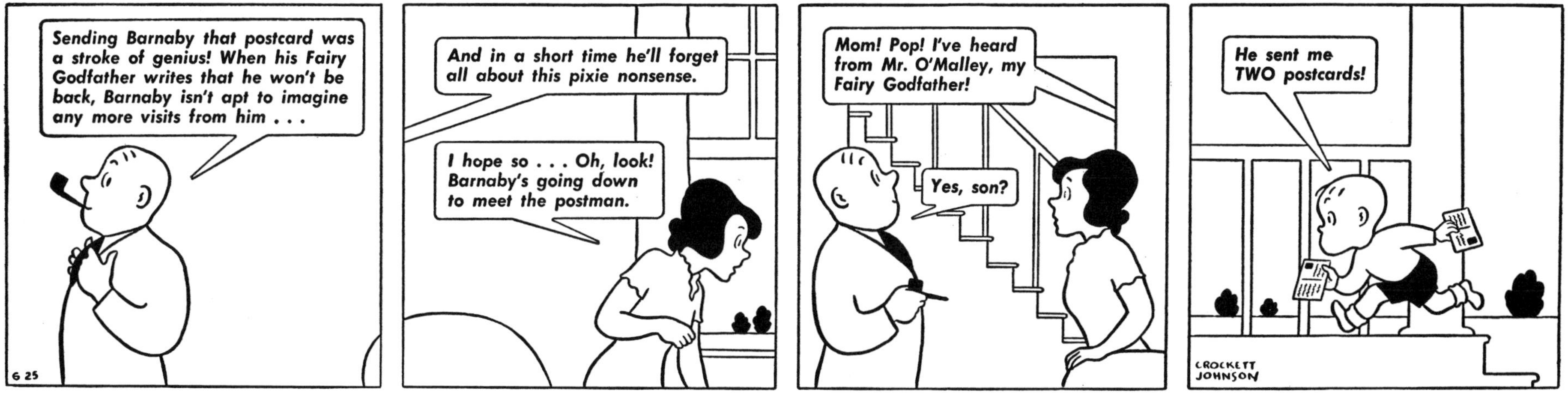

Sending Barnaby that postcard was a stroke of genius! When his Fairy Godfather writes that he won't be back, Barnaby isn't apt to imagine any more visits from him . . .
6 25
And in a short time he'll forget all about this pixie nonsense.
I hope so . . . Oh, look! Barnaby's going down to meet the postman.
Mom! Pop! I've heard from Mr. O'Malley, my Fairy Godfather!
Yes, son?
He sent me TWO postcards!
CROCKETT JOHNSON

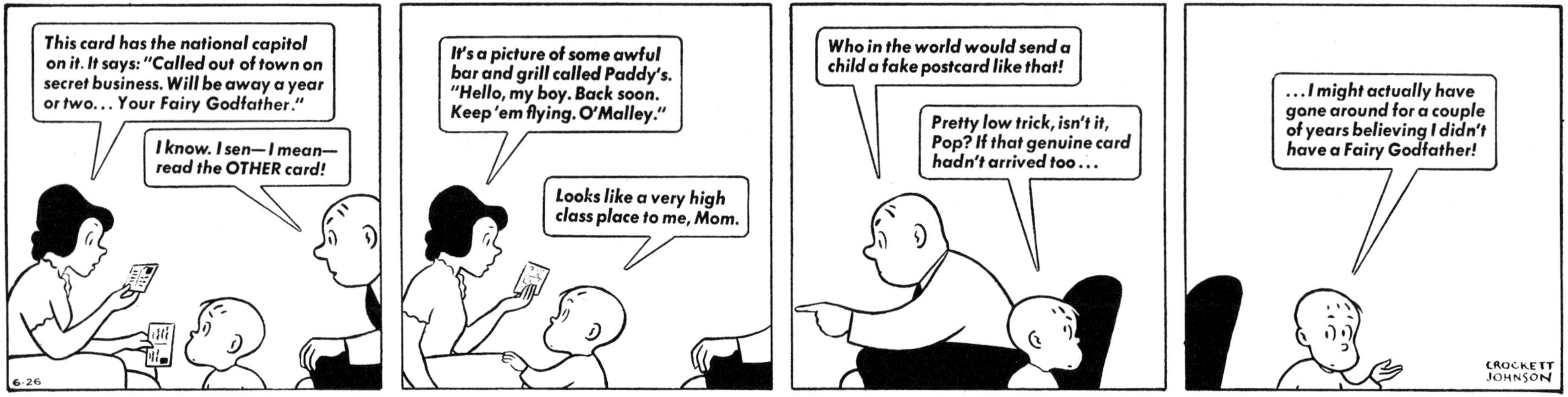
This card has the national capitol on it. It says: "Called out of town on secret business. Will be away a year or two... Your Fairy Godfather."
I know. I sen— I mean— read the OTHER card!
6-26
It's a picture of some awful bar and grill called Paddy's. "Hello, my boy. Back soon. Keep 'em flying. O'Malley."
Looks like a very high class place to me, Mom.
Who in the world would send a child a fake postcard like that!
Pretty low trick, isn't it, Pop? If that genuine card hadn't arrived too...
...I might actually have gone around for a couple of years believing I didn't have a Fairy Godfather!
CROCKETT JOHNSON

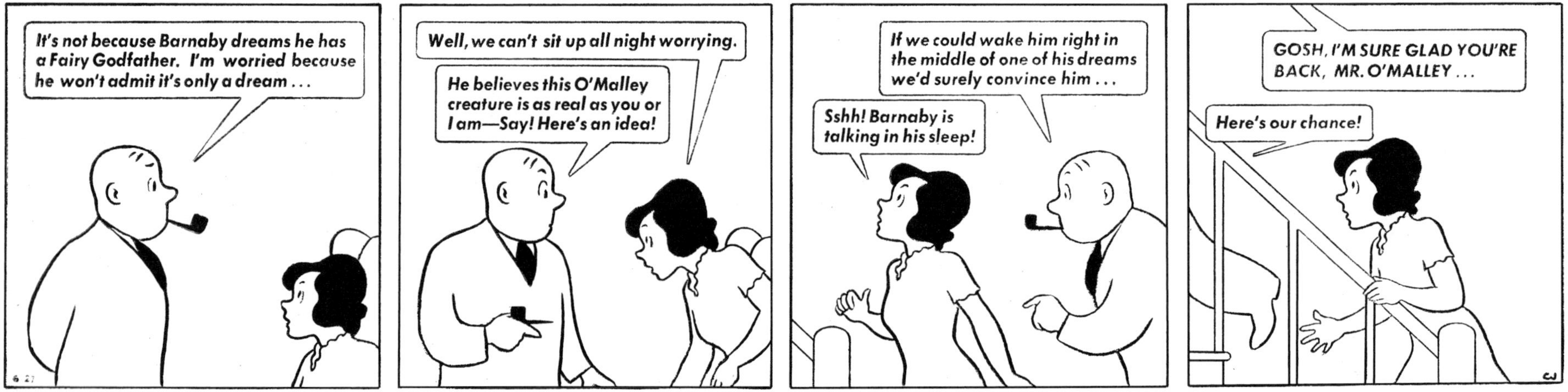
It's not because Barnaby dreams he has a Fairy Godfather. I'm worried because he won't admit it's only a dream...
Well, we can't sit up all night worrying.
He believes this O'Malley creature is as real as you or I am—Say! Here's an idea!
If we could wake him right in the middle of one of his dreams we'd surely convince him...
Sshh! Barnaby is talking in his sleep!
GOSH, I'M SURE GLAD YOU'RE BACK, MR. O'MALLEY...
Here's our chance!
CJ

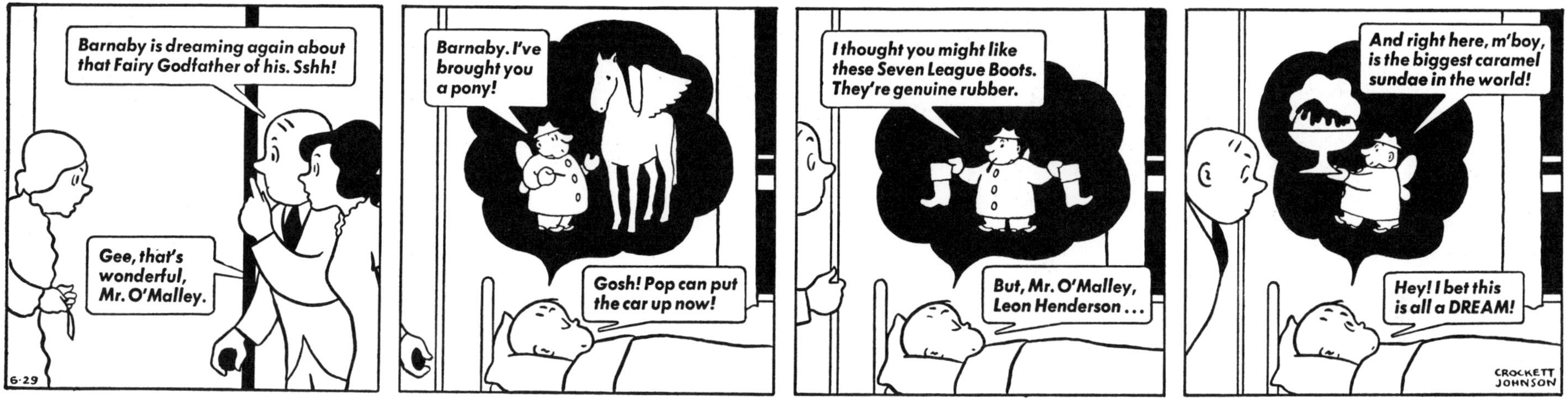
Barnaby is dreaming again about that Fairy Godfather of his. Sshh!
Gee, that's wonderful, Mr. O'Malley.
6-29
Barnaby. I've brought you a pony!
Gosh! Pop can put the car up now!
I thought you might like these Seven League Boots. They're genuine rubber.
But, Mr. O'Malley, Leon Henderson . . .
And right here, m'boy, is the biggest caramel sundae in the world!
Hey! I bet this is all a DREAM!
CROCKETT JOHNSON

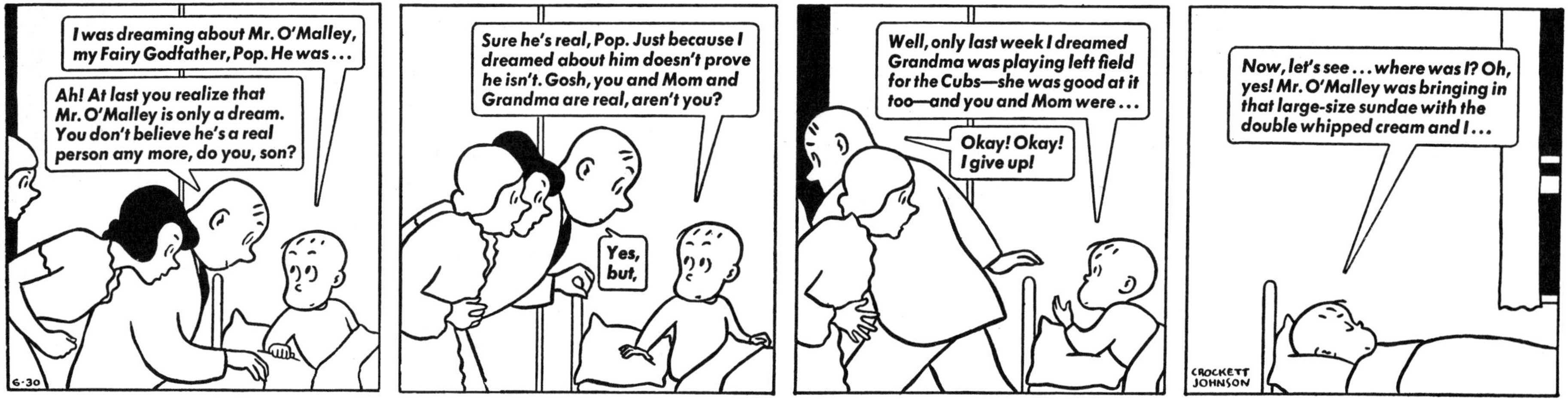
I was dreaming about Mr. O'Malley, my Fairy Godfather, Pop. He was . . .
Ah! At last you realize that Mr. O'Malley is only a dream. You don't believe he's a real person any more, do you, son?
6-30
Sure he's real, Pop. Just because I dreamed about him doesn't prove he isn't. Gosh, you and Mom and Grandma are real, aren't you?
Yes, but,
Well, only last week I dreamed Grandma was playing left field for the Cubs—she was good at it too—and you and Mom were . . .
Okay! Okay! I give up!
CROCKETT JOHNSON
Now, let's see . . . where was I? Oh, yes! Mr. O'Malley was bringing in that large-size sundae with the double whipped cream and I . . .

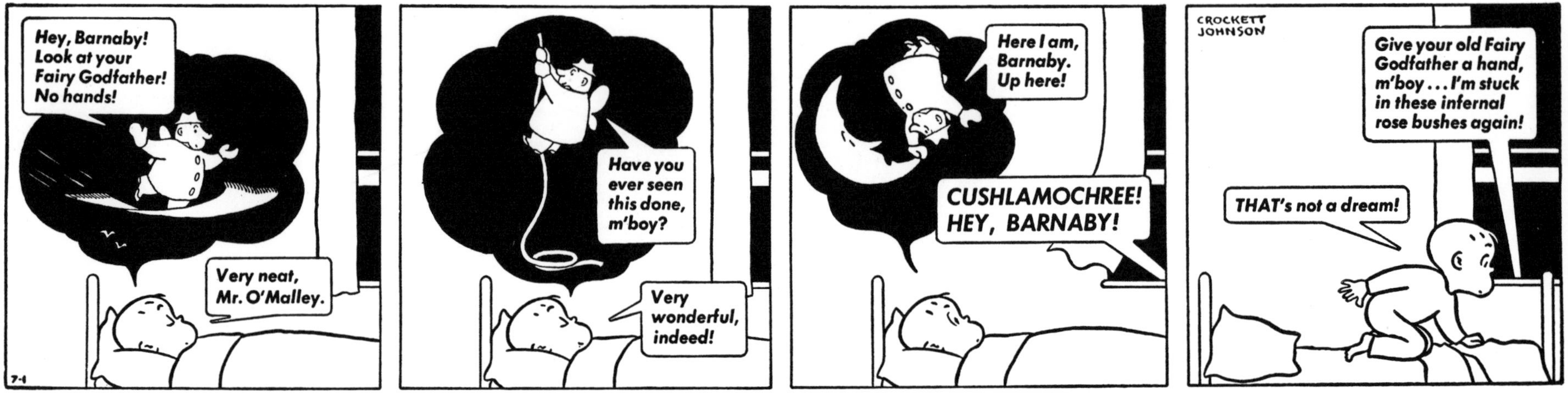
Hey, Barnaby!
Look at your
Fairy Godfather!
No hands!
Very neat,
Mr. O'Malley.
7-1
Have you
ever seen
this done,
m'boy?
Very
wonderful,
indeed!
Here I am,
Barnaby.
Up here!
CUSHLAMOCHREE!
HEY, BARNABY!
CROCKETT
JOHNSON
Give your old Fairy
Godfather a hand,
m'boy . . . I'm stuck
in these infernal
rose bushes again!
THAT's not a dream!

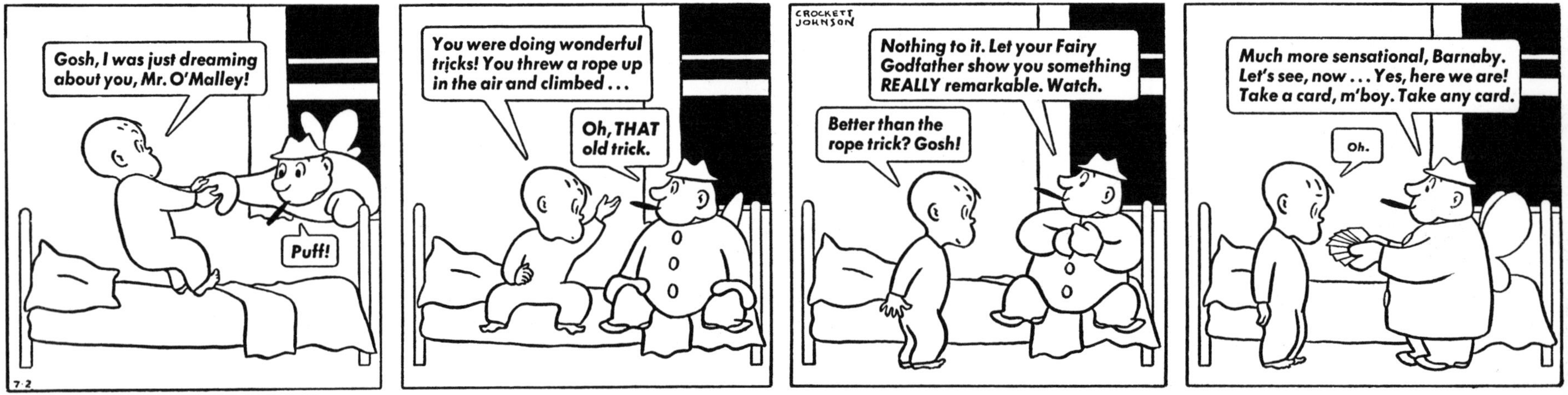
Gosh, I was just dreaming
about you, Mr. O'Malley!
Puff!
7-2
You were doing wonderful
tricks! You threw a rope up
in the air and climbed . . .
Oh, THAT
old trick.
CROCKETT
JOHNSON
Nothing to it. Let your Fairy
Godfather show you something
REALLY remarkable. Watch.
Better than the
rope trick? Gosh!
Much more sensational, Barnaby.
Let's see, now . . . Yes, here we are!
Take a card, m'boy. Take any card.
Oh.

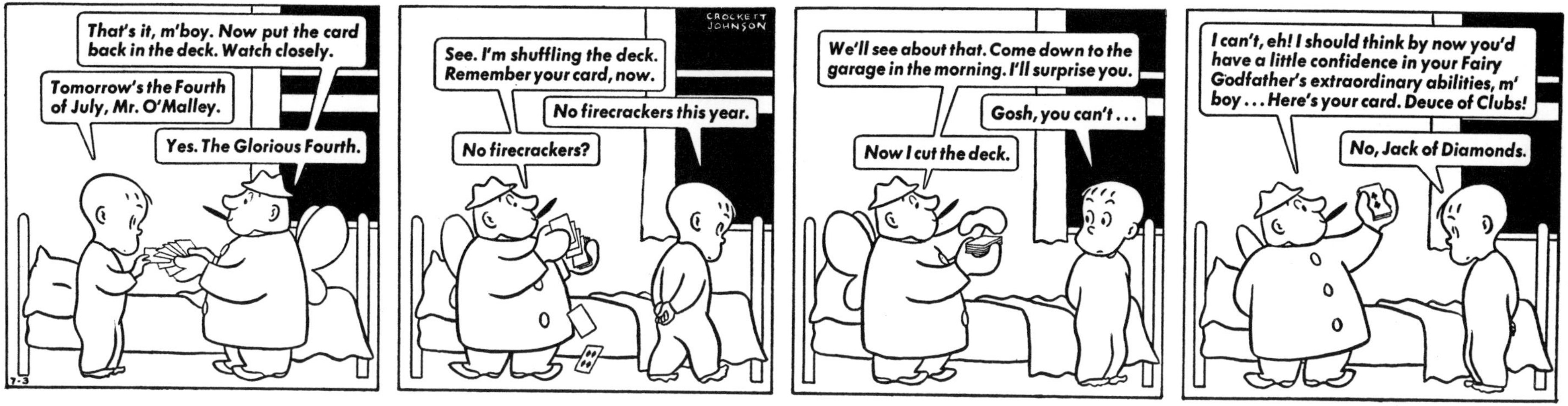
Tomorrow's the Fourth of July, Mr. O'Malley.
Yes. The Glorious Fourth.
That's it, m'boy. Now put the card back in the deck. Watch closely.
CROCKETT JOHNSON
No firecrackers?
See. I'm shuffling the deck. Remember your card, now.
No firecrackers this year.
Now I cut the deck.
We'll see about that. Come down to the garage in the morning. I'll surprise you.
Gosh, you can't . . .
I can't, eh! I should think by now you'd have a little confidence in your Fairy Godfather's extraordinary abilities, m' boy . . . Here's your card. Deuce of Clubs!
No, Jack of Diamonds.

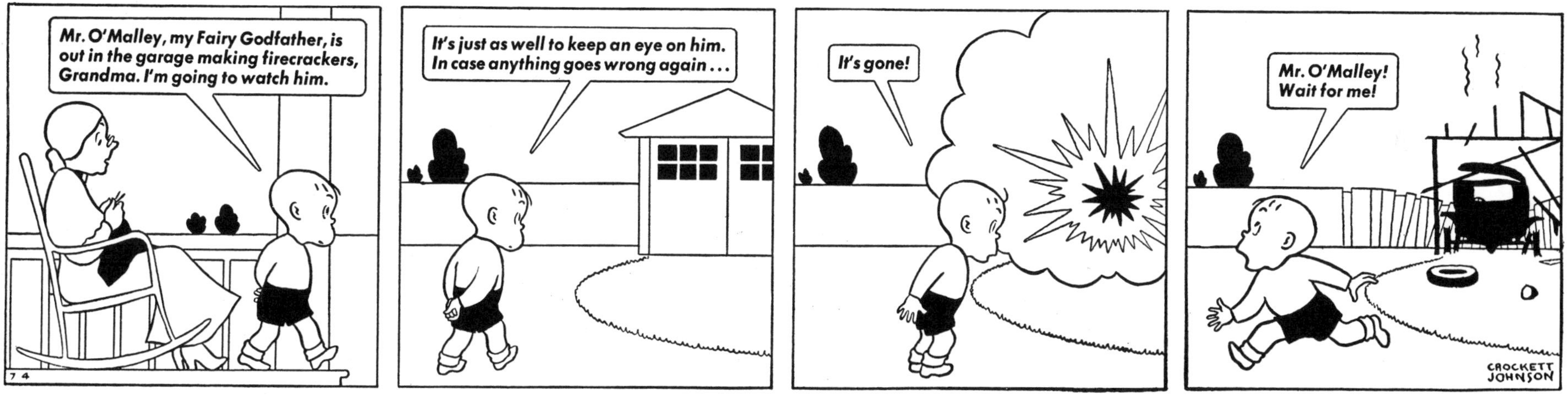
Mr. O'Malley, my Fairy Godfather, is out in the garage making firecrackers, Grandma. I'm going to watch him.
It's just as well to keep an eye on him. In case anything goes wrong again . . .
It's gone!
Mr. O'Malley! Wait for me!
CROCKETT JOHNSON

July 3 – 4

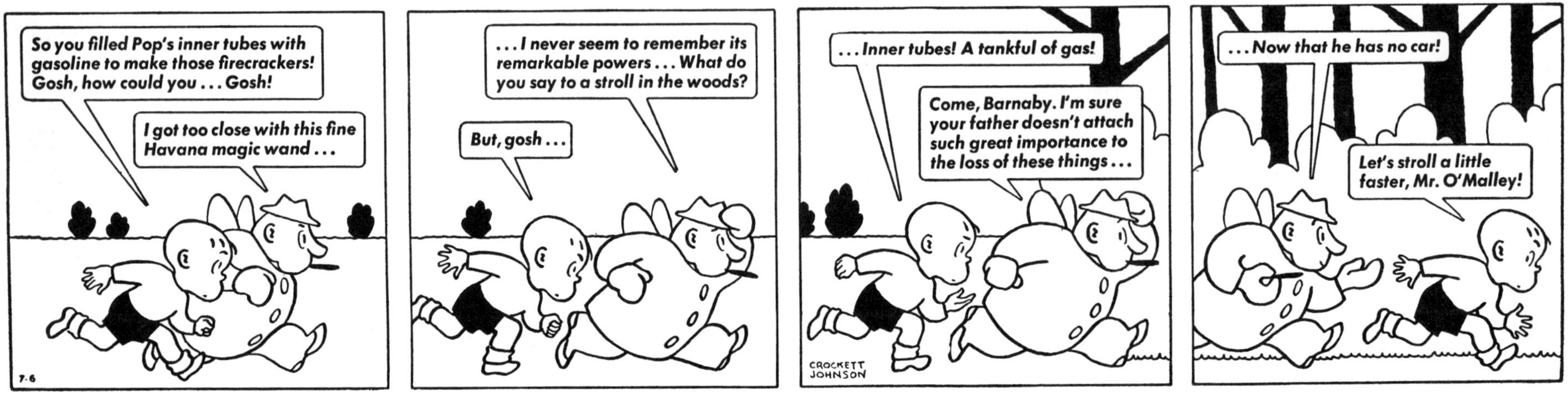
So you filled Pop's inner tubes with gasoline to make those firecrackers! Gosh, how could you . . . Gosh!
I got too close with this fine Havana magic wand . . .
7-6
But, gosh . . .
. . . I never seem to remember its remarkable powers . . . What do you say to a stroll in the woods?
. . . Inner tubes! A tankful of gas!
Come, Barnaby. I'm sure your father doesn't attach such great importance to the loss of these things . . .
CROCKETT JOHNSON
. . . Now that he has no car!
Let's stroll a little faster, Mr. O'Malley!

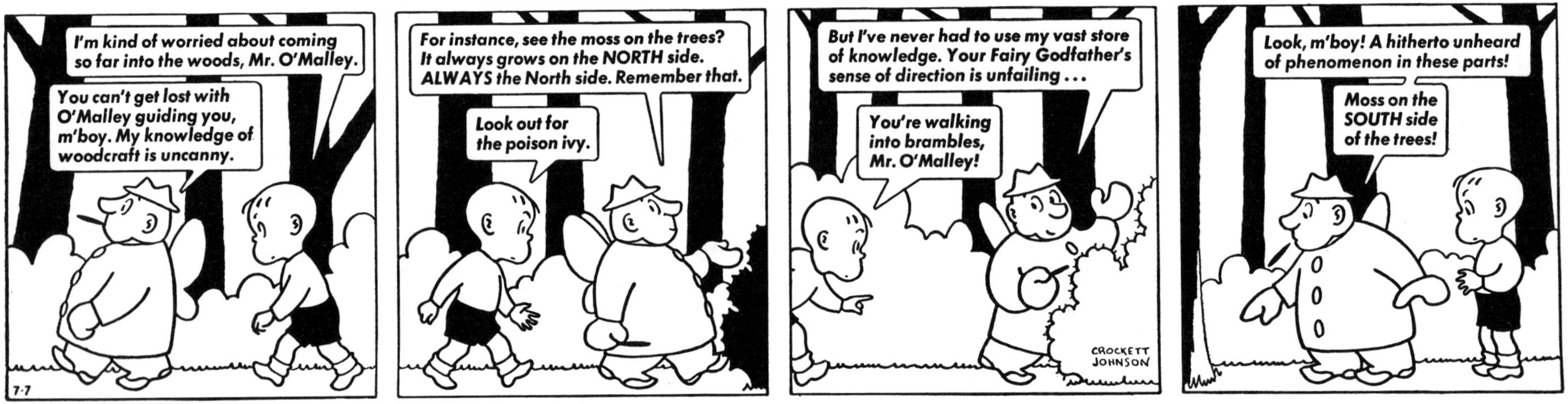
I'm kind of worried about coming so far into the woods, Mr. O'Malley.
You can't get lost with O'Malley guiding you, m'boy. My knowledge of woodcraft is uncanny.
7-7
For instance, see the moss on the trees? It always grows on the NORTH side. ALWAYS the North side. Remember that.
Look out for the poison ivy.
But I've never had to use my vast store of knowledge. Your Fairy Godfather's sense of direction is unfailing . . .
You're walking into brambles, Mr. O'Malley!
CROCKETT JOHNSON
Look, m'boy! A hitherto unheard of phenomenon in these parts!
Moss on the SOUTH side of the trees!

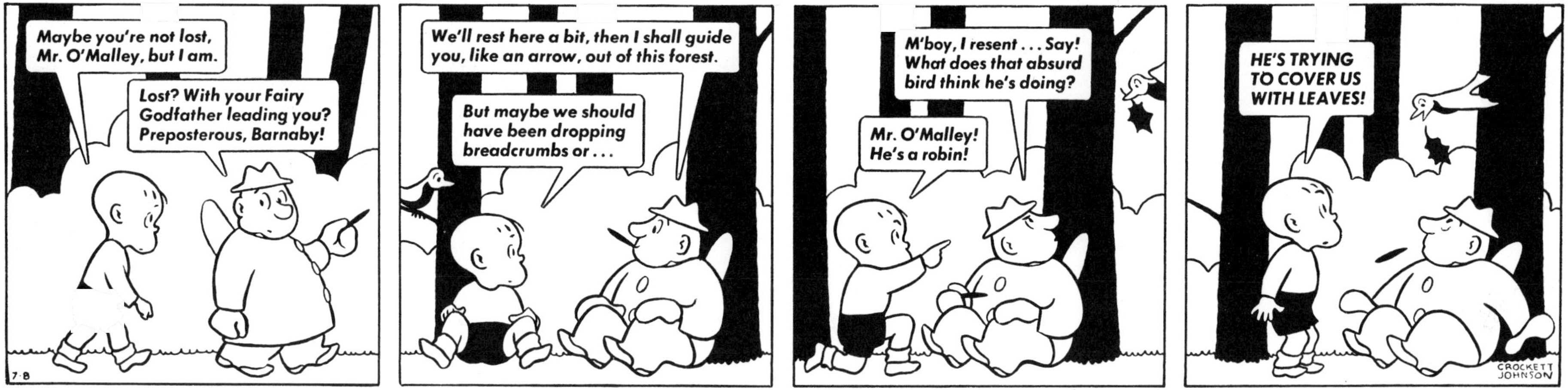
Maybe you're not lost, Mr. O'Malley, but I am.
Lost? With your Fairy Godfather leading you? Preposterous, Barnaby!
7-8
We'll rest here a bit, then I shall guide you, like an arrow, out of this forest.
But maybe we should have been dropping breadcrumbs or . . .
M'boy, I resent . . . Say! What does that absurd bird think he's doing?
Mr. O'Malley! He's a robin!
HE'S TRYING TO COVER US WITH LEAVES!
CROCKETT JOHNSON

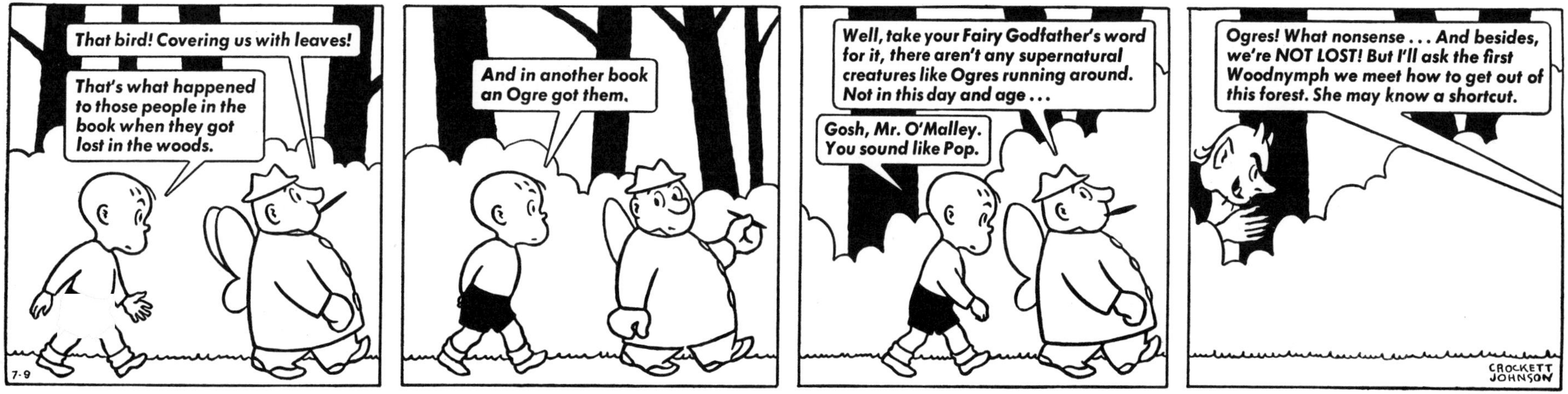
That bird! Covering us with leaves!
That's what happened to those people in the book when they got lost in the woods.
7-9
And in another book an Ogre got them.
Well, take your Fairy Godfather's word for it, there aren't any supernatural creatures like Ogres running around. Not in this day and age . . .
Gosh, Mr. O'Malley. You sound like Pop.
Ogres! What nonsense . . . And besides, we're NOT LOST! But I'll ask the first Woodnymph we meet how to get out of this forest. She may know a shortcut.
CROCKETT JOHNSON

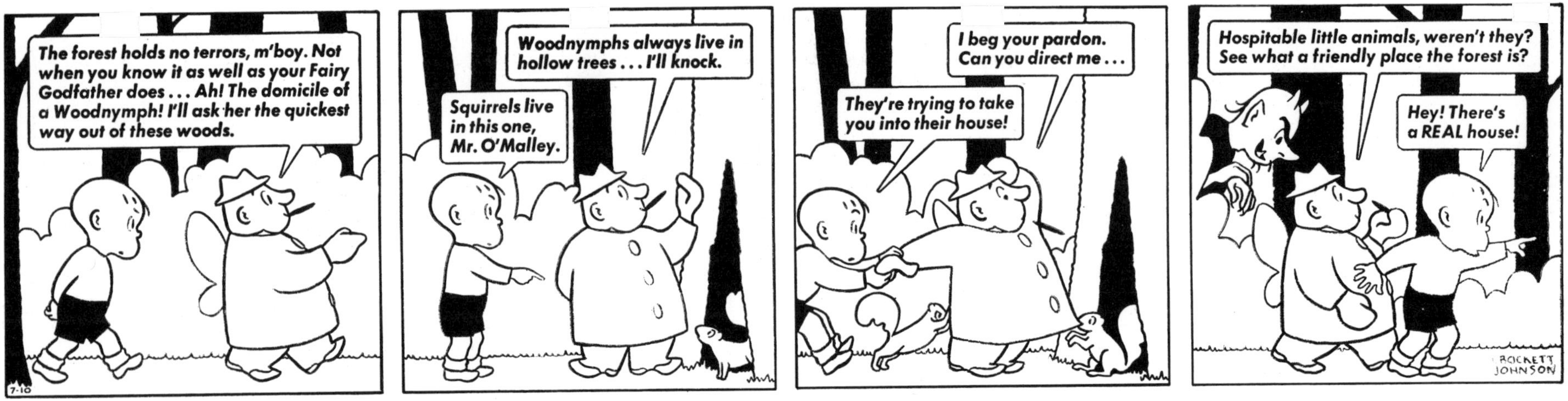
The forest holds no terrors, m'boy. Not when you know it as well as your Fairy Godfather does . . . Ah! The domicile of a Woodnymph! I'll ask her the quickest way out of these woods.
7-10
Woodnymphs always live in hollow trees . . . I'll knock.
Squirrels live in this one, Mr. O'Malley.
I beg your pardon. Can you direct me . . .
They're trying to take you into their house!
Hospitable little animals, weren't they? See what a friendly place the forest is?
Hey! There's a REAL house!
CROCKETT JOHNSON

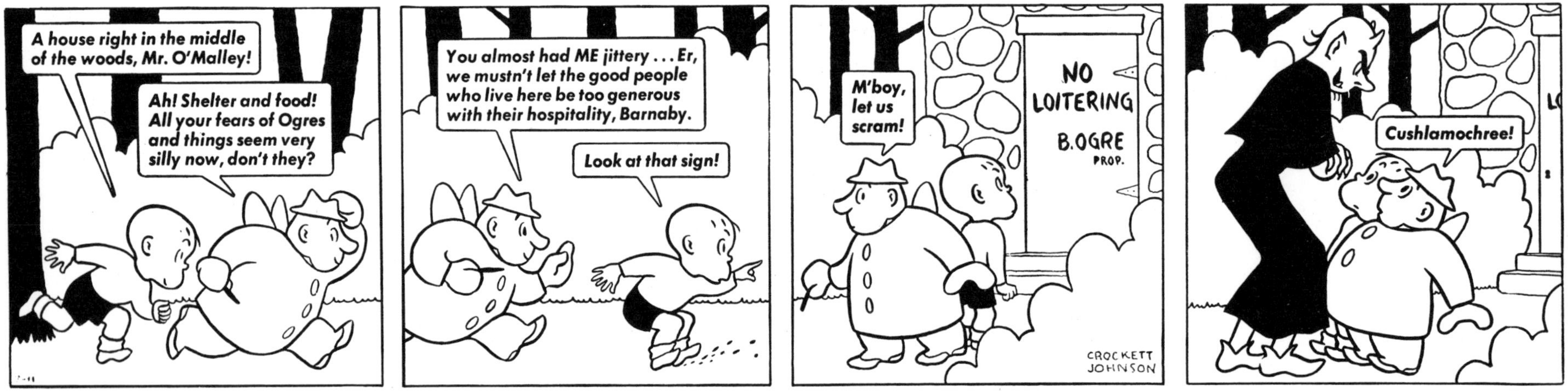
A house right in the middle of the woods, Mr. O'Malley!
Ah! Shelter and food! All your fears of Ogres and things seem very silly now, don't they?
You almost had ME jittery . . . Er, we mustn't let the good people who live here be too generous with their hospitality, Barnaby.
Look at that sign!
M'boy, let us scram!
NO LOITERING
B. OGRE PROP.
CROCKETT JOHNSON
Cushlamochree!

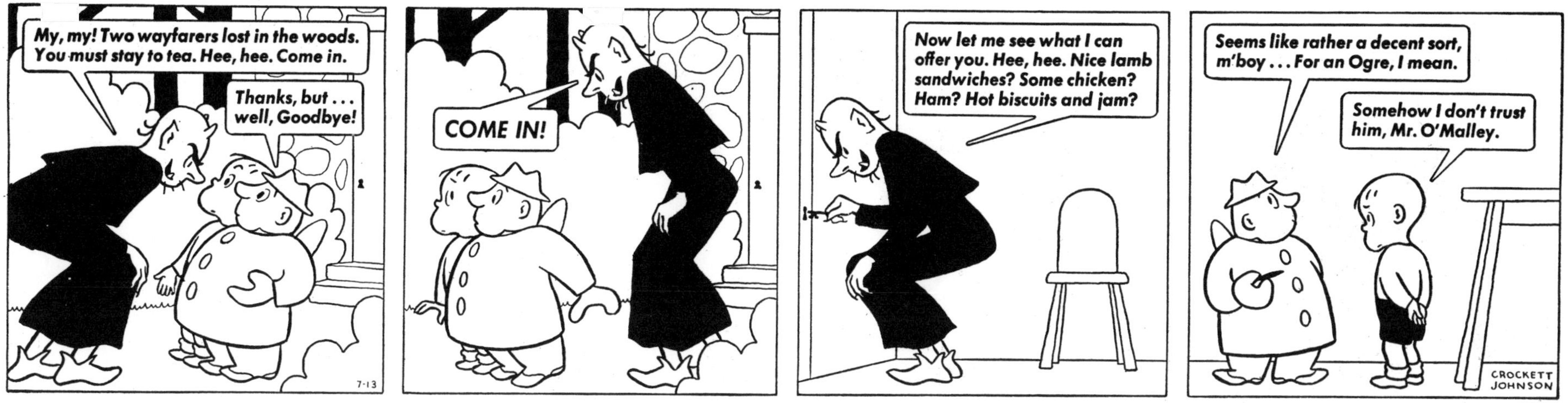
My, my! Two wayfarers lost in the woods. You must stay to tea. Hee, hee. Come in.
Thanks, but . . . well, Goodbye!
7-13
COME IN!
Now let me see what I can offer you. Hee, hee. Nice lamb sandwiches? Some chicken? Ham? Hot biscuits and jam?
Seems like rather a decent sort, m'boy . . . For an Ogre, I mean.
Somehow I don't trust him, Mr. O'Malley.
CROCKETT JOHNSON

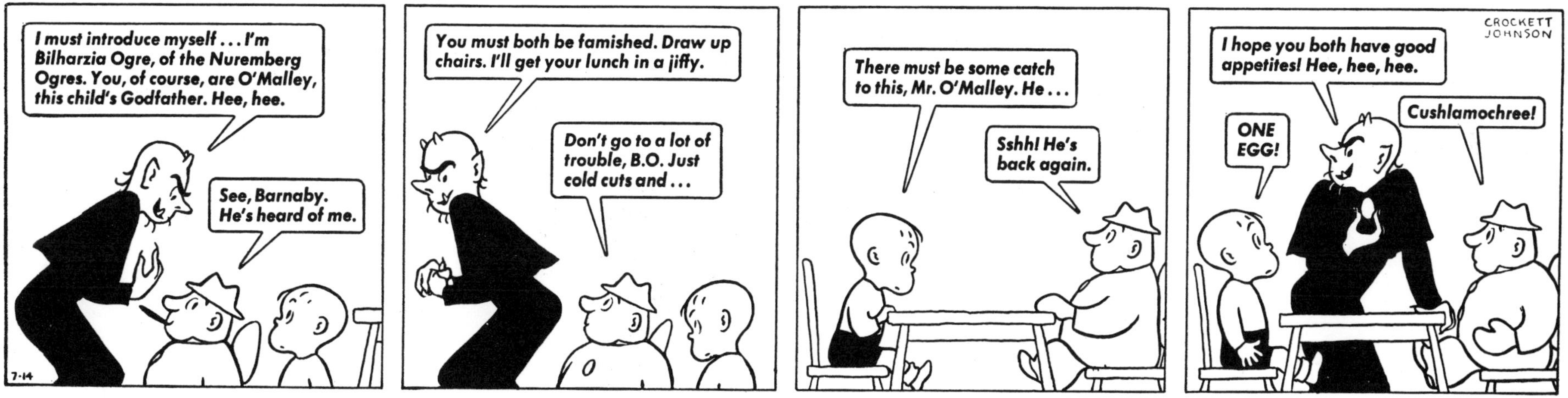
I must introduce myself . . . I'm Bilharzia Ogre, of the Nuremberg Ogres. You, of course, are O'Malley, this child's Godfather. Hee, hee.
See, Barnaby. He's heard of me.
7-14
You must both be famished. Draw up chairs. I'll get your lunch in a jiffy.
Don't go to a lot of trouble, B.O. Just cold cuts and . . .
There must be some catch to this, Mr. O'Malley. He . . .
Sshh! He's back again.
CROCKETT JOHNSON
I hope you both have good appetites! Hee, hee, hee.
ONE EGG!
Cushlamochree!

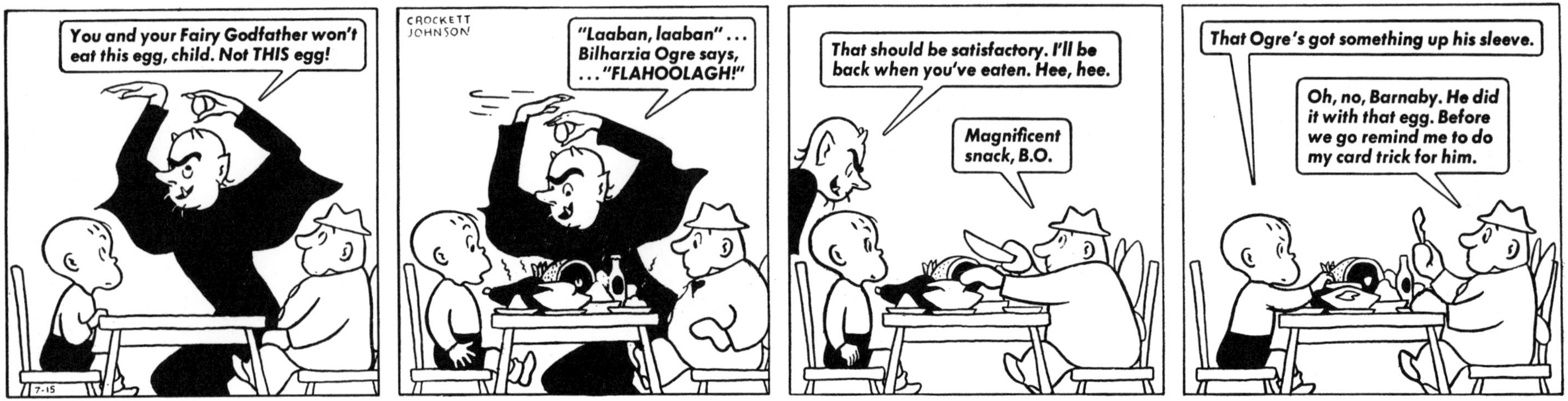
7-15
You and your Fairy Godfather won't eat this egg, child. Not THIS egg!
CROCKETT JOHNSON
"Laaban, laaban" . . . Bilharzia Ogre says, . . . "FLAHOOLAGH!"
That should be satisfactory. I'll be back when you've eaten. Hee, hee.
Magnificent snack, B.O.
That Ogre's got something up his sleeve.
Oh, no, Barnaby. He did it with that egg. Before we go remind me to do my card trick for him.

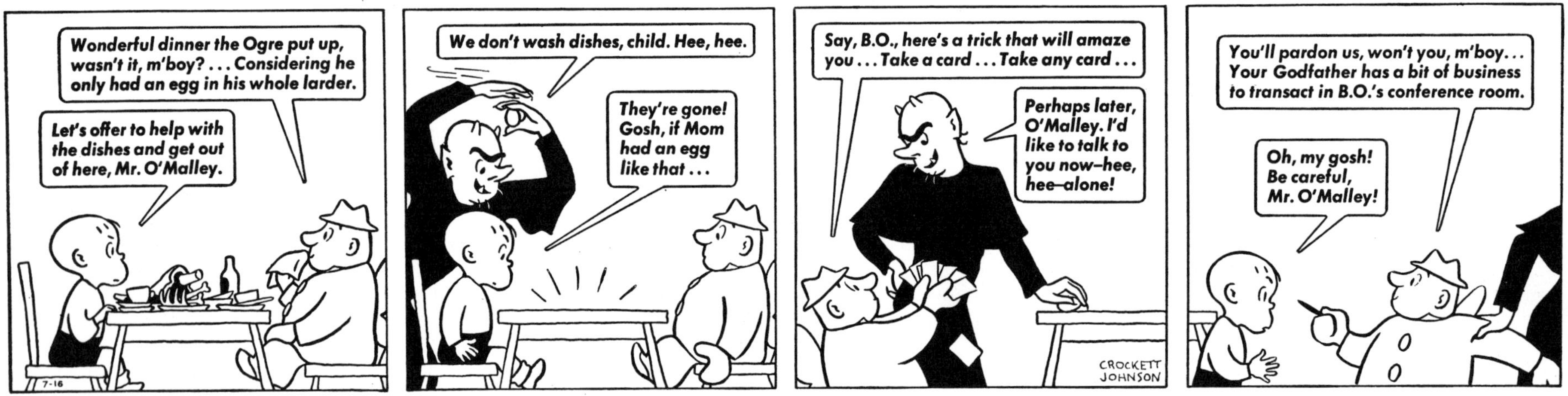
7-16
Wonderful dinner the Ogre put up, wasn't it, m'boy? . . . Considering he only had an egg in his whole larder.
Let's offer to help with the dishes and get out of here, Mr. O'Malley.
We don't wash dishes, child. Hee, hee.
They're gone! Gosh, if Mom had an egg like that . . .
Say, B.O., here's a trick that will amaze you . . . Take a card . . . Take any card . . .
Perhaps later, O'Malley. I'd like to talk to you now—hee, hee—alone!
CROCKETT JOHNSON
You'll pardon us, won't you, m'boy. . . Your Godfather has a bit of business to transact in B.O.'s conference room.
Oh, my gosh! Be careful, Mr. O'Malley!

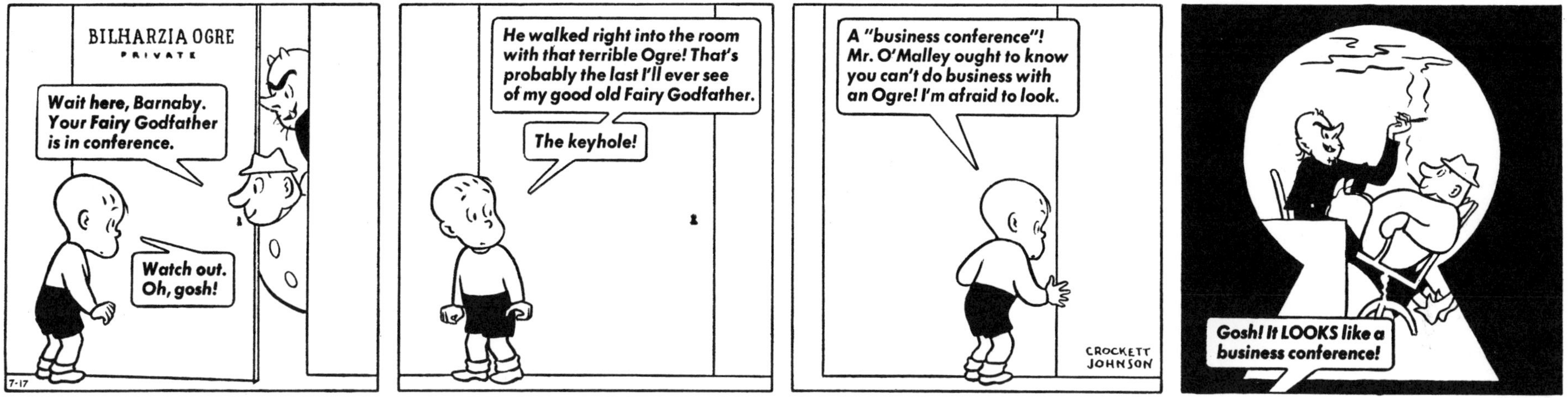
BILHARZIA OGRE
PRIVATE
Wait here, Barnaby. Your Fairy Godfather is in conference.
Watch out. Oh, gosh!
7-17
He walked right into the room with that terrible Ogre! That's probably the last I'll ever see of my good old Fairy Godfather.
The keyhole!
A "business conference"! Mr. O'Malley ought to know you can't do business with an Ogre! I'm afraid to look.
CROCKETT JOHNSON
Gosh! It LOOKS like a business conference!

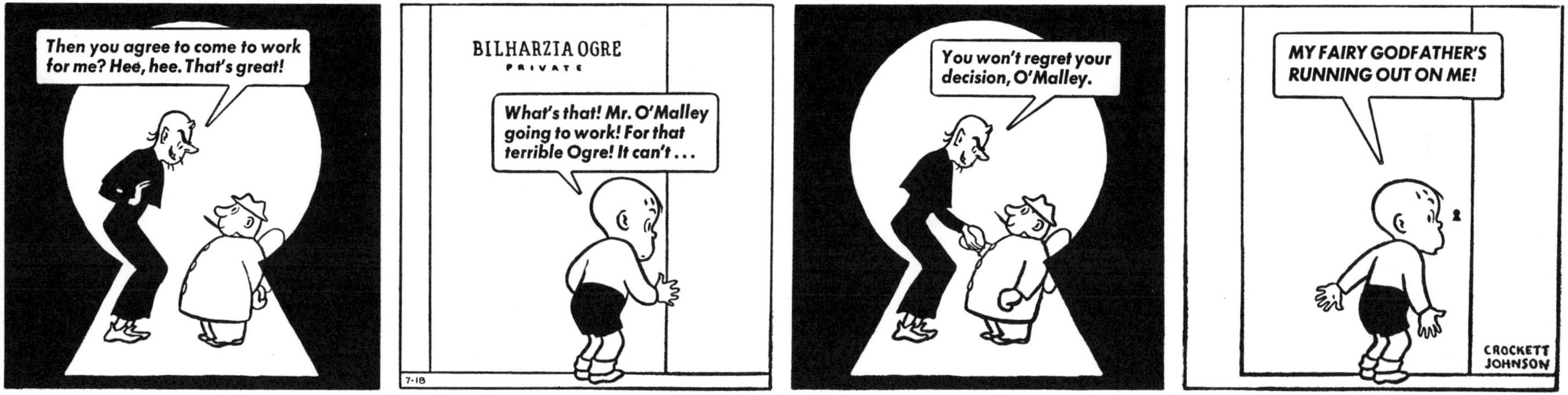
Then you agree to come to work for me? Hee, hee. That's great!
BILHARZIA OGRE
PRIVATE
What's that! Mr. O'Malley going to work! For that terrible Ogre! It can't . . .
7-18
You won't regret your decision, O'Malley.
MY FAIRY GODFATHER'S RUNNING OUT ON ME!
CROCKETT JOHNSON

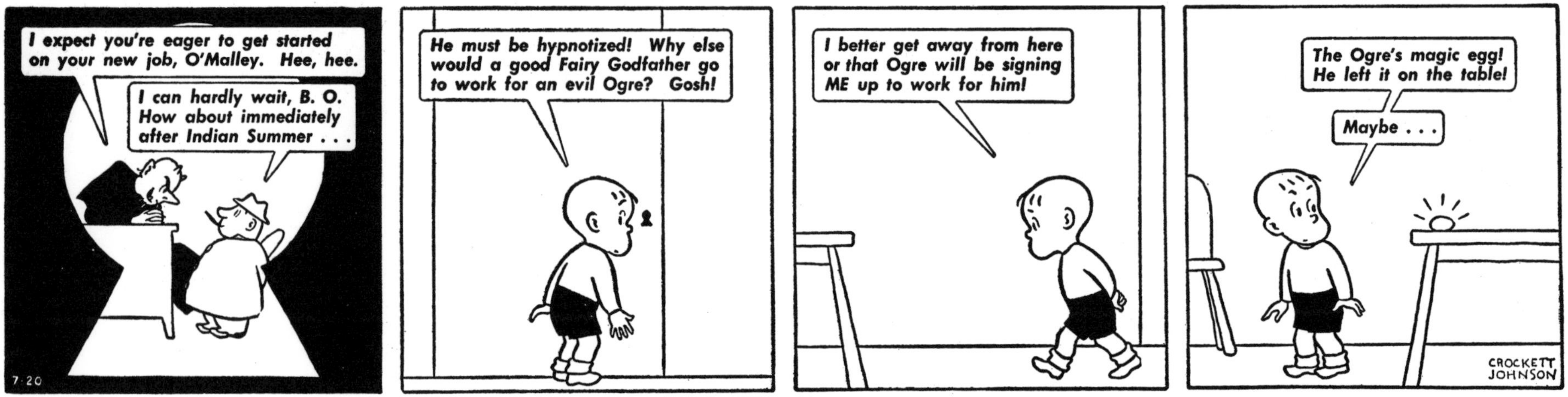

I expect you're eager to get started on your new job, O'Malley. Hee, hee.
I can hardly wait, B. O. How about immediately after Indian Summer . . .
7-20
He must be hypnotized! Why else would a good Fairy Godfather go to work for an evil Ogre? Gosh!
I better get away from here or that Ogre will be signing ME up to work for him!
The Ogre's magic egg! He left it on the table!
Maybe . . .
CROCKETT JOHNSON

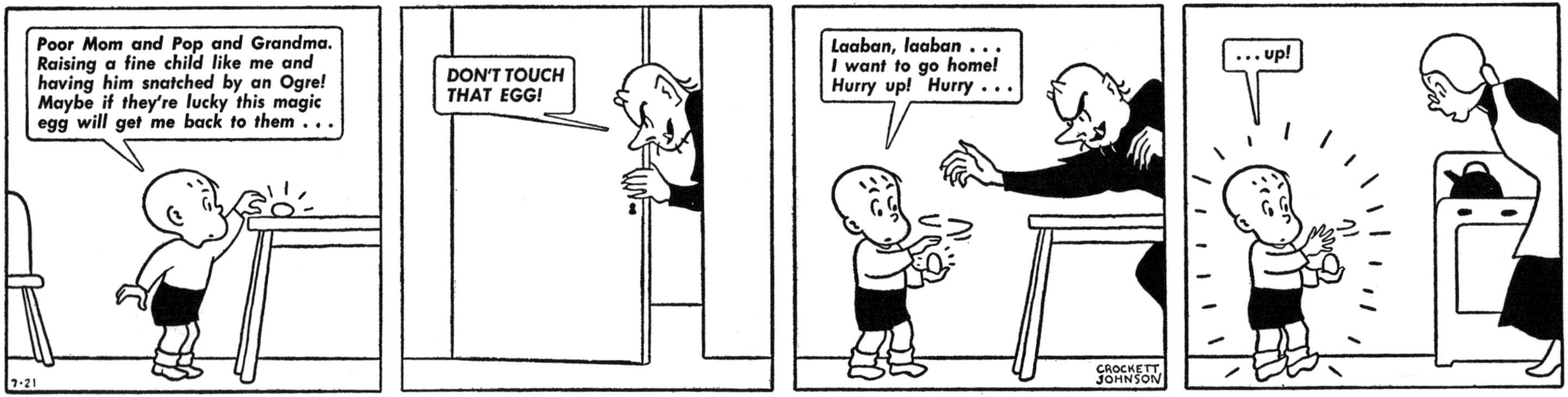

Poor Mom and Pop and Grandma. Raising a fine child like me and having him snatched by an Ogre! Maybe if they're lucky this magic egg will get me back to them . . .
7-21
DON'T TOUCH THAT EGG!
Laaban, laaban . . . I want to go home! Hurry up! Hurry . . .
CROCKETT JOHNSON
. . . up!

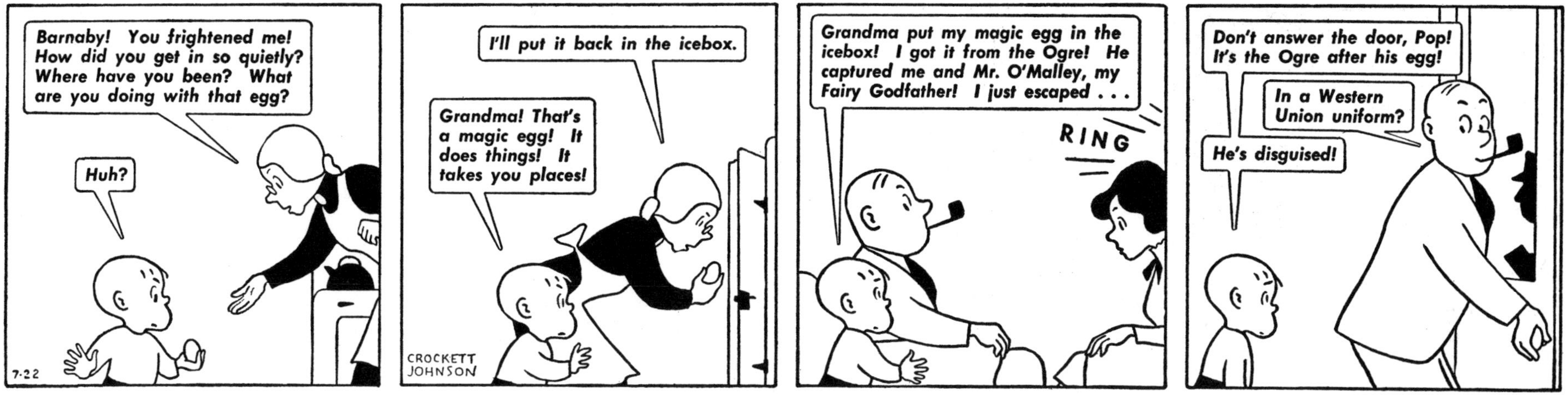
Barnaby! You frightened me! How did you get in so quietly? Where have you been? What are you doing with that egg?
Huh?
7-22
I'll put it back in the icebox.
Grandma! That's a magic egg! It does things! It takes you places!
CROCKETT JOHNSON
Grandma put my magic egg in the icebox! I got it from the Ogre! He captured me and Mr. O'Malley, my Fairy Godfather! I just escaped . . .
RING
Don't answer the door, Pop! It's the Ogre after his egg!
In a Western Union uniform?
He's disguised!

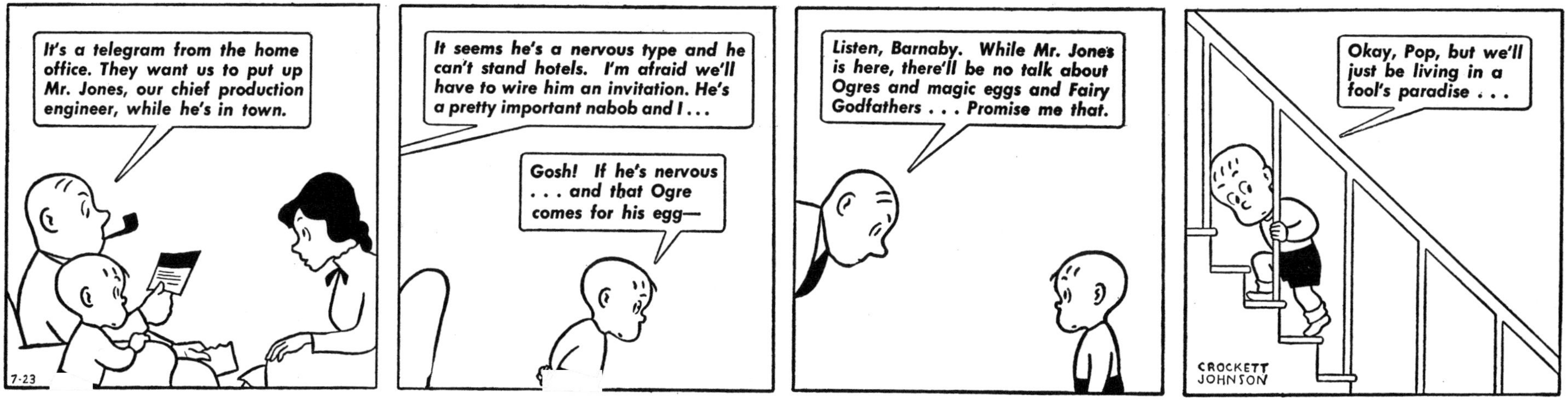
It's a telegram from the home office. They want us to put up Mr. Jones, our chief production engineer, while he's in town.
7-23
It seems he's a nervous type and he can't stand hotels. I'm afraid we'll have to wire him an invitation. He's a pretty important nabob and I . . .
Gosh! If he's nervous . . . and that Ogre comes for his egg—
Listen, Barnaby. While Mr. Jones is here, there'll be no talk about Ogres and magic eggs and Fairy Godfathers . . . Promise me that.
Okay, Pop, but we'll just be living in a fool's paradise . . .
CROCKETT JOHNSON

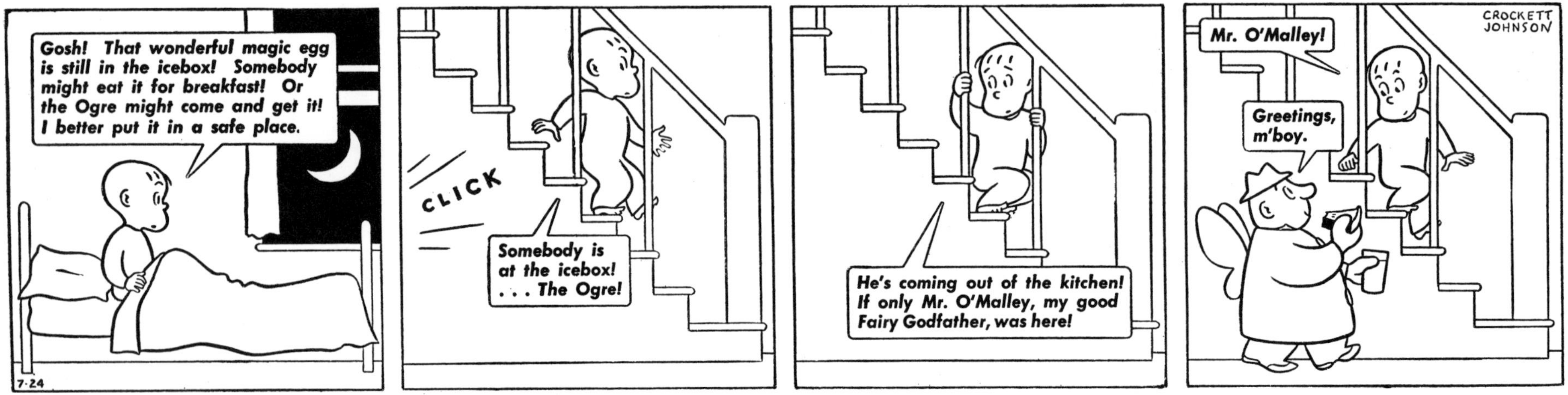
Gosh! That wonderful magic egg is still in the icebox! Somebody might eat it for breakfast! Or the Ogre might come and get it! I better put it in a safe place.
7-24
CLICK
Somebody is at the icebox! . . . The Ogre!
He's coming out of the kitchen! If only Mr. O'Malley, my good Fairy Godfather, was here!
CROCKETT JOHNSON
Mr. O'Malley!
Greetings, m'boy.

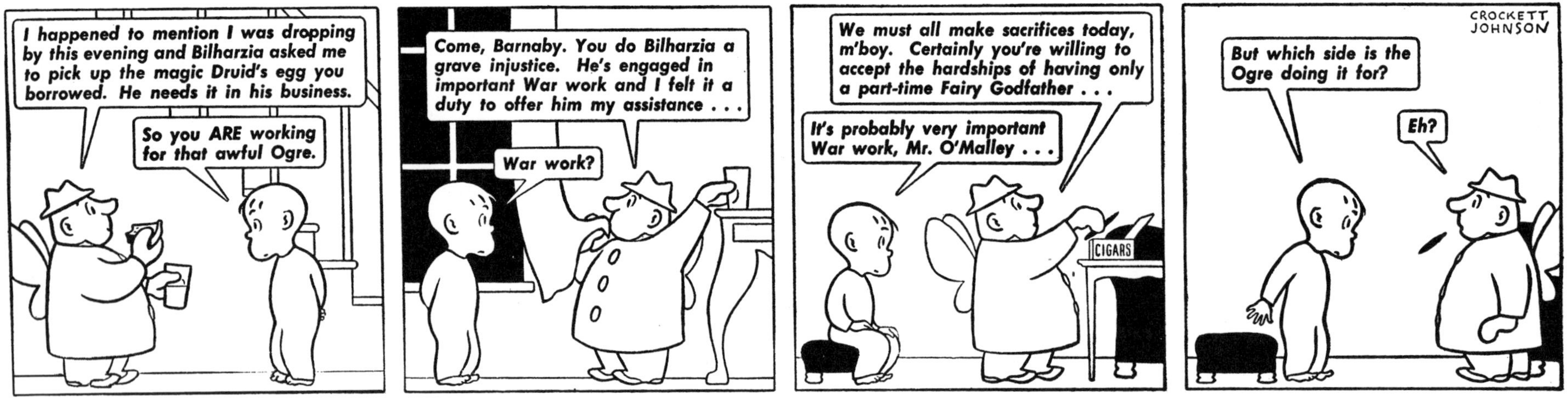
I happened to mention I was dropping by this evening and Bilharzia asked me to pick up the magic Druid's egg you borrowed. He needs it in his business.
So you ARE working for that awful Ogre.
Come, Barnaby. You do Bilharzia a grave injustice. He's engaged in important War work and I felt it a duty to offer him my assistance . . .
War work?
We must all make sacrifices today, m'boy. Certainly you're willing to accept the hardships of having only a part-time Fairy Godfather . . .
It's probably very important War work, Mr. O'Malley . . .
CIGARS
CROCKETT JOHNSON
But which side is the Ogre doing it for?
Eh?

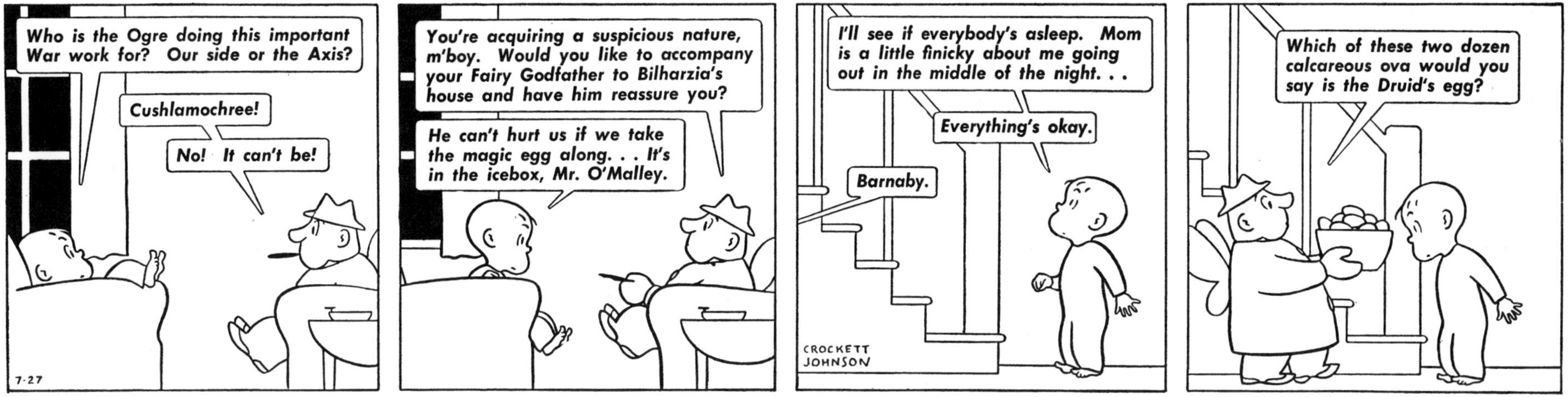
Who is the Ogre doing this important War work for? Our side or the Axis?
Cushlamochree!
No! It can't be!
7-27
You're acquiring a suspicious nature, m'boy. Would you like to accompany your Fairy Godfather to Bilharzia's house and have him reassure you?
He can't hurt us if we take the magic egg along. . . It's in the icebox, Mr. O'Malley.
I'll see if everybody's asleep. Mom is a little finicky about me going out in the middle of the night. . .
Everything's okay.
Barnaby.
CROCKETT JOHNSON
Which of these two dozen calcareous ova would you say is the Druid's egg?

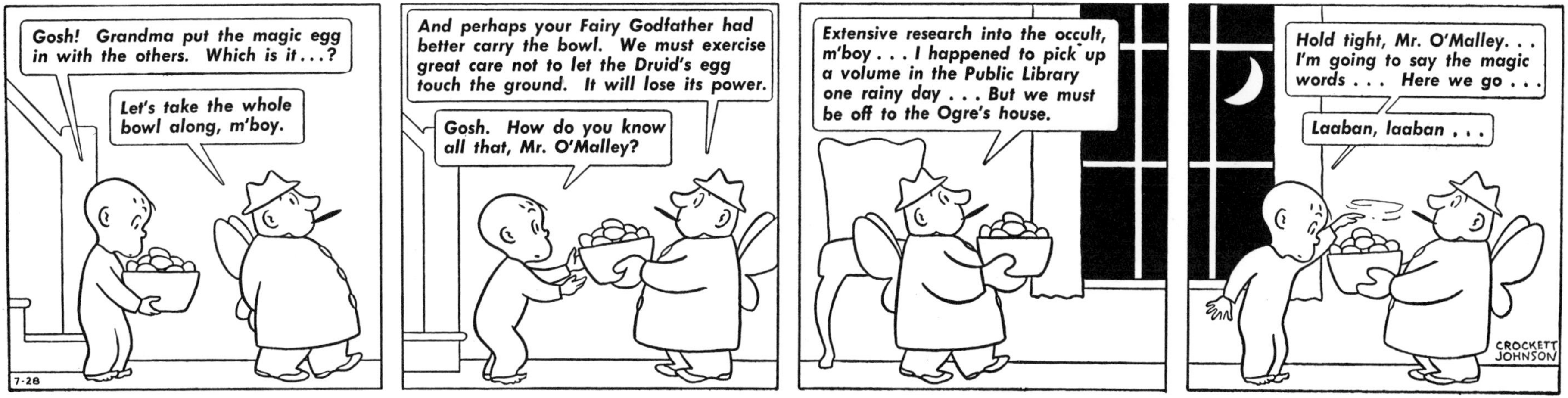
Gosh! Grandma put the magic egg in with the others. Which is it . . . ?
Let's take the whole bowl along, m'boy.
7-28
And perhaps your Fairy Godfather had better carry the bowl. We must exercise great care not to let the Druid's egg touch the ground. It will lose its power.
Gosh. How do you know all that, Mr. O'Malley?
Extensive research into the occult, m'boy . . . I happened to pick up a volume in the Public Library one rainy day . . . But we must be off to the Ogre's house.
Hold tight, Mr. O'Malley. . . I'm going to say the magic words . . . Here we go . . .
Laaban, laaban , . .
CROCKETT JOHNSON

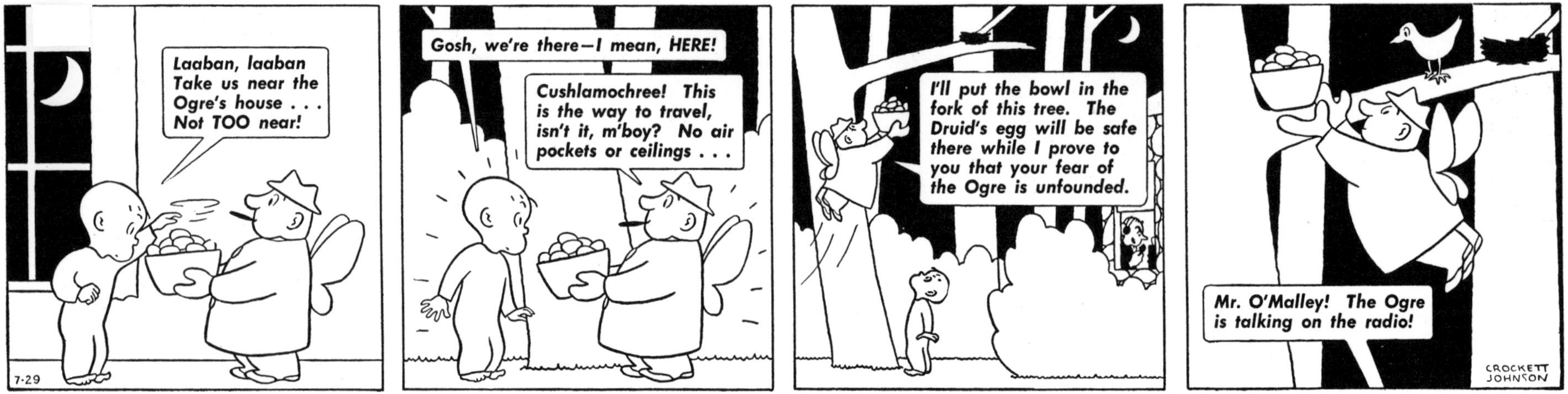
Laaban, laaban Take us near the Ogre's house . . . Not TOO near!
Gosh, we're there—I mean, HERE!
Cushlamochree! This is the way to travel, isn't it, m'boy? No air pockets or ceilings . . .
I'll put the bowl in the fork of this tree. The Druid's egg will be safe there while I prove to you that your fear of the Ogre is unfounded.
Mr. O'Malley! The Ogre is talking on the radio!
7-29
CROCKETT JOHNSON

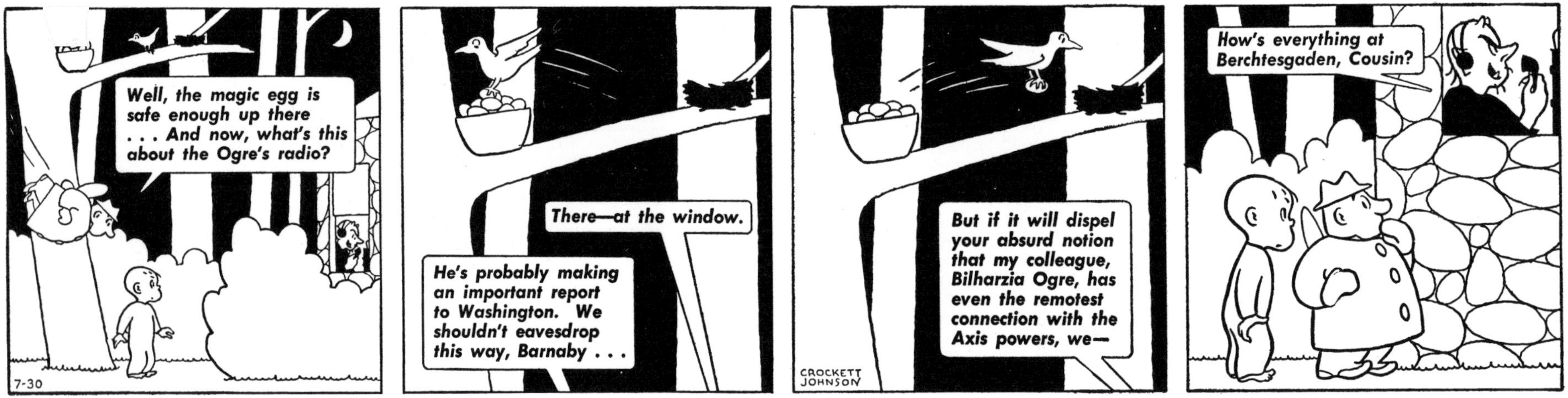
Well, the magic egg is safe enough up there . . . And now, what's this about the Ogre's radio?
There—at the window.
He's probably making an important report to Washington. We shouldn't eavesdrop this way, Barnaby . . .
But if it will dispel your absurd notion that my colleague, Bilharzia Ogre, has even the remotest connection with the Axis powers, we—
How's everything at Berchtesgaden, Cousin?
7-30
CROCKETT JOHNSON

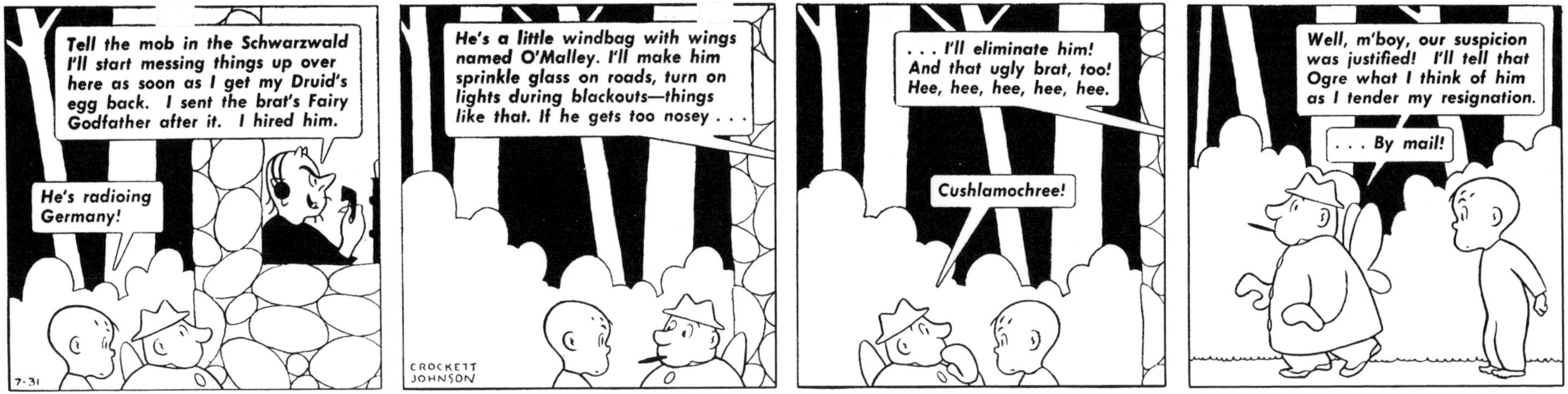
Tell the mob in the Schwarzwald I'll start messing things up over here as soon as I get my Druid's egg back. I sent the brat's Fairy Godfather after it. I hired him.
He's radioing Germany!
7-31
He's a little windbag with wings named O'Malley. I'll make him sprinkle glass on roads, turn on lights during blackouts—things like that. If he gets too nosey . . .
CROCKETT JOHNSON
. . . I'll eliminate him! And that ugly brat, too! Hee, hee, hee, hee, hee.
Cushlamochree!
Well, m'boy, our suspicion was justified! I'll tell that Ogre what I think of him as I tender my resignation.
. . . By mail!

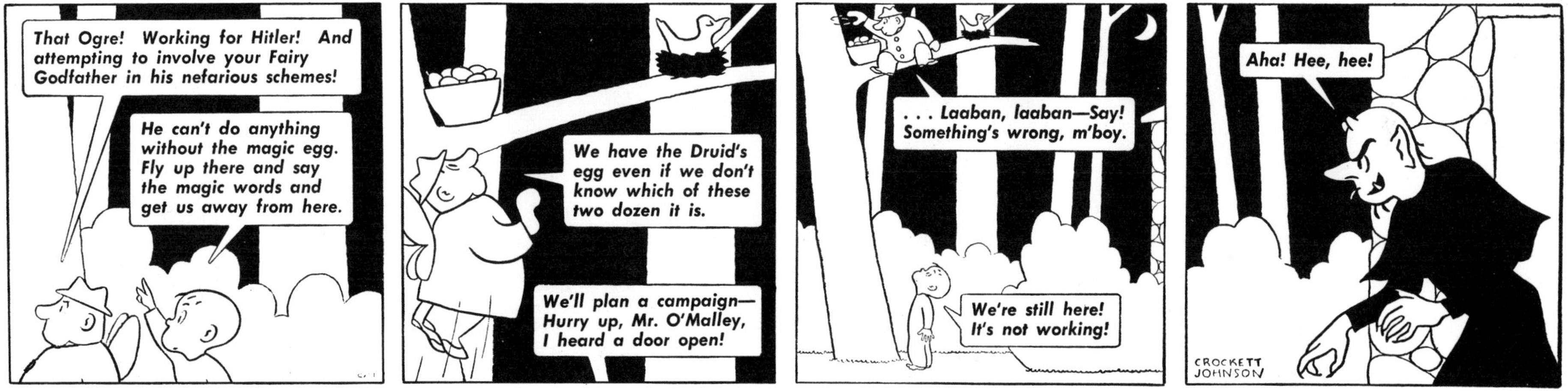
That Ogre! Working for Hitler! And attempting to involve your Fairy Godfather in his nefarious schemes!
He can't do anything without the magic egg. Fly up there and say the magic words and get us away from here.
We have the Druid's egg even if we don't know which of these two dozen it is.
We'll plan a campaign— Hurry up, Mr. O'Malley, I heard a door open!
. . . Laaban, laaban—Say! Something's wrong, m'boy.
We're still here! It's not working!
Aha! Hee, hee!
CROCKETT JOHNSON

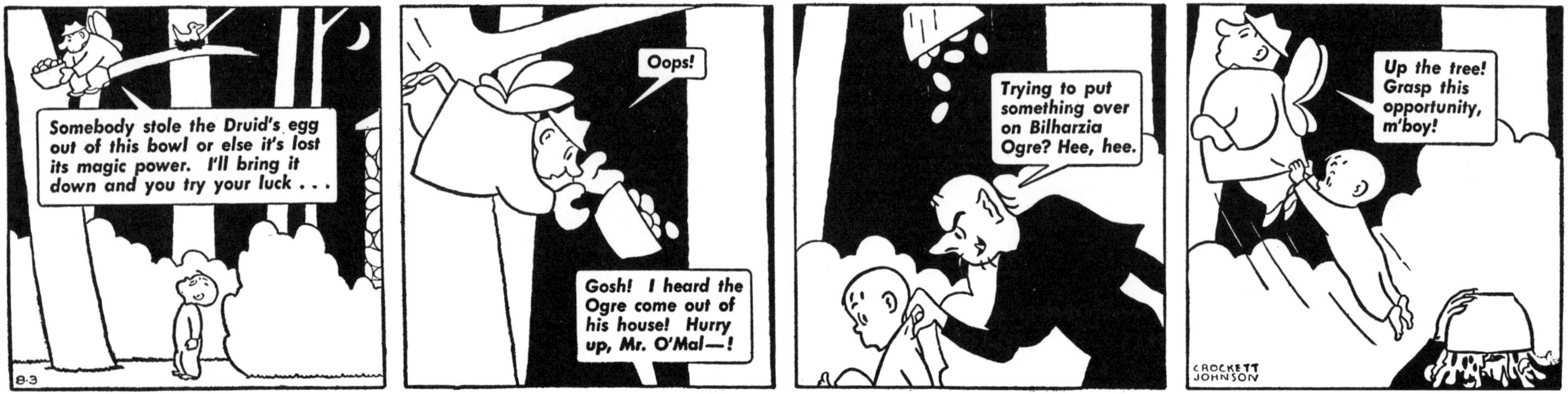
Somebody stole the Druid's egg out of this bowl or else it's lost its magic power. I'll bring it down and you try your luck . . .
8·3
Oops!
Gosh! I heard the Ogre come out of his house! Hurry up, Mr. O'Mal—!
Trying to put something over on Bilharzia Ogre? Hee, hee.
Up the tree! Grasp this opportunity, m'boy!
CROCKETT JOHNSON

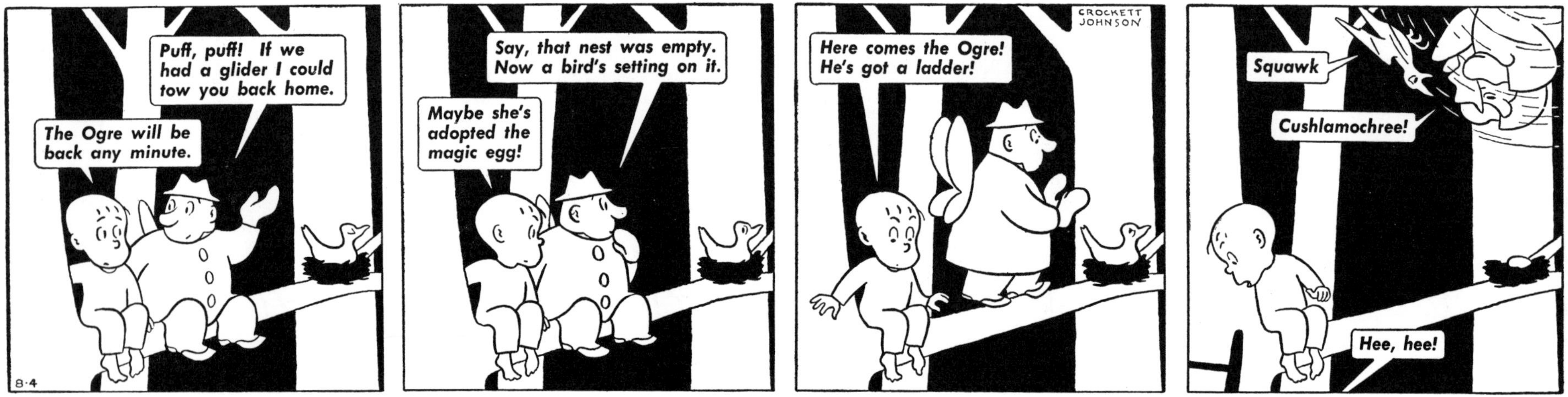
The Ogre will be back any minute.
Puff, puff! If we had a glider I could tow you back home.
8·4
Maybe she's adopted the magic egg!
Say, that nest was empty. Now a bird's setting on it.
Here comes the Ogre! He's got a ladder!
CROCKETT JOHNSON
Squawk
Cushlamochree!
Hee, hee!

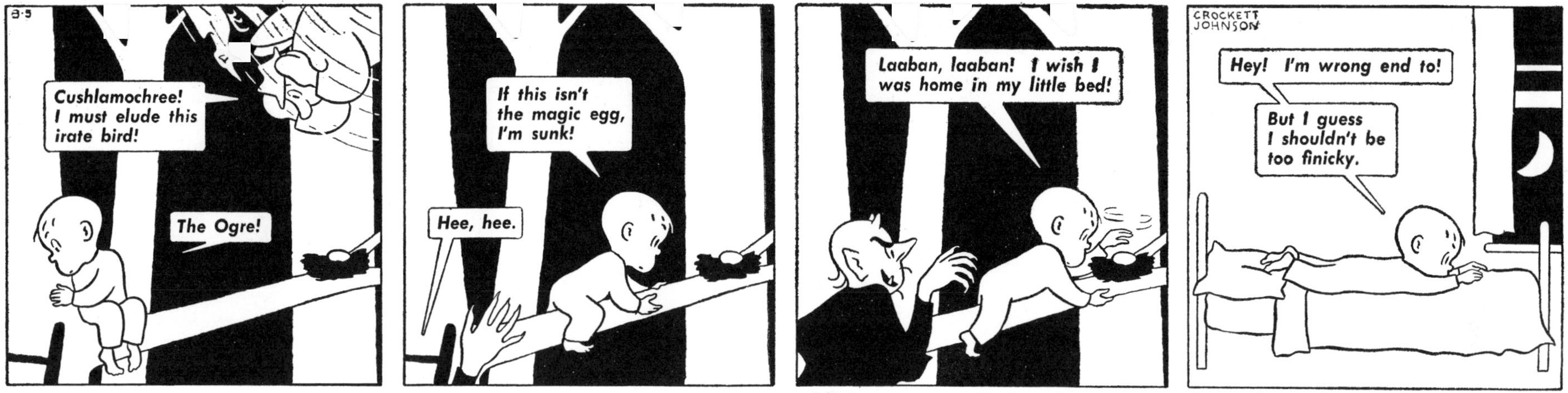
8·5
Cushlamochree! I must elude this irate bird!
The Ogre!
If this isn't the magic egg, I'm sunk!
Hee, hee.
Laaban, laaban! I wish I was home in my little bed!
CROCKETT JOHNSON
Hey! I'm wrong end to!
But I guess I shouldn't be too finicky.

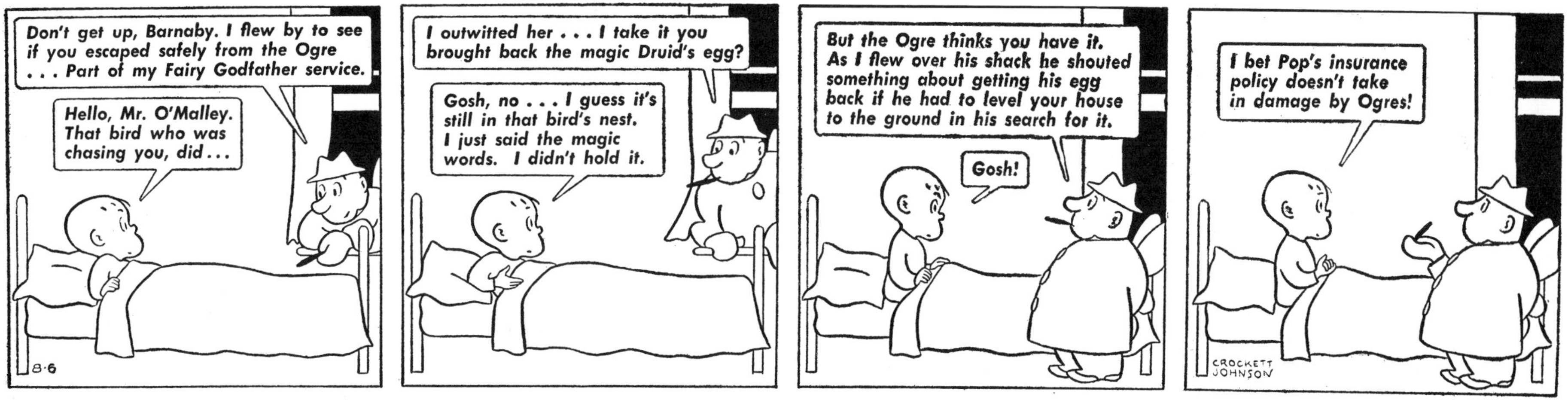
Don't get up, Barnaby. I flew by to see if you escaped safely from the Ogre . . . Part of my Fairy Godfather service.
Hello, Mr. O'Malley. That bird who was chasing you, did...
8·6
I outwitted her . . . I take it you brought back the magic Druid's egg?
Gosh, no . . . I guess it's still in that bird's nest. I just said the magic words. I didn't hold it.
But the Ogre thinks you have it. As I flew over his shack he shouted something about getting his egg back if he had to level your house to the ground in his search for it.
Gosh!
I bet Pop's insurance policy doesn't take in damage by Ogres!
CROCKETT JOHNSON

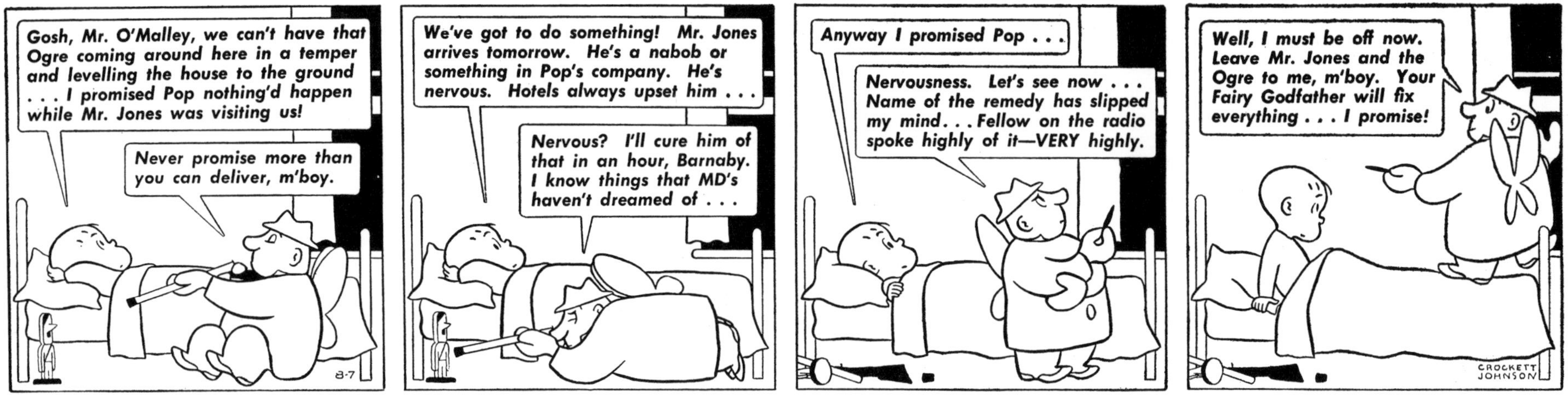
Gosh, Mr. O'Malley, we can't have that Ogre coming around here in a temper and levelling the house to the ground . . . I promised Pop nothing'd happen while Mr. Jones was visiting us!
Never promise more than you can deliver, m'boy.
8-7
We've got to do something! Mr. Jones arrives tomorrow. He's a nabob or something in Pop's company. He's nervous. Hotels always upset him . . .
Nervous? I'll cure him of that in an hour, Barnaby. I know things that MD's haven't dreamed of . . .
Anyway I promised Pop . . .
Nervousness. Let's see now . . . Name of the remedy has slipped my mind. . . Fellow on the radio spoke highly of it—VERY highly.
Well, I must be off now. Leave Mr. Jones and the Ogre to me, m'boy. Your Fairy Godfather will fix everything . . . I promise!
CROCKETT JOHNSON

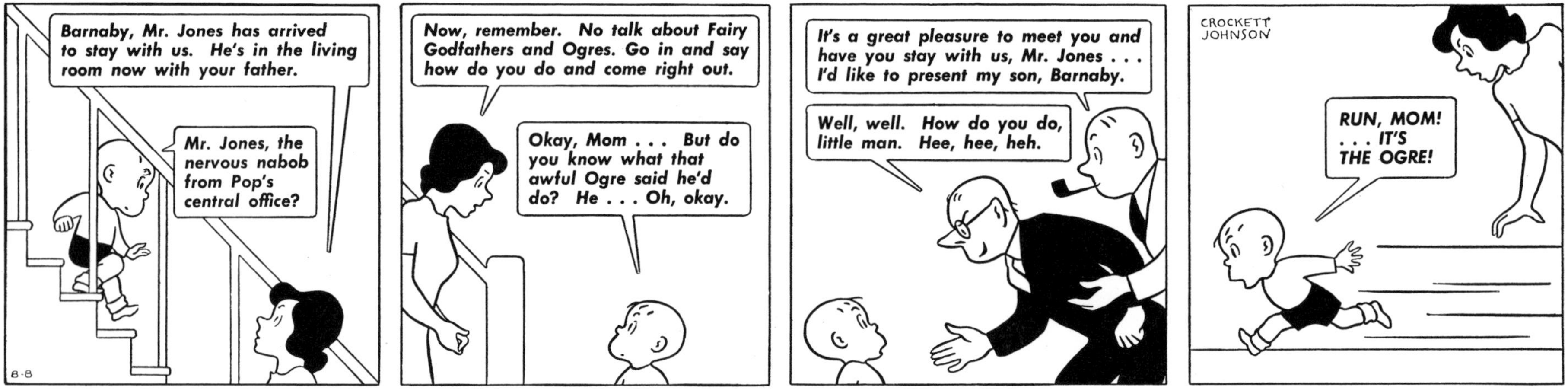
Barnaby, Mr. Jones has arrived to stay with us. He's in the living room now with your father.
Mr. Jones, the nervous nabob from Pop's central office?
8-8
Now, remember. No talk about Fairy Godfathers and Ogres. Go in and say how do you do and come right out.
Okay, Mom . . . But do you know what that awful Ogre said he'd do? He . . . Oh, okay.
It's a great pleasure to meet you and have you stay with us, Mr. Jones . . . I'd like to present my son, Barnaby.
Well, well. How do you do, little man. Hee, hee, heh.
CROCKETT JOHNSON
RUN, MOM! . . . IT'S THE OGRE!

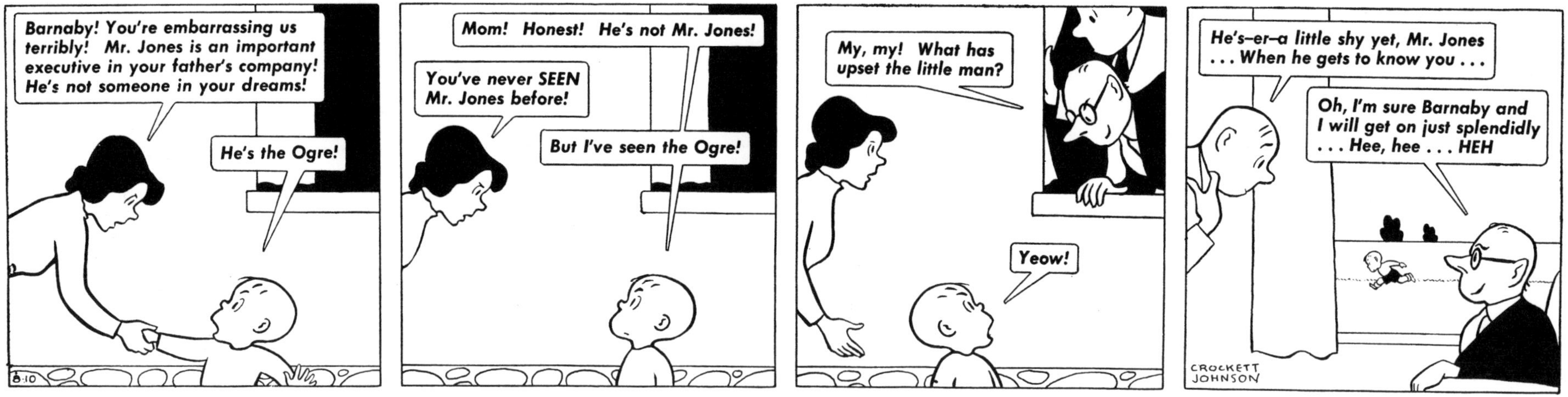
Barnaby! You're embarrassing us terribly! Mr. Jones is an important executive in your father's company! He's not someone in your dreams!
He's the Ogre!
8·10
Mom! Honest! He's not Mr. Jones!
You've never SEEN Mr. Jones before!
But I've seen the Ogre!
My, my! What has upset the little man?
Yeow!
He's–er–a little shy yet, Mr. Jones . . . When he gets to know you . . .
Oh, I'm sure Barnaby and I will get on just splendidly . . . Hee, hee . . . HEH
CROCKETT JOHNSON

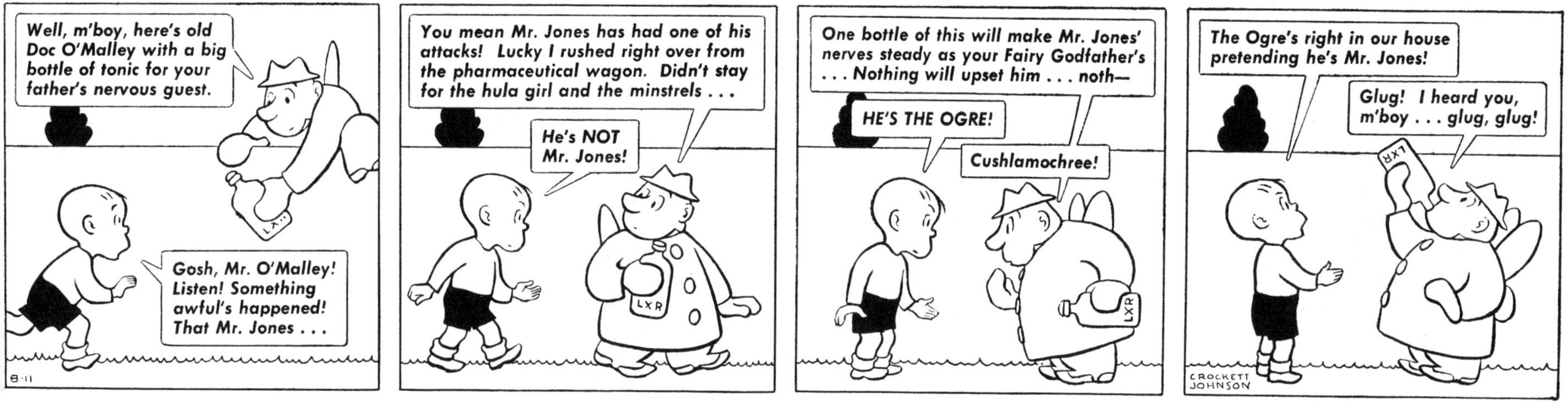
Well, m'boy, here's old Doc O'Malley with a big bottle of tonic for your father's nervous guest.
Gosh, Mr. O'Malley! Listen! Something awful's happened! That Mr. Jones . . .
8·11
You mean Mr. Jones has had one of his attacks! Lucky I rushed right over from the pharmaceutical wagon. Didn't stay for the hula girl and the minstrels . . .
He's NOT Mr. Jones!
LXR
One bottle of this will make Mr. Jones' nerves steady as your Fairy Godfather's . . . Nothing will upset him . . . noth—
HE'S THE OGRE!
Cushlamochree!
LXR
The Ogre's right in our house pretending he's Mr. Jones!
Glug! I heard you, m'boy . . . glug, glug!
LXR
CROCKETT JOHNSON

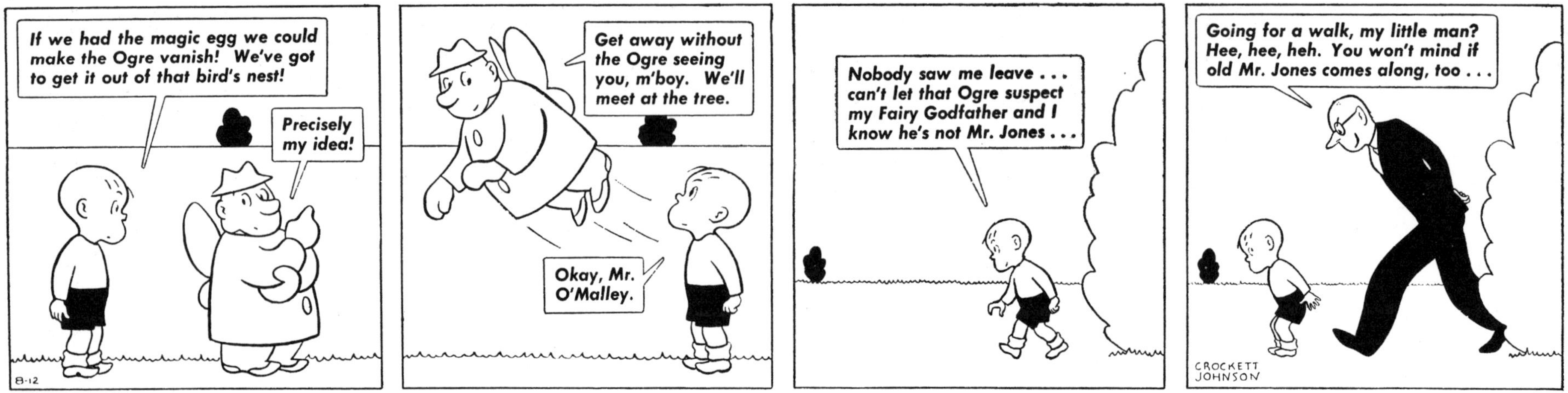
If we had the magic egg we could make the Ogre vanish! We've got to get it out of that bird's nest!
Precisely my idea!
8-12
Get away without the Ogre seeing you, m'boy. We'll meet at the tree.
Okay, Mr. O'Malley.
Nobody saw me leave . . . can't let that Ogre suspect my Fairy Godfather and I know he's not Mr. Jones . . .
Going for a walk, my little man? Hee, hee, heh. You won't mind if old Mr. Jones comes along, too . . .
CROCKETT JOHNSON

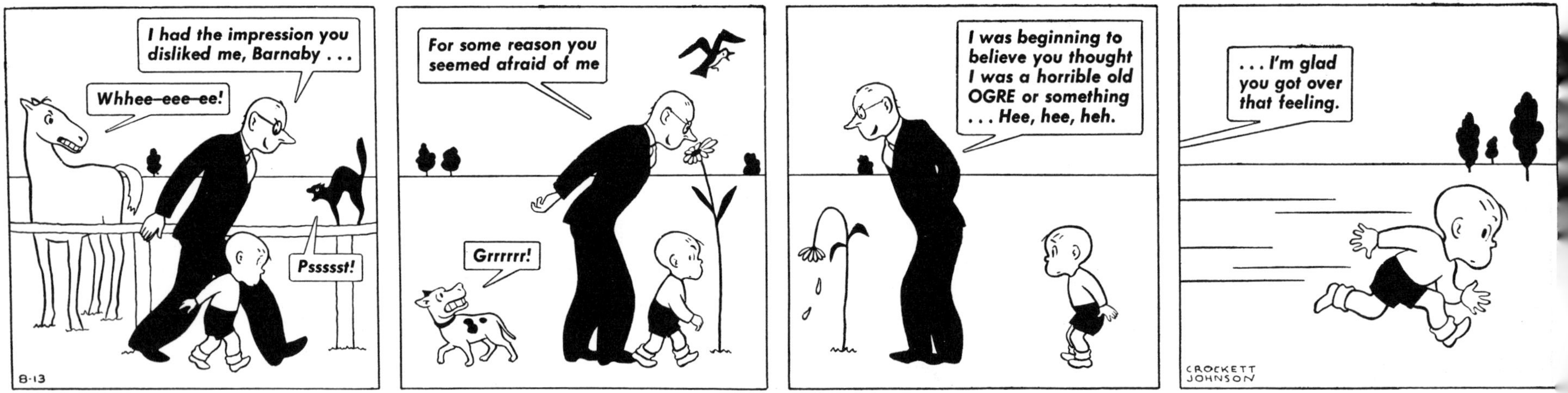
I had the impression you disliked me, Barnaby . . .
Whhee-eee-ee!
Psssssst!
8-13
For some reason you seemed afraid of me
Grrrrrr!
I was beginning to believe you thought I was a horrible old OGRE or something . . . Hee, hee, heh.
. . . I'm glad you got over that feeling.
CROCKETT JOHNSON

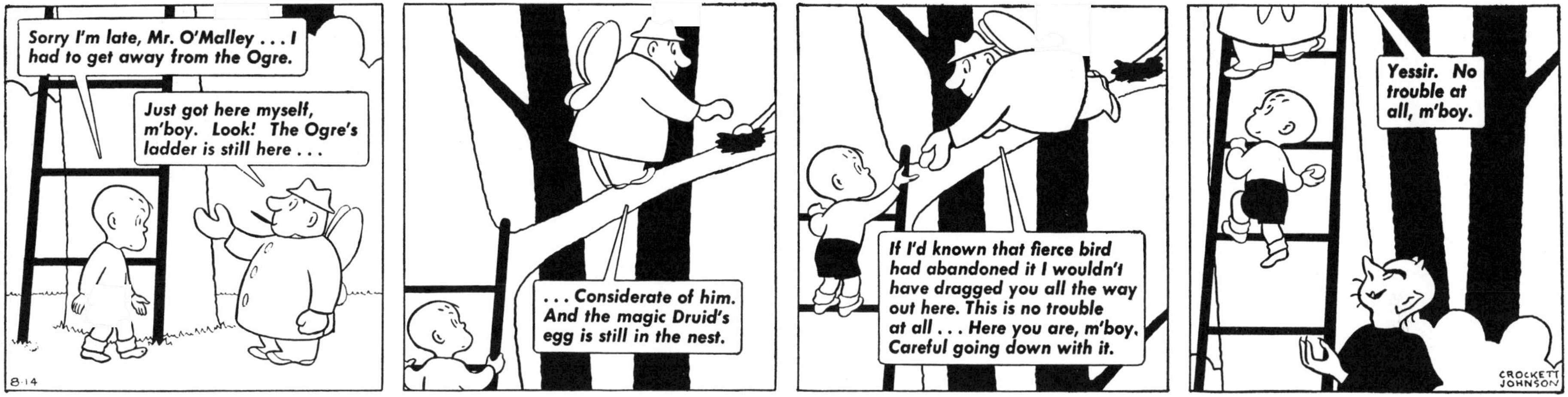
Sorry I'm late, Mr. O'Malley . . . I had to get away from the Ogre.
Just got here myself, m'boy. Look! The Ogre's ladder is still here . . .
8-14
. . . Considerate of him. And the magic Druid's egg is still in the nest.
If I'd known that fierce bird had abandoned it I wouldn't have dragged you all the way out here. This is no trouble at all . . . Here you are, m'boy. Careful going down with it.
Yessir. No trouble at all, m'boy.
CROCKETT JOHNSON

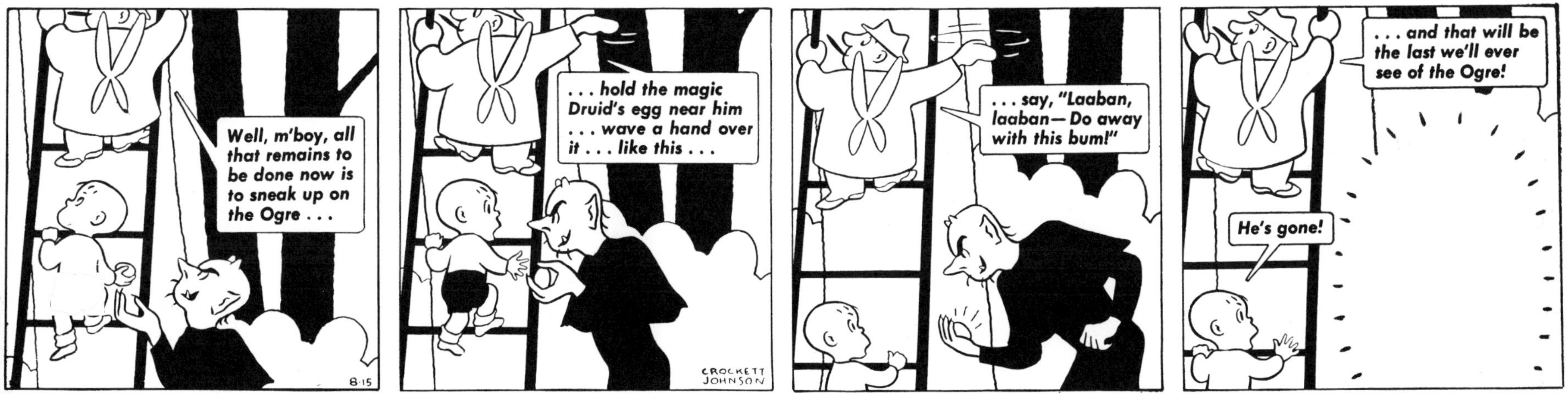
Well, m'boy, all that remains to be done now is to sneak up on the Ogre . . .
8-15
. . . hold the magic Druid's egg near him . . . wave a hand over it . . . like this . . .
CROCKETT JOHNSON
. . . say, "Laaban, laaban— Do away with this bum!"
. . . and that will be the last we'll ever see of the Ogre!
He's gone!

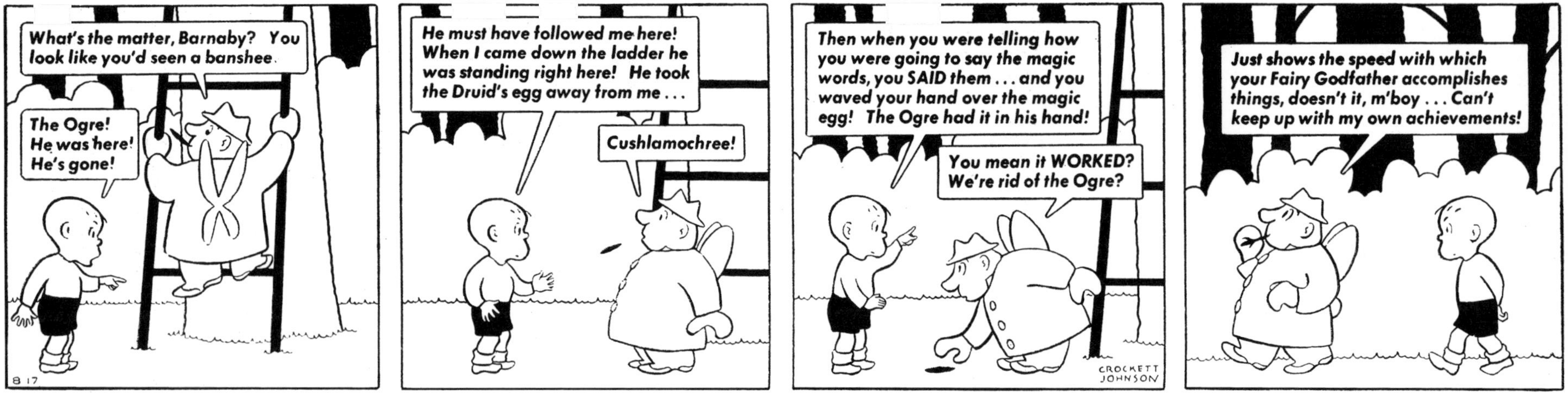
What's the matter, Barnaby? You look like you'd seen a banshee.
The Ogre! He was here! He's gone!
He must have followed me here! When I came down the ladder he was standing right here! He took the Druid's egg away from me . . .
Cushlamochree!
Then when you were telling how you were going to say the magic words, you SAID them . . . and you waved your hand over the magic egg! The Ogre had it in his hand!
You mean it WORKED? We're rid of the Ogre?
Just shows the speed with which your Fairy Godfather accomplishes things, doesn't it, m'boy . . . Can't keep up with my own achievements!
8 17
CROCKETT JOHNSON

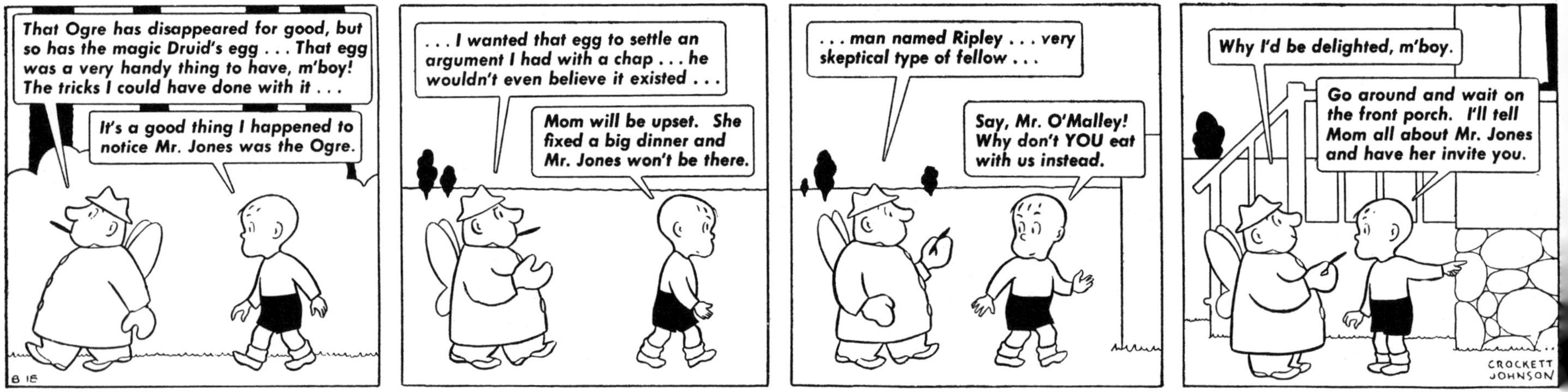
That Ogre has disappeared for good, but so has the magic Druid's egg . . . That egg was a very handy thing to have, m'boy! The tricks I could have done with it . . .
It's a good thing I happened to notice Mr. Jones was the Ogre.
. . . I wanted that egg to settle an argument I had with a chap . . . he wouldn't even believe it existed . . .
Mom will be upset. She fixed a big dinner and Mr. Jones won't be there.
. . . man named Ripley . . . very skeptical type of fellow . . .
Say, Mr. O'Malley! Why don't YOU eat with us instead.
Why I'd be delighted, m'boy.
Go around and wait on the front porch. I'll tell Mom all about Mr. Jones and have her invite you.
8 18
CROCKETT JOHNSON

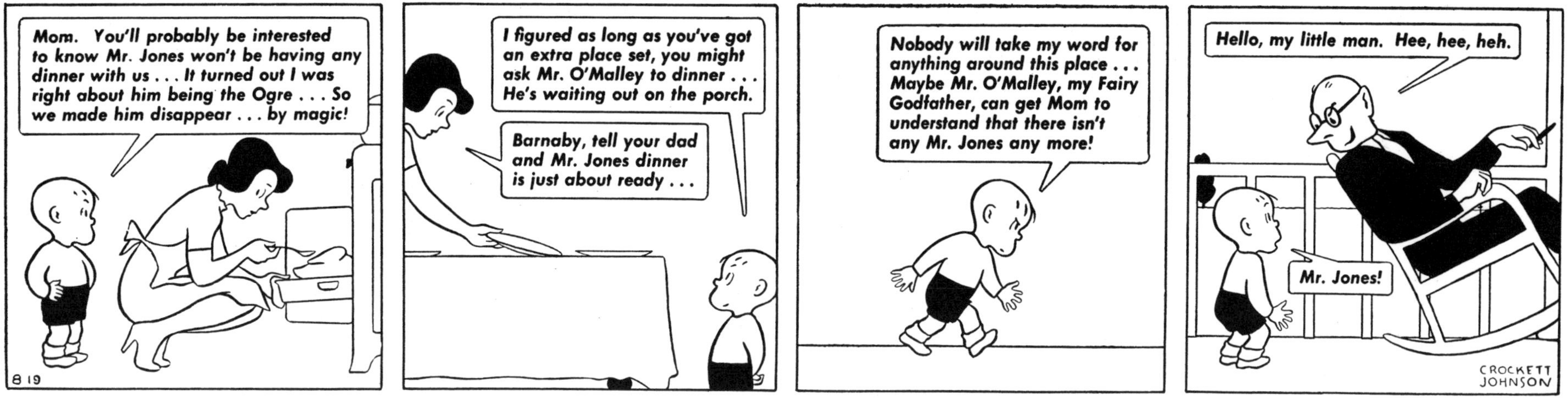
Mom. You'll probably be interested to know Mr. Jones won't be having any dinner with us . . . It turned out I was right about him being the Ogre . . . So we made him disappear . . . by magic!
8 19
I figured as long as you've got an extra place set, you might ask Mr. O'Malley to dinner . . . He's waiting out on the porch.
Barnaby, tell your dad and Mr. Jones dinner is just about ready . . .
Nobody will take my word for anything around this place . . . Maybe Mr. O'Malley, my Fairy Godfather, can get Mom to understand that there isn't any Mr. Jones any more!
Hello, my little man. Hee, hee, heh.
Mr. Jones!
CROCKETT JOHNSON

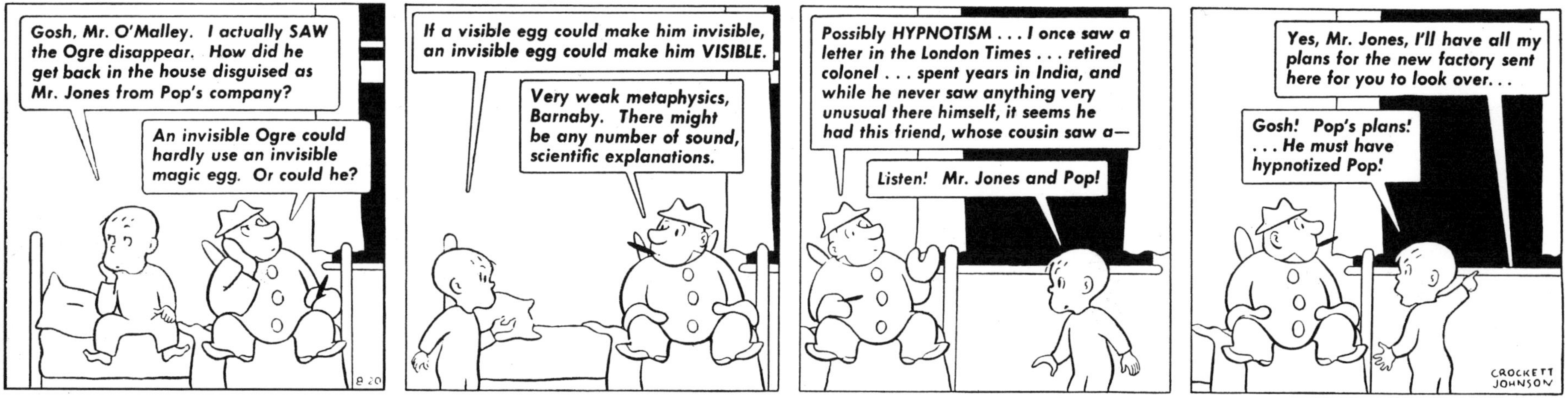
Gosh, Mr. O'Malley. I actually SAW the Ogre disappear. How did he get back in the house disguised as Mr. Jones from Pop's company?
An invisible Ogre could hardly use an invisible magic egg. Or could he?
8 20
If a visible egg could make him invisible, an invisible egg could make him VISIBLE.
Very weak metaphysics, Barnaby. There might be any number of sound, scientific explanations.
Possibly HYPNOTISM . . . I once saw a letter in the London Times . . . retired colonel . . . spent years in India, and while he never saw anything very unusual there himself, it seems he had this friend, whose cousin saw a—
Listen! Mr. Jones and Pop!
Yes, Mr. Jones, I'll have all my plans for the new factory sent here for you to look over . . .
Gosh! Pop's plans! . . . He must have hypnotized Pop!
CROCKETT JOHNSON

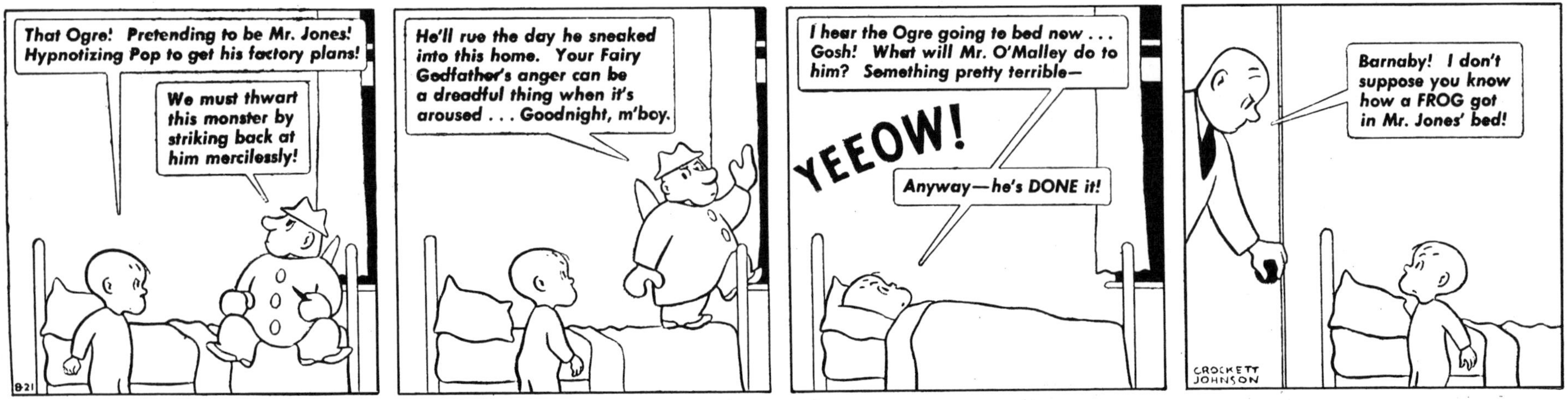
That Ogre! Pretending to be Mr. Jones! Hypnotizing Pop to get his factory plans!
We must thwart this monster by striking back at him mercilessly!
B·21
He'll rue the day he sneaked into this home. Your Fairy Godfather's anger can be a dreadful thing when it's aroused . . . Goodnight, m'boy.
I hear the Ogre going to bed now . . . Gosh! What will Mr. O'Malley do to him? Something pretty terrible—
YEEOW!
Anyway—he's DONE it!
Barnaby! I don't suppose you know how a FROG got in Mr. Jones' bed!
CROCKETT JOHNSON

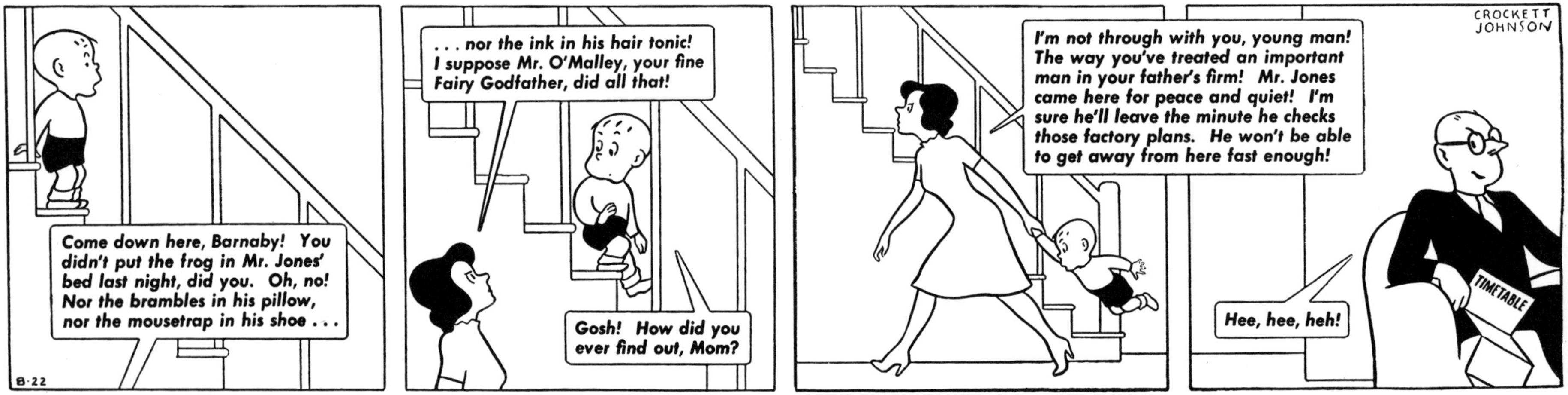
Come down here, Barnaby! You didn't put the frog in Mr. Jones' bed last night, did you. Oh, no! Nor the brambles in his pillow, nor the mousetrap in his shoe . . .
B·22
. . . nor the ink in his hair tonic! I suppose Mr. O'Malley, your fine Fairy Godfather, did all that!
Gosh! How did you ever find out, Mom?
I'm not through with you, young man! The way you've treated an important man in your father's firm! Mr. Jones came here for peace and quiet! I'm sure he'll leave the minute he checks those factory plans. He won't be able to get away from here fast enough!
CROCKETT JOHNSON
Hee, hee, heh!
TIMETABLE

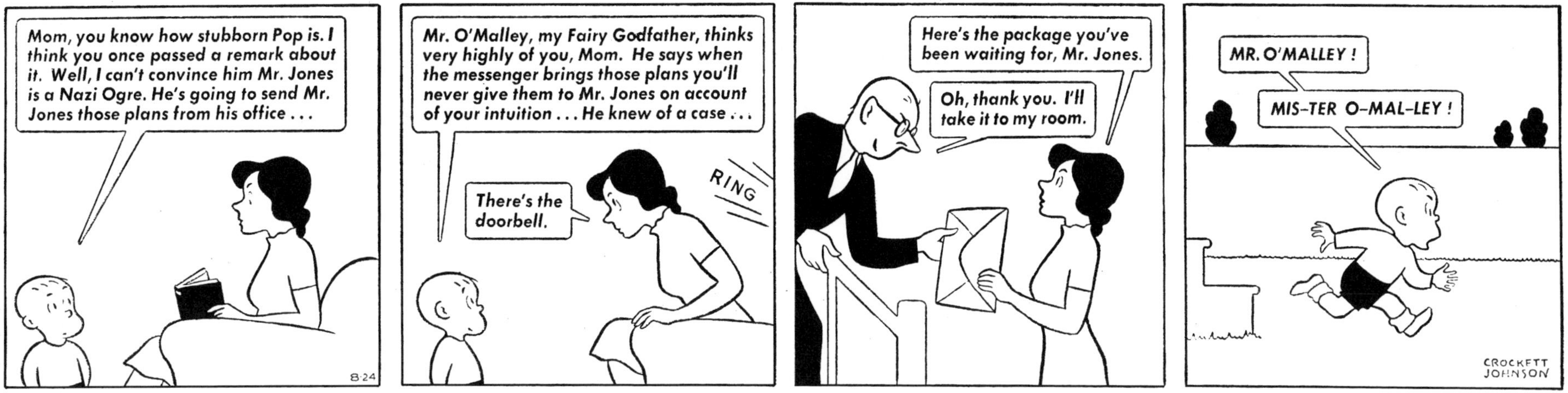
Mom, you know how stubborn Pop is. I think you once passed a remark about it. Well, I can't convince him Mr. Jones is a Nazi Ogre. He's going to send Mr. Jones those plans from his office . . .
8·24
Mr. O'Malley, my Fairy Godfather, thinks very highly of you, Mom. He says when the messenger brings those plans you'll never give them to Mr. Jones on account of your intuition . . . He knew of a case . . .
There's the doorbell.
RING
Here's the package you've been waiting for, Mr. Jones.
Oh, thank you. I'll take it to my room.
MR. O'MALLEY !
MIS-TER O-MAL-LEY !
CROCKETT JOHNSON

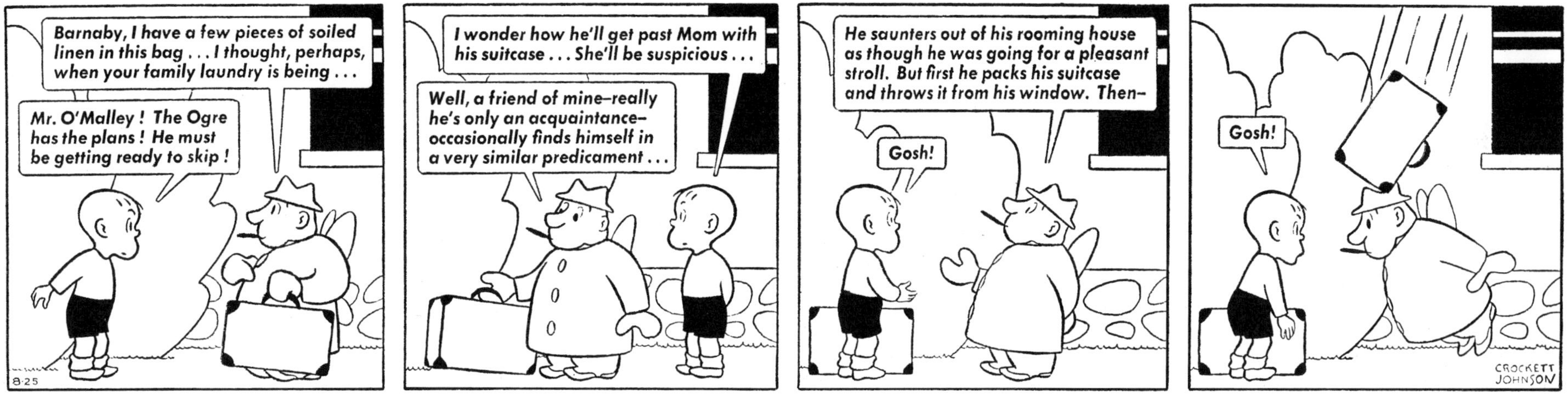
Barnaby, I have a few pieces of soiled linen in this bag . . . I thought, perhaps, when your family laundry is being . . .
Mr. O'Malley ! The Ogre has the plans ! He must be getting ready to skip !
8·25
I wonder how he'll get past Mom with his suitcase . . . She'll be suspicious . . .
Well, a friend of mine—really he's only an acquaintance—occasionally finds himself in a very similar predicament . . .
He saunters out of his rooming house as though he was going for a pleasant stroll. But first he packs his suitcase and throws it from his window. Then—
Gosh!
Gosh!
CROCKETT JOHNSON

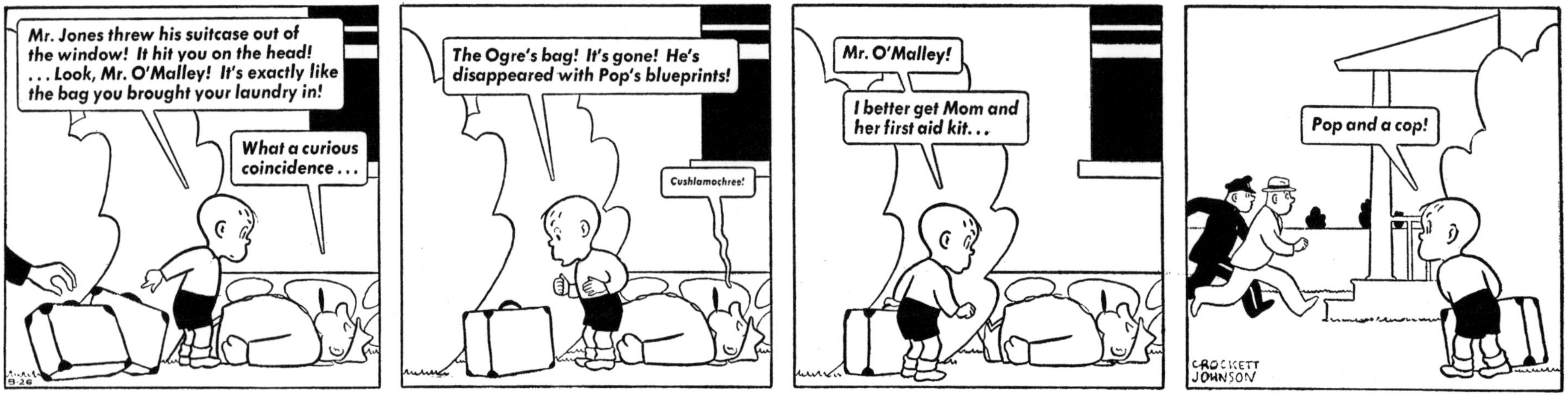
Mr. Jones threw his suitcase out of the window! It hit you on the head! . . . Look, Mr. O'Malley! It's exactly like the bag you brought your laundry in!
What a curious coincidence . . .
8-26
The Ogre's bag! It's gone! He's disappeared with Pop's blueprints!
Cushlamochree!
Mr. O'Malley!
I better get Mom and her first aid kit. . .
Pop and a cop!
CROCKETT JOHNSON

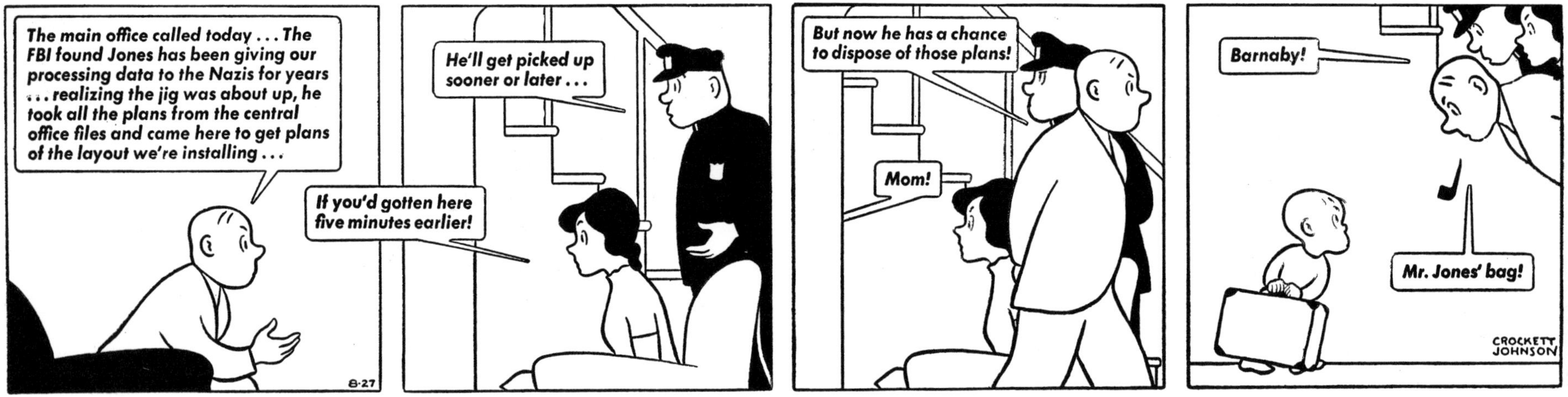
The main office called today . . . The FBI found Jones has been giving our processing data to the Nazis for years . . . realizing the jig was about up, he took all the plans from the central office files and came here to get plans of the layout we're installing . . .
8-27
If you'd gotten here five minutes earlier!
He'll get picked up sooner or later . . .
But now he has a chance to dispose of those plans!
Mom!
Barnaby!
Mr. Jones' bag!
CROCKETT JOHNSON

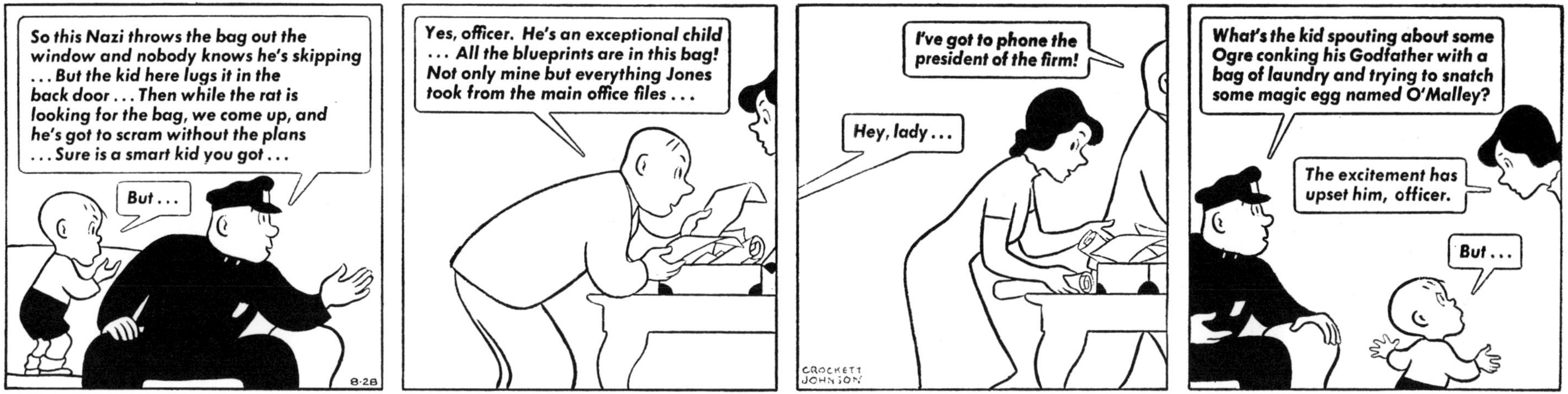
So this Nazi throws the bag out the window and nobody knows he's skipping . . . But the kid here lugs it in the back door . . . Then while the rat is looking for the bag, we come up, and he's got to scram without the plans . . . Sure is a smart kid you got . . .
But . . .
8·28
Yes, officer. He's an exceptional child . . . All the blueprints are in this bag! Not only mine but everything Jones took from the main office files . . .
I've got to phone the president of the firm!
Hey, lady . . .
CROCKETT JOHNSON
What's the kid spouting about some Ogre conking his Godfather with a bag of laundry and trying to snatch some magic egg named O'Malley?
The excitement has upset him, officer.
But . . .

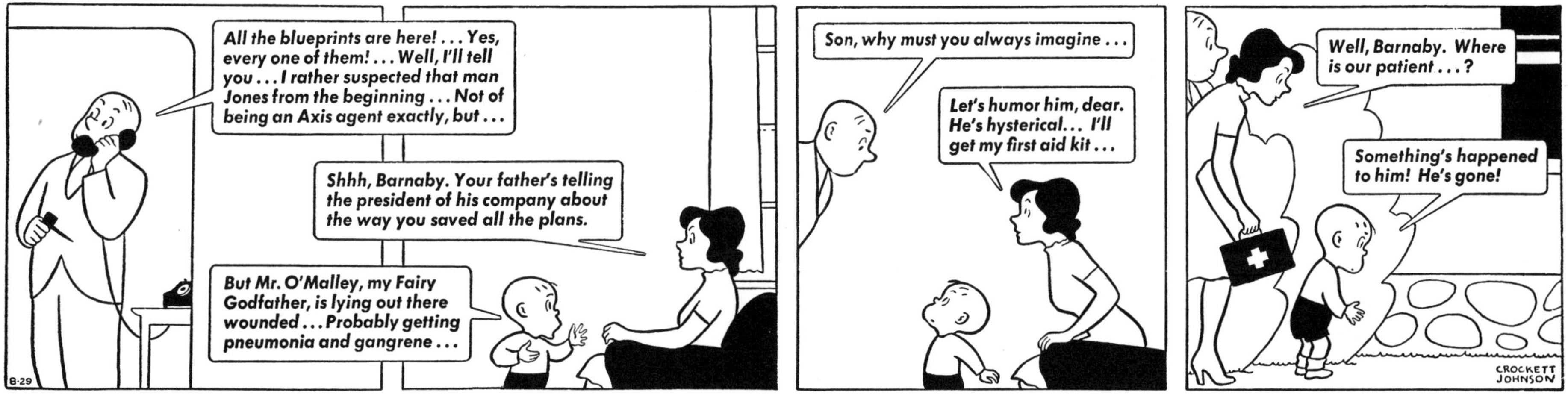
All the blueprints are here! . . . Yes, every one of them! . . . Well, I'll tell you . . . I rather suspected that man Jones from the beginning . . . Not of being an Axis agent exactly, but . . .
Shhh, Barnaby. Your father's telling the president of his company about the way you saved all the plans.
But Mr. O'Malley, my Fairy Godfather, is lying out there wounded . . . Probably getting pneumonia and gangrene . . .
8·29
Son, why must you always imagine . . .
Let's humor him, dear. He's hysterical . . . I'll get my first aid kit . . .
Well, Barnaby. Where is our patient . . . ?
Something's happened to him! He's gone!
CROCKETT JOHNSON

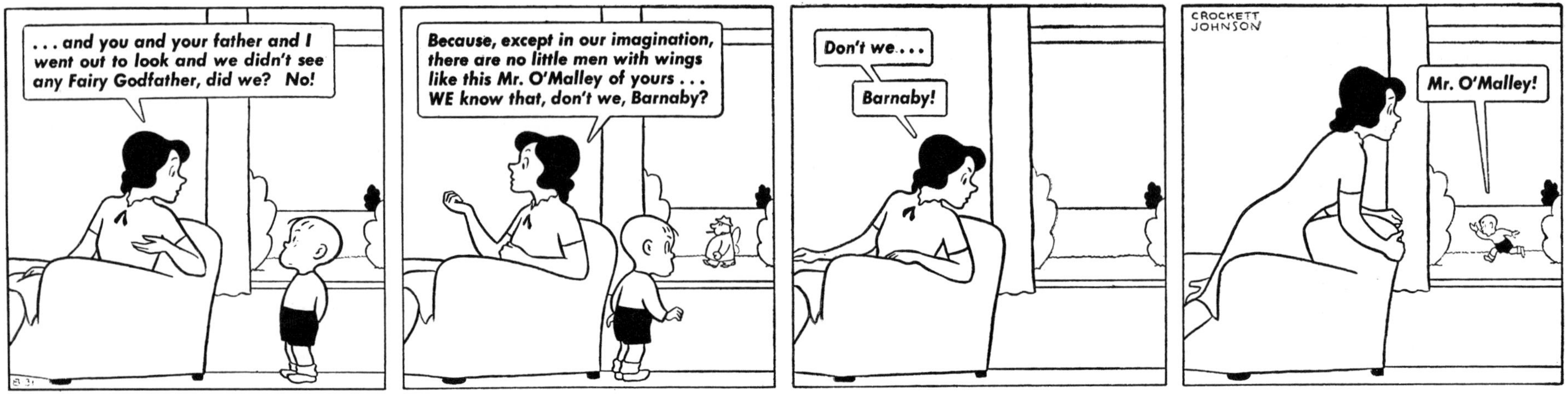

. . . and you and your father and I went out to look and we didn't see any Fairy Godfather, did we? No!
Because, except in our imagination, there are no little men with wings like this Mr. O'Malley of yours . . . WE know that, don't we, Barnaby?
Don't we. . . .
Barnaby!
CROCKETT JOHNSON
Mr. O'Malley!

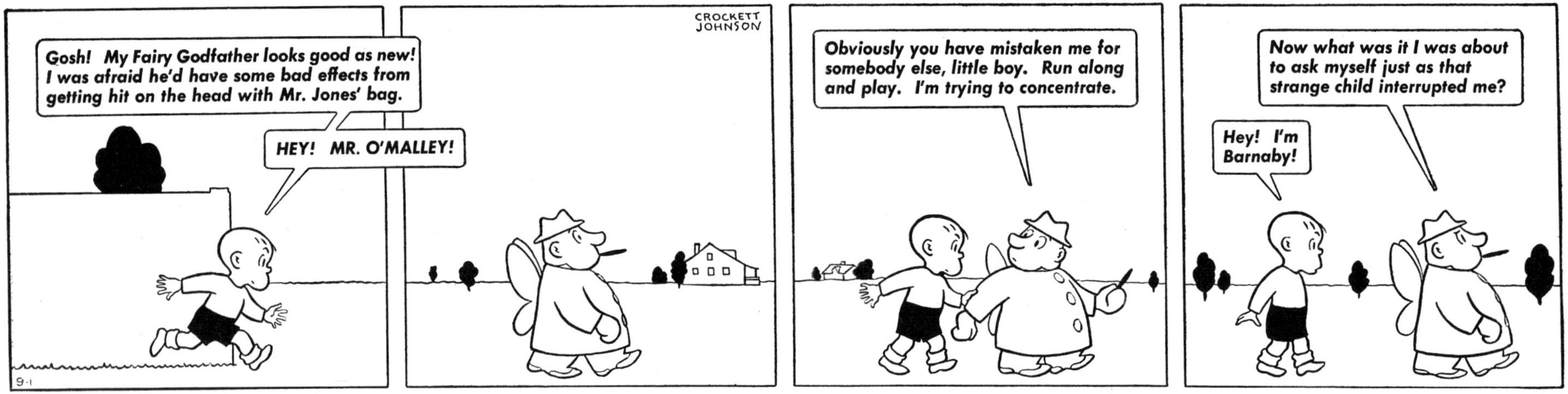

Gosh! My Fairy Godfather looks good as new! I was afraid he'd have some bad effects from getting hit on the head with Mr. Jones' bag.
HEY! MR. O'MALLEY!
CROCKETT JOHNSON
Obviously you have mistaken me for somebody else, little boy. Run along and play. I'm trying to concentrate.
Now what was it I was about to ask myself just as that strange child interrupted me?
Hey! I'm Barnaby!

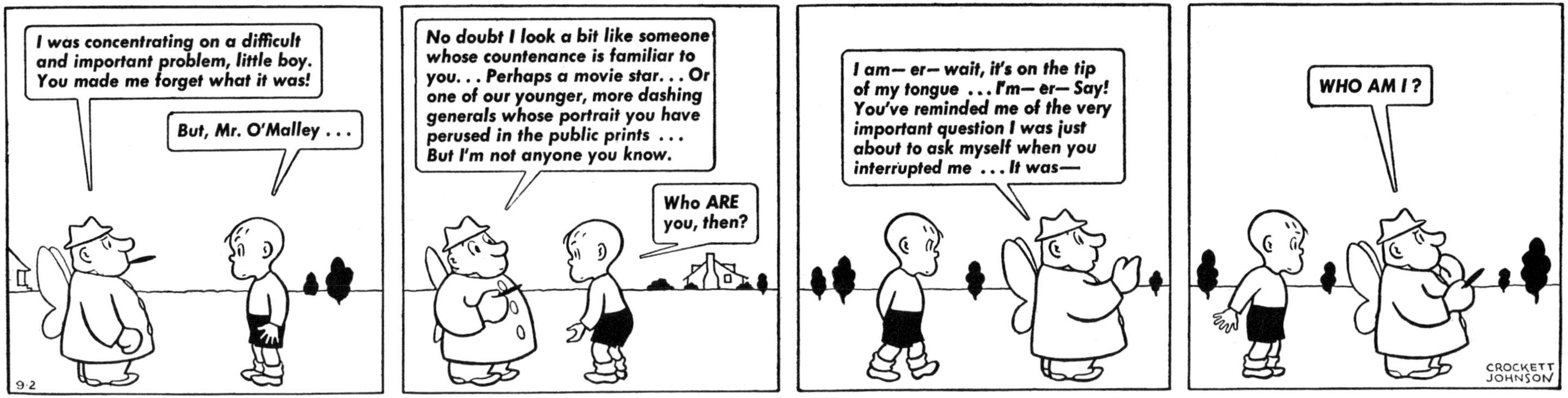
I was concentrating on a difficult and important problem, little boy. You made me forget what it was!
But, Mr. O'Malley . . .
9-2
No doubt I look a bit like someone whose countenance is familiar to you. . . Perhaps a movie star. . . Or one of our younger, more dashing generals whose portrait you have perused in the public prints . . . But I'm not anyone you know.
Who ARE you, then?
I am— er— wait, it's on the tip of my tongue . . . I'm— er— Say! You've reminded me of the very important question I was just about to ask myself when you interrupted me . . . It was—
WHO AM I?
CROCKETT JOHNSON

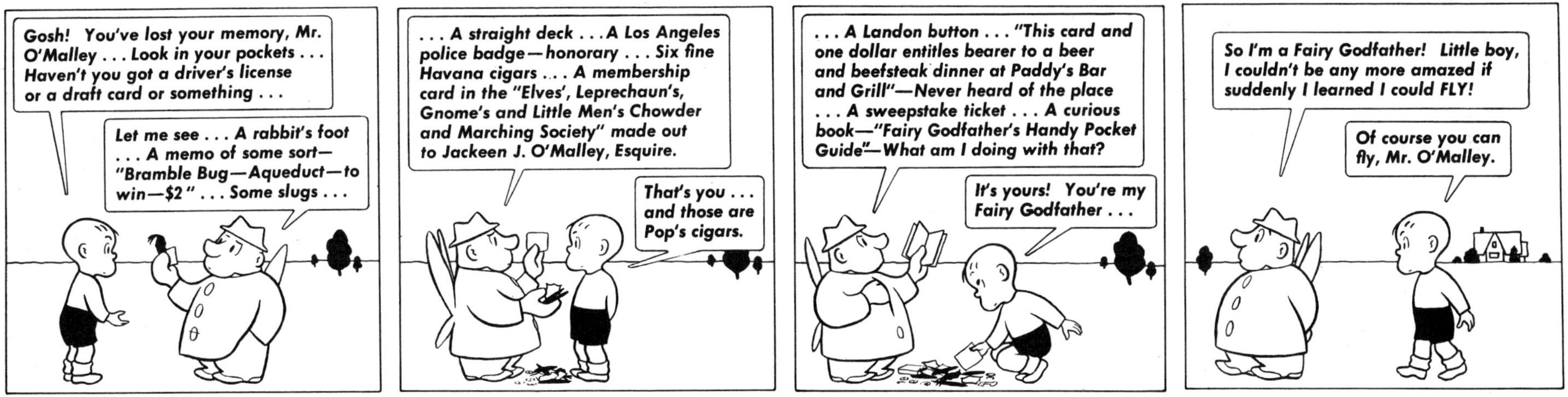
Gosh! You've lost your memory, Mr. O'Malley . . . Look in your pockets . . . Haven't you got a driver's license or a draft card or something . . .
Let me see . . . A rabbit's foot . . . A memo of some sort— "Bramble Bug—Aqueduct—to win—$2" . . . Some slugs . . .
. . . A straight deck . . . A Los Angeles police badge—honorary . . . Six fine Havana cigars . . . A membership card in the "Elves', Leprechaun's, Gnome's and Little Men's Chowder and Marching Society" made out to Jackeen J. O'Malley, Esquire.
That's you . . . and those are Pop's cigars.
. . . A Landon button . . . "This card and one dollar entitles bearer to a beer and beefsteak dinner at Paddy's Bar and Grill"—Never heard of the place . . . A sweepstake ticket . . . A curious book—"Fairy Godfather's Handy Pocket Guide"—What am I doing with that?
It's yours! You're my Fairy Godfather . . .
So I'm a Fairy Godfather! Little boy, I couldn't be any more amazed if suddenly I learned I could FLY!
Of course you can fly, Mr. O'Malley.

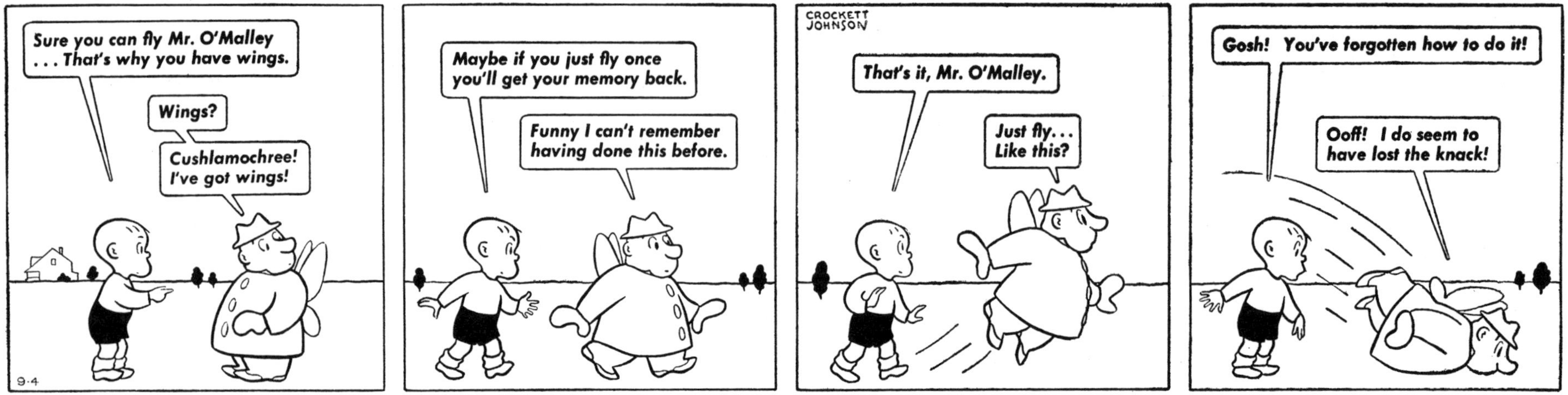
Sure you can fly Mr. O'Malley . . . That's why you have wings.
Wings?
Cushlamochree! I've got wings!
9·4
Maybe if you just fly once you'll get your memory back.
Funny I can't remember having done this before.
CROCKETT JOHNSON
That's it, Mr. O'Malley.
Just fly. . . Like this?
Gosh! You've forgotten how to do it!
Ooff! I do seem to have lost the knack!

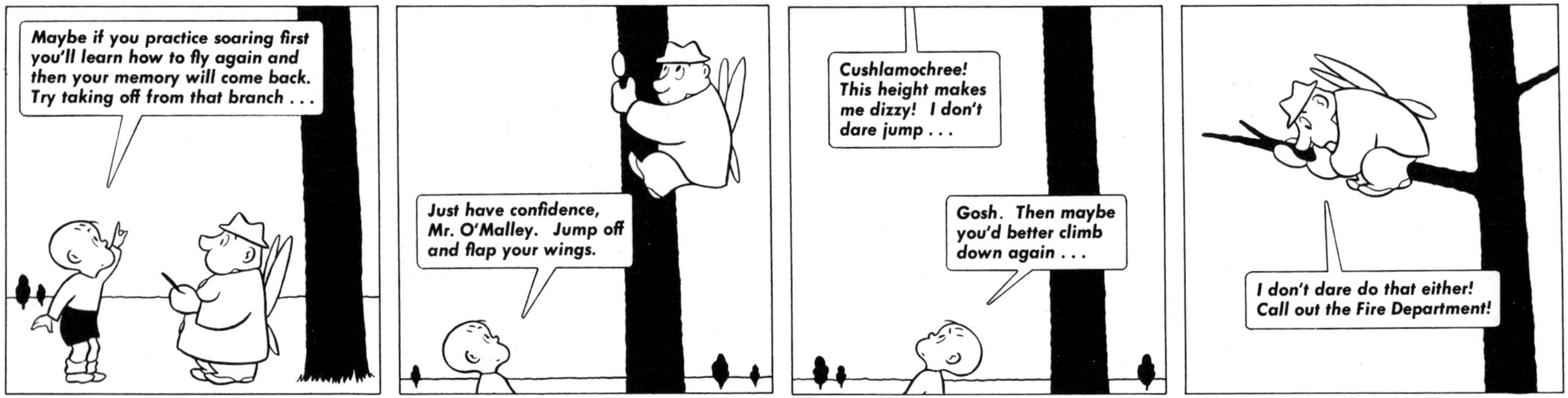
Maybe if you practice soaring first you'll learn how to fly again and then your memory will come back. Try taking off from that branch . . .
Just have confidence, Mr. O'Malley. Jump off and flap your wings.
Cushlamochree! This height makes me dizzy! I don't dare jump . . .
Gosh. Then maybe you'd better climb down again . . .
I don't dare do that either! Call out the Fire Department!

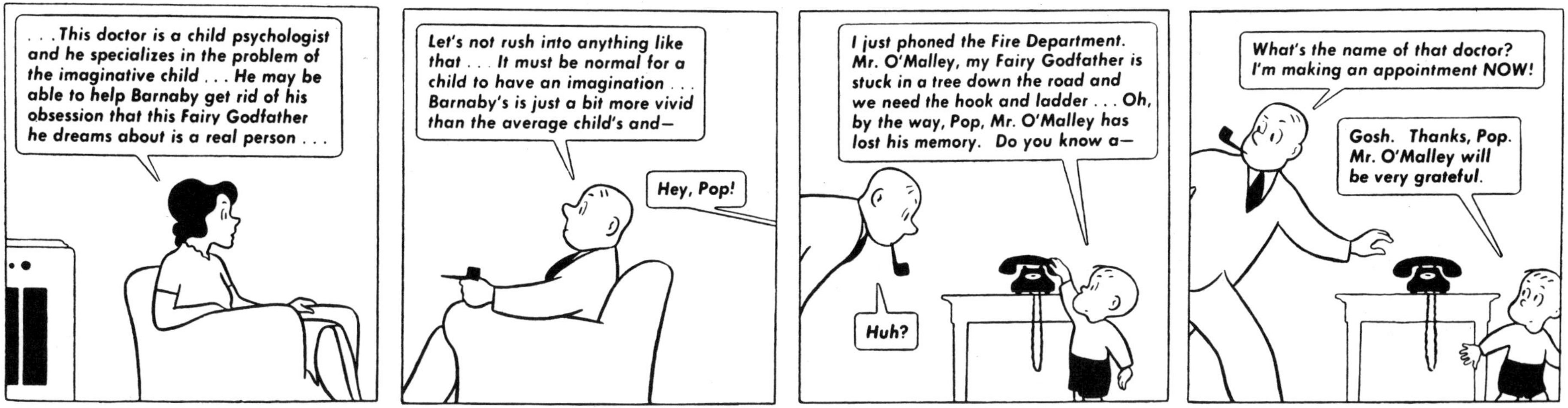
. . . This doctor is a child psychologist and he specializes in the problem of the imaginative child . . . He may be able to help Barnaby get rid of his obsession that this Fairy Godfather he dreams about is a real person . . .
Let's not rush into anything like that . . . It must be normal for a child to have an imagination . . . Barnaby's is just a bit more vivid than the average child's and—
Hey, Pop!
I just phoned the Fire Department. Mr. O'Malley, my Fairy Godfather is stuck in a tree down the road and we need the hook and ladder . . . Oh, by the way, Pop, Mr. O'Malley has lost his memory. Do you know a—
Huh?
What's the name of that doctor? I'm making an appointment NOW!
Gosh. Thanks, Pop. Mr. O'Malley will be very grateful.

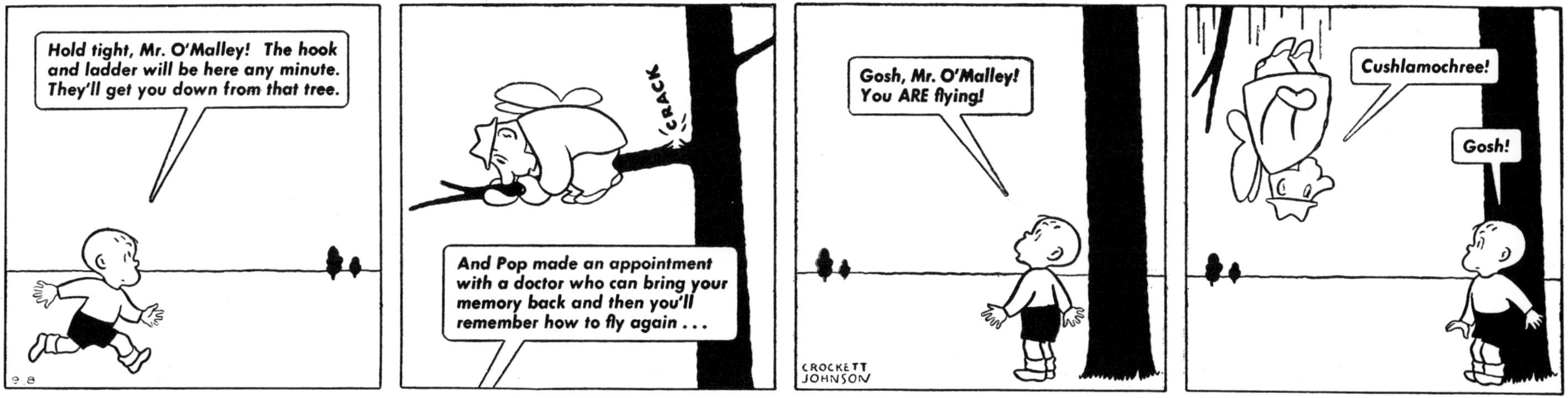
Hold tight, Mr. O'Malley! The hook and ladder will be here any minute. They'll get you down from that tree.
9.8
CRACK
And Pop made an appointment with a doctor who can bring your memory back and then you'll remember how to fly again . . .
Gosh, Mr. O'Malley! You ARE flying!
CROCKETT JOHNSON
Cushlamochree!
Gosh!

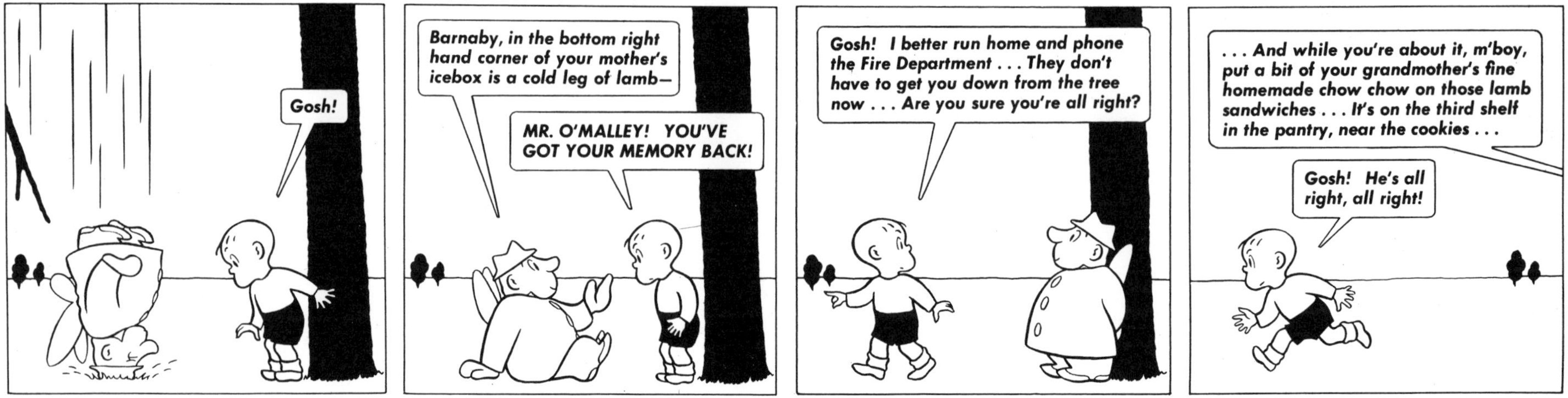
Gosh!
Barnaby, in the bottom right hand corner of your mother's icebox is a cold leg of lamb—
MR. O'MALLEY! YOU'VE GOT YOUR MEMORY BACK!
Gosh! I better run home and phone the Fire Department . . . They don't have to get you down from the tree now . . . Are you sure you're all right?
. . . And while you're about it, m'boy, put a bit of your grandmother's fine homemade chow chow on those lamb sandwiches . . . It's on the third shelf in the pantry, near the cookies . . .
Gosh! He's all right, all right!

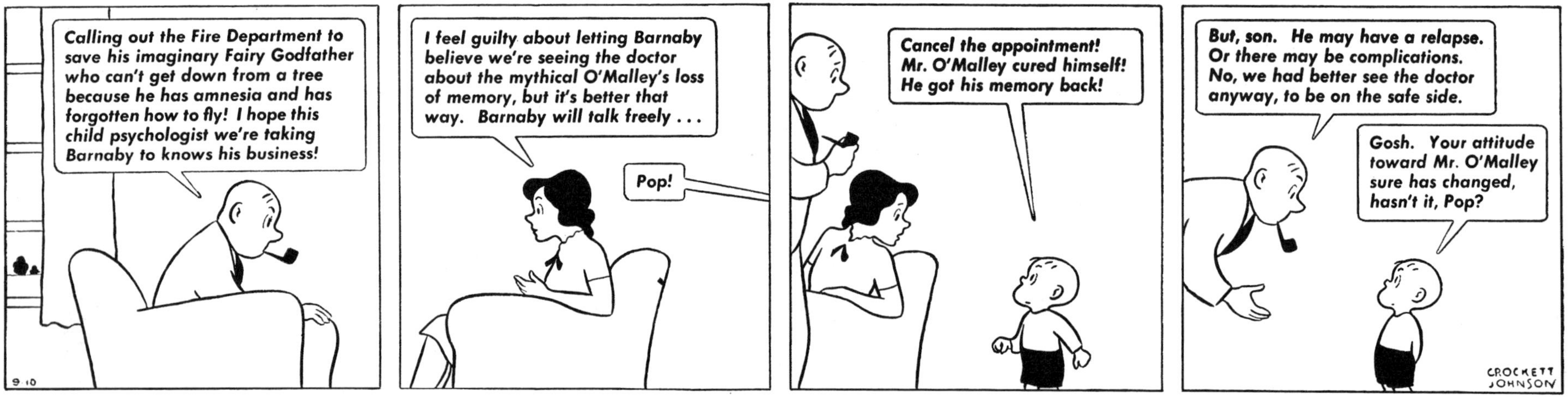
Calling out the Fire Department to save his imaginary Fairy Godfather who can't get down from a tree because he has amnesia and has forgotten how to fly! I hope this child psychologist we're taking Barnaby to knows his business!
9 10
I feel guilty about letting Barnaby believe we're seeing the doctor about the mythical O'Malley's loss of memory, but it's better that way. Barnaby will talk freely . . .
Pop!
Cancel the appointment! Mr. O'Malley cured himself! He got his memory back!
But, son. He may have a relapse. Or there may be complications. No, we had better see the doctor anyway, to be on the safe side.
Gosh. Your attitude toward Mr. O'Malley sure has changed, hasn't it, Pop?
CROCKETT JOHNSON

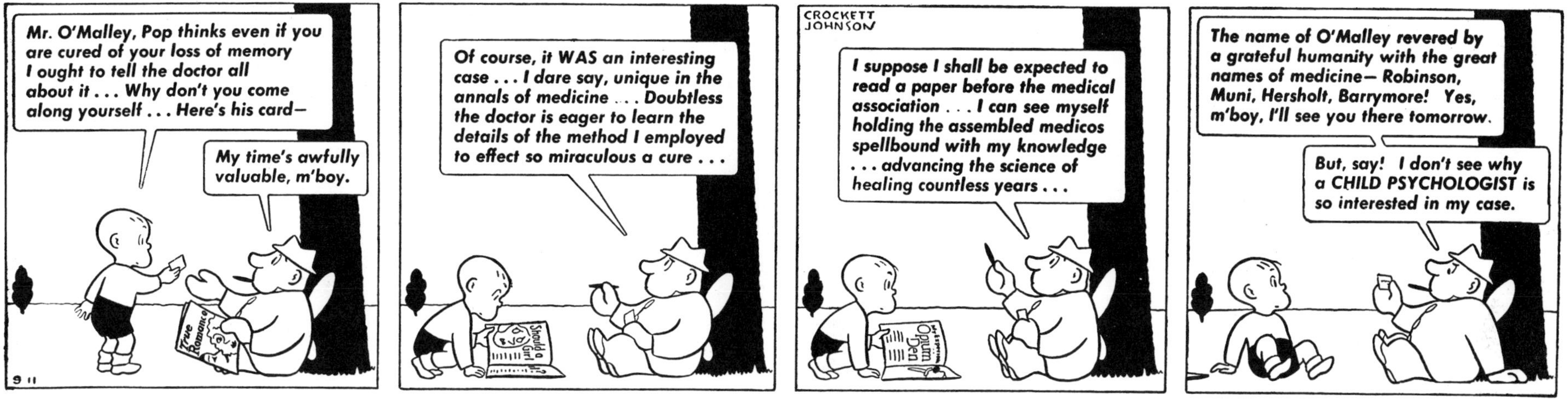
9 11
Mr. O'Malley, Pop thinks even if you are cured of your loss of memory I ought to tell the doctor all about it . . . Why don't you come along yourself . . . Here's his card—
My time's awfully valuable, m'boy.
True Romance
Of course, it WAS an interesting case . . . I dare say, unique in the annals of medicine . . . Doubtless the doctor is eager to learn the details of the method I employed to effect so miraculous a cure . . .
CROCKETT JOHNSON
I suppose I shall be expected to read a paper before the medical association . . . I can see myself holding the assembled medicos spellbound with my knowledge . . . advancing the science of healing countless years . . .
Opium Den
The name of O'Malley revered by a grateful humanity with the great names of medicine— Robinson, Muni, Hersholt, Barrymore! Yes, m'boy, I'll see you there tomorrow.
But, say! I don't see why a CHILD PSYCHOLOGIST is so interested in my case.

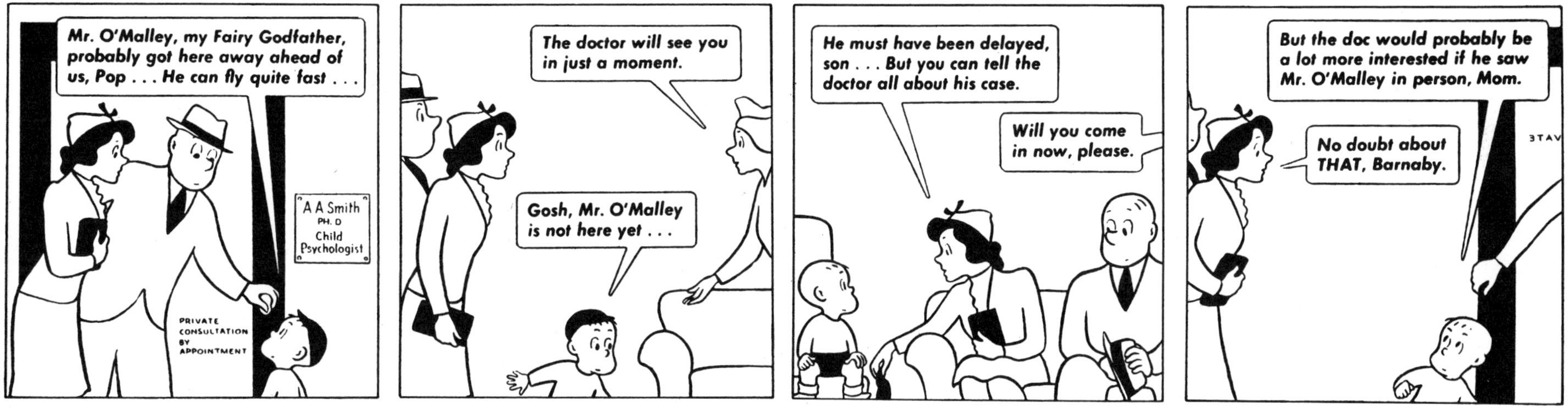
Mr. O'Malley, my Fairy Godfather, probably got here away ahead of us, Pop . . . He can fly quite fast . . .
A A Smith
PH. D
Child
Psychologist
PRIVATE CONSULTATION BY APPOINTMENT
The doctor will see you in just a moment.
Gosh, Mr. O'Malley is not here yet . . .
He must have been delayed, son . . . But you can tell the doctor all about his case.
Will you come in now, please.
But the doc would probably be a lot more interested if he saw Mr. O'Malley in person, Mom.
No doubt about THAT, Barnaby.

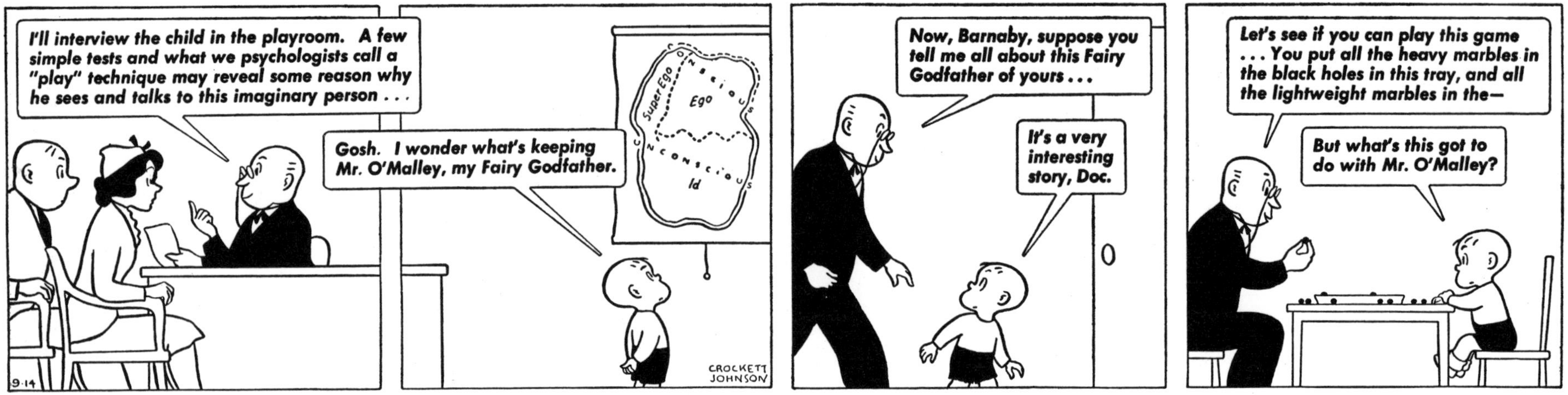
I'll interview the child in the playroom. A few simple tests and what we psychologists call a "play" technique may reveal some reason why he sees and talks to this imaginary person . . .
9-14
Gosh. I wonder what's keeping Mr. O'Malley, my Fairy Godfather.
CONSCIOUS
Super Ego
Ego
UNCONSCIOUS
Id
CROCKETT JOHNSON
Now, Barnaby, suppose you tell me all about this Fairy Godfather of yours . . .
It's a very interesting story, Doc.
Let's see if you can play this game . . . You put all the heavy marbles in the black holes in this tray, and all the lightweight marbles in the—
But what's this got to do with Mr. O'Malley?

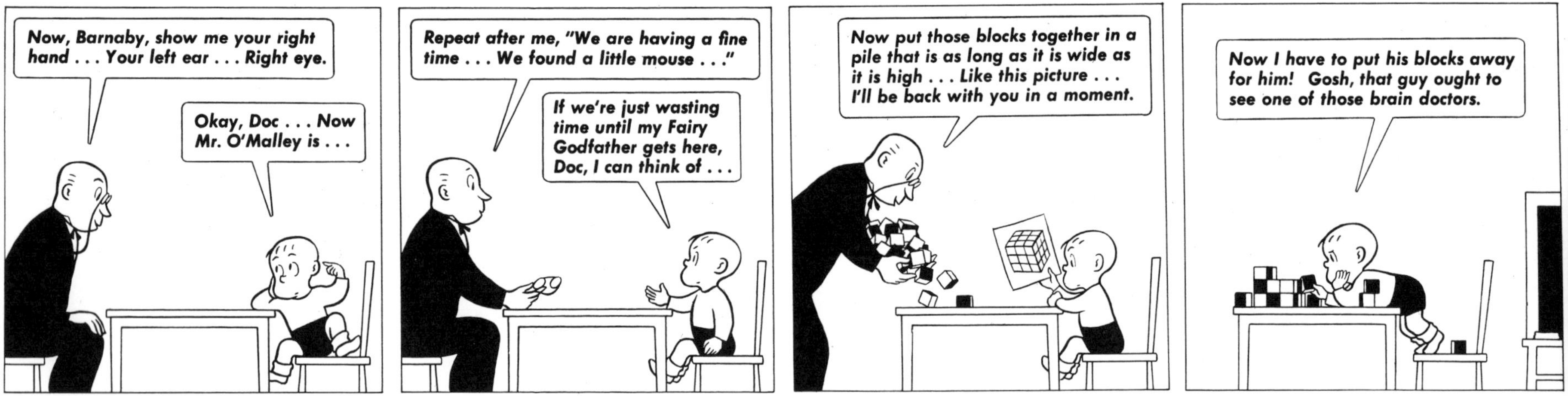
Now, Barnaby, show me your right hand . . . Your left ear . . . Right eye.
Okay, Doc . . . Now Mr. O'Malley is . . .
Repeat after me, "We are having a fine time . . . We found a little mouse . . ."
If we're just wasting time until my Fairy Godfather gets here, Doc, I can think of . . .
Now put those blocks together in a pile that is as long as it is wide as it is high . . . Like this picture . . . I'll be back with you in a moment.
Now I have to put his blocks away for him! Gosh, that guy ought to see one of those brain doctors.

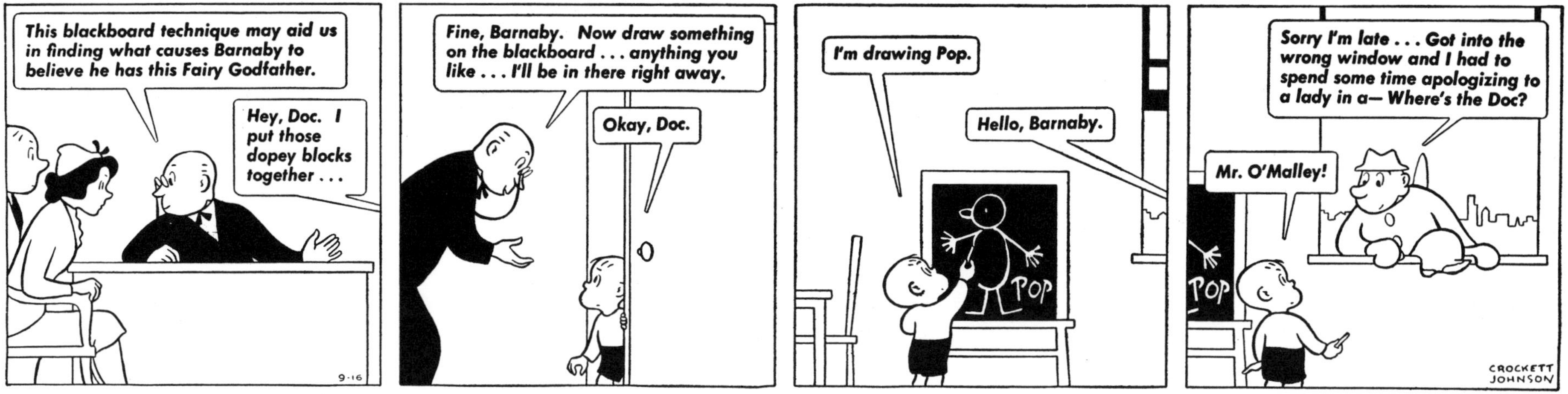
This blackboard technique may aid us in finding what causes Barnaby to believe he has this Fairy Godfather.
Hey, Doc. I put those dopey blocks together . . .
9-16
Fine, Barnaby. Now draw something on the blackboard . . . anything you like . . . I'll be in there right away.
Okay, Doc.
I'm drawing Pop.
Hello, Barnaby.
POP
Sorry I'm late . . . Got into the wrong window and I had to spend some time apologizing to a lady in a— Where's the Doc?
Mr. O'Malley!
POP
CROCKETT JOHNSON

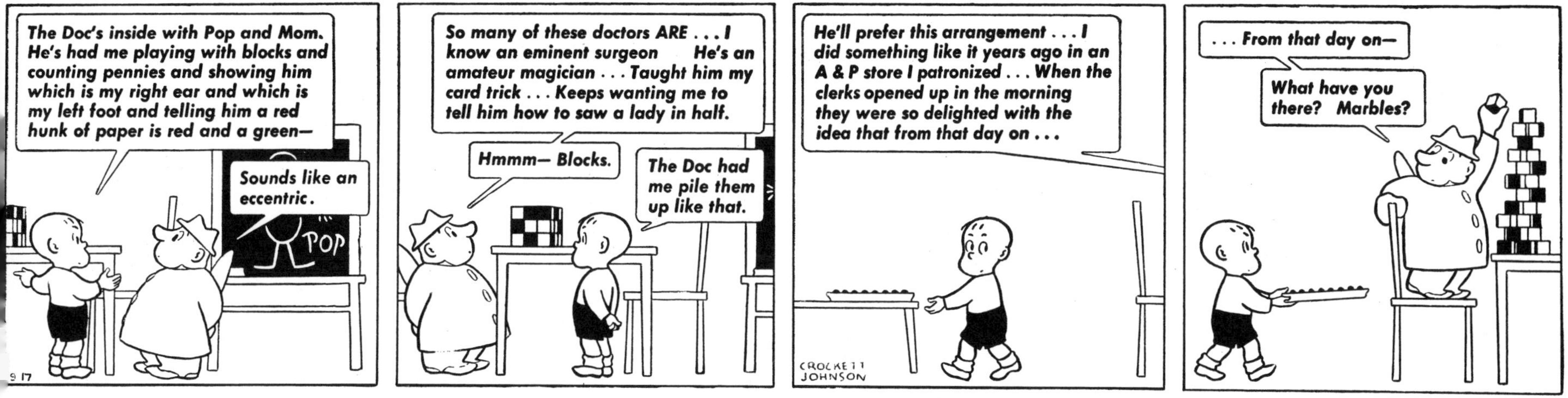
The Doc's inside with Pop and Mom. He's had me playing with blocks and counting pennies and showing him which is my right ear and which is my left foot and telling him a red hunk of paper is red and a green—
Sounds like an eccentric.
POP
9 17
So many of these doctors ARE . . . I know an eminent surgeon He's an amateur magician . . . Taught him my card trick . . . Keeps wanting me to tell him how to saw a lady in half.
Hmmm— Blocks.
The Doc had me pile them up like that.
He'll prefer this arrangement . . . I did something like it years ago in an A & P store I patronized . . . When the clerks opened up in the morning they were so delighted with the idea that from that day on . . .
CROCKETT JOHNSON
. . . From that day on—
What have you there? Marbles?

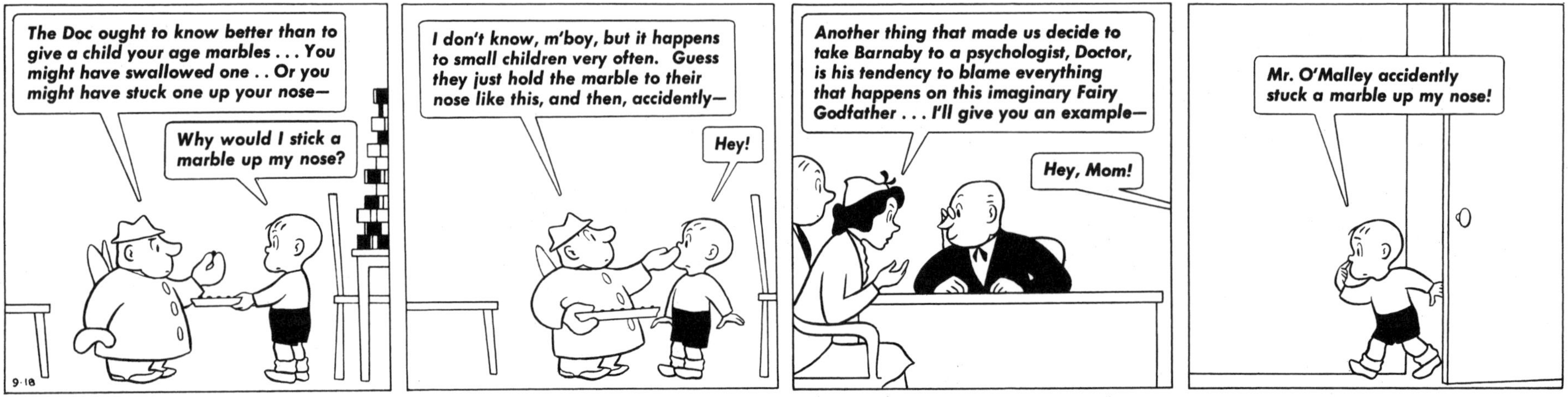
The Doc ought to know better than to give a child your age marbles . . . You might have swallowed one . . Or you might have stuck one up your nose—
Why would I stick a marble up my nose?
9-18
I don't know, m'boy, but it happens to small children very often. Guess they just hold the marble to their nose like this, and then, accidently—
Hey!
Another thing that made us decide to take Barnaby to a psychologist, Doctor, is his tendency to blame everything that happens on this imaginary Fairy Godfather . . . I'll give you an example—
Hey, Mom!
Mr. O'Malley accidently stuck a marble up my nose!

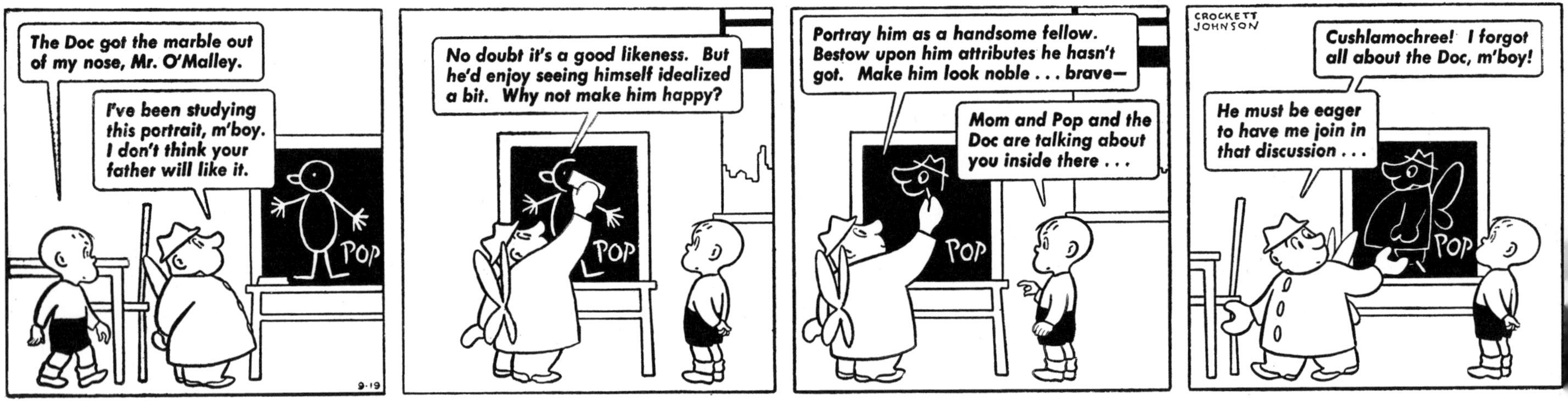
The Doc got the marble out of my nose, Mr. O'Malley.
I've been studying this portrait, m'boy. I don't think your father will like it.
POP
9-19
No doubt it's a good likeness. But he'd enjoy seeing himself idealized a bit. Why not make him happy?
POP
Portray him as a handsome fellow. Bestow upon him attributes he hasn't got. Make him look noble . . . brave—
Mom and Pop and the Doc are talking about you inside there . . .
POP
CROCKETT JOHNSON
Cushlamochree! I forgot all about the Doc, m'boy!
He must be eager to have me join in that discussion . . .
POP

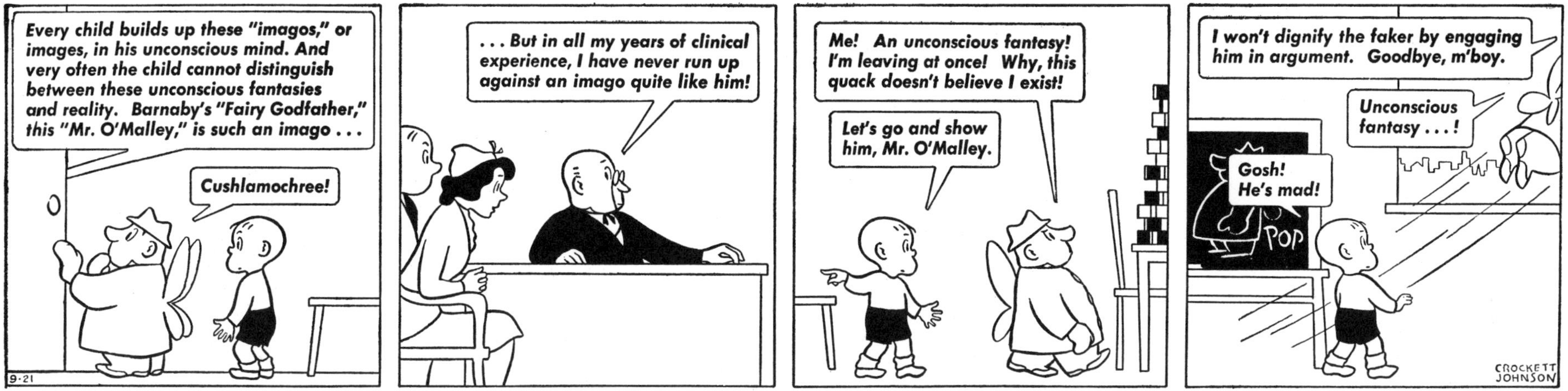

Every child builds up these "imagos," or images, in his unconscious mind. And very often the child cannot distinguish between these unconscious fantasies and reality. Barnaby's "Fairy Godfather," this "Mr. O'Malley," is such an imago . . .
Cushlamochree!
9·21
. . . But in all my years of clinical experience, I have never run up against an imago quite like him!
Me! An unconscious fantasy! I'm leaving at once! Why, this quack doesn't believe I exist!
Let's go and show him, Mr. O'Malley.
I won't dignify the faker by engaging him in argument. Goodbye, m'boy.
Unconscious fantasy . . . !
Gosh! He's mad!
POP
CROCKETT JOHNSON

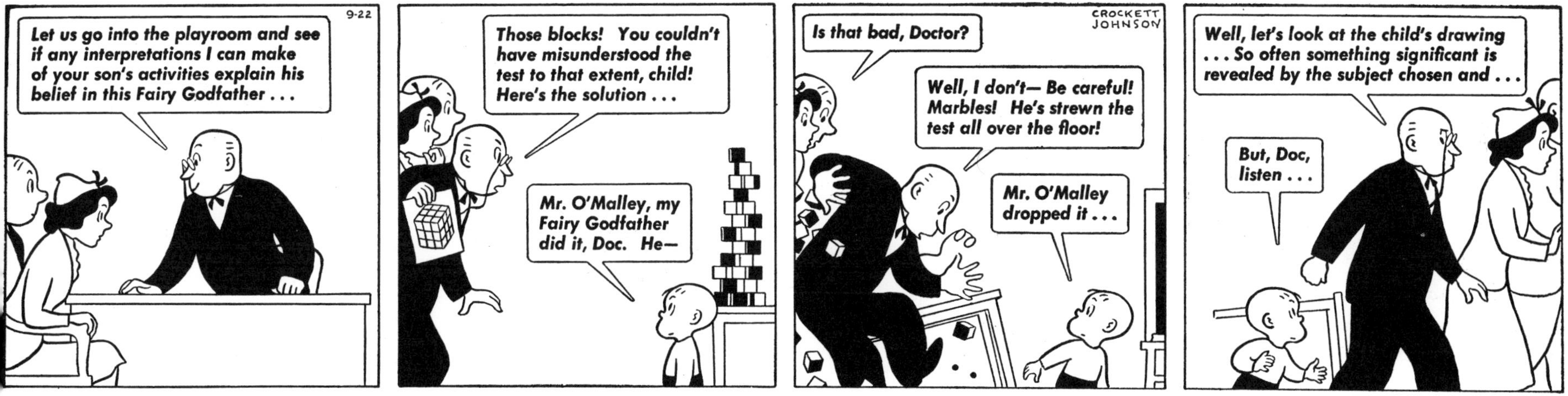

9·22
Let us go into the playroom and see if any interpretations I can make of your son's activities explain his belief in this Fairy Godfather . . .
Those blocks! You couldn't have misunderstood the test to that extent, child! Here's the solution . . .
Mr. O'Malley, my Fairy Godfather did it, Doc. He—
CROCKETT JOHNSON
Is that bad, Doctor?
Well, I don't— Be careful! Marbles! He's strewn the test all over the floor!
Mr. O'Malley dropped it . . .
Well, let's look at the child's drawing . . . So often something significant is revealed by the subject chosen and . . .
But, Doc, listen . . .

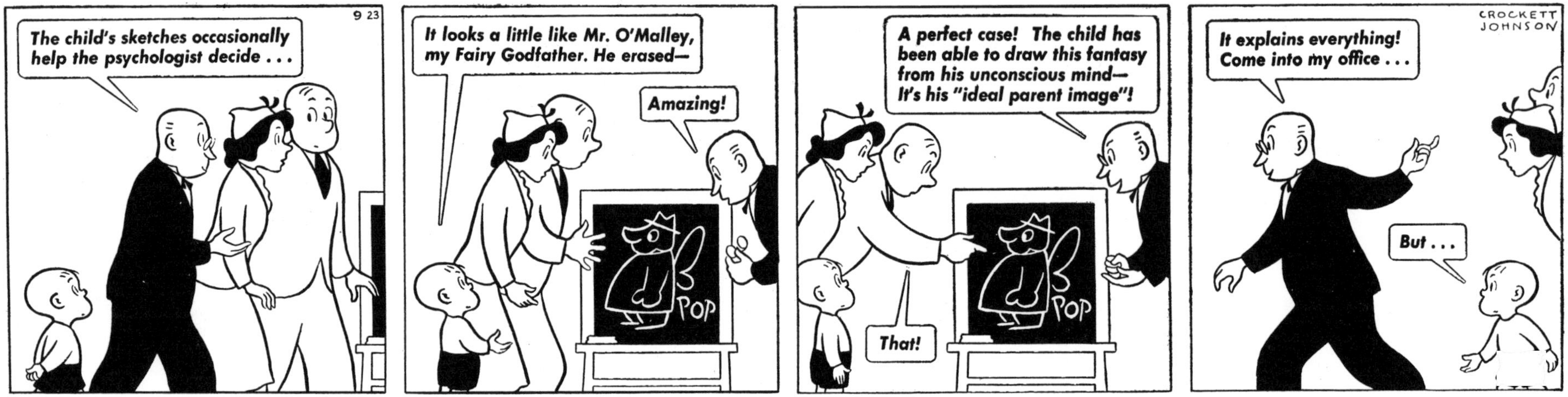
9 23
The child's sketches occasionally help the psychologist decide . . .
It looks a little like Mr. O'Malley, my Fairy Godfather. He erased—
Amazing!
POP
A perfect case! The child has been able to draw this fantasy from his unconscious mind— It's his "ideal parent image"!
That!
POP
CROCKETT JOHNSON
It explains everything! Come into my office . . .
But . . .

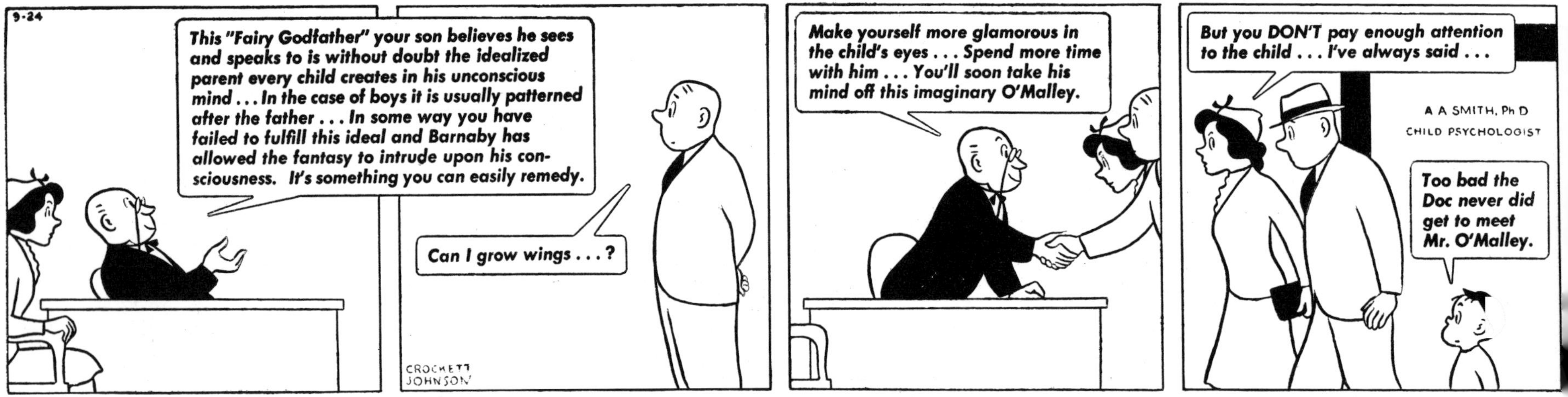
9-24
This "Fairy Godfather" your son believes he sees and speaks to is without doubt the idealized parent every child creates in his unconscious mind . . . In the case of boys it is usually patterned after the father . . . In some way you have failed to fulfill this ideal and Barnaby has allowed the fantasy to intrude upon his consciousness. It's something you can easily remedy.
Can I grow wings . . . ?
CROCKETT JOHNSON
Make yourself more glamorous in the child's eyes . . . Spend more time with him . . . You'll soon take his mind off this imaginary O'Malley.
But you DON'T pay enough attention to the child . . . I've always said . . .
A A SMITH, Ph D
CHILD PSYCHOLOGIST
Too bad the Doc never did get to meet Mr. O'Malley.

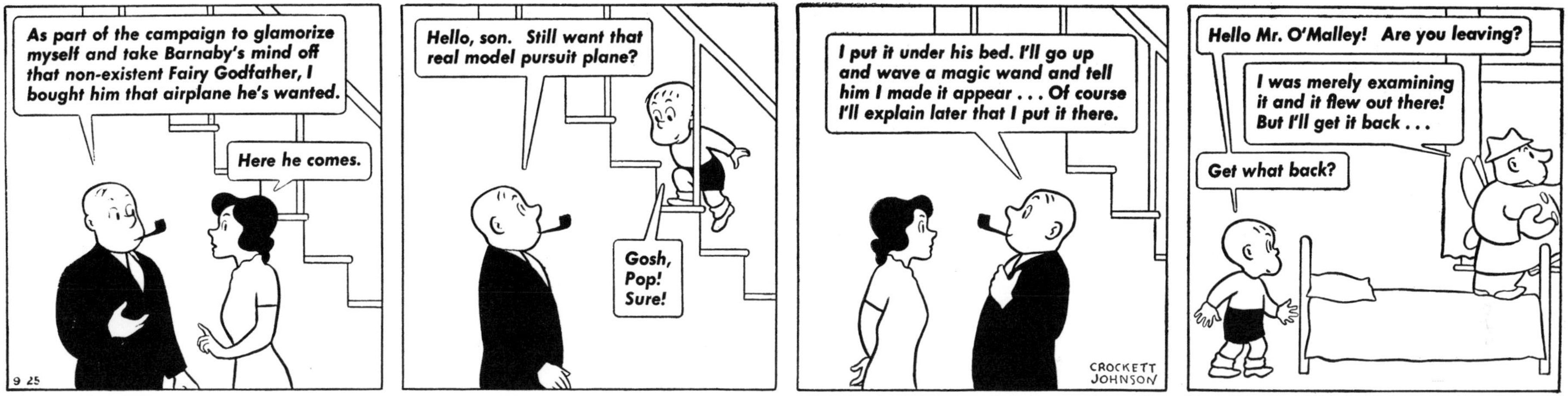
As part of the campaign to glamorize myself and take Barnaby's mind off that non-existent Fairy Godfather, I bought him that airplane he's wanted.
Here he comes.
9 25
Hello, son. Still want that real model pursuit plane?
Gosh, Pop! Sure!
I put it under his bed. I'll go up and wave a magic wand and tell him I made it appear . . . Of course I'll explain later that I put it there.
CROCKETT JOHNSON
Hello Mr. O'Malley! Are you leaving?
I was merely examining it and it flew out there! But I'll get it back . . .
Get what back?

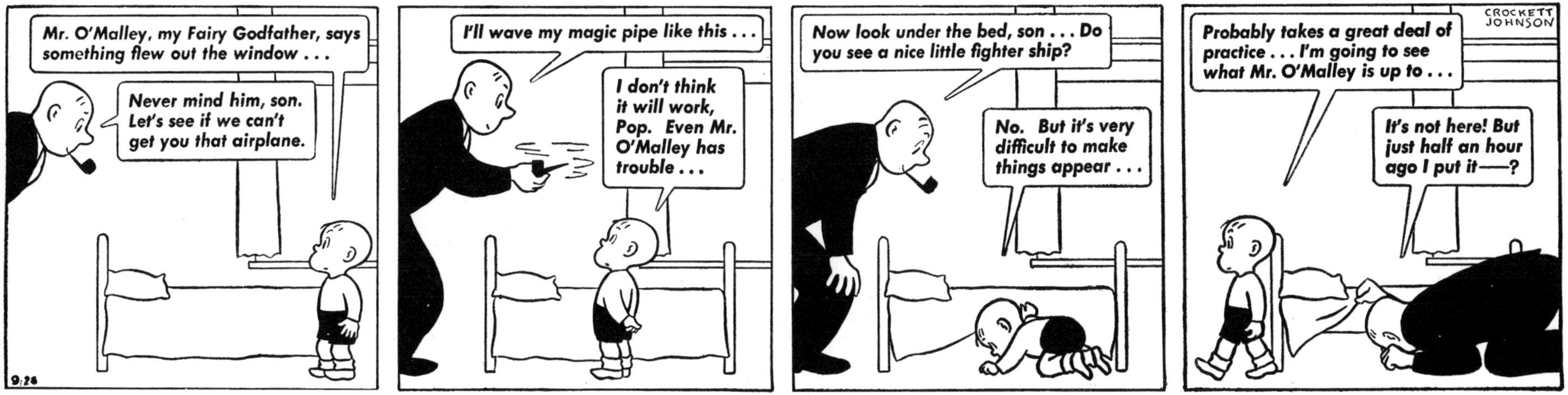
Mr. O'Malley, my Fairy Godfather, says something flew out the window . . .
Never mind him, son. Let's see if we can't get you that airplane.
9 26
I'll wave my magic pipe like this . . .
I don't think it will work, Pop. Even Mr. O'Malley has trouble . . .
Now look under the bed, son . . . Do you see a nice little fighter ship?
No. But it's very difficult to make things appear . . .
CROCKETT JOHNSON
Probably takes a great deal of practice . . . I'm going to see what Mr. O'Malley is up to . . .
It's not here! But just half an hour ago I put it—?

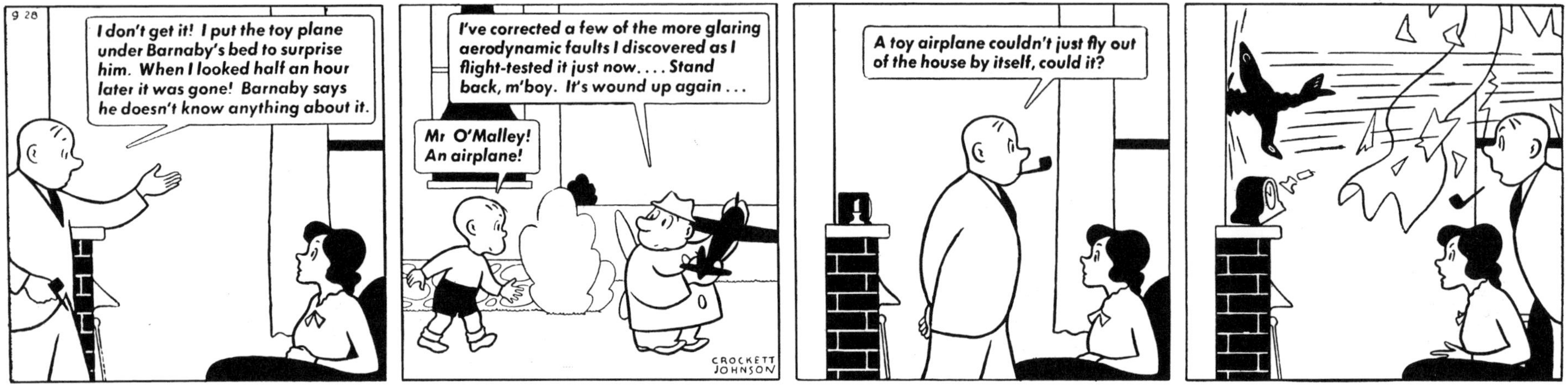
9 28
I don't get it! I put the toy plane under Barnaby's bed to surprise him. When I looked half an hour later it was gone! Barnaby says he doesn't know anything about it.
I've corrected a few of the more glaring aerodynamic faults I discovered as I flight-tested it just now.... Stand back, m'boy. It's wound up again...
Mr O'Malley! An airplane!
CROCKETT JOHNSON
A toy airplane couldn't just fly out of the house by itself, could it?

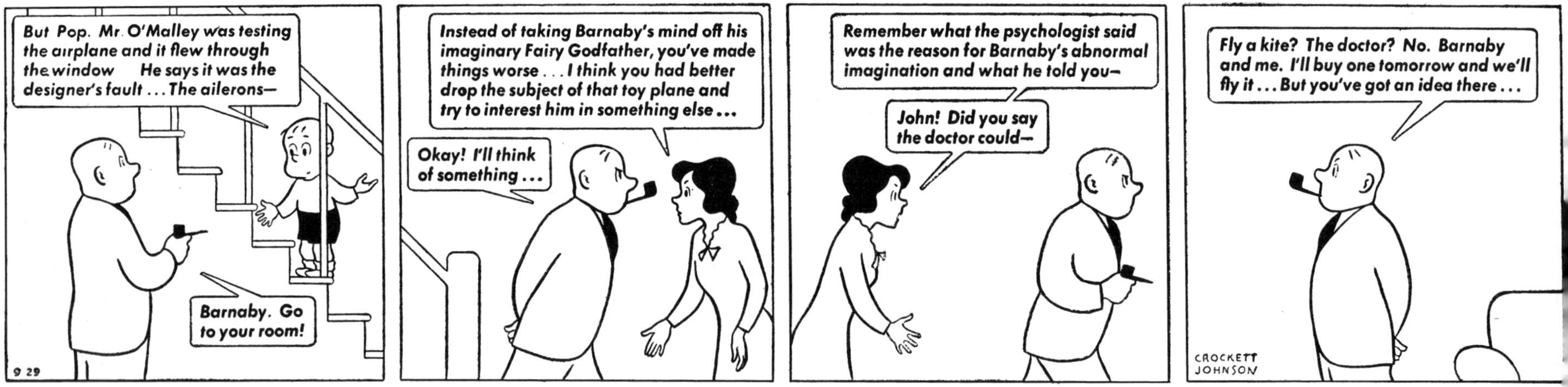
But Pop. Mr. O'Malley was testing the airplane and it flew through the window He says it was the designer's fault ... The ailerons—
Barnaby. Go to your room!
9 29
Instead of taking Barnaby's mind off his imaginary Fairy Godfather, you've made things worse ... I think you had better drop the subject of that toy plane and try to interest him in something else ...
Okay! I'll think of something ...
Remember what the psychologist said was the reason for Barnaby's abnormal imagination and what he told you—
John! Did you say the doctor could—
Fly a kite? The doctor? No. Barnaby and me. I'll buy one tomorrow and we'll fly it ... But you've got an idea there ...
CROCKETT JOHNSON

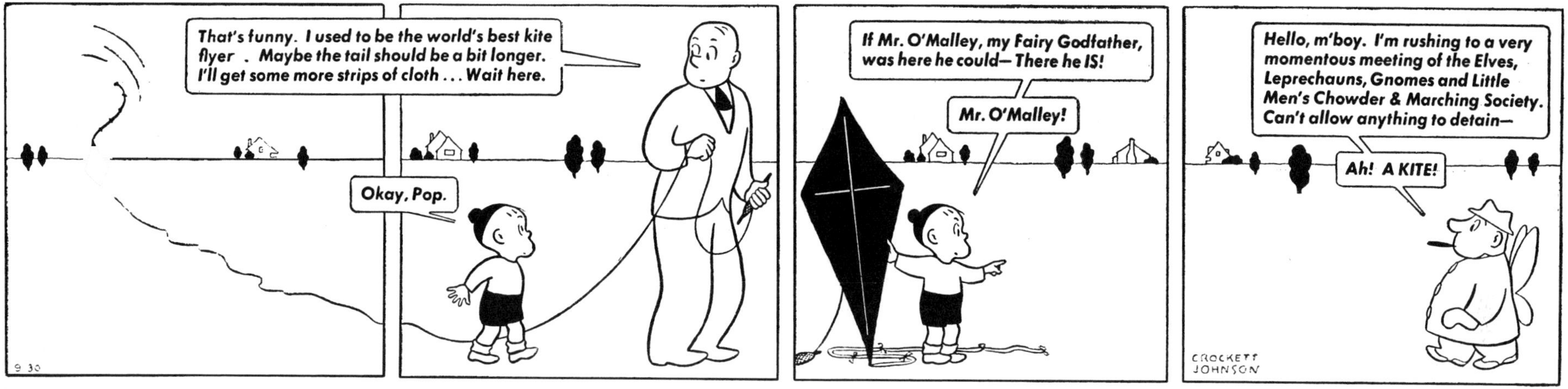
That's funny. I used to be the world's best kite flyer . Maybe the tail should be a bit longer. I'll get some more strips of cloth . . . Wait here.
Okay, Pop.
If Mr. O'Malley, my Fairy Godfather, was here he could— There he IS!
Mr. O'Malley!
Hello, m'boy. I'm rushing to a very momentous meeting of the Elves, Leprechauns, Gnomes and Little Men's Chowder & Marching Society. Can't allow anything to detain—
Ah! A KITE!
CROCKETT JOHNSON

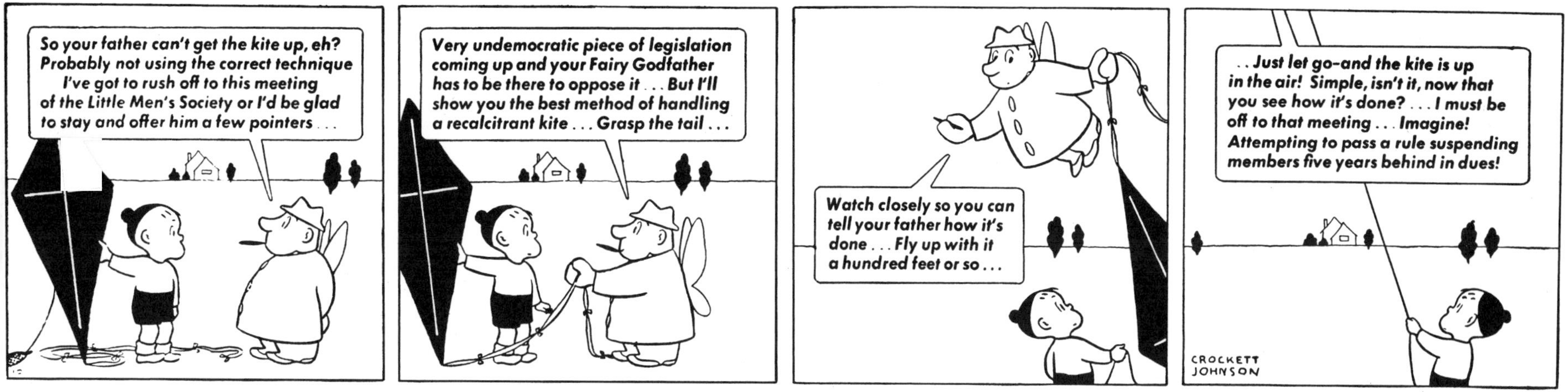
So your father can't get the kite up, eh? Probably not using the correct technique I've got to rush off to this meeting of the Little Men's Society or I'd be glad to stay and offer him a few pointers . . .
Very undemocratic piece of legislation coming up and your Fairy Godfather has to be there to oppose it . . . But I'll show you the best method of handling a recalcitrant kite . . . Grasp the tail . . .
Watch closely so you can tell your father how it's done . . . Fly up with it a hundred feet or so . . .
. . Just let go–and the kite is up in the air! Simple, isn't it, now that you see how it's done? . . . I must be off to that meeting . . . Imagine! Attempting to pass a rule suspending members five years behind in dues!
CROCKETT JOHNSON

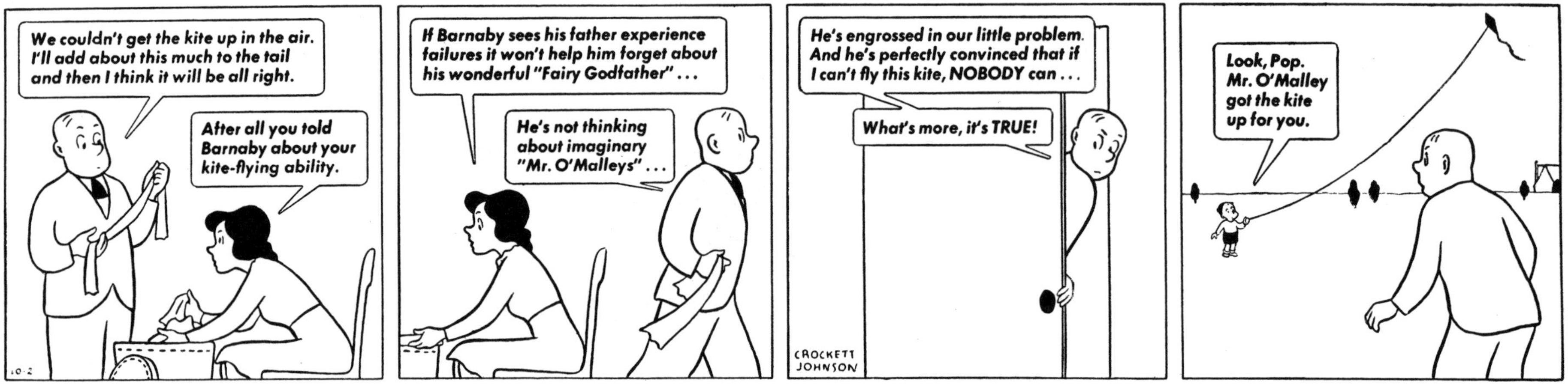
We couldn't get the kite up in the air. I'll add about this much to the tail and then I think it will be all right.
After all you told Barnaby about your kite-flying ability.
10-2
If Barnaby sees his father experience failures it won't help him forget about his wonderful "Fairy Godfather" . . .
He's not thinking about imaginary "Mr. O'Malleys" . . .
He's engrossed in our little problem. And he's perfectly convinced that if I can't fly this kite, NOBODY can . . .
What's more, it's TRUE!
CROCKETT JOHNSON
Look, Pop. Mr. O'Malley got the kite up for you.

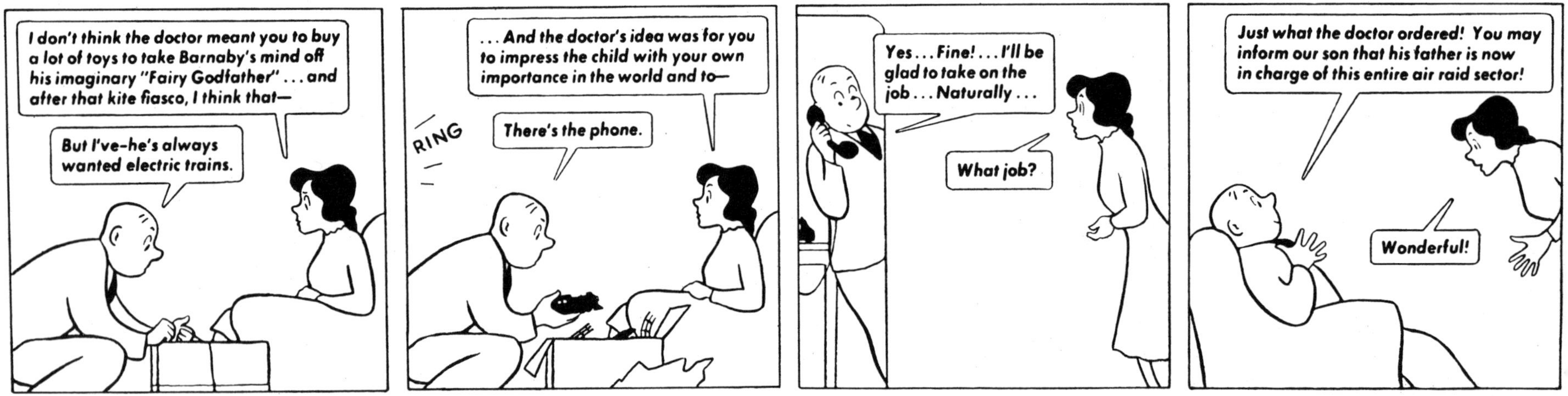
I don't think the doctor meant you to buy a lot of toys to take Barnaby's mind off his imaginary "Fairy Godfather" . . . and after that kite fiasco, I think that—
But I've–he's always wanted electric trains.
. . . And the doctor's idea was for you to impress the child with your own importance in the world and to—
RING
There's the phone.
Yes . . . Fine! . . . I'll be glad to take on the job . . . Naturally . . .
What job?
Just what the doctor ordered! You may inform our son that his father is now in charge of this entire air raid sector!
Wonderful!

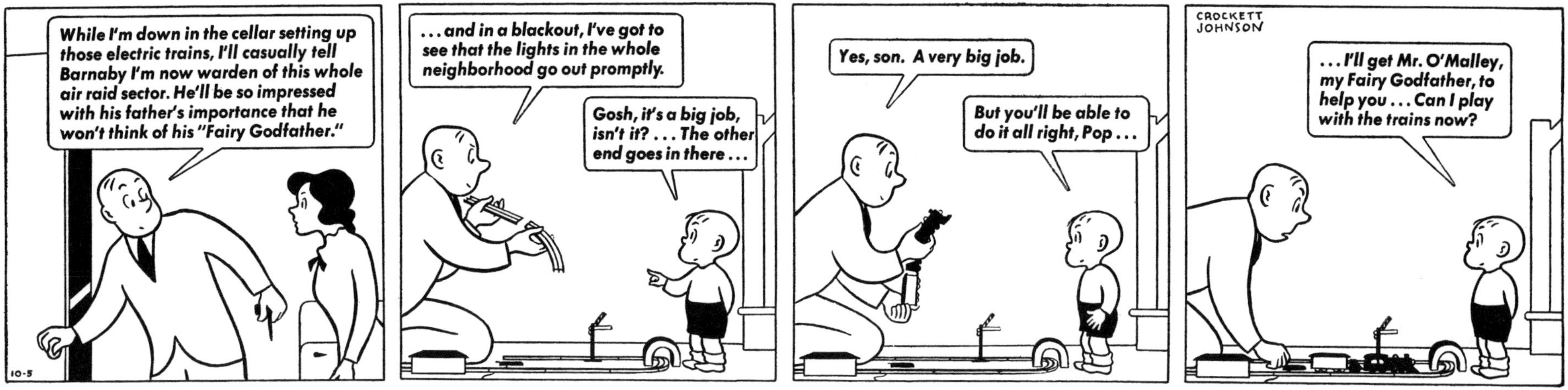
While I'm down in the cellar setting up those electric trains, I'll casually tell Barnaby I'm now warden of this whole air raid sector. He'll be so impressed with his father's importance that he won't think of his "Fairy Godfather."
10-5
. . . and in a blackout, I've got to see that the lights in the whole neighborhood go out promptly.
Gosh, it's a big job, isn't it? . . . The other end goes in there . . .
Yes, son. A very big job.
But you'll be able to do it all right, Pop . . .
CROCKETT JOHNSON
. . . I'll get Mr. O'Malley, my Fairy Godfather, to help you . . . Can I play with the trains now?

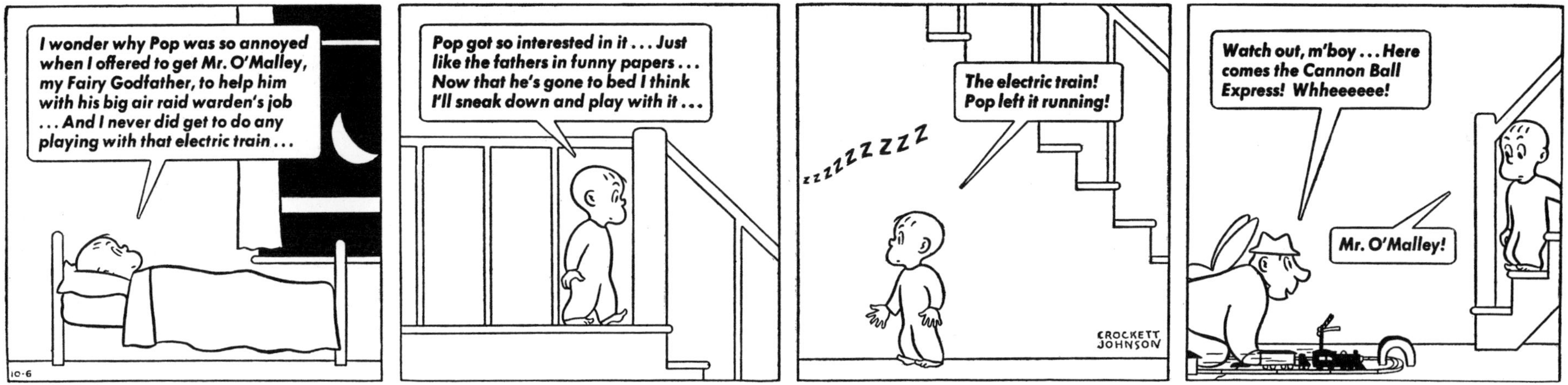
I wonder why Pop was so annoyed when I offered to get Mr. O'Malley, my Fairy Godfather, to help him with his big air raid warden's job . . . And I never did get to do any playing with that electric train . . .
10-6
Pop got so interested in it . . . Just like the fathers in funny papers . . . Now that he's gone to bed I think I'll sneak down and play with it . . .
zzzZZZZZ
The electric train! Pop left it running!
CROCKETT JOHNSON
Watch out, m'boy . . . Here comes the Cannon Ball Express! Whheeeeee!
Mr. O'Malley!

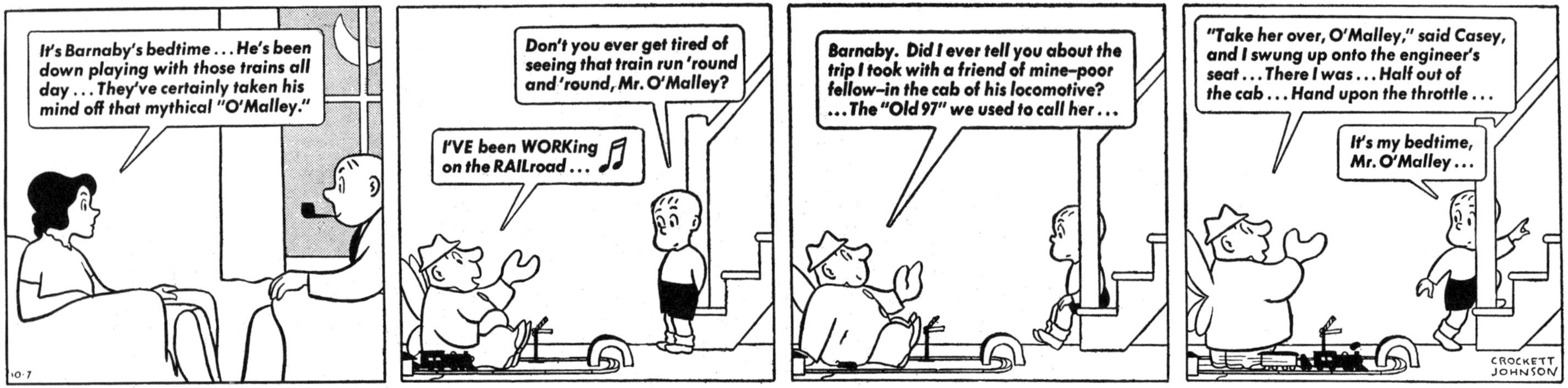
10-7
It's Barnaby's bedtime . . . He's been down playing with those trains all day . . . They've certainly taken his mind off that mythical "O'Malley."
Don't you ever get tired of seeing that train run 'round and 'round, Mr. O'Malley?
I'VE been WORKing on the RAILroad . . .
Barnaby. Did I ever tell you about the trip I took with a friend of mine–poor fellow–in the cab of his locomotive? . . . The "Old 97" we used to call her . . .
"Take her over, O'Malley," said Casey, and I swung up onto the engineer's seat . . . There I was . . . Half out of the cab . . . Hand upon the throttle . . .
It's my bedtime, Mr. O'Malley . . .
CROCKETT JOHNSON

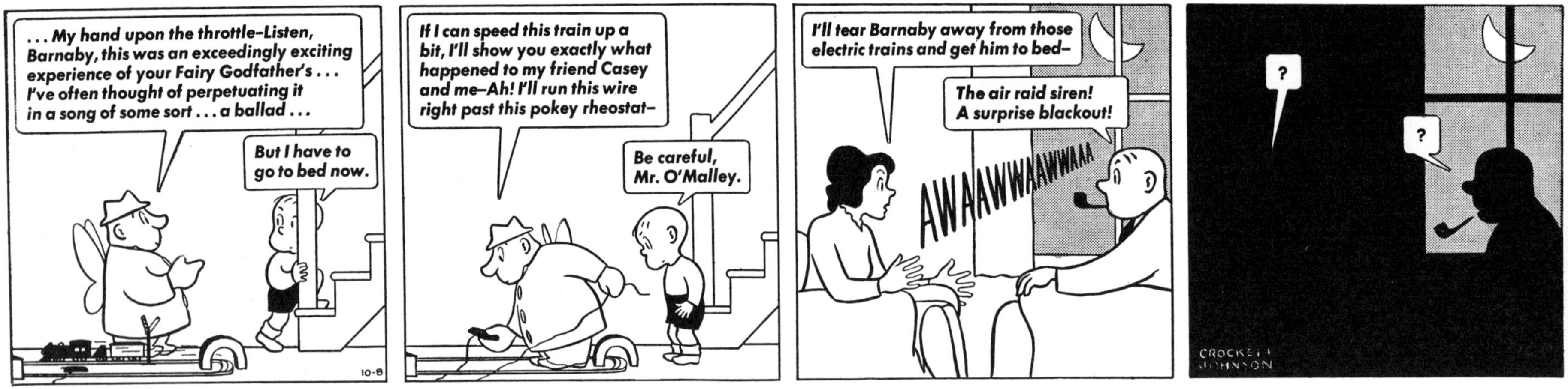
. . . My hand upon the throttle–Listen, Barnaby, this was an exceedingly exciting experience of your Fairy Godfather's . . . I've often thought of perpetuating it in a song of some sort . . . a ballad . . .
But I have to go to bed now.
10-8
If I can speed this train up a bit, I'll show you exactly what happened to my friend Casey and me–Ah! I'll run this wire right past this pokey rheostat–
Be careful, Mr. O'Malley.
I'll tear Barnaby away from those electric trains and get him to bed–
The air raid siren! A surprise blackout!
AWAAWWAAWWAAA
?
?
CROCKETT JOHNSON

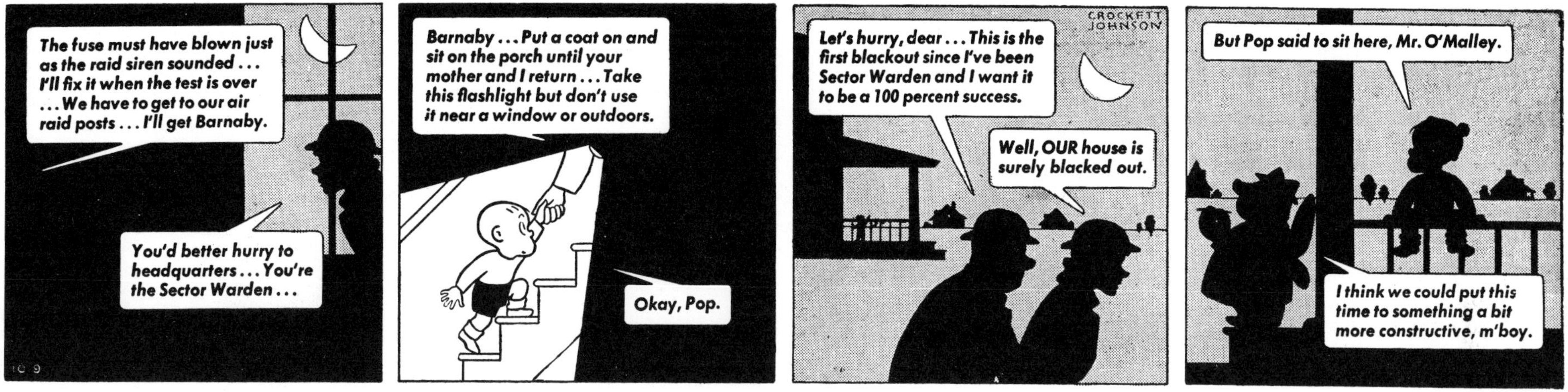
The fuse must have blown just as the raid siren sounded . . . I'll fix it when the test is over . . . We have to get to our air raid posts . . . I'll get Barnaby.
You'd better hurry to headquarters . . . You're the Sector Warden . . .
Barnaby . . . Put a coat on and sit on the porch until your mother and I return . . . Take this flashlight but don't use it near a window or outdoors.
Okay, Pop.
CROCKETT JOHNSON
Let's hurry, dear . . . This is the first blackout since I've been Sector Warden and I want it to be a 100 percent success.
Well, OUR house is surely blacked out.
But Pop said to sit here, Mr. O'Malley.
I think we could put this time to something a bit more constructive, m'boy.

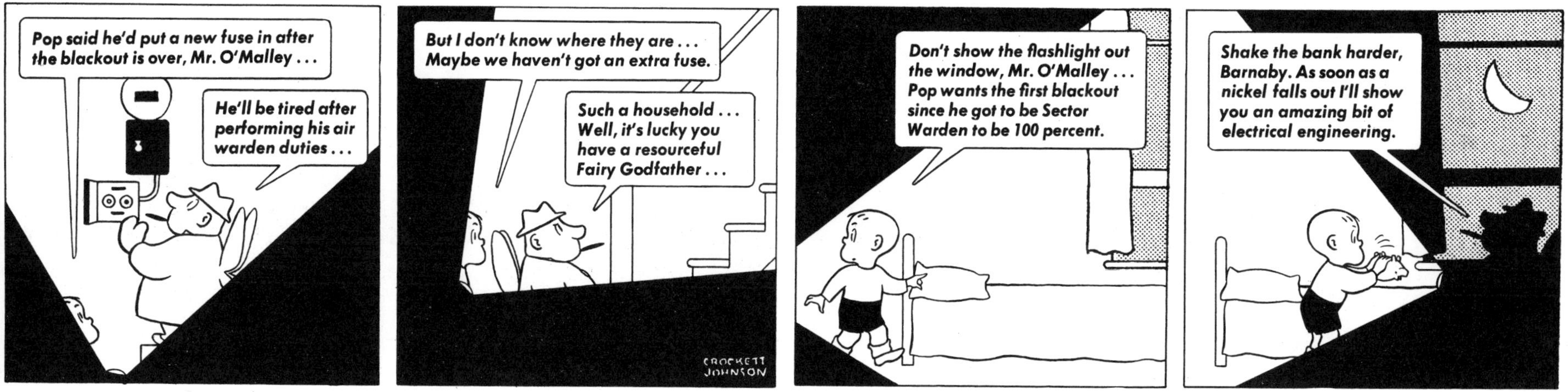
Pop said he'd put a new fuse in after the blackout is over, Mr. O'Malley . . .
He'll be tired after performing his air warden duties . . .
But I don't know where they are . . . Maybe we haven't got an extra fuse.
Such a household . . . Well, it's lucky you have a resourceful Fairy Godfather . . .
CROCKETT JOHNSON
Don't show the flashlight out the window, Mr. O'Malley . . . Pop wants the first blackout since he got to be Sector Warden to be 100 percent.
Shake the bank harder, Barnaby. As soon as a nickel falls out I'll show you an amazing bit of electrical engineering.

October 9 – 10

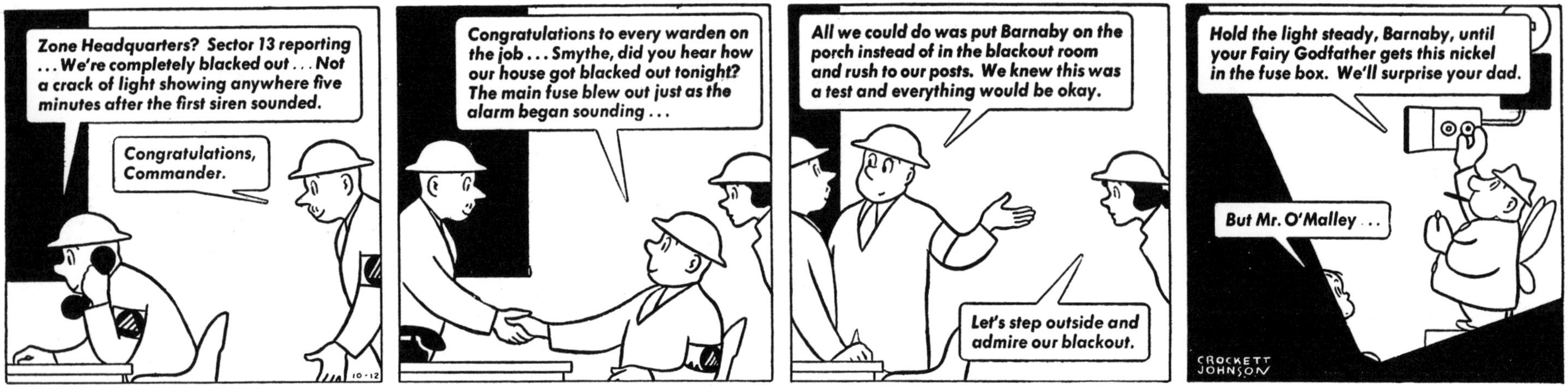
Zone Headquarters? Sector 13 reporting . . . We're completely blacked out . . . Not a crack of light showing anywhere five minutes after the first siren sounded.
Congratulations, Commander.
10-12
Congratulations to every warden on the job . . . Smythe, did you hear how our house got blacked out tonight? The main fuse blew out just as the alarm began sounding . . .
All we could do was put Barnaby on the porch instead of in the blackout room and rush to our posts. We knew this was a test and everything would be okay.
Let's step outside and admire our blackout.
Hold the light steady, Barnaby, until your Fairy Godfather gets this nickel in the fuse box. We'll surprise your dad.
But Mr. O'Malley . . .
CROCKETT JOHNSON

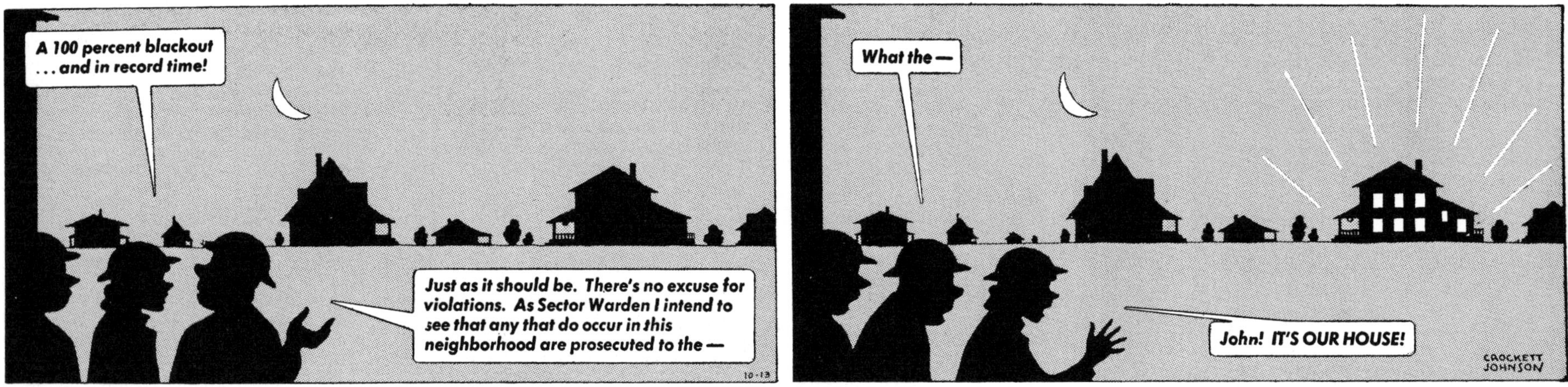
A 100 percent blackout . . . and in record time!
Just as it should be. There's no excuse for violations. As Sector Warden I intend to see that any that do occur in this neighborhood are prosecuted to the —
10-13
What the —
John! IT'S OUR HOUSE!
CROCKETT JOHNSON

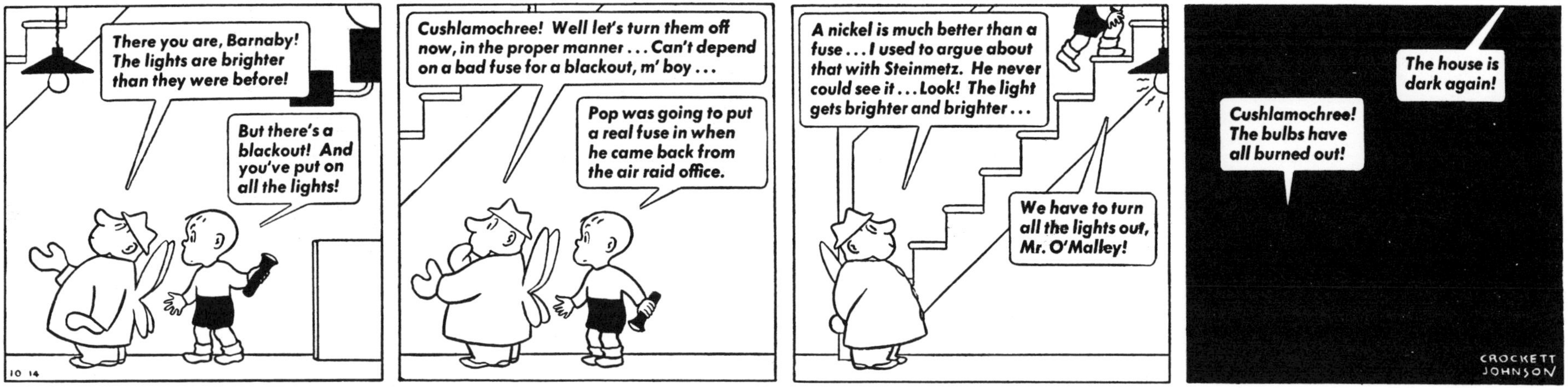
10 14
There you are, Barnaby! The lights are brighter than they were before!
But there's a blackout! And you've put on all the lights!
Cushlamochree! Well let's turn them off now, in the proper manner . . . Can't depend on a bad fuse for a blackout, m' boy . . .
Pop was going to put a real fuse in when he came back from the air raid office.
A nickel is much better than a fuse . . . I used to argue about that with Steinmetz. He never could see it . . . Look! The light gets brighter and brighter . . .
We have to turn all the lights out, Mr. O'Malley!
The house is dark again!
Cushlamochree! The bulbs have all burned out!
CROCKETT JOHNSON

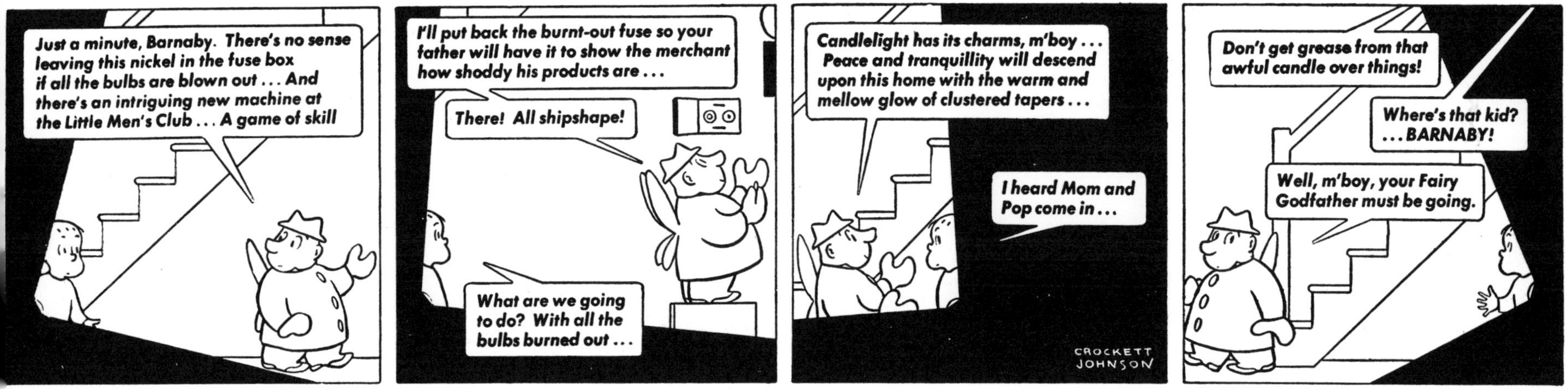
Just a minute, Barnaby. There's no sense leaving this nickel in the fuse box if all the bulbs are blown out . . . And there's an intriguing new machine at the Little Men's Club . . . A game of skill
I'll put back the burnt-out fuse so your father will have it to show the merchant how shoddy his products are . . .
There! All shipshape!
What are we going to do? With all the bulbs burned out . . .
Candlelight has its charms, m'boy . . . Peace and tranquillity will descend upon this home with the warm and mellow glow of clustered tapers . . .
I heard Mom and Pop come in . . .
CROCKETT JOHNSON
Don't get grease from that awful candle over things!
Where's that kid? . . . BARNABY!
Well, m'boy, your Fairy Godfather must be going.

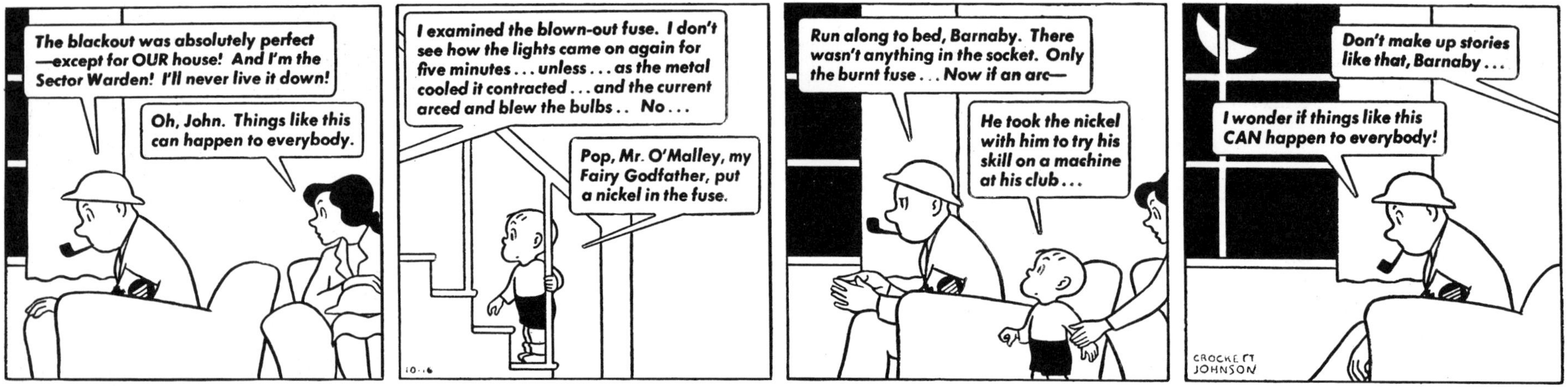
The blackout was absolutely perfect —except for OUR house! And I'm the Sector Warden! I'll never live it down!
Oh, John. Things like this can happen to everybody.
I examined the blown-out fuse. I don't see how the lights came on again for five minutes . . . unless . . . as the metal cooled it contracted . . . and the current arced and blew the bulbs . . No . . .
Pop, Mr. O'Malley, my Fairy Godfather, put a nickel in the fuse.
Run along to bed, Barnaby. There wasn't anything in the socket. Only the burnt fuse . . . Now if an arc—
He took the nickel with him to try his skill on a machine at his club . . .
Don't make up stories like that, Barnaby . . .
I wonder if things like this CAN happen to everybody!
CROCKETT JOHNSON

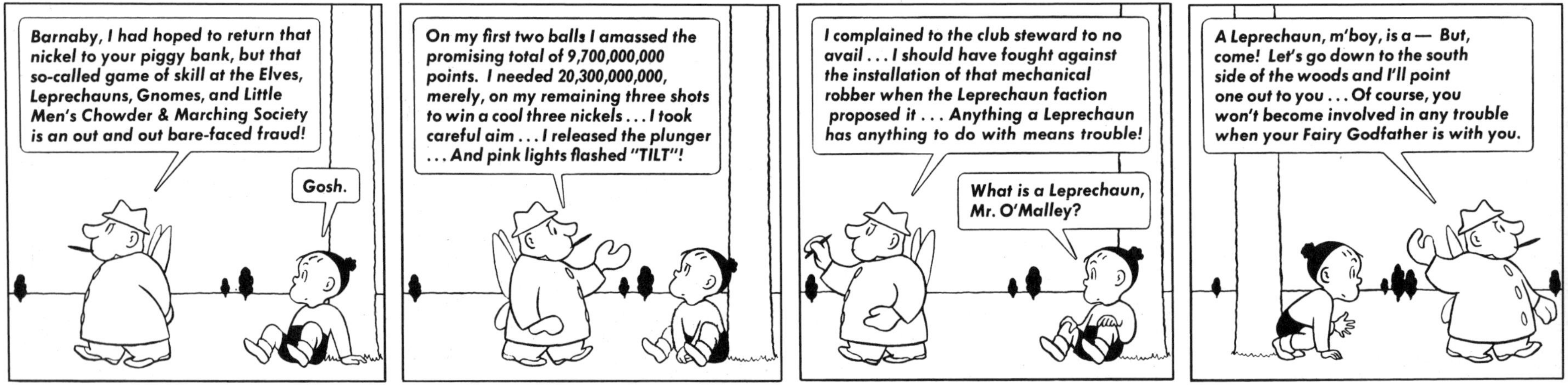
Barnaby, I had hoped to return that nickel to your piggy bank, but that so-called game of skill at the Elves, Leprechauns, Gnomes, and Little Men's Chowder & Marching Society is an out and out bare-faced fraud!
Gosh.
On my first two balls I amassed the promising total of 9,700,000,000 points. I needed 20,300,000,000, merely, on my remaining three shots to win a cool three nickels . . . I took careful aim . . . I released the plunger . . . And pink lights flashed "TILT"!
I complained to the club steward to no avail . . . I should have fought against the installation of that mechanical robber when the Leprechaun faction proposed it . . . Anything a Leprechaun has anything to do with means trouble!
What is a Leprechaun, Mr. O'Malley?
A Leprechaun, m'boy, is a— But, come! Let's go down to the south side of the woods and I'll point one out to you . . . Of course, you won't become involved in any trouble when your Fairy Godfather is with you.

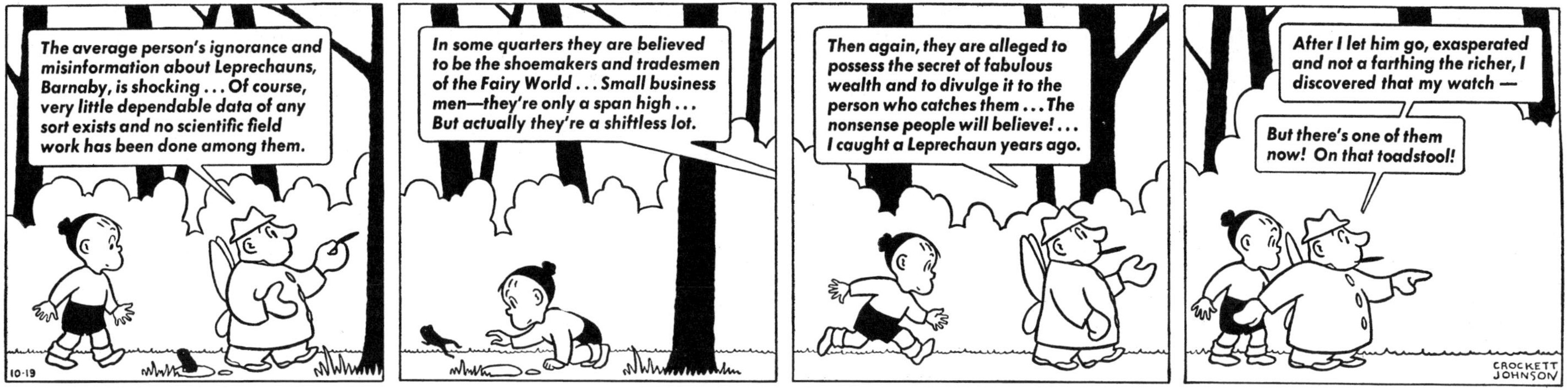
10-19
The average person's ignorance and misinformation about Leprechauns, Barnaby, is shocking . . . Of course, very little dependable data of any sort exists and no scientific field work has been done among them.
In some quarters they are believed to be the shoemakers and tradesmen of the Fairy World . . . Small business men—they're only a span high . . . But actually they're a shiftless lot.
Then again, they are alleged to possess the secret of fabulous wealth and to divulge it to the person who catches them . . . The nonsense people will believe! . . . I caught a Leprechaun years ago.
After I let him go, exasperated and not a farthing the richer, I discovered that my watch —
But there's one of them now! On that toadstool!
CROCKETT JOHNSON

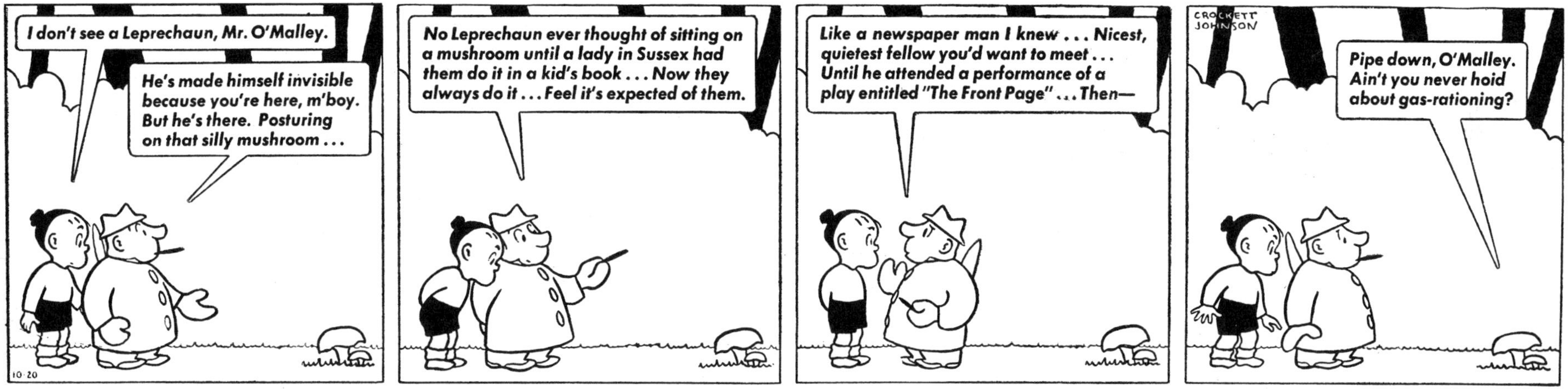
10-20
I don't see a Leprechaun, Mr. O'Malley.
He's made himself invisible because you're here, m'boy. But he's there. Posturing on that silly mushroom . . .
No Leprechaun ever thought of sitting on a mushroom until a lady in Sussex had them do it in a kid's book . . . Now they always do it . . . Feel it's expected of them.
Like a newspaper man I knew . . . Nicest, quietest fellow you'd want to meet . . . Until he attended a performance of a play entitled "The Front Page" . . . Then—
CROCKETT JOHNSON
Pipe down, O'Malley. Ain't you never hoid about gas-rationing?

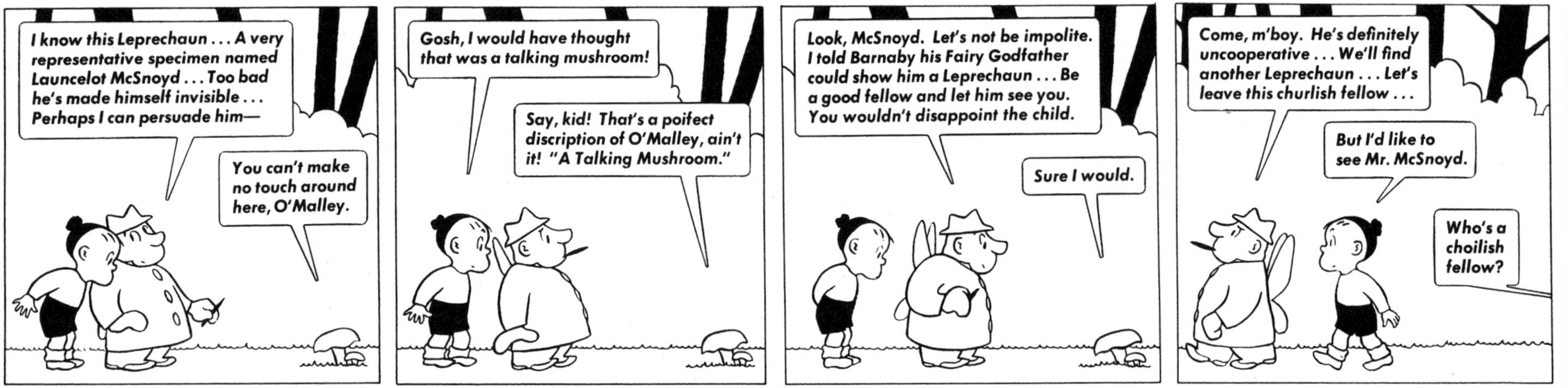
I know this Leprechaun . . . A very representative specimen named Launcelot McSnoyd . . . Too bad he's made himself invisible . . . Perhaps I can persuade him—
You can't make no touch around here, O'Malley.
Gosh, I would have thought that was a talking mushroom!
Say, kid! That's a poifect discription of O'Malley, ain't it! "A Talking Mushroom."
Look, McSnoyd. Let's not be impolite. I told Barnaby his Fairy Godfather could show him a Leprechaun . . . Be a good fellow and let him see you. You wouldn't disappoint the child.
Sure I would.
Come, m'boy. He's definitely uncooperative . . . We'll find another Leprechaun . . . Let's leave this churlish fellow . . .
But I'd like to see Mr. McSnoyd.
Who's a choilish fellow?

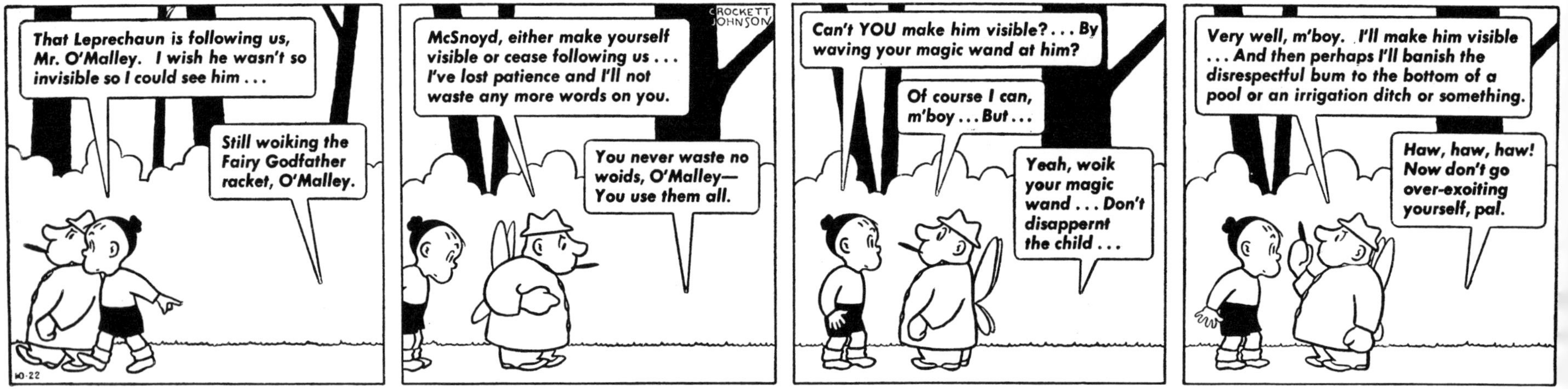
That Leprechaun is following us, Mr. O'Malley. I wish he wasn't so invisible so I could see him . . .
Still woiking the Fairy Godfather racket, O'Malley.
10-22
CROCKETT JOHNSON
McSnoyd, either make yourself visible or cease following us . . . I've lost patience and I'll not waste any more words on you.
You never waste no woids, O'Malley— You use them all.
Can't YOU make him visible? . . . By waving your magic wand at him?
Of course I can, m'boy . . . But . . .
Yeah, woik your magic wand . . . Don't disappernt the child . . .
Very well, m'boy. I'll make him visible . . . And then perhaps I'll banish the disrespectful bum to the bottom of a pool or an irrigation ditch or something.
Haw, haw, haw! Now don't go over-exoiting yourself, pal.

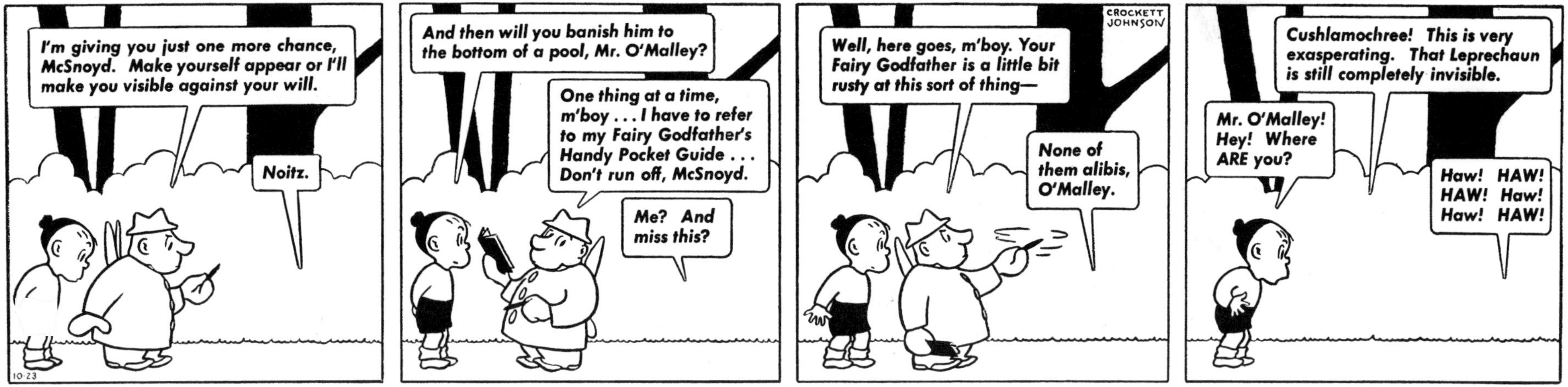
10-23
I'm giving you just one more chance, McSnoyd. Make yourself appear or I'll make you visible against your will.
Noitz.
And then will you banish him to the bottom of a pool, Mr. O'Malley?
One thing at a time, m'boy . . . I have to refer to my Fairy Godfather's Handy Pocket Guide . . . Don't run off, McSnoyd.
Me? And miss this?
CROCKETT JOHNSON
Well, here goes, m'boy. Your Fairy Godfather is a little bit rusty at this sort of thing—
None of them alibis, O'Malley.
Cushlamochree! This is very exasperating. That Leprechaun is still completely invisible.
Mr. O'Malley! Hey! Where ARE you?
Haw! HAW! HAW! Haw! Haw! HAW!

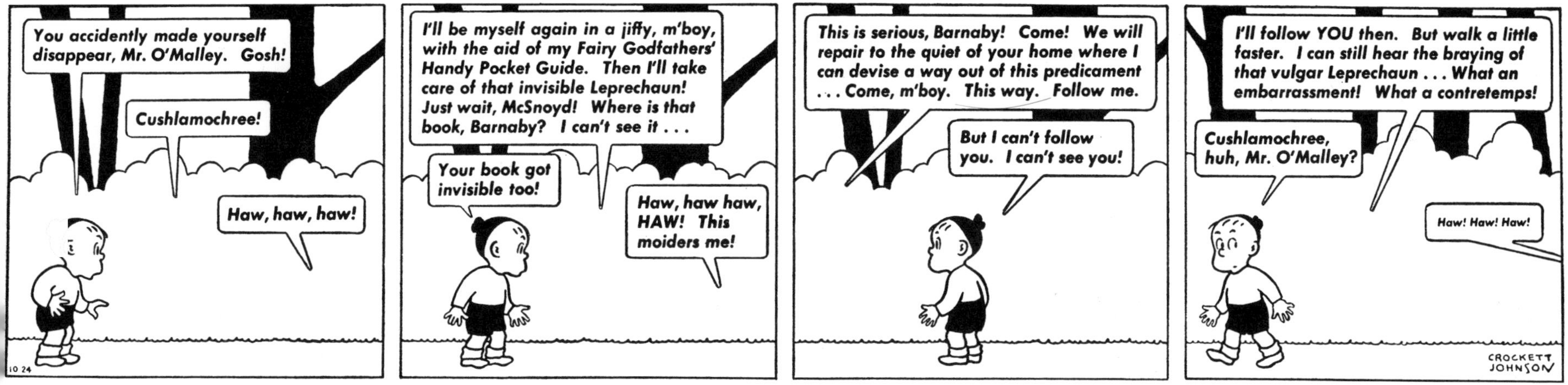
10-24
You accidently made yourself disappear, Mr. O'Malley. Gosh!
Cushlamochree!
Haw, haw, haw!
I'll be myself again in a jiffy, m'boy, with the aid of my Fairy Godfathers' Handy Pocket Guide. Then I'll take care of that invisible Leprechaun! Just wait, McSnoyd! Where is that book, Barnaby? I can't see it . . .
Your book got invisible too!
Haw, haw haw, HAW! This moiders me!
This is serious, Barnaby! Come! We will repair to the quiet of your home where I can devise a way out of this predicament . . . Come, m'boy. This way. Follow me.
But I can't follow you. I can't see you!
I'll follow YOU then. But walk a little faster. I can still hear the braying of that vulgar Leprechaun . . . What an embarrassment! What a contretemps!
Cushlamochree, huh, Mr. O'Malley?
Haw! Haw! Haw!
CROCKETT JOHNSON

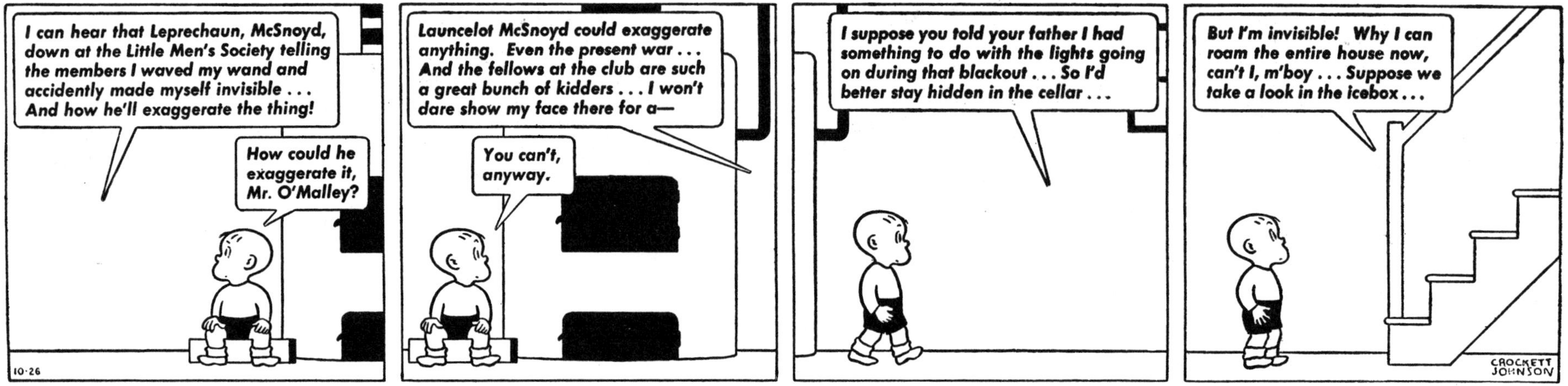
I can hear that Leprechaun, McSnoyd, down at the Little Men's Society telling the members I waved my wand and accidently made myself invisible . . . And how he'll exaggerate the thing!
How could he exaggerate it, Mr. O'Malley?
10·26
Launcelot McSnoyd could exaggerate anything. Even the present war . . . And the fellows at the club are such a great bunch of kidders . . . I won't dare show my face there for a—
You can't, anyway.
I suppose you told your father I had something to do with the lights going on during that blackout . . . So I'd better stay hidden in the cellar . . .
But I'm invisible! Why I can roam the entire house now, can't I, m'boy . . . Suppose we take a look in the icebox . . .
CROCKETT JOHNSON

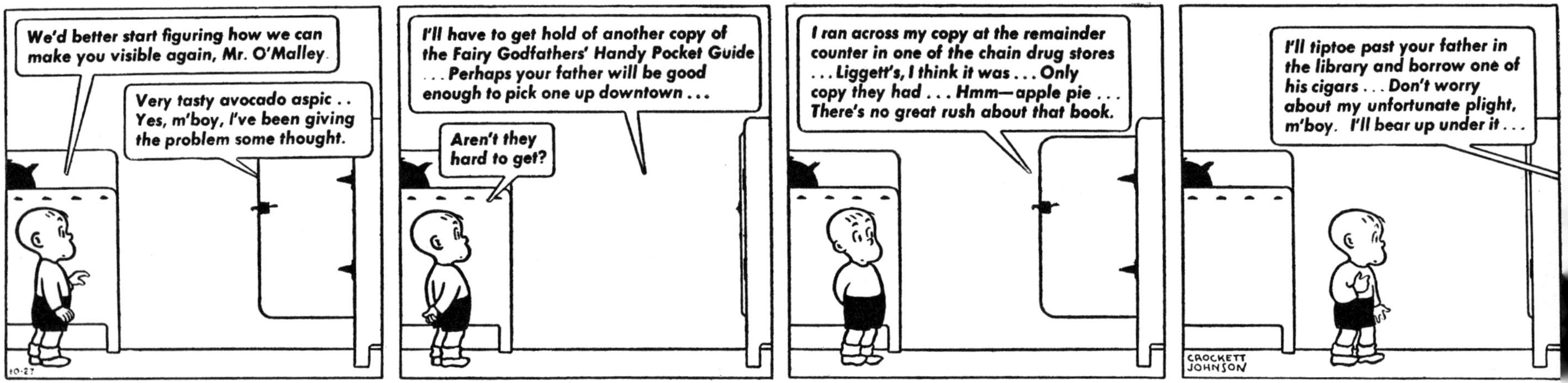
We'd better start figuring how we can make you visible again, Mr. O'Malley.
Very tasty avocado aspic . . Yes, m'boy, I've been giving the problem some thought.
10·27
I'll have to get hold of another copy of the Fairy Godfathers' Handy Pocket Guide . . . Perhaps your father will be good enough to pick one up downtown . . .
Aren't they hard to get?
I ran across my copy at the remainder counter in one of the chain drug stores . . . Liggett's, I think it was . . . Only copy they had . . . Hmm—apple pie . . . There's no great rush about that book.
I'll tiptoe past your father in the library and borrow one of his cigars . . . Don't worry about my unfortunate plight, m'boy. I'll bear up under it . . .
CROCKETT JOHNSON

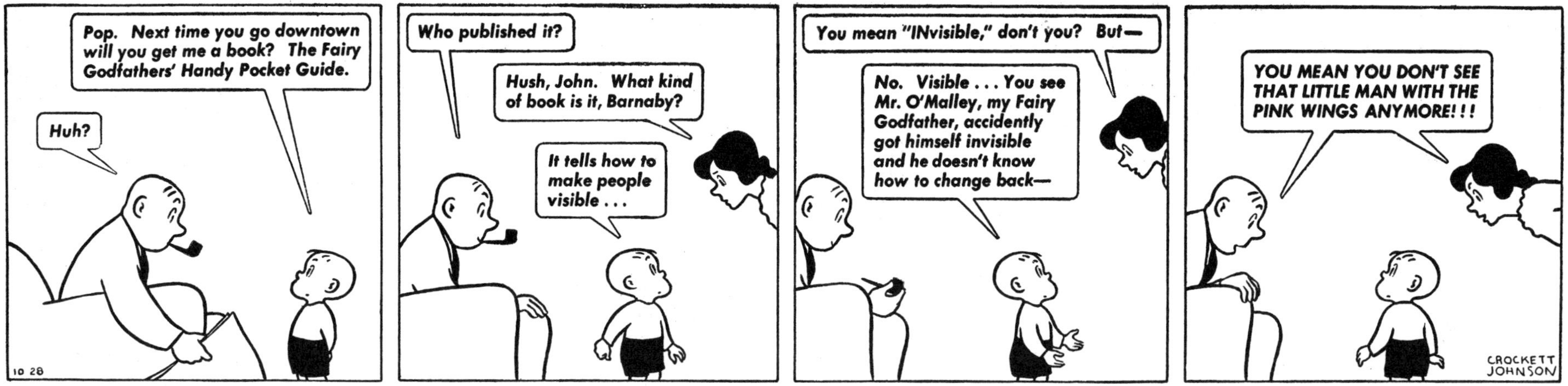
Pop. Next time you go downtown will you get me a book? The Fairy Godfathers' Handy Pocket Guide.
Huh?
10 28
Who published it?
Hush, John. What kind of book is it, Barnaby?
It tells how to make people visible . . .
You mean "INvisible," don't you? But—
No. Visible . . . You see Mr. O'Malley, my Fairy Godfather, accidently got himself invisible and he doesn't know how to change back—
YOU MEAN YOU DON'T SEE THAT LITTLE MAN WITH THE PINK WINGS ANYMORE!!!
CROCKETT JOHNSON

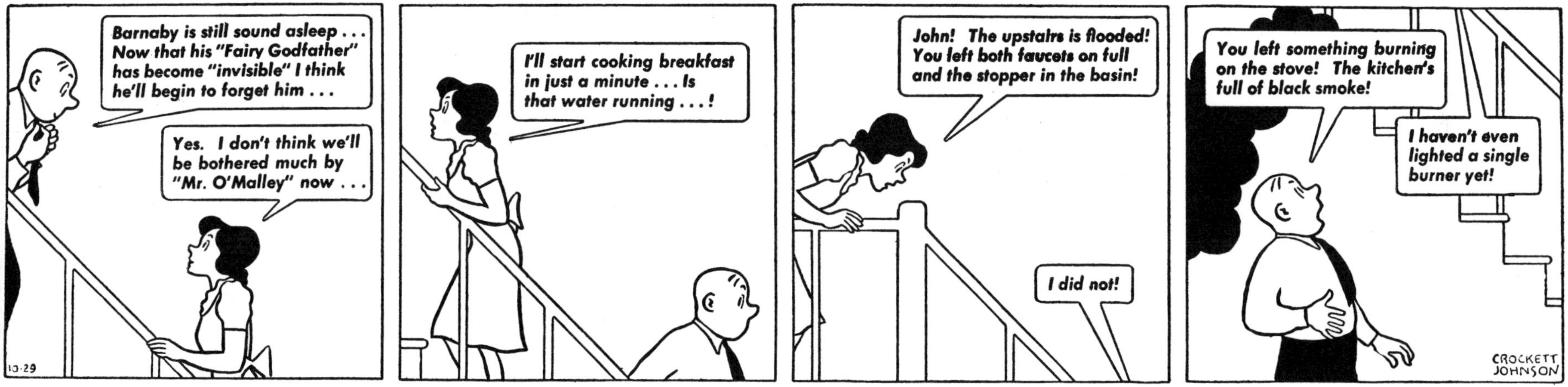
Barnaby is still sound asleep . . . Now that his "Fairy Godfather" has become "invisible" I think he'll begin to forget him . . .
Yes. I don't think we'll be bothered much by "Mr. O'Malley" now . . .
10·29
I'll start cooking breakfast in just a minute . . . Is that water running . . . !
John! The upstairs is flooded! You left both faucets on full and the stopper in the basin!
I did not!
You left something burning on the stove! The kitchen's full of black smoke!
I haven't even lighted a single burner yet!
CROCKETT JOHNSON

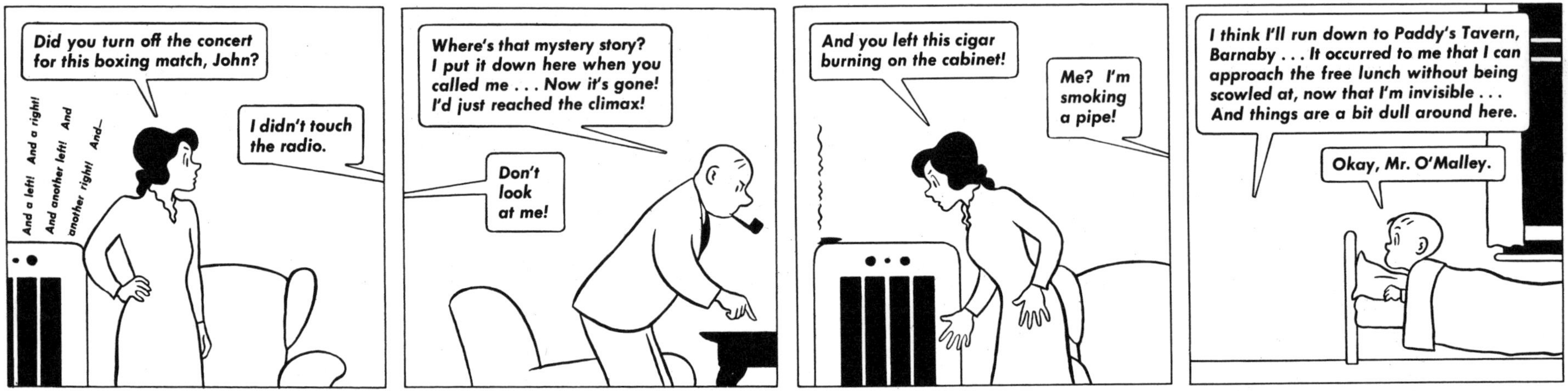
Did you turn off the concert for this boxing match, John?
And a left! And a right! And another left! And another right! And—
I didn't touch the radio.
Where's that mystery story? I put it down here when you called me . . . Now it's gone! I'd just reached the climax!
Don't look at me!
And you left this cigar burning on the cabinet!
Me? I'm smoking a pipe!
I think I'll run down to Paddy's Tavern, Barnaby . . . It occurred to me that I can approach the free lunch without being scowled at, now that I'm invisible . . . And things are a bit dull around here.
Okay, Mr. O'Malley.

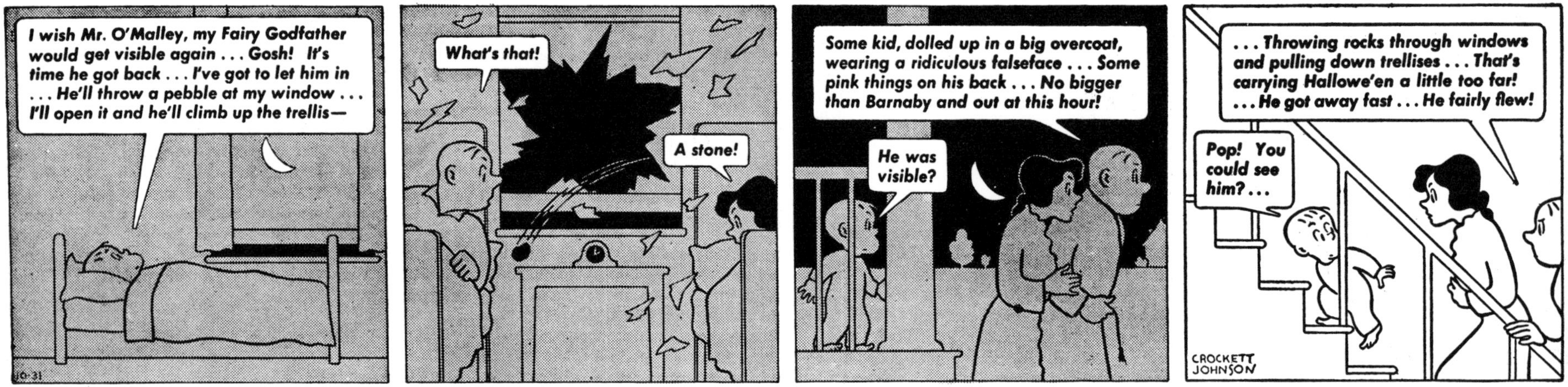
I wish Mr. O'Malley, my Fairy Godfather would get visible again . . . Gosh! It's time he got back . . . I've got to let him in . . . He'll throw a pebble at my window . . . I'll open it and he'll climb up the trellis—
10-31
What's that!
A stone!
Some kid, dolled up in a big overcoat, wearing a ridiculous falseface . . . Some pink things on his back . . . No bigger than Barnaby and out at this hour!
He was visible?
. . . Throwing rocks through windows and pulling down trellises . . . That's carrying Hallowe'en a little too far! . . . He got away fast . . . He fairly flew!
Pop! You could see him? . . .
CROCKETT JOHNSON

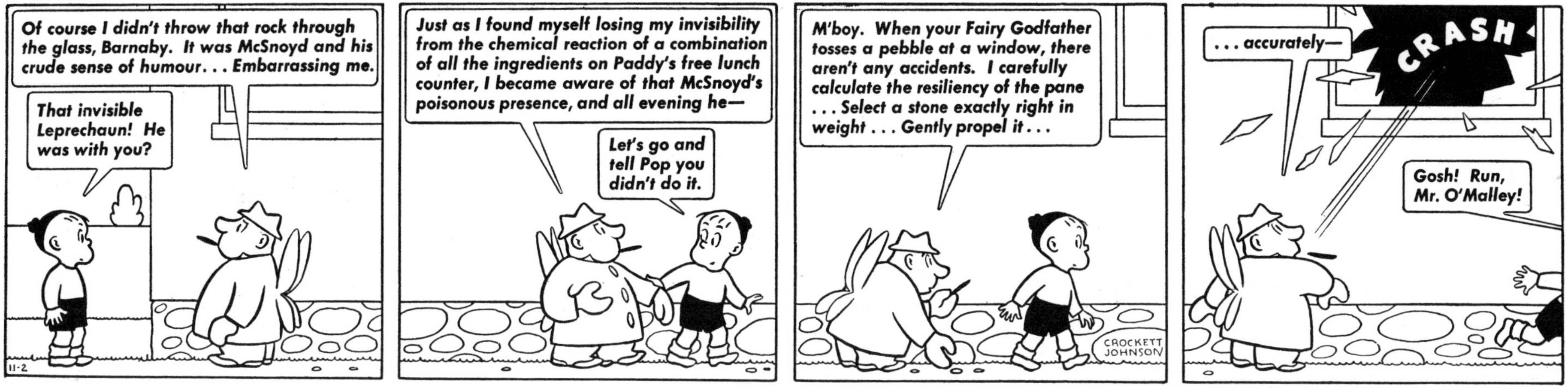
Of course I didn't throw that rock through the glass, Barnaby. It was McSnoyd and his crude sense of humour . . . Embarrassing me.
That invisible Leprechaun! He was with you?
11-2
Just as I found myself losing my invisibility from the chemical reaction of a combination of all the ingredients on Paddy's free lunch counter, I became aware of that McSnoyd's poisonous presence, and all evening he—
Let's go and tell Pop you didn't do it.
M'boy. When your Fairy Godfather tosses a pebble at a window, there aren't any accidents. I carefully calculate the resiliency of the pane . . . Select a stone exactly right in weight . . . Gently propel it . . .
CROCKETT JOHNSON
. . . accurately—
CRASH
Gosh! Run, Mr. O'Malley!

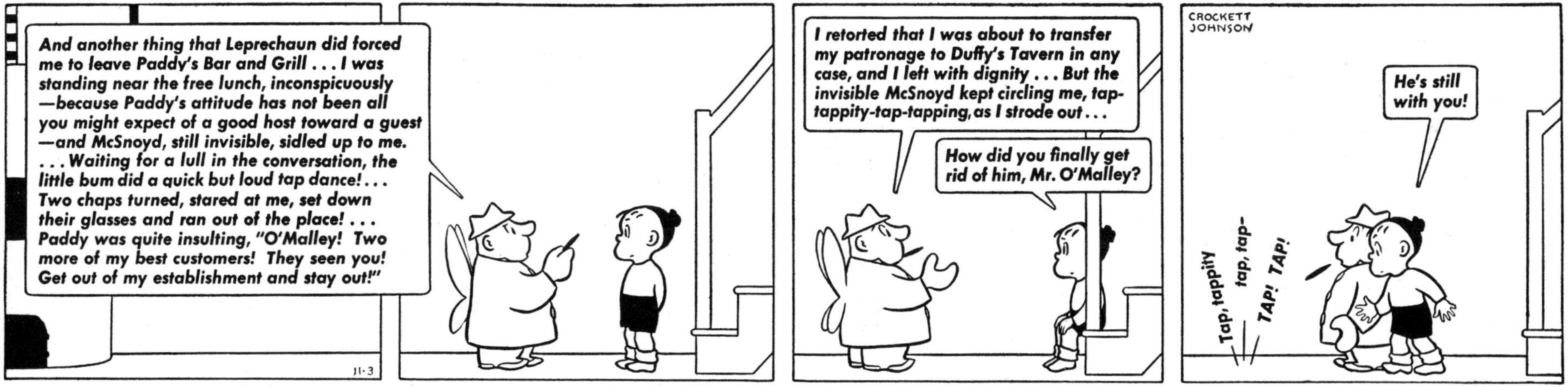
And another thing that Leprechaun did forced me to leave Paddy's Bar and Grill . . . I was standing near the free lunch, inconspicuously —because Paddy's attitude has not been all you might expect of a good host toward a guest —and McSnoyd, still invisible, sidled up to me. . . . Waiting for a lull in the conversation, the little bum did a quick but loud tap dance! . . . Two chaps turned, stared at me, set down their glasses and ran out of the place! . . . Paddy was quite insulting, "O'Malley! Two more of my best customers! They seen you! Get out of my establishment and stay out!"
11-3
I retorted that I was about to transfer my patronage to Duffy's Tavern in any case, and I left with dignity . . . But the invisible McSnoyd kept circling me, tap-tappity-tap-tapping, as I strode out . . .
How did you finally get rid of him, Mr. O'Malley?
CROCKETT JOHNSON
He's still with you!
Tap, tappity
tap, tap-
TAP! TAP!

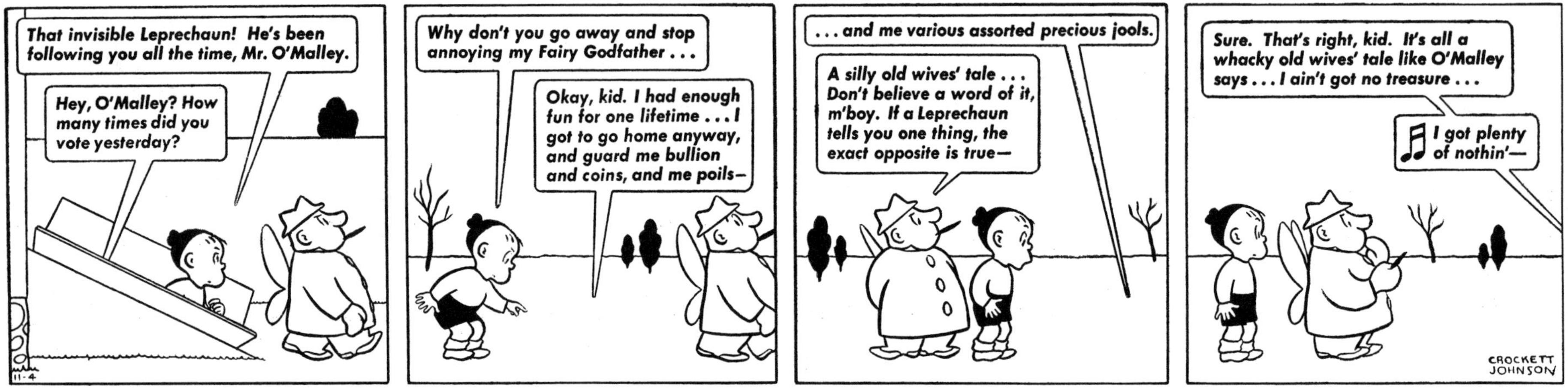
That invisible Leprechaun! He's been following you all the time, Mr. O'Malley.
Hey, O'Malley? How many times did you vote yesterday?
11-4
Why don't you go away and stop annoying my Fairy Godfather . . .
Okay, kid. I had enough fun for one lifetime . . . I got to go home anyway, and guard me bullion and coins, and me poils–
. . . and me various assorted precious jools.
A silly old wives' tale . . . Don't believe a word of it, m'boy. If a Leprechaun tells you one thing, the exact opposite is true—
Sure. That's right, kid. It's all a whacky old wives' tale like O'Malley says . . . I ain't got no treasure . . .
I got plenty of nothin'—
CROCKETT JOHNSON

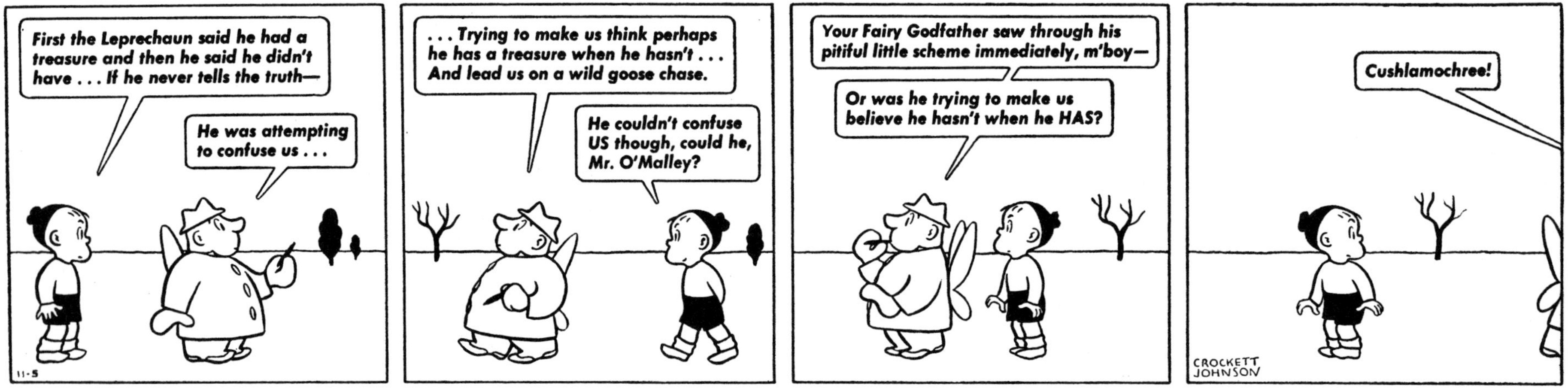
First the Leprechaun said he had a treasure and then he said he didn't have . . . If he never tells the truth—
He was attempting to confuse us . . .
11-5
. . . Trying to make us think perhaps he has a treasure when he hasn't . . . And lead us on a wild goose chase.
He couldn't confuse US though, could he, Mr. O'Malley?
Your Fairy Godfather saw through his pitiful little scheme immediately, m'boy—
Or was he trying to make us believe he hasn't when he HAS?
Cushlamochree!
CROCKETT JOHNSON

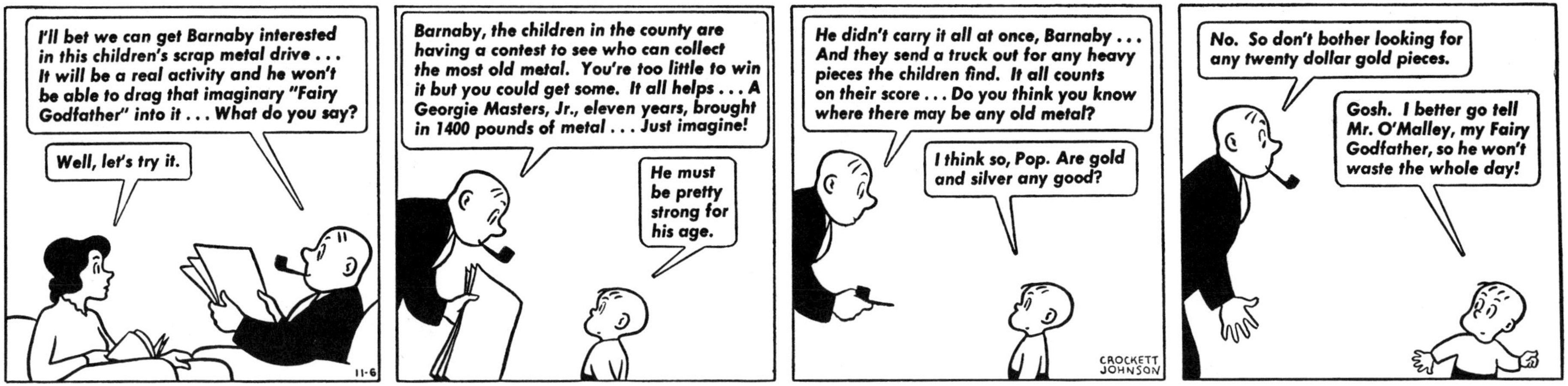

I'll bet we can get Barnaby interested in this children's scrap metal drive . . . It will be a real activity and he won't be able to drag that imaginary "Fairy Godfather" into it . . . What do you say?
Well, let's try it.
11-6
Barnaby, the children in the county are having a contest to see who can collect the most old metal. You're too little to win it but you could get some. It all helps . . . A Georgie Masters, Jr., eleven years, brought in 1400 pounds of metal . . . Just imagine!
He must be pretty strong for his age.
He didn't carry it all at once, Barnaby . . . And they send a truck out for any heavy pieces the children find. It all counts on their score . . . Do you think you know where there may be any old metal?
I think so, Pop. Are gold and silver any good?
CROCKETT JOHNSON
No. So don't bother looking for any twenty dollar gold pieces.
Gosh. I better go tell Mr. O'Malley, my Fairy Godfather, so he won't waste the whole day!

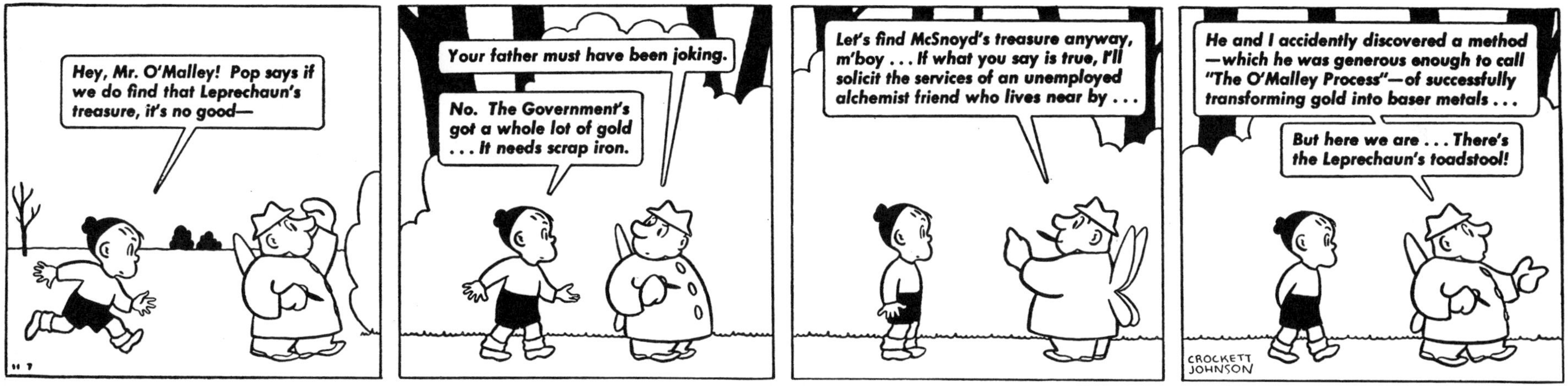

Hey, Mr. O'Malley! Pop says if we do find that Leprechaun's treasure, it's no good—
Your father must have been joking.
No. The Government's got a whole lot of gold . . . It needs scrap iron.
Let's find McSnoyd's treasure anyway, m'boy . . . If what you say is true, I'll solicit the services of an unemployed alchemist friend who lives near by . . .
He and I accidently discovered a method —which he was generous enough to call "The O'Malley Process"—of successfully transforming gold into baser metals . . .
But here we are . . . There's the Leprechaun's toadstool!
CROCKETT JOHNSON

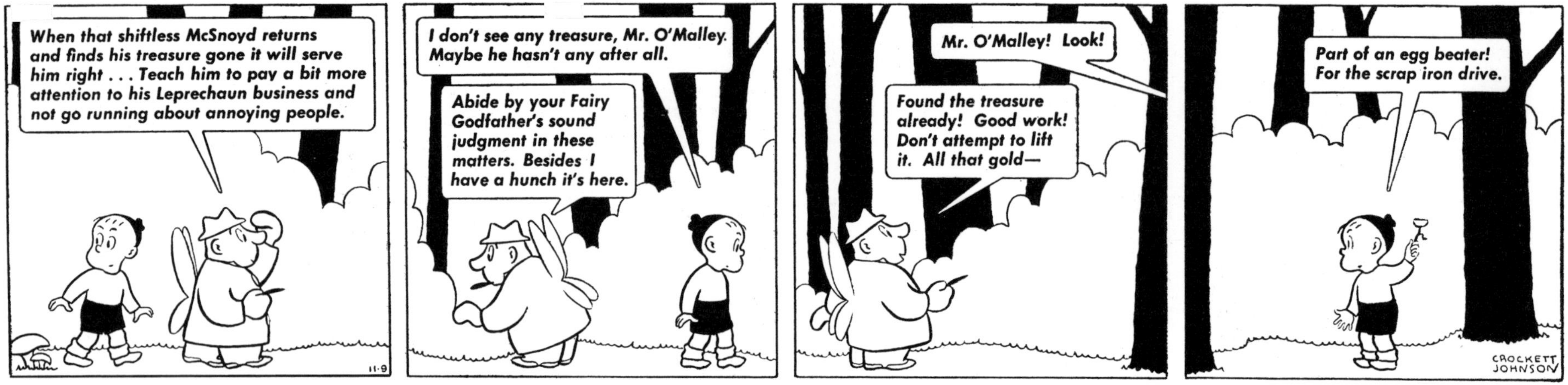
When that shiftless McSnoyd returns and finds his treasure gone it will serve him right . . . Teach him to pay a bit more attention to his Leprechaun business and not go running about annoying people.
11·9
I don't see any treasure, Mr. O'Malley. Maybe he hasn't any after all.
Abide by your Fairy Godfather's sound judgment in these matters. Besides I have a hunch it's here.
Mr. O'Malley! Look!
Found the treasure already! Good work! Don't attempt to lift it. All that gold—
Part of an egg beater! For the scrap iron drive.
CROCKETT JOHNSON

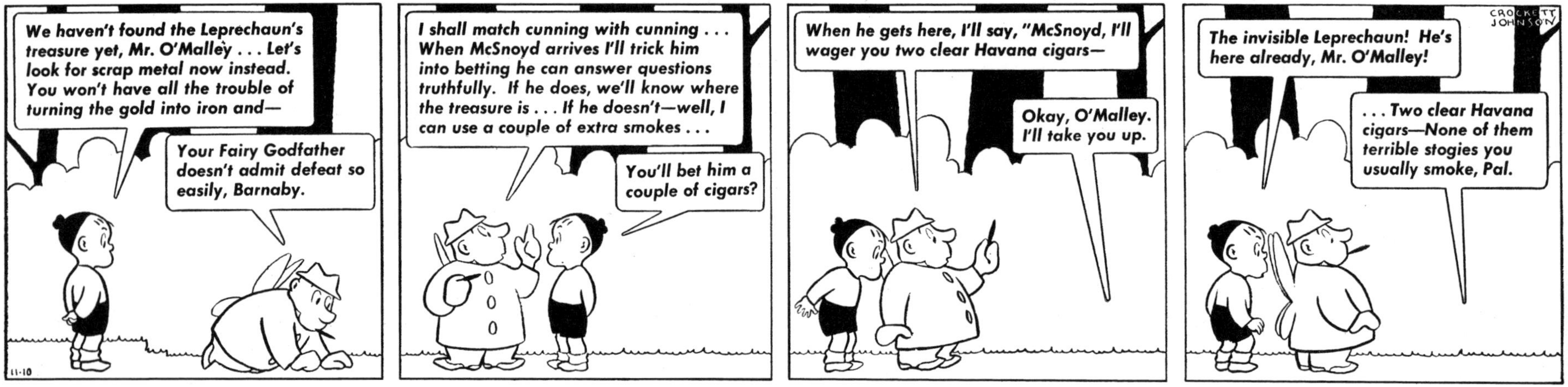
We haven't found the Leprechaun's treasure yet, Mr. O'Malley . . . Let's look for scrap metal now instead. You won't have all the trouble of turning the gold into iron and—
Your Fairy Godfather doesn't admit defeat so easily, Barnaby.
11·10
I shall match cunning with cunning . . . When McSnoyd arrives I'll trick him into betting he can answer questions truthfully. If he does, we'll know where the treasure is . . . If he doesn't—well, I can use a couple of extra smokes . . .
You'll bet him a couple of cigars?
When he gets here, I'll say, "McSnoyd, I'll wager you two clear Havana cigars—
Okay, O'Malley. I'll take you up.
CROCKETT JOHNSON
The invisible Leprechaun! He's here already, Mr. O'Malley!
. . . Two clear Havana cigars—None of them terrible stogies you usually smoke, Pal.

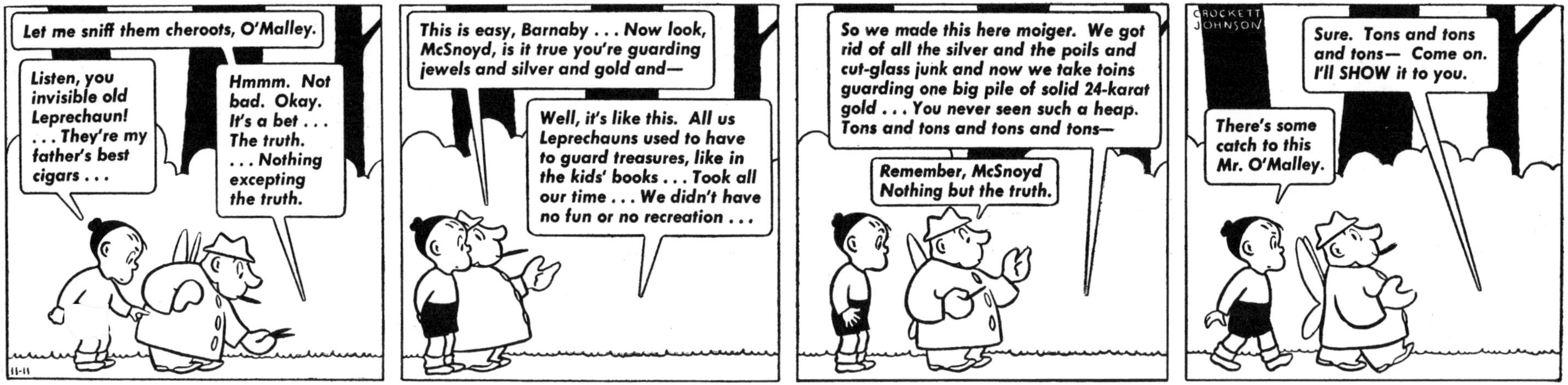
Let me sniff them cheroots, O'Malley.
Listen, you invisible old Leprechaun! . . . They're my father's best cigars . . .
Hmmm. Not bad. Okay. It's a bet . . . The truth. . . . Nothing excepting the truth.
11-11
This is easy, Barnaby . . . Now look, McSnoyd, is it true you're guarding jewels and silver and gold and—
Well, it's like this. All us Leprechauns used to have to guard treasures, like in the kids' books . . . Took all our time . . . We didn't have no fun or no recreation . . .
So we made this here moiger. We got rid of all the silver and the poils and cut-glass junk and now we take toins guarding one big pile of solid 24-karat gold . . . You never seen such a heap. Tons and tons and tons and tons—
Remember, McSnoyd Nothing but the truth.
CROCKETT JOHNSON
Sure. Tons and tons and tons— Come on. I'll SHOW it to you.
There's some catch to this Mr. O'Malley.

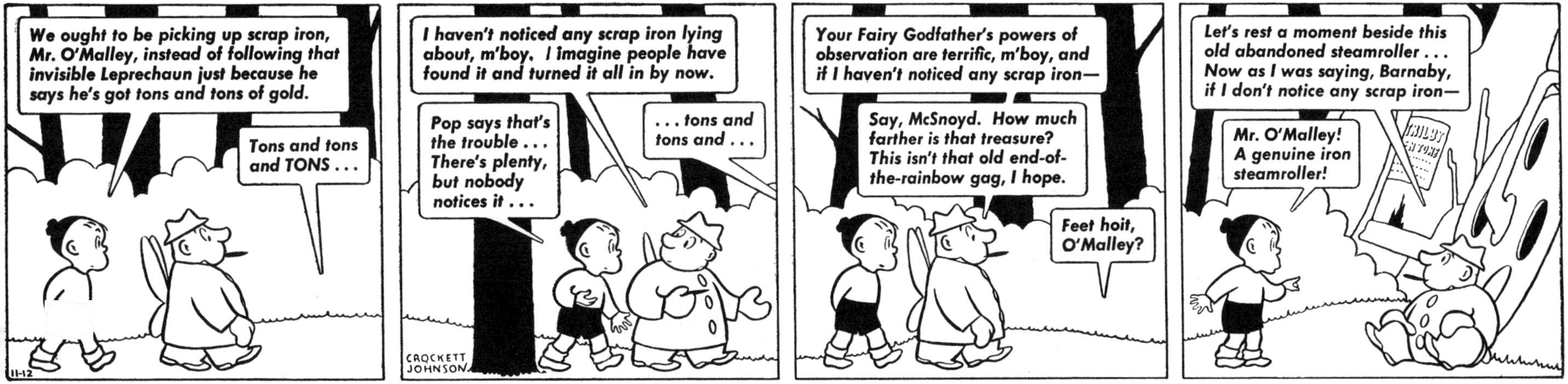
We ought to be picking up scrap iron, Mr. O'Malley, instead of following that invisible Leprechaun just because he says he's got tons and tons of gold.
Tons and tons and TONS . . .
11-12
I haven't noticed any scrap iron lying about, m'boy. I imagine people have found it and turned it all in by now.
Pop says that's the trouble . . . There's plenty, but nobody notices it . . .
. . . tons and tons and . . .
CROCKETT JOHNSON
Your Fairy Godfather's powers of observation are terrific, m'boy, and if I haven't noticed any scrap iron—
Say, McSnoyd. How much farther is that treasure? This isn't that old end-of-the-rainbow gag, I hope.
Feet hoit, O'Malley?
Let's rest a moment beside this old abandoned steamroller . . . Now as I was saying, Barnaby, if I don't notice any scrap iron—
Mr. O'Malley! A genuine iron steamroller!

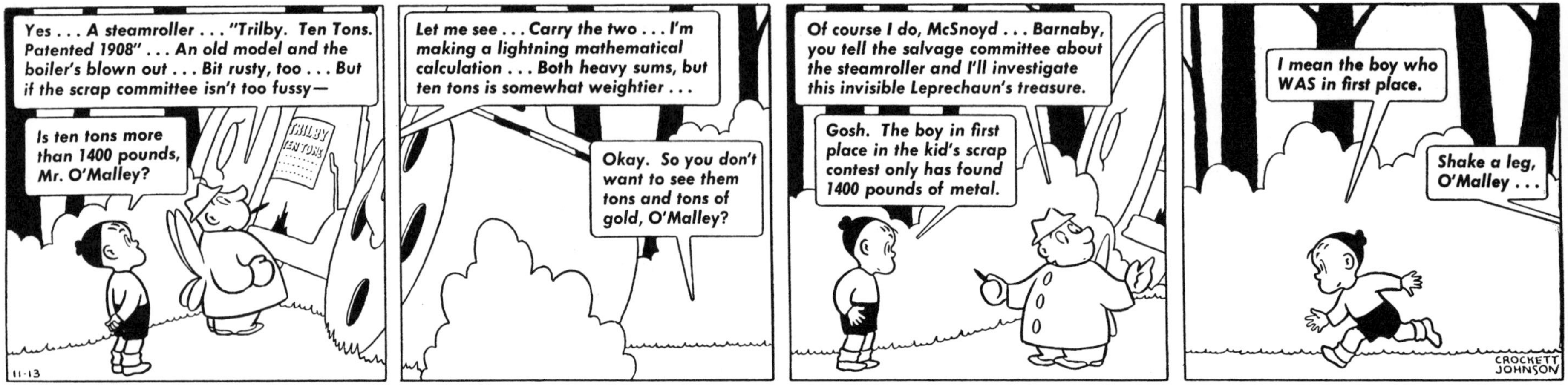
Yes . . . A steamroller . . . "Trilby. Ten Tons. Patented 1908" . . . An old model and the boiler's blown out . . . Bit rusty, too . . . But if the scrap committee isn't too fussy—
Is ten tons more than 1400 pounds, Mr. O'Malley?
TRILBY
TEN TONS
11-13
Let me see . . . Carry the two . . . I'm making a lightning mathematical calculation . . . Both heavy sums, but ten tons is somewhat weightier . . .
Okay. So you don't want to see them tons and tons of gold, O'Malley?
Of course I do, McSnoyd . . . Barnaby, you tell the salvage committee about the steamroller and I'll investigate this invisible Leprechaun's treasure.
Gosh. The boy in first place in the kid's scrap contest only has found 1400 pounds of metal.
I mean the boy who WAS in first place.
Shake a leg, O'Malley . . .
CROCKETT JOHNSON

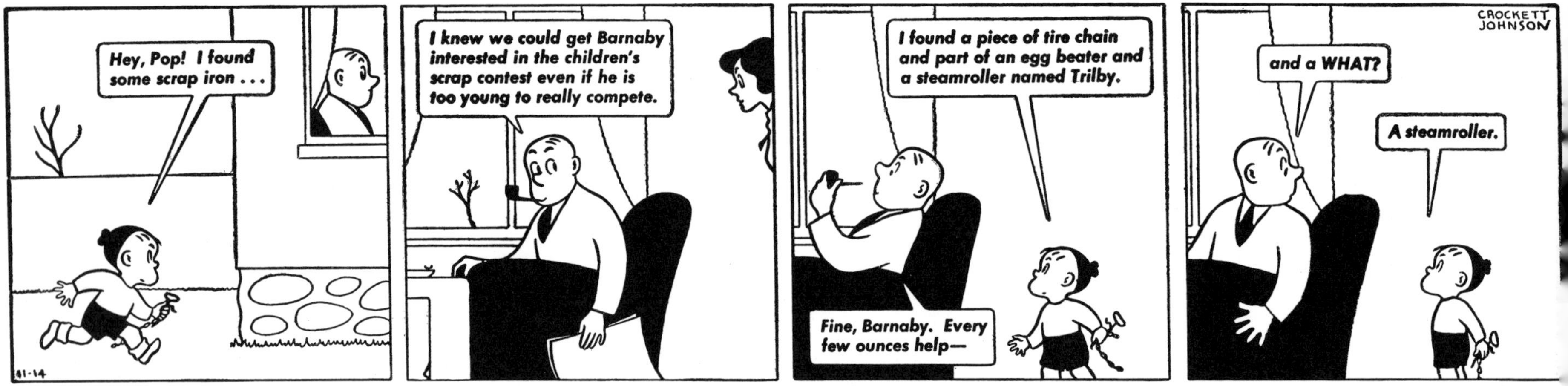
Hey, Pop! I found some scrap iron . . .
11-14
I knew we could get Barnaby interested in the children's scrap contest even if he is too young to really compete.
I found a piece of tire chain and part of an egg beater and a steamroller named Trilby.
Fine, Barnaby. Every few ounces help—
CROCKETT JOHNSON
and a WHAT?
A steamroller.

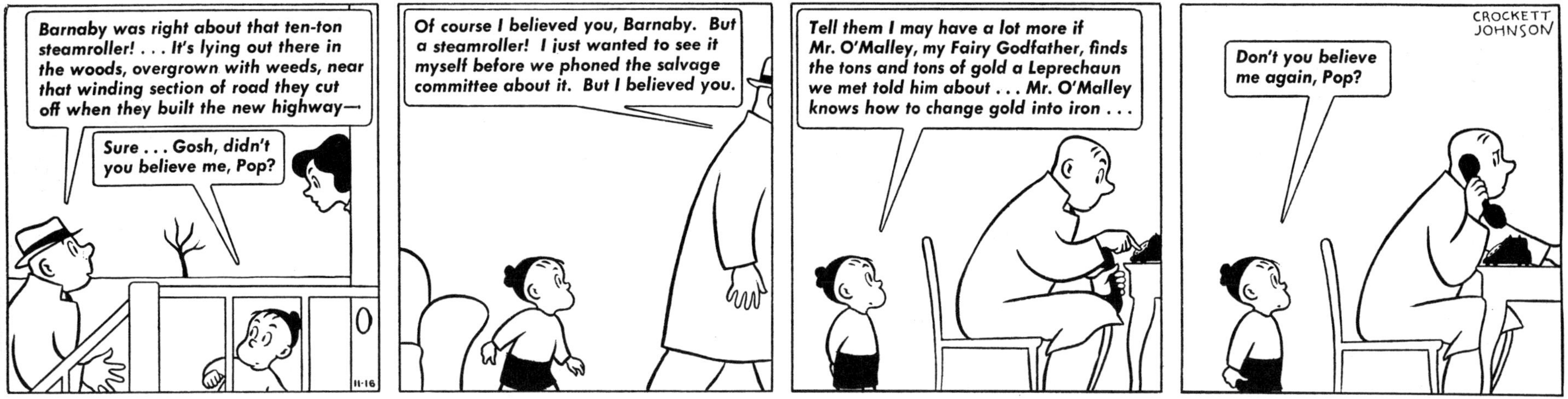
Barnaby was right about that ten-ton steamroller! . . . It's lying out there in the woods, overgrown with weeds, near that winding section of road they cut off when they built the new highway—
Sure . . . Gosh, didn't you believe me, Pop?
11-16
Of course I believed you, Barnaby. But a steamroller! I just wanted to see it myself before we phoned the salvage committee about it. But I believed you.
Tell them I may have a lot more if Mr. O'Malley, my Fairy Godfather, finds the tons and tons of gold a Leprechaun we met told him about . . . Mr. O'Malley knows how to change gold into iron . . .
CROCKETT JOHNSON
Don't you believe me again, Pop?

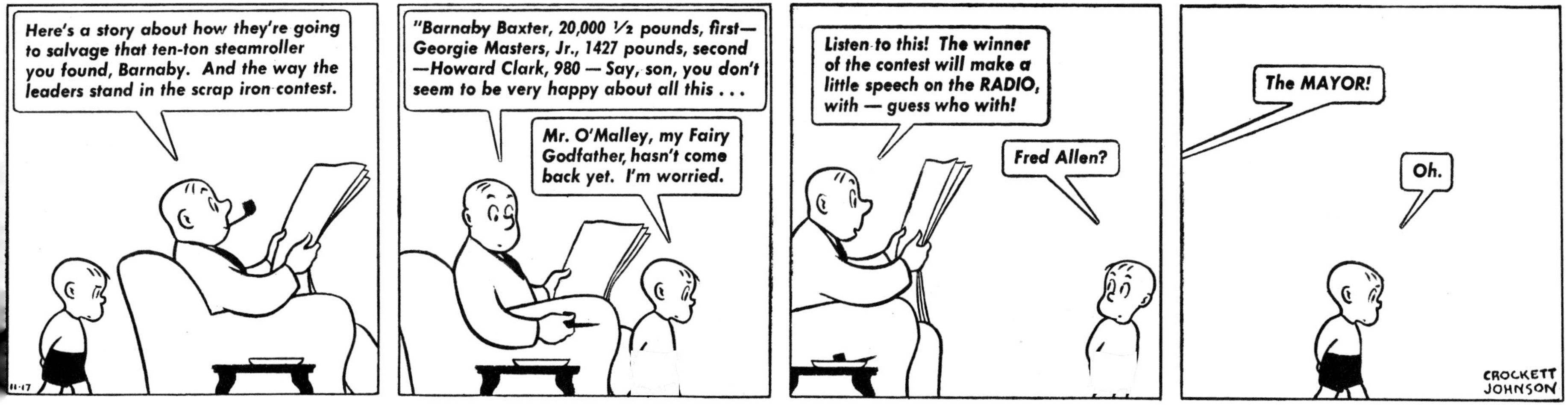
Here's a story about how they're going to salvage that ten-ton steamroller you found, Barnaby. And the way the leaders stand in the scrap iron contest.
11-17
"Barnaby Baxter, 20,000 ½ pounds, first—Georgie Masters, Jr., 1427 pounds, second—Howard Clark, 980 — Say, son, you don't seem to be very happy about all this . . .
Mr. O'Malley, my Fairy Godfather, hasn't come back yet. I'm worried.
Listen to this! The winner of the contest will make a little speech on the RADIO, with — guess who with!
Fred Allen?
The MAYOR!
Oh.
CROCKETT JOHNSON

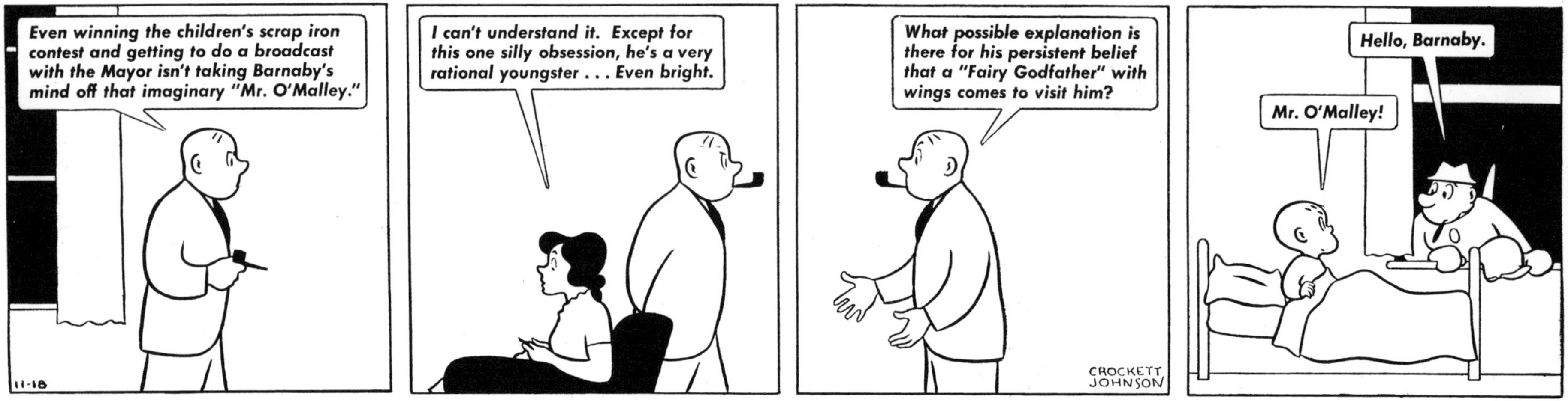
Even winning the children's scrap iron contest and getting to do a broadcast with the Mayor isn't taking Barnaby's mind off that imaginary "Mr. O'Malley."
11-18
I can't understand it. Except for this one silly obsession, he's a very rational youngster . . . Even bright.
What possible explanation is there for his persistent belief that a "Fairy Godfather" with wings comes to visit him?
CROCKETT JOHNSON
Mr. O'Malley!
Hello, Barnaby.

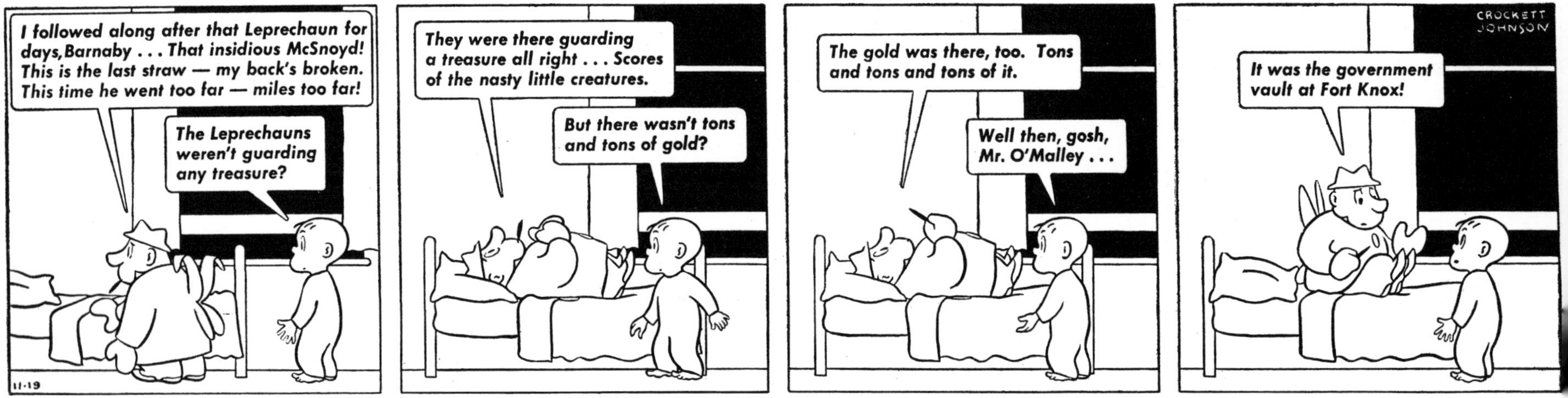
I followed along after that Leprechaun for days, Barnaby . . . That insidious McSnoyd! This is the last straw — my back's broken. This time he went too far — miles too far!
The Leprechauns weren't guarding any treasure?
11-19
They were there guarding a treasure all right . . . Scores of the nasty little creatures.
But there wasn't tons and tons of gold?
The gold was there, too. Tons and tons and tons of it.
Well then, gosh, Mr. O'Malley . . .
CROCKETT JOHNSON
It was the government vault at Fort Knox!

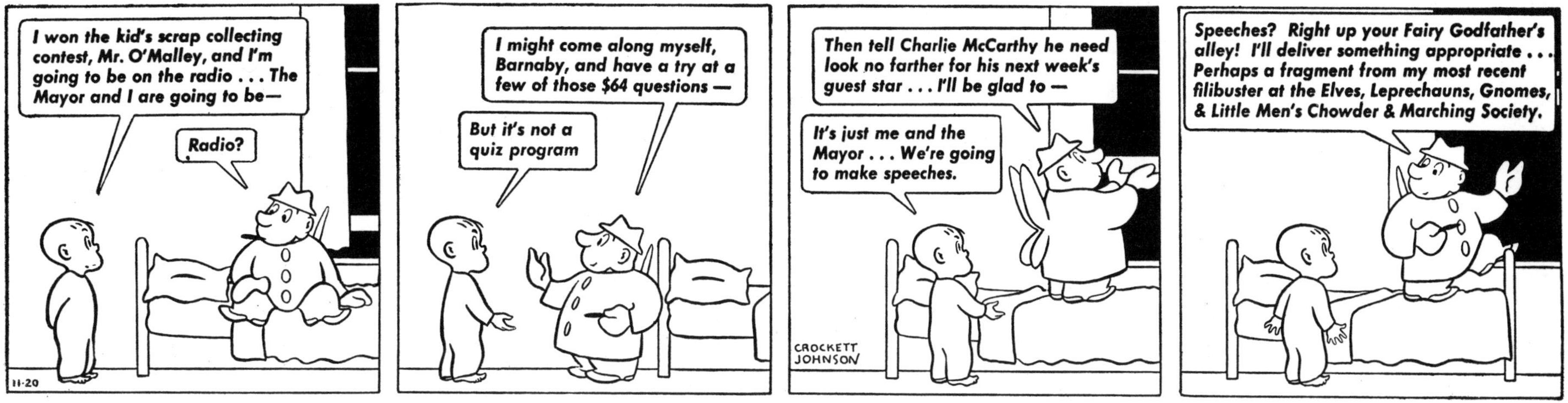
I won the kid's scrap collecting contest, Mr. O'Malley, and I'm going to be on the radio . . . The Mayor and I are going to be—
Radio?
11·20
I might come along myself, Barnaby, and have a try at a few of those $64 questions —
But it's not a quiz program
Then tell Charlie McCarthy he need look no farther for his next week's guest star . . . I'll be glad to —
It's just me and the Mayor . . . We're going to make speeches.
CROCKETT JOHNSON
Speeches? Right up your Fairy Godfather's alley! I'll deliver something appropriate . . . Perhaps a fragment from my most recent filibuster at the Elves, Leprechauns, Gnomes, & Little Men's Chowder & Marching Society.

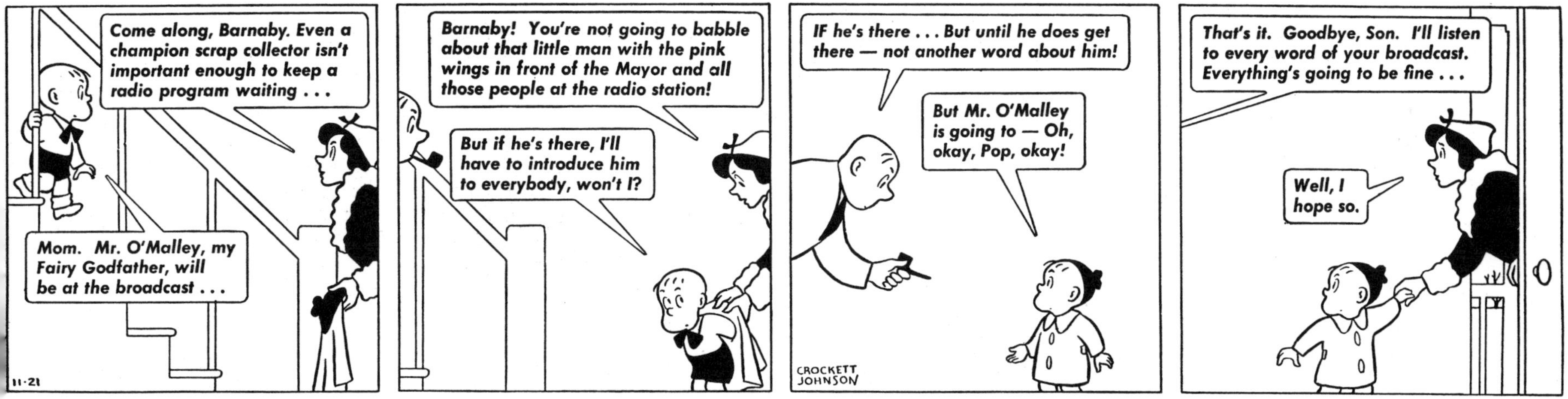
Come along, Barnaby. Even a champion scrap collector isn't important enough to keep a radio program waiting . . .
Mom. Mr. O'Malley, my Fairy Godfather, will be at the broadcast . . .
11·21
Barnaby! You're not going to babble about that little man with the pink wings in front of the Mayor and all those people at the radio station!
But if he's there, I'll have to introduce him to everybody, won't I?
IF he's there . . . But until he does get there — not another word about him!
But Mr. O'Malley is going to — Oh, okay, Pop, okay!
CROCKETT JOHNSON
That's it. Goodbye, Son. I'll listen to every word of your broadcast. Everything's going to be fine . . .
Well, I hope so.

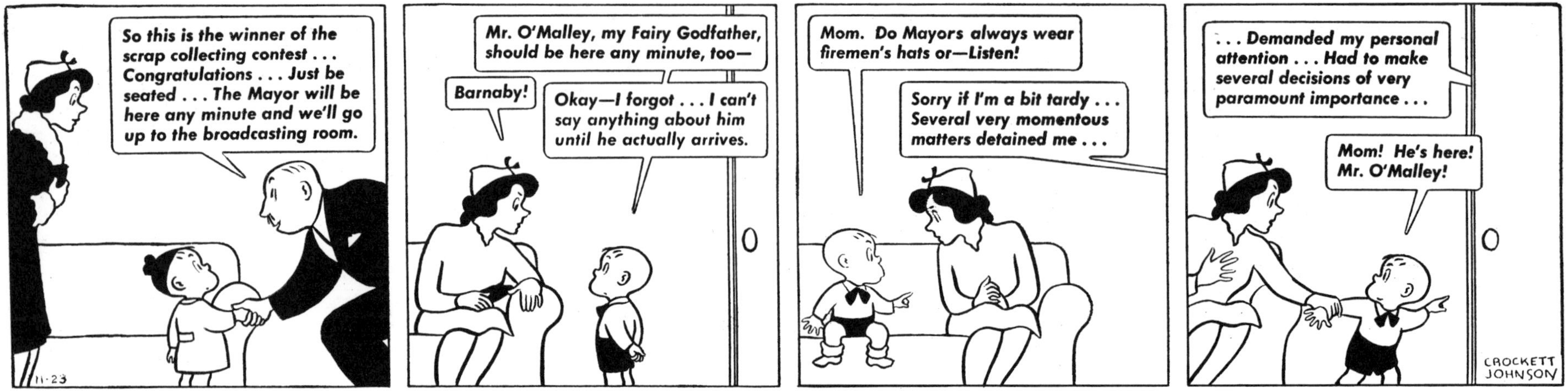
So this is the winner of the scrap collecting contest . . . Congratulations . . . Just be seated . . . The Mayor will be here any minute and we'll go up to the broadcasting room.
11·23
Mr. O'Malley, my Fairy Godfather, should be here any minute, too—
Barnaby!
Okay—I forgot . . . I can't say anything about him until he actually arrives.
Mom. Do Mayors always wear firemen's hats or—Listen!
Sorry if I'm a bit tardy . . . Several very momentous matters detained me . . .
. . . Demanded my personal attention . . . Had to make several decisions of very paramount importance . . .
Mom! He's here! Mr. O'Malley!
CROCKETT JOHNSON

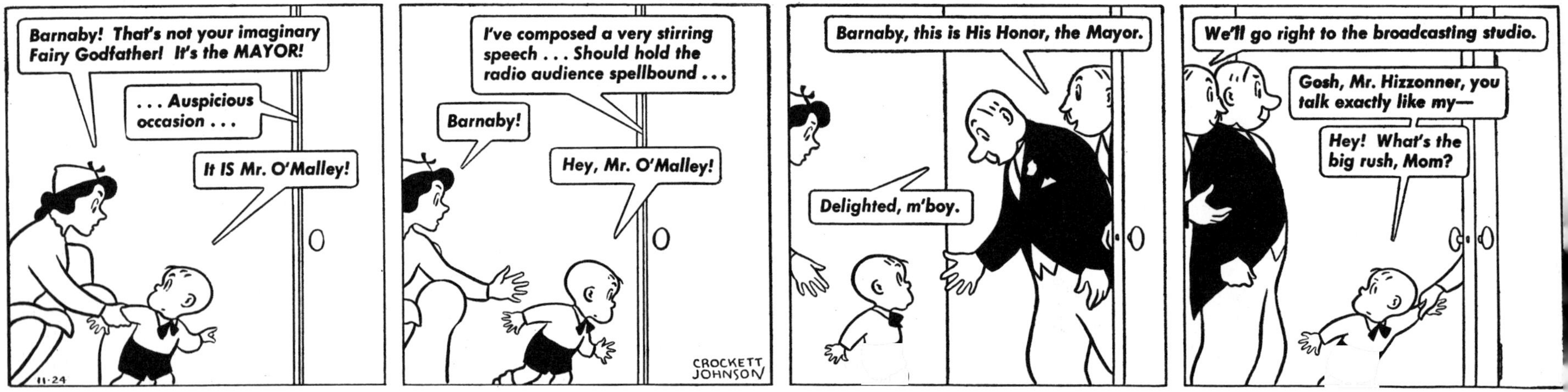
Barnaby! That's not your imaginary Fairy Godfather! It's the MAYOR!
. . . Auspicious occasion . . .
It IS Mr. O'Malley!
11·24
I've composed a very stirring speech . . . Should hold the radio audience spellbound . . .
Barnaby!
Hey, Mr. O'Malley!
CROCKETT JOHNSON
Barnaby, this is His Honor, the Mayor.
Delighted, m'boy.
We'll go right to the broadcasting studio.
Gosh, Mr. Hizzonner, you talk exactly like my—
Hey! What's the big rush, Mom?

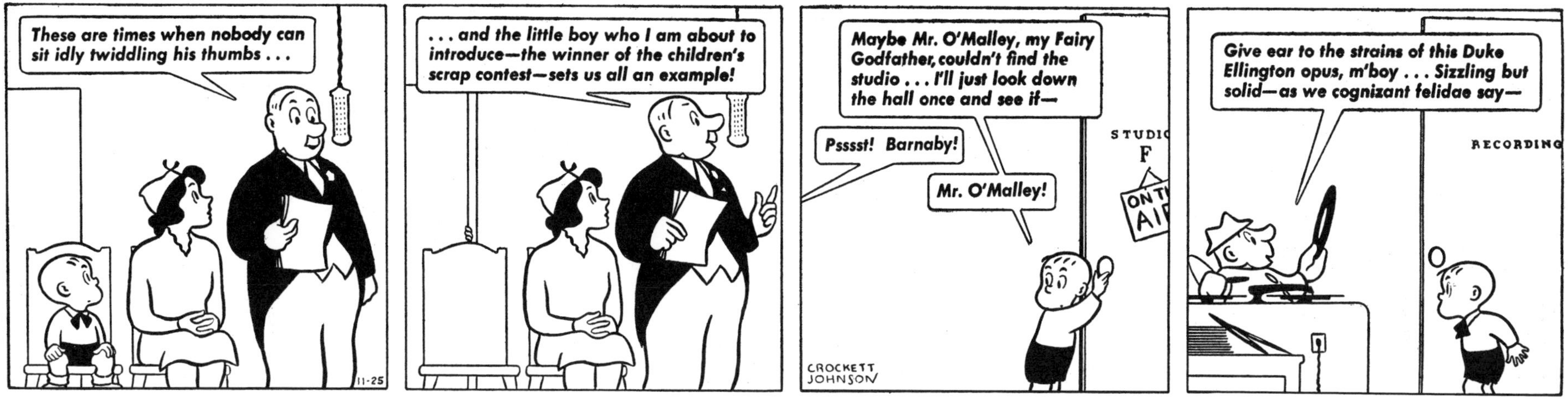
These are times when nobody can sit idly twiddling his thumbs . . .
11-25
. . . and the little boy who I am about to introduce—the winner of the children's scrap contest—sets us all an example!
Maybe Mr. O'Malley, my Fairy Godfather, couldn't find the studio . . . I'll just look down the hall once and see if—
Psssst! Barnaby!
Mr. O'Malley!
CROCKETT JOHNSON
Give ear to the strains of this Duke Ellington opus, m'boy . . . Sizzling but solid—as we cognizant felidae say—
RECORDING

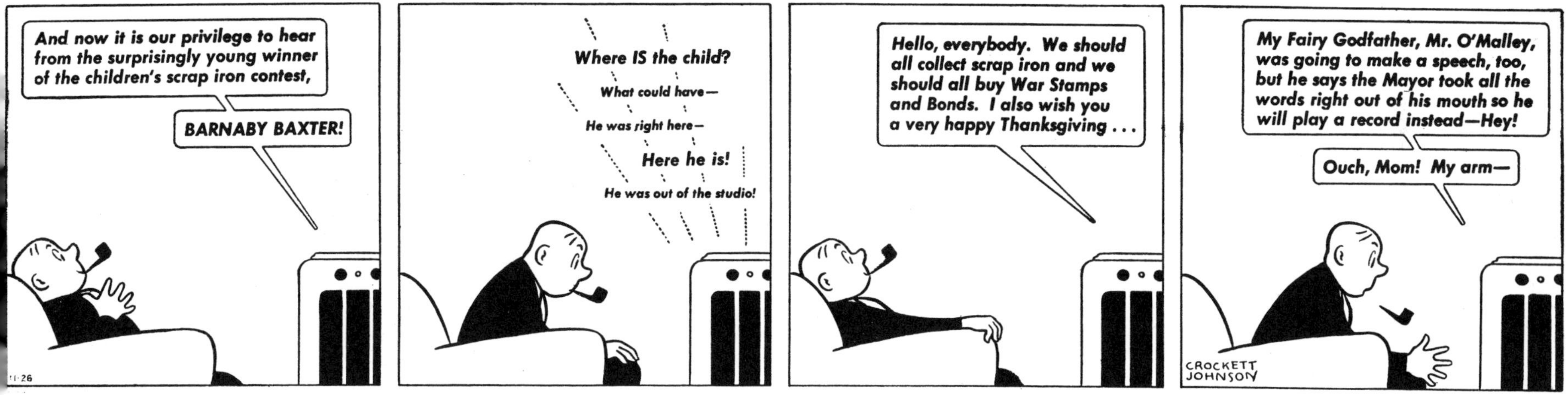
And now it is our privilege to hear from the surprisingly young winner of the children's scrap iron contest,
BARNABY BAXTER!
11-26
Where IS the child?
What could have—
He was right here—
Here he is!
He was out of the studio!
Hello, everybody. We should all collect scrap iron and we should all buy War Stamps and Bonds. I also wish you a very happy Thanksgiving . . .
My Fairy Godfather, Mr. O'Malley, was going to make a speech, too, but he says the Mayor took all the words right out of his mouth so he will play a record instead—Hey!
Ouch, Mom! My arm—
CROCKETT JOHNSON

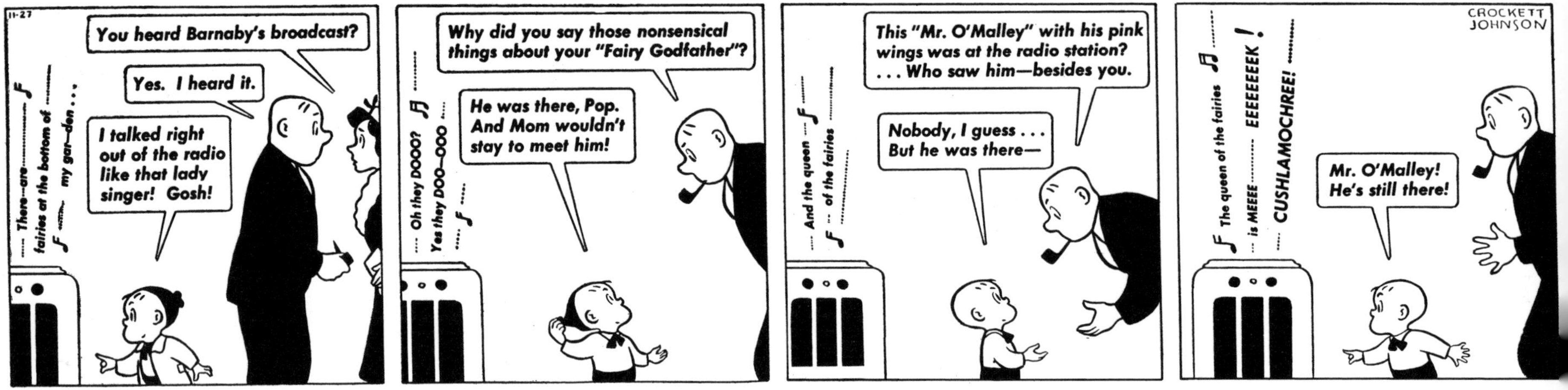
11-27
You heard Barnaby's broadcast?
Yes. I heard it.
I talked right out of the radio like that lady singer! Gosh!
There—are—— fairies at the bottom of —— my gar—den . . .
Why did you say those nonsensical things about your "Fairy Godfather"?
He was there, Pop. And Mom wouldn't stay to meet him!
Oh they DOOO? Yes they DOO—OOO
This "Mr. O'Malley" with his pink wings was at the radio station? . . . Who saw him—besides you.
Nobody, I guess . . . But he was there—
And the queen — of the fairies
CROCKETT JOHNSON
The queen of the fairies
is MEEEE .... EEEEEEEK!
CUSHLAMOCHREE!
Mr. O'Malley! He's still there!

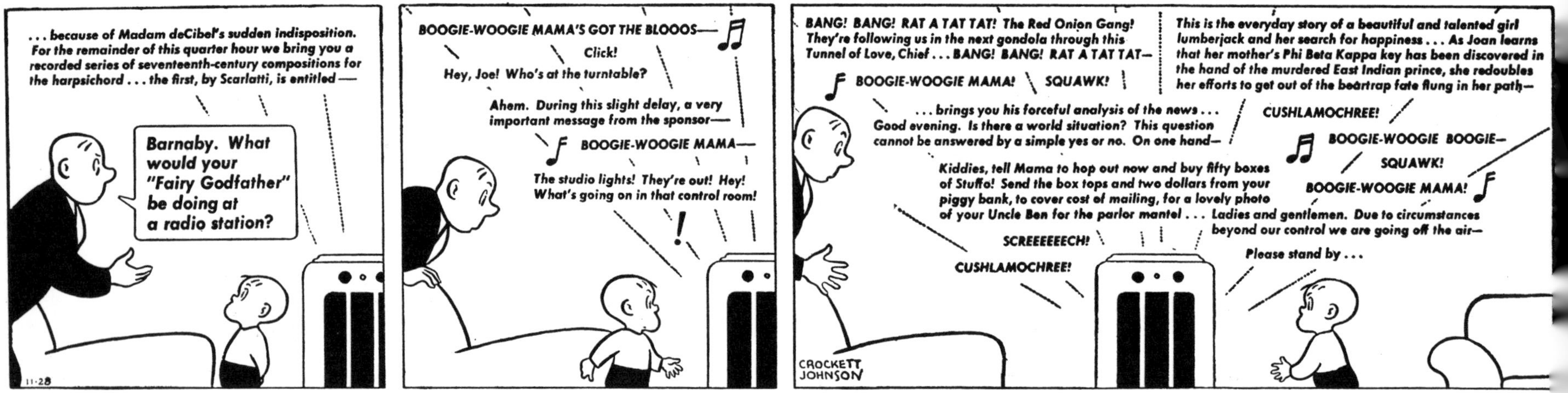
. . . because of Madam deCibel's sudden indisposition. For the remainder of this quarter hour we bring you a recorded series of seventeenth-century compositions for the harpsichord . . . the first, by Scarlatti, is entitled —
Barnaby. What would your "Fairy Godfather" be doing at a radio station?
11-28
BOOGIE-WOOGIE MAMA'S GOT THE BLOOOS—
Click!
Hey, Joe! Who's at the turntable?
Ahem. During this slight delay, a very important message from the sponsor—
BOOGIE-WOOGIE MAMA—
The studio lights! They're out! Hey! What's going on in that control room!
!
BANG! BANG! RAT A TAT TAT! The Red Onion Gang! They're following us in the next gondola through this Tunnel of Love, Chief . . . BANG! BANG! RAT A TAT TAT—
This is the everyday story of a beautiful and talented girl lumberjack and her search for happiness . . . As Joan learns that her mother's Phi Beta Kappa key has been discovered in the hand of the murdered East Indian prince, she redoubles her efforts to get out of the beartrap fate flung in her path—
BOOGIE-WOOGIE MAMA!
SQUAWK!
. . . brings you his forceful analysis of the news . . . Good evening. Is there a world situation? This question cannot be answered by a simple yes or no. On one hand—
CUSHLAMOCHREE!
BOOGIE-WOOGIE BOOGIE—
SQUAWK!
BOOGIE-WOOGIE MAMA!
Kiddies, tell Mama to hop out now and buy fifty boxes of Stuffo! Send the box tops and two dollars from your piggy bank, to cover cost of mailing, for a lovely photo of your Uncle Ben for the parlor mantel . . . Ladies and gentlemen. Due to circumstances beyond our control we are going off the air—
SCREEEEEECH!
Please stand by . . .
CUSHLAMOCHREE!
CROCKETT JOHNSON

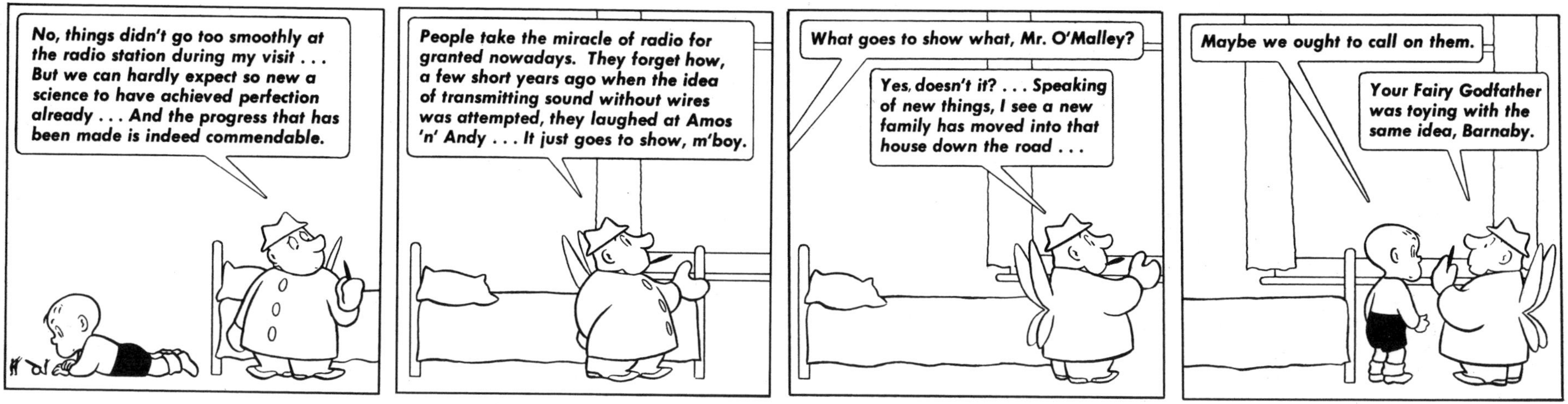
No, things didn't go too smoothly at the radio station during my visit . . . But we can hardly expect so new a science to have achieved perfection already . . . And the progress that has been made is indeed commendable.
People take the miracle of radio for granted nowadays. They forget how, a few short years ago when the idea of transmitting sound without wires was attempted, they laughed at Amos 'n' Andy . . . It just goes to show, m'boy.
What goes to show what, Mr. O'Malley?
Yes, doesn't it? . . . Speaking of new things, I see a new family has moved into that house down the road . . .
Maybe we ought to call on them.
Your Fairy Godfather was toying with the same idea, Barnaby.

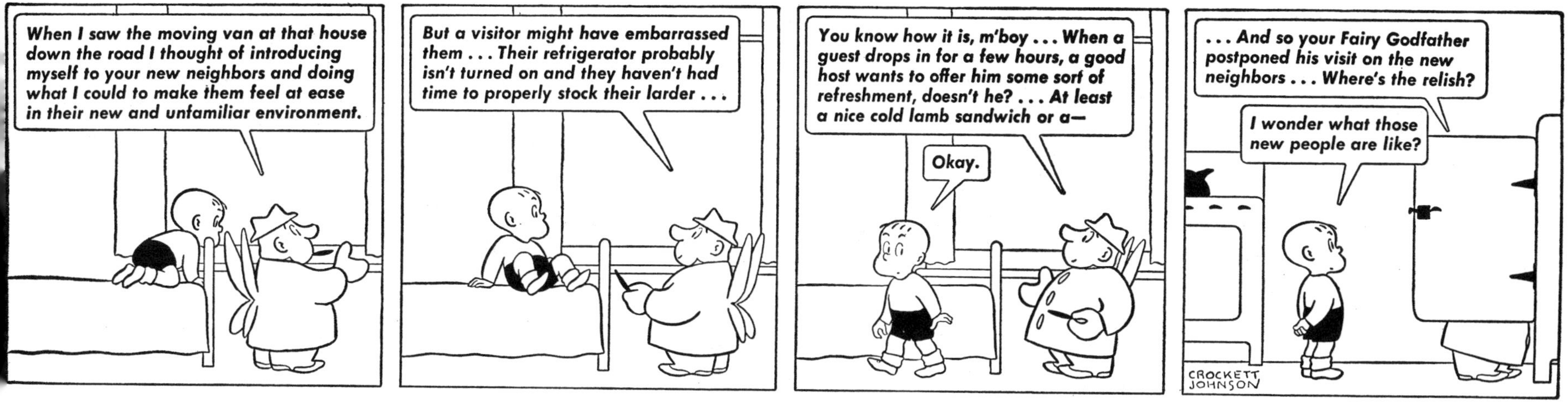
When I saw the moving van at that house down the road I thought of introducing myself to your new neighbors and doing what I could to make them feel at ease in their new and unfamiliar environment.
But a visitor might have embarrassed them . . . Their refrigerator probably isn't turned on and they haven't had time to properly stock their larder . . .
You know how it is, m'boy . . . When a guest drops in for a few hours, a good host wants to offer him some sort of refreshment, doesn't he? . . . At least a nice cold lamb sandwich or a—
Okay.
. . . And so your Fairy Godfather postponed his visit on the new neighbors . . . Where's the relish?
I wonder what those new people are like?
CROCKETT JOHNSON

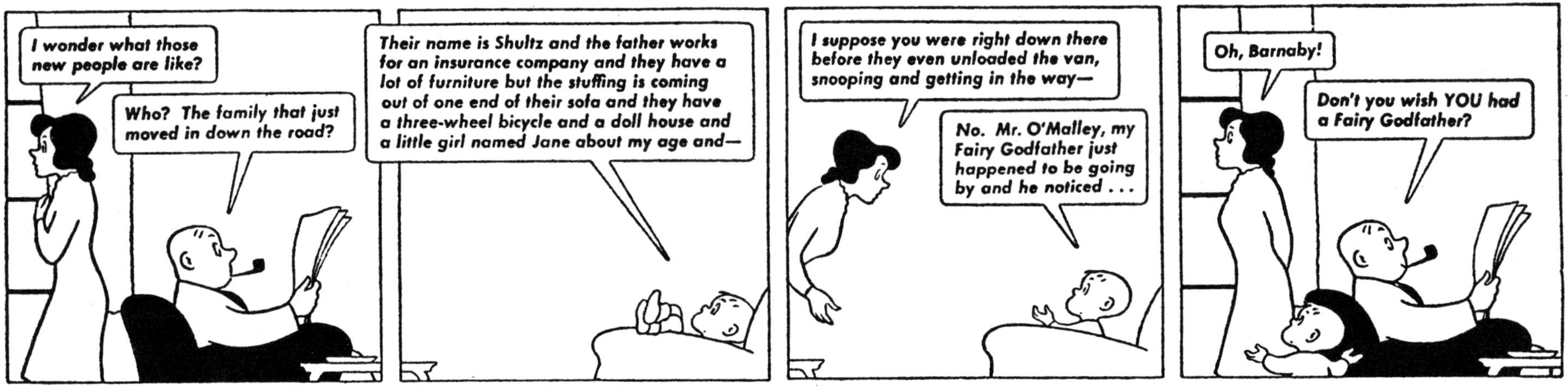
I wonder what those new people are like?
Who? The family that just moved in down the road?
Their name is Shultz and the father works for an insurance company and they have a lot of furniture but the stuffing is coming out of one end of their sofa and they have a three-wheel bicycle and a doll house and a little girl named Jane about my age and—
I suppose you were right down there before they even unloaded the van, snooping and getting in the way—
No. Mr. O'Malley, my Fairy Godfather just happened to be going by and he noticed . . .
Oh, Barnaby!
Don't you wish YOU had a Fairy Godfather?

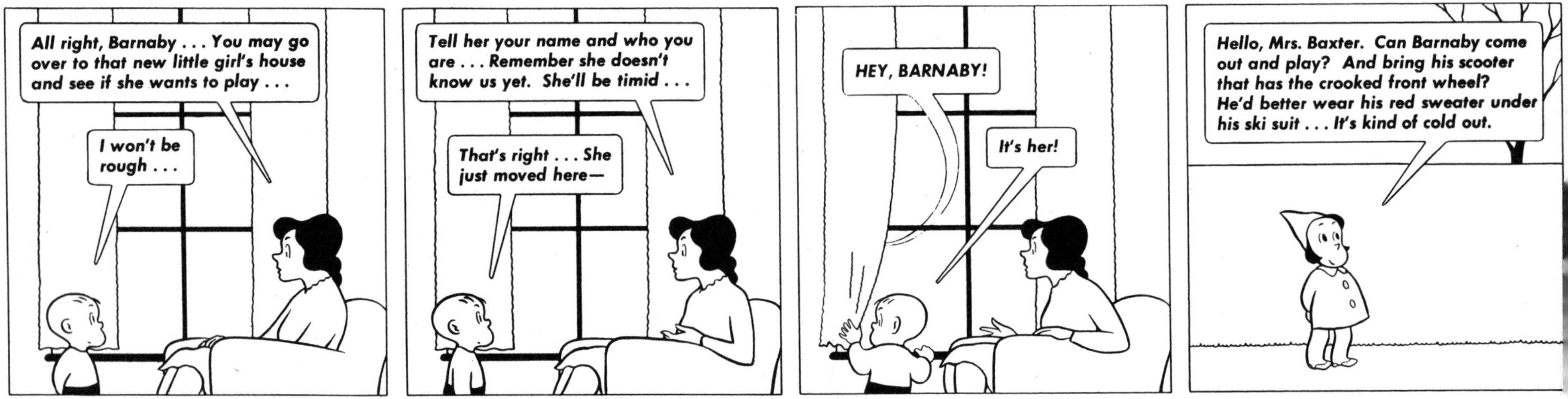
All right, Barnaby . . . You may go over to that new little girl's house and see if she wants to play . . .
I won't be rough . . .
Tell her your name and who you are . . . Remember she doesn't know us yet. She'll be timid . . .
That's right . . . She just moved here—
HEY, BARNABY!
It's her!
Hello, Mrs. Baxter. Can Barnaby come out and play? And bring his scooter that has the crooked front wheel? He'd better wear his red sweater under his ski suit . . . It's kind of cold out.

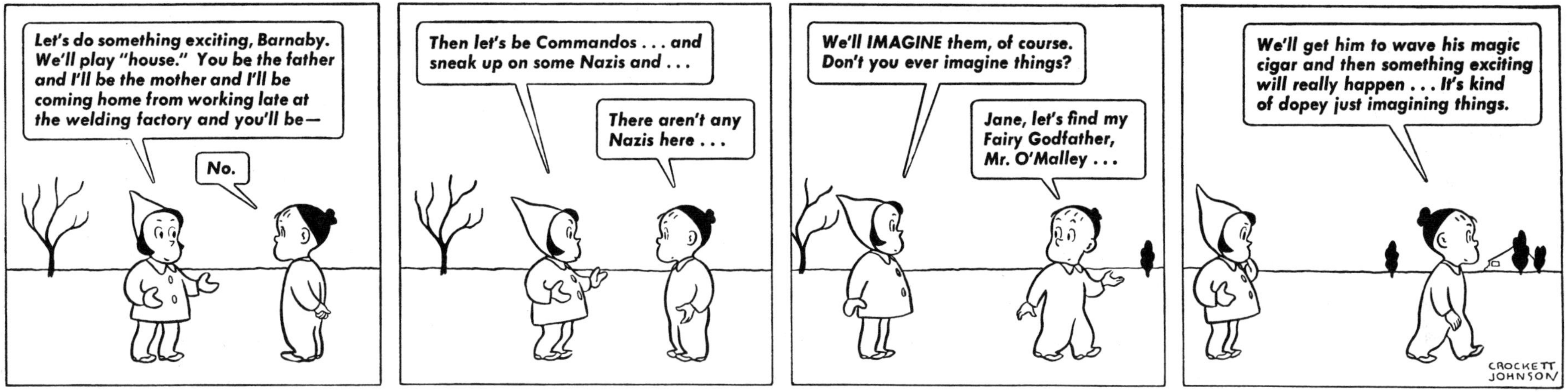
Let's do something exciting, Barnaby. We'll play "house." You be the father and I'll be the mother and I'll be coming home from working late at the welding factory and you'll be—
No.
Then let's be Commandos . . . and sneak up on some Nazis and . . .
There aren't any Nazis here . . .
We'll IMAGINE them, of course. Don't you ever imagine things?
Jane, let's find my Fairy Godfather, Mr. O'Malley . . .
We'll get him to wave his magic cigar and then something exciting will really happen . . . It's kind of dopey just imagining things.
CROCKETT JOHNSON

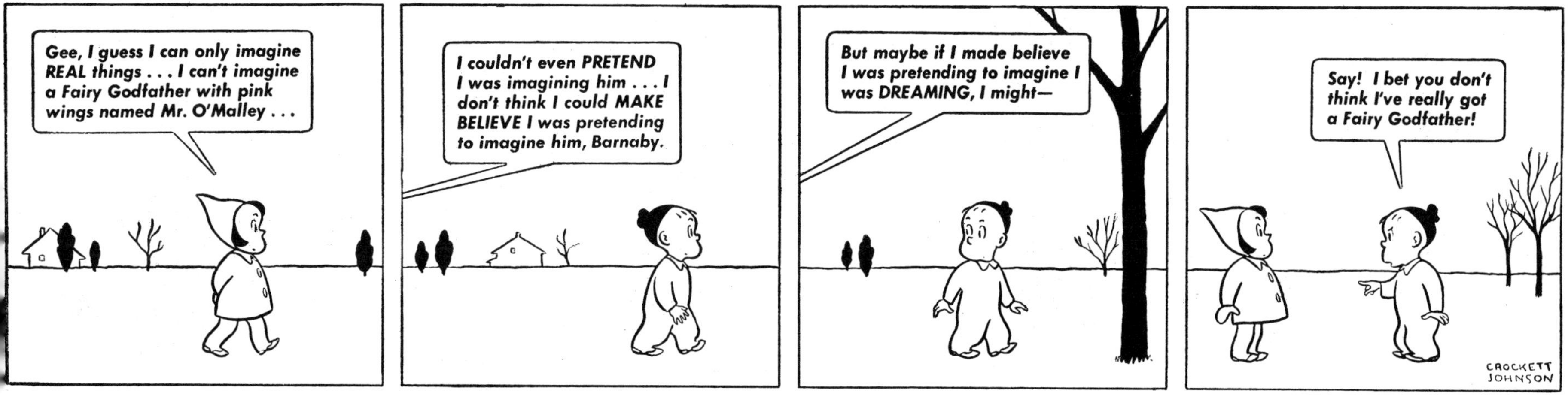
Gee, I guess I can only imagine REAL things . . . I can't imagine a Fairy Godfather with pink wings named Mr. O'Malley . . .
I couldn't even PRETEND I was imagining him . . . I don't think I could MAKE BELIEVE I was pretending to imagine him, Barnaby.
But maybe if I made believe I was pretending to imagine I was DREAMING, I might—
Say! I bet you don't think I've really got a Fairy Godfather!
CROCKETT JOHNSON

December 4 – 5

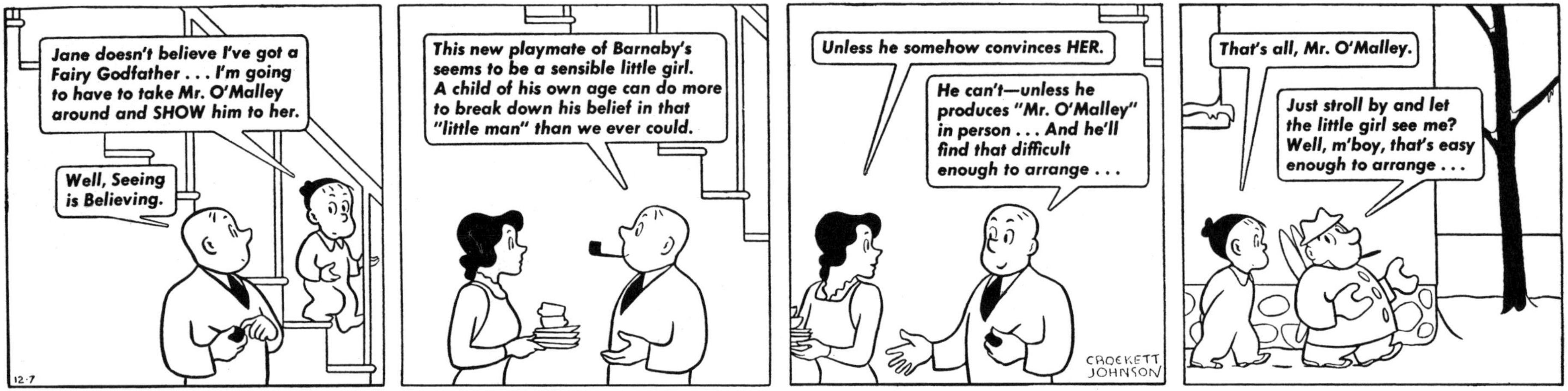
Jane doesn't believe I've got a Fairy Godfather . . . I'm going to have to take Mr. O'Malley around and SHOW him to her.
Well, Seeing is Believing.
12·7
This new playmate of Barnaby's seems to be a sensible little girl. A child of his own age can do more to break down his belief in that "little man" than we ever could.
Unless he somehow convinces HER.
He can't—unless he produces "Mr. O'Malley" in person . . . And he'll find that difficult enough to arrange . . .
CROCKETT JOHNSON
That's all, Mr. O'Malley.
Just stroll by and let the little girl see me? Well, m'boy, that's easy enough to arrange . . .

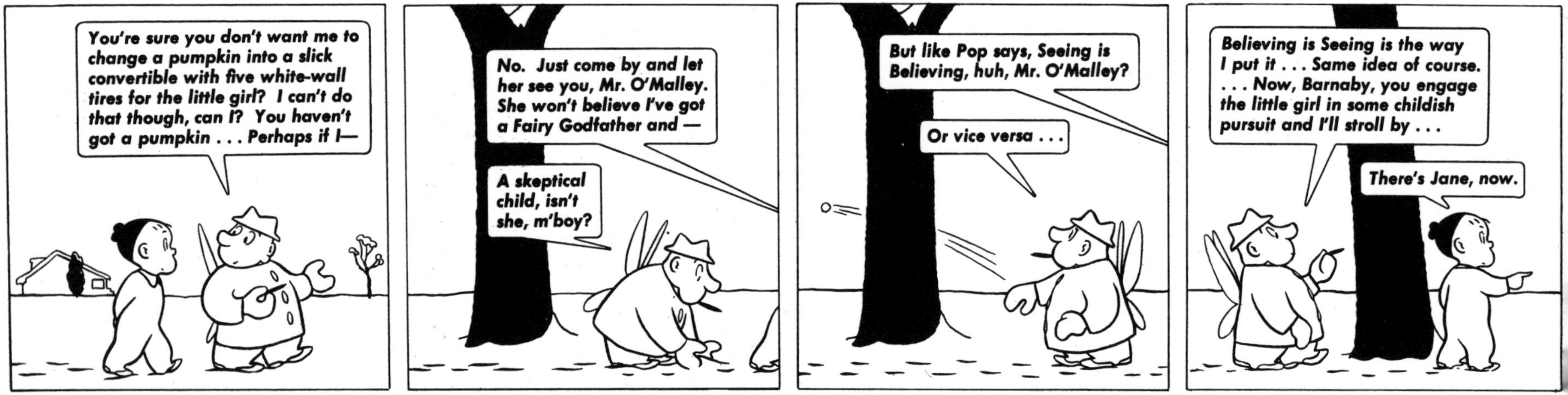
You're sure you don't want me to change a pumpkin into a slick convertible with five white-wall tires for the little girl? I can't do that though, can I? You haven't got a pumpkin . . . Perhaps if I—
No. Just come by and let her see you, Mr. O'Malley. She won't believe I've got a Fairy Godfather and —
A skeptical child, isn't she, m'boy?
But like Pop says, Seeing is Believing, huh, Mr. O'Malley?
Or vice versa . . .
Believing is Seeing is the way I put it . . . Same idea of course. . . . Now, Barnaby, you engage the little girl in some childish pursuit and I'll stroll by . . .
There's Jane, now.

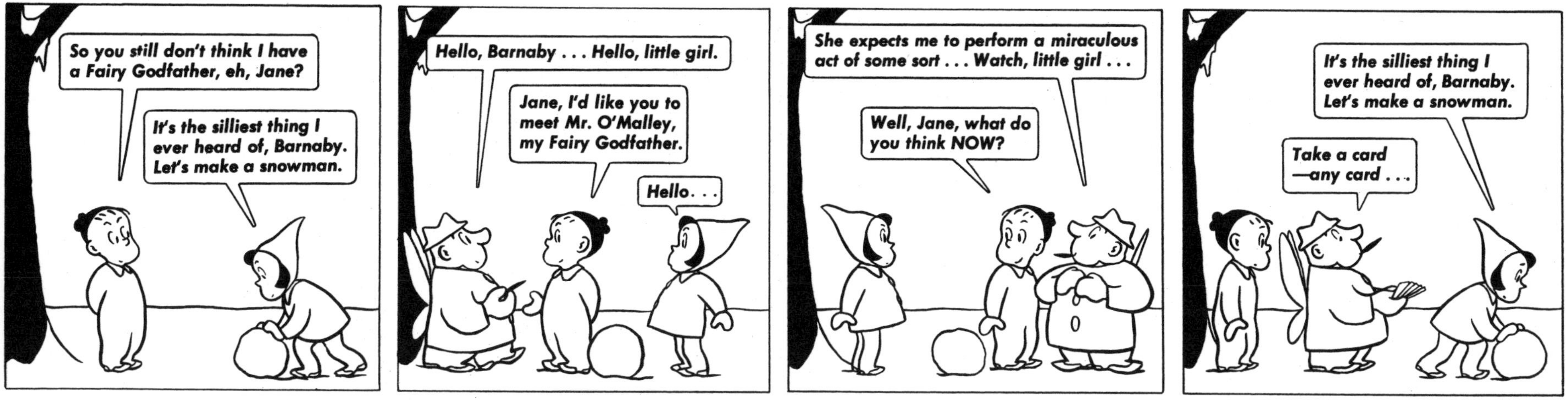
So you still don't think I have a Fairy Godfather, eh, Jane?
It's the silliest thing I ever heard of, Barnaby. Let's make a snowman.
Hello, Barnaby . . . Hello, little girl.
Jane, I'd like you to meet Mr. O'Malley, my Fairy Godfather.
Hello. . .
She expects me to perform a miraculous act of some sort . . . Watch, little girl . . .
Well, Jane, what do you think NOW?
It's the silliest thing I ever heard of, Barnaby. Let's make a snowman.
Take a card —any card . . .

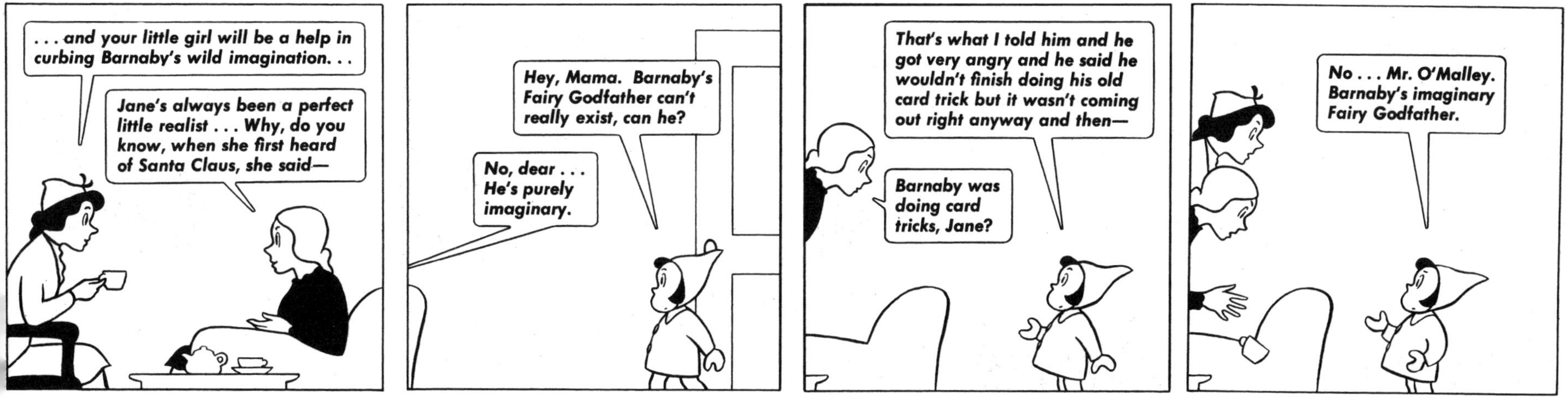
. . . and your little girl will be a help in curbing Barnaby's wild imagination. . .
Jane's always been a perfect little realist . . . Why, do you know, when she first heard of Santa Claus, she said—
Hey, Mama. Barnaby's Fairy Godfather can't really exist, can he?
No, dear . . . He's purely imaginary.
That's what I told him and he got very angry and he said he wouldn't finish doing his old card trick but it wasn't coming out right anyway and then—
Barnaby was doing card tricks, Jane?
No . . . Mr. O'Malley. Barnaby's imaginary Fairy Godfather.

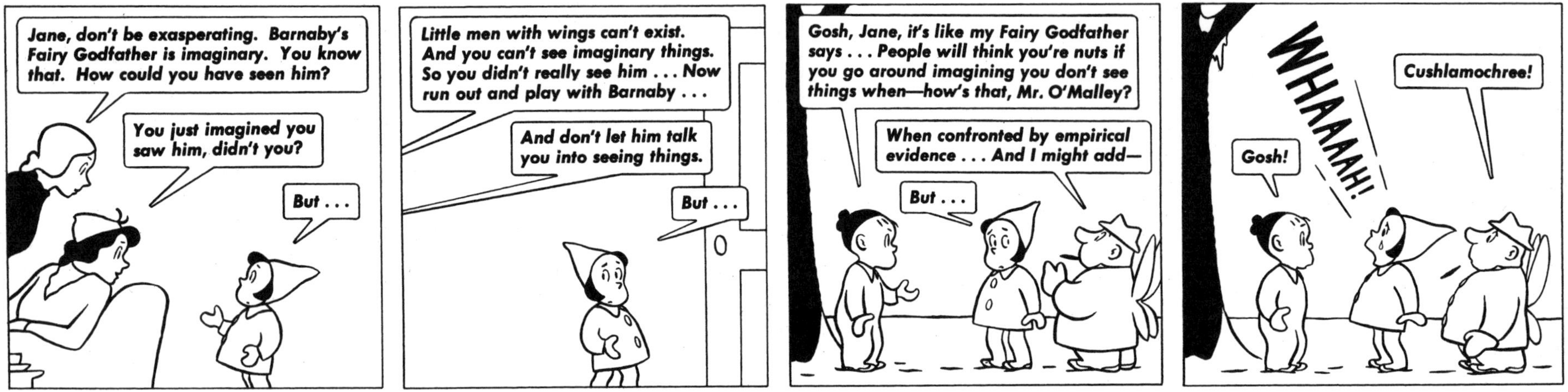
Jane, don't be exasperating. Barnaby's Fairy Godfather is imaginary. You know that. How could you have seen him?
You just imagined you saw him, didn't you?
But . . .
Little men with wings can't exist. And you can't see imaginary things. So you didn't really see him . . . Now run out and play with Barnaby . . .
And don't let him talk you into seeing things.
But . . .
Gosh, Jane, it's like my Fairy Godfather says . . . People will think you're nuts if you go around imagining you don't see things when—how's that, Mr. O'Malley?
When confronted by empirical evidence . . . And I might add—
But . . .
WHAAAAH!
Gosh!
Cushlamochree!

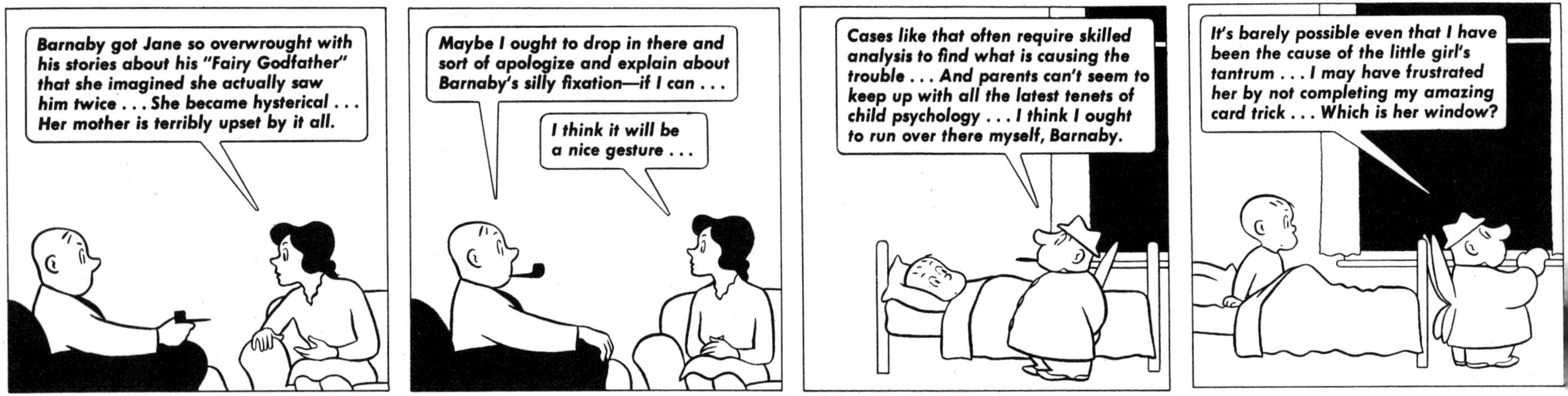
Barnaby got Jane so overwrought with his stories about his "Fairy Godfather" that she imagined she actually saw him twice . . . She became hysterical . . . Her mother is terribly upset by it all.
Maybe I ought to drop in there and sort of apologize and explain about Barnaby's silly fixation—if I can . . .
I think it will be a nice gesture . . .
Cases like that often require skilled analysis to find what is causing the trouble . . . And parents can't seem to keep up with all the latest tenets of child psychology . . . I think I ought to run over there myself, Barnaby.
It's barely possible even that I have been the cause of the little girl's tantrum . . . I may have frustrated her by not completing my amazing card trick . . . Which is her window?

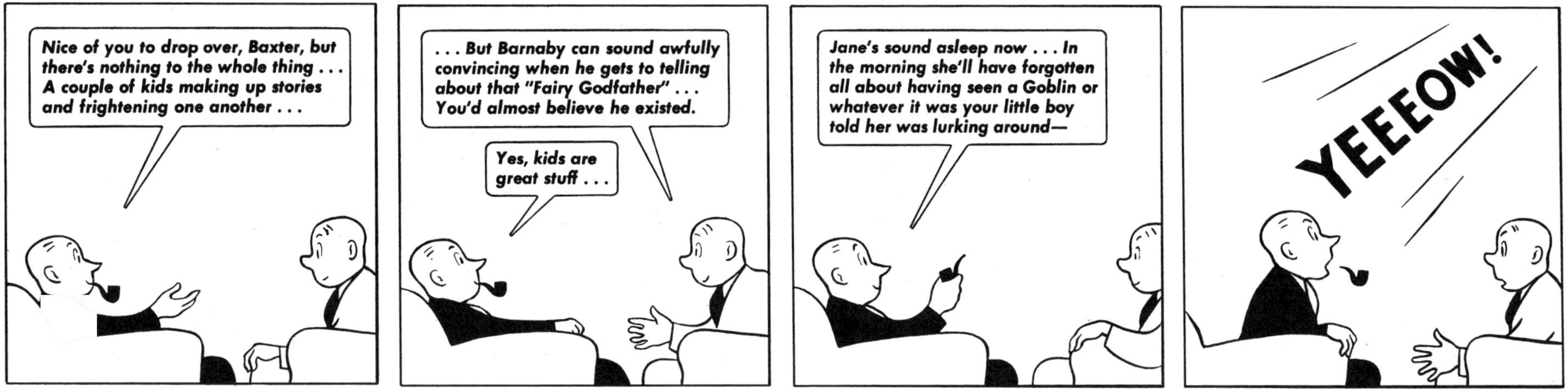
Nice of you to drop over, Baxter, but there's nothing to the whole thing . . . A couple of kids making up stories and frightening one another . . .
. . . But Barnaby can sound awfully convincing when he gets to telling about that "Fairy Godfather" . . . You'd almost believe he existed.
Yes, kids are great stuff . . .
Jane's sound asleep now . . . In the morning she'll have forgotten all about having seen a Goblin or whatever it was your little boy told her was lurking around—
YEEEOW!

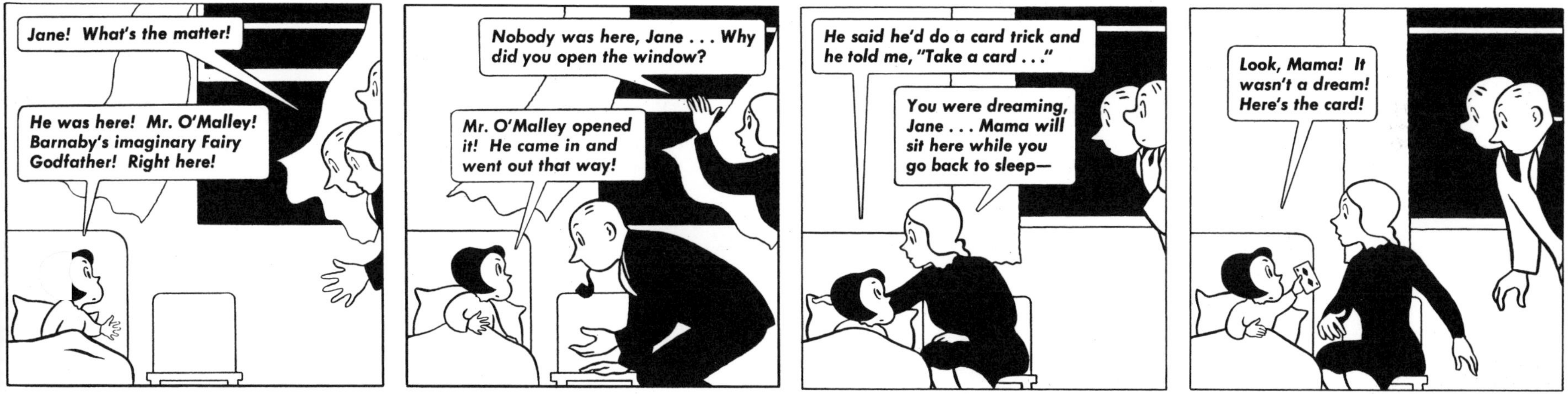
Jane! What's the matter!
He was here! Mr. O'Malley! Barnaby's imaginary Fairy Godfather! Right here!
Nobody was here, Jane . . . Why did you open the window?
Mr. O'Malley opened it! He came in and went out that way!
He said he'd do a card trick and he told me, "Take a card . . ."
You were dreaming, Jane . . . Mama will sit here while you go back to sleep—
Look, Mama! It wasn't a dream! Here's the card!

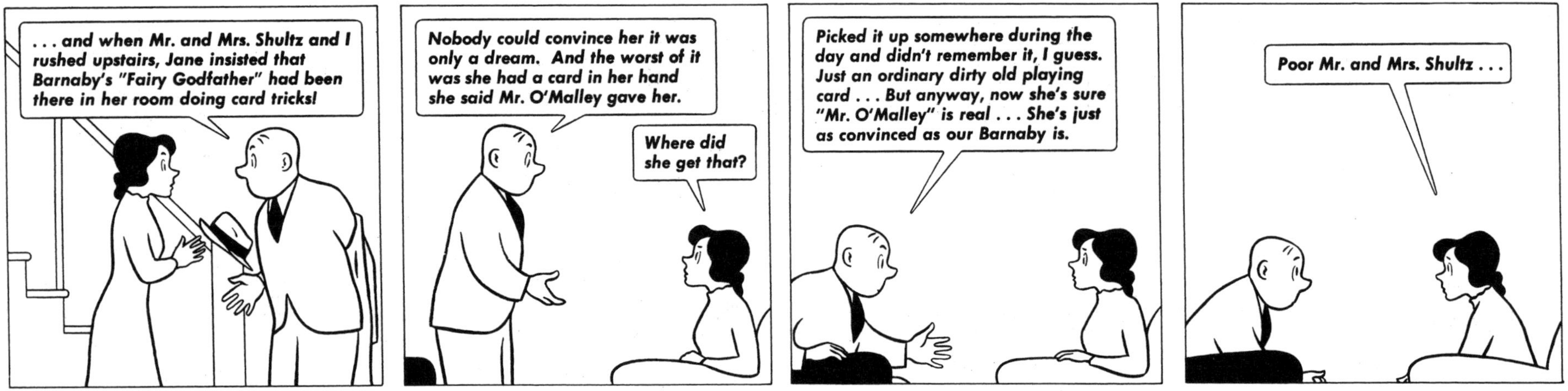
. . . and when Mr. and Mrs. Shultz and I rushed upstairs, Jane insisted that Barnaby's "Fairy Godfather" had been there in her room doing card tricks!
Nobody could convince her it was only a dream. And the worst of it was she had a card in her hand she said Mr. O'Malley gave her.
Where did she get that?
Picked it up somewhere during the day and didn't remember it, I guess. Just an ordinary dirty old playing card . . . But anyway, now she's sure "Mr. O'Malley" is real . . . She's just as convinced as our Barnaby is.
Poor Mr. and Mrs. Shultz . . .

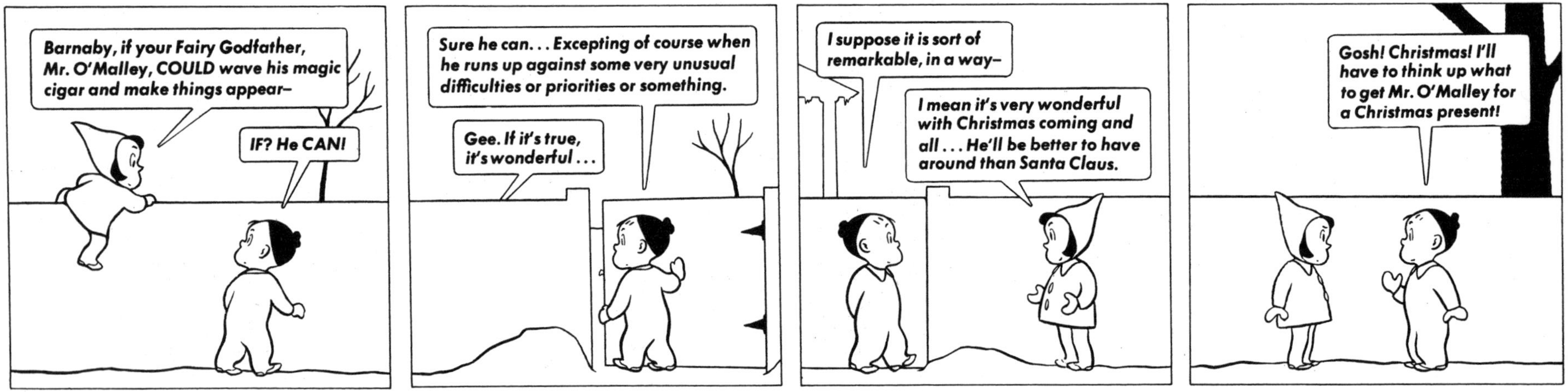
Barnaby, if your Fairy Godfather, Mr. O'Malley, COULD wave his magic cigar and make things appear–
IF? He CAN!
Sure he can. . . Excepting of course when he runs up against some very unusual difficulties or priorities or something.
Gee. If it's true, it's wonderful . . .
I suppose it is sort of remarkable, in a way–
I mean it's very wonderful with Christmas coming and all . . . He'll be better to have around than Santa Claus.
Gosh! Christmas! I'll have to think up what to get Mr. O'Malley for a Christmas present!

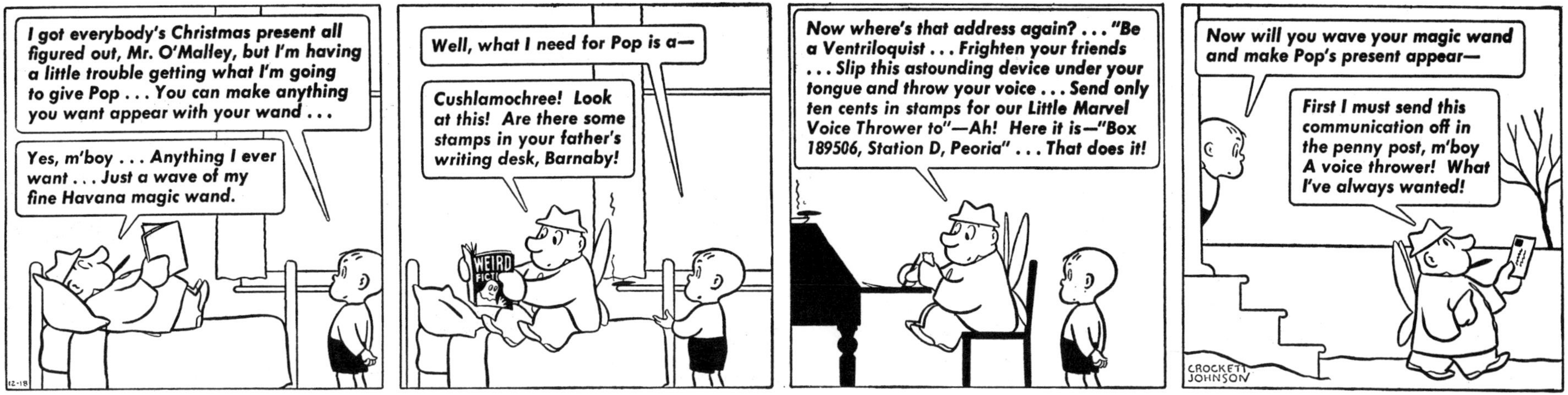
12-18
I got everybody's Christmas present all figured out, Mr. O'Malley, but I'm having a little trouble getting what I'm going to give Pop . . . You can make anything you want appear with your wand . . .
Yes, m'boy . . . Anything I ever want . . . Just a wave of my fine Havana magic wand.
Well, what I need for Pop is a—
Cushlamochree! Look at this! Are there some stamps in your father's writing desk, Barnaby!
WEIRD FICTI
Now where's that address again? . . . "Be a Ventriloquist . . . Frighten your friends . . . Slip this astounding device under your tongue and throw your voice . . . Send only ten cents in stamps for our Little Marvel Voice Thrower to"—Ah! Here it is—"Box 189506, Station D, Peoria" . . . That does it!
Now will you wave your magic wand and make Pop's present appear—
First I must send this communication off in the penny post, m'boy A voice thrower! What I've always wanted!
CROCKETT JOHNSON

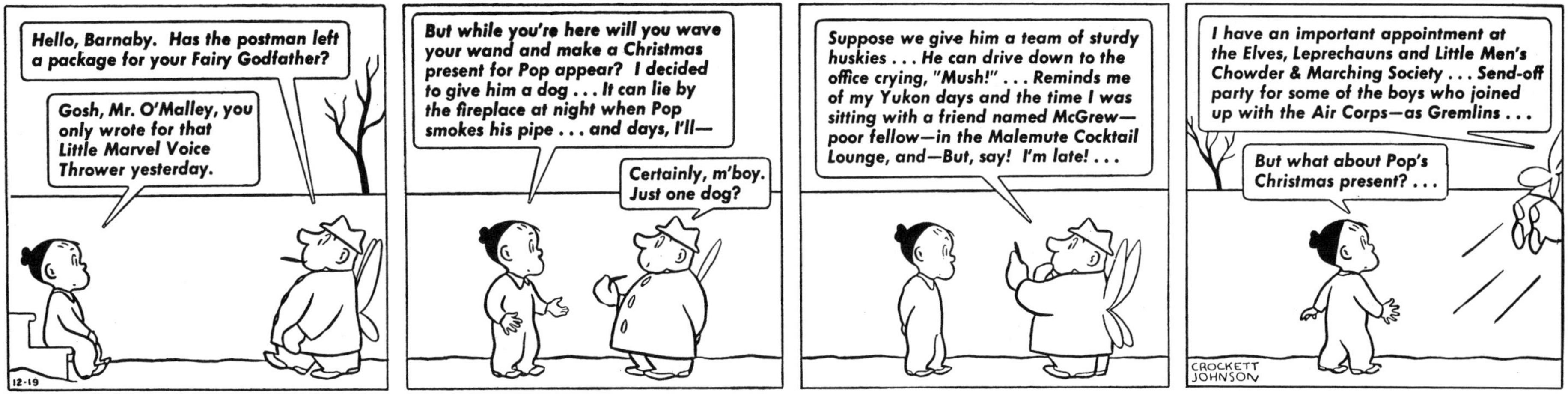
Hello, Barnaby. Has the postman left a package for your Fairy Godfather?
Gosh, Mr. O'Malley, you only wrote for that Little Marvel Voice Thrower yesterday.
12-19
But while you're here will you wave your wand and make a Christmas present for Pop appear? I decided to give him a dog . . . It can lie by the fireplace at night when Pop smokes his pipe . . . and days, I'll—
Certainly, m'boy. Just one dog?
Suppose we give him a team of sturdy huskies . . . He can drive down to the office crying, "Mush!" . . . Reminds me of my Yukon days and the time I was sitting with a friend named McGrew—poor fellow—in the Malemute Cocktail Lounge, and—But, say! I'm late! . . .
I have an important appointment at the Elves, Leprechauns and Little Men's Chowder & Marching Society . . . Send-off party for some of the boys who joined up with the Air Corps—as Gremlins . . .
But what about Pop's Christmas present? . . .
CROCKETT JOHNSON

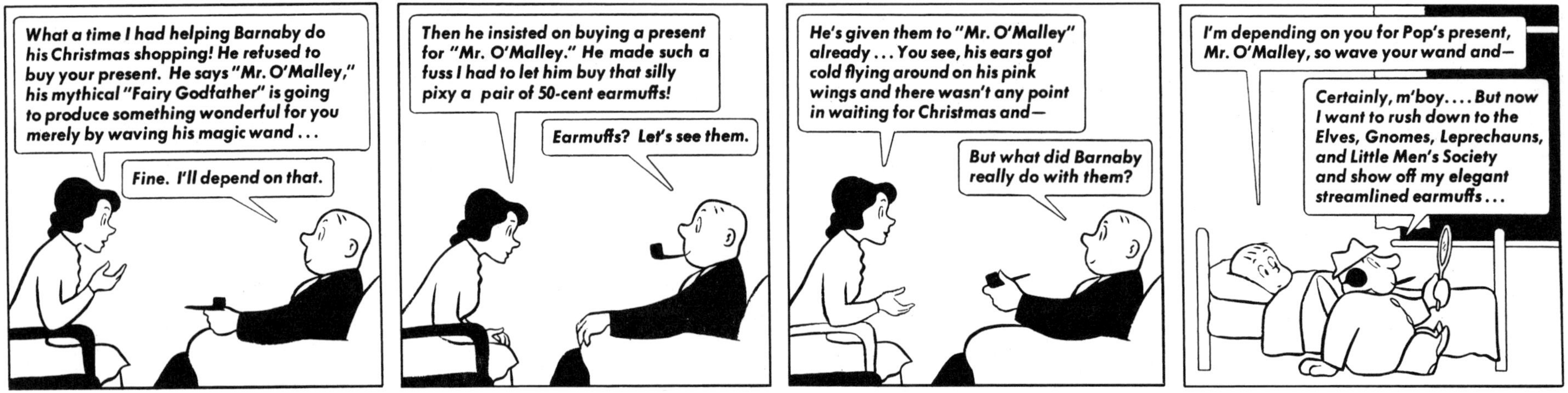
What a time I had helping Barnaby do his Christmas shopping! He refused to buy your present. He says "Mr. O'Malley," his mythical "Fairy Godfather" is going to produce something wonderful for you merely by waving his magic wand . . .
Fine. I'll depend on that.
Then he insisted on buying a present for "Mr. O'Malley." He made such a fuss I had to let him buy that silly pixy a pair of 50-cent earmuffs!
Earmuffs? Let's see them.
He's given them to "Mr. O'Malley" already . . . You see, his ears got cold flying around on his pink wings and there wasn't any point in waiting for Christmas and—
But what did Barnaby really do with them?
I'm depending on you for Pop's present, Mr. O'Malley, so wave your wand and—
Certainly, m'boy. . . . But now I want to rush down to the Elves, Gnomes, Leprechauns, and Little Men's Society and show off my elegant streamlined earmuffs . . .

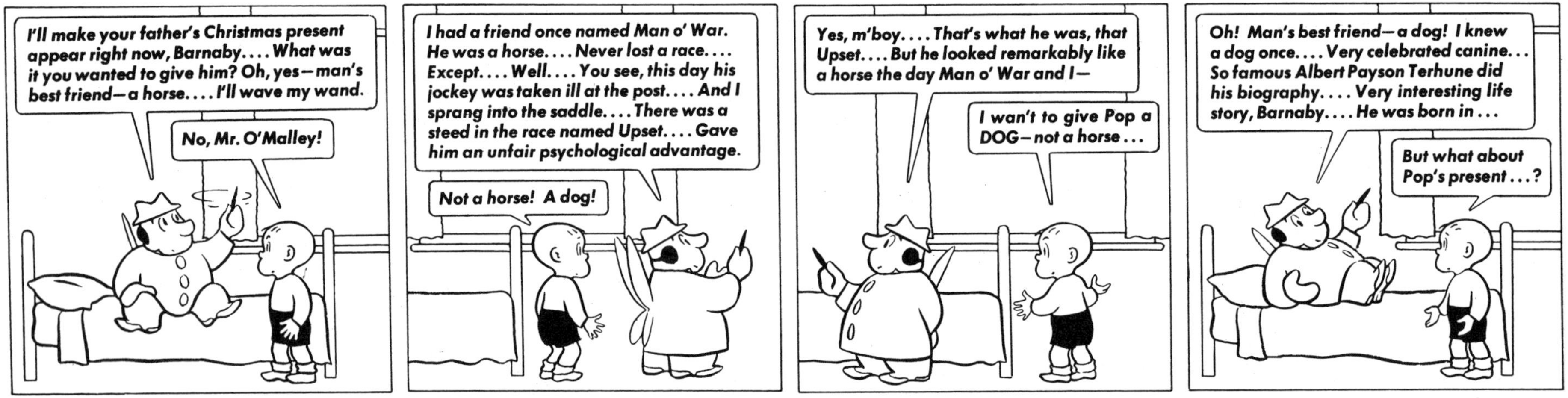
I'll make your father's Christmas present appear right now, Barnaby. . . . What was it you wanted to give him? Oh, yes—man's best friend—a horse. . . . I'll wave my wand.
No, Mr. O'Malley!
I had a friend once named Man o' War. He was a horse. . . . Never lost a race. . . . Except. . . . Well. . . . You see, this day his jockey was taken ill at the post. . . . And I sprang into the saddle. . . . There was a steed in the race named Upset. . . . Gave him an unfair psychological advantage.
Not a horse! A dog!
Yes, m'boy. . . . That's what he was, that Upset. . . . But he looked remarkably like a horse the day Man o' War and I—
I wan't to give Pop a DOG—not a horse . . .
Oh! Man's best friend—a dog! I knew a dog once. . . . Very celebrated canine. . . So famous Albert Payson Terhune did his biography. . . . Very interesting life story, Barnaby. . . . He was born in . . .
But what about Pop's present . . . ?

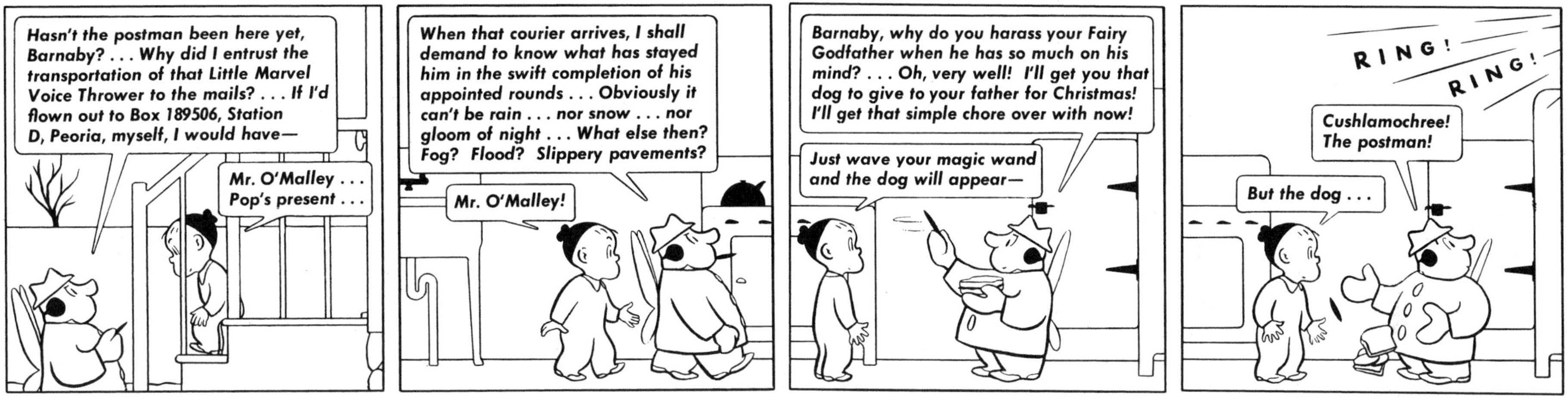
Hasn't the postman been here yet, Barnaby? . . . Why did I entrust the transportation of that Little Marvel Voice Thrower to the mails? . . . If I'd flown out to Box 189506, Station D, Peoria, myself, I would have—
Mr. O'Malley . . . Pop's present . . .
When that courier arrives, I shall demand to know what has stayed him in the swift completion of his appointed rounds . . . Obviously it can't be rain . . . nor snow . . . nor gloom of night . . . What else then? Fog? Flood? Slippery pavements?
Mr. O'Malley!
Barnaby, why do you harass your Fairy Godfather when he has so much on his mind? . . . Oh, very well! I'll get you that dog to give to your father for Christmas! I'll get that simple chore over with now!
Just wave your magic wand and the dog will appear—
RING! RING!
Cushlamochree! The postman!
But the dog . . .

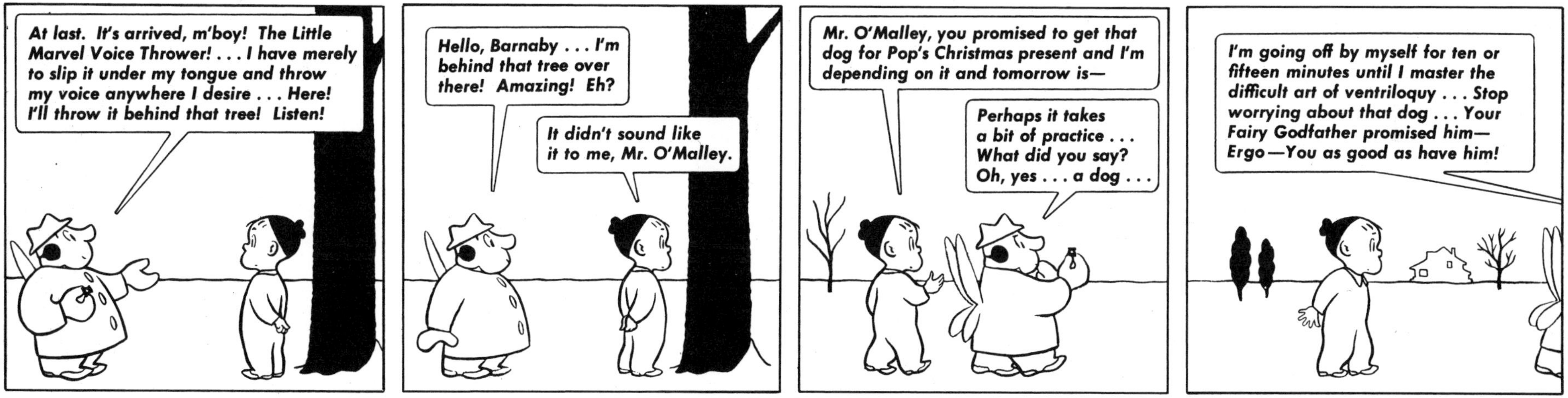
At last. It's arrived, m'boy! The Little Marvel Voice Thrower! . . . I have merely to slip it under my tongue and throw my voice anywhere I desire . . . Here! I'll throw it behind that tree! Listen!
Hello, Barnaby . . . I'm behind that tree over there! Amazing! Eh?
It didn't sound like it to me, Mr. O'Malley.
Mr. O'Malley, you promised to get that dog for Pop's Christmas present and I'm depending on it and tomorrow is—
Perhaps it takes a bit of practice . . . What did you say? Oh, yes . . . a dog . . .
I'm going off by myself for ten or fifteen minutes until I master the difficult art of ventriloquy . . . Stop worrying about that dog . . . Your Fairy Godfather promised him—Ergo—You as good as have him!

December 23 – 24

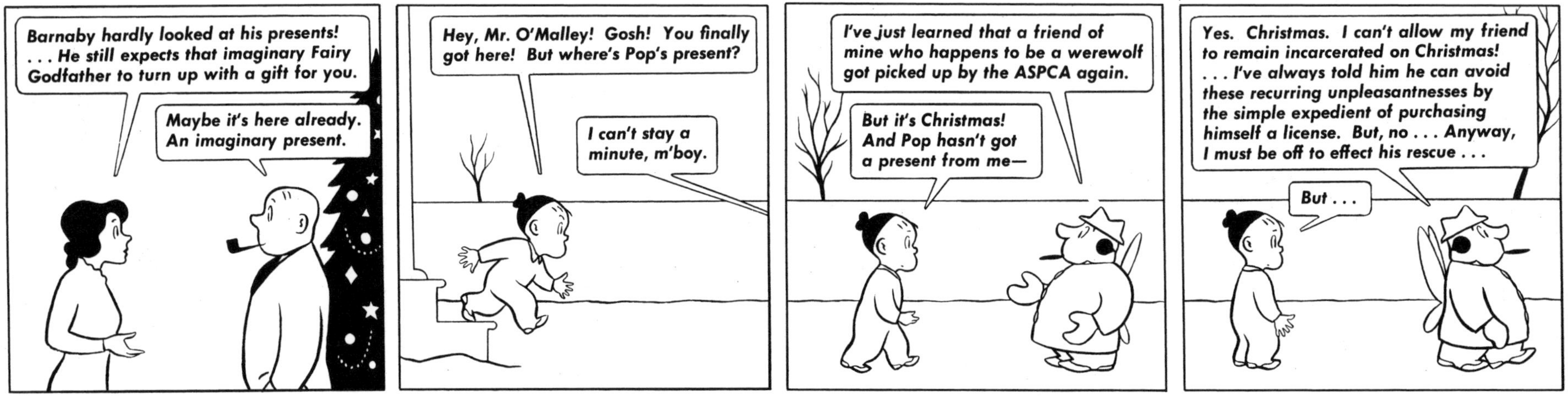
Barnaby hardly looked at his presents! . . . He still expects that imaginary Fairy Godfather to turn up with a gift for you.
Maybe it's here already. An imaginary present.
Hey, Mr. O'Malley! Gosh! You finally got here! But where's Pop's present?
I can't stay a minute, m'boy.
I've just learned that a friend of mine who happens to be a werewolf got picked up by the ASPCA again.
But it's Christmas! And Pop hasn't got a present from me—
Yes. Christmas. I can't allow my friend to remain incarcerated on Christmas! . . . I've always told him he can avoid these recurring unpleasantnesses by the simple expedient of purchasing himself a license. But, no . . . Anyway, I must be off to effect his rescue . . .
But . . .

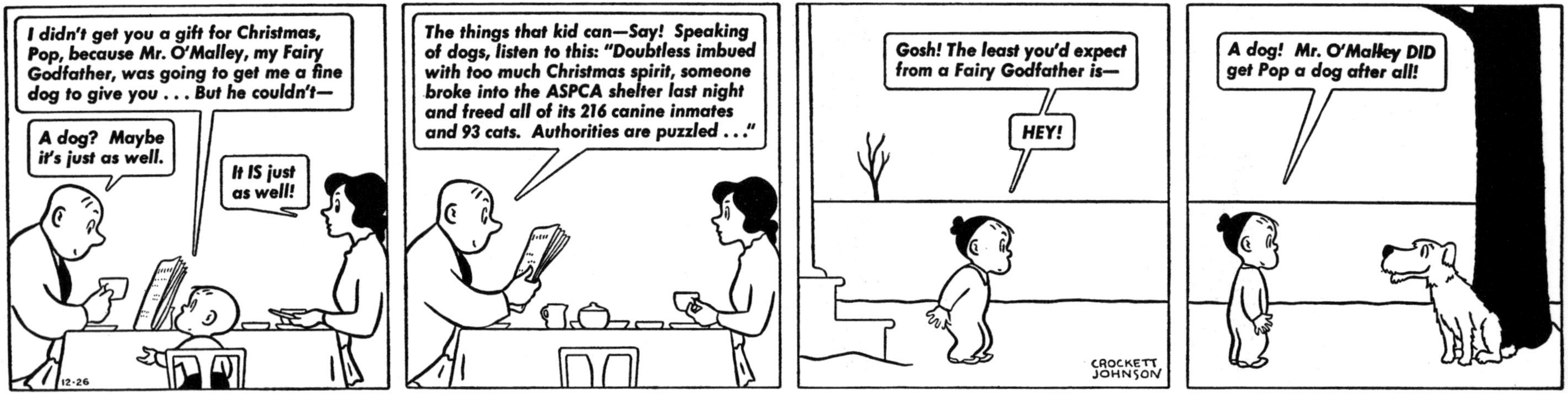
I didn't get you a gift for Christmas, Pop, because Mr. O'Malley, my Fairy Godfather, was going to get me a fine dog to give you . . . But he couldn't—
A dog? Maybe it's just as well.
It IS just as well!
12-26
The things that kid can—Say! Speaking of dogs, listen to this: "Doubtless imbued with too much Christmas spirit, someone broke into the ASPCA shelter last night and freed all of its 216 canine inmates and 93 cats. Authorities are puzzled . . ."
Gosh! The least you'd expect from a Fairy Godfather is—
HEY!
CROCKETT JOHNSON
A dog! Mr. O'Malley DID get Pop a dog after all!

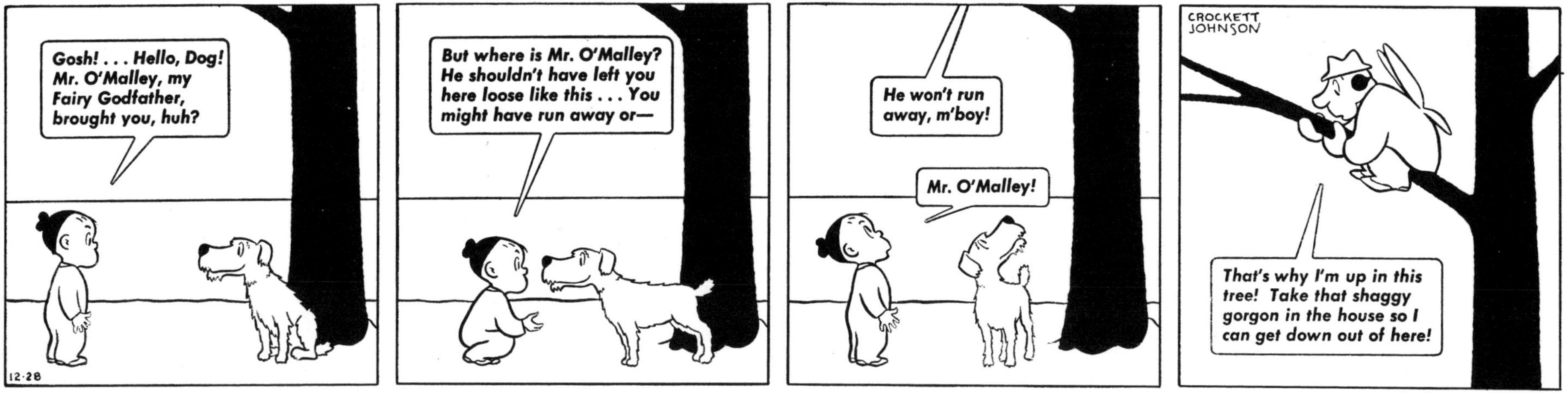
Gosh! . . . Hello, Dog! Mr. O'Malley, my Fairy Godfather, brought you, huh?
12·28
But where is Mr. O'Malley? He shouldn't have left you here loose like this . . . You might have run away or—
He won't run away, m'boy!
Mr. O'Malley!
CROCKETT JOHNSON
That's why I'm up in this tree! Take that shaggy gorgon in the house so I can get down out of here!

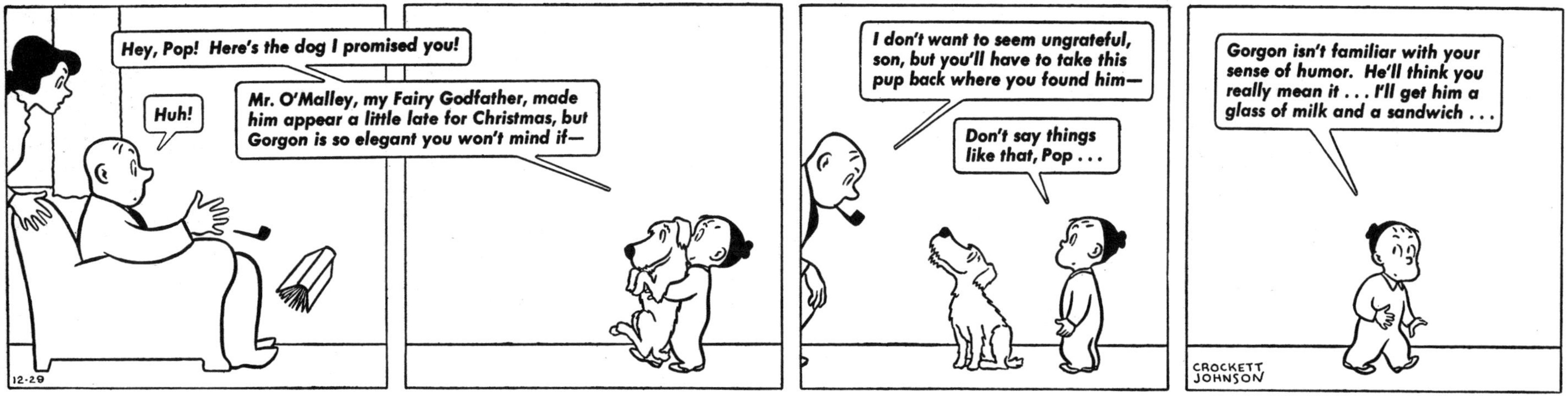
Hey, Pop! Here's the dog I promised you!
Huh!
Mr. O'Malley, my Fairy Godfather, made him appear a little late for Christmas, but Gorgon is so elegant you won't mind if—
12·29
I don't want to seem ungrateful, son, but you'll have to take this pup back where you found him—
Don't say things like that, Pop . . .
Gorgon isn't familiar with your sense of humor. He'll think you really mean it . . . I'll get him a glass of milk and a sandwich . . .
CROCKETT JOHNSON

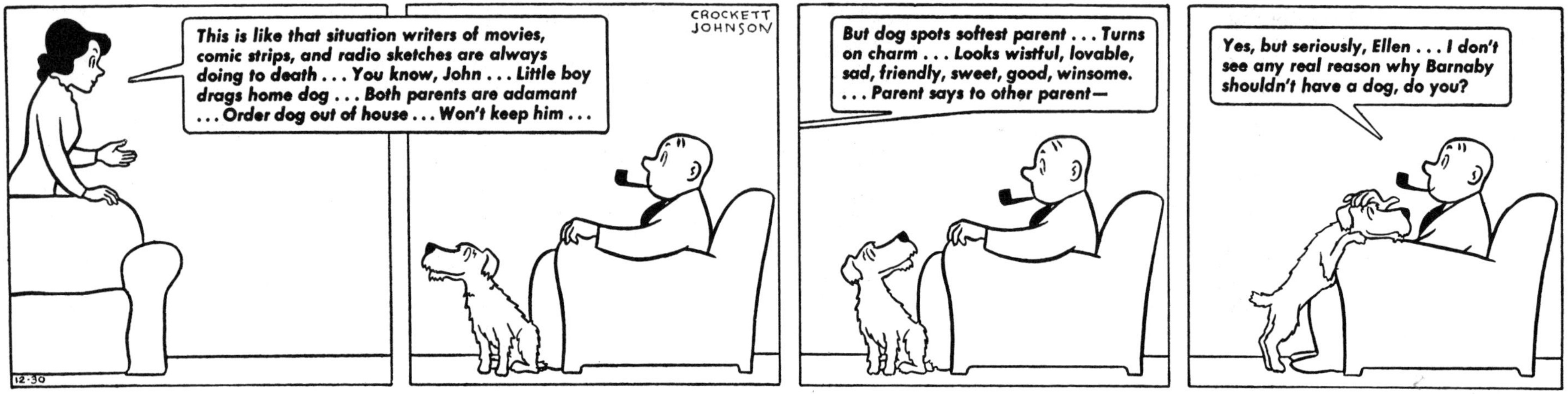
This is like that situation writers of movies, comic strips, and radio sketches are always doing to death . . . You know, John . . . Little boy drags home dog . . . Both parents are adamant . . . Order dog out of house . . . Won't keep him . . .
CROCKETT JOHNSON
12·30
But dog spots softest parent . . . Turns on charm . . . Looks wistful, lovable, sad, friendly, sweet, good, winsome. . . . Parent says to other parent—
Yes, but seriously, Ellen . . . I don't see any real reason why Barnaby shouldn't have a dog, do you?

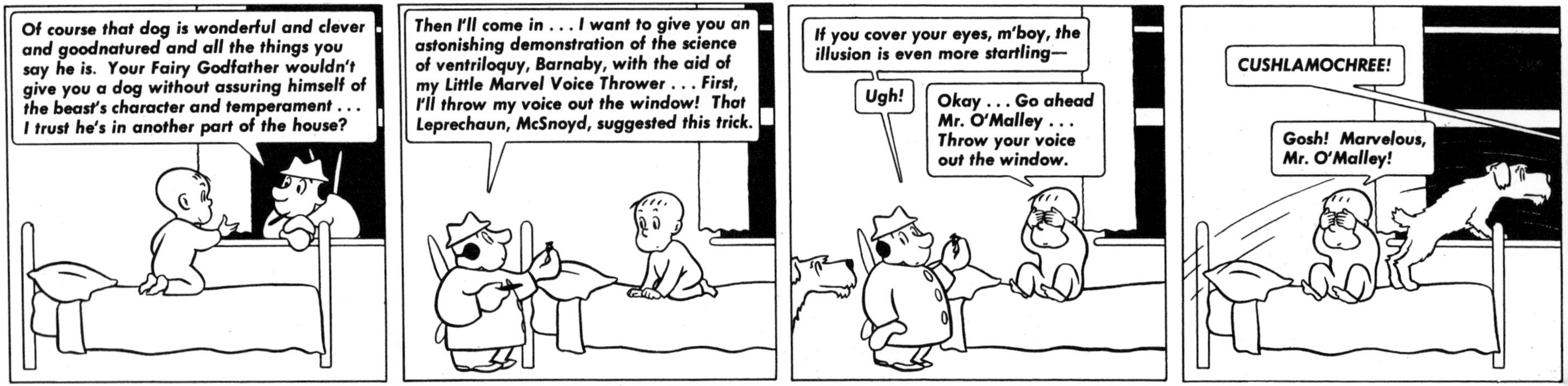
Of course that dog is wonderful and clever and goodnatured and all the things you say he is. Your Fairy Godfather wouldn't give you a dog without assuring himself of the beast's character and temperament . . . I trust he's in another part of the house?
Then I'll come in . . . I want to give you an astonishing demonstration of the science of ventriloquy, Barnaby, with the aid of my Little Marvel Voice Thrower . . . First, I'll throw my voice out the window! That Leprechaun, McSnoyd, suggested this trick.
If you cover your eyes, m'boy, the illusion is even more startling—
Ugh!
Okay . . . Go ahead Mr. O'Malley . . . Throw your voice out the window.
CUSHLAMOCHREE!
Gosh! Marvelous, Mr. O'Malley!

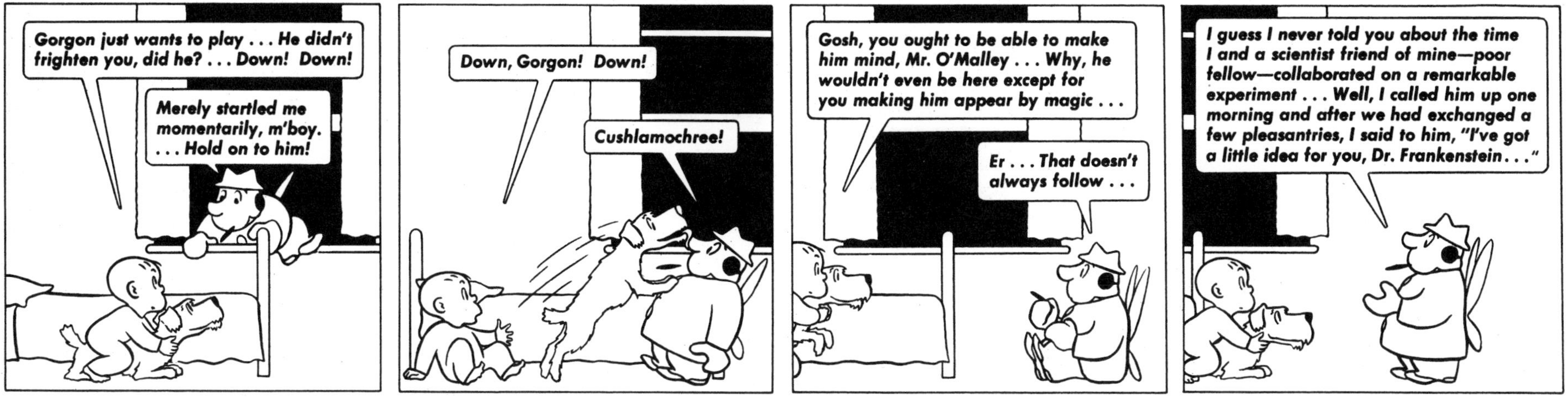
Gorgon just wants to play . . . He didn't frighten you, did he? . . . Down! Down!
Merely startled me momentarily, m'boy. . . . Hold on to him!
Down, Gorgon! Down!
Cushlamochree!
Gosh, you ought to be able to make him mind, Mr. O'Malley . . . Why, he wouldn't even be here except for you making him appear by magic . . .
Er . . . That doesn't always follow . . .
I guess I never told you about the time I and a scientist friend of mine—poor fellow—collaborated on a remarkable experiment . . . Well, I called him up one morning and after we had exchanged a few pleasantries, I said to him, "I've got a little idea for you, Dr. Frankenstein . . ."

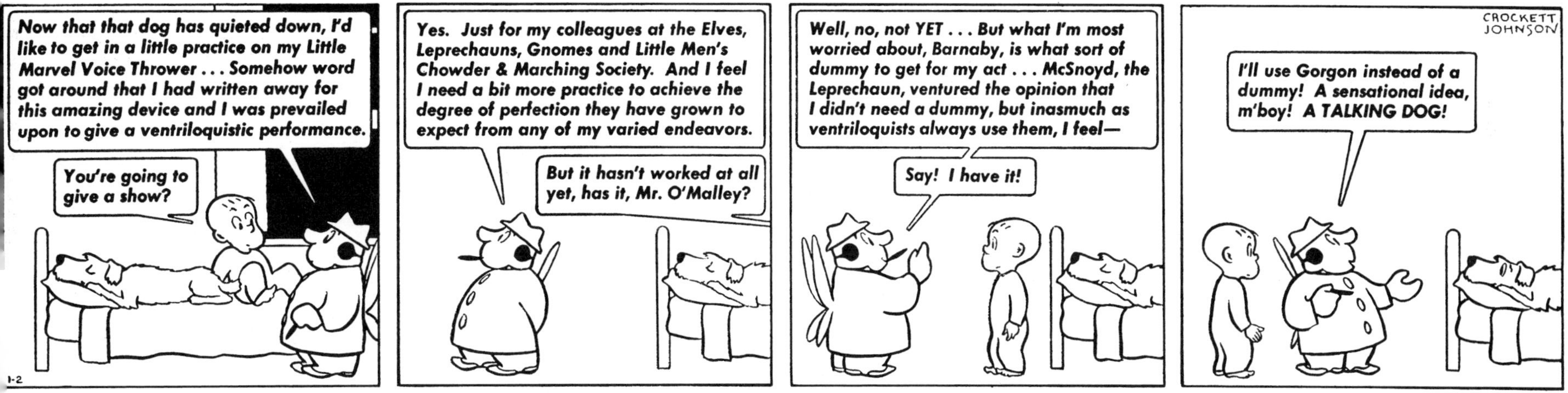
Now that that dog has quieted down, I'd like to get in a little practice on my Little Marvel Voice Thrower . . . Somehow word got around that I had written away for this amazing device and I was prevailed upon to give a ventriloquistic performance.
You're going to give a show?
1-2
Yes. Just for my colleagues at the Elves, Leprechauns, Gnomes and Little Men's Chowder & Marching Society. And I feel I need a bit more practice to achieve the degree of perfection they have grown to expect from any of my varied endeavors.
But it hasn't worked at all yet, has it, Mr. O'Malley?
Well, no, not YET . . . But what I'm most worried about, Barnaby, is what sort of dummy to get for my act . . . McSnoyd, the Leprechaun, ventured the opinion that I didn't need a dummy, but inasmuch as ventriloquists always use them, I feel—
Say! I have it!
CROCKETT JOHNSON
I'll use Gorgon instead of a dummy! A sensational idea, m'boy! A TALKING DOG!

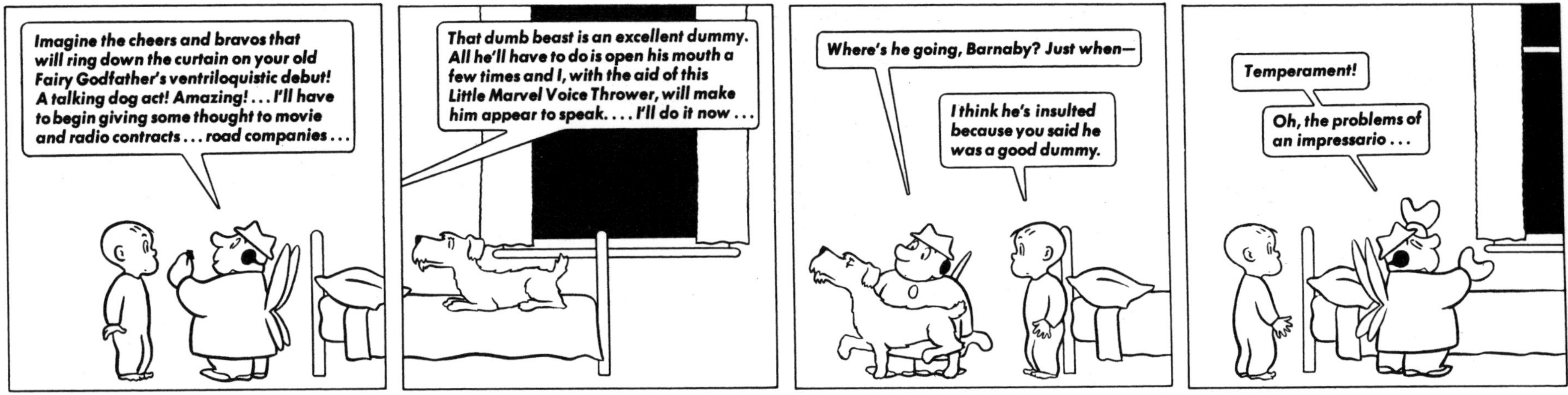
Imagine the cheers and bravos that will ring down the curtain on your old Fairy Godfather's ventriloquistic debut! A talking dog act! Amazing! . . . I'll have to begin giving some thought to movie and radio contracts . . . road companies . . .
That dumb beast is an excellent dummy. All he'll have to do is open his mouth a few times and I, with the aid of this Little Marvel Voice Thrower, will make him appear to speak. . . . I'll do it now . . .
Where's he going, Barnaby? Just when—
I think he's insulted because you said he was a good dummy.
Temperament!
Oh, the problems of an impressario . . .

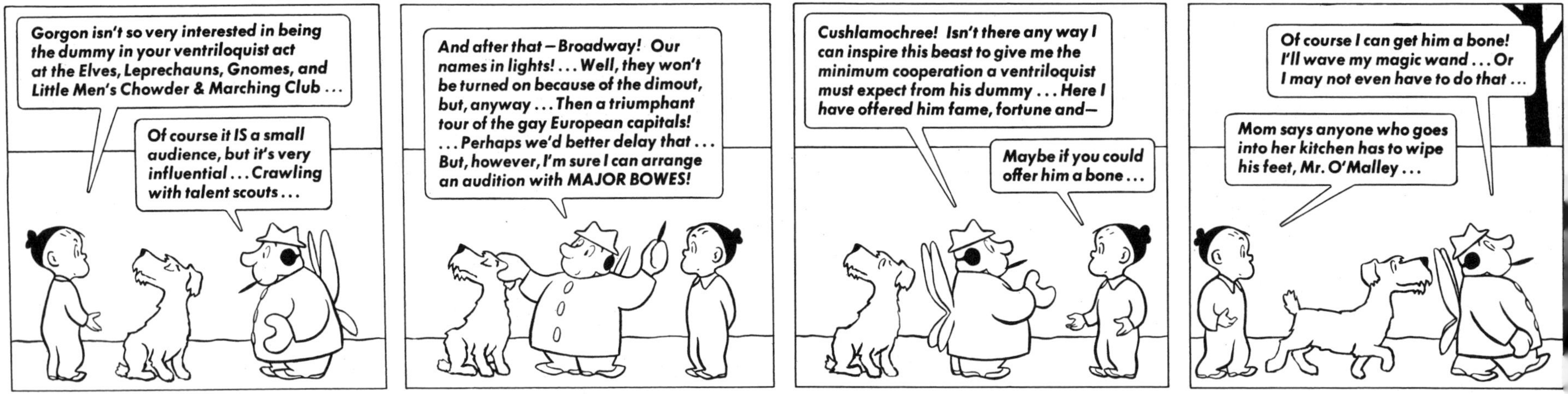
Gorgon isn't so very interested in being the dummy in your ventriloquist act at the Elves, Leprechauns, Gnomes, and Little Men's Chowder & Marching Club . . .
Of course it IS a small audience, but it's very influential . . . Crawling with talent scouts . . .
And after that — Broadway! Our names in lights! . . . Well, they won't be turned on because of the dimout, but, anyway . . . Then a triumphant tour of the gay European capitals! . . . Perhaps we'd better delay that . . . But, however, I'm sure I can arrange an audition with MAJOR BOWES!
Cushlamochree! Isn't there any way I can inspire this beast to give me the minimum cooperation a ventriloquist must expect from his dummy . . . Here I have offered him fame, fortune and—
Maybe if you could offer him a bone . . .
Of course I can get him a bone! I'll wave my magic wand . . . Or I may not even have to do that . . .
Mom says anyone who goes into her kitchen has to wipe his feet, Mr. O'Malley . . .

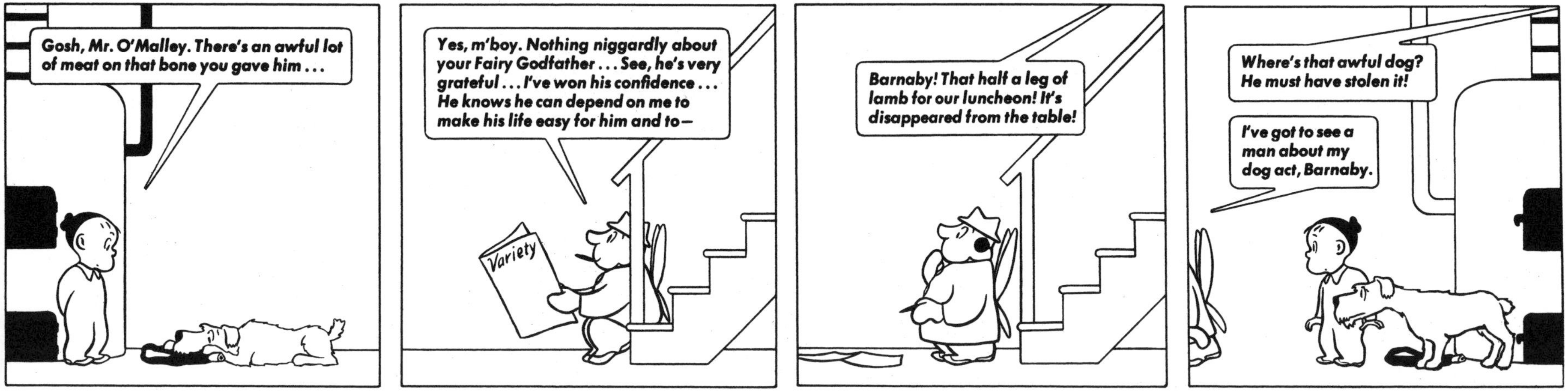
Gosh, Mr. O'Malley. There's an awful lot of meat on that bone you gave him . . .
Yes, m'boy. Nothing niggardly about your Fairy Godfather . . . See, he's very grateful . . . I've won his confidence . . . He knows he can depend on me to make his life easy for him and to—
Variety
Barnaby! That half a leg of lamb for our luncheon! It's disappeared from the table!
Where's that awful dog? He must have stolen it!
I've got to see a man about my dog act, Barnaby.

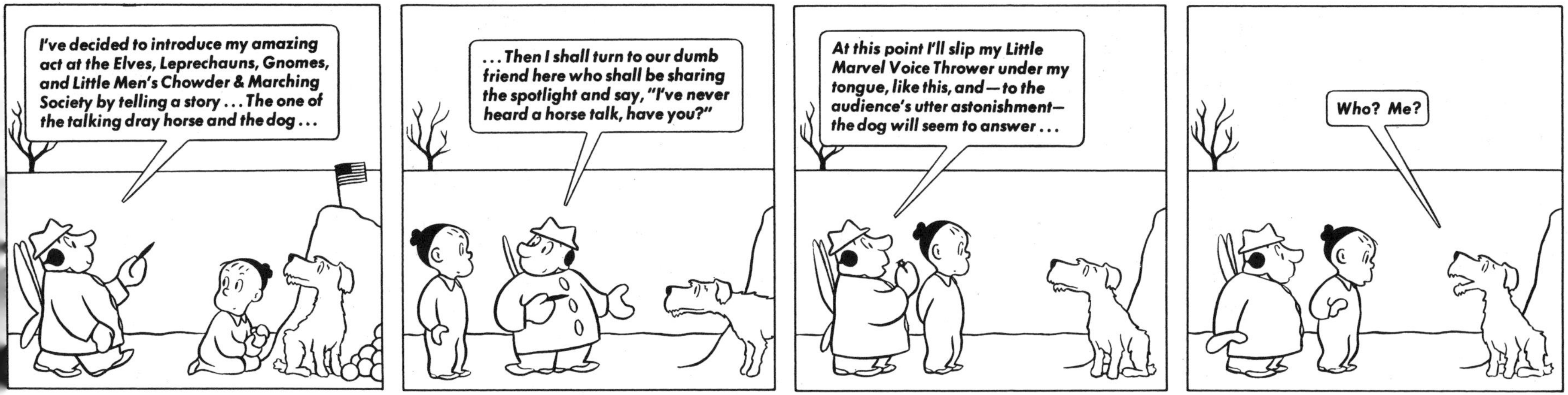
I've decided to introduce my amazing act at the Elves, Leprechauns, Gnomes, and Little Men's Chowder & Marching Society by telling a story . . . The one of the talking dray horse and the dog . . .
. . . Then I shall turn to our dumb friend here who shall be sharing the spotlight and say, "I've never heard a horse talk, have you?"
At this point I'll slip my Little Marvel Voice Thrower under my tongue, like this, and — to the audience's utter astonishment— the dog will seem to answer . . .
Who? Me?

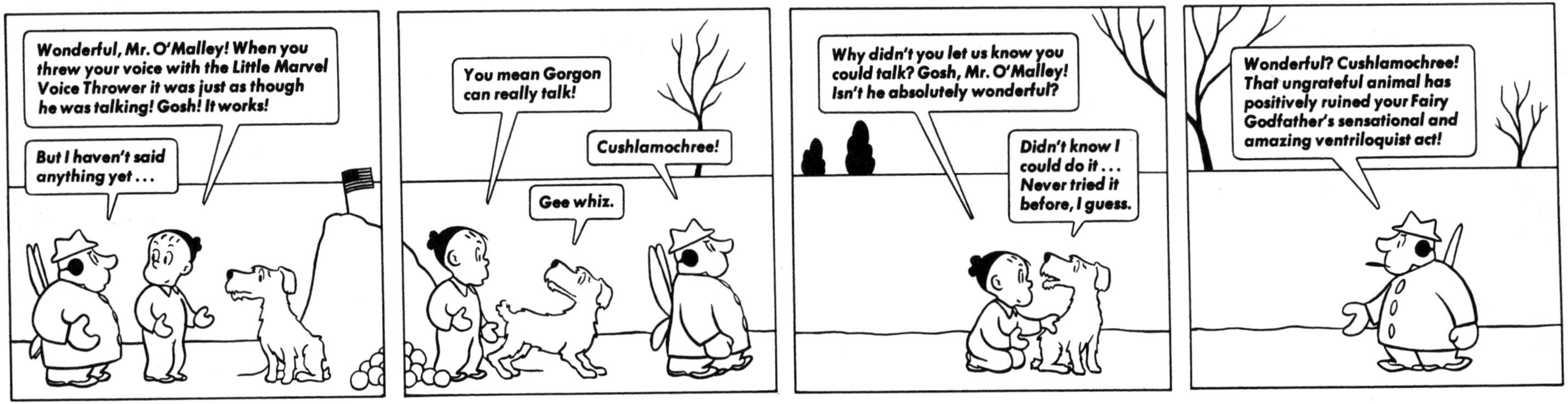
Wonderful, Mr. O'Malley! When you threw your voice with the Little Marvel Voice Thrower it was just as though he was talking! Gosh! It works!
But I haven't said anything yet . . .
You mean Gorgon can really talk!
Cushlamochree!
Gee whiz.
Why didn't you let us know you could talk? Gosh, Mr. O'Malley! Isn't he absolutely wonderful?
Didn't know I could do it . . . Never tried it before, I guess.
Wonderful? Cushlamochree! That ungrateful animal has positively ruined your Fairy Godfather's sensational and amazing ventriloquist act!

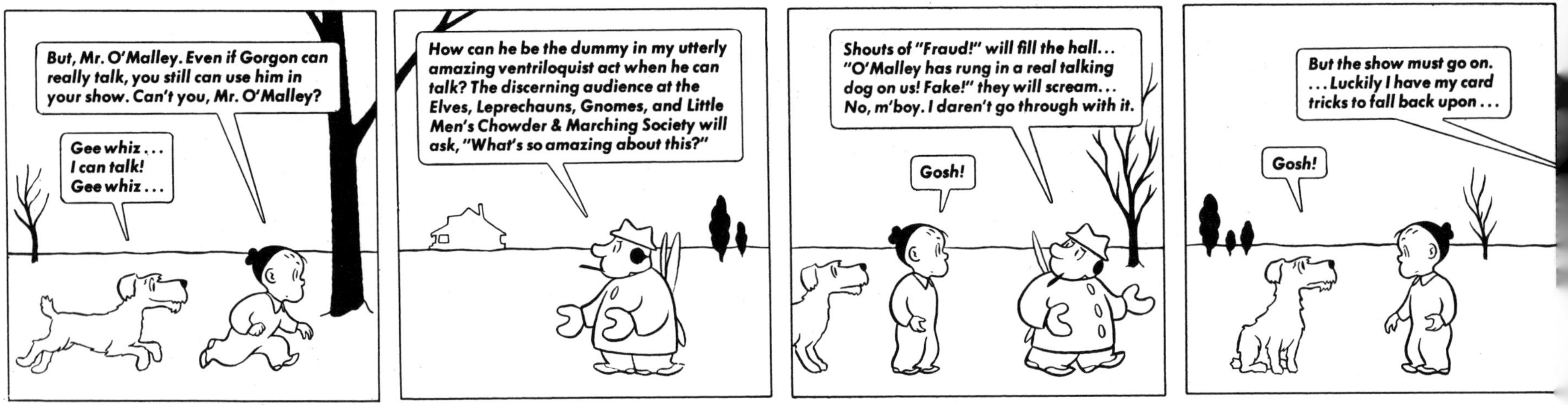
But, Mr. O'Malley. Even if Gorgon can really talk, you still can use him in your show. Can't you, Mr. O'Malley?
Gee whiz . . . I can talk! Gee whiz . . .
How can he be the dummy in my utterly amazing ventriloquist act when he can talk? The discerning audience at the Elves, Leprechauns, Gnomes, and Little Men's Chowder & Marching Society will ask, "What's so amazing about this?"
Shouts of "Fraud!" will fill the hall . . . "O'Malley has rung in a real talking dog on us! Fake!" they will scream . . . No, m'boy. I daren't go through with it.
Gosh!
But the show must go on. . . . Luckily I have my card tricks to fall back upon . . .
Gosh!

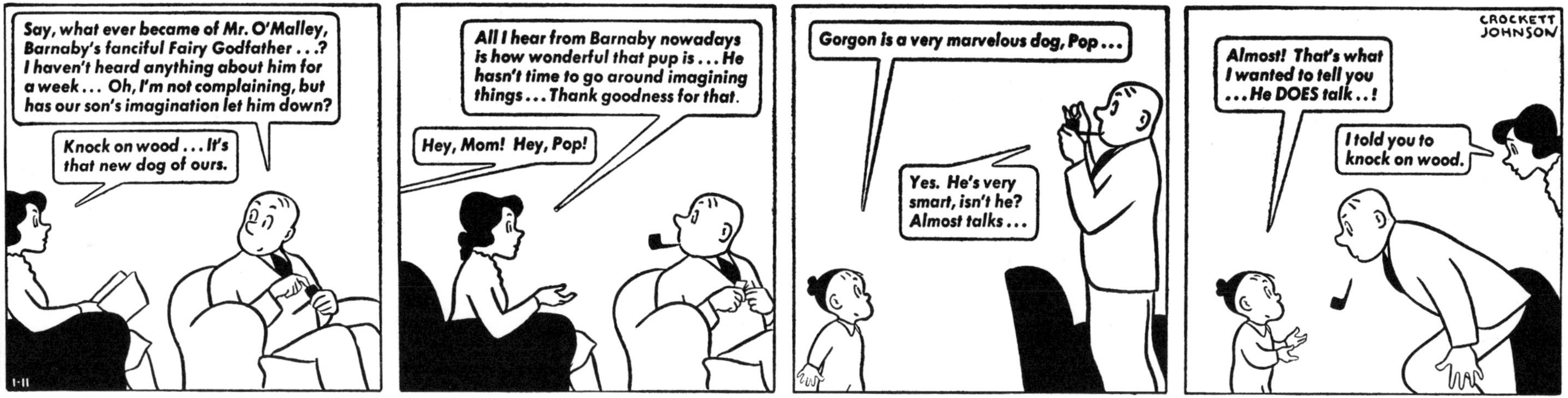
1-11
Say, what ever became of Mr. O'Malley, Barnaby's fanciful Fairy Godfather . . .? I haven't heard anything about him for a week . . . Oh, I'm not complaining, but has our son's imagination let him down?
Knock on wood . . . It's that new dog of ours.
All I hear from Barnaby nowadays is how wonderful that pup is . . . He hasn't time to go around imagining things . . . Thank goodness for that.
Hey, Mom! Hey, Pop!
Gorgon is a very marvelous dog, Pop . . .
Yes. He's very smart, isn't he? Almost talks . . .
CROCKETT JOHNSON
Almost! That's what I wanted to tell you . . . He DOES talk . . !
I told you to knock on wood.

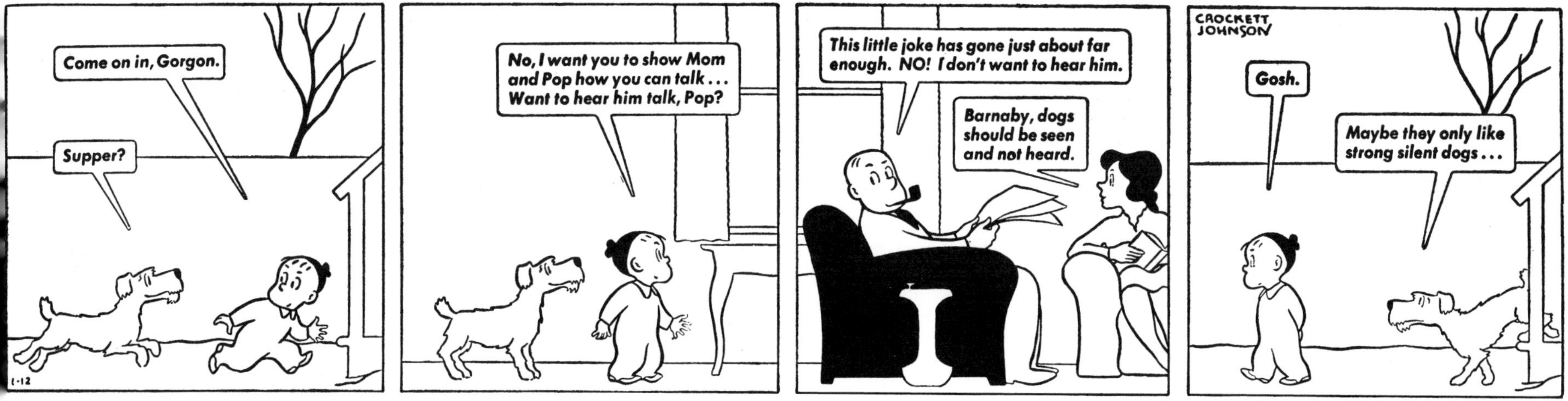
1-12
Come on in, Gorgon.
Supper?
No, I want you to show Mom and Pop how you can talk . . . Want to hear him talk, Pop?
This little joke has gone just about far enough. NO! I don't want to hear him.
Barnaby, dogs should be seen and not heard.
CROCKETT JOHNSON
Gosh.
Maybe they only like strong silent dogs . . .

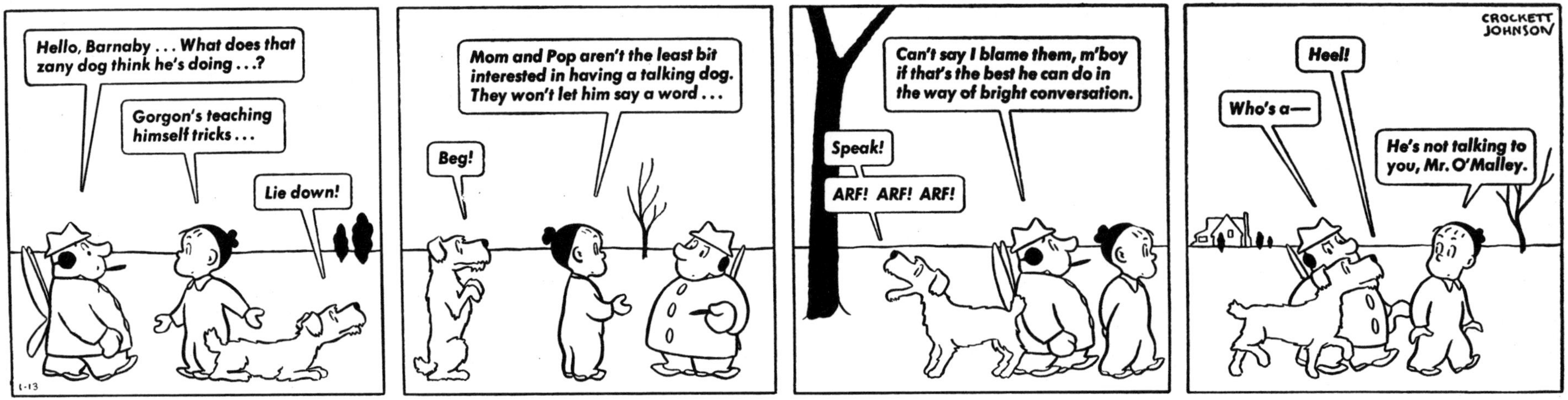
Hello, Barnaby . . . What does that zany dog think he's doing . . .?
Gorgon's teaching himself tricks . . .
Lie down!
1-13
Mom and Pop aren't the least bit interested in having a talking dog. They won't let him say a word . . .
Beg!
Can't say I blame them, m'boy if that's the best he can do in the way of bright conversation.
Speak!
ARF! ARF! ARF!
CROCKETT JOHNSON
Heel!
Who's a—
He's not talking to you, Mr. O'Malley.

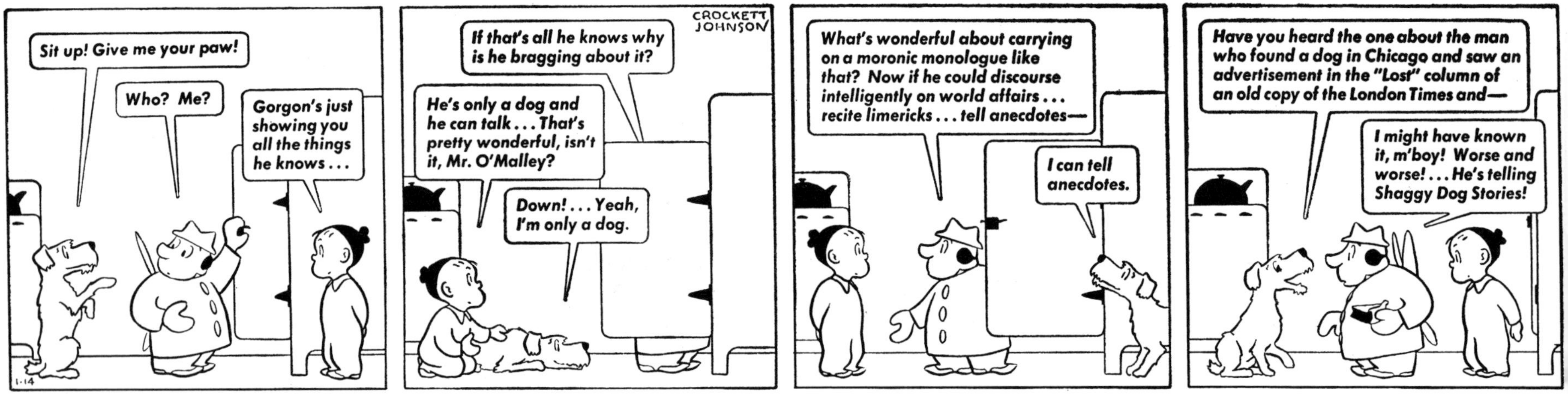
Sit up! Give me your paw!
Who? Me?
Gorgon's just showing you all the things he knows . . .
1-14
CROCKETT JOHNSON
If that's all he knows why is he bragging about it?
He's only a dog and he can talk . . . That's pretty wonderful, isn't it, Mr. O'Malley?
Down! . . . Yeah, I'm only a dog.
What's wonderful about carrying on a moronic monologue like that? Now if he could discourse intelligently on world affairs . . . recite limericks . . . tell anecdotes—
I can tell anecdotes.
Have you heard the one about the man who found a dog in Chicago and saw an advertisement in the "Lost" column of an old copy of the London Times and—
I might have known it, m'boy! Worse and worse! . . . He's telling Shaggy Dog Stories!

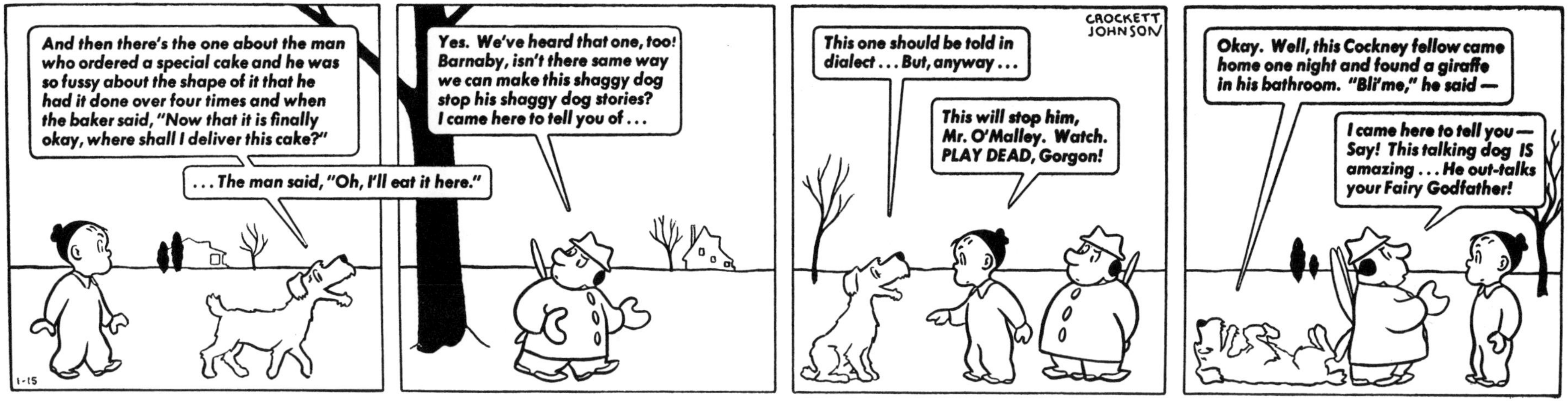

And then there's the one about the man who ordered a special cake and he was so fussy about the shape of it that he had it done over four times and when the baker said, "Now that it is finally okay, where shall I deliver this cake?"
... The man said, "Oh, I'll eat it here."
1-15
Yes. We've heard that one, too! Barnaby, isn't there same way we can make this shaggy dog stop his shaggy dog stories? I came here to tell you of ...
CROCKETT JOHNSON
This one should be told in dialect ... But, anyway ...
This will stop him, Mr. O'Malley. Watch. PLAY DEAD, Gorgon!
Okay. Well, this Cockney fellow came home one night and found a giraffe in his bathroom. "Bli'me," he said —
I came here to tell you — Say! This talking dog IS amazing ... He out-talks your Fairy Godfather!

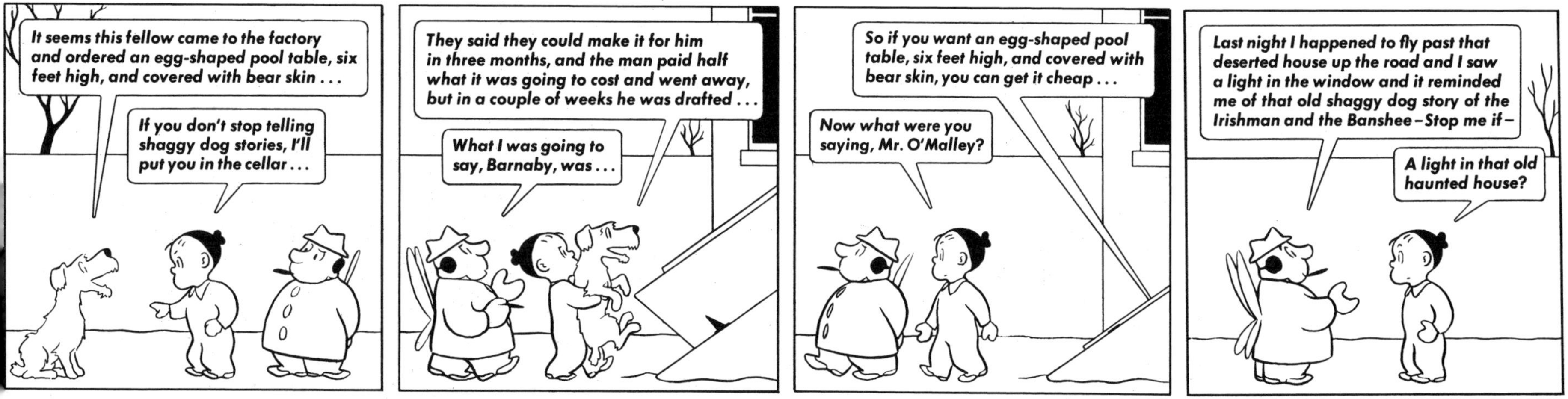

It seems this fellow came to the factory and ordered an egg-shaped pool table, six feet high, and covered with bear skin ...
If you don't stop telling shaggy dog stories, I'll put you in the cellar ...
They said they could make it for him in three months, and the man paid half what it was going to cost and went away, but in a couple of weeks he was drafted ...
What I was going to say, Barnaby, was ...
So if you want an egg-shaped pool table, six feet high, and covered with bear skin, you can get it cheap ...
Now what were you saying, Mr. O'Malley?
Last night I happened to fly past that deserted house up the road and I saw a light in the window and it reminded me of that old shaggy dog story of the Irishman and the Banshee – Stop me if –
A light in that old haunted house?

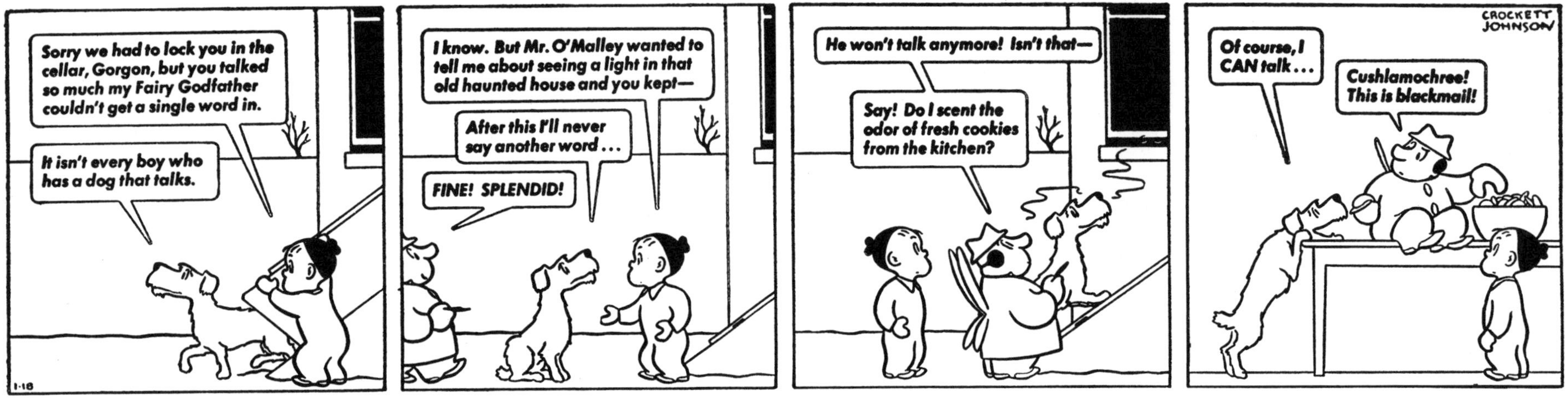
Sorry we had to lock you in the cellar, Gorgon, but you talked so much my Fairy Godfather couldn't get a single word in.
It isn't every boy who has a dog that talks.
1-18
I know. But Mr. O'Malley wanted to tell me about seeing a light in that old haunted house and you kept—
After this I'll never say another word . . .
FINE! SPLENDID!
He won't talk anymore! Isn't that—
Say! Do I scent the odor of fresh cookies from the kitchen?
CROCKETT JOHNSON
Of course, I CAN talk . . .
Cushlamochree! This is blackmail!

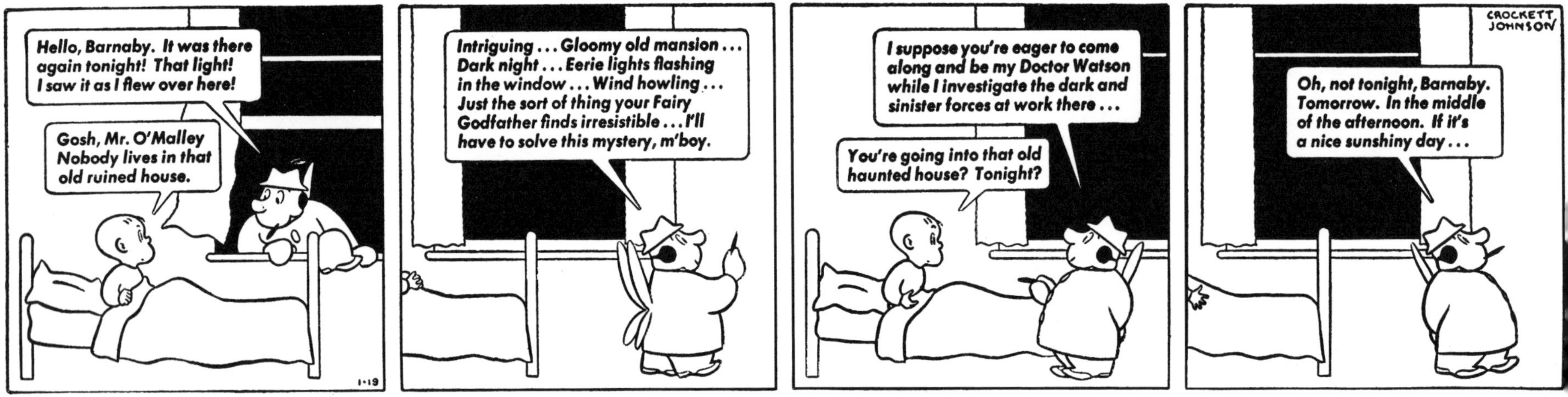
Hello, Barnaby. It was there again tonight! That light! I saw it as I flew over here!
Gosh, Mr. O'Malley Nobody lives in that old ruined house.
1-19
Intriguing . . . Gloomy old mansion . . . Dark night . . . Eerie lights flashing in the window . . . Wind howling . . . Just the sort of thing your Fairy Godfather finds irresistible . . . I'll have to solve this mystery, m'boy.
I suppose you're eager to come along and be my Doctor Watson while I investigate the dark and sinister forces at work there . . .
You're going into that old haunted house? Tonight?
CROCKETT JOHNSON
Oh, not tonight, Barnaby. Tomorrow. In the middle of the afternoon. If it's a nice sunshiny day . . .

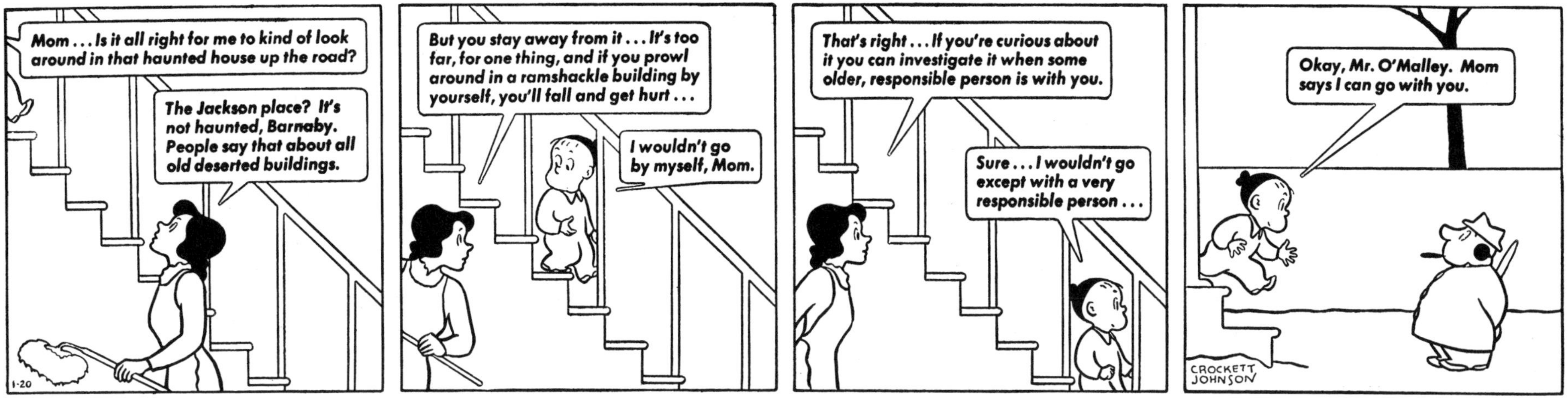
1-20
Mom . . . Is it all right for me to kind of look around in that haunted house up the road?
The Jackson place? It's not haunted, Barnaby. People say that about all old deserted buildings.
But you stay away from it . . . It's too far, for one thing, and if you prowl around in a ramshackle building by yourself, you'll fall and get hurt . . .
I wouldn't go by myself, Mom.
That's right . . . If you're curious about it you can investigate it when some older, responsible person is with you.
Sure . . . I wouldn't go except with a very responsible person . . .
Okay, Mr. O'Malley. Mom says I can go with you.
CROCKETT JOHNSON

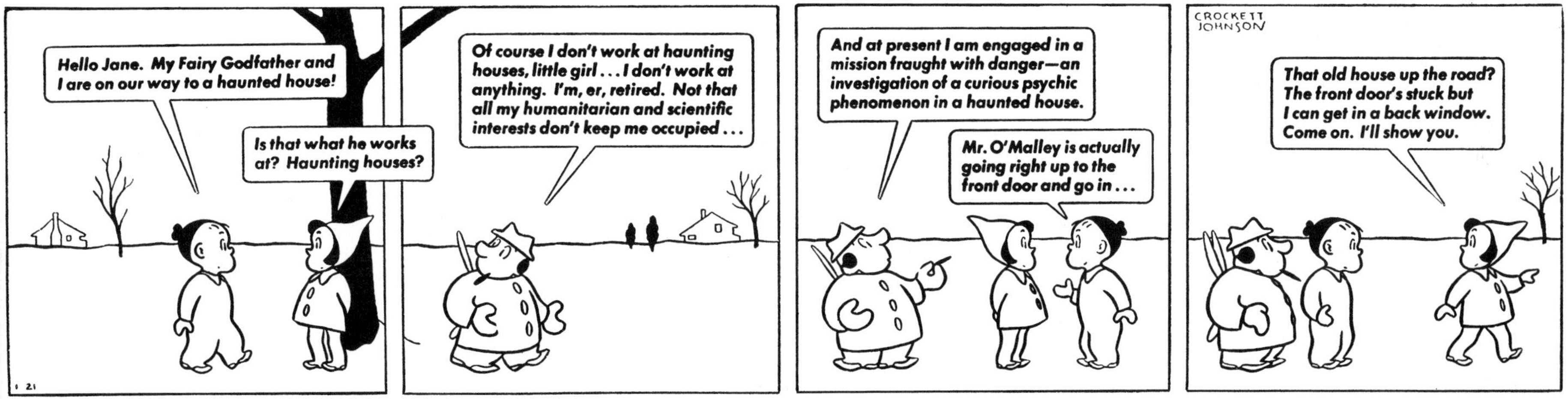
1 21
Hello Jane. My Fairy Godfather and I are on our way to a haunted house!
Is that what he works at? Haunting houses?
Of course I don't work at haunting houses, little girl . . . I don't work at anything. I'm, er, retired. Not that all my humanitarian and scientific interests don't keep me occupied . . .
And at present I am engaged in a mission fraught with danger—an investigation of a curious psychic phenomenon in a haunted house.
Mr. O'Malley is actually going right up to the front door and go in . . .
CROCKETT JOHNSON
That old house up the road? The front door's stuck but I can get in a back window. Come on. I'll show you.

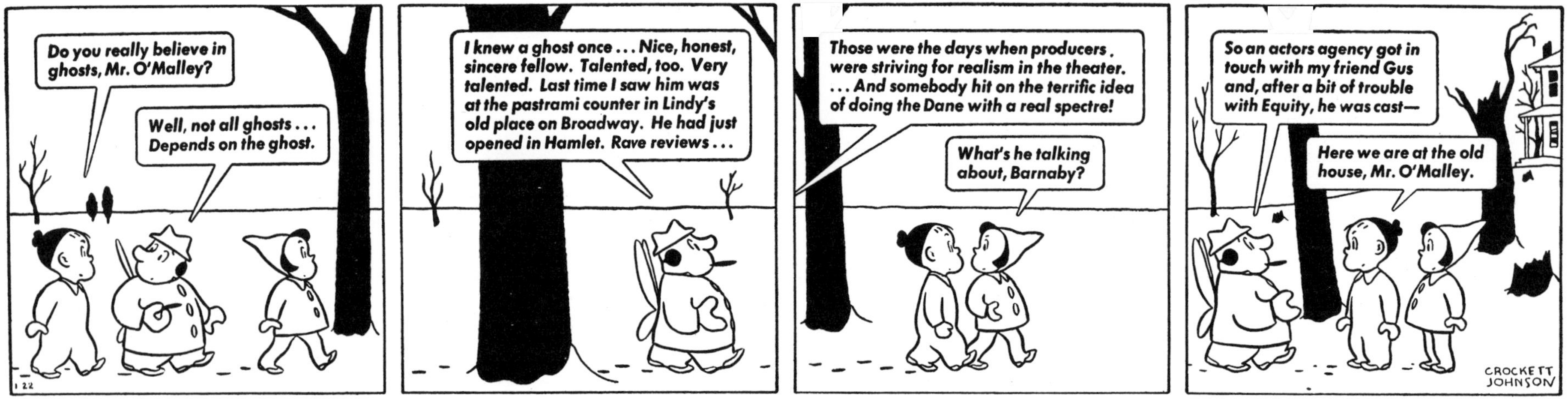
Do you really believe in ghosts, Mr. O'Malley?
Well, not all ghosts . . . Depends on the ghost.
1 22
I knew a ghost once . . . Nice, honest, sincere fellow. Talented, too. Very talented. Last time I saw him was at the pastrami counter in Lindy's old place on Broadway. He had just opened in Hamlet. Rave reviews . . .
Those were the days when producers were striving for realism in the theater. . . . And somebody hit on the terrific idea of doing the Dane with a real spectre!
What's he talking about, Barnaby?
So an actors agency got in touch with my friend Gus and, after a bit of trouble with Equity, he was cast—
Here we are at the old house, Mr. O'Malley.
CROCKETT JOHNSON

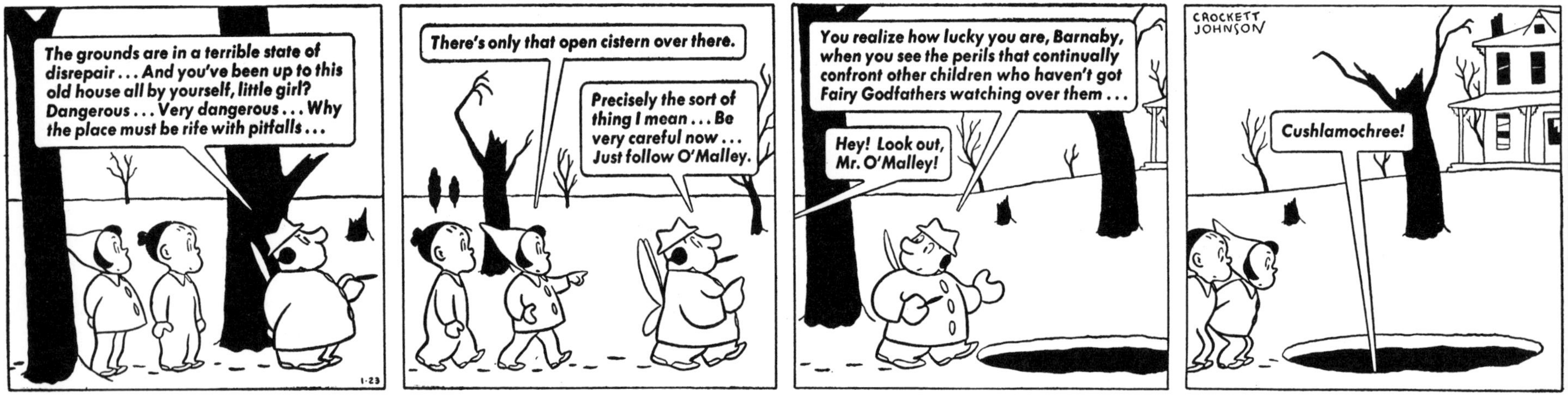
The grounds are in a terrible state of disrepair . . . And you've been up to this old house all by yourself, little girl? Dangerous . . . Very dangerous . . . Why the place must be rife with pitfalls . . .
1-23
There's only that open cistern over there.
Precisely the sort of thing I mean . . . Be very careful now . . . Just follow O'Malley.
You realize how lucky you are, Barnaby, when you see the perils that continually confront other children who haven't got Fairy Godfathers watching over them . . .
Hey! Look out, Mr. O'Malley!
CROCKETT JOHNSON
Cushlamochree!

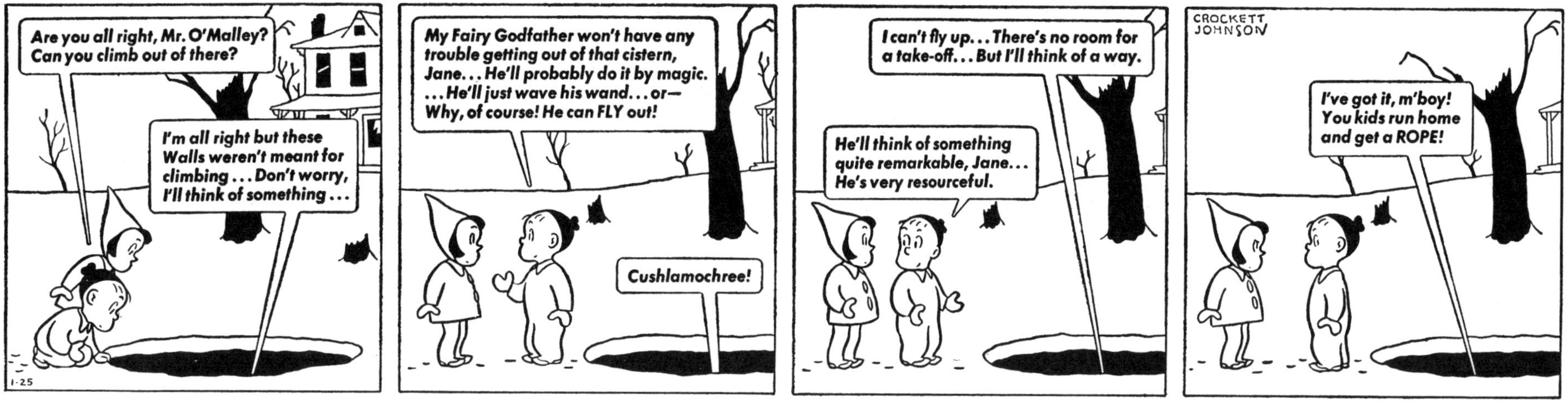
Are you all right, Mr. O'Malley? Can you climb out of there?
I'm all right but these Walls weren't meant for climbing . . . Don't worry, I'll think of something . . .
1·25
My Fairy Godfather won't have any trouble getting out of that cistern, Jane. . . He'll probably do it by magic. . . . He'll just wave his wand. . . or— Why, of course! He can FLY out!
Cushlamochree!
I can't fly up. . . There's no room for a take-off. . . But I'll think of a way.
He'll think of something quite remarkable, Jane. . . He's very resourceful.
CROCKETT JOHNSON
I've got it, m'boy! You kids run home and get a ROPE!

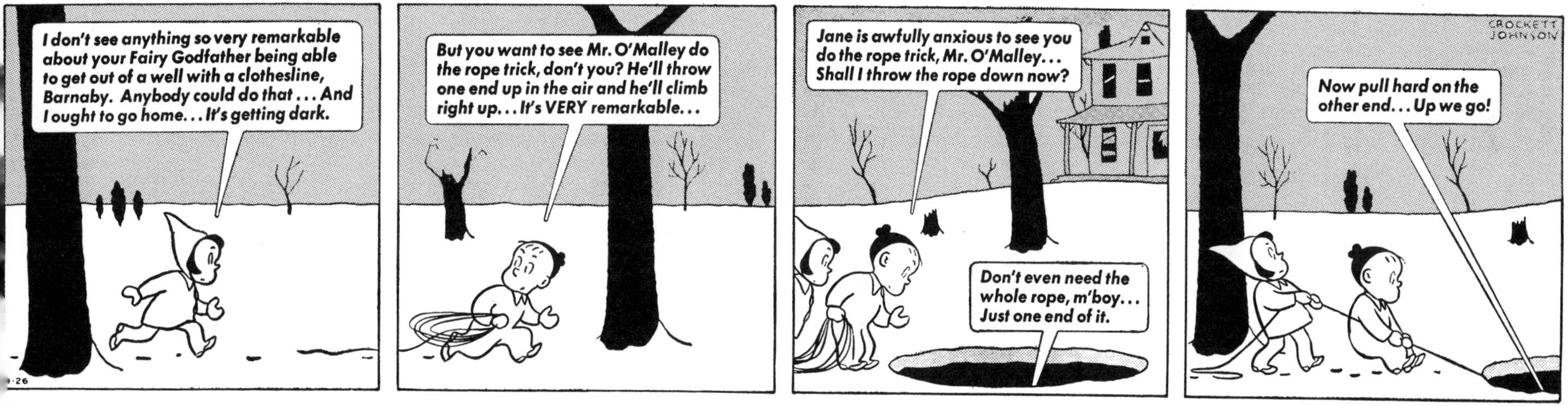
I don't see anything so very remarkable about your Fairy Godfather being able to get out of a well with a clothesline, Barnaby. Anybody could do that . . . And I ought to go home. . . It's getting dark.
1·26
But you want to see Mr. O'Malley do the rope trick, don't you? He'll throw one end up in the air and he'll climb right up. . . It's VERY remarkable. . .
Jane is awfully anxious to see you do the rope trick, Mr. O'Malley. . . Shall I throw the rope down now?
Don't even need the whole rope, m'boy. . . Just one end of it.
CROCKETT JOHNSON
Now pull hard on the other end. . . Up we go!

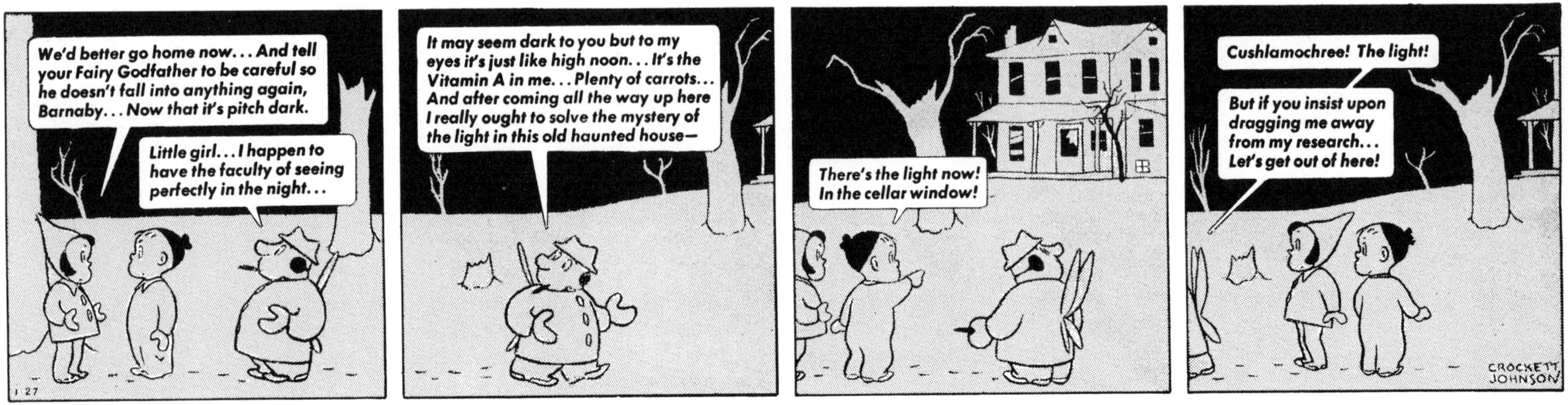

We'd better go home now... And tell your Fairy Godfather to be careful so he doesn't fall into anything again, Barnaby... Now that it's pitch dark.
Little girl... I happen to have the faculty of seeing perfectly in the night...
1-27
It may seem dark to you but to my eyes it's just like high noon... It's the Vitamin A in me... Plenty of carrots... And after coming all the way up here I really ought to solve the mystery of the light in this old haunted house—
There's the light now! In the cellar window!
Cushlamochree! The light!
But if you insist upon dragging me away from my research... Let's get out of here!
CROCKETT JOHNSON

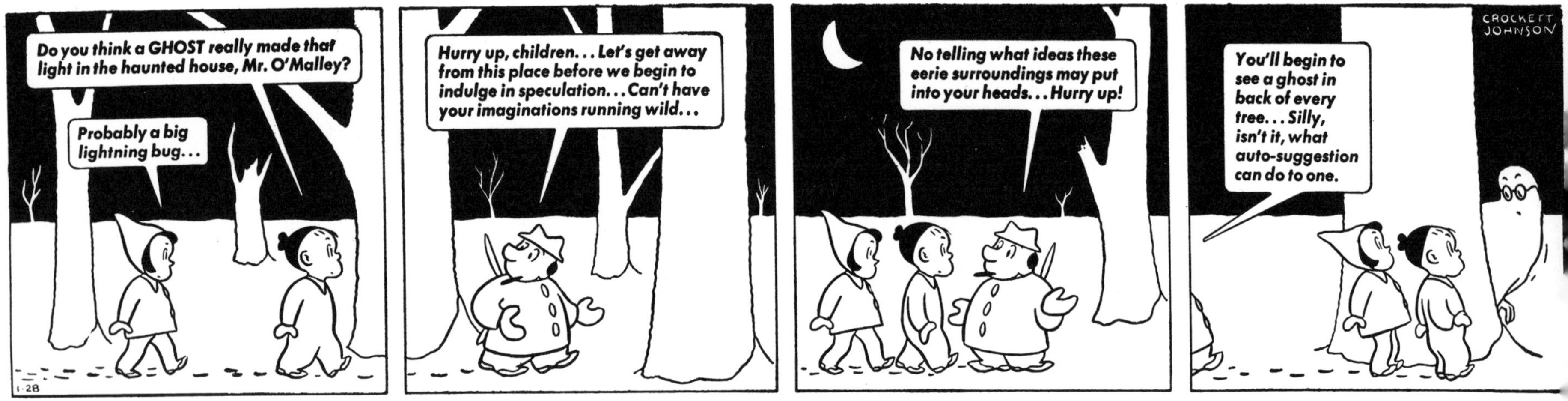

Do you think a GHOST really made that light in the haunted house, Mr. O'Malley?
Probably a big lightning bug...
1-28
Hurry up, children... Let's get away from this place before we begin to indulge in speculation... Can't have your imaginations running wild...
No telling what ideas these eerie surroundings may put into your heads... Hurry up!
CROCKETT JOHNSON
You'll begin to see a ghost in back of every tree... Silly, isn't it, what auto-suggestion can do to one.

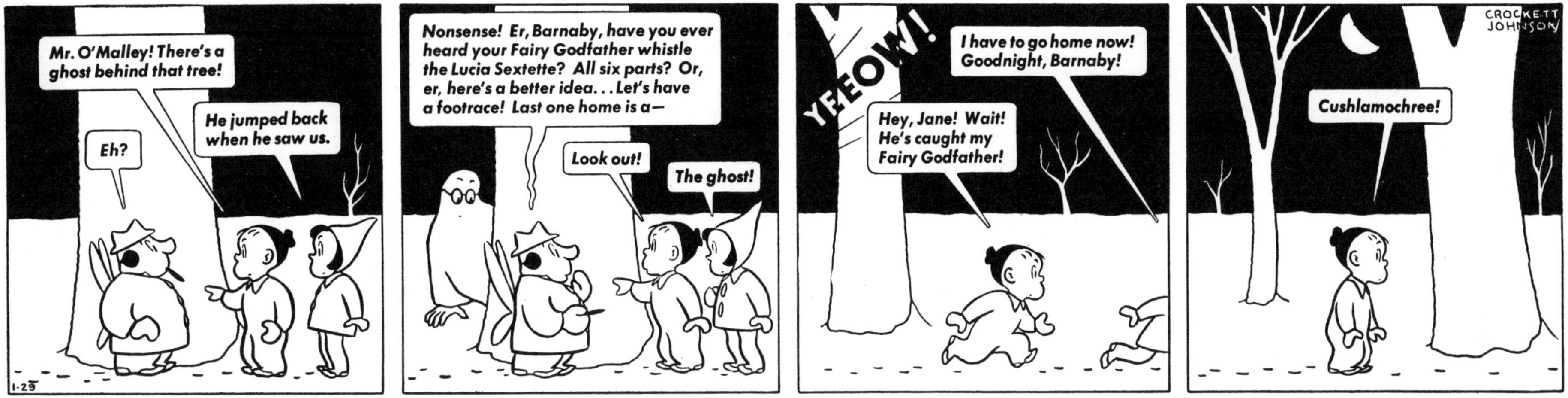
Mr. O'Malley! There's a ghost behind that tree!
Eh?
He jumped back when he saw us.
1-29
Nonsense! Er, Barnaby, have you ever heard your Fairy Godfather whistle the Lucia Sextette? All six parts? Or, er, here's a better idea. . . Let's have a footrace! Last one home is a—
Look out!
The ghost!
YEEOW!
I have to go home now! Goodnight, Barnaby!
Hey, Jane! Wait! He's caught my Fairy Godfather!
CROCKETT JOHNSON
Cushlamochree!

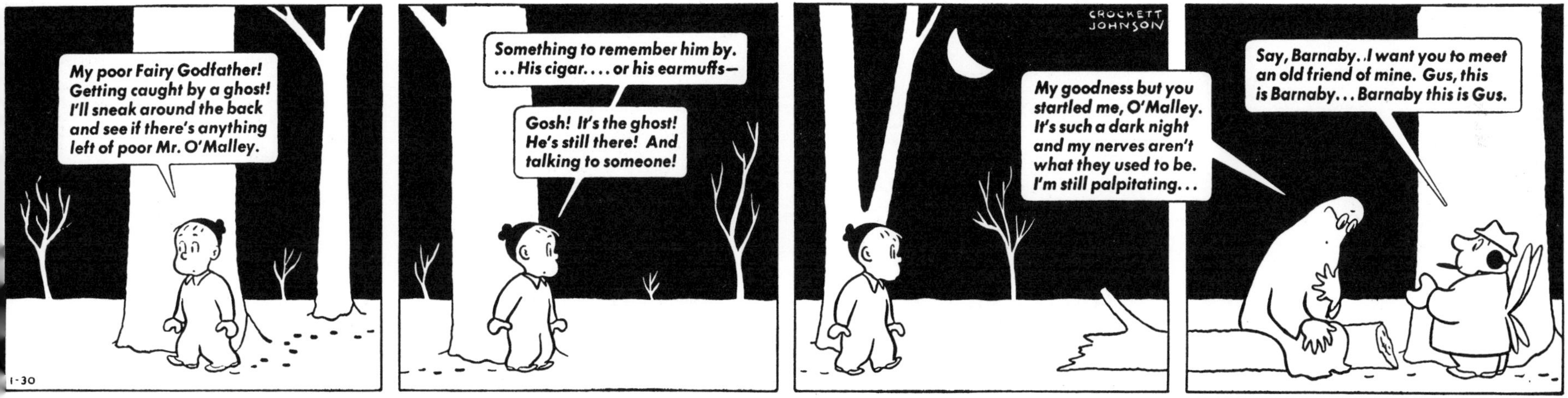
My poor Fairy Godfather! Getting caught by a ghost! I'll sneak around the back and see if there's anything left of poor Mr. O'Malley.
1-30
Something to remember him by. . . . His cigar. . . . or his earmuffs—
Gosh! It's the ghost! He's still there! And talking to someone!
CROCKETT JOHNSON
My goodness but you startled me, O'Malley. It's such a dark night and my nerves aren't what they used to be. I'm still palpitating. . .
Say, Barnaby. .I want you to meet an old friend of mine. Gus, this is Barnaby. . . Barnaby this is Gus.

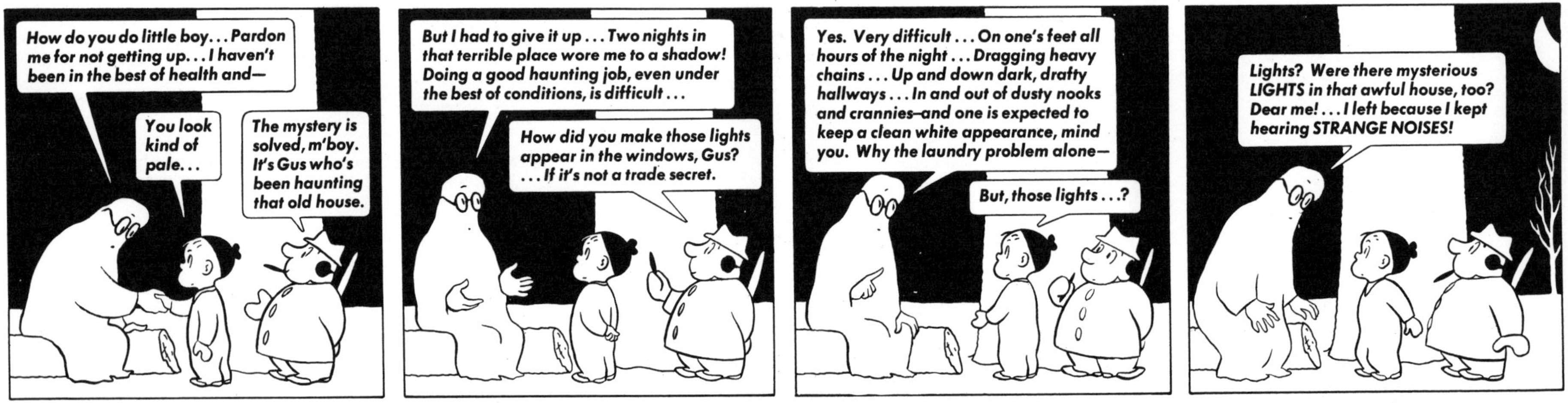
How do you do little boy... Pardon me for not getting up... I haven't been in the best of health and—
You look kind of pale...
The mystery is solved, m'boy. It's Gus who's been haunting that old house.
But I had to give it up... Two nights in that terrible place wore me to a shadow! Doing a good haunting job, even under the best of conditions, is difficult...
How did you make those lights appear in the windows, Gus? ... If it's not a trade secret.
Yes. Very difficult... On one's feet all hours of the night... Dragging heavy chains... Up and down dark, drafty hallways... In and out of dusty nooks and crannies—and one is expected to keep a clean white appearance, mind you. Why the laundry problem alone—
But, those lights...?
Lights? Were there mysterious LIGHTS in that awful house, too? Dear me!... I left because I kept hearing STRANGE NOISES!

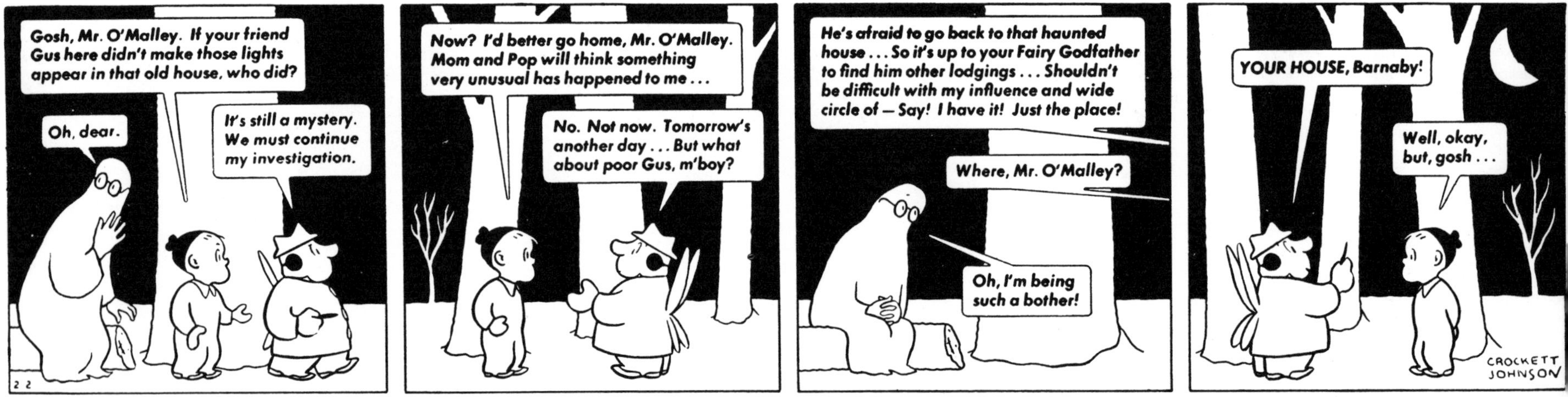
Gosh, Mr. O'Malley. If your friend Gus here didn't make those lights appear in that old house, who did?
Oh, dear.
It's still a mystery. We must continue my investigation.
2 2
Now? I'd better go home, Mr. O'Malley. Mom and Pop will think something very unusual has happened to me...
No. Not now. Tomorrow's another day... But what about poor Gus, m'boy?
He's afraid to go back to that haunted house... So it's up to your Fairy Godfather to find him other lodgings... Shouldn't be difficult with my influence and wide circle of — Say! I have it! Just the place!
Where, Mr. O'Malley?
Oh, I'm being such a bother!
YOUR HOUSE, Barnaby!
Well, okay, but, gosh...
CROCKETT JOHNSON

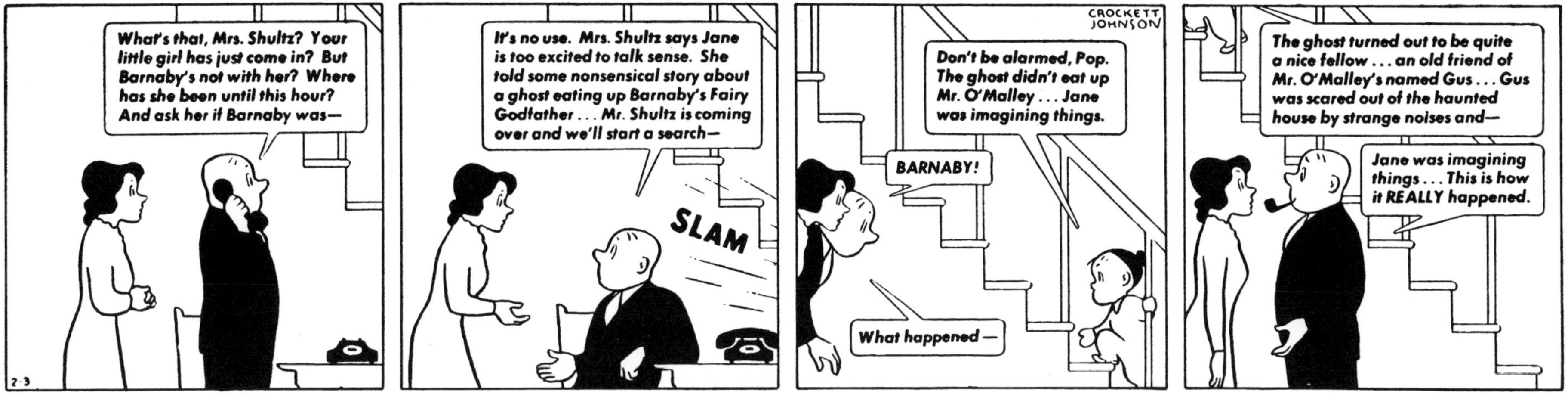
What's that, Mrs. Shultz? Your little girl has just come in? But Barnaby's not with her? Where has she been until this hour? And ask her if Barnaby was—
2-3
It's no use. Mrs. Shultz says Jane is too excited to talk sense. She told some nonsensical story about a ghost eating up Barnaby's Fairy Godfather . . . Mr. Shultz is coming over and we'll start a search—
SLAM
CROCKETT JOHNSON
BARNABY!
What happened —
Don't be alarmed, Pop. The ghost didn't eat up Mr. O'Malley . . . Jane was imagining things.
The ghost turned out to be quite a nice fellow . . . an old friend of Mr. O'Malley's named Gus . . . Gus was scared out of the haunted house by strange noises and—
Jane was imagining things . . . This is how it REALLY happened.

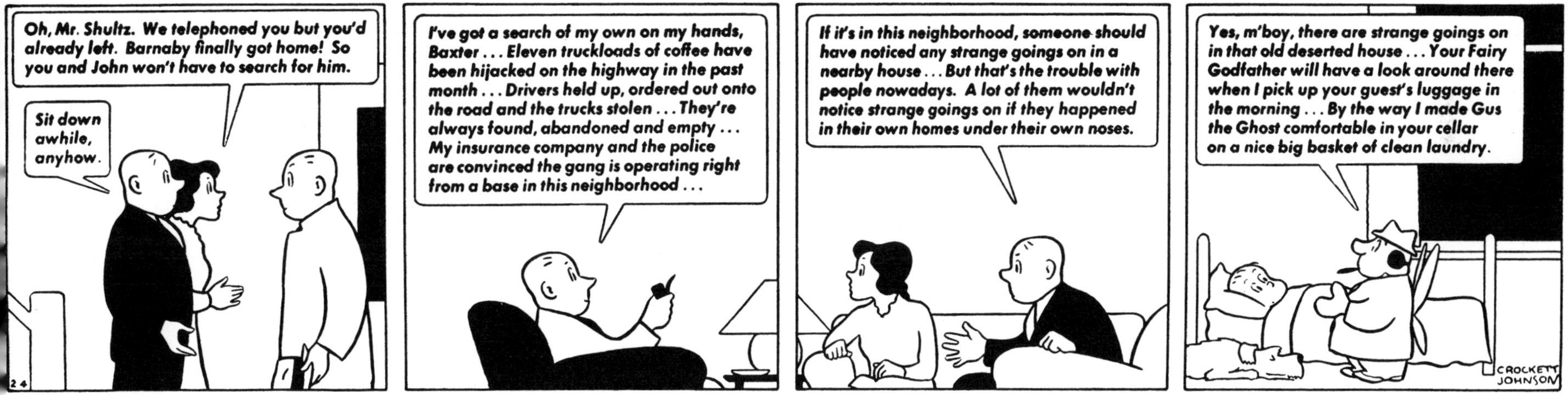
Oh, Mr. Shultz. We telephoned you but you'd already left. Barnaby finally got home! So you and John won't have to search for him.
Sit down awhile, anyhow.
2-4
I've got a search of my own on my hands, Baxter . . . Eleven truckloads of coffee have been hijacked on the highway in the past month . . . Drivers held up, ordered out onto the road and the trucks stolen . . . They're always found, abandoned and empty . . . My insurance company and the police are convinced the gang is operating right from a base in this neighborhood . . .
If it's in this neighborhood, someone should have noticed any strange goings on in a nearby house . . . But that's the trouble with people nowadays. A lot of them wouldn't notice strange goings on if they happened in their own homes under their own noses.
Yes, m'boy, there are strange goings on in that old deserted house . . . Your Fairy Godfather will have a look around there when I pick up your guest's luggage in the morning . . . By the way I made Gus the Ghost comfortable in your cellar on a nice big basket of clean laundry.
CROCKETT JOHNSON

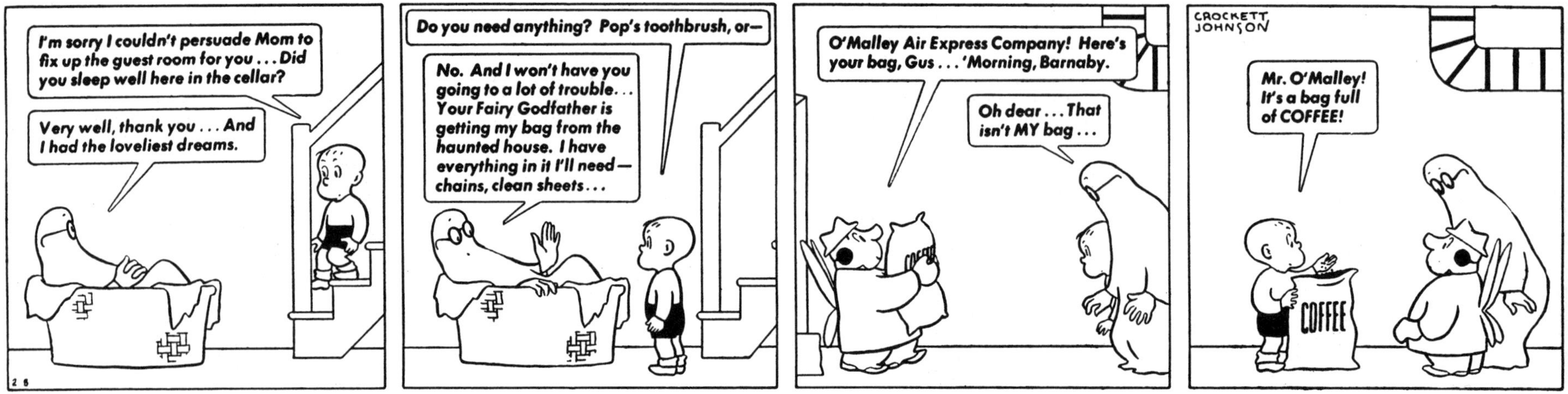
I'm sorry I couldn't persuade Mom to fix up the guest room for you . . . Did you sleep well here in the cellar?
Very well, thank you . . . And I had the loveliest dreams.
2 5
Do you need anything? Pop's toothbrush, or—
No. And I won't have you going to a lot of trouble. . . Your Fairy Godfather is getting my bag from the haunted house. I have everything in it I'll need—chains, clean sheets . . .
O'Malley Air Express Company! Here's your bag, Gus . . . 'Morning, Barnaby.
Oh dear . . . That isn't MY bag . . .
CROCKETT JOHNSON
Mr. O'Malley! It's a bag full of COFFEE!
COFFEE

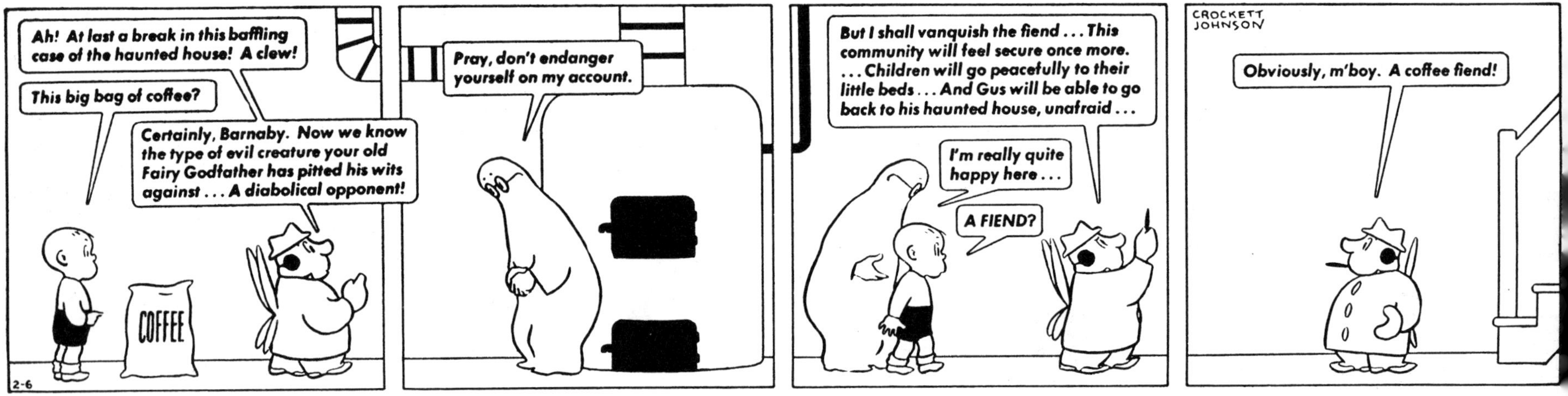
Ah! At last a break in this baffling case of the haunted house! A clew!
This big bag of coffee?
Certainly, Barnaby. Now we know the type of evil creature your old Fairy Godfather has pitted his wits against . . . A diabolical opponent!
COFFEE
2-6
Pray, don't endanger yourself on my account.
But I shall vanquish the fiend . . . This community will feel secure once more. . . . Children will go peacefully to their little beds . . . And Gus will be able to go back to his haunted house, unafraid . . .
I'm really quite happy here . . .
A FIEND?
CROCKETT JOHNSON
Obviously, m'boy. A coffee fiend!

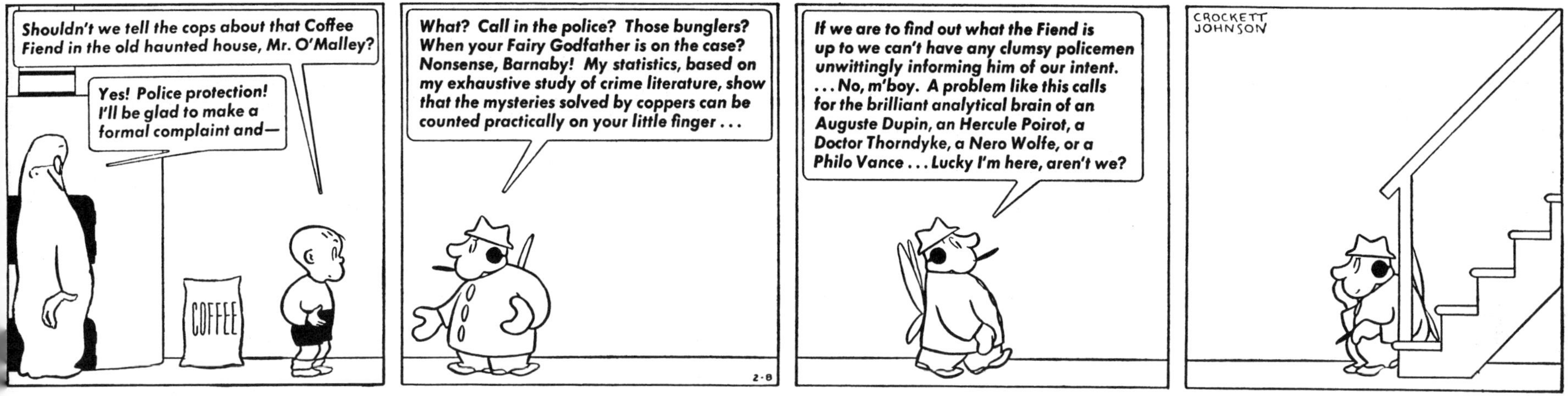
Shouldn't we tell the cops about that Coffee Fiend in the old haunted house, Mr. O'Malley?
Yes! Police protection! I'll be glad to make a formal complaint and—
COFFEE
What? Call in the police? Those bunglers? When your Fairy Godfather is on the case? Nonsense, Barnaby! My statistics, based on my exhaustive study of crime literature, show that the mysteries solved by coppers can be counted practically on your little finger . . .
2-8
If we are to find out what the Fiend is up to we can't have any clumsy policemen unwittingly informing him of our intent. . . . No, m'boy. A problem like this calls for the brilliant analytical brain of an Auguste Dupin, an Hercule Poirot, a Doctor Thorndyke, a Nero Wolfe, or a Philo Vance . . . Lucky I'm here, aren't we?
CROCKETT JOHNSON

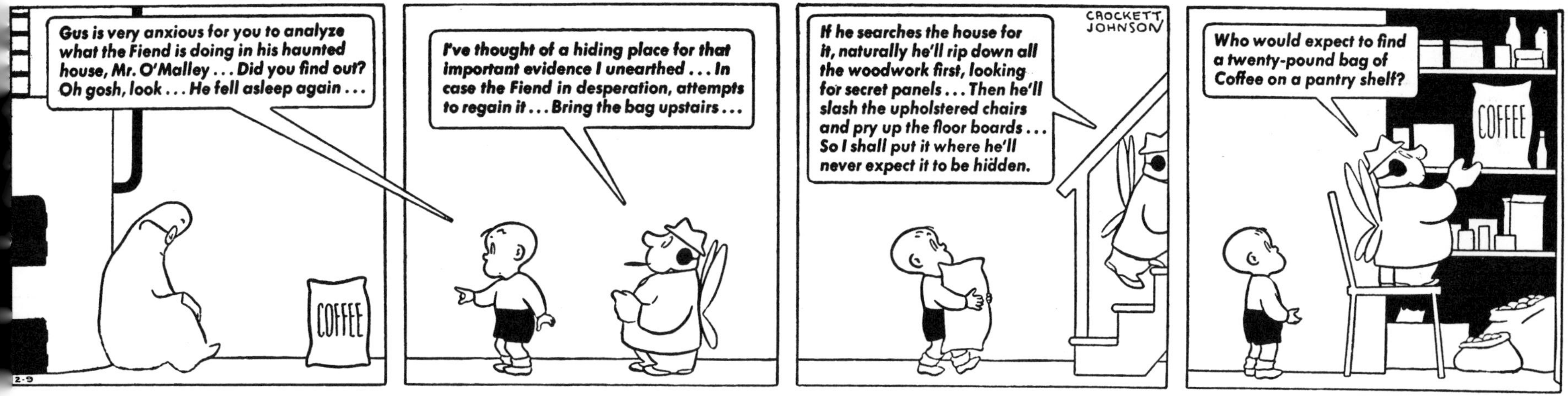
Gus is very anxious for you to analyze what the Fiend is doing in his haunted house, Mr. O'Malley . . . Did you find out? Oh gosh, look . . . He fell asleep again . . .
COFFEE
2-9
I've thought of a hiding place for that important evidence I unearthed . . . In case the Fiend in desperation, attempts to regain it . . . Bring the bag upstairs . . .
CROCKETT JOHNSON
If he searches the house for it, naturally he'll rip down all the woodwork first, looking for secret panels . . . Then he'll slash the upholstered chairs and pry up the floor boards . . . So I shall put it where he'll never expect it to be hidden.
Who would expect to find a twenty-pound bag of Coffee on a pantry shelf?
COFFEE

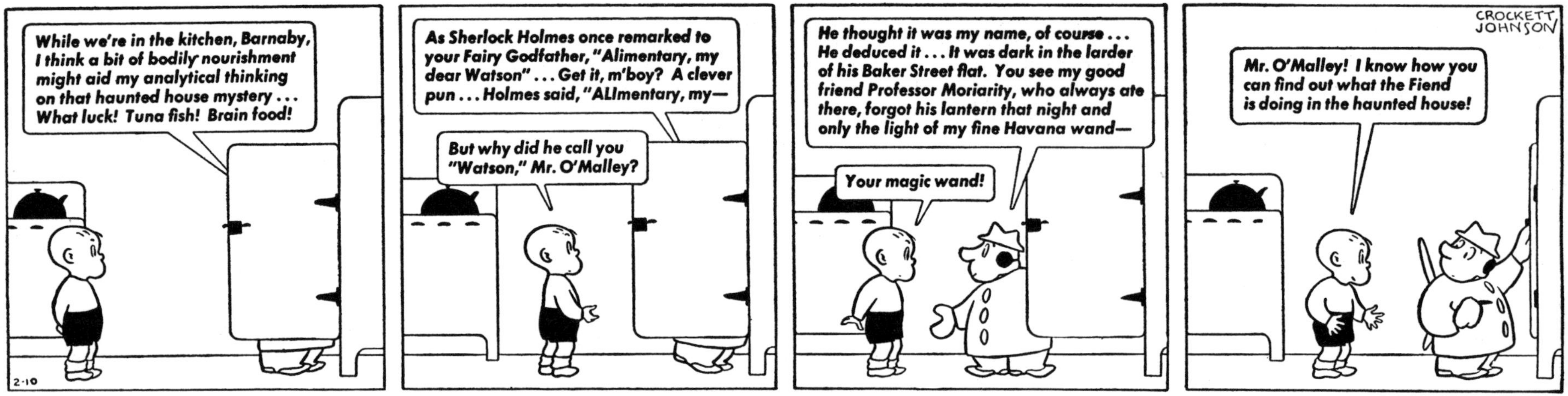
While we're in the kitchen, Barnaby, I think a bit of bodily nourishment might aid my analytical thinking on that haunted house mystery . . . What luck! Tuna fish! Brain food!
2-10
As Sherlock Holmes once remarked to your Fairy Godfather, "Alimentary, my dear Watson" . . . Get it, m'boy? A clever pun . . . Holmes said, "ALImentary, my—
But why did he call you "Watson," Mr. O'Malley?
He thought it was my name, of course . . . He deduced it . . . It was dark in the larder of his Baker Street flat. You see my good friend Professor Moriarity, who always ate there, forgot his lantern that night and only the light of my fine Havana wand—
Your magic wand!
CROCKETT JOHNSON
Mr. O'Malley! I know how you can find out what the Fiend is doing in the haunted house!

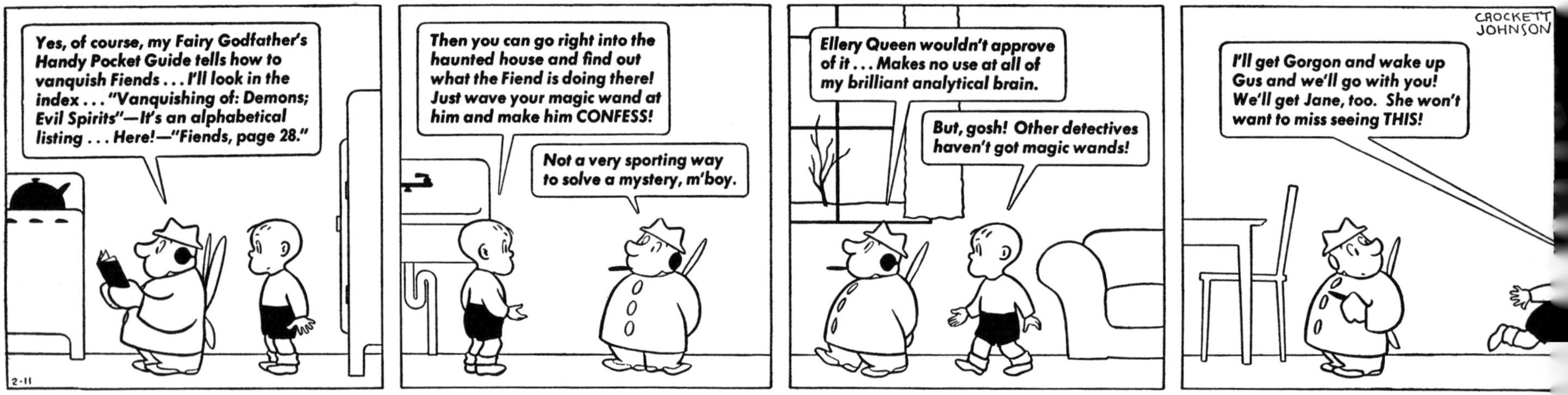
Yes, of course, my Fairy Godfather's Handy Pocket Guide tells how to vanquish Fiends . . . I'll look in the index . . . "Vanquishing of: Demons; Evil Spirits"—It's an alphabetical listing . . . Here!—"Fiends, page 28."
2-11
Then you can go right into the haunted house and find out what the Fiend is doing there! Just wave your magic wand at him and make him CONFESS!
Not a very sporting way to solve a mystery, m'boy.
Ellery Queen wouldn't approve of it . . . Makes no use at all of my brilliant analytical brain.
But, gosh! Other detectives haven't got magic wands!
CROCKETT JOHNSON
I'll get Gorgon and wake up Gus and we'll go with you! We'll get Jane, too. She won't want to miss seeing THIS!

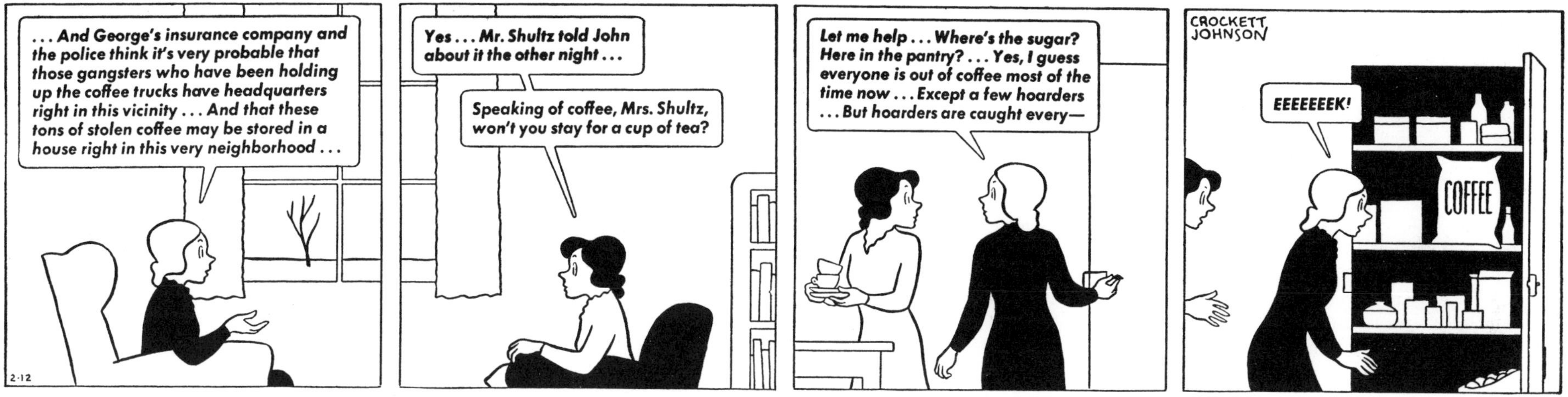

. . . And George's insurance company and the police think it's very probable that those gangsters who have been holding up the coffee trucks have headquarters right in this vicinity . . . And that these tons of stolen coffee may be stored in a house right in this very neighborhood . . .
2-12
Yes . . . Mr. Shultz told John about it the other night . . .
Speaking of coffee, Mrs. Shultz, won't you stay for a cup of tea?
Let me help . . . Where's the sugar? Here in the pantry? . . . Yes, I guess everyone is out of coffee most of the time now . . . Except a few hoarders . . . But hoarders are caught every—
CROCKETT JOHNSON
EEEEEEEK!
COFFEE

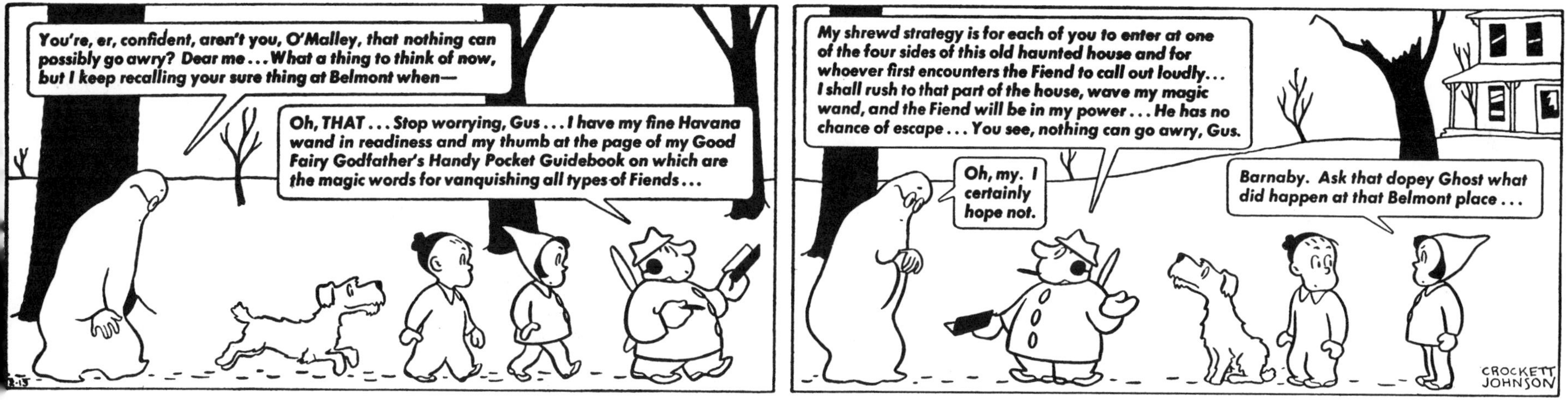

You're, er, confident, aren't you, O'Malley, that nothing can possibly go awry? Dear me . . . What a thing to think of now, but I keep recalling your sure thing at Belmont when—
Oh, THAT . . . Stop worrying, Gus . . . I have my fine Havana wand in readiness and my thumb at the page of my Good Fairy Godfather's Handy Pocket Guidebook on which are the magic words for vanquishing all types of Fiends . . .
2-13
My shrewd strategy is for each of you to enter at one of the four sides of this old haunted house and for whoever first encounters the Fiend to call out loudly . . . I shall rush to that part of the house, wave my magic wand, and the Fiend will be in my power . . . He has no chance of escape . . . You see, nothing can go awry, Gus.
Oh, my. I certainly hope not.
Barnaby. Ask that dopey Ghost what did happen at that Belmont place . . .
CROCKETT JOHNSON

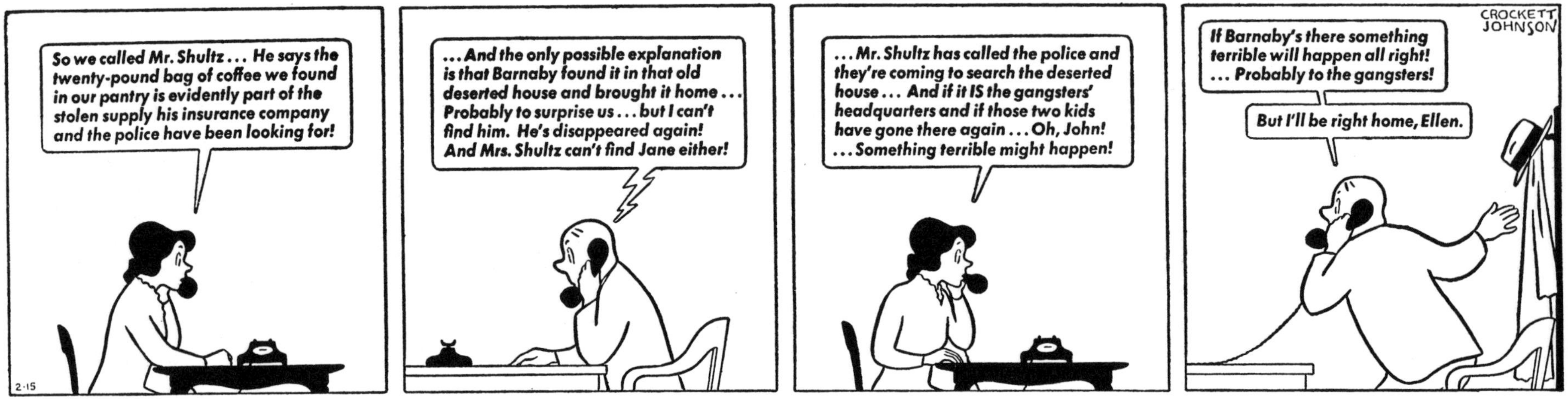
So we called Mr. Shultz . . . He says the twenty-pound bag of coffee we found in our pantry is evidently part of the stolen supply his insurance company and the police have been looking for!
2-15
. . . And the only possible explanation is that Barnaby found it in that old deserted house and brought it home . . . Probably to surprise us . . . but I can't find him. He's disappeared again! And Mrs. Shultz can't find Jane either!
. . . Mr. Shultz has called the police and they're coming to search the deserted house . . . And if it IS the gangsters' headquarters and if those two kids have gone there again . . . Oh, John! . . . Something terrible might happen!
CROCKETT JOHNSON
If Barnaby's there something terrible will happen all right! . . . Probably to the gangsters!
But I'll be right home, Ellen.

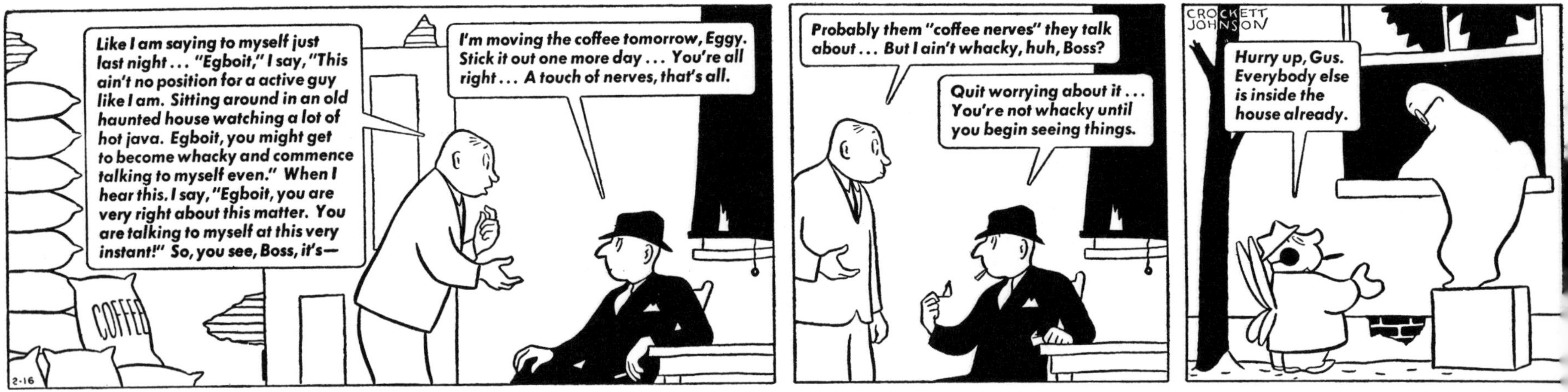
Like I am saying to myself just last night . . . "Egboit," I say, "This ain't no position for a active guy like I am. Sitting around in an old haunted house watching a lot of hot java. Egboit, you might get to become whacky and commence talking to myself even." When I hear this, I say, "Egboit, you are very right about this matter. You are talking to myself at this very instant!" So, you see, Boss, it's—
I'm moving the coffee tomorrow, Eggy. Stick it out one more day . . . You're all right . . . A touch of nerves, that's all.
COFFEE
2-16
Probably them "coffee nerves" they talk about . . . But I ain't whacky, huh, Boss?
Quit worrying about it . . . You're not whacky until you begin seeing things.
CROCKETT JOHNSON
Hurry up, Gus. Everybody else is inside the house already.

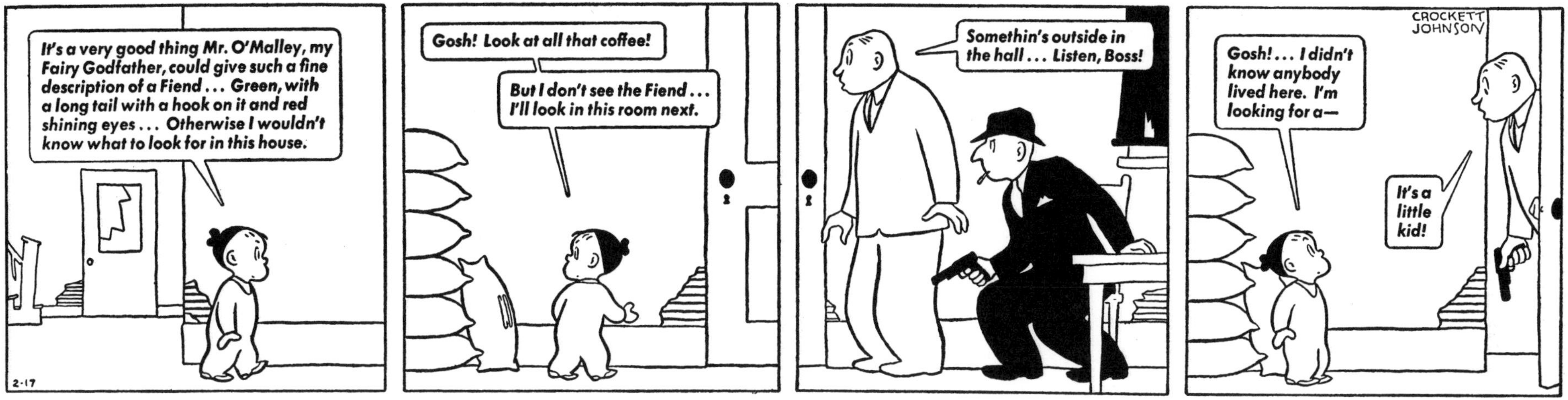
It's a very good thing Mr. O'Malley, my Fairy Godfather, could give such a fine description of a Fiend . . . Green, with a long tail with a hook on it and red shining eyes . . . Otherwise I wouldn't know what to look for in this house.
2-17
Gosh! Look at all that coffee!
But I don't see the Fiend . . . I'll look in this room next.
Somethin's outside in the hall . . . Listen, Boss!
CROCKETT JOHNSON
Gosh! . . . I didn't know anybody lived here. I'm looking for a—
It's a little kid!

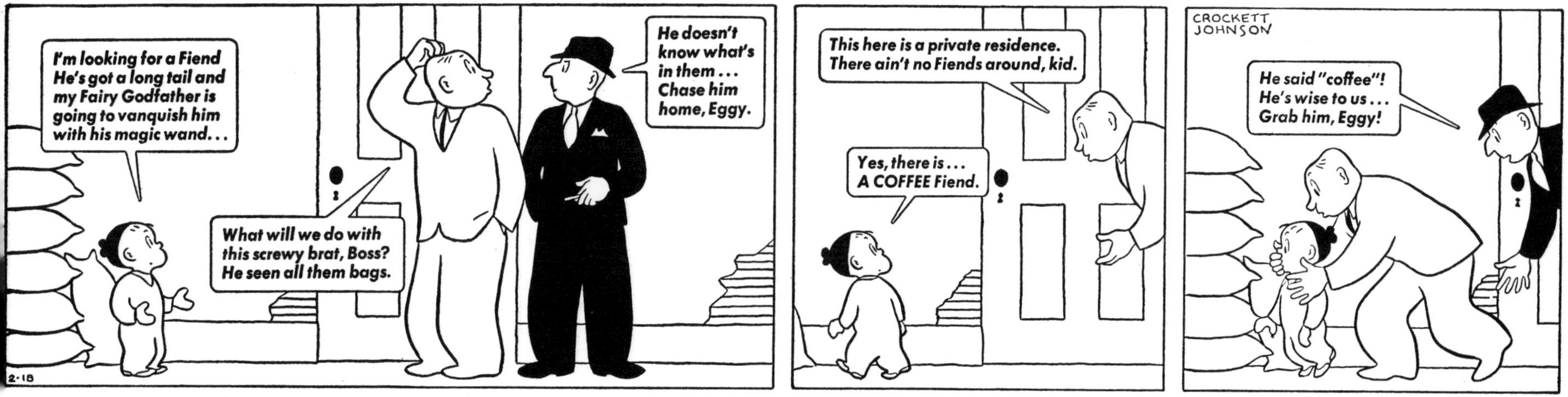
I'm looking for a Fiend He's got a long tail and my Fairy Godfather is going to vanquish him with his magic wand . . .
What will we do with this screwy brat, Boss? He seen all them bags.
He doesn't know what's in them . . . Chase him home, Eggy.
2-18
This here is a private residence. There ain't no Fiends around, kid.
Yes, there is . . . A COFFEE Fiend.
CROCKETT JOHNSON
He said "coffee"! He's wise to us . . . Grab him, Eggy!

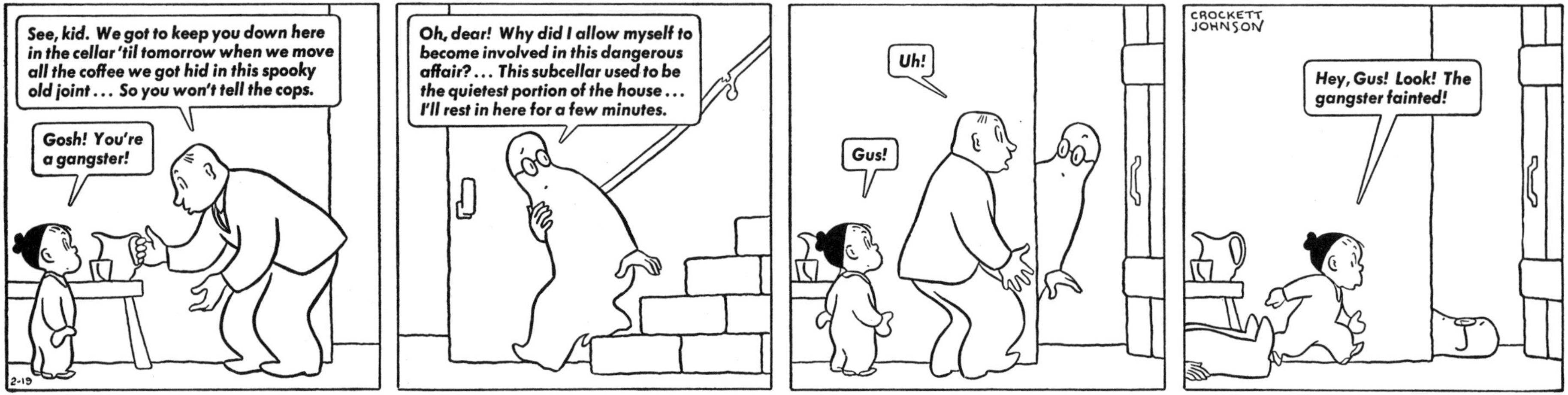
See, kid. We got to keep you down here in the cellar 'til tomorrow when we move all the coffee we got hid in this spooky old joint . . . So you won't tell the cops.
Gosh! You're a gangster!
2-19
Oh, dear! Why did I allow myself to become involved in this dangerous affair? . . . This subcellar used to be the quietest portion of the house . . . I'll rest in here for a few minutes.
Uh!
Gus!
CROCKETT JOHNSON
Hey, Gus! Look! The gangster fainted!

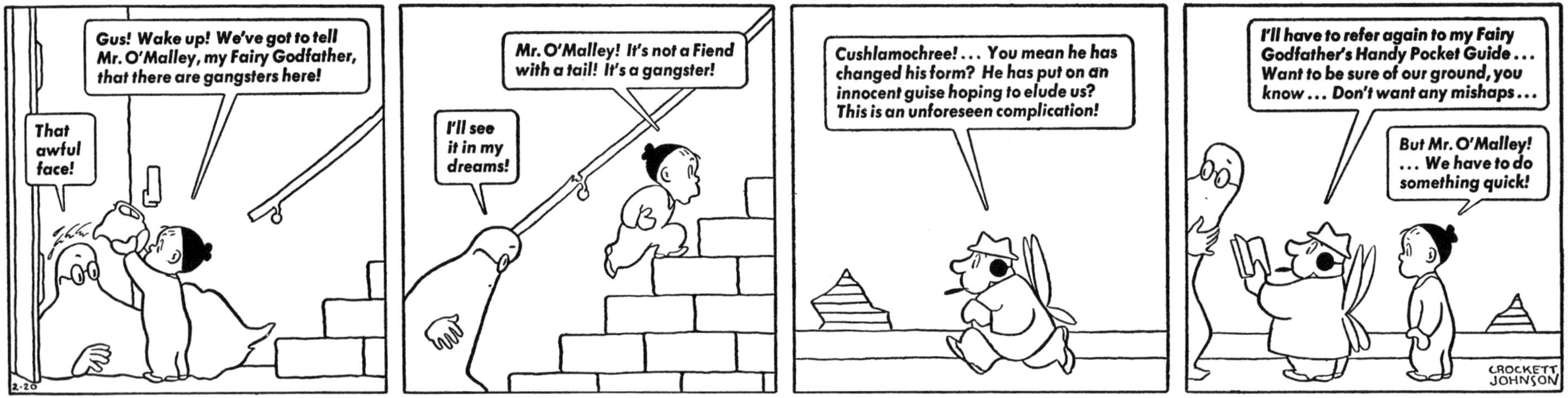
Gus! Wake up! We've got to tell Mr. O'Malley, my Fairy Godfather, that there are gangsters here!
That awful face!
2-20
Mr. O'Malley! It's not a Fiend with a tail! It's a gangster!
I'll see it in my dreams!
Cushlamochree! . . . You mean he has changed his form? He has put on an innocent guise hoping to elude us? This is an unforeseen complication!
I'll have to refer again to my Fairy Godfather's Handy Pocket Guide . . . Want to be sure of our ground, you know . . . Don't want any mishaps . . .
But Mr. O'Malley! . . . We have to do something quick!
CROCKETT JOHNSON

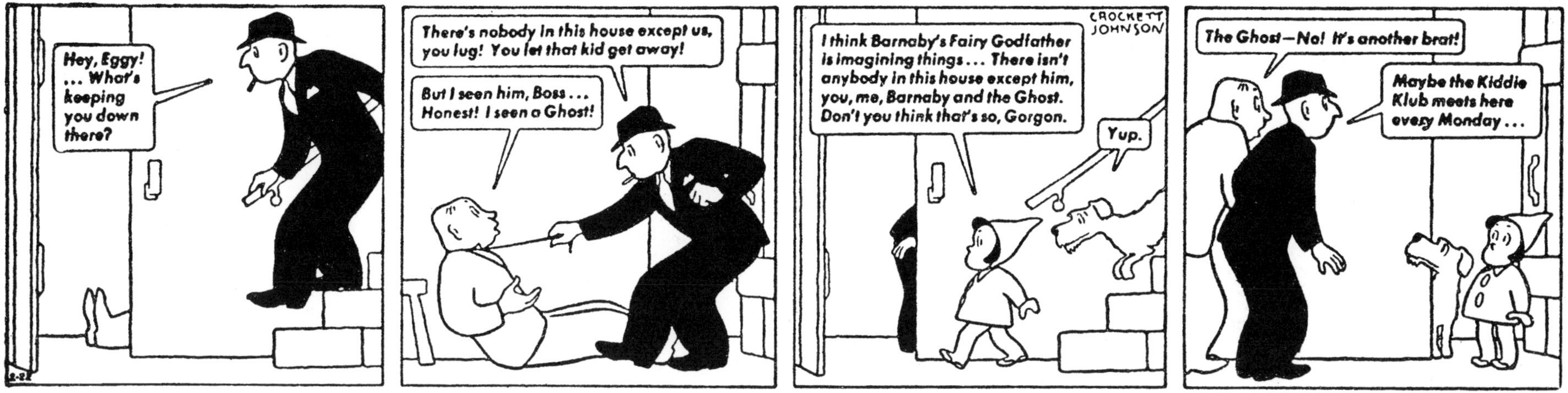
Hey, Eggy! ... What's keeping you down there?
There's nobody in this house except us, you lug! You let that kid get away!
But I seen him, Boss ... Honest! I seen a Ghost!
CROCKETT JOHNSON
I think Barnaby's Fairy Godfather is imagining things ... There isn't anybody in this house except him, you, me, Barnaby and the Ghost. Don't you think that's so, Gorgon.
Yup.
The Ghost—No! It's another brat!
Maybe the Kiddie Klub meets here every Monday ...

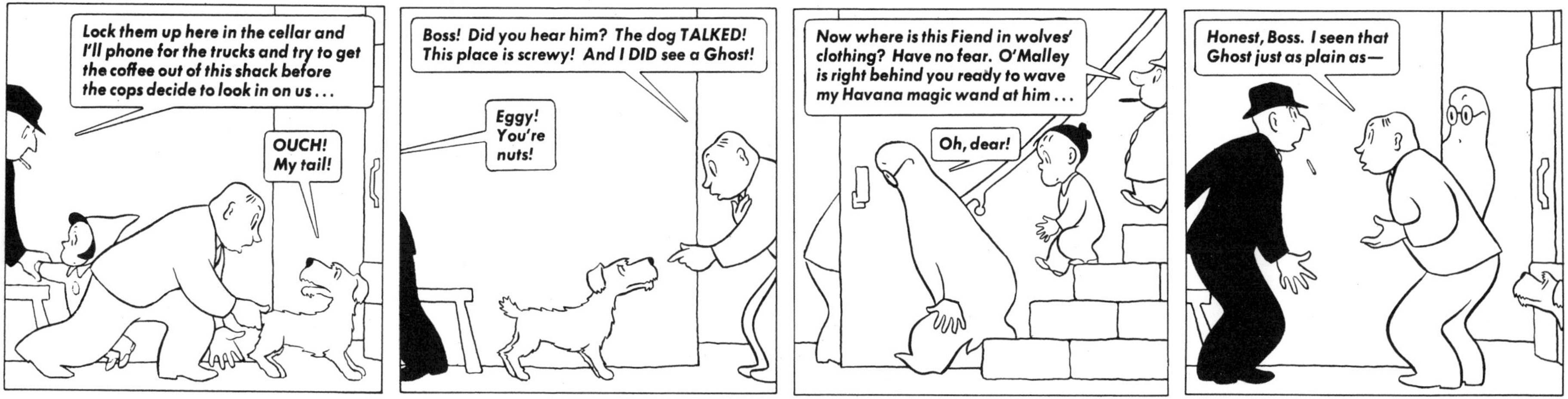
Lock them up here in the cellar and I'll phone for the trucks and try to get the coffee out of this shack before the cops decide to look in on us ...
OUCH! My tail!
Boss! Did you hear him? The dog TALKED! This place is screwy! And I DID see a Ghost!
Eggy! You're nuts!
Now where is this Fiend in wolves' clothing? Have no fear. O'Malley is right behind you ready to wave my Havana magic wand at him ...
Oh, dear!
Honest, Boss. I seen that Ghost just as plain as—

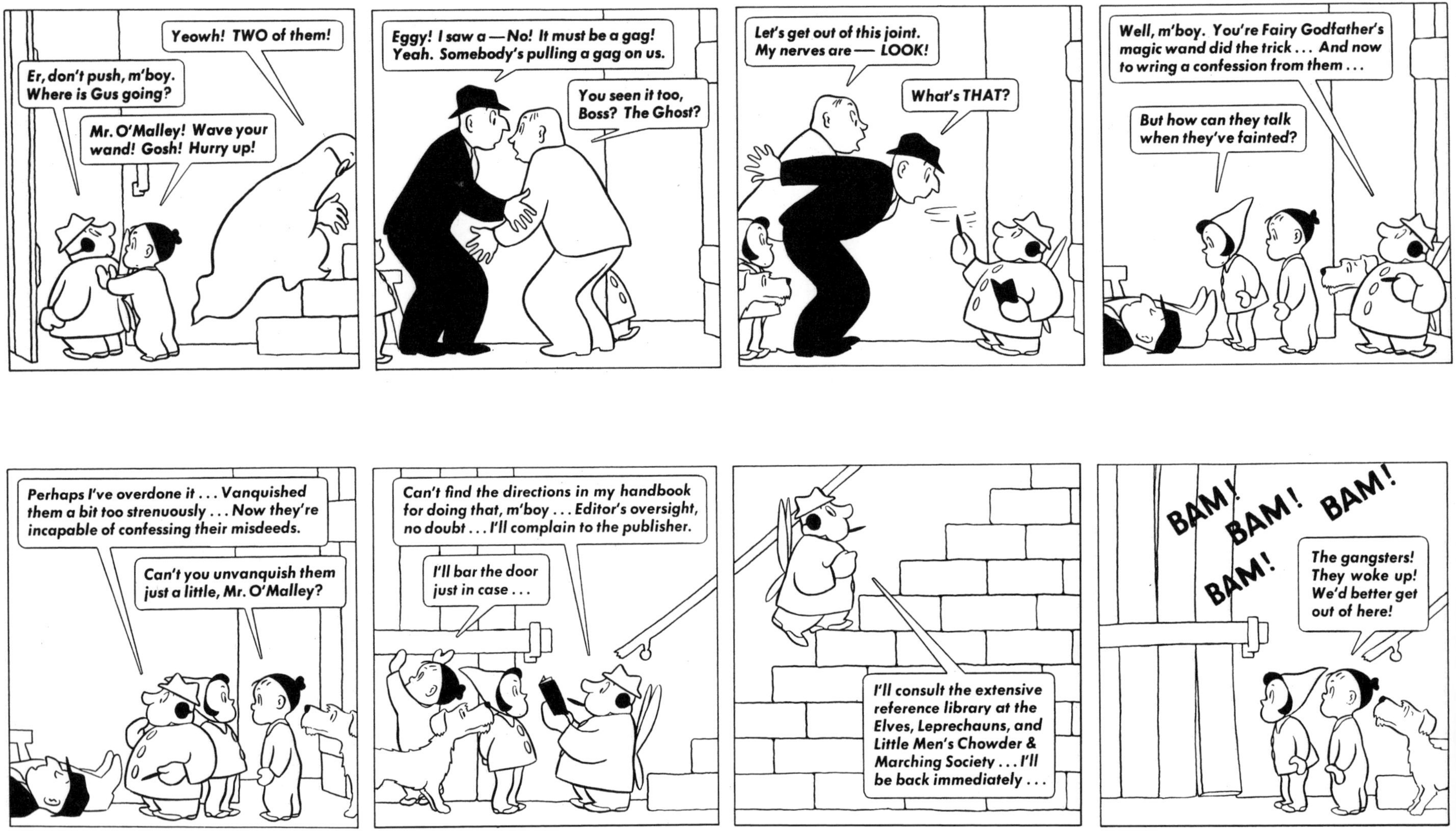
Yeowh! TWO of them!
Er, don't push, m'boy. Where is Gus going?
Mr. O'Malley! Wave your wand! Gosh! Hurry up!
Eggy! I saw a—No! It must be a gag! Yeah. Somebody's pulling a gag on us.
You seen it too, Boss? The Ghost?
Let's get out of this joint. My nerves are— LOOK!
What's THAT?
Well, m'boy. You're Fairy Godfather's magic wand did the trick . . . And now to wring a confession from them . . .
But how can they talk when they've fainted?
Perhaps I've overdone it . . . Vanquished them a bit too strenuously . . . Now they're incapable of confessing their misdeeds.
Can't you unvanquish them just a little, Mr. O'Malley?
Can't find the directions in my handbook for doing that, m'boy . . . Editor's oversight, no doubt . . . I'll complain to the publisher.
I'll bar the door just in case . . .
I'll consult the extensive reference library at the Elves, Leprechauns, and Little Men's Chowder & Marching Society . . . I'll be back immediately . . .
BAM! BAM! BAM! BAM!
The gangsters! They woke up! We'd better get out of here!

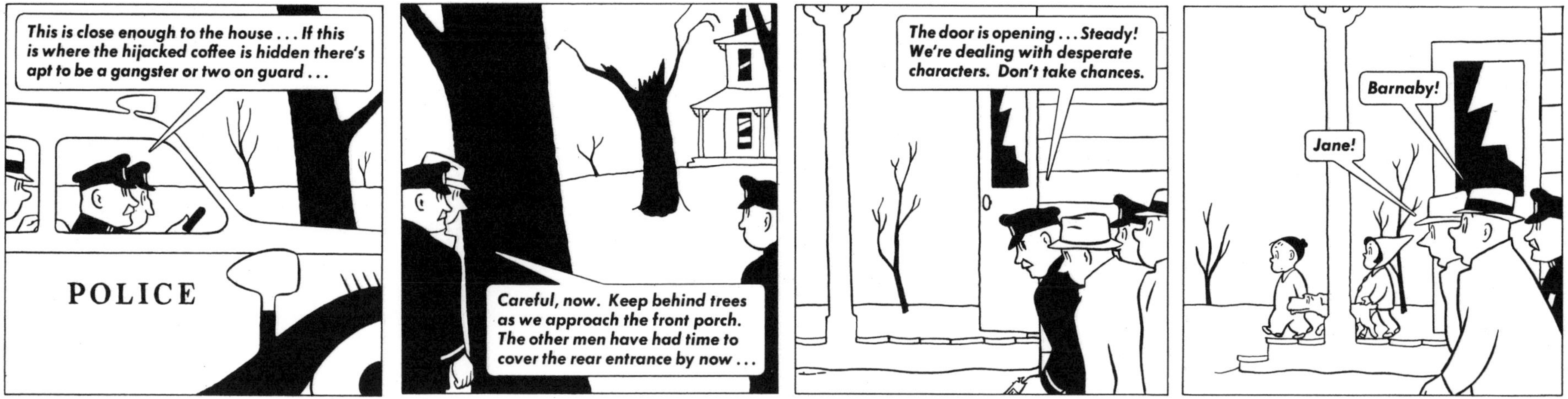
POLICE
This is close enough to the house . . . If this is where the hijacked coffee is hidden there's apt to be a gangster or two on guard . . .
Careful, now. Keep behind trees as we approach the front porch. The other men have had time to cover the rear entrance by now . . .
The door is opening . . . Steady! We're dealing with desperate characters. Don't take chances.
Barnaby!
Jane!

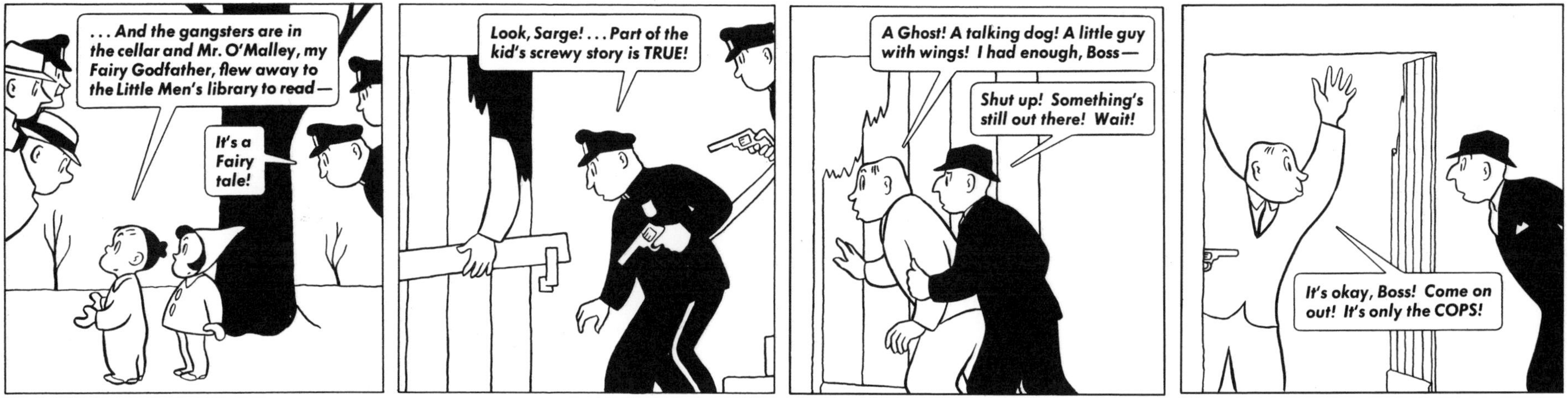
. . . And the gangsters are in the cellar and Mr. O'Malley, my Fairy Godfather, flew away to the Little Men's library to read—
It's a Fairy tale!
Look, Sarge! . . . Part of the kid's screwy story is TRUE!
A Ghost! A talking dog! A little guy with wings! I had enough, Boss—
Shut up! Something's still out there! Wait!
It's okay, Boss! Come on out! It's only the COPS!

February 26 – 27

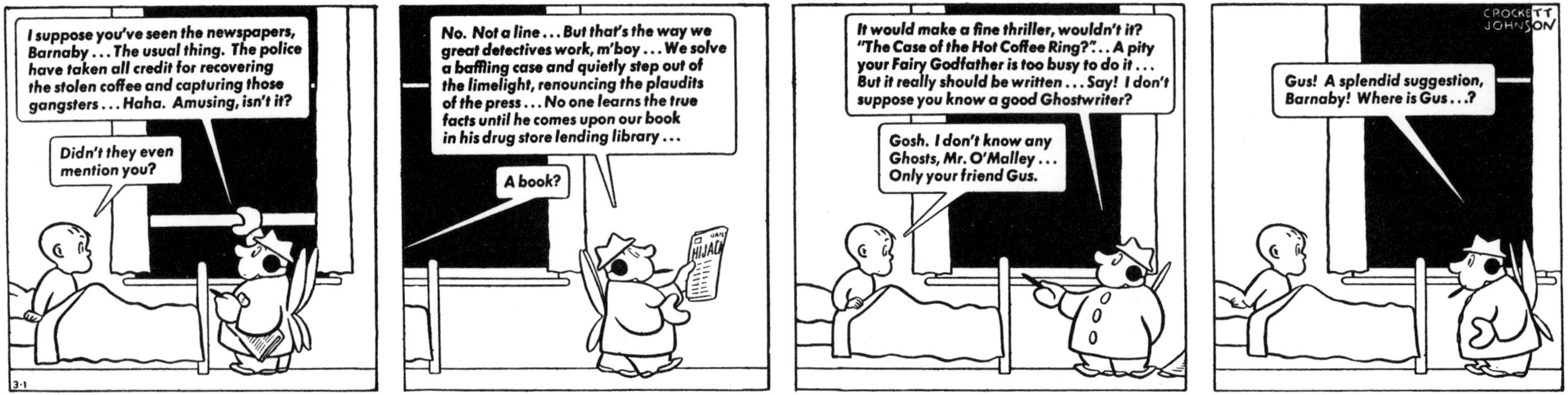
I suppose you've seen the newspapers, Barnaby . . . The usual thing. The police have taken all credit for recovering the stolen coffee and capturing those gangsters . . . Haha. Amusing, isn't it?
Didn't they even mention you?
No. Not a line . . . But that's the way we great detectives work, m'boy . . . We solve a baffling case and quietly step out of the limelight, renouncing the plaudits of the press . . . No one learns the true facts until he comes upon our book in his drug store lending library . . .
A book?
HIJACK
It would make a fine thriller, wouldn't it? "The Case of the Hot Coffee Ring?" . . A pity your Fairy Godfather is too busy to do it . . . But it really should be written . . . Say! I don't suppose you know a good Ghostwriter?
Gosh. I don't know any Ghosts, Mr. O'Malley . . . Only your friend Gus.
CROCKETT JOHNSON
Gus! A splendid suggestion, Barnaby! Where is Gus . . .?
3-1

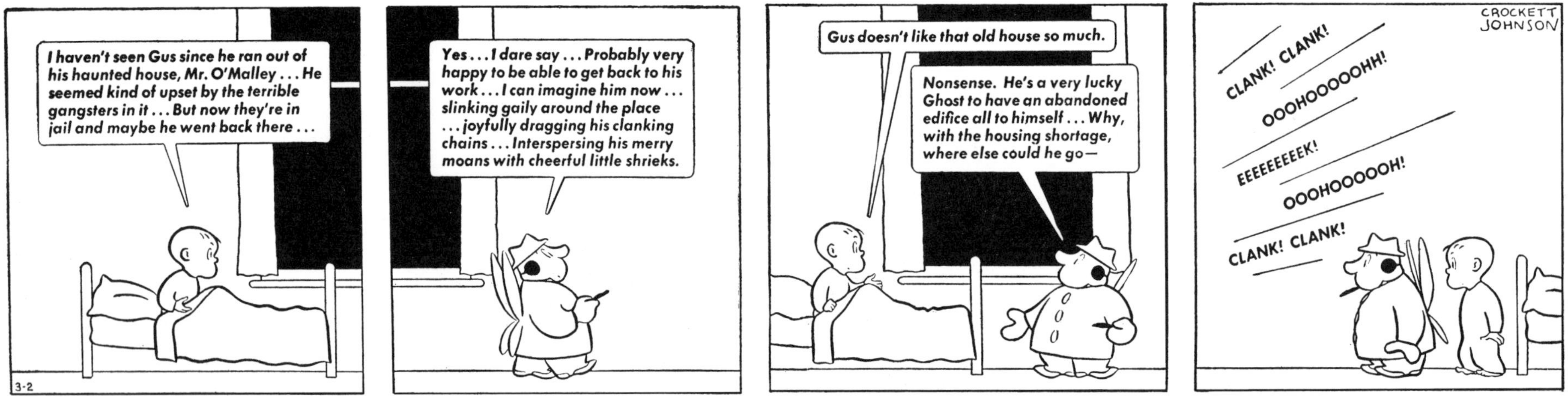
I haven't seen Gus since he ran out of his haunted house, Mr. O'Malley . . . He seemed kind of upset by the terrible gangsters in it . . . But now they're in jail and maybe he went back there . . .
Yes . . . I dare say . . . Probably very happy to be able to get back to his work . . . I can imagine him now . . . slinking gaily around the place . . . joyfully dragging his clanking chains . . . Interspersing his merry moans with cheerful little shrieks.
Gus doesn't like that old house so much.
Nonsense. He's a very lucky Ghost to have an abandoned edifice all to himself . . . Why, with the housing shortage, where else could he go—
CROCKETT JOHNSON
CLANK! CLANK!
OOOHOOOOOHH!
EEEEEEEEEK!
OOOHOOOOOH!
CLANK! CLANK!
3-2

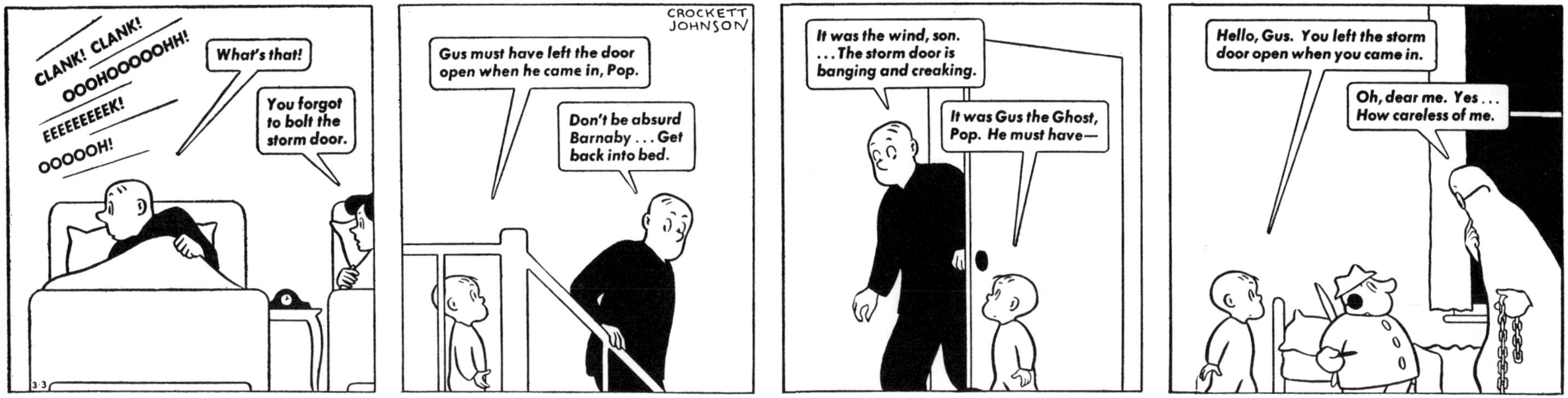
CLANK! CLANK!
OOOHOOOOOHH!
EEEEEEEEEK!
OOOOOH!
What's that!
You forgot to bolt the storm door.
3·3
CROCKETT JOHNSON
Gus must have left the door open when he came in, Pop.
Don't be absurd Barnaby . . . Get back into bed.
It was the wind, son. . . . The storm door is banging and creaking.
It was Gus the Ghost, Pop. He must have—
Hello, Gus. You left the storm door open when you came in.
Oh, dear me. Yes . . . How careless of me.

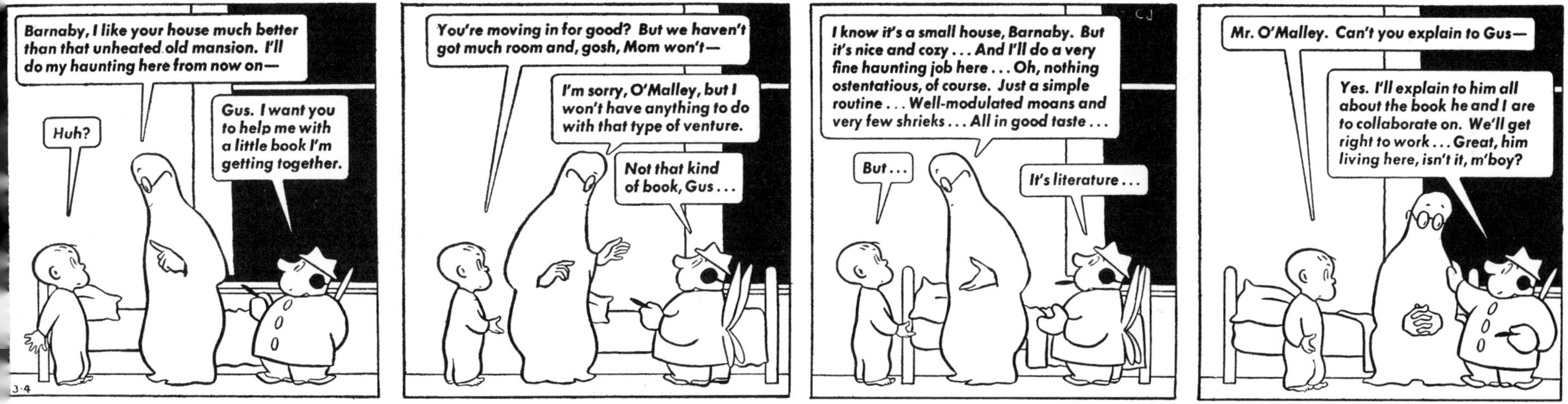
Barnaby, I like your house much better than that unheated old mansion. I'll do my haunting here from now on—
Huh?
Gus. I want you to help me with a little book I'm getting together.
3·4
You're moving in for good? But we haven't got much room and, gosh, Mom won't—
I'm sorry, O'Malley, but I won't have anything to do with that type of venture.
Not that kind of book, Gus . . .
CJ
I know it's a small house, Barnaby. But it's nice and cozy . . . And I'll do a very fine haunting job here . . . Oh, nothing ostentatious, of course. Just a simple routine . . . Well-modulated moans and very few shrieks . . . All in good taste . . .
But . . .
It's literature . . .
Mr. O'Malley. Can't you explain to Gus—
Yes. I'll explain to him all about the book he and I are to collaborate on. We'll get right to work . . . Great, him living here, isn't it, m'boy?

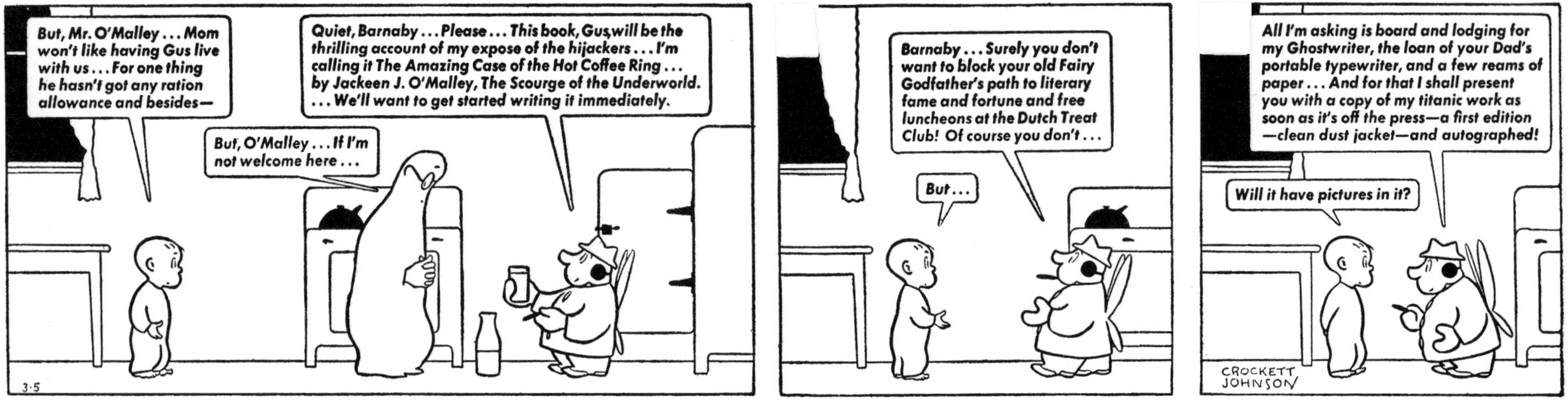
But, Mr. O'Malley . . . Mom won't like having Gus live with us . . . For one thing he hasn't got any ration allowance and besides—
Quiet, Barnaby . . . Please . . . This book, Gus, will be the thrilling account of my expose of the hijackers . . . I'm calling it The Amazing Case of the Hot Coffee Ring . . . by Jackeen J. O'Malley, The Scourge of the Underworld. . . . We'll want to get started writing it immediately.
But, O'Malley . . . If I'm not welcome here . . .
3·5
Barnaby . . . Surely you don't want to block your old Fairy Godfather's path to literary fame and fortune and free luncheons at the Dutch Treat Club! Of course you don't . . .
But . . .
All I'm asking is board and lodging for my Ghostwriter, the loan of your Dad's portable typewriter, and a few reams of paper . . . And for that I shall present you with a copy of my titanic work as soon as it's off the press—a first edition —clean dust jacket—and autographed!
Will it have pictures in it?
CROCKETT JOHNSON

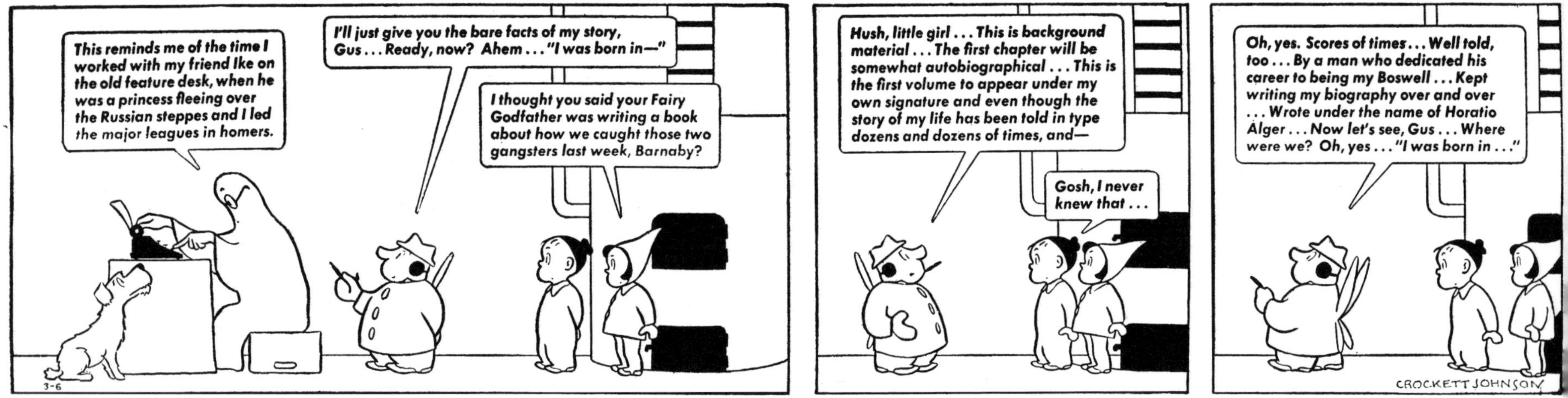
This reminds me of the time I worked with my friend Ike on the old feature desk, when he was a princess fleeing over the Russian steppes and I led the major leagues in homers.
I'll just give you the bare facts of my story, Gus . . . Ready, now? Ahem . . . "I was born in—"
I thought you said your Fairy Godfather was writing a book about how we caught those two gangsters last week, Barnaby?
3-6
Hush, little girl . . . This is background material . . . The first chapter will be somewhat autobiographical . . . This is the first volume to appear under my own signature and even though the story of my life has been told in type dozens and dozens of times, and—
Gosh, I never knew that . . .
Oh, yes. Scores of times . . . Well told, too . . . By a man who dedicated his career to being my Boswell . . . Kept writing my biography over and over . . . Wrote under the name of Horatio Alger . . . Now let's see, Gus . . . Where were we? Oh, yes . . . "I was born in . . ."
CROCKETT JOHNSON

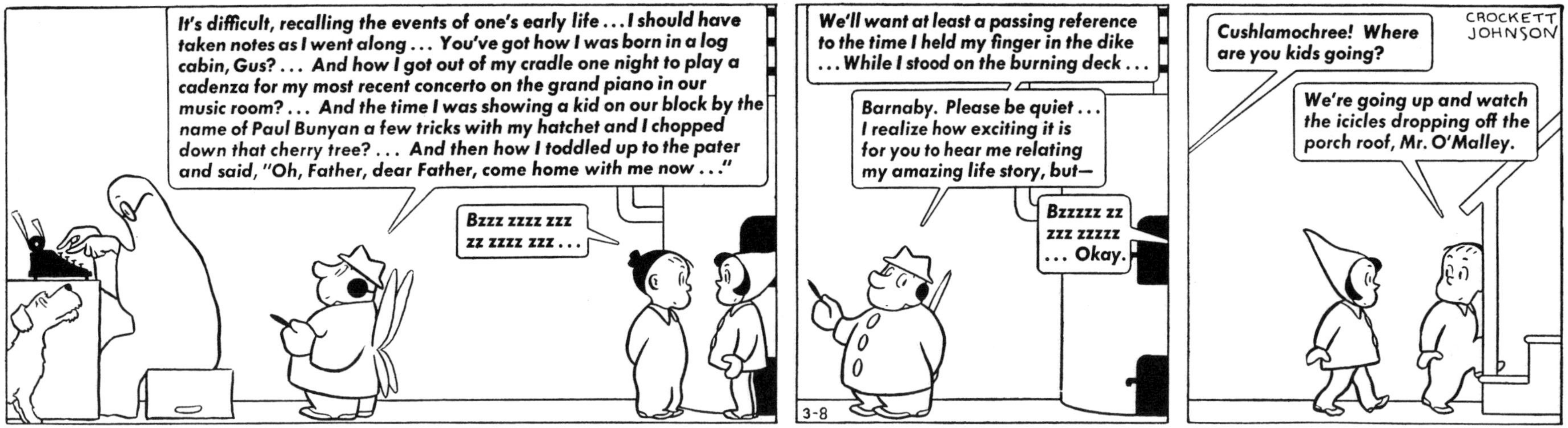
It's difficult, recalling the events of one's early life . . . I should have taken notes as I went along . . . You've got how I was born in a log cabin, Gus? . . . And how I got out of my cradle one night to play a cadenza for my most recent concerto on the grand piano in our music room? . . . And the time I was showing a kid on our block by the name of Paul Bunyan a few tricks with my hatchet and I chopped down that cherry tree? . . . And then how I toddled up to the pater and said, "Oh, Father, dear Father, come home with me now . . ."
Bzzz zzzz zzz zz zzzz zzz . . .
We'll want at least a passing reference to the time I held my finger in the dike . . . While I stood on the burning deck . . .
Barnaby. Please be quiet . . . I realize how exciting it is for you to hear me relating my amazing life story, but—
Bzzzzz zz zzz zzzzz . . . Okay.
3-8
CROCKETT JOHNSON
Cushlamochree! Where are you kids going?
We're going up and watch the icicles dropping off the porch roof, Mr. O'Malley.

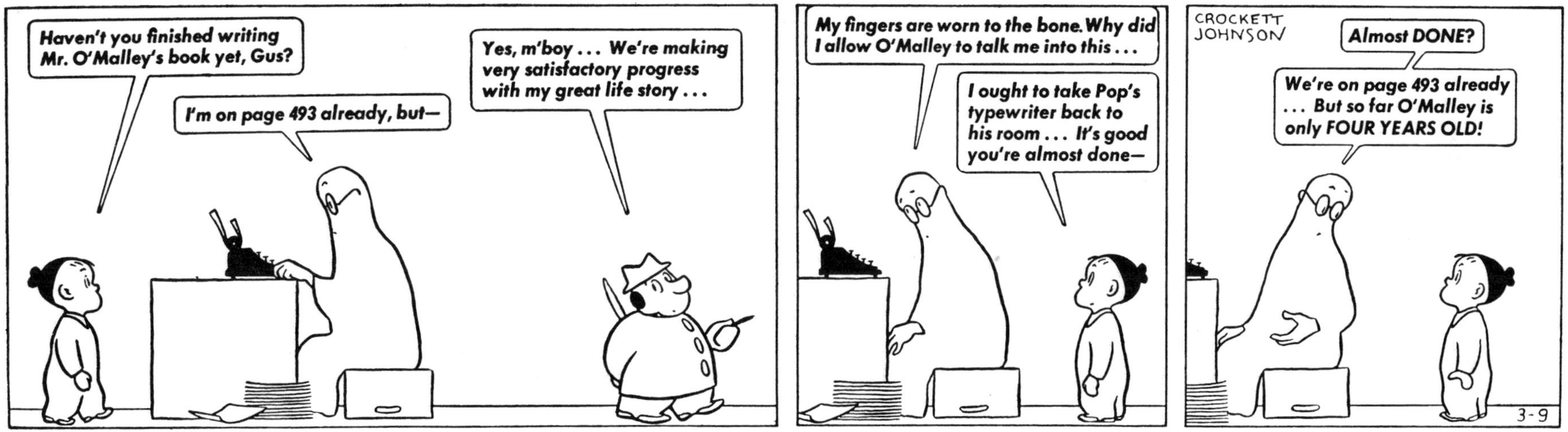
Haven't you finished writing Mr. O'Malley's book yet, Gus?
I'm on page 493 already, but—
Yes, m'boy . . . We're making very satisfactory progress with my great life story . . .
My fingers are worn to the bone. Why did I allow O'Malley to talk me into this . . .
I ought to take Pop's typewriter back to his room . . . It's good you're almost done—
CROCKETT JOHNSON
Almost DONE?
We're on page 493 already . . . But so far O'Malley is only FOUR YEARS OLD!
3-9

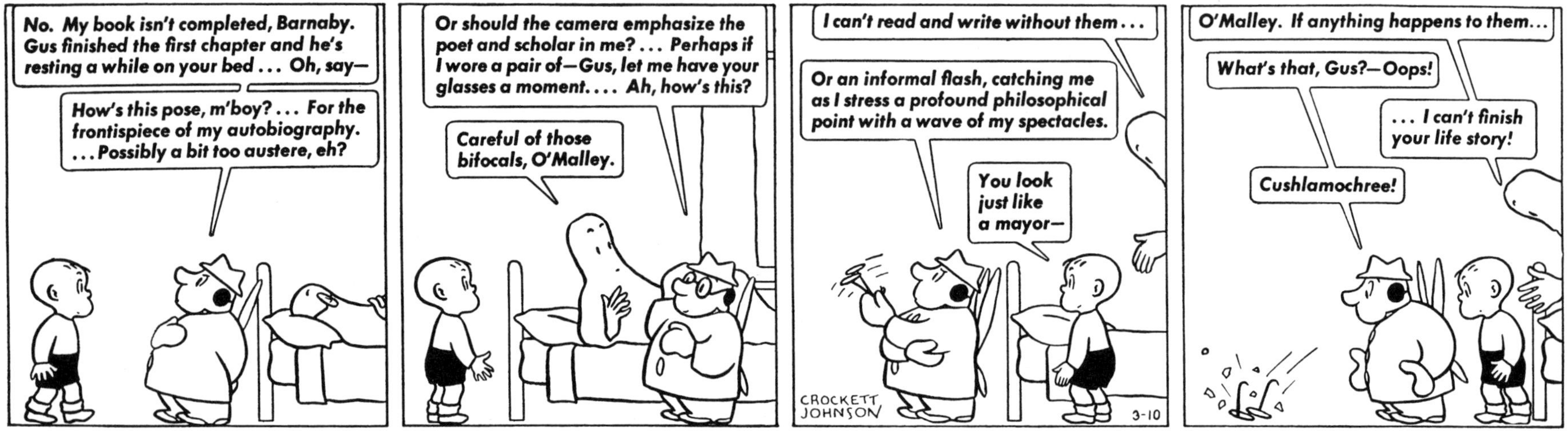
No. My book isn't completed, Barnaby. Gus finished the first chapter and he's resting a while on your bed ... Oh, say—
How's this pose, m'boy? ... For the frontispiece of my autobiography. ... Possibly a bit too austere, eh?
Or should the camera emphasize the poet and scholar in me? ... Perhaps if I wore a pair of—Gus, let me have your glasses a moment.... Ah, how's this?
Careful of those bifocals, O'Malley.
I can't read and write without them ...
Or an informal flash, catching me as I stress a profound philosophical point with a wave of my spectacles.
You look just like a mayor—
CROCKETT JOHNSON
3-10
O'Malley. If anything happens to them...
What's that, Gus?—Oops!
... I can't finish your life story!
Cushlamochree!

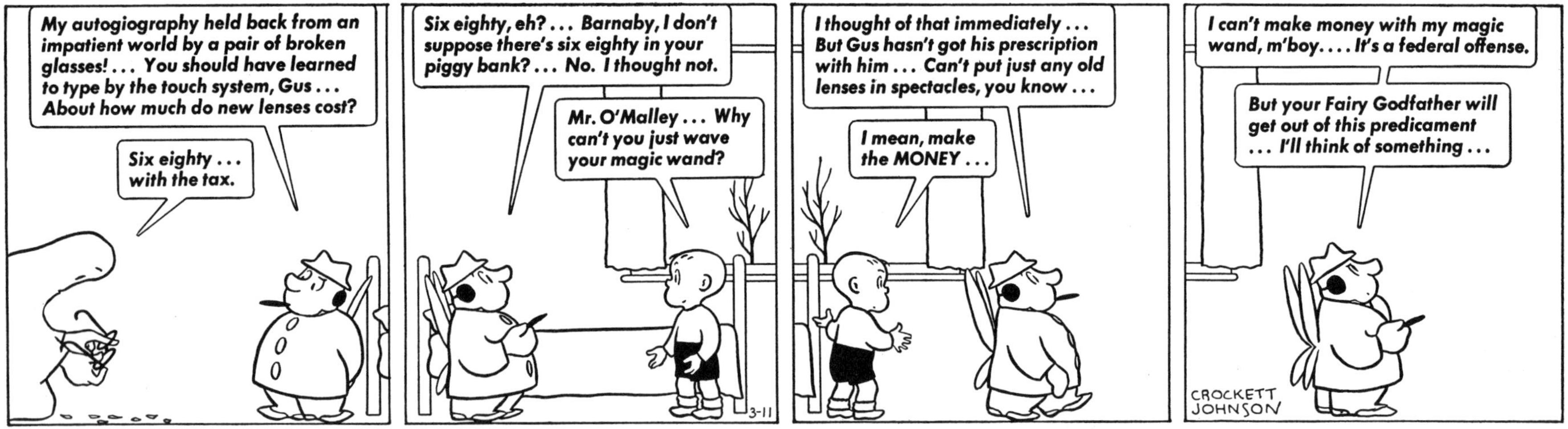
My autogiography held back from an impatient world by a pair of broken glasses! ... You should have learned to type by the touch system, Gus ... About how much do new lenses cost?
Six eighty ... with the tax.
Six eighty, eh? ... Barnaby, I don't suppose there's six eighty in your piggy bank? ... No. I thought not.
Mr. O'Malley ... Why can't you just wave your magic wand?
3-11
I thought of that immediately ... But Gus hasn't got his prescription with him ... Can't put just any old lenses in spectacles, you know ...
I mean, make the MONEY ...
I can't make money with my magic wand, m'boy.... It's a federal offense.
But your Fairy Godfather will get out of this predicament ... I'll think of something ...
CROCKETT JOHNSON

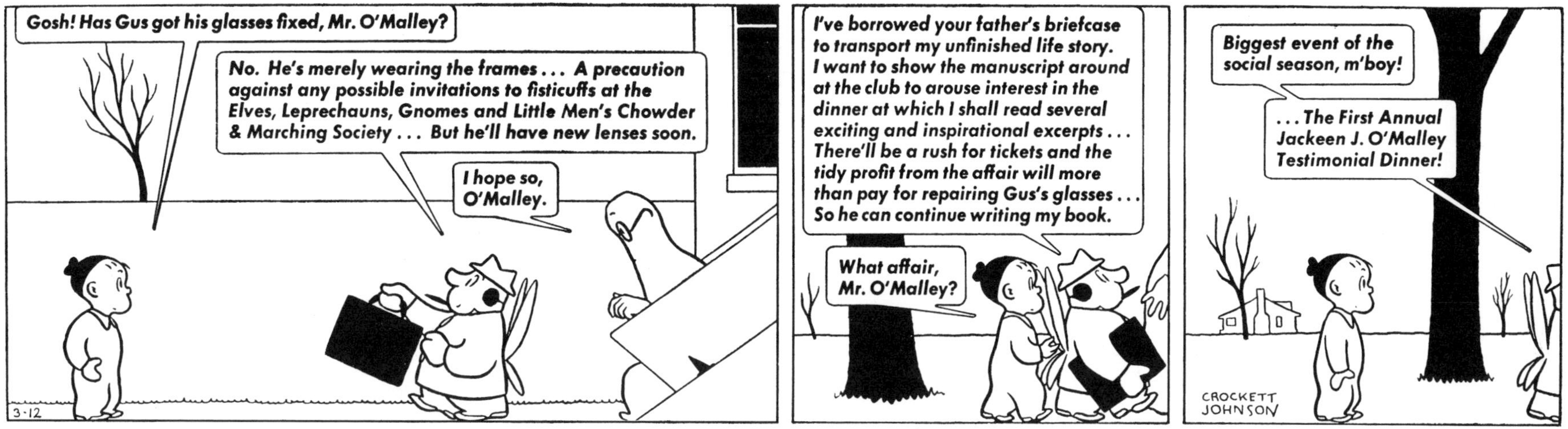
Gosh! Has Gus got his glasses fixed, Mr. O'Malley?
No. He's merely wearing the frames . . . A precaution against any possible invitations to fisticuffs at the Elves, Leprechauns, Gnomes and Little Men's Chowder & Marching Society . . . But he'll have new lenses soon.
I hope so, O'Malley.
3·12
I've borrowed your father's briefcase to transport my unfinished life story. I want to show the manuscript around at the club to arouse interest in the dinner at which I shall read several exciting and inspirational excerpts . . . There'll be a rush for tickets and the tidy profit from the affair will more than pay for repairing Gus's glasses . . . So he can continue writing my book.
What affair, Mr. O'Malley?
Biggest event of the social season, m'boy!
. . . The First Annual Jackeen J. O'Malley Testimonial Dinner!
CROCKETT JOHNSON

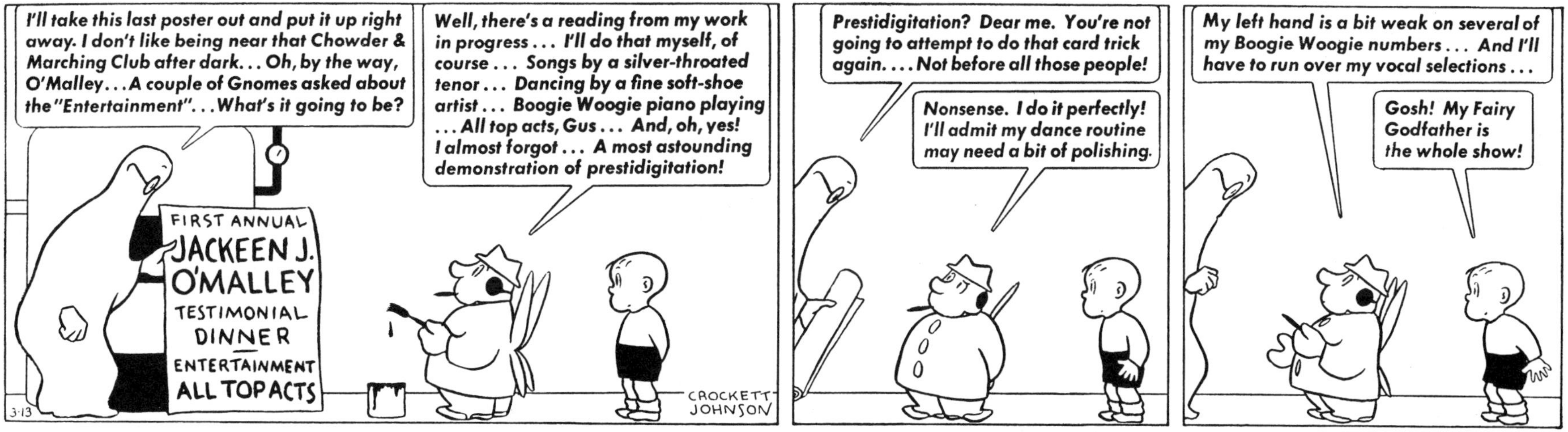
I'll take this last poster out and put it up right away. I don't like being near that Chowder & Marching Club after dark. . . Oh, by the way, O'Malley. . . A couple of Gnomes asked about the "Entertainment". . . What's it going to be?
FIRST ANNUAL
JACKEEN J. O'MALLEY
TESTIMONIAL
DINNER
ENTERTAINMENT
ALL TOP ACTS
3·13
Well, there's a reading from my work in progress . . . I'll do that myself, of course . . . Songs by a silver-throated tenor . . . Dancing by a fine soft-shoe artist . . . Boogie Woogie piano playing . . . All top acts, Gus . . . And, oh, yes! I almost forgot . . . A most astounding demonstration of prestidigitation!
CROCKETT JOHNSON
Prestidigitation? Dear me. You're not going to attempt to do that card trick again. . . . Not before all those people!
Nonsense. I do it perfectly! I'll admit my dance routine may need a bit of polishing.
My left hand is a bit weak on several of my Boogie Woogie numbers . . . And I'll have to run over my vocal selections . . .
Gosh! My Fairy Godfather is the whole show!

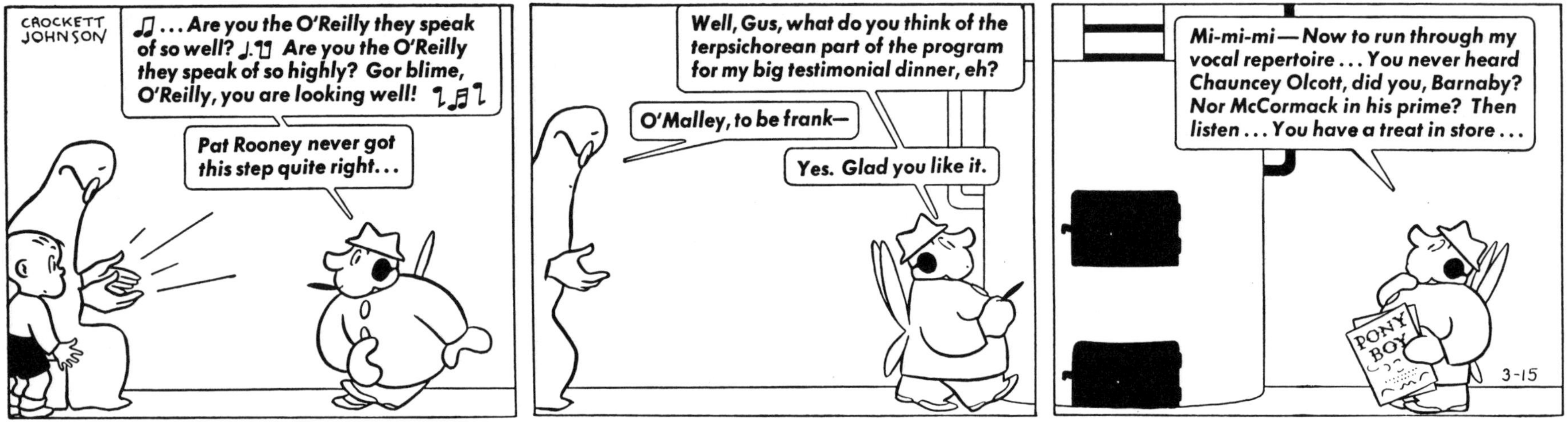
CROCKETT JOHNSON
♫ . . . Are you the O'Reilly they speak of so well? ♩.♪ Are you the O'Reilly they speak of so highly? Gor blime, O'Reilly, you are looking well! ♪♫♪
Pat Rooney never got this step quite right . . .
Well, Gus, what do you think of the terpsichorean part of the program for my big testimonial dinner, eh?
O'Malley, to be frank—
Yes. Glad you like it.
Mi-mi-mi—Now to run through my vocal repertoire . . . You never heard Chauncey Olcott, did you, Barnaby? Nor McCormack in his prime? Then listen . . . You have a treat in store . . .
PONY BOY
3-15

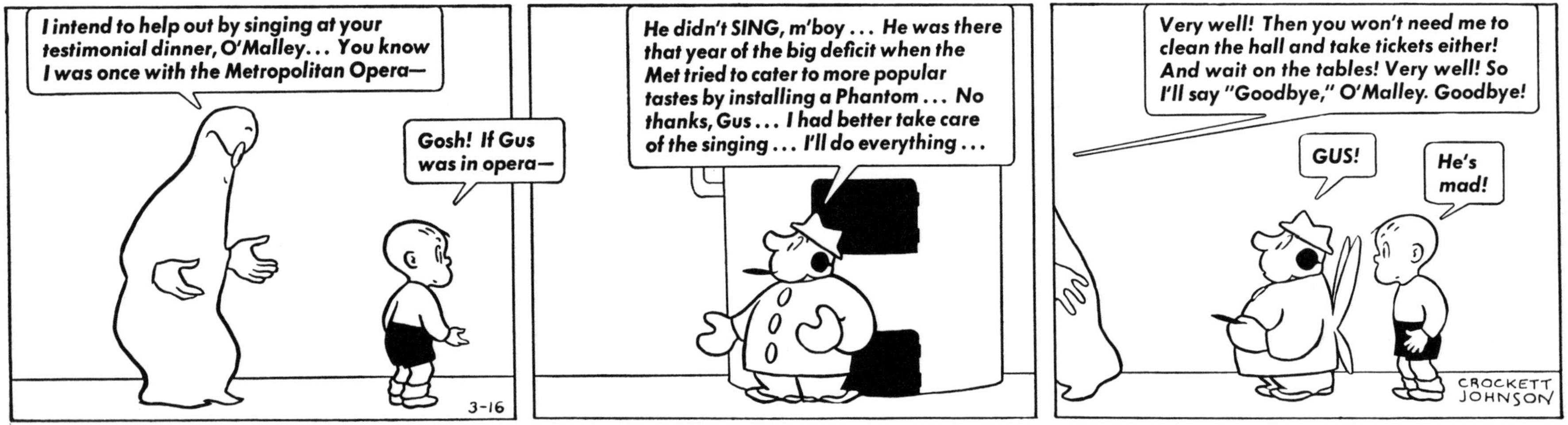
I intend to help out by singing at your testimonial dinner, O'Malley . . . You know I was once with the Metropolitan Opera—
Gosh! If Gus was in opera—
3-16
He didn't SING, m'boy . . . He was there that year of the big deficit when the Met tried to cater to more popular tastes by installing a Phantom . . . No thanks, Gus . . . I had better take care of the singing . . . I'll do everything . . .
Very well! Then you won't need me to clean the hall and take tickets either! And wait on the tables! Very well! So I'll say "Goodbye," O'Malley. Goodbye!
GUS!
He's mad!
CROCKETT JOHNSON

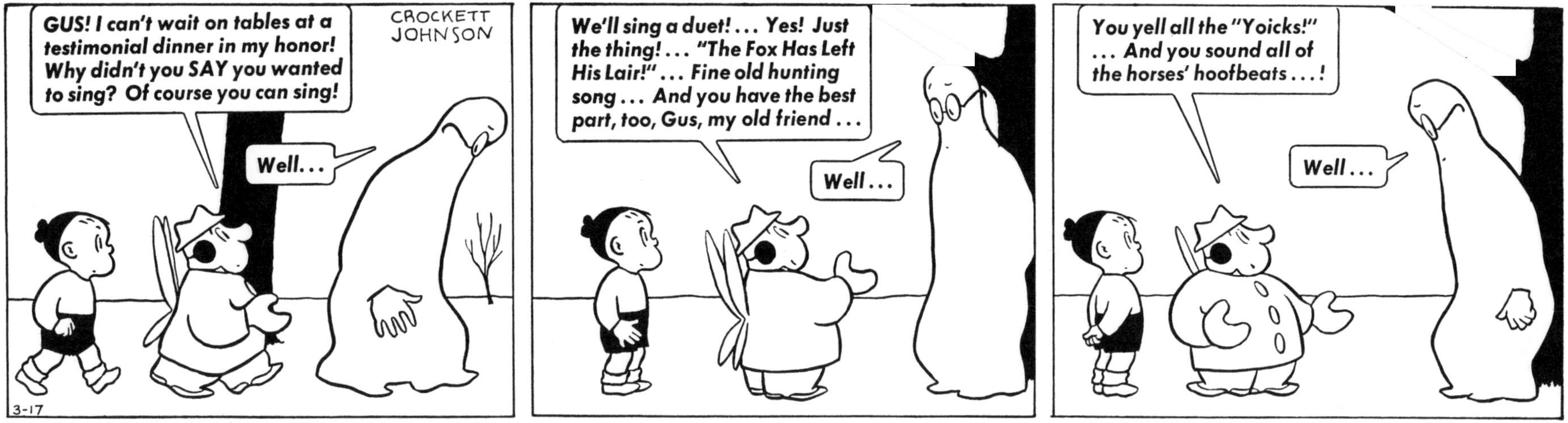
CROCKETT JOHNSON
GUS! I can't wait on tables at a testimonial dinner in my honor! Why didn't you SAY you wanted to sing? Of course you can sing!
Well...
3-17
We'll sing a duet! ... Yes! Just the thing! ... "The Fox Has Left His Lair!" ... Fine old hunting song ... And you have the best part, too, Gus, my old friend ...
Well ...
You yell all the "Yoicks!" ... And you sound all of the horses' hoofbeats ...!
Well ...

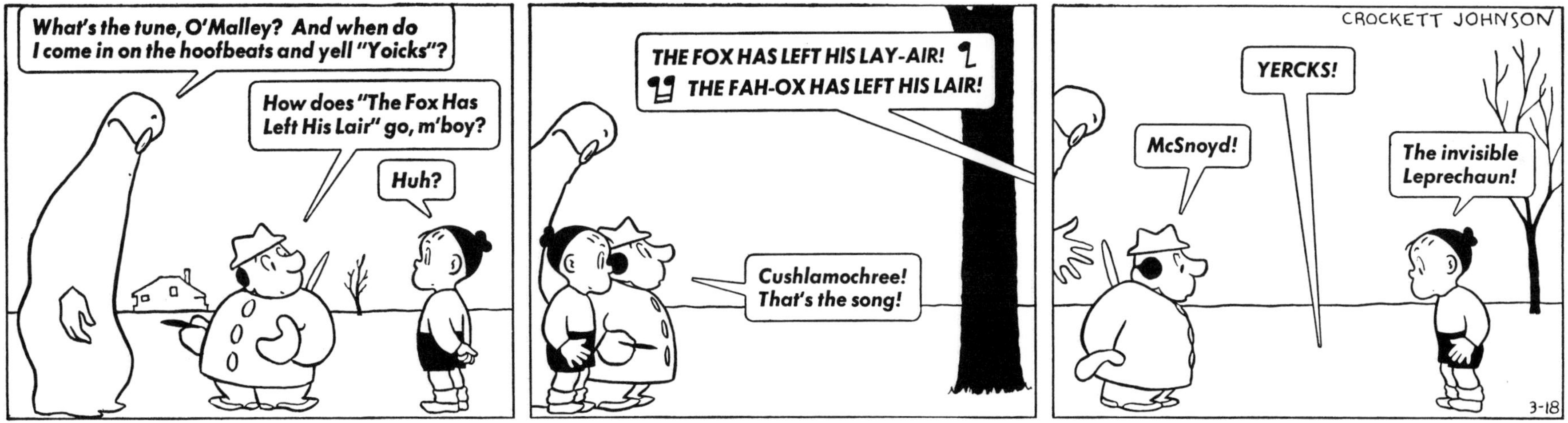
What's the tune, O'Malley? And when do I come in on the hoofbeats and yell "Yoicks"?
How does "The Fox Has Left His Lair" go, m'boy?
Huh?
THE FOX HAS LEFT HIS LAY-AIR!
THE FAH-OX HAS LEFT HIS LAIR!
Cushlamochree! That's the song!
CROCKETT JOHNSON
YERCKS!
McSnoyd!
The invisible Leprechaun!
3-18

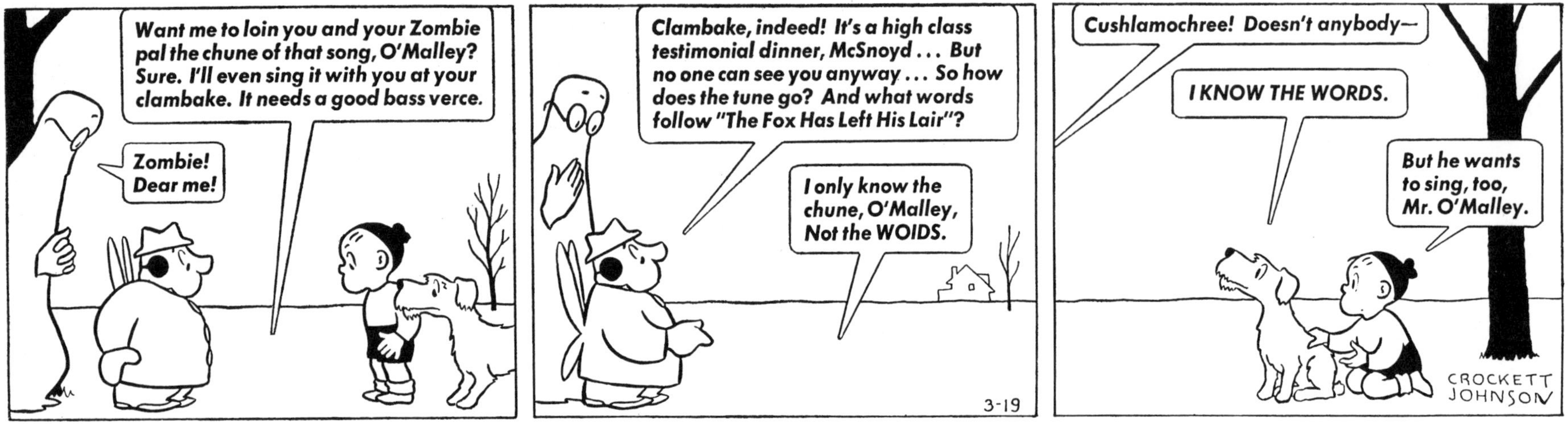
Want me to loin you and your Zombie pal the chune of that song, O'Malley? Sure. I'll even sing it with you at your clambake. It needs a good bass verce.
Zombie! Dear me!
Clambake, indeed! It's a high class testimonial dinner, McSnoyd . . . But no one can see you anyway . . . So how does the tune go? And what words follow "The Fox Has Left His Lair"?
I only know the chune, O'Malley, Not the WOIDS.
3-19
Cushlamochree! Doesn't anybody—
I KNOW THE WORDS.
But he wants to sing, too, Mr. O'Malley.
CROCKETT JOHNSON

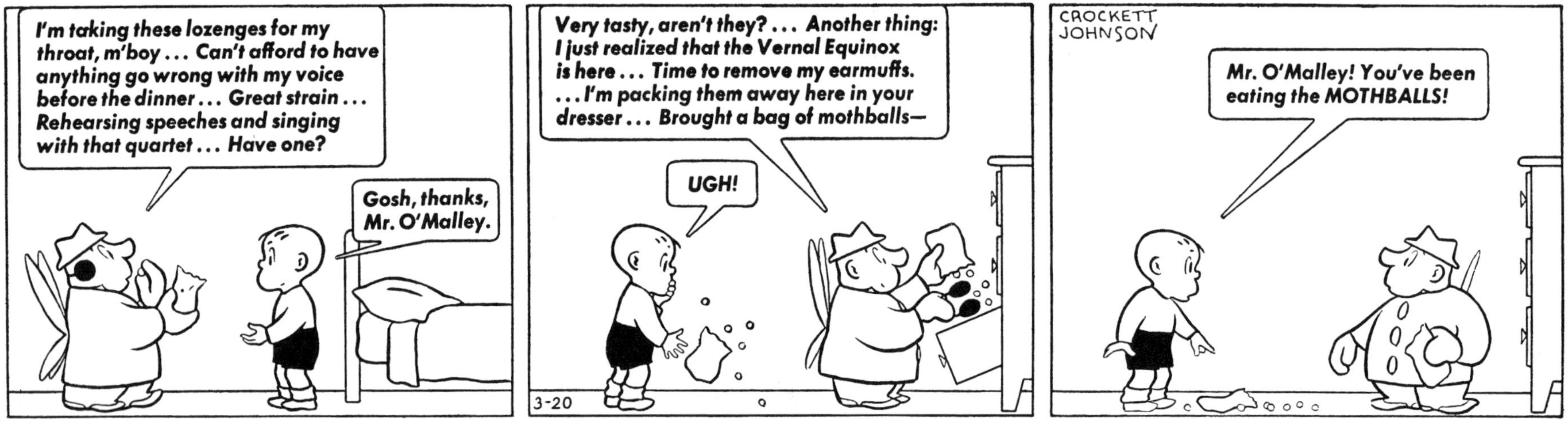
I'm taking these lozenges for my throat, m'boy . . . Can't afford to have anything go wrong with my voice before the dinner . . . Great strain . . . Rehearsing speeches and singing with that quartet . . . Have one?
Gosh, thanks, Mr. O'Malley.
Very tasty, aren't they? . . . Another thing: I just realized that the Vernal Equinox is here . . . Time to remove my earmuffs. . . . I'm packing them away here in your dresser . . . Brought a bag of mothballs—
UGH!
3-20
CROCKETT JOHNSON
Mr. O'Malley! You've been eating the MOTHBALLS!

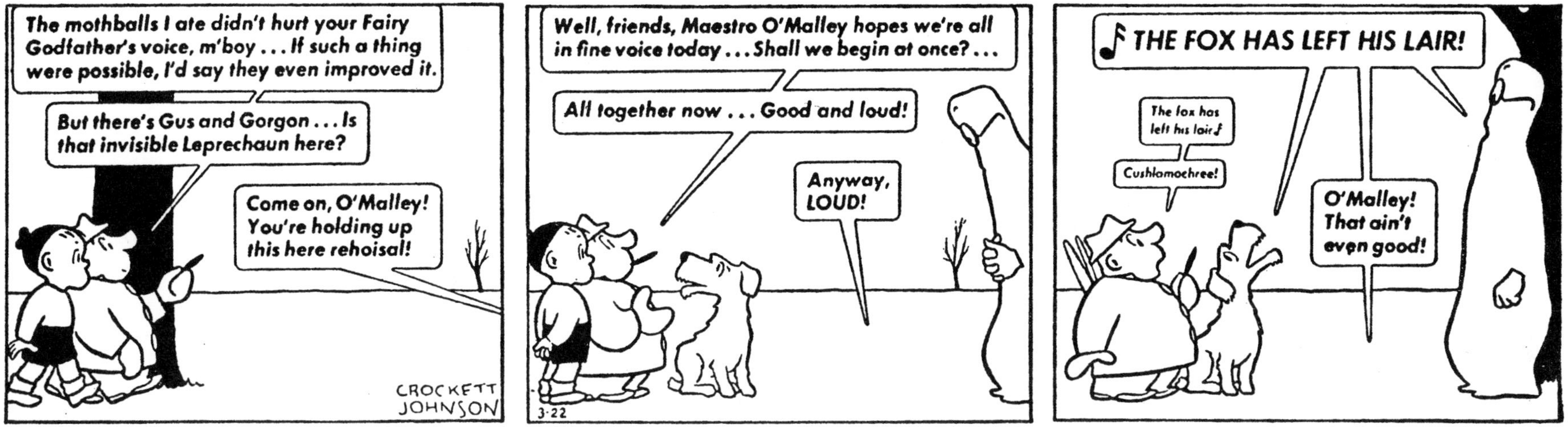

The mothballs I ate didn't hurt your Fairy Godfather's voice, m'boy . . . If such a thing were possible, I'd say they even improved it.
But there's Gus and Gorgon . . . Is that invisible Leprechaun here?
Come on, O'Malley! You're holding up this here rehoisal!
CROCKETT JOHNSON
Well, friends, Maestro O'Malley hopes we're all in fine voice today . . . Shall we begin at once? . . .
All together now . . . Good and loud!
Anyway, LOUD!
3·22
THE FOX HAS LEFT HIS LAIR!
The fox has left his lair
Cushlamochree!
O'Malley! That ain't even good!

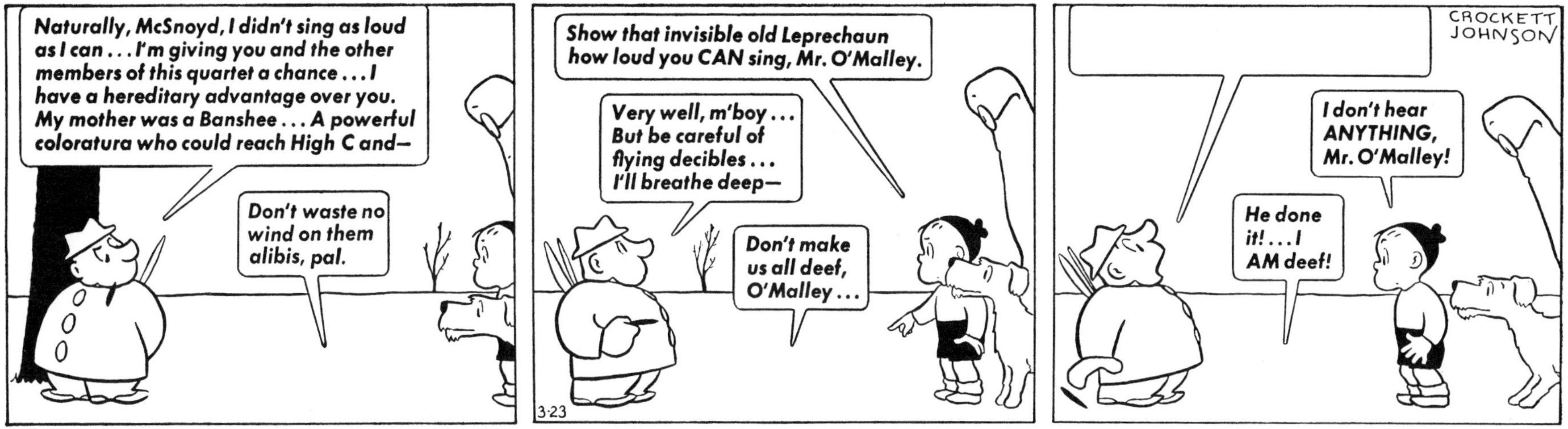

Naturally, McSnoyd, I didn't sing as loud as I can . . . I'm giving you and the other members of this quartet a chance . . . I have a hereditary advantage over you. My mother was a Banshee . . . A powerful coloratura who could reach High C and—
Don't waste no wind on them alibis, pal.
Show that invisible old Leprechaun how loud you CAN sing, Mr. O'Malley.
Very well, m'boy . . . But be careful of flying decibles . . . I'll breathe deep—
Don't make us all deef, O'Malley . . .
3·23
CROCKETT JOHNSON
I don't hear ANYTHING, Mr. O'Malley!
He done it! . . . I AM deef!

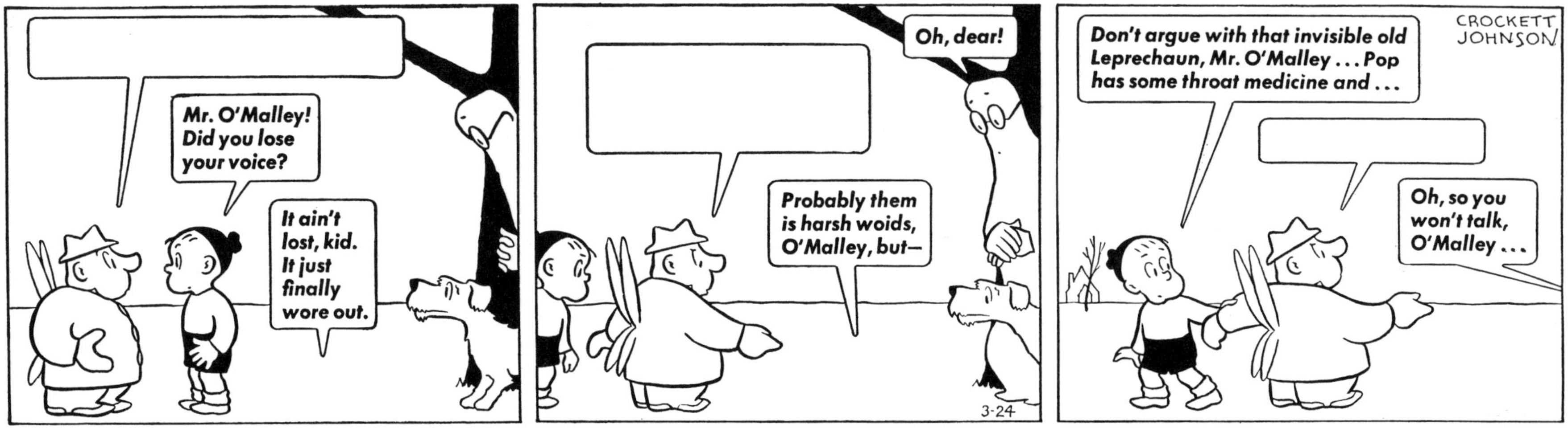
Mr. O'Malley! Did you lose your voice?
It ain't lost, kid. It just finally wore out.
Oh, dear!
Probably them is harsh woids, O'Malley, but—
3-24
CROCKETT JOHNSON
Don't argue with that invisible old Leprechaun, Mr. O'Malley . . . Pop has some throat medicine and . . .
Oh, so you won't talk, O'Malley . . .

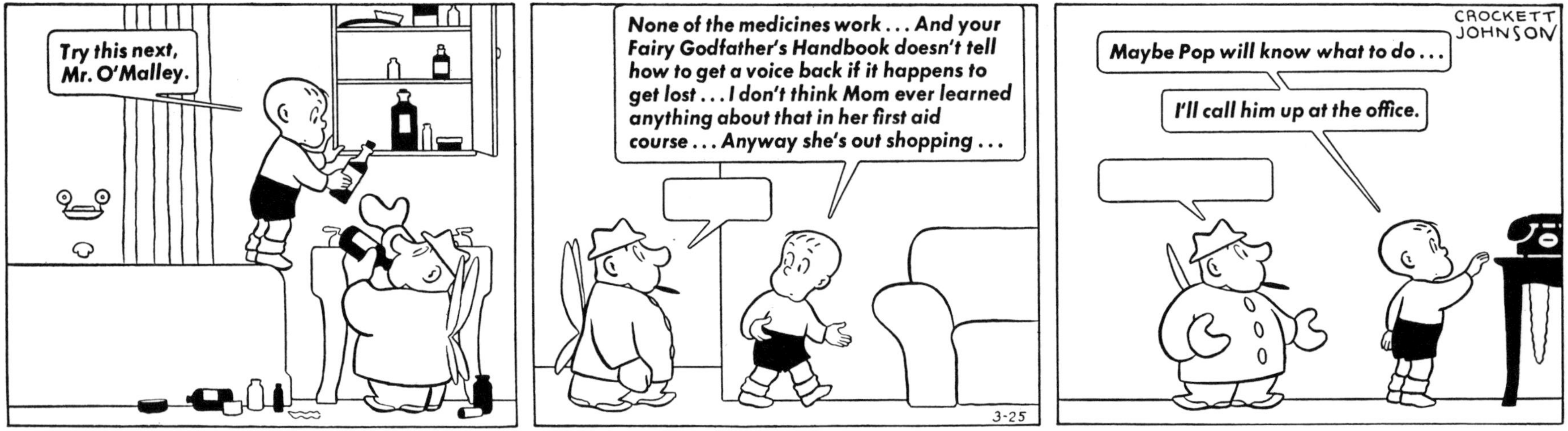
Try this next, Mr. O'Malley.
None of the medicines work . . . And your Fairy Godfather's Handbook doesn't tell how to get a voice back if it happens to get lost . . . I don't think Mom ever learned anything about that in her first aid course . . . Anyway she's out shopping . . .
3-25
CROCKETT JOHNSON
Maybe Pop will know what to do . . .
I'll call him up at the office.

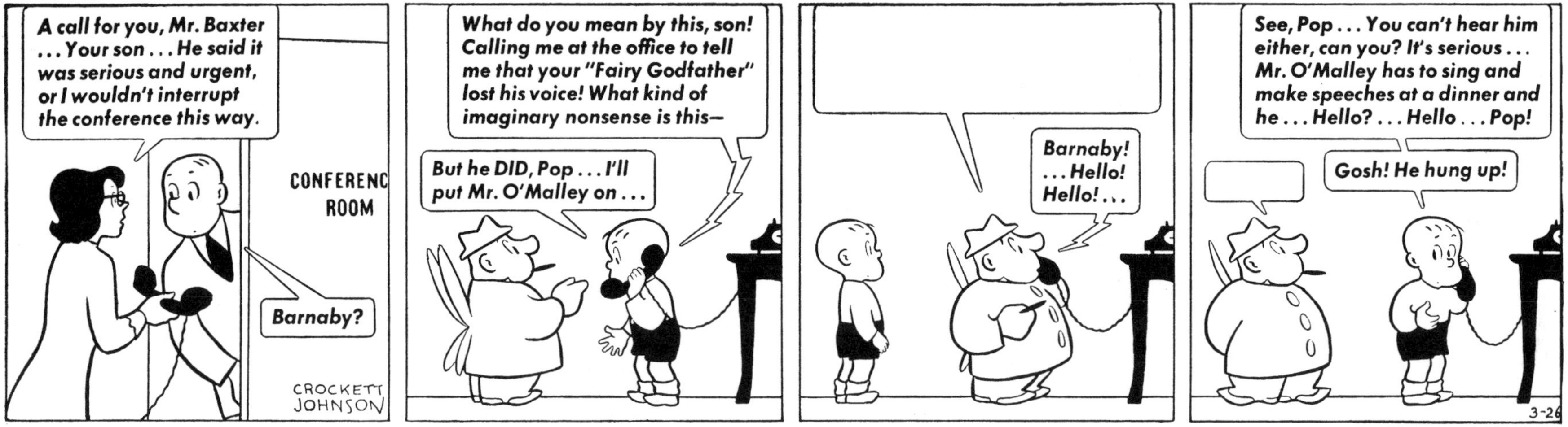
A call for you, Mr. Baxter . . . Your son . . . He said it was serious and urgent, or I wouldn't interrupt the conference this way.
CONFERENC ROOM
Barnaby?
CROCKETT JOHNSON
What do you mean by this, son! Calling me at the office to tell me that your "Fairy Godfather" lost his voice! What kind of imaginary nonsense is this—
But he DID, Pop . . . I'll put Mr. O'Malley on . . .
Barnaby! . . . Hello! Hello! . . .
See, Pop . . . You can't hear him either, can you? It's serious . . . Mr. O'Malley has to sing and make speeches at a dinner and he . . . Hello? . . . Hello . . . Pop!
Gosh! He hung up!
3-26

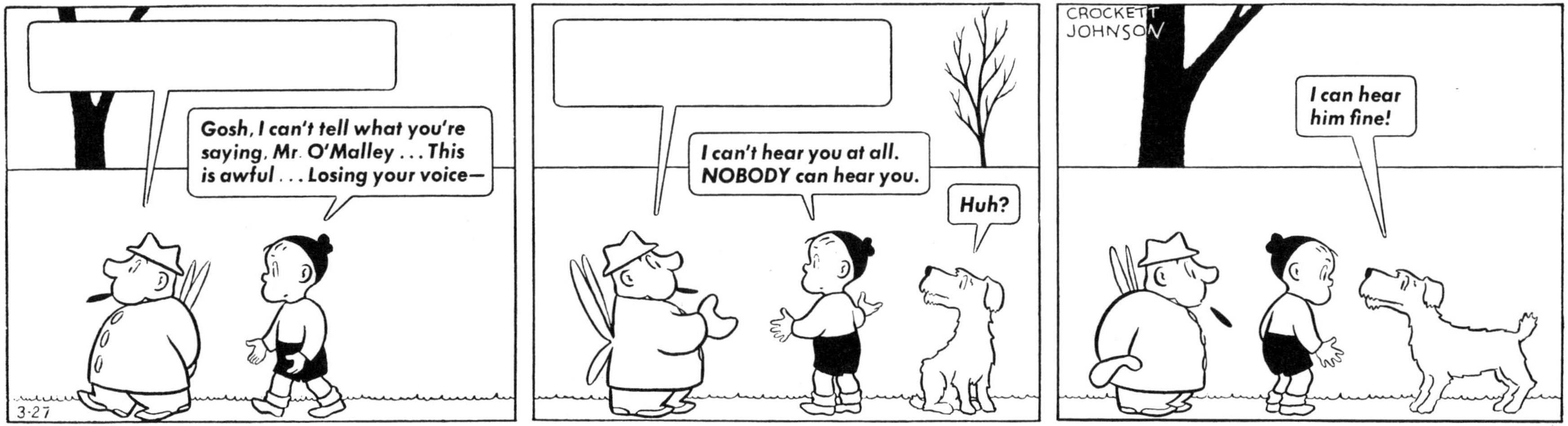
Gosh, I can't tell what you're saying, Mr. O'Malley . . . This is awful . . . Losing your voice—
3-27
I can't hear you at all. NOBODY can hear you.
Huh?
CROCKETT JOHNSON
I can hear him fine!

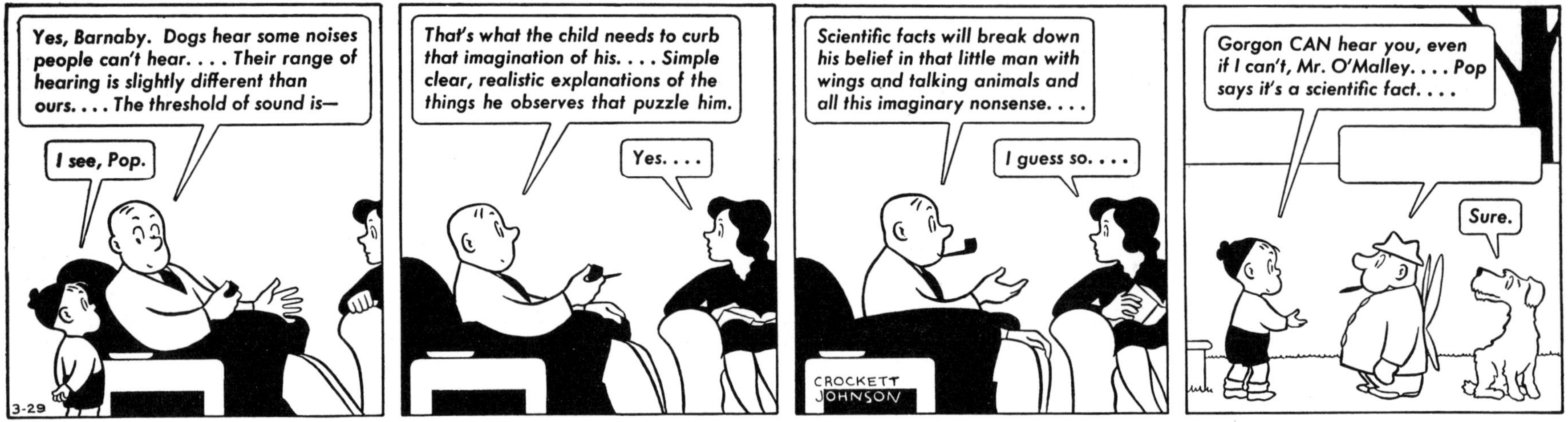
Yes, Barnaby. Dogs hear some noises people can't hear. . . . Their range of hearing is slightly different than ours. . . . The threshold of sound is—
I see, Pop.
3-29
That's what the child needs to curb that imagination of his. . . . Simple clear, realistic explanations of the things he observes that puzzle him.
Yes. . . .
Scientific facts will break down his belief in that little man with wings and talking animals and all this imaginary nonsense. . . .
I guess so. . . .
CROCKETT JOHNSON
Gorgon CAN hear you, even if I can't, Mr. O'Malley. . . . Pop says it's a scientific fact. . . .
Sure.

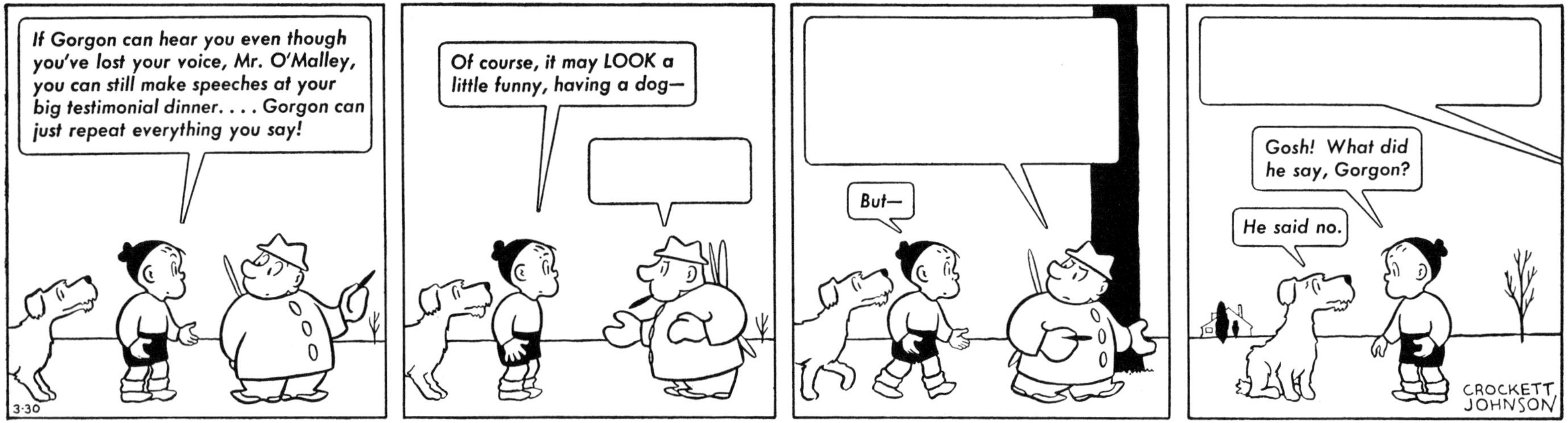
If Gorgon can hear you even though you've lost your voice, Mr. O'Malley, you can still make speeches at your big testimonial dinner. . . . Gorgon can just repeat everything you say!
3-30
Of course, it may LOOK a little funny, having a dog—
But—
Gosh! What did he say, Gorgon?
He said no.
CROCKETT JOHNSON

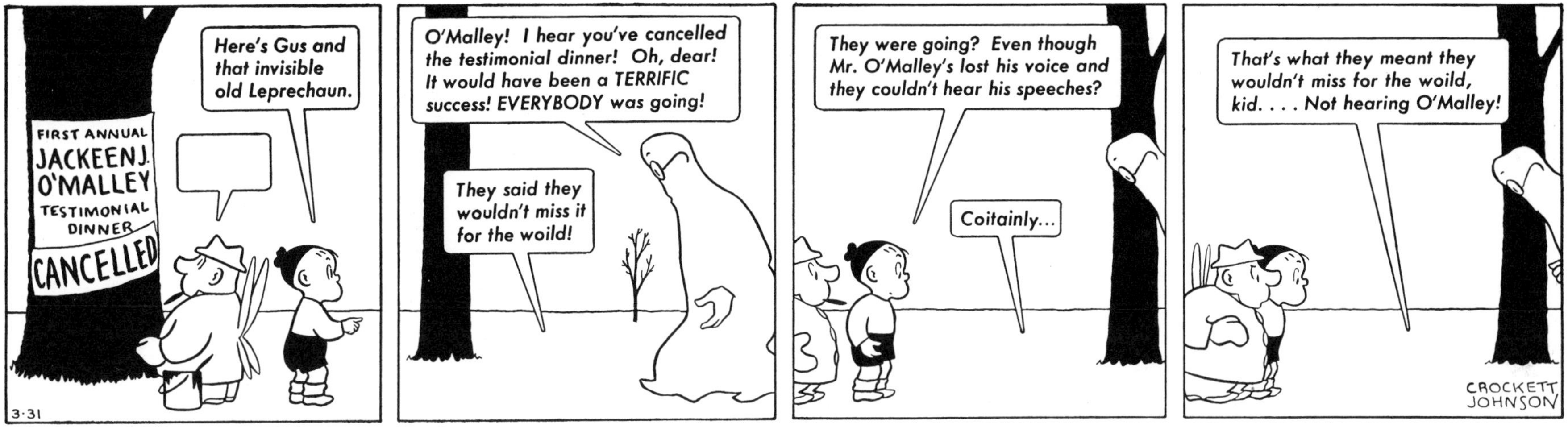
Here's Gus and that invisible old Leprechaun.
FIRST ANNUAL JACKEEN J. O'MALLEY TESTIMONIAL DINNER
CANCELLED
3-31
O'Malley! I hear you've cancelled the testimonial dinner! Oh, dear! It would have been a TERRIFIC success! EVERYBODY was going!
They said they wouldn't miss it for the woild!
They were going? Even though Mr. O'Malley's lost his voice and they couldn't hear his speeches?
Coitainly...
That's what they meant they wouldn't miss for the woild, kid. . . . Not hearing O'Malley!
CROCKETT JOHNSON

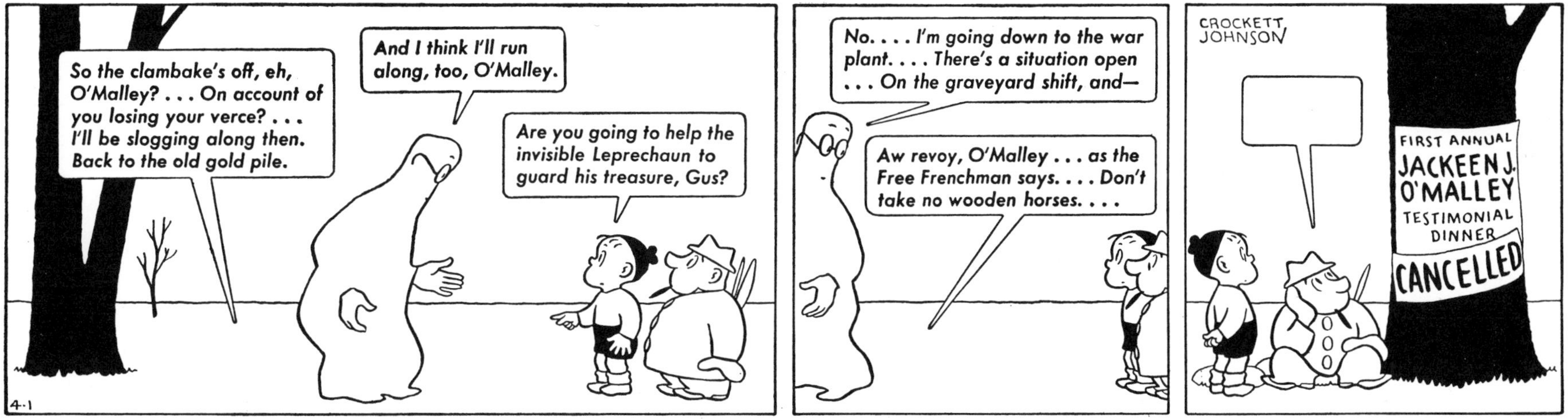
So the clambake's off, eh, O'Malley? . . . On account of you losing your verce? . . . I'll be slogging along then. Back to the old gold pile.
And I think I'll run along, too, O'Malley.
Are you going to help the invisible Leprechaun to guard his treasure, Gus?
4-1
No. . . . I'm going down to the war plant. . . . There's a situation open . . . On the graveyard shift, and—
Aw revoy, O'Malley . . . as the Free Frenchman says. . . . Don't take no wooden horses. . . .
CROCKETT JOHNSON
FIRST ANNUAL JACKEEN J. O'MALLEY TESTIMONIAL DINNER
CANCELLED

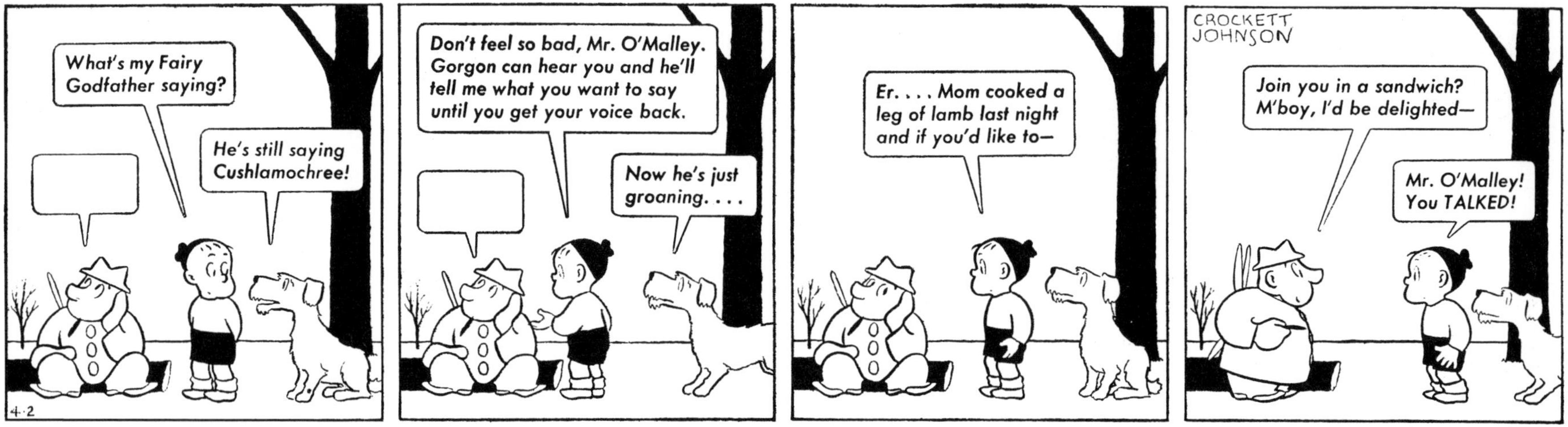
What's my Fairy Godfather saying?
He's still saying Cushlamochree!
4·2
Don't feel so bad, Mr. O'Malley. Gorgon can hear you and he'll tell me what you want to say until you get your voice back.
Now he's just groaning. . . .
Er. . . . Mom cooked a leg of lamb last night and if you'd like to—
CROCKETT JOHNSON
Join you in a sandwich? M'boy, I'd be delighted—
Mr. O'Malley! You TALKED!

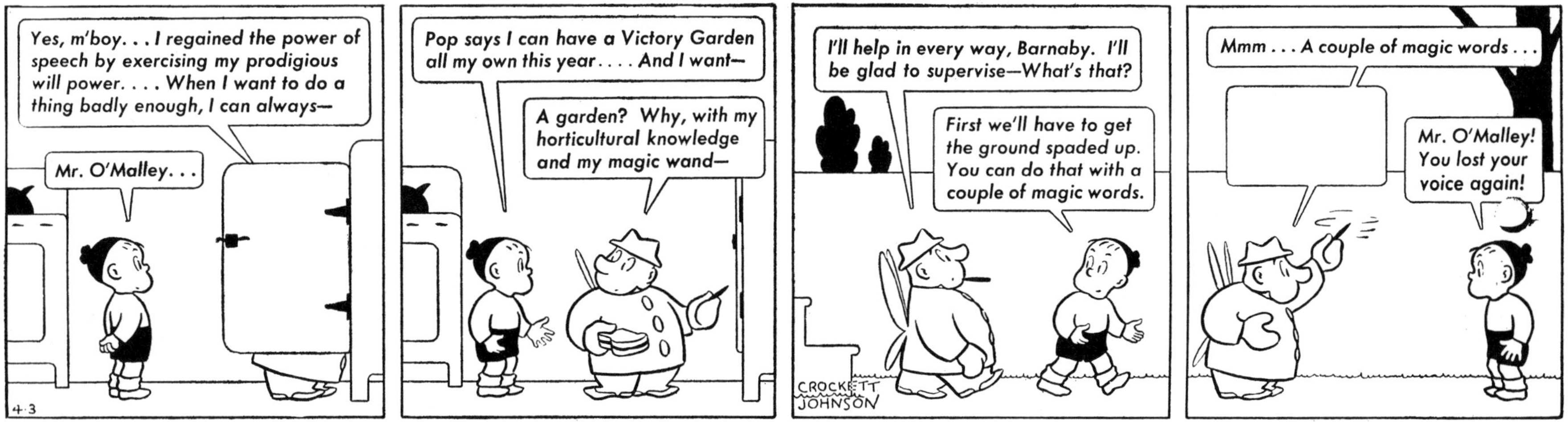
Yes, m'boy. . . I regained the power of speech by exercising my prodigious will power. . . . When I want to do a thing badly enough, I can always—
Mr. O'Malley. . .
4·3
Pop says I can have a Victory Garden all my own this year. . . . And I want—
A garden? Why, with my horticultural knowledge and my magic wand—
I'll help in every way, Barnaby. I'll be glad to supervise—What's that?
First we'll have to get the ground spaded up. You can do that with a couple of magic words.
CROCKETT JOHNSON
Mmm . . . A couple of magic words . . .
Mr. O'Malley! You lost your voice again!

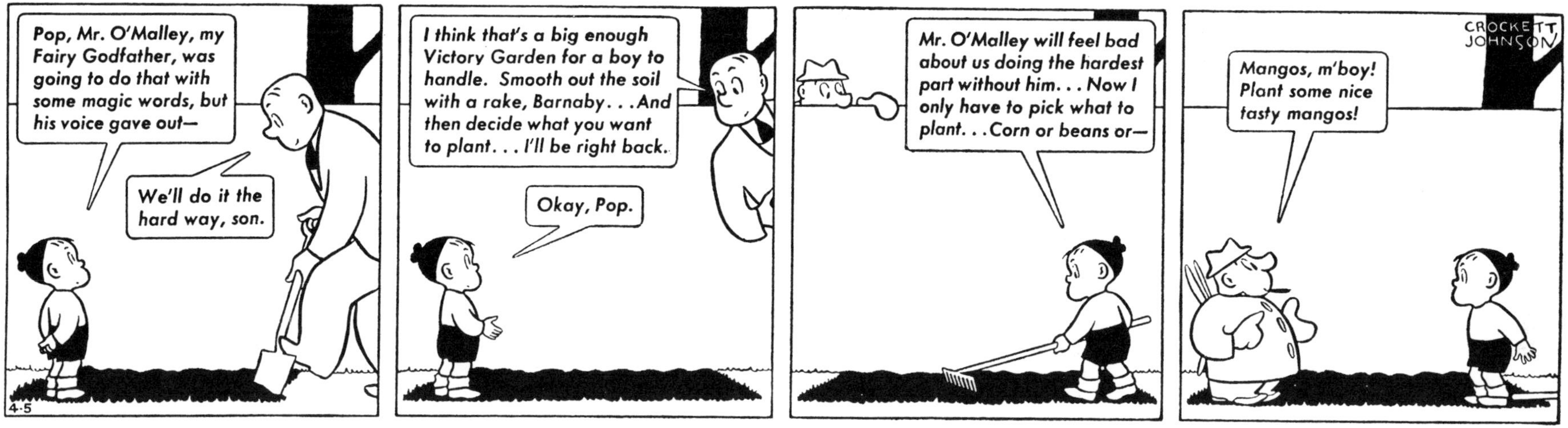
Pop, Mr. O'Malley, my Fairy Godfather, was going to do that with some magic words, but his voice gave out—
We'll do it the hard way, son.
4·5
I think that's a big enough Victory Garden for a boy to handle. Smooth out the soil with a rake, Barnaby. . . And then decide what you want to plant. . . I'll be right back.
Okay, Pop.
Mr. O'Malley will feel bad about us doing the hardest part without him. . . Now I only have to pick what to plant. . . Corn or beans or—
CROCKETT JOHNSON
Mangos, m'boy! Plant some nice tasty mangos!

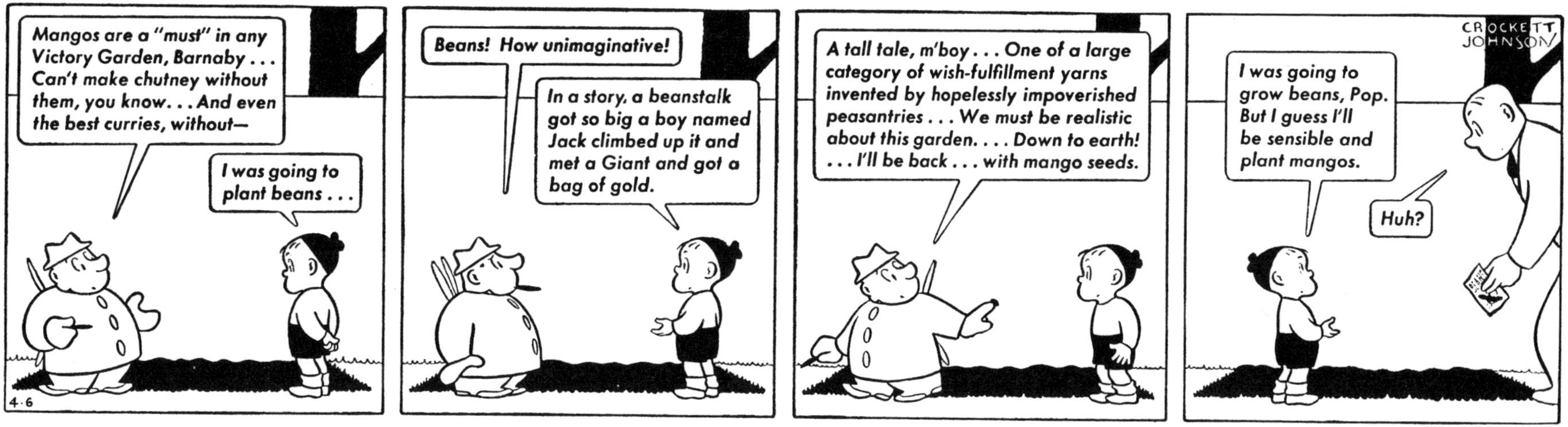
Mangos are a "must" in any Victory Garden, Barnaby . . . Can't make chutney without them, you know. . . And even the best curries, without—
I was going to plant beans . . .
4·6
Beans! How unimaginative!
In a story, a beanstalk got so big a boy named Jack climbed up it and met a Giant and got a bag of gold.
A tall tale, m'boy . . . One of a large category of wish-fulfillment yarns invented by hopelessly impoverished peasantries . . . We must be realistic about this garden. . . . Down to earth! . . . I'll be back . . . with mango seeds.
CROCKETT JOHNSON
I was going to grow beans, Pop. But I guess I'll be sensible and plant mangos.
Huh?

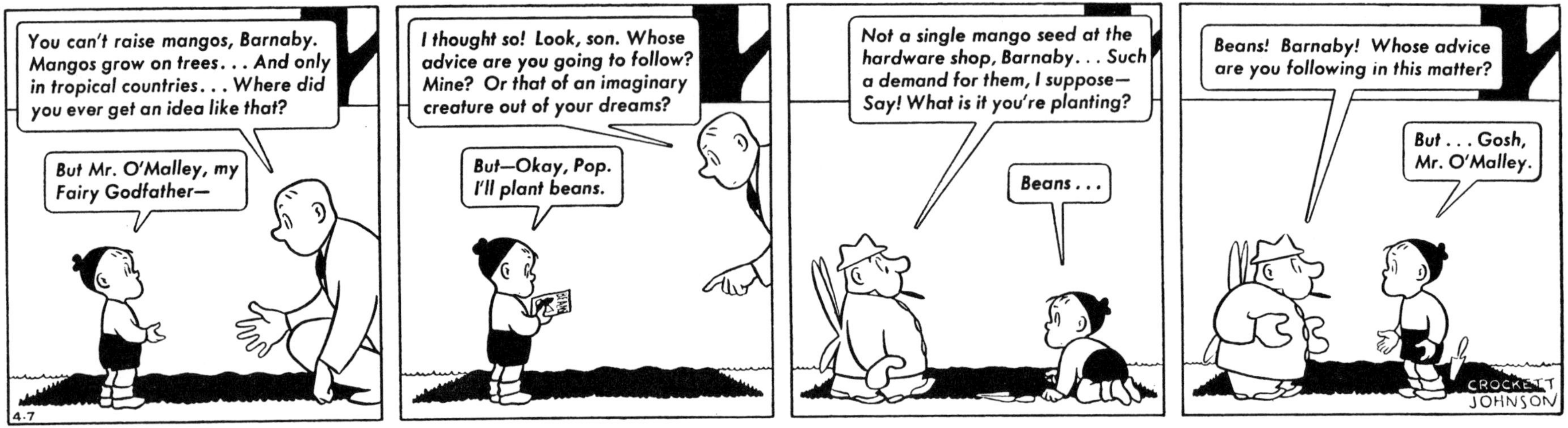

You can't raise mangos, Barnaby. Mangos grow on trees. . . And only in tropical countries. . . Where did you ever get an idea like that?
But Mr. O'Malley, my Fairy Godfather—
I thought so! Look, son. Whose advice are you going to follow? Mine? Or that of an imaginary creature out of your dreams?
But—Okay, Pop. I'll plant beans.
Not a single mango seed at the hardware shop, Barnaby. . . Such a demand for them, I suppose— Say! What is it you're planting?
Beans . . .
Beans! Barnaby! Whose advice are you following in this matter?
But . . . Gosh, Mr. O'Malley.
CROCKETT JOHNSON
4-7

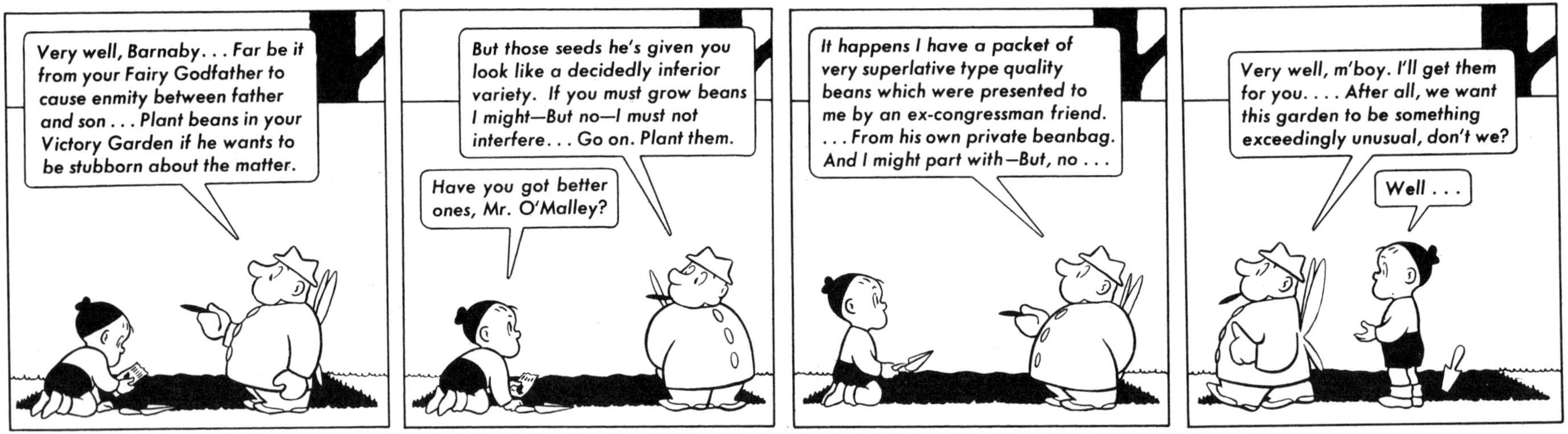

Very well, Barnaby. . . Far be it from your Fairy Godfather to cause enmity between father and son . . . Plant beans in your Victory Garden if he wants to be stubborn about the matter.
But those seeds he's given you look like a decidedly inferior variety. If you must grow beans I might—But no—I must not interfere. . . Go on. Plant them.
Have you got better ones, Mr. O'Malley?
It happens I have a packet of very superlative type quality beans which were presented to me by an ex-congressman friend. . . . From his own private beanbag. And I might part with—But, no . . .
Very well, m'boy. I'll get them for you. . . . After all, we want this garden to be something exceedingly unusual, don't we?
Well . . .

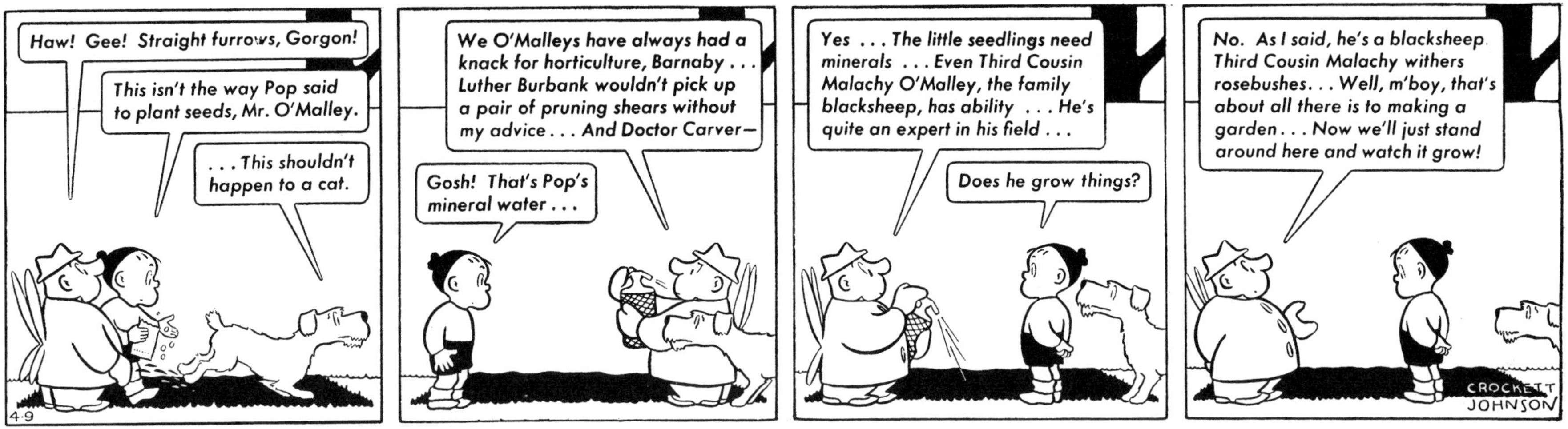
Haw! Gee! Straight furrows, Gorgon!
This isn't the way Pop said to plant seeds, Mr. O'Malley.
. . . This shouldn't happen to a cat.
4-9
We O'Malleys have always had a knack for horticulture, Barnaby . . . Luther Burbank wouldn't pick up a pair of pruning shears without my advice . . . And Doctor Carver—
Gosh! That's Pop's mineral water . . .
Yes . . . The little seedlings need minerals . . . Even Third Cousin Malachy O'Malley, the family blacksheep, has ability . . . He's quite an expert in his field . . .
Does he grow things?
No. As I said, he's a blacksheep. Third Cousin Malachy withers rosebushes. . . Well, m'boy, that's about all there is to making a garden . . . Now we'll just stand around here and watch it grow!
CROCKETT JOHNSON

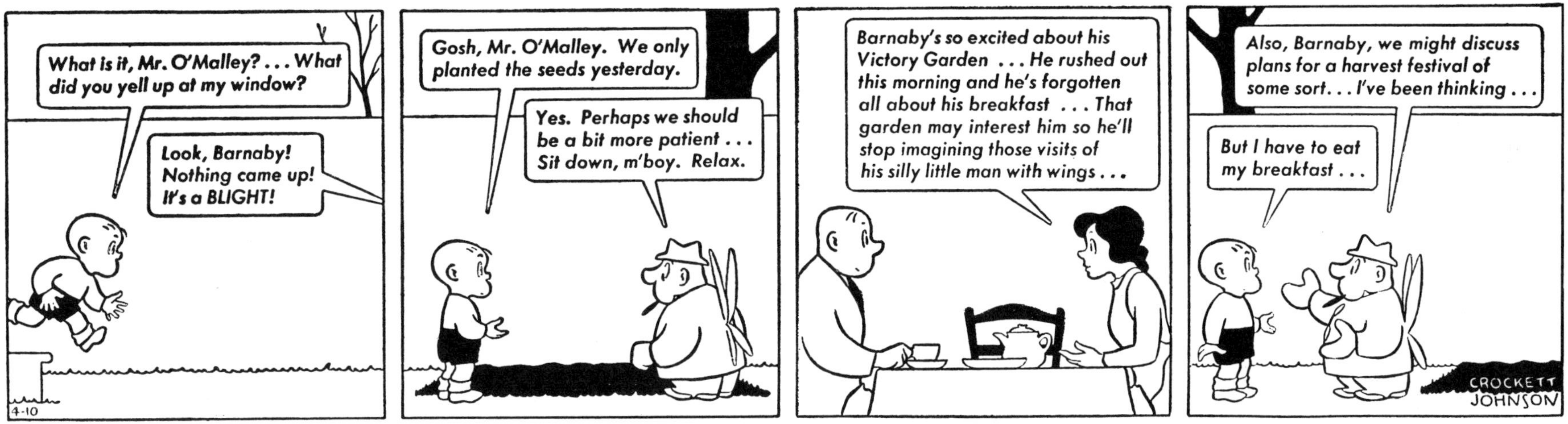
What is it, Mr. O'Malley? . . . What did you yell up at my window?
Look, Barnaby! Nothing came up! It's a BLIGHT!
4-10
Gosh, Mr. O'Malley. We only planted the seeds yesterday.
Yes. Perhaps we should be a bit more patient . . . Sit down, m'boy. Relax.
Barnaby's so excited about his Victory Garden . . . He rushed out this morning and he's forgotten all about his breakfast . . . That garden may interest him so he'll stop imagining those visits of his silly little man with wings . . .
Also, Barnaby, we might discuss plans for a harvest festival of some sort. . . I've been thinking . . .
But I have to eat my breakfast . . .
CROCKETT JOHNSON

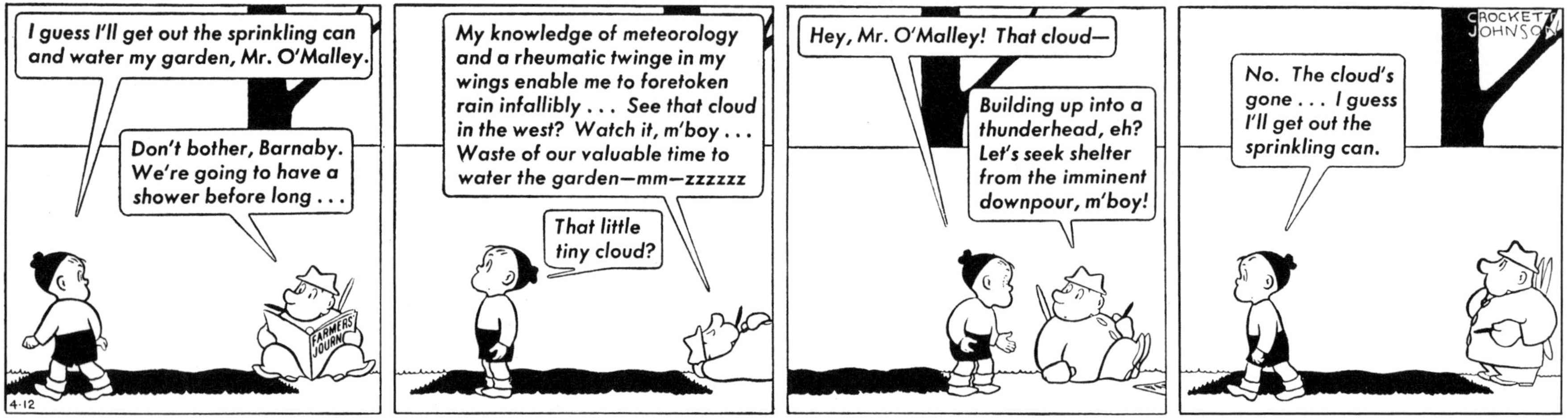
I guess I'll get out the sprinkling can and water my garden, Mr. O'Malley.
Don't bother, Barnaby. We're going to have a shower before long . . .
FARMERS' JOURN
4·12
My knowledge of meteorology and a rheumatic twinge in my wings enable me to foretoken rain infallibly . . . See that cloud in the west? Watch it, m'boy . . . Waste of our valuable time to water the garden—mm—zzzzzz
That little tiny cloud?
Hey, Mr. O'Malley! That cloud—
Building up into a thunderhead, eh? Let's seek shelter from the imminent downpour, m'boy!
CROCKETT JOHNSON
No. The cloud's gone . . . I guess I'll get out the sprinkling can.

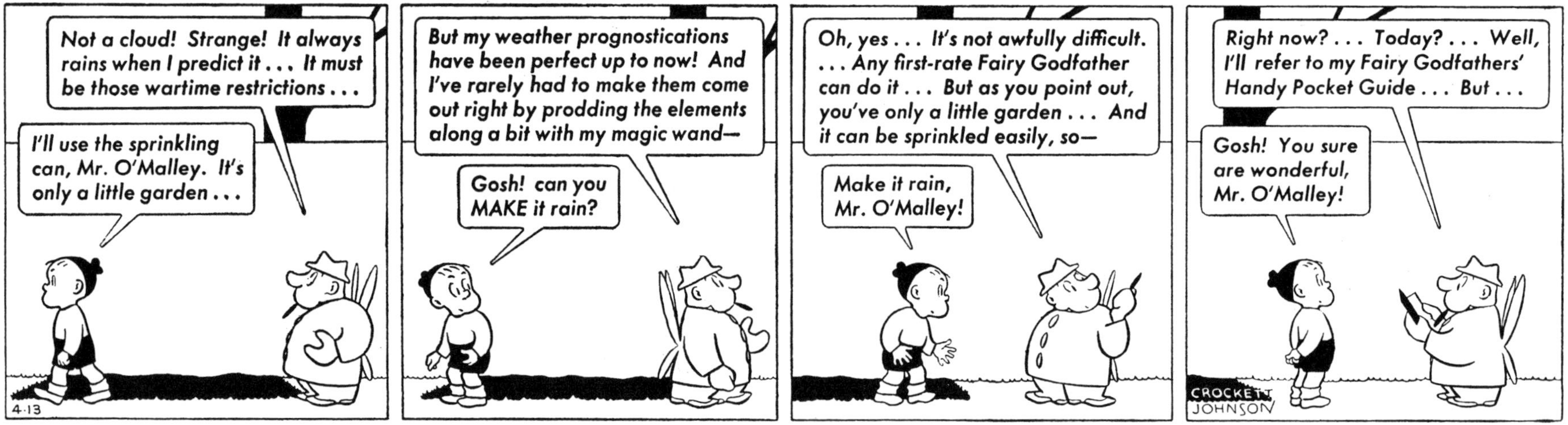
Not a cloud! Strange! It always rains when I predict it . . . It must be those wartime restrictions . . .
I'll use the sprinkling can, Mr. O'Malley. It's only a little garden . . .
4·13
But my weather prognostications have been perfect up to now! And I've rarely had to make them come out right by prodding the elements along a bit with my magic wand—
Gosh! can you MAKE it rain?
Oh, yes . . . It's not awfully difficult. . . . Any first-rate Fairy Godfather can do it . . . But as you point out, you've only a little garden . . . And it can be sprinkled easily, so—
Make it rain, Mr. O'Malley!
Right now? . . . Today? . . . Well, I'll refer to my Fairy Godfathers' Handy Pocket Guide . . . But . . .
Gosh! You sure are wonderful, Mr. O'Malley!
CROCKETT JOHNSON

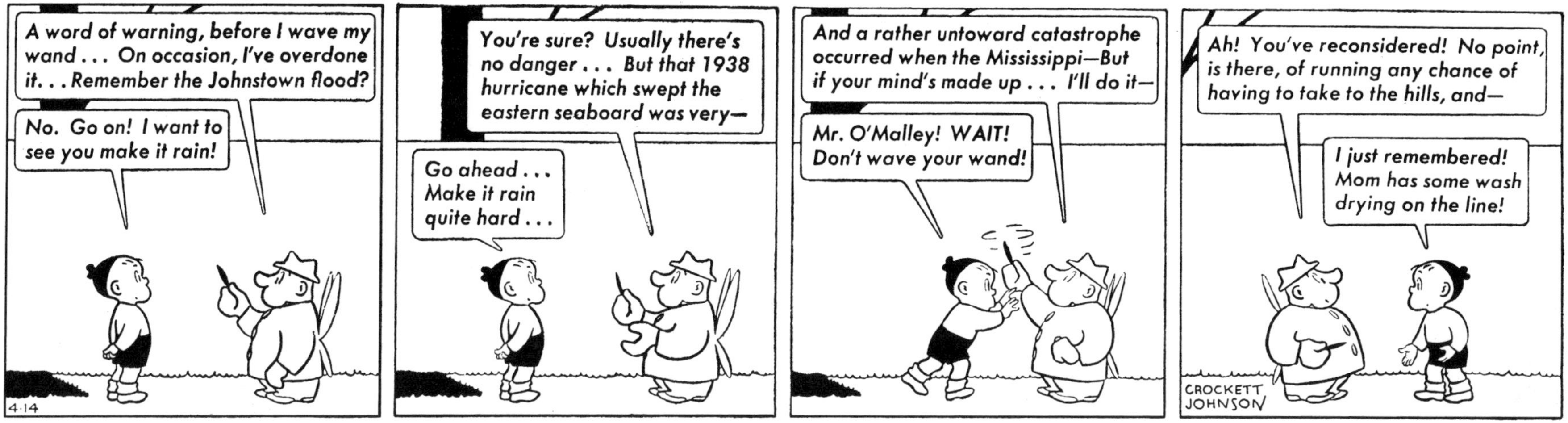
A word of warning, before I wave my wand . . . On occasion, I've overdone it. . . Remember the Johnstown flood?
No. Go on! I want to see you make it rain!
You're sure? Usually there's no danger . . . But that 1938 hurricane which swept the eastern seaboard was very—
Go ahead . . . Make it rain quite hard . . .
And a rather untoward catastrophe occurred when the Mississippi—But if your mind's made up . . . I'll do it—
Mr. O'Malley! WAIT! Don't wave your wand!
Ah! You've reconsidered! No point, is there, of running any chance of having to take to the hills, and—
I just remembered! Mom has some wash drying on the line!
4·14
CROCKETT JOHNSON

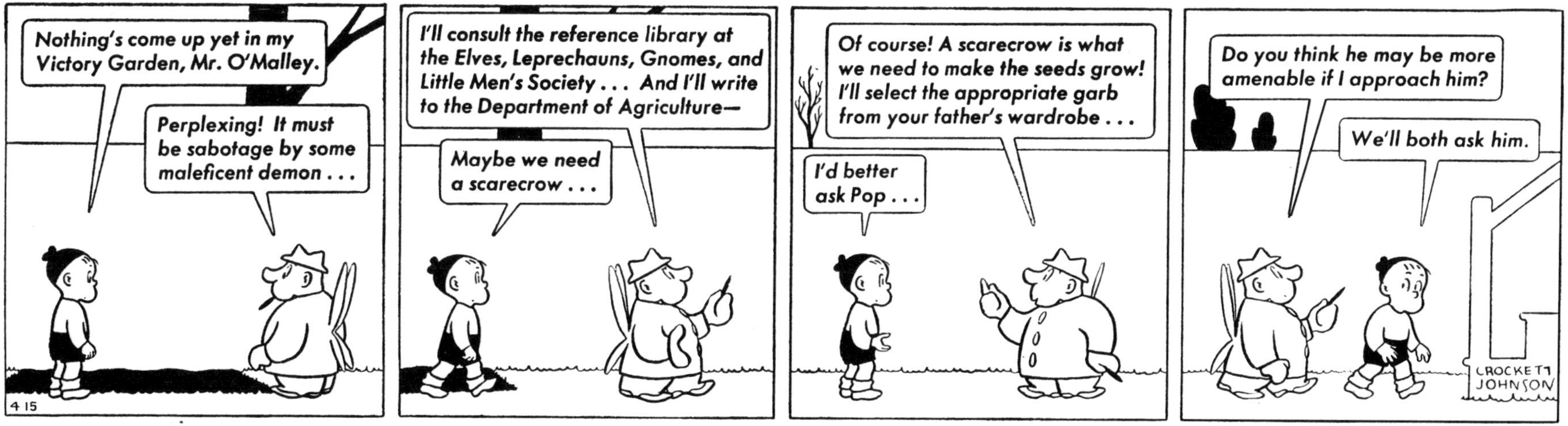
Nothing's come up yet in my Victory Garden, Mr. O'Malley.
Perplexing! It must be sabotage by some maleficent demon . . .
I'll consult the reference library at the Elves, Leprechauns, Gnomes, and Little Men's Society . . . And I'll write to the Department of Agriculture—
Maybe we need a scarecrow . . .
Of course! A scarecrow is what we need to make the seeds grow! I'll select the appropriate garb from your father's wardrobe . . .
I'd better ask Pop . . .
Do you think he may be more amenable if I approach him?
We'll both ask him.
4·15
CROCKETT JOHNSON

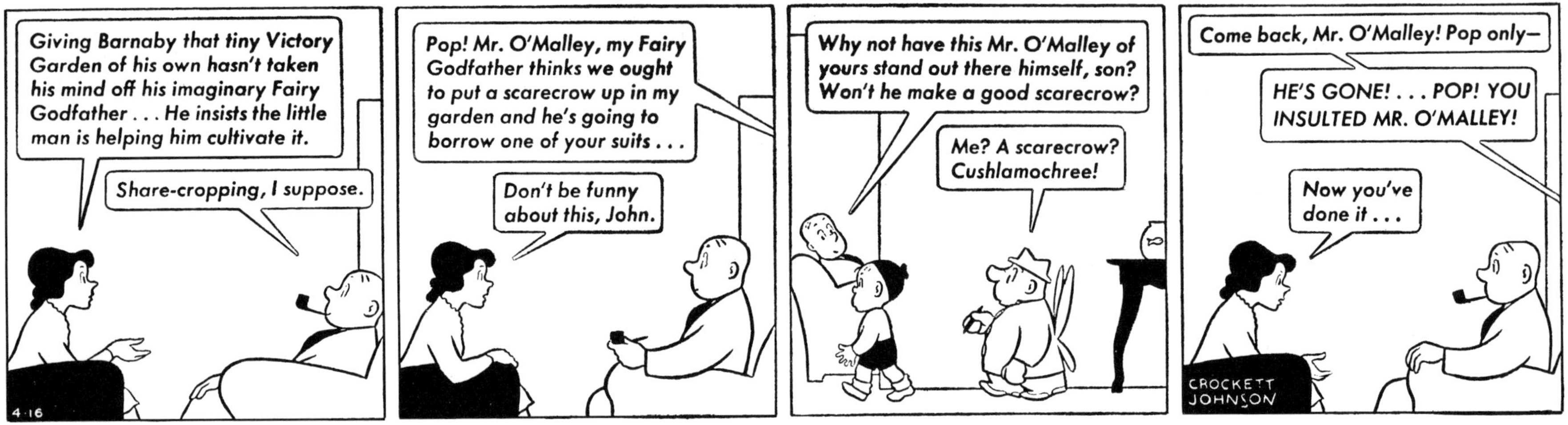
Giving Barnaby that tiny Victory Garden of his own hasn't taken his mind off his imaginary Fairy Godfather . . . He insists the little man is helping him cultivate it.
Share-cropping, I suppose.
4·16
Pop! Mr. O'Malley, my Fairy Godfather thinks we ought to put a scarecrow up in my garden and he's going to borrow one of your suits . . .
Don't be funny about this, John.
Why not have this Mr. O'Malley of yours stand out there himself, son? Won't he make a good scarecrow?
Me? A scarecrow? Cushlamochree!
Come back, Mr. O'Malley! Pop only—
HE'S GONE! . . . POP! YOU INSULTED MR. O'MALLEY!
Now you've done it . . .
CROCKETT JOHNSON

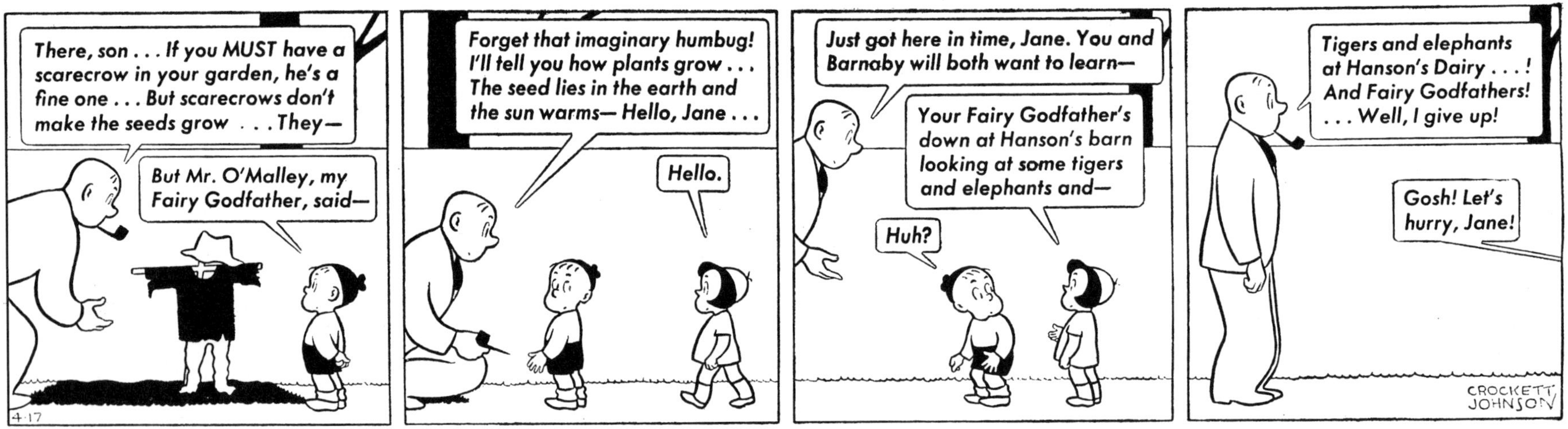
There, son . . . If you MUST have a scarecrow in your garden, he's a fine one . . . But scarecrows don't make the seeds grow . . . They—
But Mr. O'Malley, my Fairy Godfather, said—
4·17
Forget that imaginary humbug! I'll tell you how plants grow . . . The seed lies in the earth and the sun warms— Hello, Jane . . .
Hello.
Just got here in time, Jane. You and Barnaby will both want to learn—
Your Fairy Godfather's down at Hanson's barn looking at some tigers and elephants and—
Huh?
Tigers and elephants at Hanson's Dairy . . . ! And Fairy Godfathers! . . . Well, I give up!
Gosh! Let's hurry, Jane!
CROCKETT JOHNSON

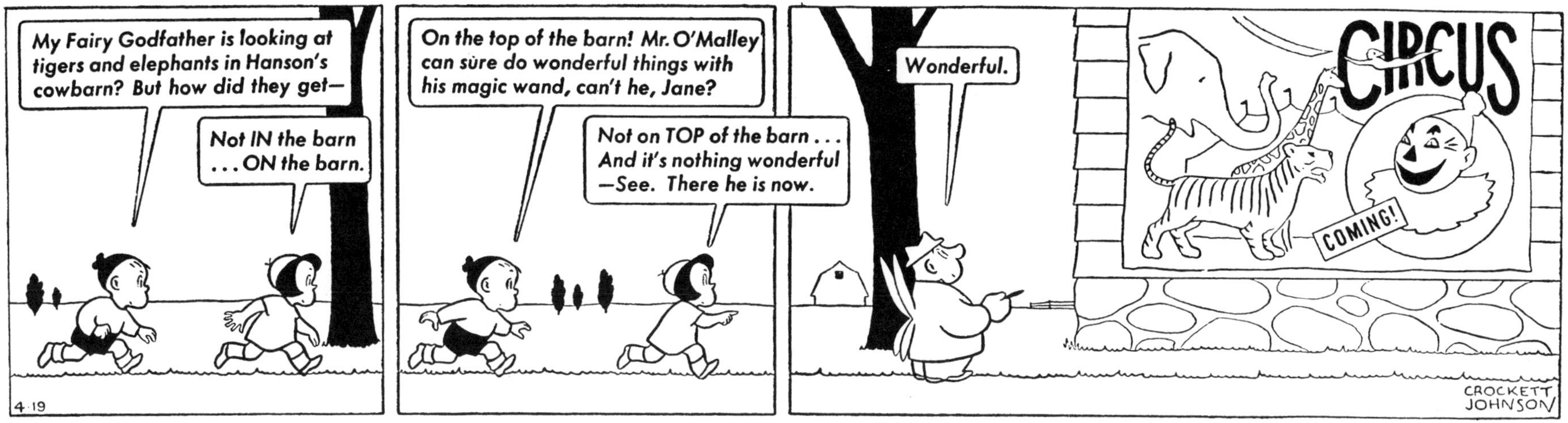
My Fairy Godfather is looking at tigers and elephants in Hanson's cowbarn? But how did they get—
Not IN the barn . . . ON the barn.
On the top of the barn! Mr. O'Malley can sure do wonderful things with his magic wand, can't he, Jane?
Not on TOP of the barn . . . And it's nothing wonderful —See. There he is now.
Wonderful.
CIRCUS
COMING!
4·19
CROCKETT JOHNSON

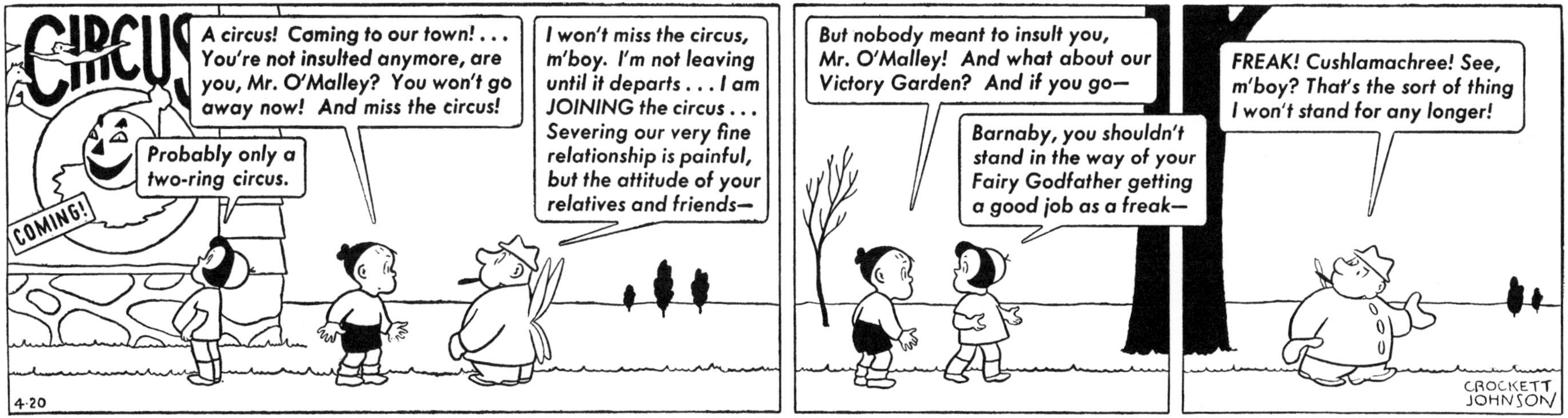
CIRCUS
COMING!
Probably only a two-ring circus.
A circus! Coming to our town! . . . You're not insulted anymore, are you, Mr. O'Malley? You won't go away now! And miss the circus!
I won't miss the circus, m'boy. I'm not leaving until it departs . . . I am JOINING the circus . . . Severing our very fine relationship is painful, but the attitude of your relatives and friends—
But nobody meant to insult you, Mr. O'Malley! And what about our Victory Garden? And if you go—
Barnaby, you shouldn't stand in the way of your Fairy Godfather getting a good job as a freak—
FREAK! Cushlamachree! See, m'boy? That's the sort of thing I won't stand for any longer!
4·20
CROCKETT JOHNSON

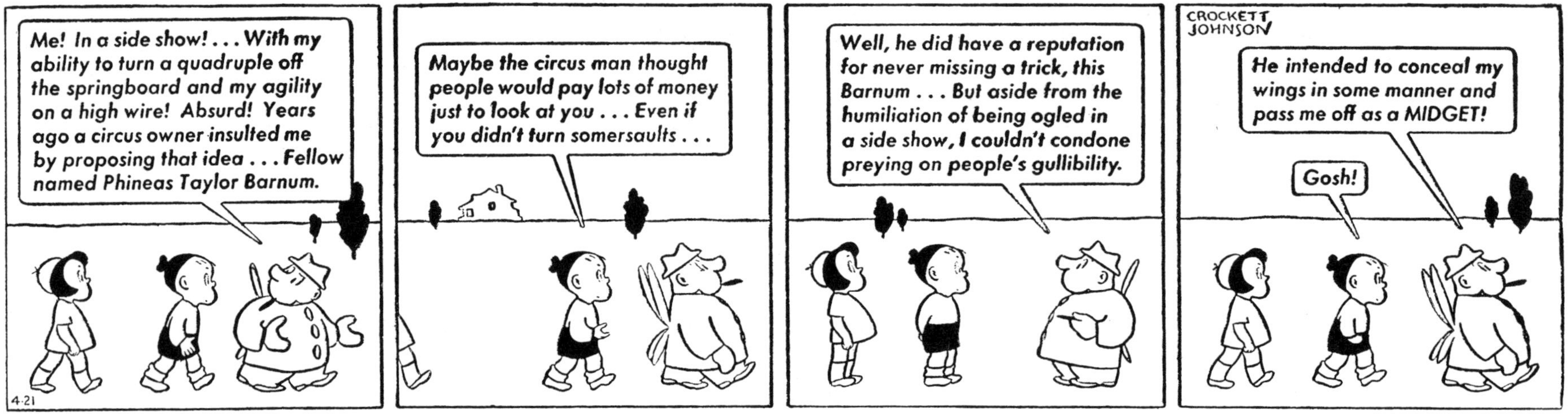
Me! In a side show! . . . With my ability to turn a quadruple off the springboard and my agility on a high wire! Absurd! Years ago a circus owner insulted me by proposing that idea . . . Fellow named Phineas Taylor Barnum.
4·21
Maybe the circus man thought people would pay lots of money just to look at you . . . Even if you didn't turn somersaults . . .
Well, he did have a reputation for never missing a trick, this Barnum . . . But aside from the humiliation of being ogled in a side show, I couldn't condone preying on people's gullibility.
CROCKETT JOHNSON
He intended to conceal my wings in some manner and pass me off as a MIDGET!
Gosh!

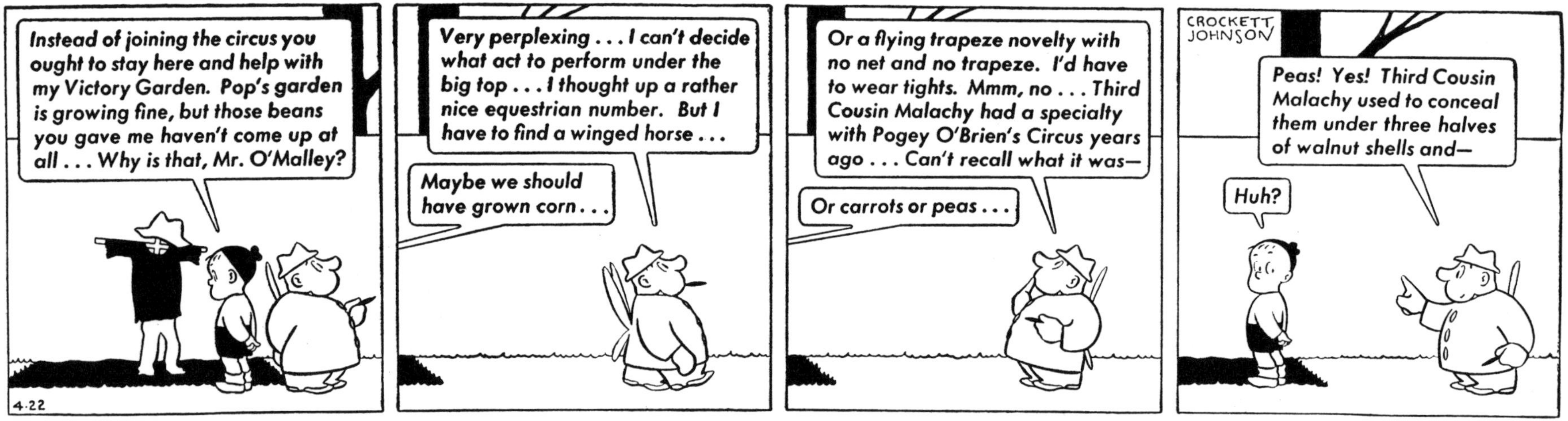
Instead of joining the circus you ought to stay here and help with my Victory Garden. Pop's garden is growing fine, but those beans you gave me haven't come up at all . . . Why is that, Mr. O'Malley?
4·22
Very perplexing . . . I can't decide what act to perform under the big top . . . I thought up a rather nice equestrian number. But I have to find a winged horse . . .
Maybe we should have grown corn . . .
Or a flying trapeze novelty with no net and no trapeze. I'd have to wear tights. Mmm, no . . . Third Cousin Malachy had a specialty with Pogey O'Brien's Circus years ago . . . Can't recall what it was—
Or carrots or peas . . .
CROCKETT JOHNSON
Peas! Yes! Third Cousin Malachy used to conceal them under three halves of walnut shells and—
Huh?

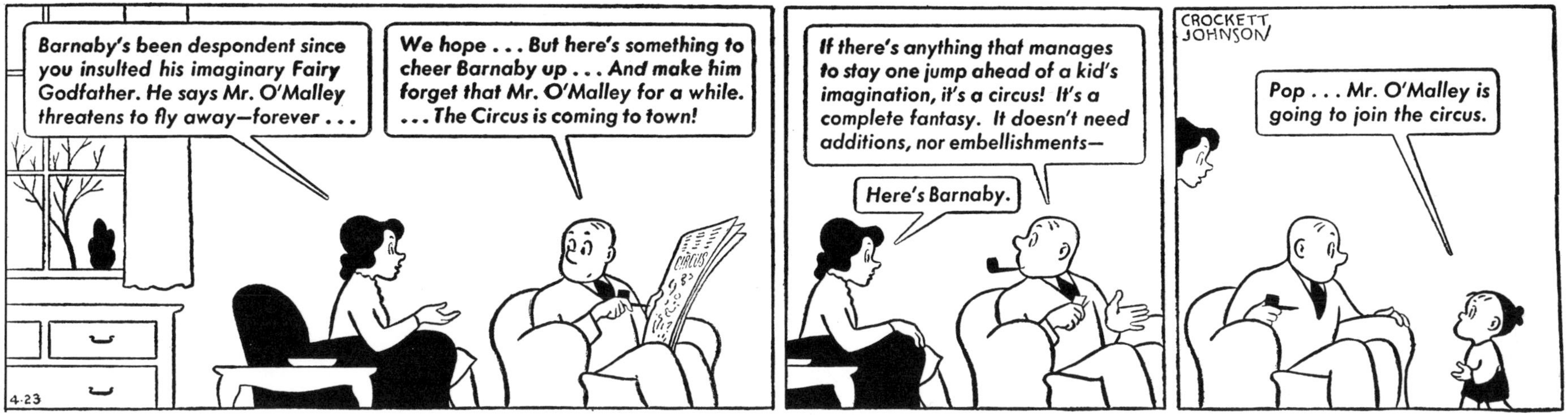
4·23
Barnaby's been despondent since you insulted his imaginary Fairy Godfather. He says Mr. O'Malley threatens to fly away—forever . . .
We hope . . . But here's something to cheer Barnaby up . . . And make him forget that Mr. O'Malley for a while. . . . The Circus is coming to town!
CIRCUS
If there's anything that manages to stay one jump ahead of a kid's imagination, it's a circus! It's a complete fantasy. It doesn't need additions, nor embellishments—
Here's Barnaby.
CROCKETT JOHNSON
Pop . . . Mr. O'Malley is going to join the circus.

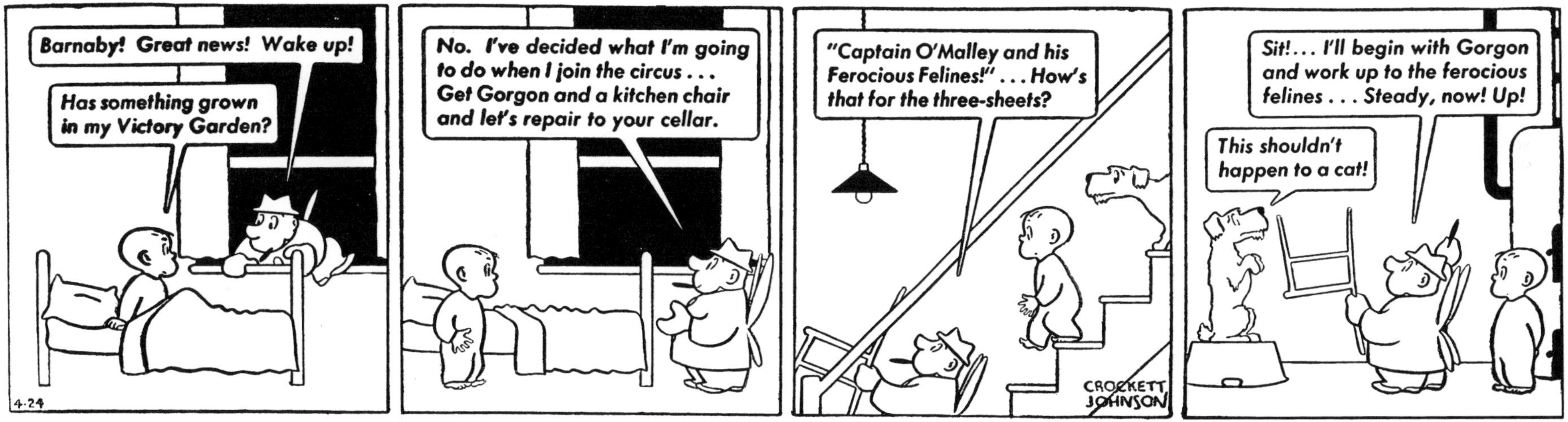
4·24
Barnaby! Great news! Wake up!
Has something grown in my Victory Garden?
No. I've decided what I'm going to do when I join the circus . . . Get Gorgon and a kitchen chair and let's repair to your cellar.
"Captain O'Malley and his Ferocious Felines!" . . . How's that for the three-sheets?
CROCKETT JOHNSON
Sit! . . . I'll begin with Gorgon and work up to the ferocious felines . . . Steady, now! Up!
This shouldn't happen to a cat!

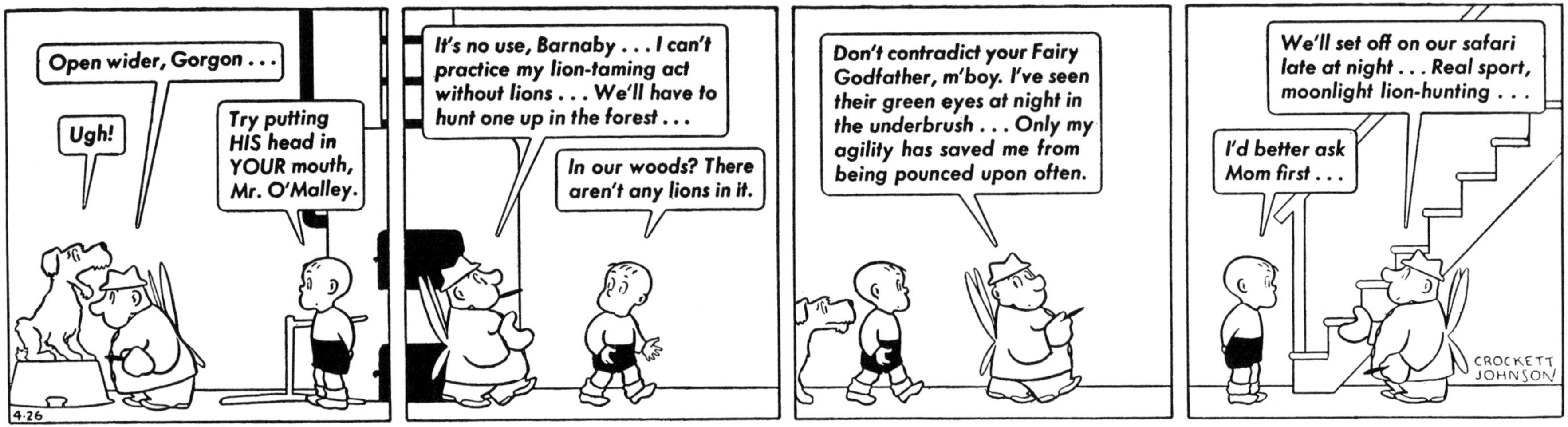
Open wider, Gorgon . . .
Ugh!
Try putting HIS head in YOUR mouth, Mr. O'Malley.
It's no use, Barnaby . . . I can't practice my lion-taming act without lions . . . We'll have to hunt one up in the forest . . .
In our woods? There aren't any lions in it.
Don't contradict your Fairy Godfather, m'boy. I've seen their green eyes at night in the underbrush . . . Only my agility has saved me from being pounced upon often.
We'll set off on our safari late at night . . . Real sport, moonlight lion-hunting . . .
I'd better ask Mom first . . .
CROCKETT JOHNSON
4·26

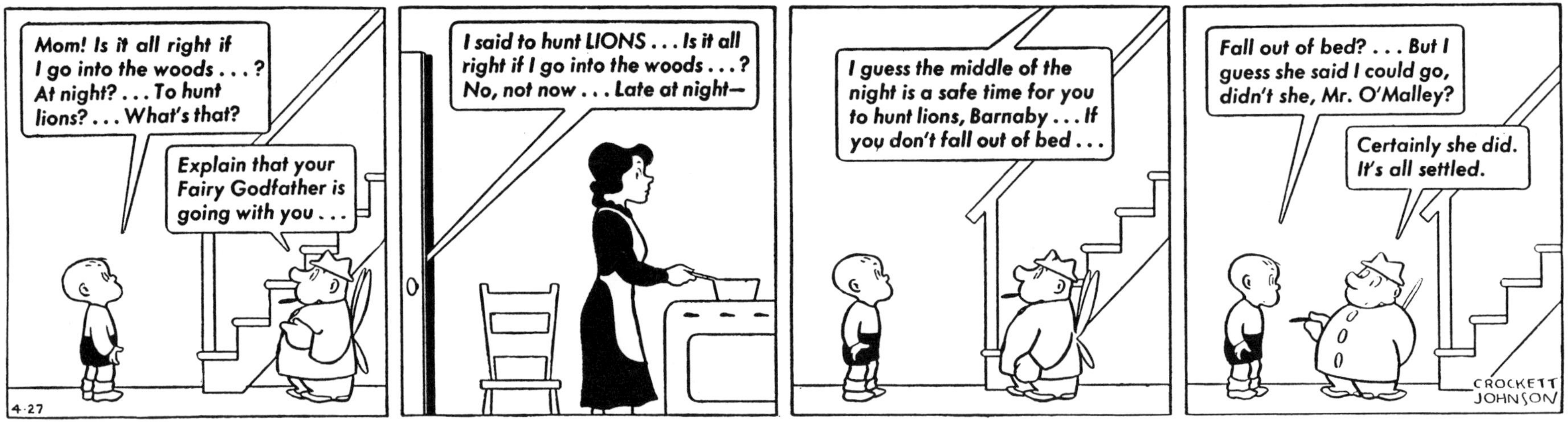
Mom! Is it all right if I go into the woods . . . ? At night? . . . To hunt lions? . . . What's that?
Explain that your Fairy Godfather is going with you . . .
I said to hunt LIONS . . . Is it all right if I go into the woods . . . ? No, not now . . . Late at night—
I guess the middle of the night is a safe time for you to hunt lions, Barnaby . . . If you don't fall out of bed . . .
Fall out of bed? . . . But I guess she said I could go, didn't she, Mr. O'Malley?
Certainly she did. It's all settled.
CROCKETT JOHNSON
4·27

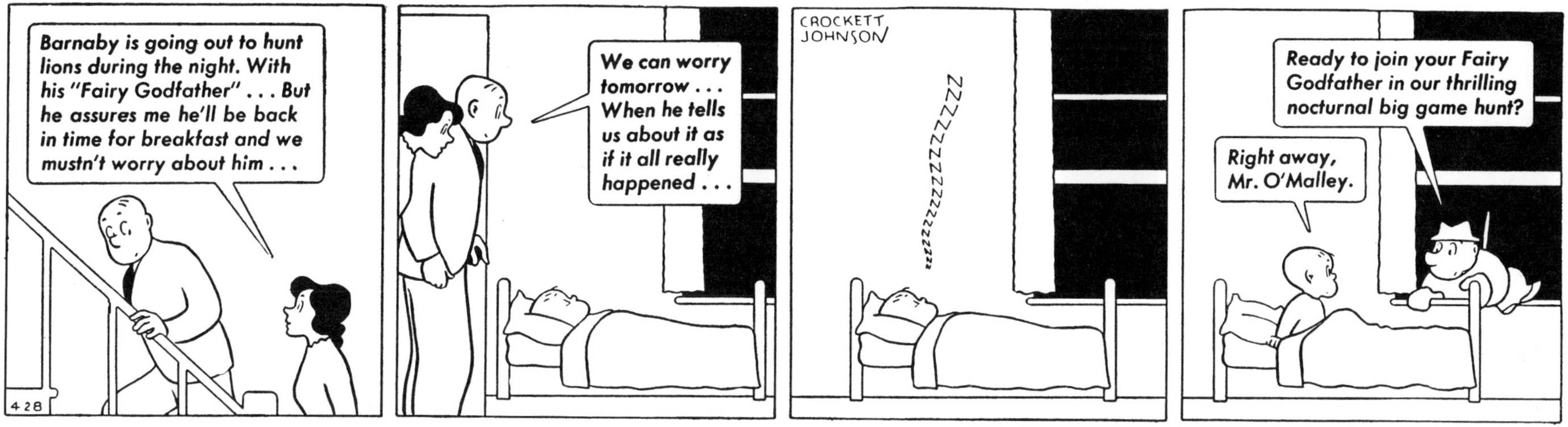
Barnaby is going out to hunt lions during the night. With his "Fairy Godfather" . . . But he assures me he'll be back in time for breakfast and we mustn't worry about him . . .
4 28
We can worry tomorrow . . . When he tells us about it as if it all really happened . . .
CROCKETT JOHNSON
ZZZZZZZZZZZZZZZZZ
Ready to join your Fairy Godfather in our thrilling nocturnal big game hunt?
Right away, Mr. O'Malley.

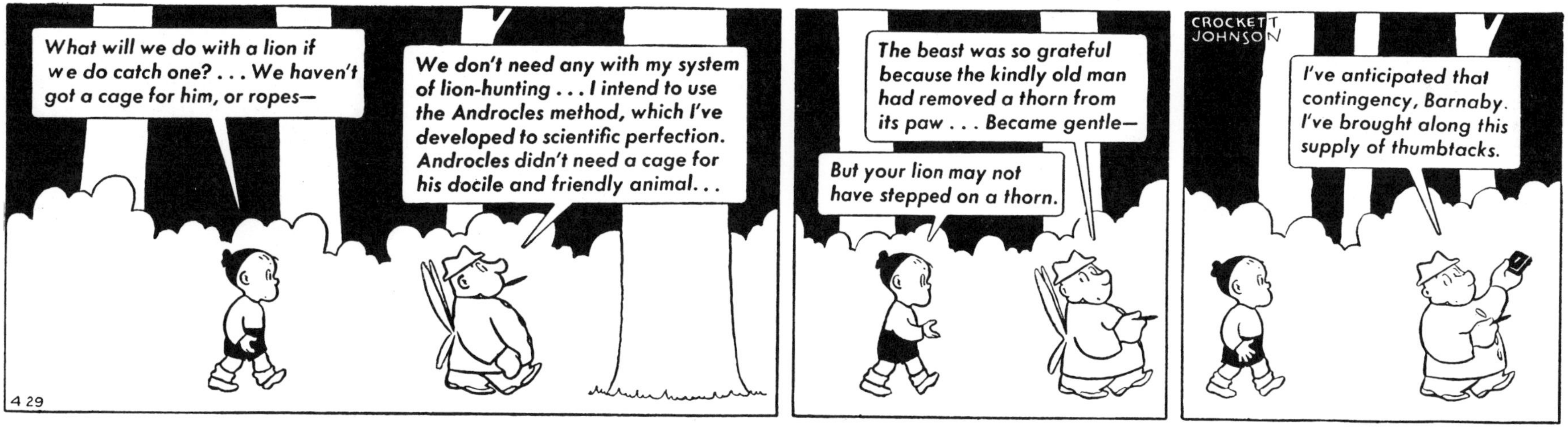
What will we do with a lion if we do catch one? . . . We haven't got a cage for him, or ropes—
We don't need any with my system of lion-hunting . . . I intend to use the Androcles method, which I've developed to scientific perfection. Androcles didn't need a cage for his docile and friendly animal. . .
4 29
The beast was so grateful because the kindly old man had removed a thorn from its paw . . . Became gentle—
But your lion may not have stepped on a thorn.
CROCKETT JOHNSON
I've anticipated that contingency, Barnaby. I've brought along this supply of thumbtacks.

April 28 – 29

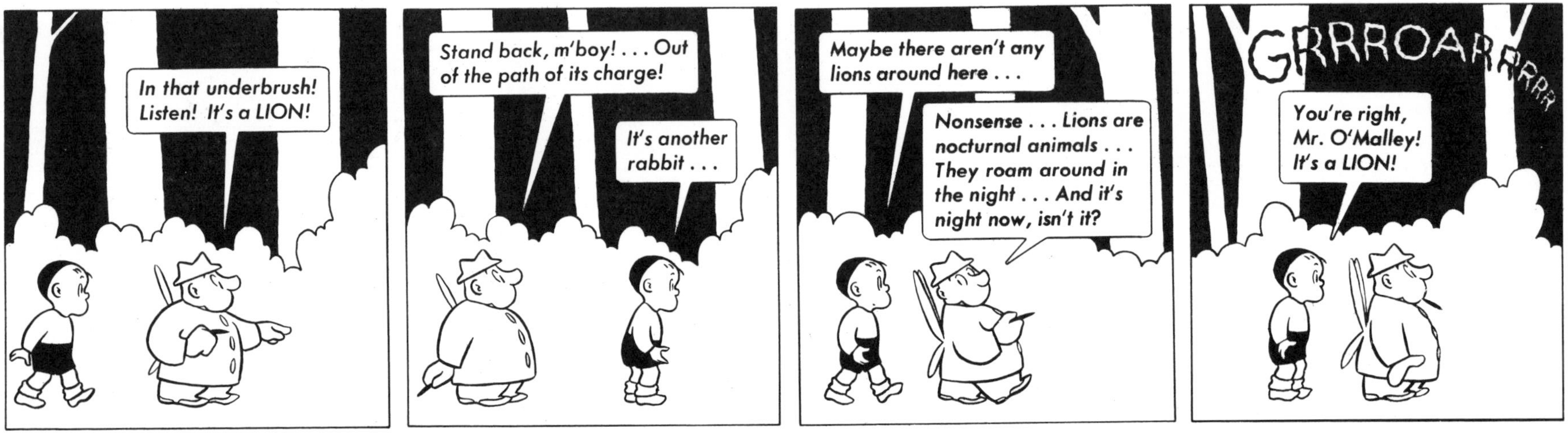
In that underbrush! Listen! It's a LION!
Stand back, m'boy! . . . Out of the path of its charge!
It's another rabbit . . .
Maybe there aren't any lions around here . . .
Nonsense . . . Lions are nocturnal animals . . . They roam around in the night . . . And it's night now, isn't it?
GRRROARRRRR
You're right, Mr. O'Malley! It's a LION!

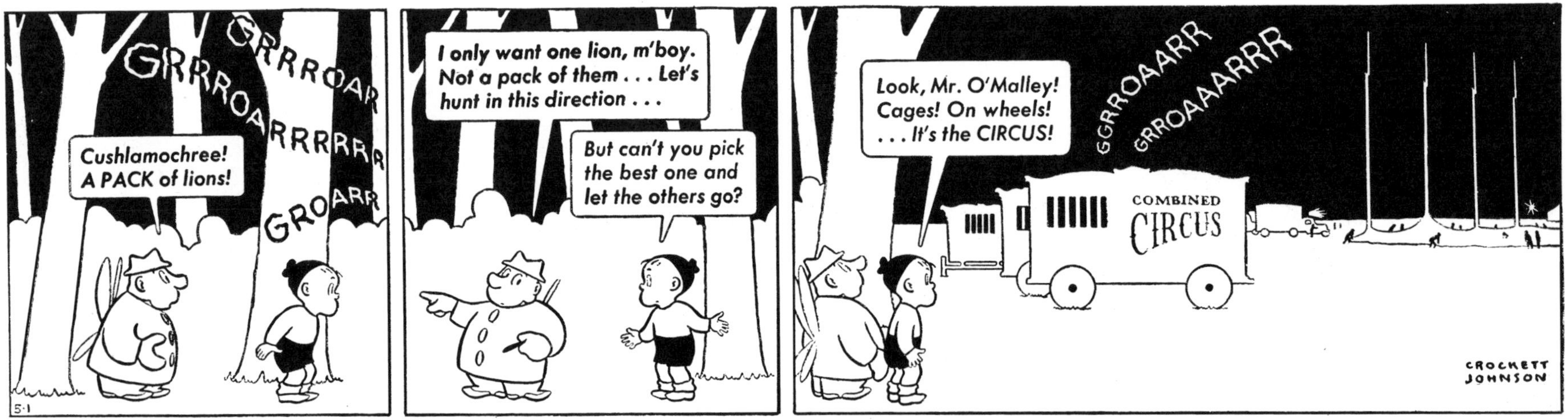
GRRROARRRRRRR
GRRROAR
Cushlamochree! A PACK of lions!
GROARR
5·1
I only want one lion, m'boy. Not a pack of them . . . Let's hunt in this direction . . .
But can't you pick the best one and let the others go?
Look, Mr. O'Malley! Cages! On wheels! . . . It's the CIRCUS!
GGRROAARR
GRROAAARRRR
COMBINED CIRCUS
CROCKETT JOHNSON

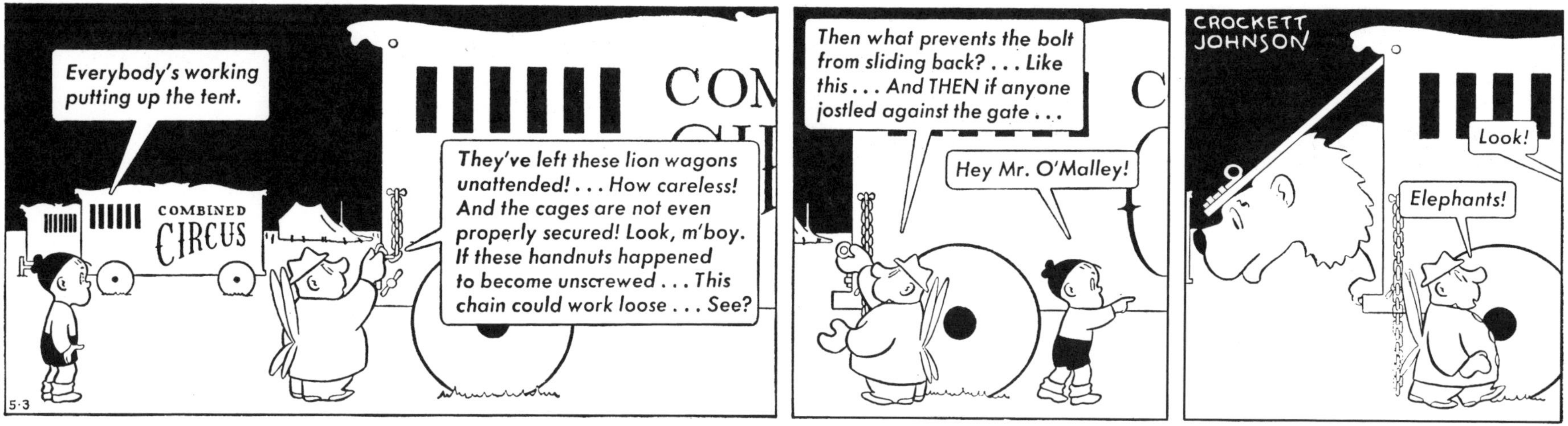
Everybody's working putting up the tent.
COMBINED CIRCUS
They've left these lion wagons unattended! . . . How careless! And the cages are not even properly secured! Look, m'boy. If these handnuts happened to become unscrewed . . . This chain could work loose . . . See?
5·3
Then what prevents the bolt from sliding back? . . . Like this . . . And THEN if anyone jostled against the gate . . .
Hey Mr. O'Malley!
CROCKETT JOHNSON
Look!
Elephants!

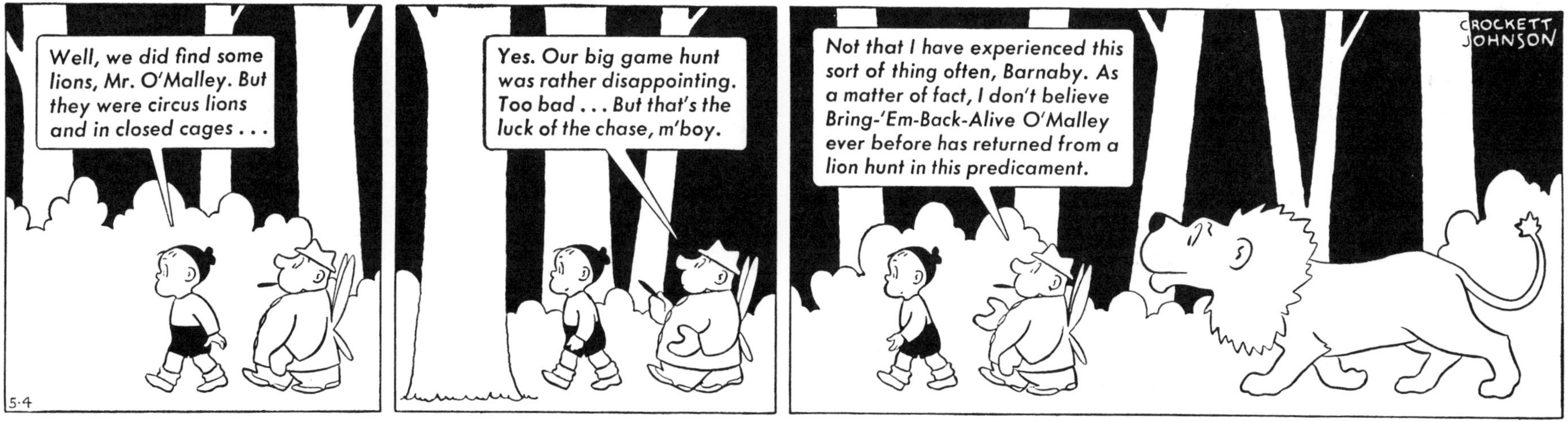
Well, we did find some lions, Mr. O'Malley. But they were circus lions and in closed cages . . .
5·4
Yes. Our big game hunt was rather disappointing. Too bad . . . But that's the luck of the chase, m'boy.
Not that I have experienced this sort of thing often, Barnaby. As a matter of fact, I don't believe Bring-'Em-Back-Alive O'Malley ever before has returned from a lion hunt in this predicament.
CROCKETT JOHNSON

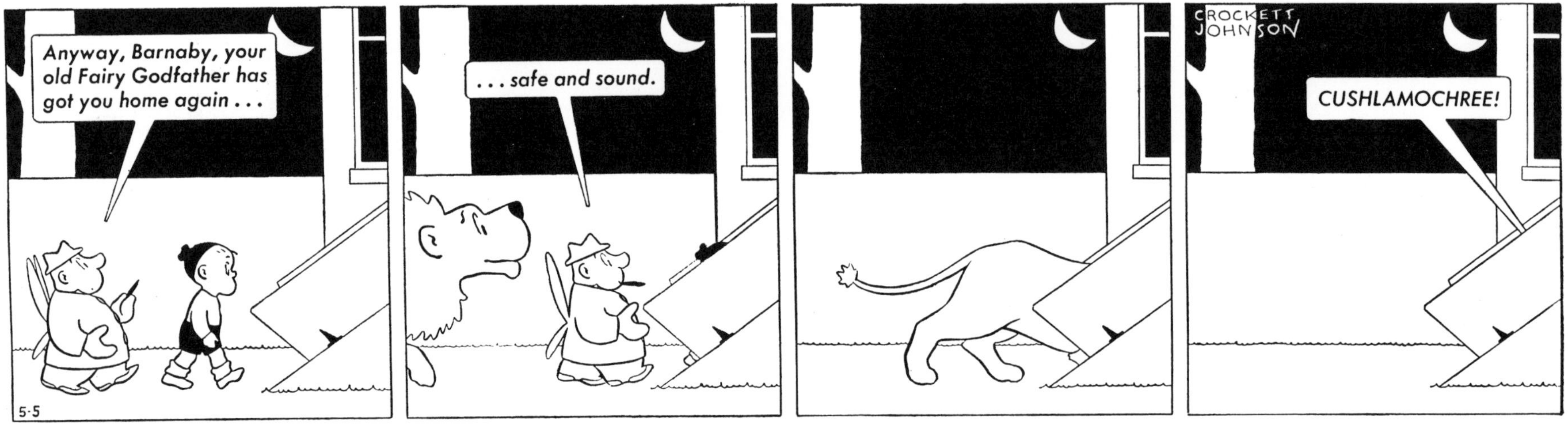
Anyway, Barnaby, your old Fairy Godfather has got you home again . . .
. . . safe and sound.
CROCKETT JOHNSON
CUSHLAMOCHREE!
5-5

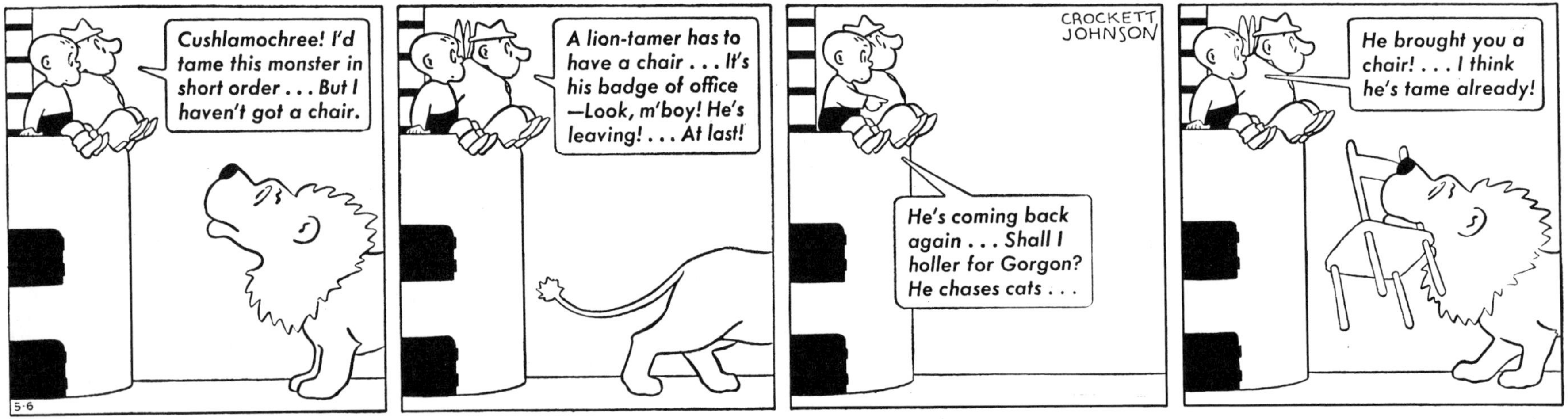
Cushlamochree! I'd tame this monster in short order . . . But I haven't got a chair.
A lion-tamer has to have a chair . . . It's his badge of office —Look, m'boy! He's leaving! . . . At last!
CROCKETT JOHNSON
He's coming back again . . . Shall I holler for Gorgon? He chases cats . . .
He brought you a chair! . . . I think he's tame already!
5-6

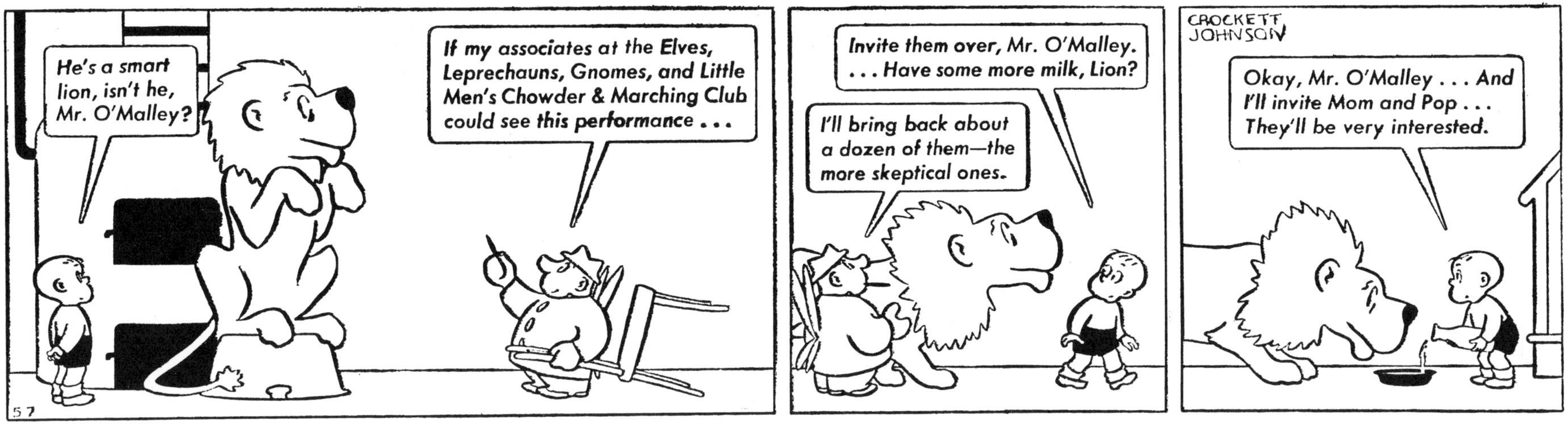
He's a smart lion, isn't he, Mr. O'Malley?
If my associates at the Elves, Leprechauns, Gnomes, and Little Men's Chowder & Marching Club could see this performance . . .
Invite them over, Mr. O'Malley. . . . Have some more milk, Lion?
I'll bring back about a dozen of them—the more skeptical ones.
CROCKETT JOHNSON
Okay, Mr. O'Malley . . . And I'll invite Mom and Pop . . . They'll be very interested.
5 7

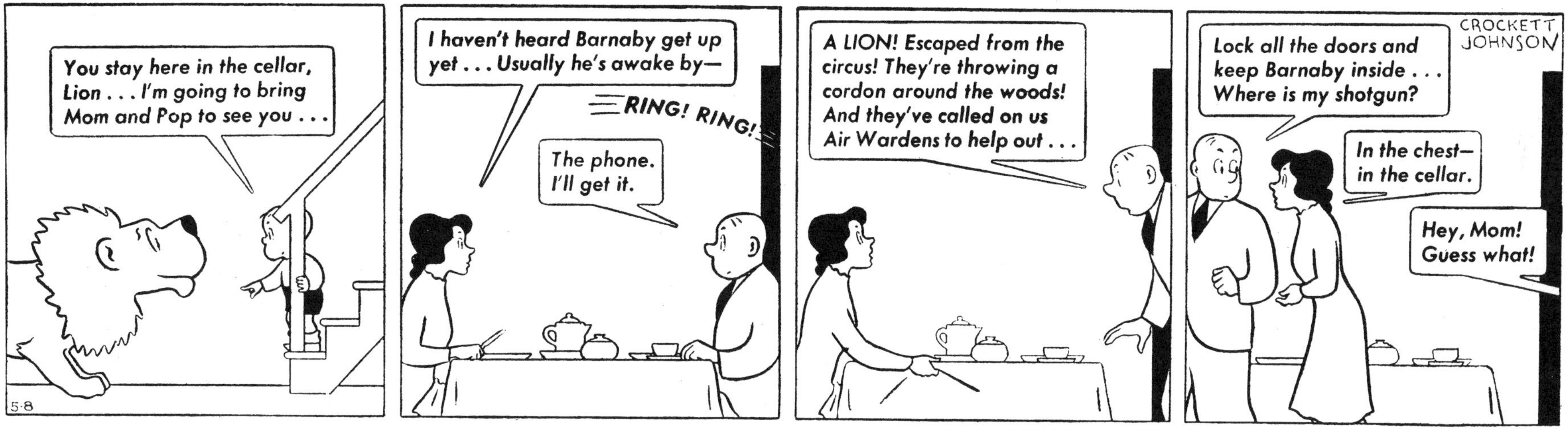
You stay here in the cellar, Lion . . . I'm going to bring Mom and Pop to see you . . .
5·8
I haven't heard Barnaby get up yet . . . Usually he's awake by—
RING! RING!
The phone. I'll get it.
A LION! Escaped from the circus! They're throwing a cordon around the woods! And they've called on us Air Wardens to help out . . .
CROCKETT JOHNSON
Lock all the doors and keep Barnaby inside . . . Where is my shotgun?
In the chest—in the cellar.
Hey, Mom! Guess what!

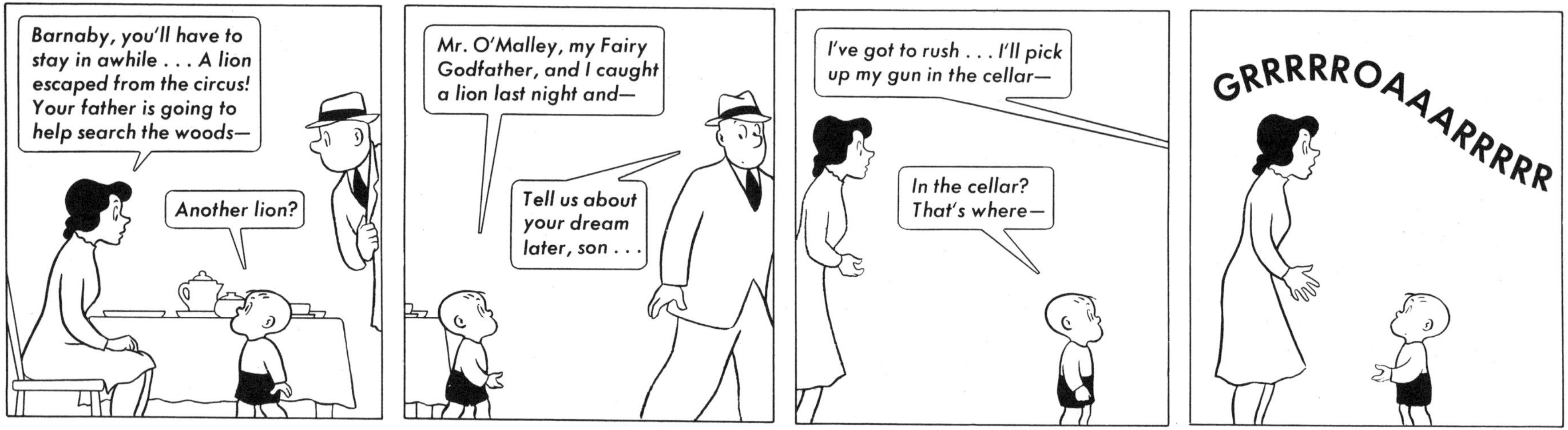
Barnaby, you'll have to stay in awhile . . . A lion escaped from the circus! Your father is going to help search the woods—
Another lion?
Mr. O'Malley, my Fairy Godfather, and I caught a lion last night and—
Tell us about your dream later, son . . .
I've got to rush . . . I'll pick up my gun in the cellar—
In the cellar? That's where—
GRRRRROAAAARRRRRR

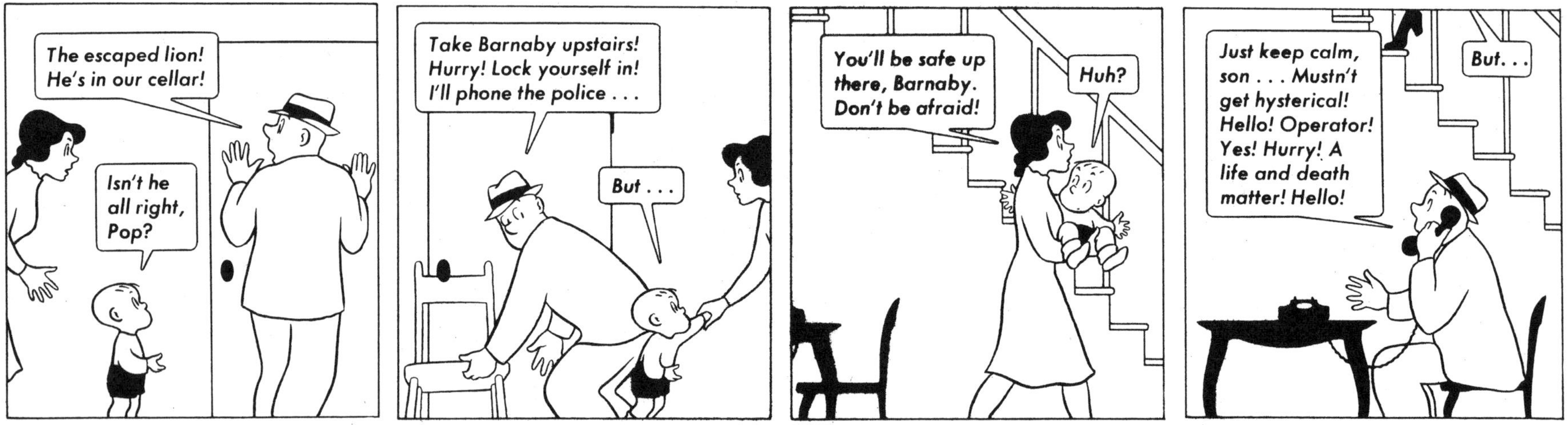
The escaped lion! He's in our cellar!
Isn't he all right, Pop?
Take Barnaby upstairs! Hurry! Lock yourself in! I'll phone the police . . .
But . . .
You'll be safe up there, Barnaby. Don't be afraid!
Huh?
Just keep calm, son . . . Mustn't get hysterical! Hello! Operator! Yes! Hurry! A life and death matter! Hello!
But. . .

May 10 – 11

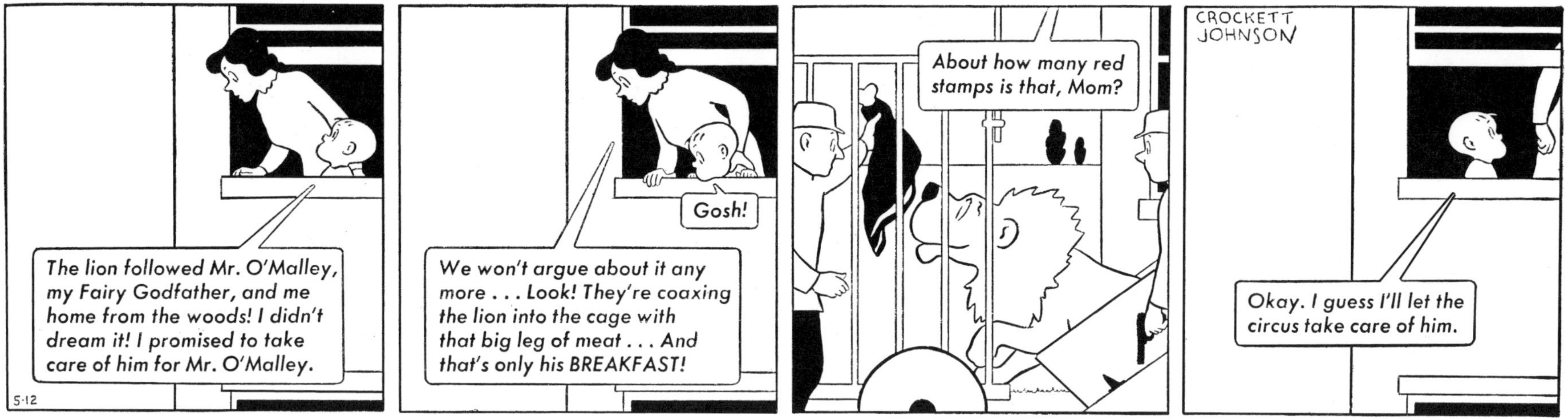
The lion followed Mr. O'Malley, my Fairy Godfather, and me home from the woods! I didn't dream it! I promised to take care of him for Mr. O'Malley.
5·12
We won't argue about it any more . . . Look! They're coaxing the lion into the cage with that big leg of meat . . . And that's only his BREAKFAST!
Gosh!
About how many red stamps is that, Mom?
CROCKETT JOHNSON
Okay. I guess I'll let the circus take care of him.

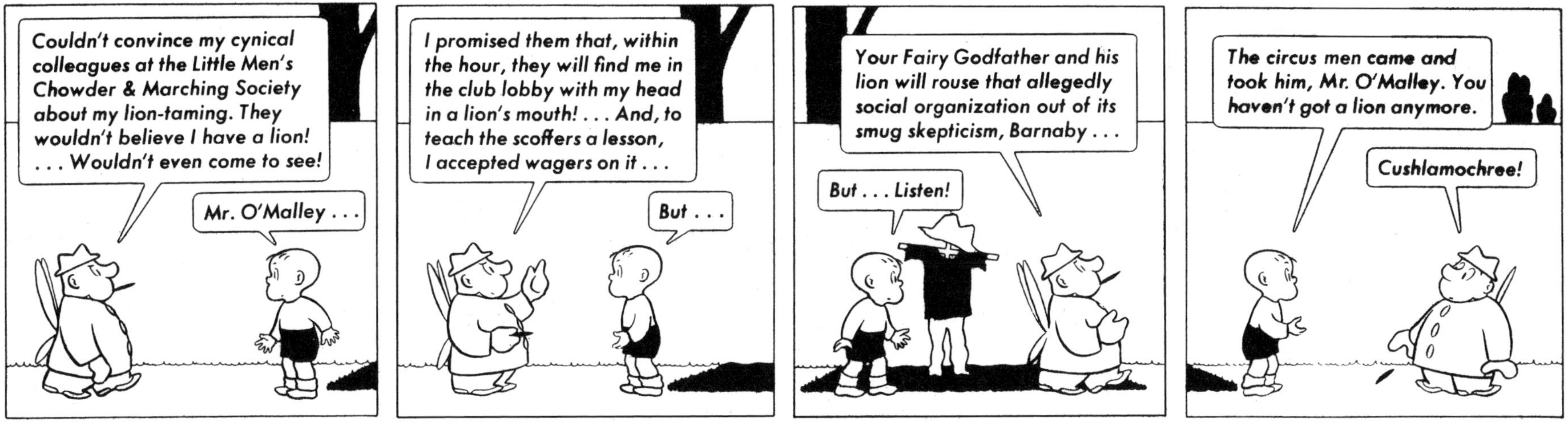
Couldn't convince my cynical colleagues at the Little Men's Chowder & Marching Society about my lion-taming. They wouldn't believe I have a lion! . . . Wouldn't even come to see!
Mr. O'Malley . . .
I promised them that, within the hour, they will find me in the club lobby with my head in a lion's mouth! . . . And, to teach the scoffers a lesson, I accepted wagers on it . . .
But . . .
Your Fairy Godfather and his lion will rouse that allegedly social organization out of its smug skepticism, Barnaby . . .
But . . . Listen!
The circus men came and took him, Mr. O'Malley. You haven't got a lion anymore.
Cushlamochree!

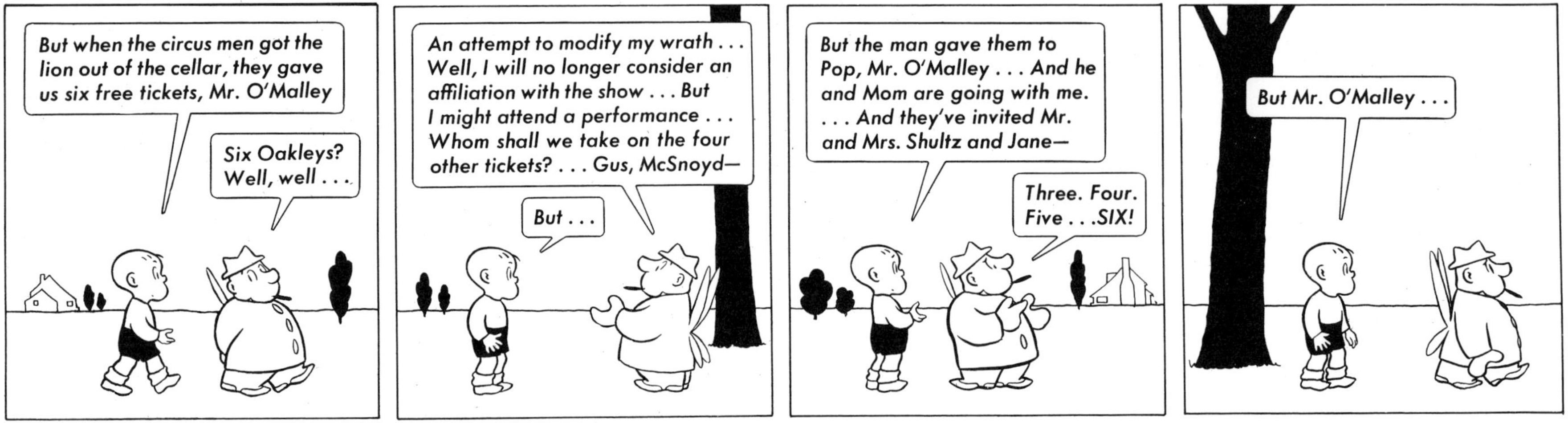

But when the circus men got the lion out of the cellar, they gave us six free tickets, Mr. O'Malley
Six Oakleys? Well, well . . .
An attempt to modify my wrath . . . Well, I will no longer consider an affiliation with the show . . . But I might attend a performance . . . Whom shall we take on the four other tickets? . . . Gus, McSnoyd—
But . . .
But the man gave them to Pop, Mr. O'Malley . . . And he and Mom are going with me. . . . And they've invited Mr. and Mrs. Shultz and Jane—
Three. Four. Five . . .SIX!
But Mr. O'Malley . . .

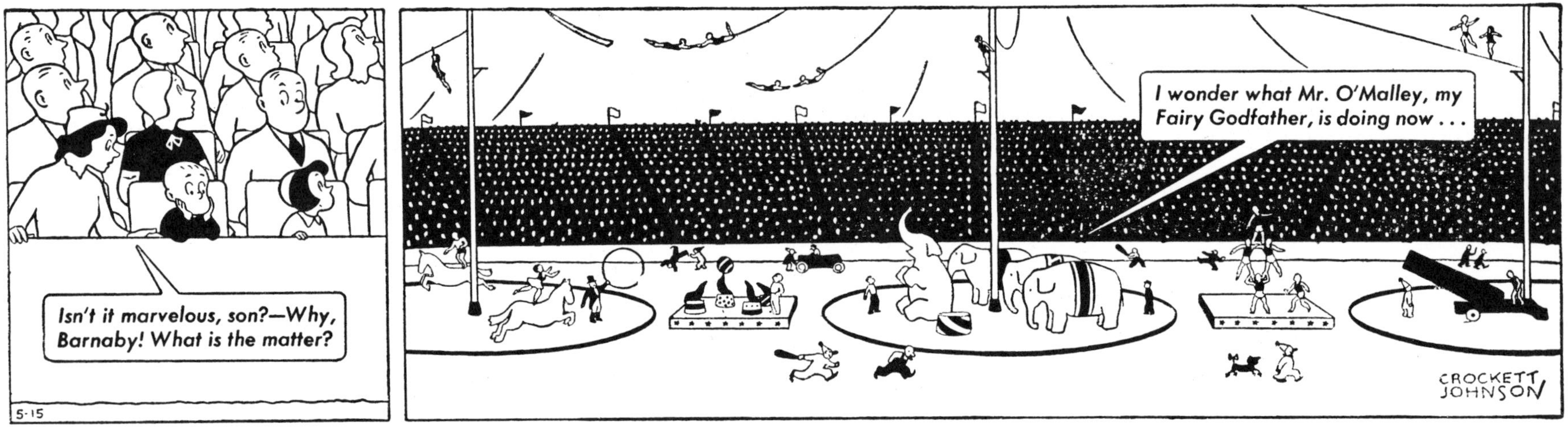

Isn't it marvelous, son?—Why, Barnaby! What is the matter?
5-15
I wonder what Mr. O'Malley, my Fairy Godfather, is doing now . . .
CROCKETT JOHNSON

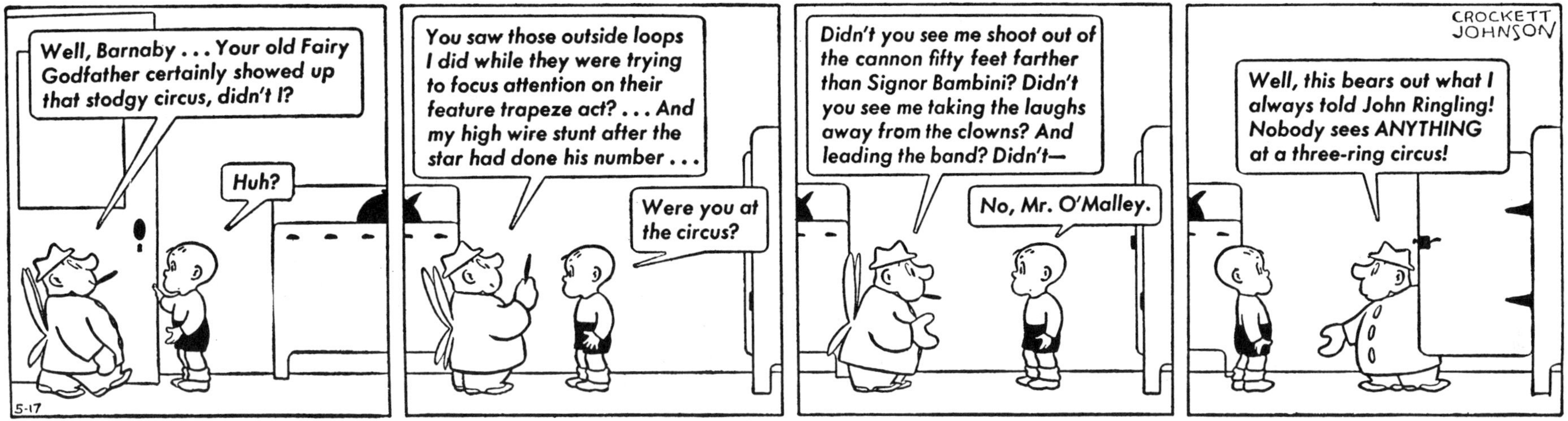
Well, Barnaby . . . Your old Fairy Godfather certainly showed up that stodgy circus, didn't I?
Huh?
5-17
You saw those outside loops I did while they were trying to focus attention on their feature trapeze act? . . . And my high wire stunt after the star had done his number . . .
Were you at the circus?
Didn't you see me shoot out of the cannon fifty feet farther than Signor Bambini? Didn't you see me taking the laughs away from the clowns? And leading the band? Didn't—
No, Mr. O'Malley.
CROCKETT JOHNSON
Well, this bears out what I always told John Ringling! Nobody sees ANYTHING at a three-ring circus!

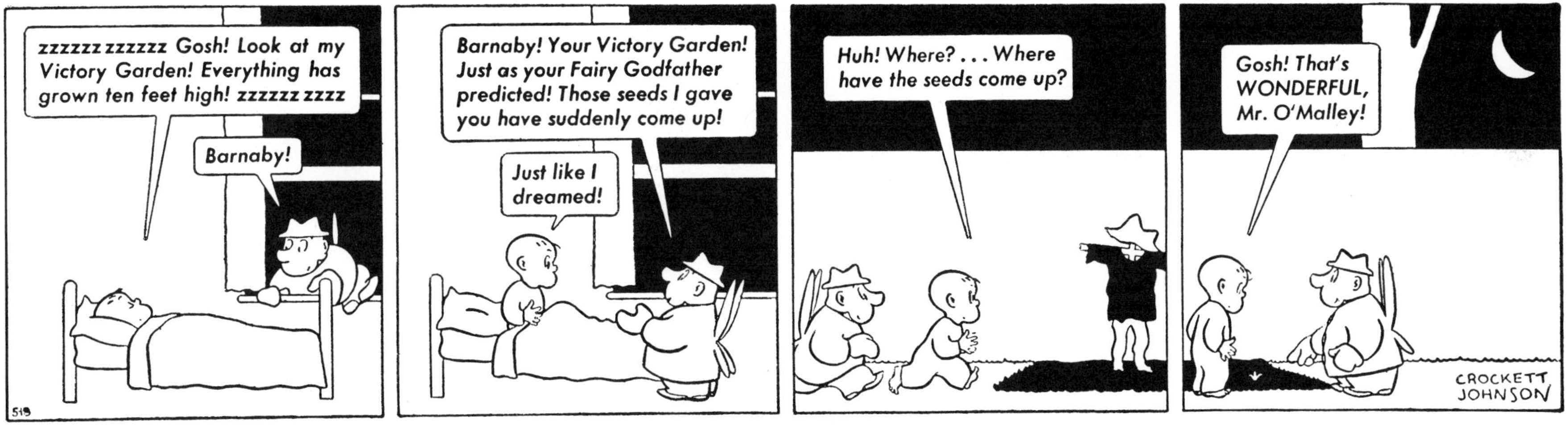
zzzzzz zzzzzz Gosh! Look at my Victory Garden! Everything has grown ten feet high! zzzzzz zzzz
Barnaby!
Barnaby! Your Victory Garden! Just as your Fairy Godfather predicted! Those seeds I gave you have suddenly come up!
Just like I dreamed!
Huh! Where? . . . Where have the seeds come up?
Gosh! That's WONDERFUL, Mr. O'Malley!
CROCKETT JOHNSON

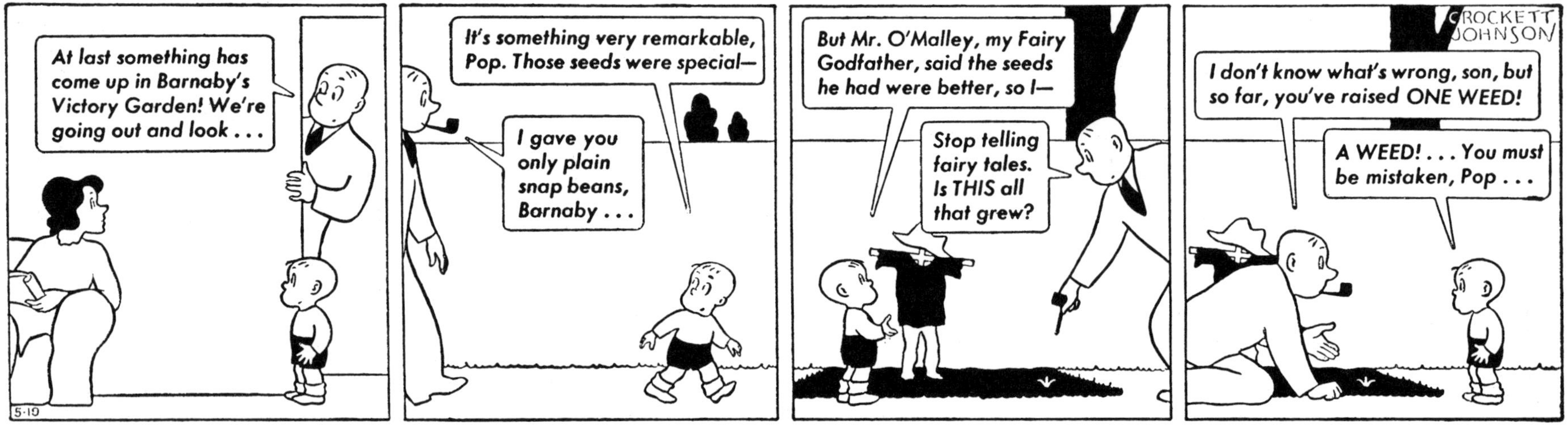
At last something has come up in Barnaby's Victory Garden! We're going out and look . . .
It's something very remarkable, Pop. Those seeds were special—
I gave you only plain snap beans, Barnaby . . .
But Mr. O'Malley, my Fairy Godfather, said the seeds he had were better, so I—
Stop telling fairy tales. Is THIS all that grew?
CROCKETT JOHNSON
I don't know what's wrong, son, but so far, you've raised ONE WEED!
A WEED! . . . You must be mistaken, Pop . . .
5-19

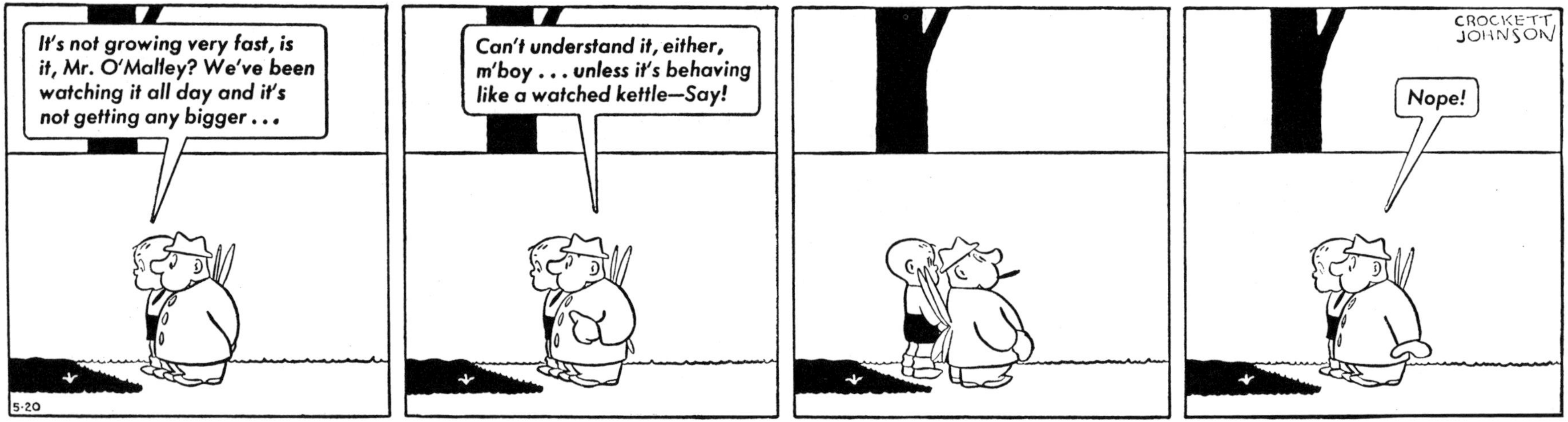
It's not growing very fast, is it, Mr. O'Malley? We've been watching it all day and it's not getting any bigger . . .
Can't understand it, either, m'boy . . . unless it's behaving like a watched kettle—Say!
CROCKETT JOHNSON
Nope!
5-20

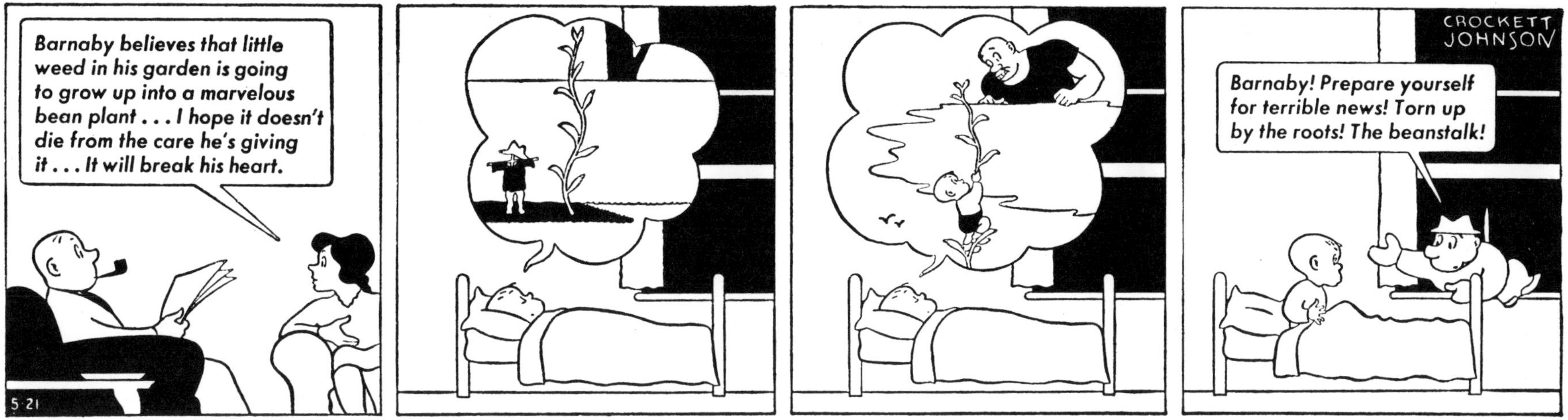
Barnaby believes that little weed in his garden is going to grow up into a marvelous bean plant . . . I hope it doesn't die from the care he's giving it . . . It will break his heart.
5·21
CROCKETT JOHNSON
Barnaby! Prepare yourself for terrible news! Torn up by the roots! The beanstalk!

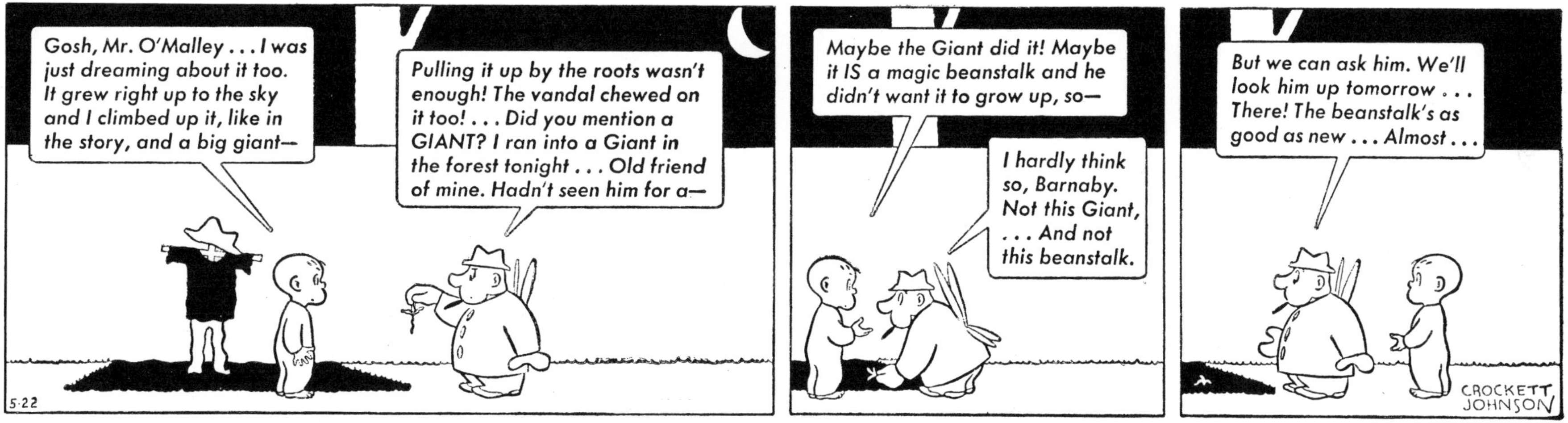
Gosh, Mr. O'Malley . . . I was just dreaming about it too. It grew right up to the sky and I climbed up it, like in the story, and a big giant—
Pulling it up by the roots wasn't enough! The vandal chewed on it too! . . . Did you mention a GIANT? I ran into a Giant in the forest tonight . . . Old friend of mine. Hadn't seen him for a—
5·22
Maybe the Giant did it! Maybe it IS a magic beanstalk and he didn't want it to grow up, so—
I hardly think so, Barnaby. Not this Giant, . . . And not this beanstalk.
But we can ask him. We'll look him up tomorrow . . . There! The beanstalk's as good as new . . . Almost . . .
CROCKETT JOHNSON

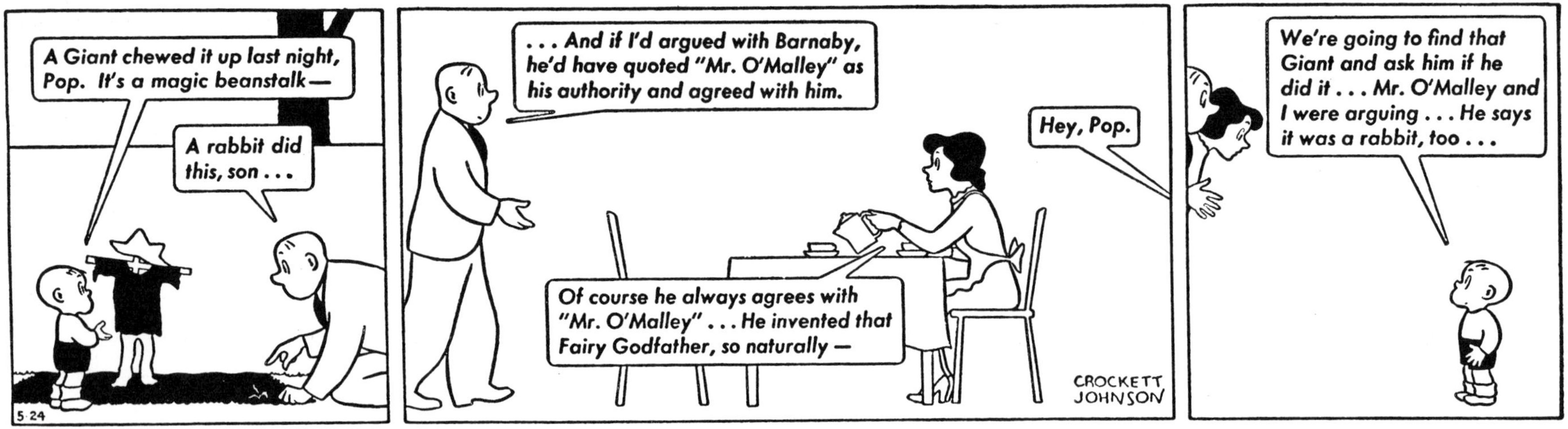
A Giant chewed it up last night, Pop. It's a magic beanstalk—
A rabbit did this, son . . .
5.24
. . . And if I'd argued with Barnaby, he'd have quoted "Mr. O'Malley" as his authority and agreed with him.
Of course he always agrees with "Mr. O'Malley" . . . He invented that Fairy Godfather, so naturally —
Hey, Pop.
CROCKETT JOHNSON
We're going to find that Giant and ask him if he did it . . . Mr. O'Malley and I were arguing . . . He says it was a rabbit, too . . .

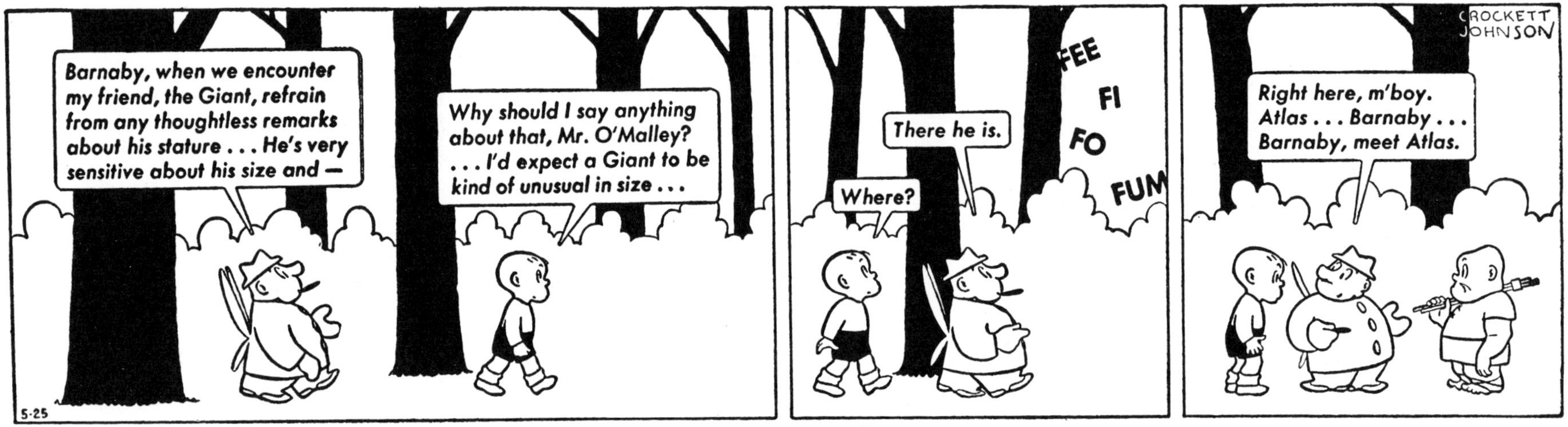
Barnaby, when we encounter my friend, the Giant, refrain from any thoughtless remarks about his stature . . . He's very sensitive about his size and —
Why should I say anything about that, Mr. O'Malley? . . . I'd expect a Giant to be kind of unusual in size . . .
5.25
There he is.
Where?
FEE
FI
FO
FUM
CROCKETT JOHNSON
Right here, m'boy. Atlas . . . Barnaby . . . Barnaby, meet Atlas.

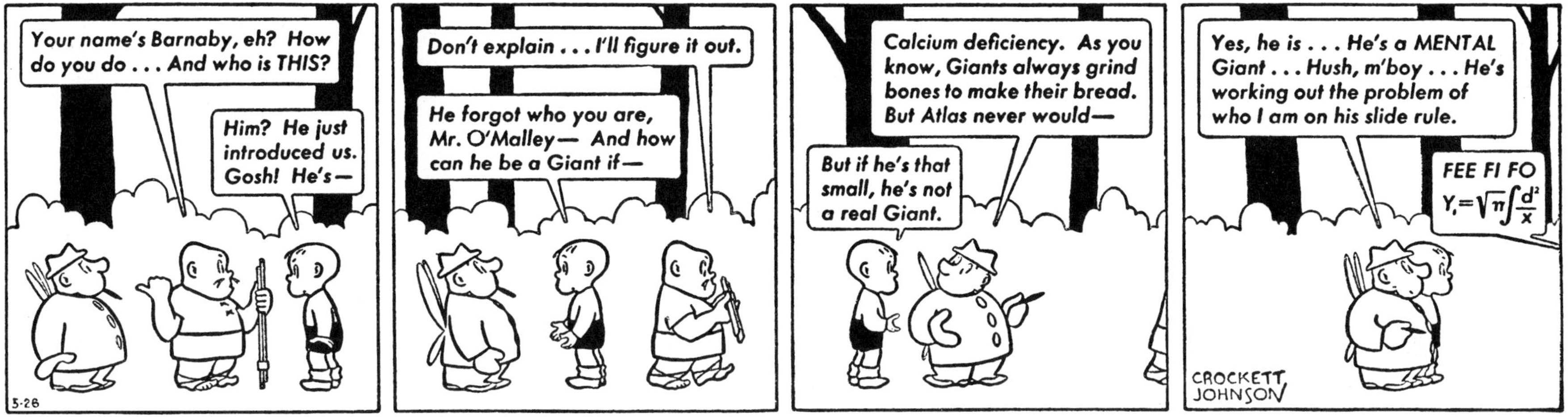

Your name's Barnaby, eh? How do you do . . . And who is THIS?
Him? He just introduced us. Gosh! He's—
5·26
Don't explain . . . I'll figure it out.
He forgot who you are, Mr. O'Malley— And how can he be a Giant if—
Calcium deficiency. As you know, Giants always grind bones to make their bread. But Atlas never would—
But if he's that small, he's not a real Giant.
Yes, he is . . . He's a MENTAL Giant . . . Hush, m'boy . . . He's working out the problem of who I am on his slide rule.
FEE FI FO
$Y_1=\sqrt{\pi}\int\frac{d^2}{x}$
CROCKETT JOHNSON

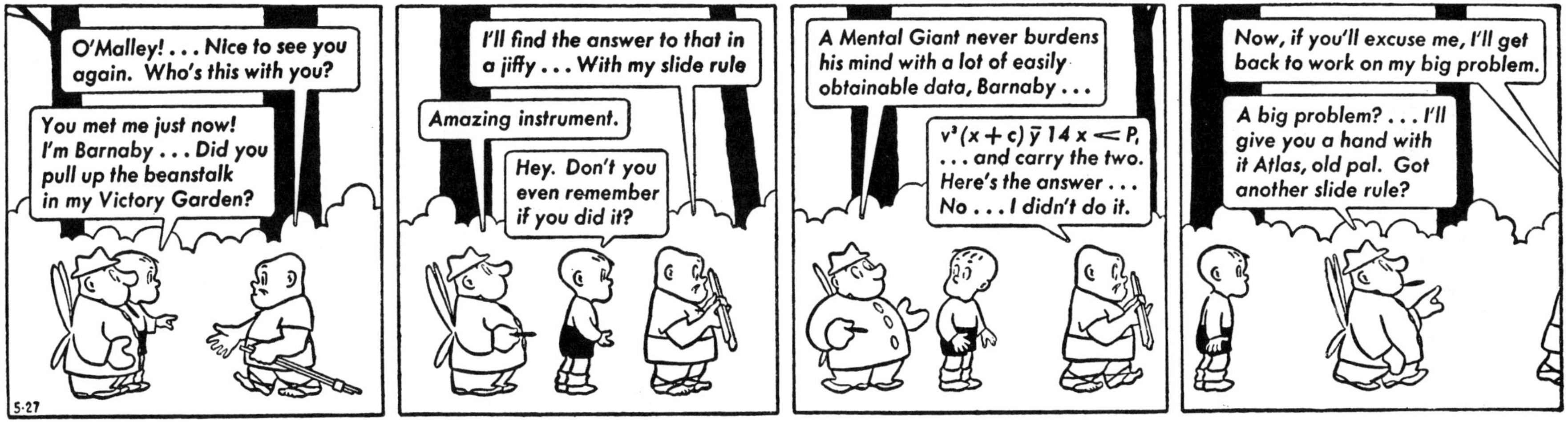

O'Malley! . . . Nice to see you again. Who's this with you?
You met me just now! I'm Barnaby . . . Did you pull up the beanstalk in my Victory Garden?
5·27
I'll find the answer to that in a jiffy . . . With my slide rule
Amazing instrument.
Hey. Don't you even remember if you did it?
A Mental Giant never burdens his mind with a lot of easily obtainable data, Barnaby . . .
$v^3(x+c)\,\bar{y}\,14\,x < P_1$ . . . and carry the two. Here's the answer . . . No . . . I didn't do it.
Now, if you'll excuse me, I'll get back to work on my big problem.
A big problem? . . . I'll give you a hand with it Atlas, old pal. Got another slide rule?

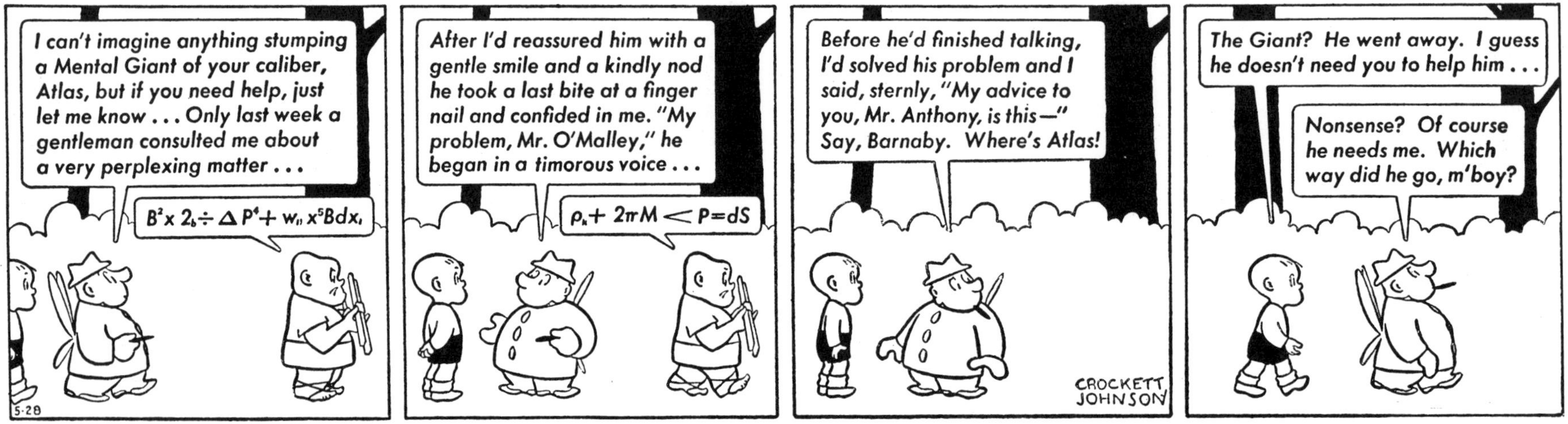

I can't imagine anything stumping a Mental Giant of your caliber, Atlas, but if you need help, just let me know . . . Only last week a gentleman consulted me about a very perplexing matter . . .
$B^2 x\ 2_b \div \Delta P^4 + w_{11}\ x^5 Bdx,$
After I'd reassured him with a gentle smile and a kindly nod he took a last bite at a finger nail and confided in me. "My problem, Mr. O'Malley," he began in a timorous voice . . .
$\rho_x + 2\pi M < P = dS$
Before he'd finished talking, I'd solved his problem and I said, sternly, "My advice to you, Mr. Anthony, is this—" Say, Barnaby. Where's Atlas!
CROCKETT JOHNSON
The Giant? He went away. I guess he doesn't need you to help him . . .
Nonsense? Of course he needs me. Which way did he go, m'boy?
5-28

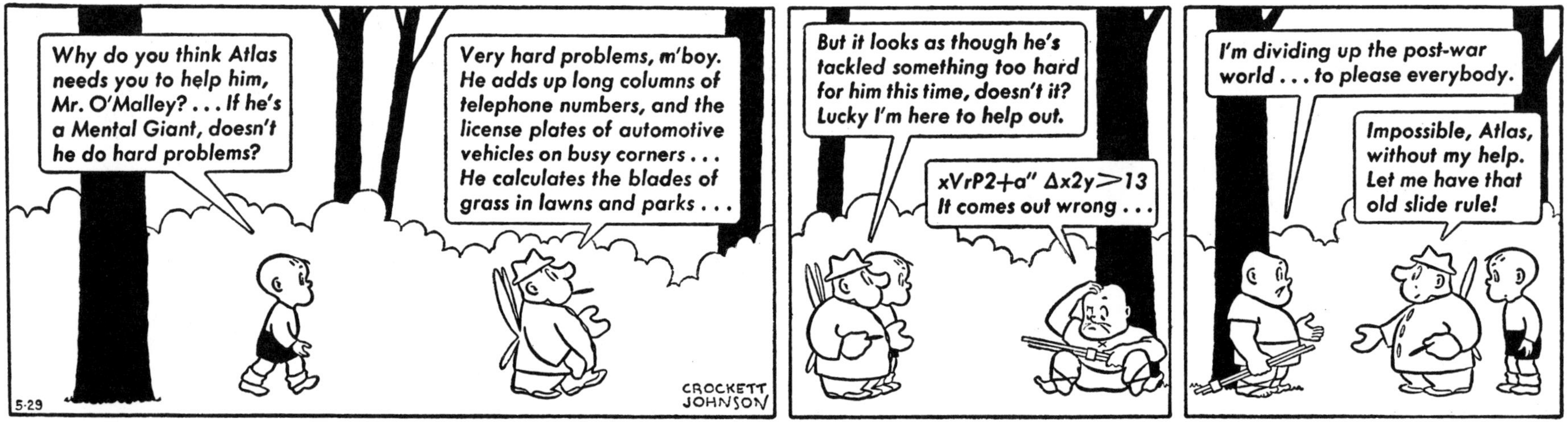

Why do you think Atlas needs you to help him, Mr. O'Malley? . . . If he's a Mental Giant, doesn't he do hard problems?
Very hard problems, m'boy. He adds up long columns of telephone numbers, and the license plates of automotive vehicles on busy corners . . . He calculates the blades of grass in lawns and parks . . .
CROCKETT JOHNSON
But it looks as though he's tackled something too hard for him this time, doesn't it? Lucky I'm here to help out.
xVrP2+a" Δx2y>13 It comes out wrong . . .
I'm dividing up the post-war world . . . to please everybody.
Impossible, Atlas, without my help. Let me have that old slide rule!
5-29

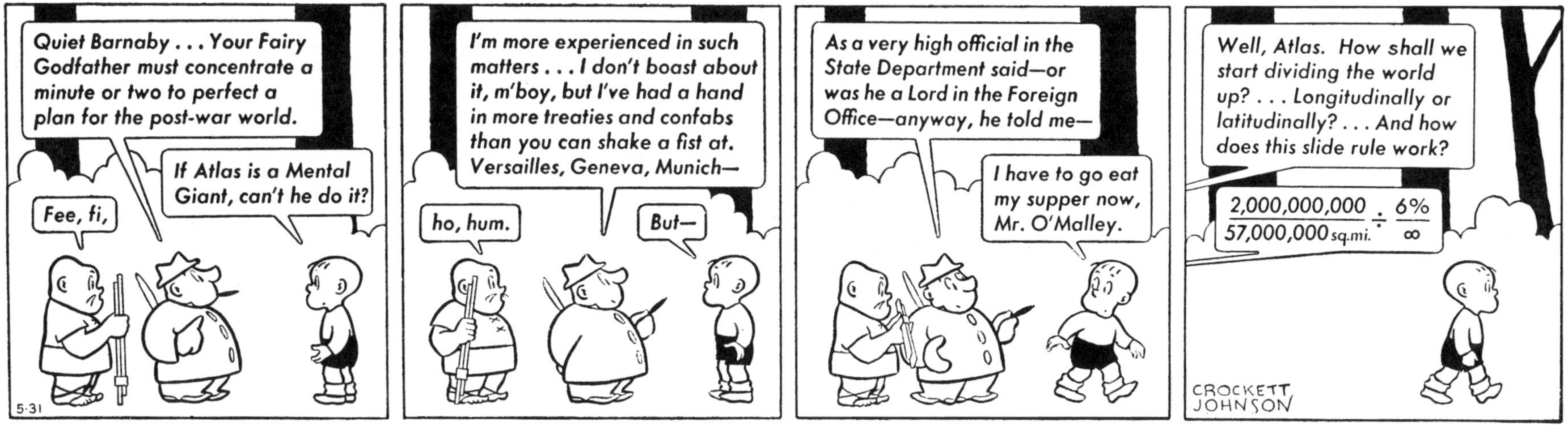
Quiet Barnaby . . . Your Fairy Godfather must concentrate a minute or two to perfect a plan for the post-war world.
If Atlas is a Mental Giant, can't he do it?
Fee, fi,
5·31
I'm more experienced in such matters . . . I don't boast about it, m'boy, but I've had a hand in more treaties and confabs than you can shake a fist at. Versailles, Geneva, Munich—
ho, hum.
But—
As a very high official in the State Department said—or was he a Lord in the Foreign Office—anyway, he told me—
I have to go eat my supper now, Mr. O'Malley.
Well, Atlas. How shall we start dividing the world up? . . . Longitudinally or latitudinally? . . . And how does this slide rule work?
2,000,000,000 / 57,000,000 sq.mi. ÷ 6% / ∞
CROCKETT JOHNSON

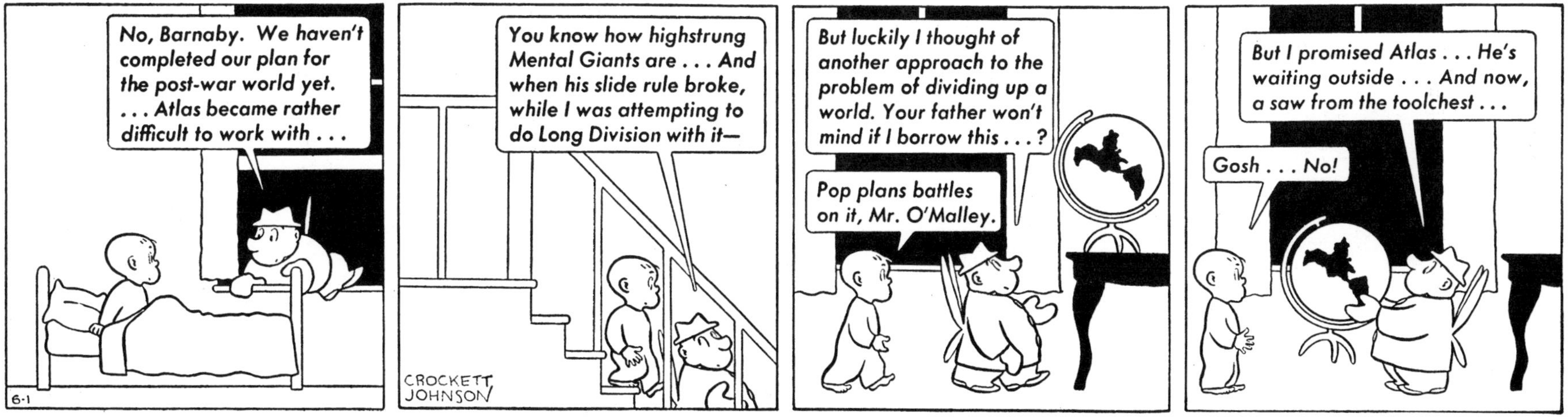
No, Barnaby. We haven't completed our plan for the post-war world yet. . . . Atlas became rather difficult to work with . . .
6·1
You know how highstrung Mental Giants are . . . And when his slide rule broke, while I was attempting to do Long Division with it—
CROCKETT JOHNSON
But luckily I thought of another approach to the problem of dividing up a world. Your father won't mind if I borrow this . . . ?
Pop plans battles on it, Mr. O'Malley.
But I promised Atlas . . . He's waiting outside . . . And now, a saw from the toolchest . . .
Gosh . . . No!

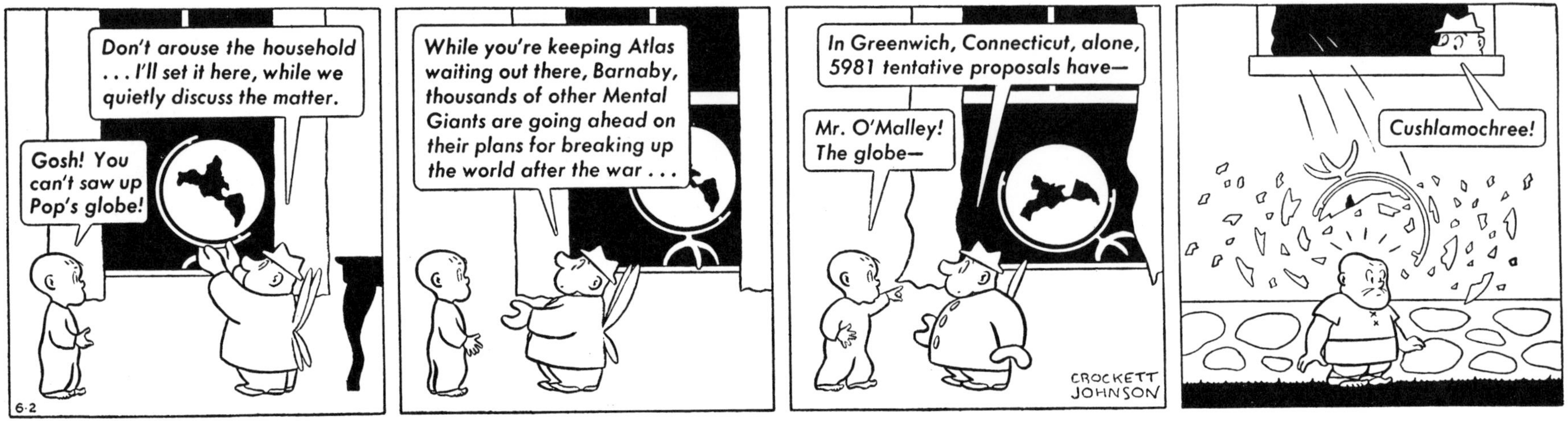
Don't arouse the household . . . I'll set it here, while we quietly discuss the matter.
Gosh! You can't saw up Pop's globe!
6·2
While you're keeping Atlas waiting out there, Barnaby, thousands of other Mental Giants are going ahead on their plans for breaking up the world after the war . . .
In Greenwich, Connecticut, alone, 5981 tentative proposals have—
Mr. O'Malley! The globe—
CROCKETT JOHNSON
Cushlamochree!

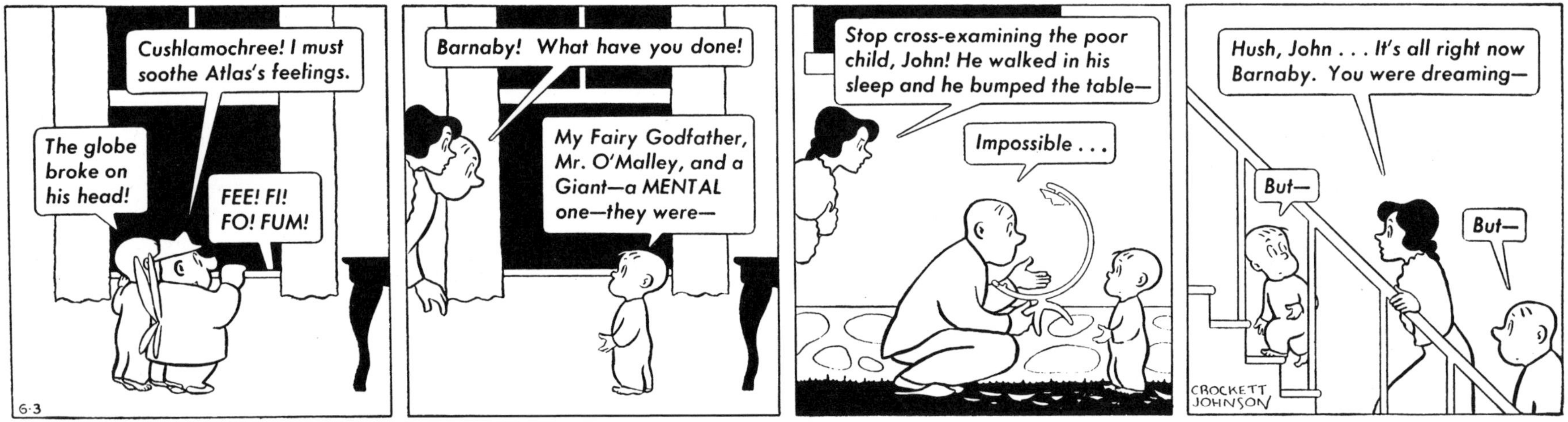
Cushlamochree! I must soothe Atlas's feelings.
The globe broke on his head!
FEE! FI! FO! FUM!
6·3
Barnaby! What have you done!
My Fairy Godfather, Mr. O'Malley, and a Giant—a MENTAL one—they were—
Stop cross-examining the poor child, John! He walked in his sleep and he bumped the table—
Impossible . . .
Hush, John . . . It's all right now Barnaby. You were dreaming—
But—
But—
CROCKETT JOHNSON

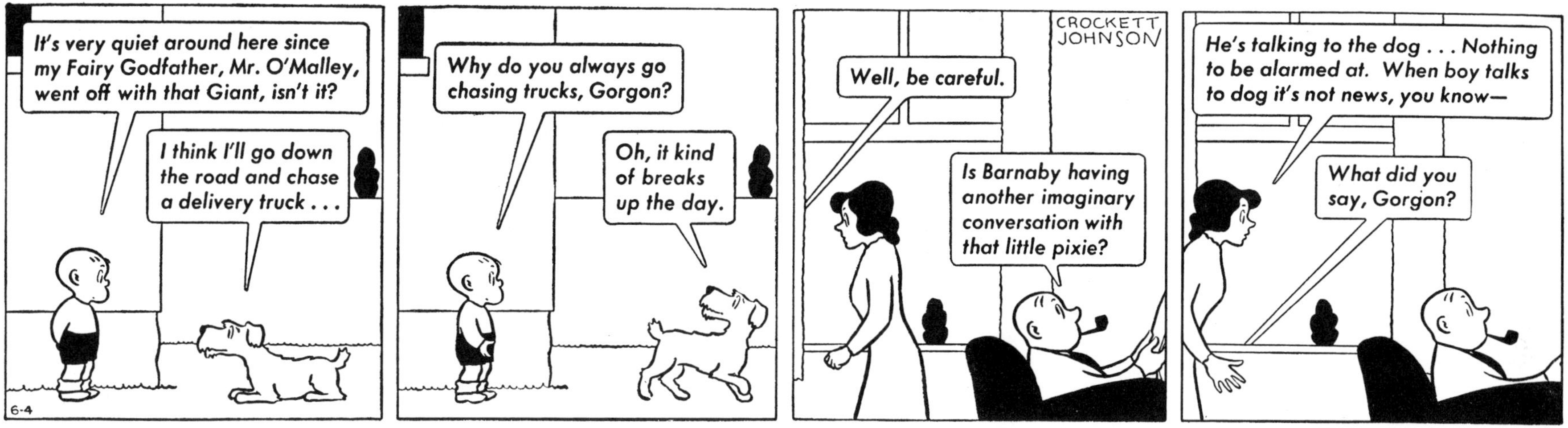
6-4
It's very quiet around here since my Fairy Godfather, Mr. O'Malley, went off with that Giant, isn't it?
I think I'll go down the road and chase a delivery truck . . .
Why do you always go chasing trucks, Gorgon?
Oh, it kind of breaks up the day.
CROCKETT JOHNSON
Well, be careful.
Is Barnaby having another imaginary conversation with that little pixie?
He's talking to the dog . . . Nothing to be alarmed at. When boy talks to dog it's not news, you know—
What did you say, Gorgon?

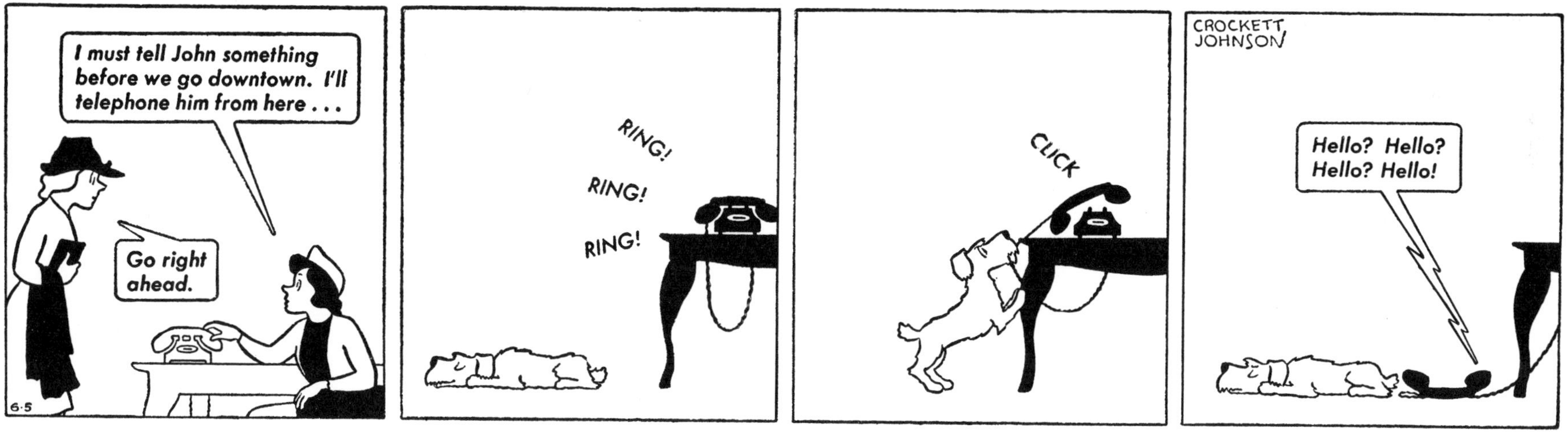
6-5
I must tell John something before we go downtown. I'll telephone him from here . . .
Go right ahead.
RING!
RING!
RING!
CLICK
CROCKETT JOHNSON
Hello? Hello? Hello? Hello!

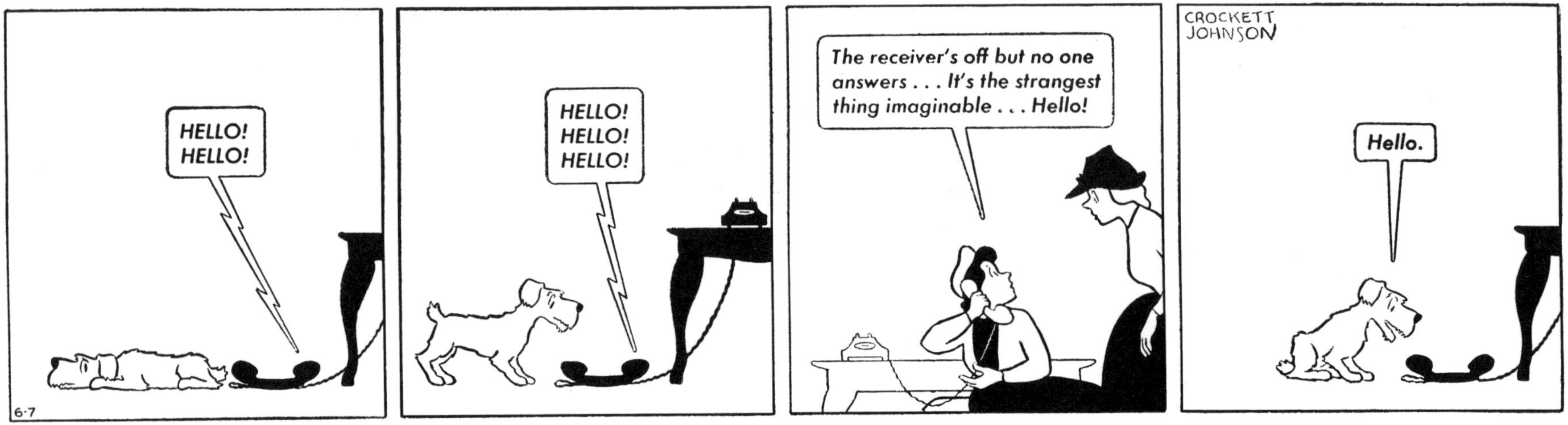
HELLO!
HELLO!
6·7
HELLO!
HELLO!
HELLO!
The receiver's off but no one answers . . . It's the strangest thing imaginable . . . Hello!
CROCKETT JOHNSON
Hello.

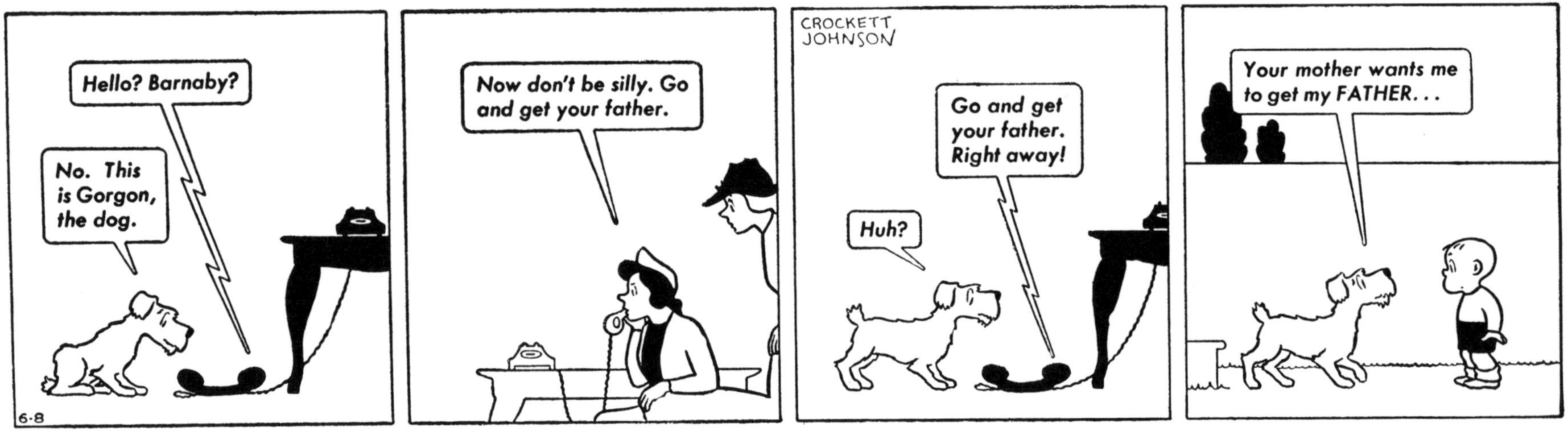
Hello? Barnaby?
No. This is Gorgon, the dog.
6·8
Now don't be silly. Go and get your father.
CROCKETT JOHNSON
Huh?
Go and get your father. Right away!
Your mother wants me to get my FATHER. . .

June 7 – 8

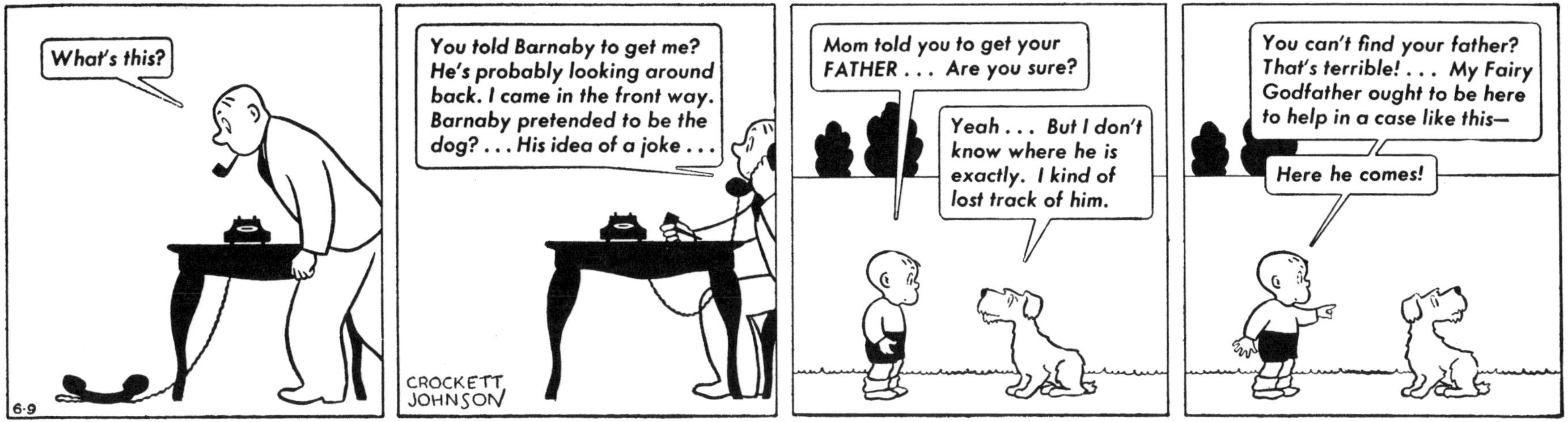
What's this?
You told Barnaby to get me? He's probably looking around back. I came in the front way. Barnaby pretended to be the dog? . . . His idea of a joke . . .
CROCKETT JOHNSON
Mom told you to get your FATHER . . . Are you sure?
Yeah . . . But I don't know where he is exactly. I kind of lost track of him.
You can't find your father? That's terrible! . . . My Fairy Godfather ought to be here to help in a case like this—
Here he comes!
6·9

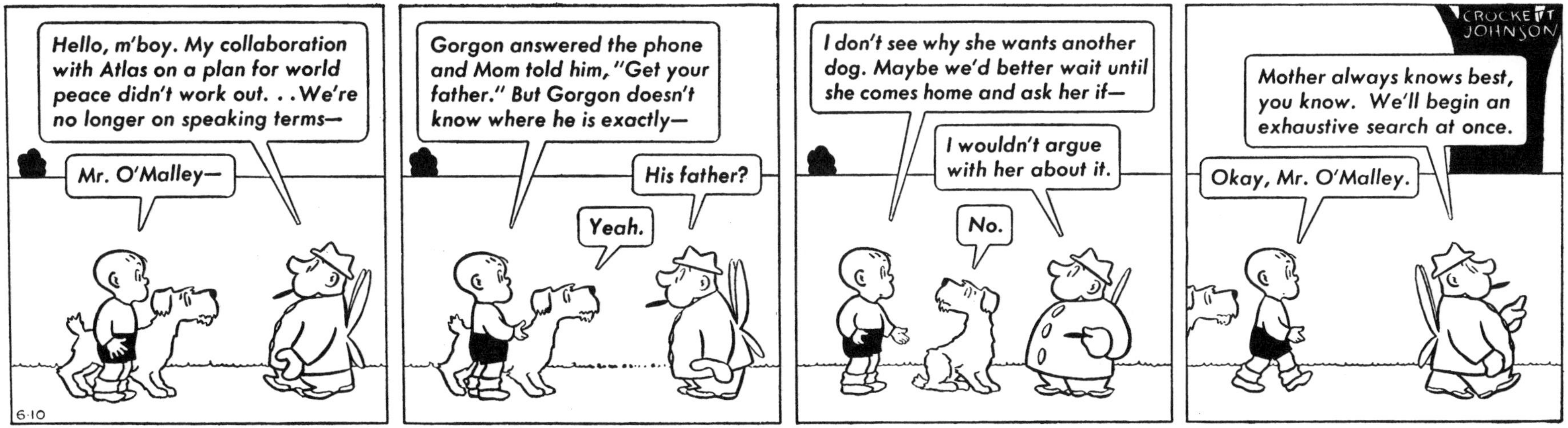
Hello, m'boy. My collaboration with Atlas on a plan for world peace didn't work out. . . We're no longer on speaking terms—
Mr. O'Malley—
Gorgon answered the phone and Mom told him, "Get your father." But Gorgon doesn't know where he is exactly—
His father?
Yeah.
I don't see why she wants another dog. Maybe we'd better wait until she comes home and ask her if—
I wouldn't argue with her about it.
No.
CROCKETT JOHNSON
Mother always knows best, you know. We'll begin an exhaustive search at once.
Okay, Mr. O'Malley.
6·10

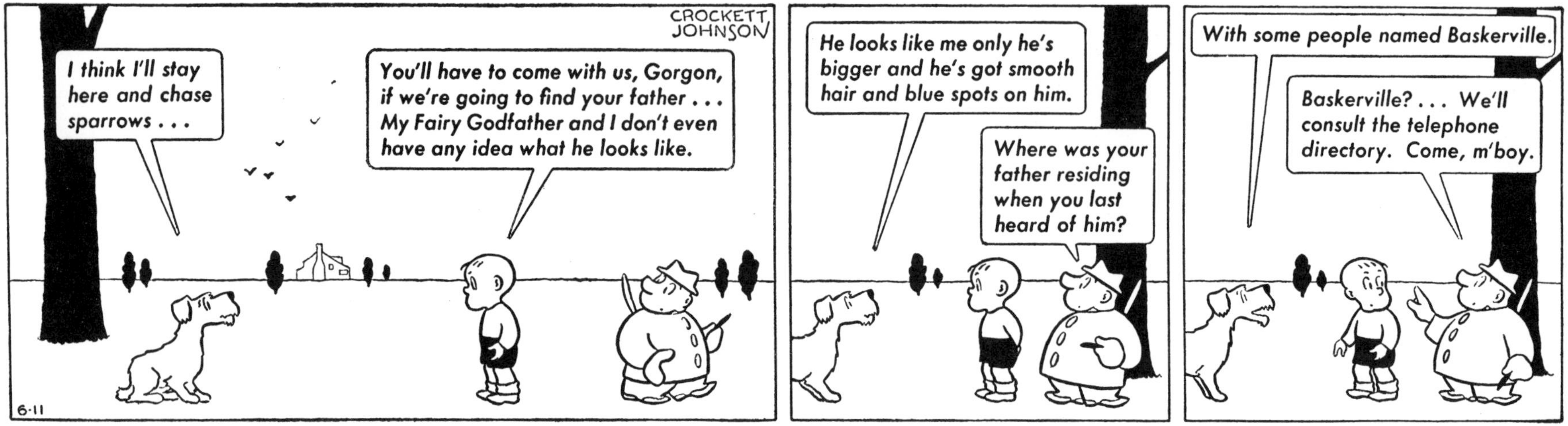
CROCKETT JOHNSON
I think I'll stay here and chase sparrows . . .
You'll have to come with us, Gorgon, if we're going to find your father . . . My Fairy Godfather and I don't even have any idea what he looks like.
6-11
He looks like me only he's bigger and he's got smooth hair and blue spots on him.
Where was your father residing when you last heard of him?
With some people named Baskerville.
Baskerville? . . . We'll consult the telephone directory. Come, m'boy.

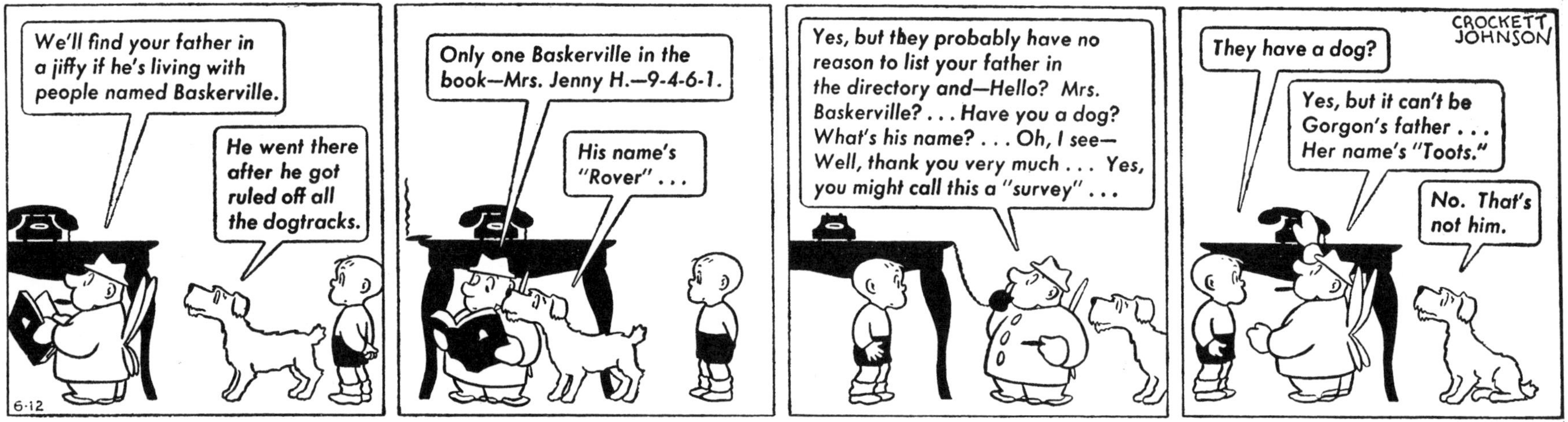
We'll find your father in a jiffy if he's living with people named Baskerville.
He went there after he got ruled off all the dogtracks.
6-12
Only one Baskerville in the book—Mrs. Jenny H.—9-4-6-1.
His name's "Rover" . . .
Yes, but they probably have no reason to list your father in the directory and—Hello? Mrs. Baskerville? . . . Have you a dog? What's his name? . . . Oh, I see— Well, thank you very much . . . Yes, you might call this a "survey" . . .
CROCKETT JOHNSON
They have a dog?
Yes, but it can't be Gorgon's father . . . Her name's "Toots."
No. That's not him.

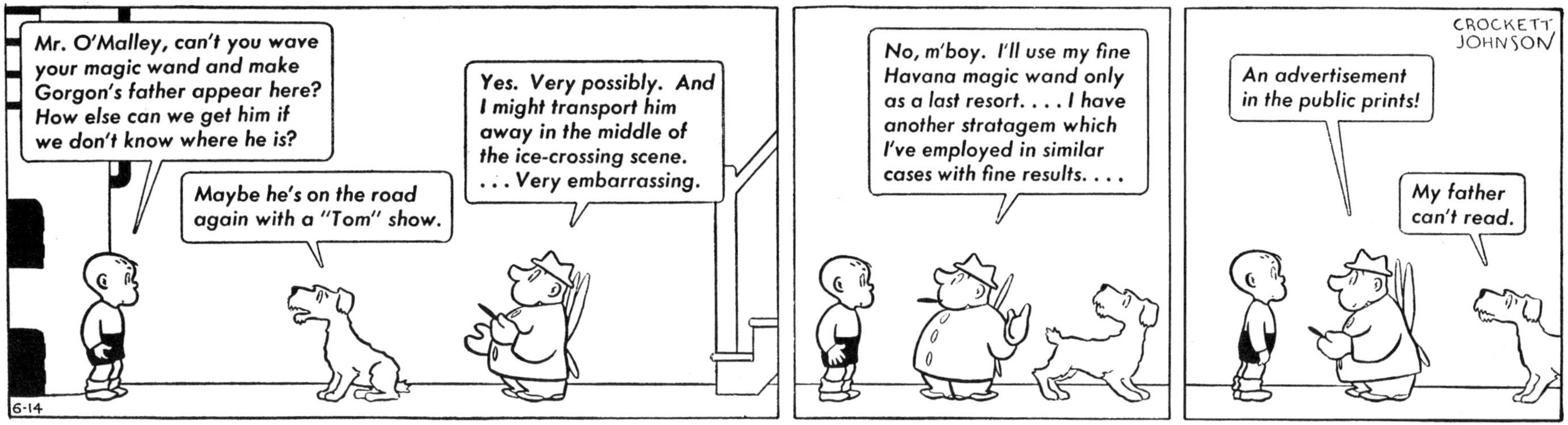
6-14
Mr. O'Malley, can't you wave your magic wand and make Gorgon's father appear here? How else can we get him if we don't know where he is?
Maybe he's on the road again with a "Tom" show.
Yes. Very possibly. And I might transport him away in the middle of the ice-crossing scene. . . . Very embarrassing.
No, m'boy. I'll use my fine Havana magic wand only as a last resort. . . . I have another stratagem which I've employed in similar cases with fine results. . . .
CROCKETT JOHNSON
An advertisement in the public prints!
My father can't read.

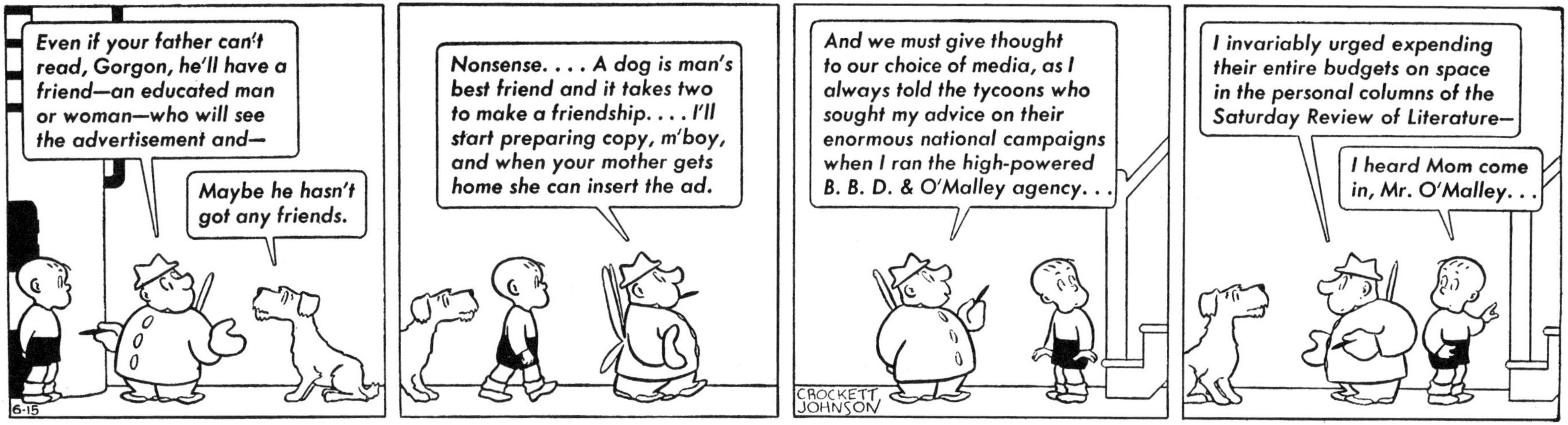
6-15
Even if your father can't read, Gorgon, he'll have a friend—an educated man or woman—who will see the advertisement and—
Maybe he hasn't got any friends.
Nonsense. . . . A dog is man's best friend and it takes two to make a friendship. . . . I'll start preparing copy, m'boy, and when your mother gets home she can insert the ad.
And we must give thought to our choice of media, as I always told the tycoons who sought my advice on their enormous national campaigns when I ran the high-powered B. B. D. & O'Malley agency. . .
CROCKETT JOHNSON
I invariably urged expending their entire budgets on space in the personal columns of the Saturday Review of Literature—
I heard Mom come in, Mr. O'Malley. . .

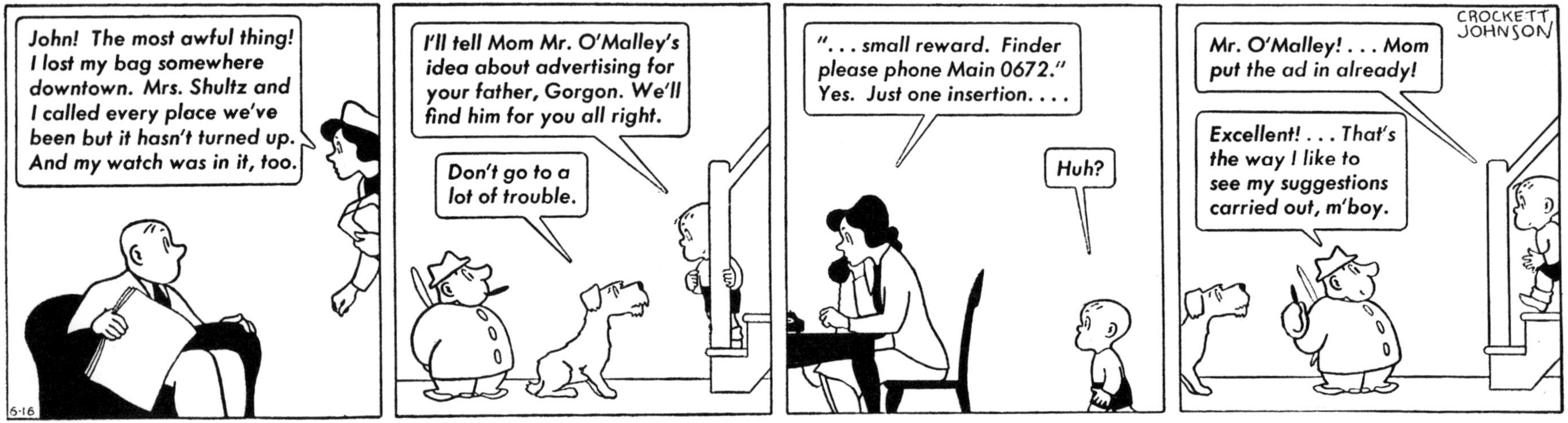
John! The most awful thing! I lost my bag somewhere downtown. Mrs. Shultz and I called every place we've been but it hasn't turned up. And my watch was in it, too.
6·16
I'll tell Mom Mr. O'Malley's idea about advertising for your father, Gorgon. We'll find him for you all right.
Don't go to a lot of trouble.
". . . small reward. Finder please phone Main 0672." Yes. Just one insertion. . . .
Huh?
CROCKETT JOHNSON
Mr. O'Malley! . . . Mom put the ad in already!
Excellent! . . . That's the way I like to see my suggestions carried out, m'boy.

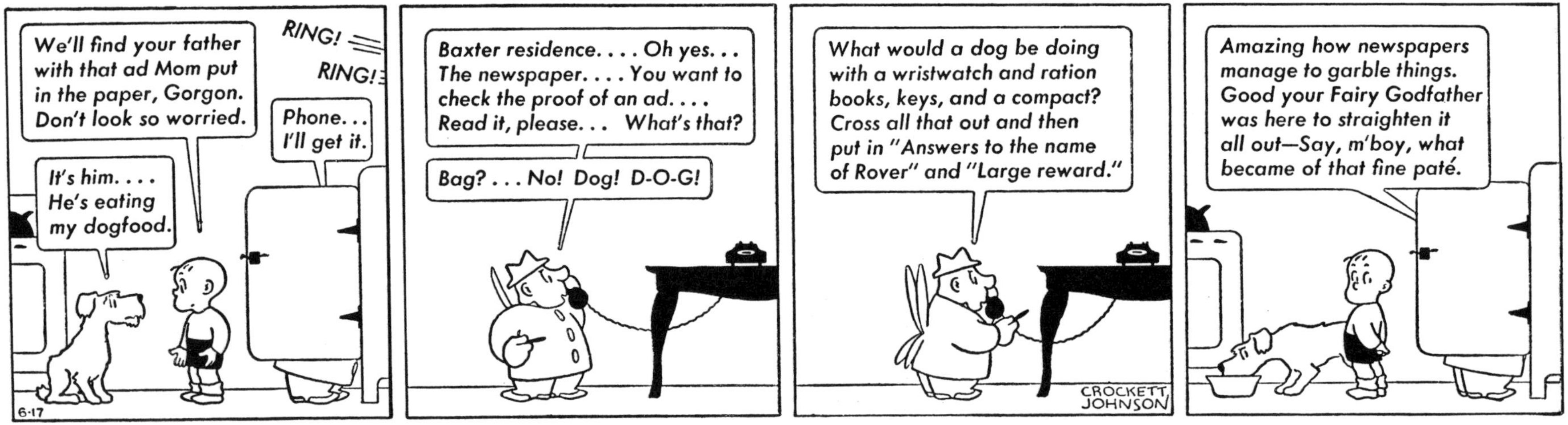
We'll find your father with that ad Mom put in the paper, Gorgon. Don't look so worried.
RING!
RING!
Phone. . . I'll get it.
It's him. . . . He's eating my dogfood.
6·17
Baxter residence. . . . Oh yes. . . The newspaper. . . . You want to check the proof of an ad. . . . Read it, please. . . What's that?
Bag? . . . No! Dog! D-O-G!
What would a dog be doing with a wristwatch and ration books, keys, and a compact? Cross all that out and then put in "Answers to the name of Rover" and "Large reward."
CROCKETT JOHNSON
Amazing how newspapers manage to garble things. Good your Fairy Godfather was here to straighten it all out—Say, m'boy, what became of that fine paté.

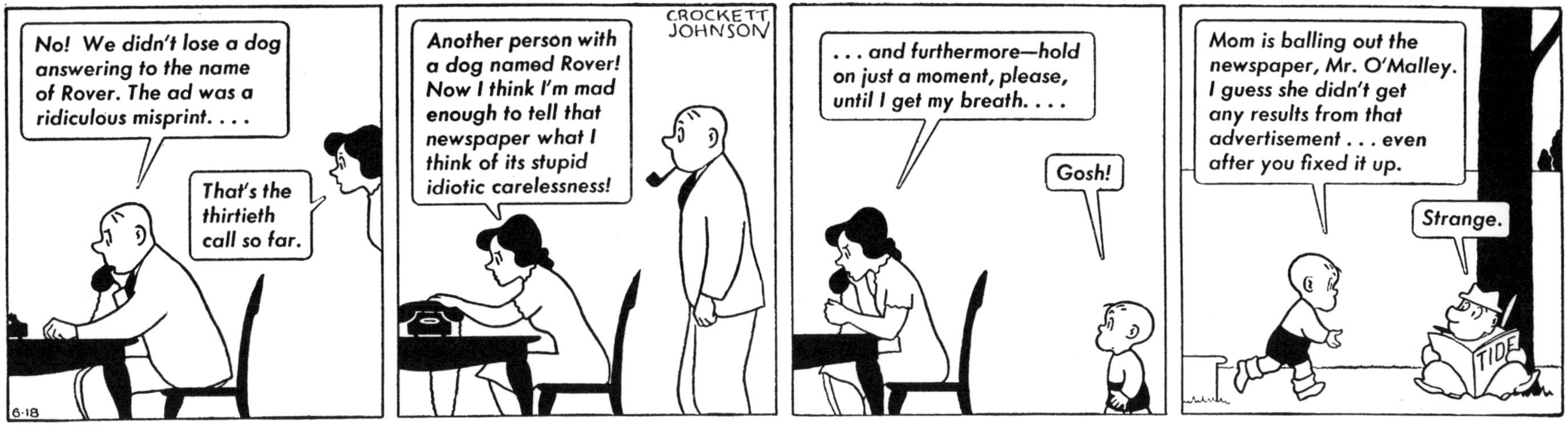
No! We didn't lose a dog answering to the name of Rover. The ad was a ridiculous misprint. . . .
That's the thirtieth call so far.
CROCKETT JOHNSON
Another person with a dog named Rover! Now I think I'm mad enough to tell that newspaper what I think of its stupid idiotic carelessness!
. . . and furthermore—hold on just a moment, please, until I get my breath. . . .
Gosh!
Mom is balling out the newspaper, Mr. O'Malley. I guess she didn't get any results from that advertisement . . . even after you fixed it up.
Strange.
TIDE
6·18

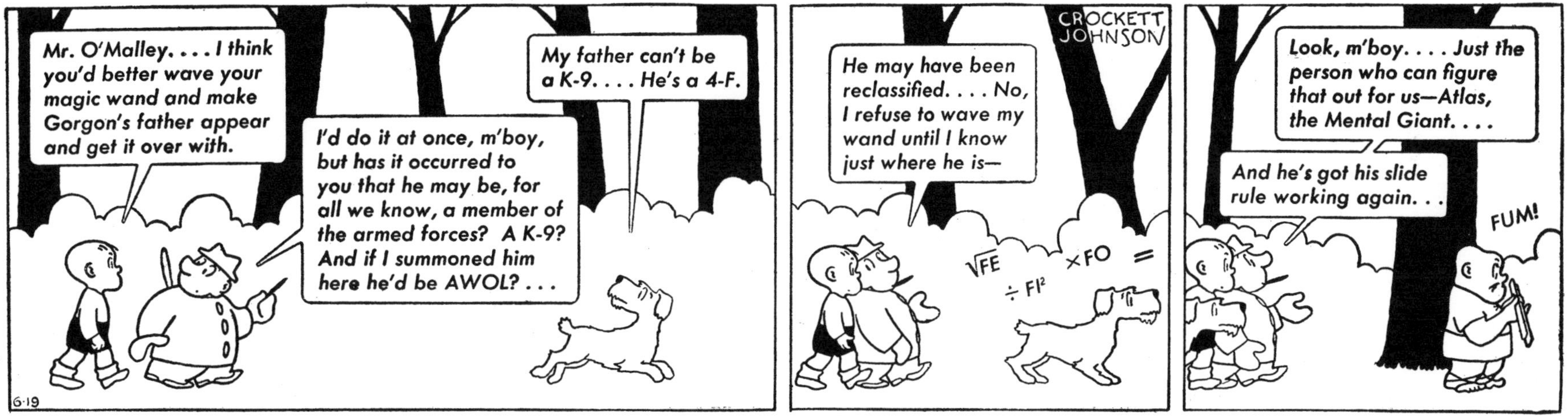
Mr. O'Malley. . . . I think you'd better wave your magic wand and make Gorgon's father appear and get it over with.
I'd do it at once, m'boy, but has it occurred to you that he may be, for all we know, a member of the armed forces? A K-9? And if I summoned him here he'd be AWOL? . . .
My father can't be a K-9. . . . He's a 4-F.
CROCKETT JOHNSON
He may have been reclassified. . . . No, I refuse to wave my wand until I know just where he is—
√FE ÷ FI² ×FO =
Look, m'boy. . . . Just the person who can figure that out for us—Atlas, the Mental Giant. . . .
And he's got his slide rule working again. . .
FUM!
6·19

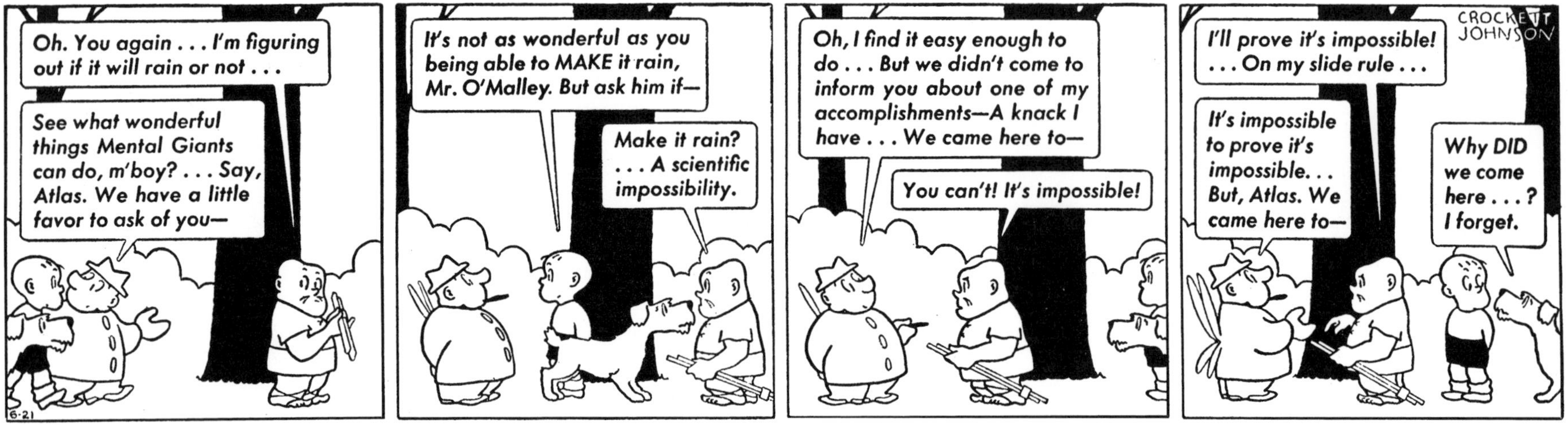
Oh. You again . . . I'm figuring out if it will rain or not . . .
See what wonderful things Mental Giants can do, m'boy? . . . Say, Atlas. We have a little favor to ask of you—
6-21
It's not as wonderful as you being able to MAKE it rain, Mr. O'Malley. But ask him if—
Make it rain? . . . A scientific impossibility.
Oh, I find it easy enough to do . . . But we didn't come to inform you about one of my accomplishments—A knack I have . . . We came here to—
You can't! It's impossible!
CROCKETT JOHNSON
I'll prove it's impossible! . . . On my slide rule . . .
It's impossible to prove it's impossible. . . But, Atlas. We came here to—
Why DID we come here . . . ? I forget.

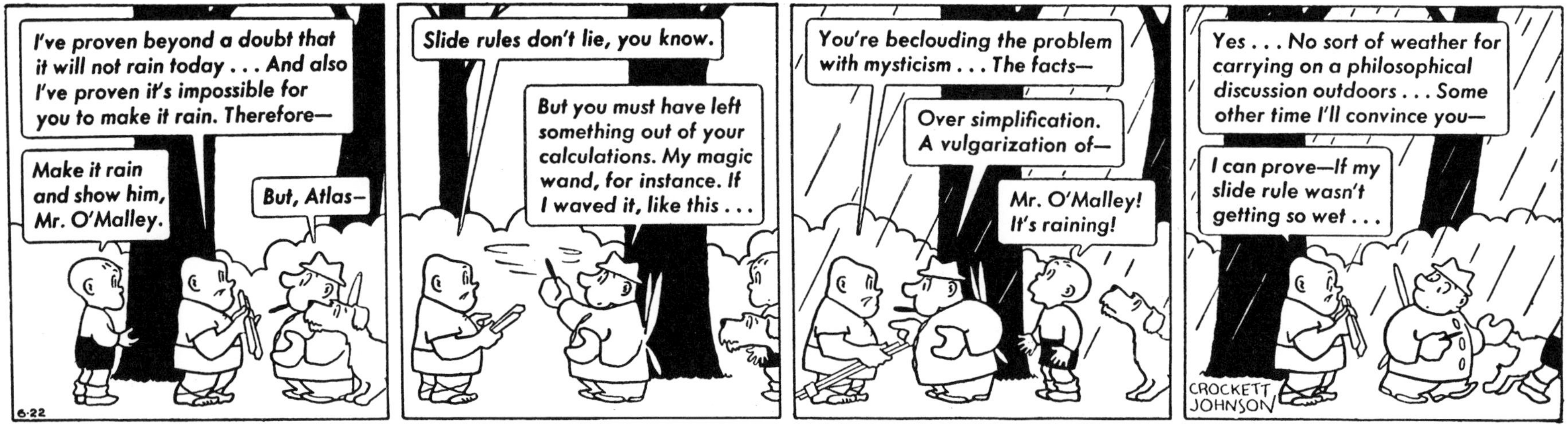
I've proven beyond a doubt that it will not rain today . . . And also I've proven it's impossible for you to make it rain. Therefore—
Make it rain and show him, Mr. O'Malley.
But, Atlas—
6-22
Slide rules don't lie, you know.
But you must have left something out of your calculations. My magic wand, for instance. If I waved it, like this . . .
You're beclouding the problem with mysticism . . . The facts—
Over simplification. A vulgarization of—
Mr. O'Malley! It's raining!
Yes . . . No sort of weather for carrying on a philosophical discussion outdoors . . . Some other time I'll convince you—
I can prove—If my slide rule wasn't getting so wet . . .
CROCKETT JOHNSON

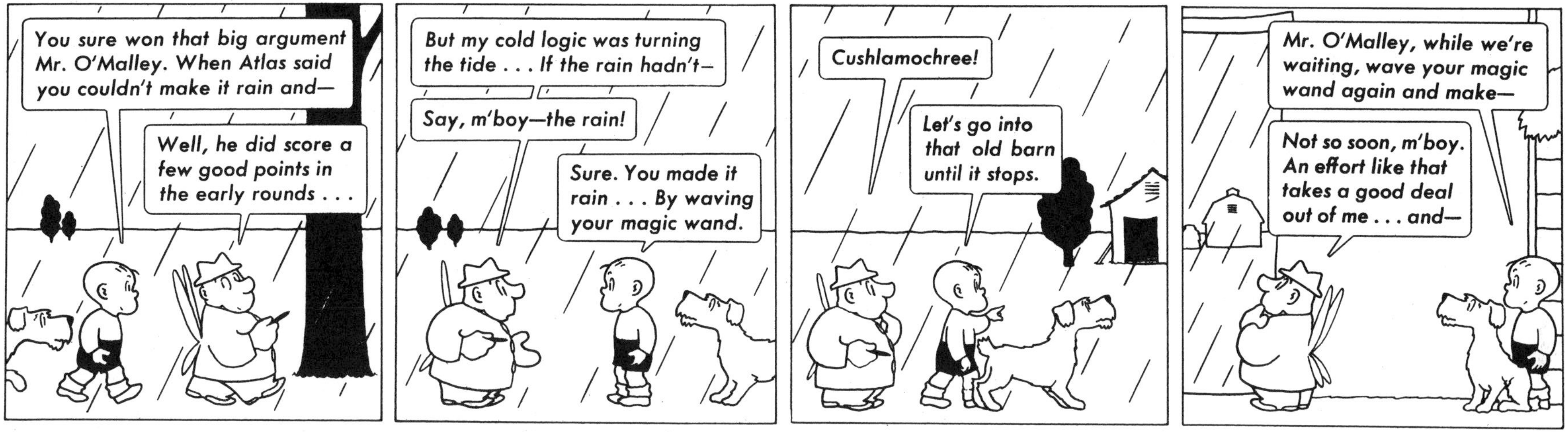
You sure won that big argument Mr. O'Malley. When Atlas said you couldn't make it rain and—
Well, he did score a few good points in the early rounds . . .
But my cold logic was turning the tide . . . If the rain hadn't—
Say, m'boy—the rain!
Sure. You made it rain . . . By waving your magic wand.
Cushlamochree!
Let's go into that old barn until it stops.
Mr. O'Malley, while we're waiting, wave your magic wand again and make—
Not so soon, m'boy. An effort like that takes a good deal out of me . . . and—

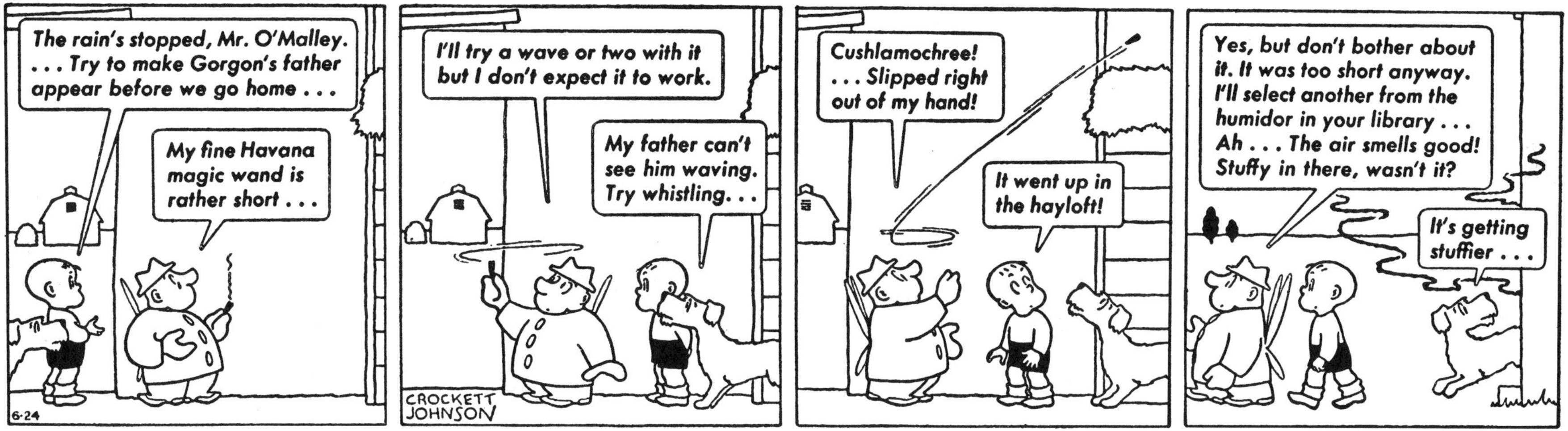
The rain's stopped, Mr. O'Malley. . . . Try to make Gorgon's father appear before we go home . . .
My fine Havana magic wand is rather short . . .
6-24
I'll try a wave or two with it but I don't expect it to work.
My father can't see him waving. Try whistling. . .
CROCKETT JOHNSON
Cushlamochree! . . . Slipped right out of my hand!
It went up in the hayloft!
Yes, but don't bother about it. It was too short anyway. I'll select another from the humidor in your library . . . Ah . . . The air smells good! Stuffy in there, wasn't it?
It's getting stuffier . . .

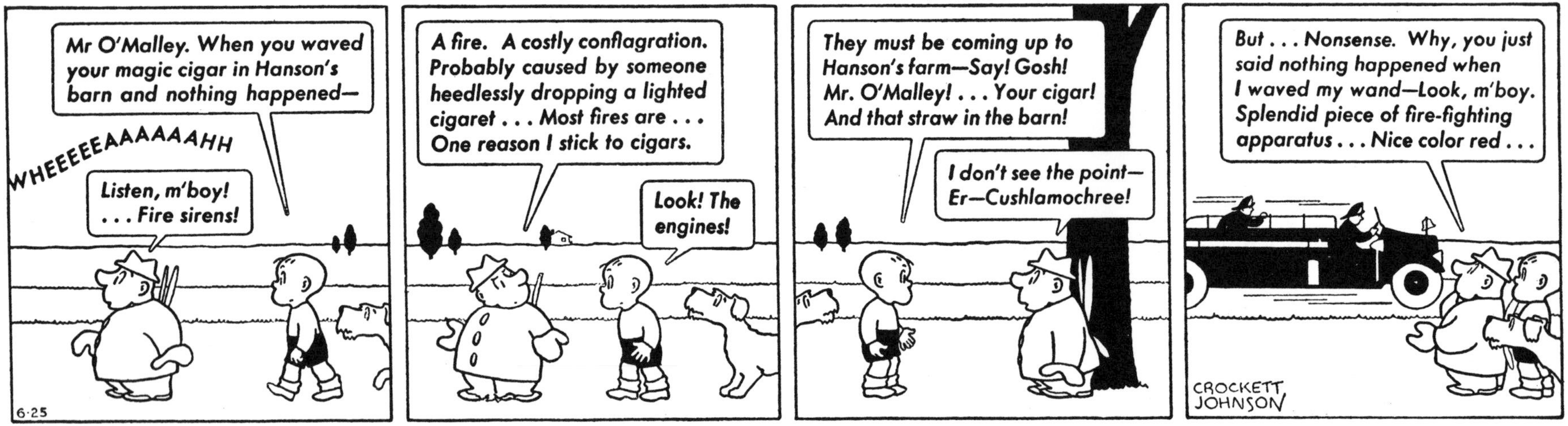

6·25
Mr O'Malley. When you waved your magic cigar in Hanson's barn and nothing happened—
WHEEEEEAAAAAAHH
Listen, m'boy! . . . Fire sirens!
A fire. A costly conflagration. Probably caused by someone heedlessly dropping a lighted cigaret . . . Most fires are . . . One reason I stick to cigars.
Look! The engines!
They must be coming up to Hanson's farm—Say! Gosh! Mr. O'Malley! . . . Your cigar! And that straw in the barn!
I don't see the point— Er—Cushlamochree!
But . . . Nonsense. Why, you just said nothing happened when I waved my wand—Look, m'boy. Splendid piece of fire-fighting apparatus . . . Nice color red . . .
CROCKETT JOHNSON

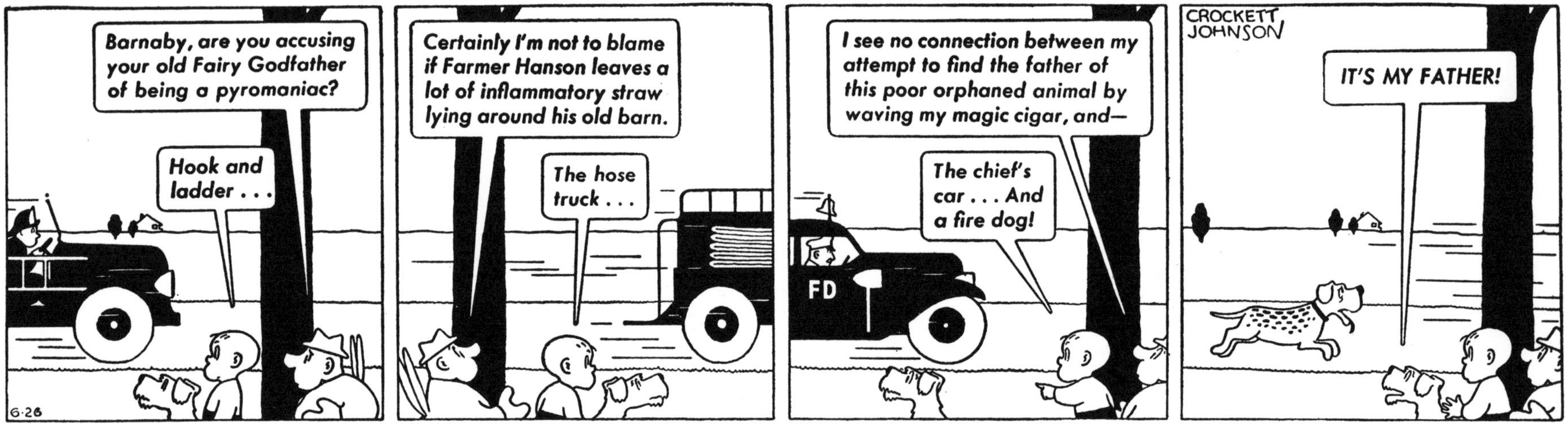

6·26
Barnaby, are you accusing your old Fairy Godfather of being a pyromaniac?
Hook and ladder . . .
Certainly I'm not to blame if Farmer Hanson leaves a lot of inflammatory straw lying around his old barn.
The hose truck . . .
I see no connection between my attempt to find the father of this poor orphaned animal by waving my magic cigar, and—
The chief's car . . . And a fire dog!
FD
CROCKETT JOHNSON
IT'S MY FATHER!

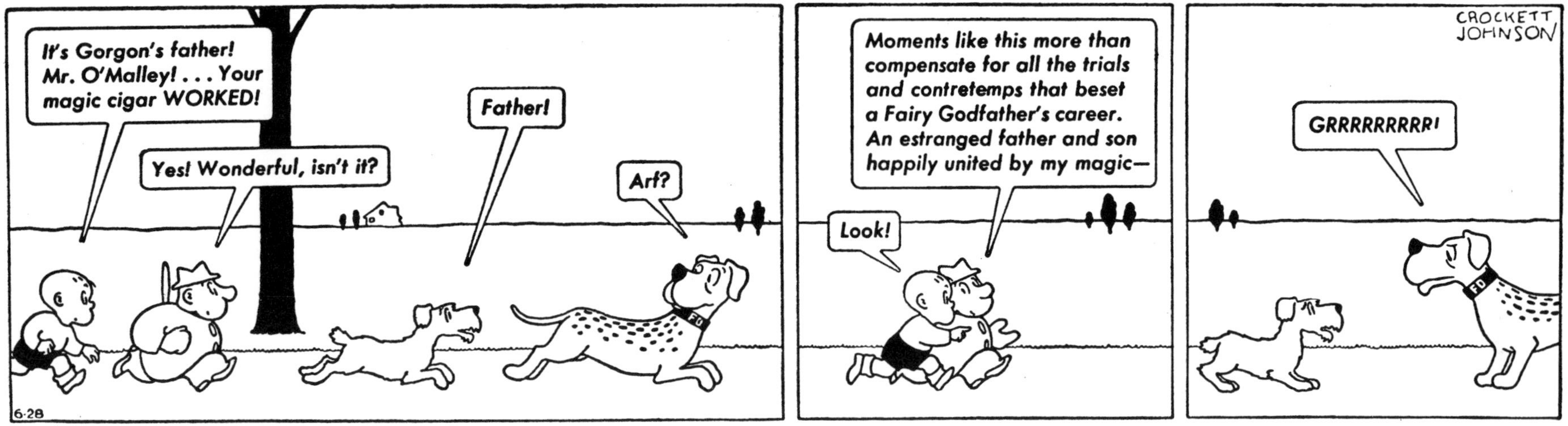
It's Gorgon's father! Mr. O'Malley! . . . Your magic cigar WORKED!
Yes! Wonderful, isn't it?
Father!
Arf?
Moments like this more than compensate for all the trials and contretemps that beset a Fairy Godfather's career. An estranged father and son happily united by my magic—
Look!
CROCKETT JOHNSON
GRRRRRRRRR!
6·28

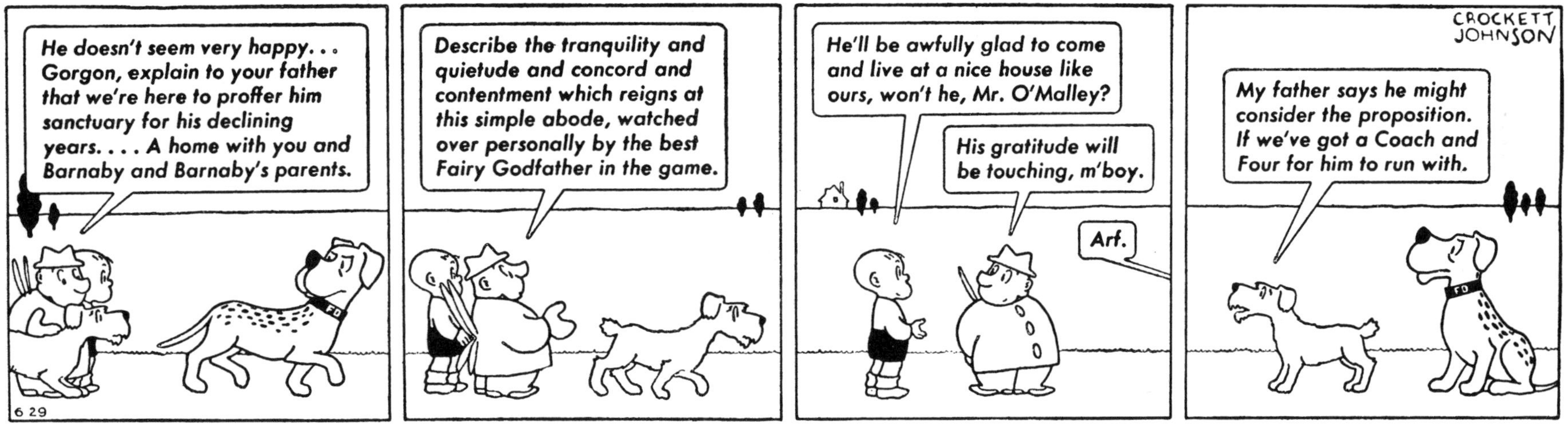
He doesn't seem very happy. . . Gorgon, explain to your father that we're here to proffer him sanctuary for his declining years. . . . A home with you and Barnaby and Barnaby's parents.
Describe the tranquility and quietude and concord and contentment which reigns at this simple abode, watched over personally by the best Fairy Godfather in the game.
He'll be awfully glad to come and live at a nice house like ours, won't he, Mr. O'Malley?
His gratitude will be touching, m'boy.
Arf.
CROCKETT JOHNSON
My father says he might consider the proposition. If we've got a Coach and Four for him to run with.
6 29

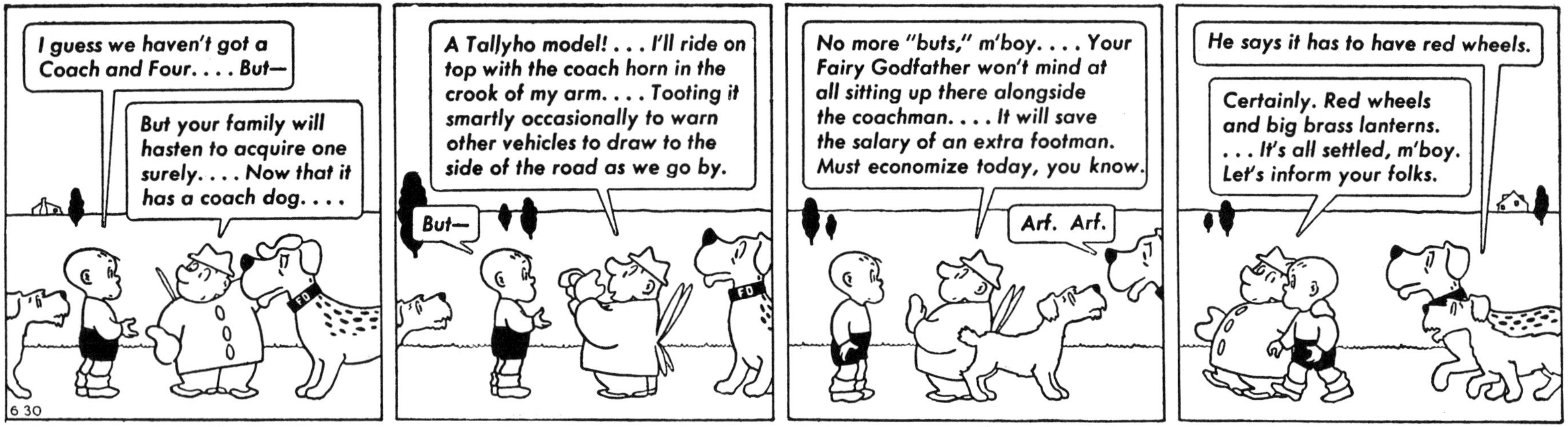
I guess we haven't got a Coach and Four. . . . But—
But your family will hasten to acquire one surely. . . . Now that it has a coach dog. . . .
6 30
A Tallyho model! . . . I'll ride on top with the coach horn in the crook of my arm. . . . Tooting it smartly occasionally to warn other vehicles to draw to the side of the road as we go by.
But—
No more "buts," m'boy. . . . Your Fairy Godfather won't mind at all sitting up there alongside the coachman. . . . It will save the salary of an extra footman. Must economize today, you know.
Arf. Arf.
He says it has to have red wheels.
Certainly. Red wheels and big brass lanterns. . . . It's all settled, m'boy. Let's inform your folks.
FD

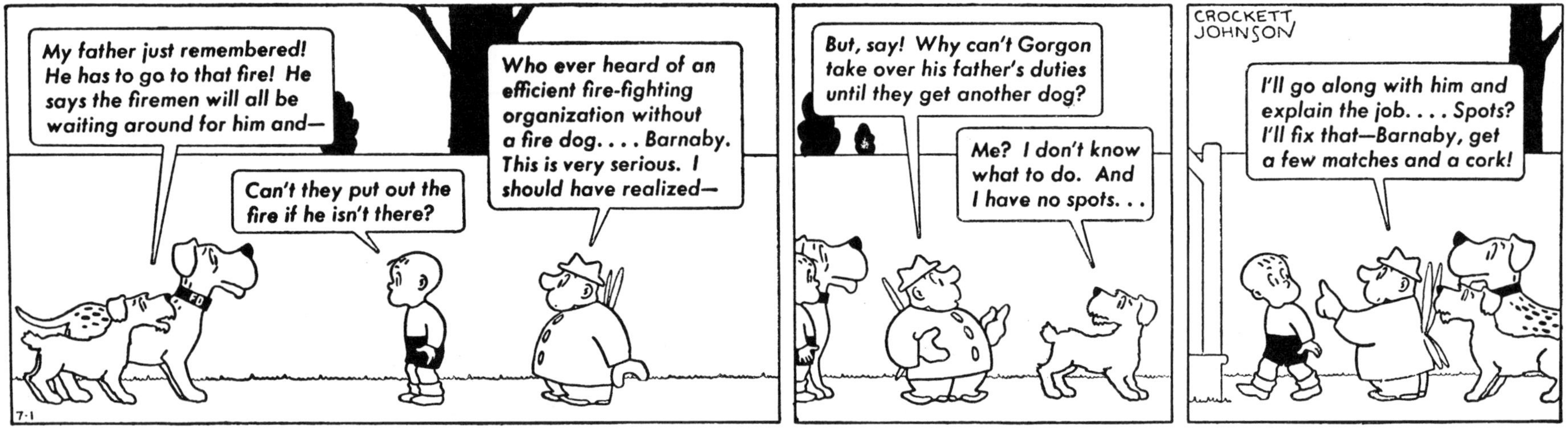
My father just remembered! He has to go to that fire! He says the firemen will all be waiting around for him and—
Can't they put out the fire if he isn't there?
Who ever heard of an efficient fire-fighting organization without a fire dog. . . . Barnaby. This is very serious. I should have realized—
7-1
But, say! Why can't Gorgon take over his father's duties until they get another dog?
Me? I don't know what to do. And I have no spots. . .
CROCKETT JOHNSON
I'll go along with him and explain the job. . . . Spots? I'll fix that—Barnaby, get a few matches and a cork!
FD

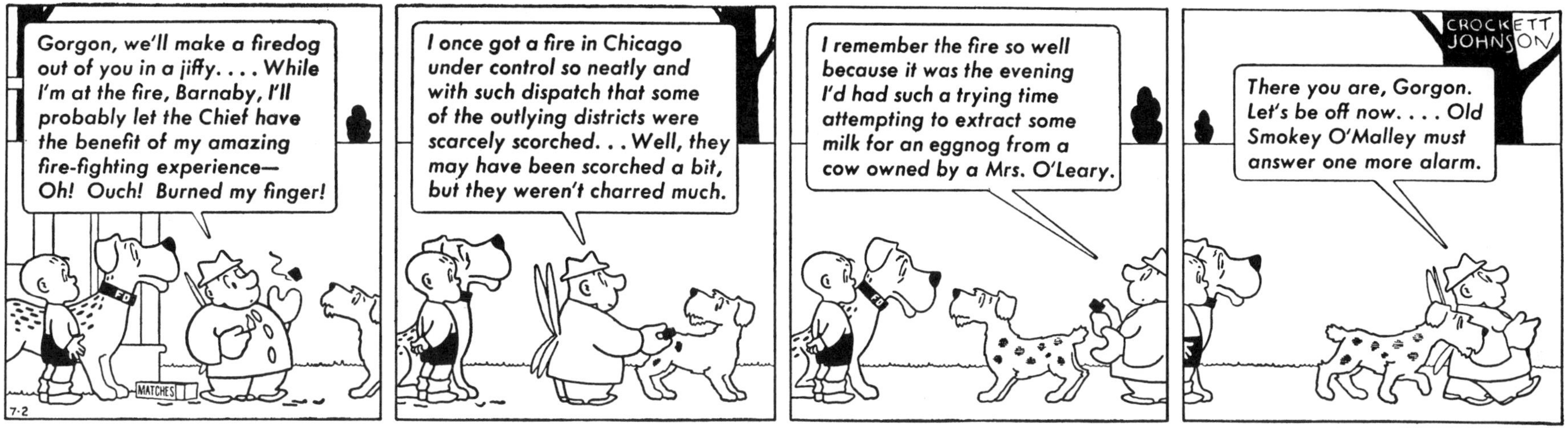
Gorgon, we'll make a firedog out of you in a jiffy. . . . While I'm at the fire, Barnaby, I'll probably let the Chief have the benefit of my amazing fire-fighting experience— Oh! Ouch! Burned my finger!
FD
MATCHES
7·2
I once got a fire in Chicago under control so neatly and with such dispatch that some of the outlying districts were scarcely scorched. . . Well, they may have been scorched a bit, but they weren't charred much.
I remember the fire so well because it was the evening I'd had such a trying time attempting to extract some milk for an eggnog from a cow owned by a Mrs. O'Leary.
CROCKETT JOHNSON
There you are, Gorgon. Let's be off now. . . . Old Smokey O'Malley must answer one more alarm.

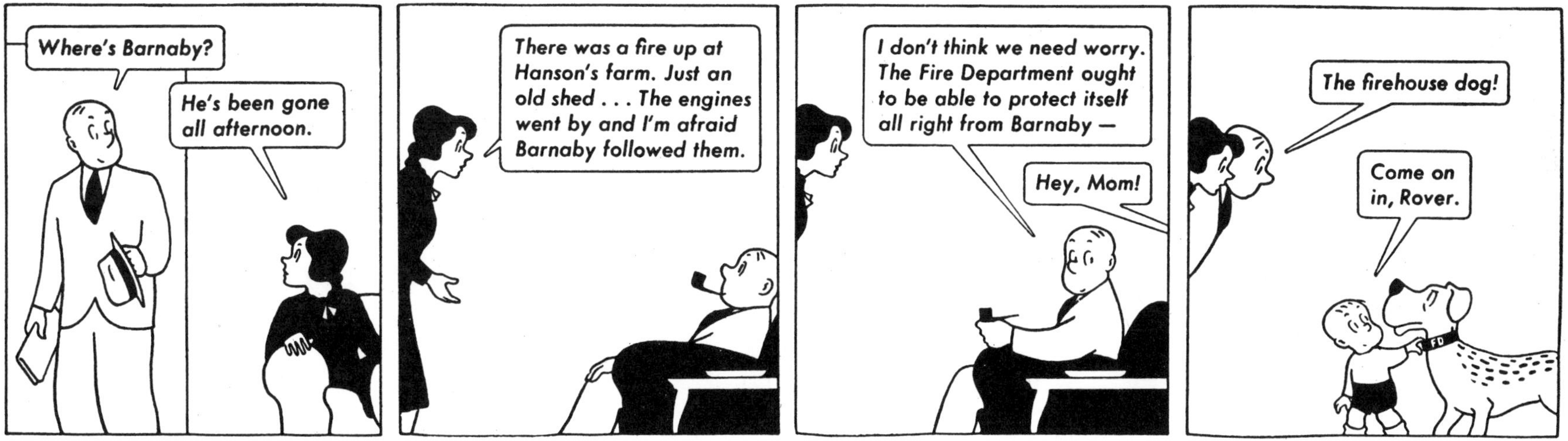
Where's Barnaby?
He's been gone all afternoon.
There was a fire up at Hanson's farm. Just an old shed . . . The engines went by and I'm afraid Barnaby followed them.
I don't think we need worry. The Fire Department ought to be able to protect itself all right from Barnaby —
Hey, Mom!
The firehouse dog!
Come on in, Rover.
FD

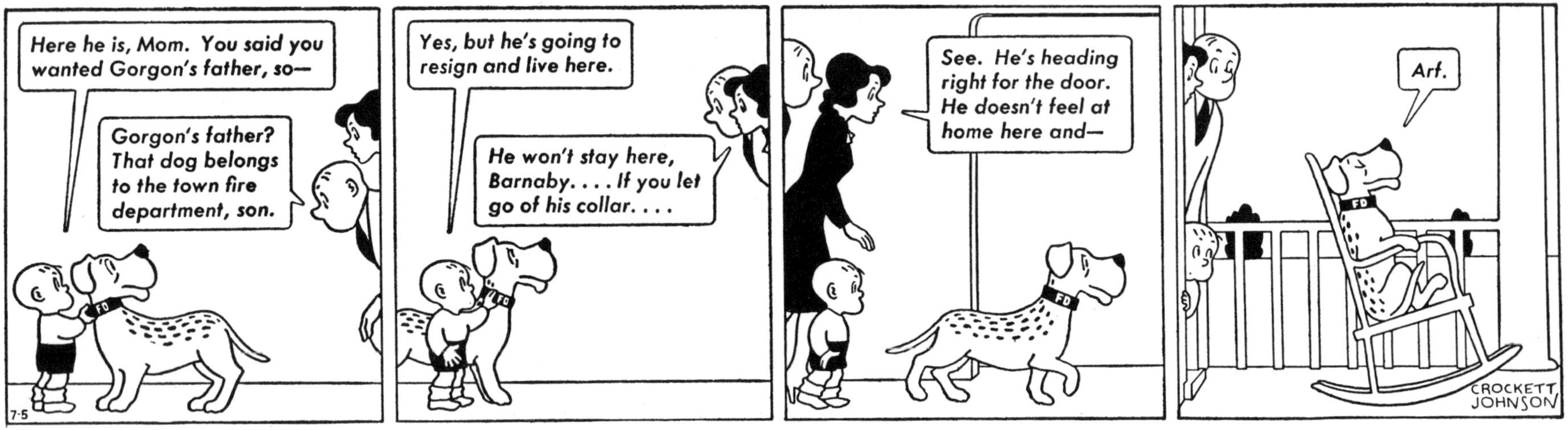
Here he is, Mom. You said you wanted Gorgon's father, so—
Gorgon's father? That dog belongs to the town fire department, son.
7·5
Yes, but he's going to resign and live here.
He won't stay here, Barnaby. . . . If you let go of his collar. . . .
See. He's heading right for the door. He doesn't feel at home here and—
Arf.
CROCKETT JOHNSON

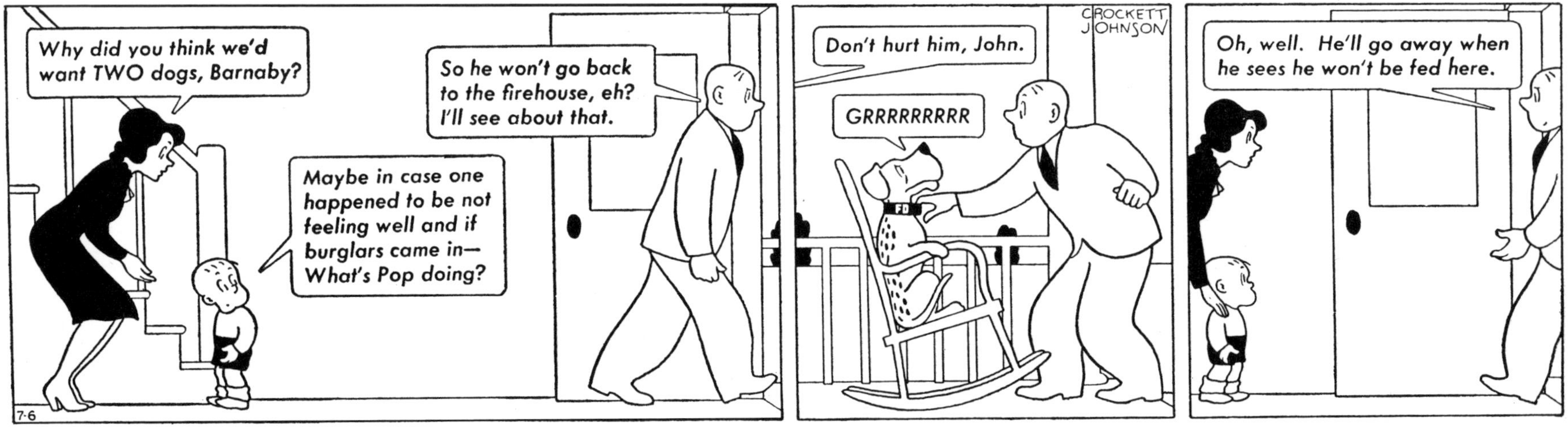
Why did you think we'd want TWO dogs, Barnaby?
Maybe in case one happened to be not feeling well and if burglars came in— What's Pop doing?
So he won't go back to the firehouse, eh? I'll see about that.
7·6
Don't hurt him, John.
GRRRRRRRRR
CROCKETT JOHNSON
Oh, well. He'll go away when he sees he won't be fed here.

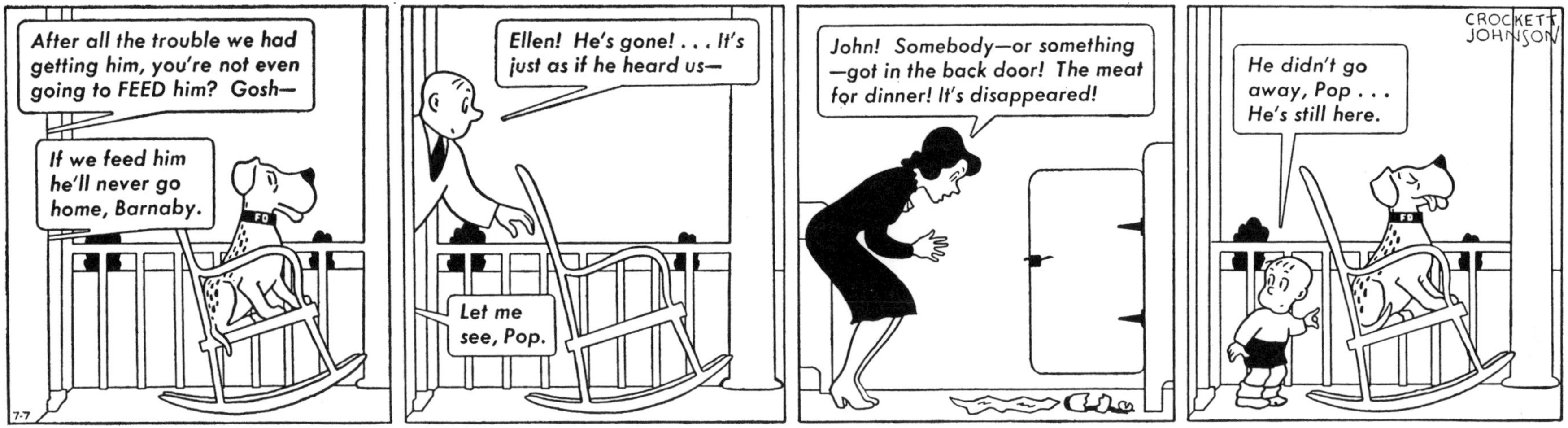
After all the trouble we had getting him, you're not even going to FEED him? Gosh—
If we feed him he'll never go home, Barnaby.
FO
7-7
Ellen! He's gone! . . . It's just as if he heard us—
Let me see, Pop.
John! Somebody—or something—got in the back door! The meat for dinner! It's disappeared!
CROCKETT JOHNSON
He didn't go away, Pop . . . He's still here.
FO

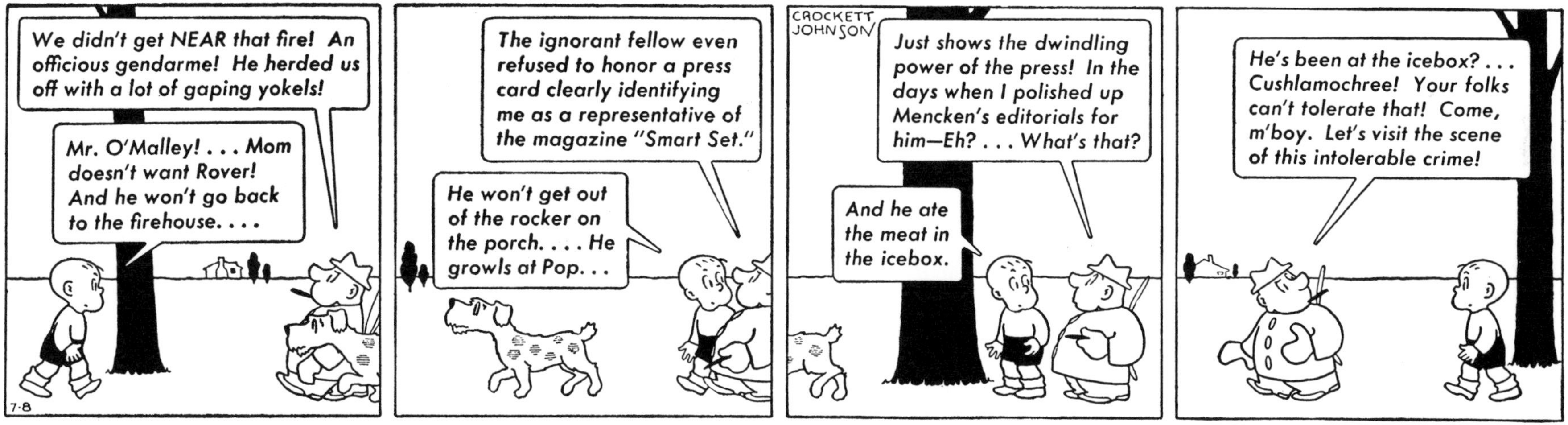
We didn't get NEAR that fire! An officious gendarme! He herded us off with a lot of gaping yokels!
Mr. O'Malley! . . . Mom doesn't want Rover! And he won't go back to the firehouse. . . .
7-8
The ignorant fellow even refused to honor a press card clearly identifying me as a representative of the magazine "Smart Set."
He won't get out of the rocker on the porch. . . . He growls at Pop. . .
CROCKETT JOHNSON
Just shows the dwindling power of the press! In the days when I polished up Mencken's editorials for him—Eh? . . . What's that?
And he ate the meat in the icebox.
He's been at the icebox? . . . Cushlamochree! Your folks can't tolerate that! Come, m'boy. Let's visit the scene of this intolerable crime!

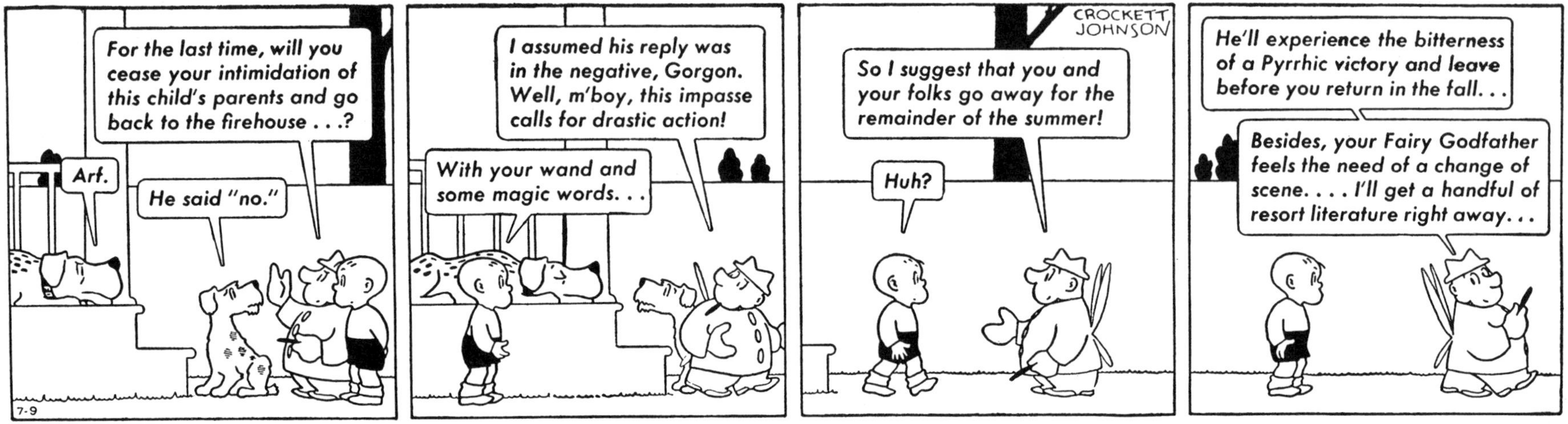
For the last time, will you cease your intimidation of this child's parents and go back to the firehouse . . .?
Arf.
He said "no."
I assumed his reply was in the negative, Gorgon. Well, m'boy, this impasse calls for drastic action!
With your wand and some magic words. . .
CROCKETT JOHNSON
So I suggest that you and your folks go away for the remainder of the summer!
Huh?
He'll experience the bitterness of a Pyrrhic victory and leave before you return in the fall. . .
Besides, your Fairy Godfather feels the need of a change of scene. . . . I'll get a handful of resort literature right away. . .
7-9

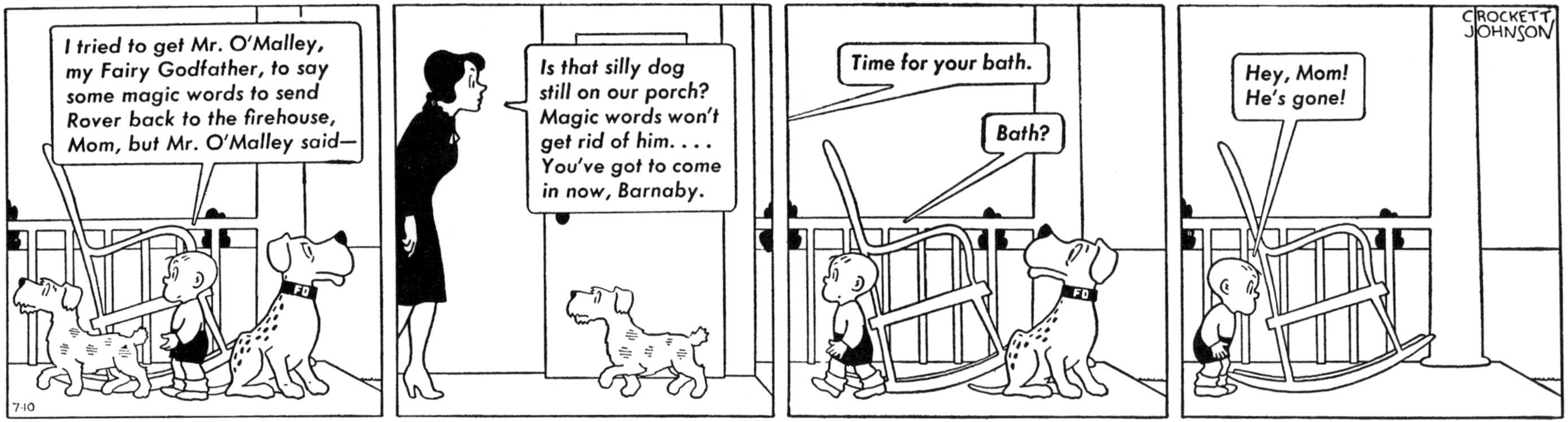
I tried to get Mr. O'Malley, my Fairy Godfather, to say some magic words to send Rover back to the firehouse, Mom, but Mr. O'Malley said—
FD
Is that silly dog still on our porch? Magic words won't get rid of him. . . . You've got to come in now, Barnaby.
Time for your bath.
Bath?
FD
CROCKETT JOHNSON
Hey, Mom! He's gone!
7-10

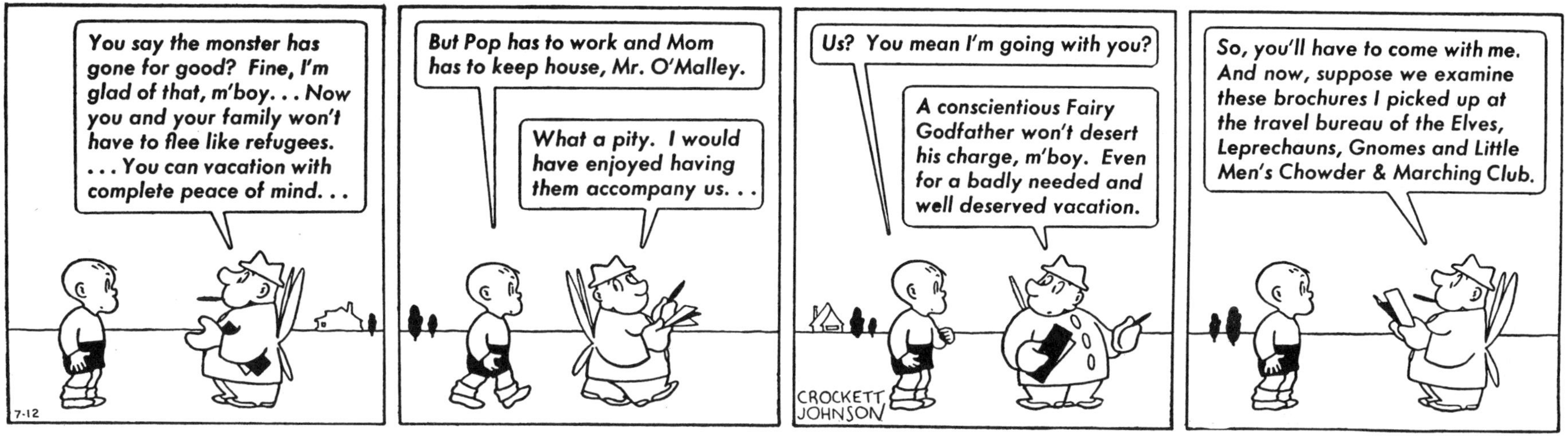
7-12
You say the monster has gone for good? Fine, I'm glad of that, m'boy. . . Now you and your family won't have to flee like refugees. . . . You can vacation with complete peace of mind. . .
But Pop has to work and Mom has to keep house, Mr. O'Malley.
What a pity. I would have enjoyed having them accompany us. . .
Us? You mean I'm going with you?
A conscientious Fairy Godfather won't desert his charge, m'boy. Even for a badly needed and well deserved vacation.
CROCKETT JOHNSON
So, you'll have to come with me. And now, suppose we examine these brochures I picked up at the travel bureau of the Elves, Leprechauns, Gnomes and Little Men's Chowder & Marching Club.

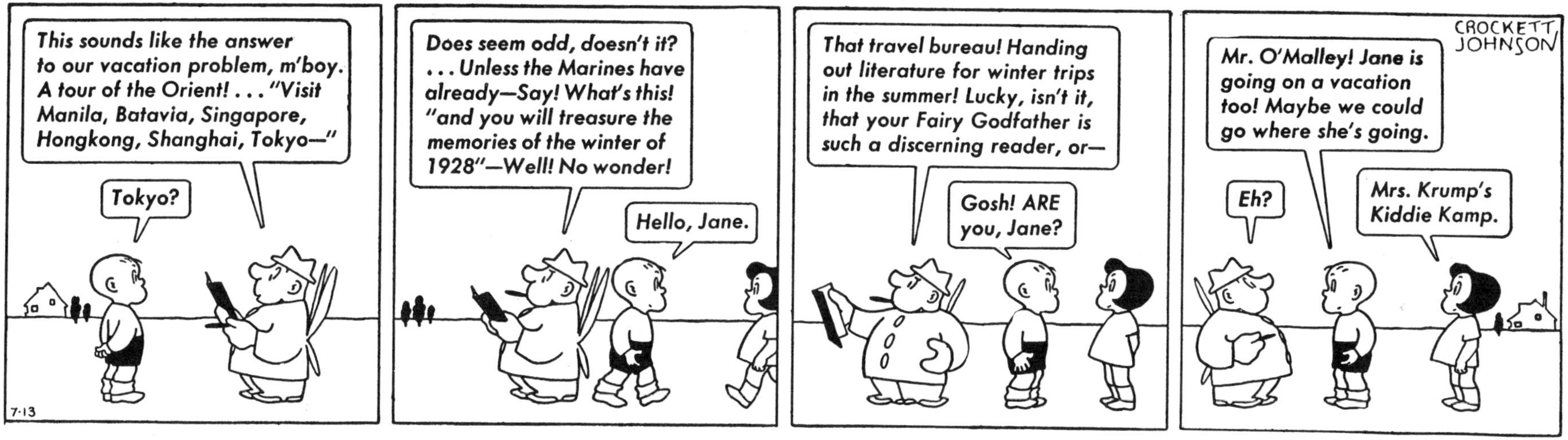
7-13
This sounds like the answer to our vacation problem, m'boy. A tour of the Orient! . . . "Visit Manila, Batavia, Singapore, Hongkong, Shanghai, Tokyo—"
Tokyo?
Does seem odd, doesn't it? . . . Unless the Marines have already—Say! What's this! "and you will treasure the memories of the winter of 1928"—Well! No wonder!
Hello, Jane.
That travel bureau! Handing out literature for winter trips in the summer! Lucky, isn't it, that your Fairy Godfather is such a discerning reader, or—
Gosh! ARE you, Jane?
CROCKETT JOHNSON
Mr. O'Malley! Jane is going on a vacation too! Maybe we could go where she's going.
Eh?
Mrs. Krump's Kiddie Kamp.

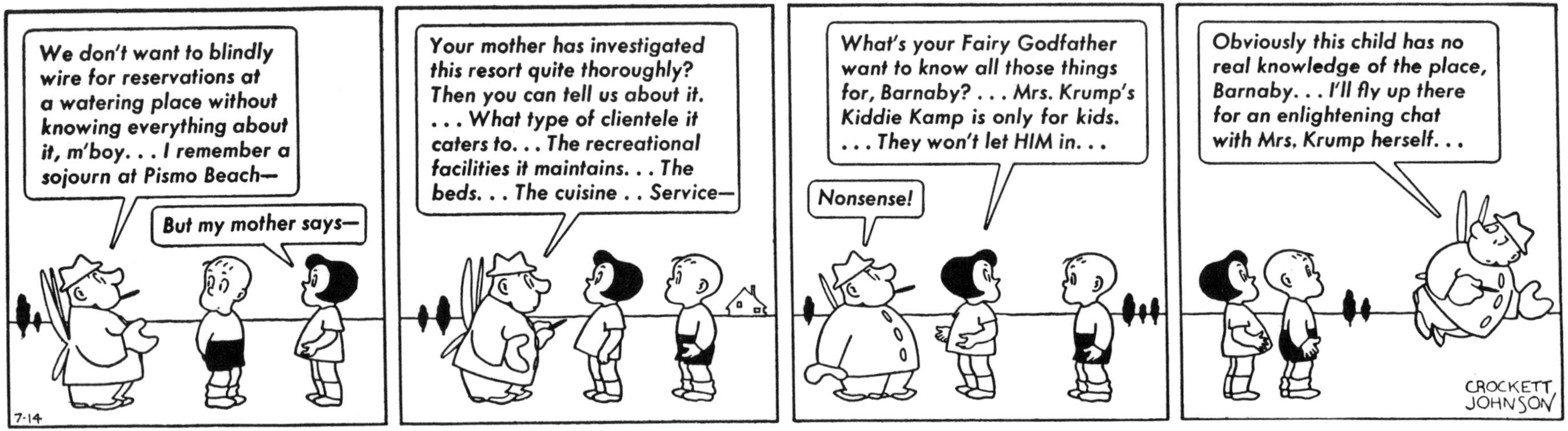
We don't want to blindly wire for reservations at a watering place without knowing everything about it, m'boy. . . I remember a sojourn at Pismo Beach—
But my mother says—
7-14
Your mother has investigated this resort quite thoroughly? Then you can tell us about it. . . . What type of clientele it caters to. . . The recreational facilities it maintains. . . The beds. . . The cuisine . . Service—
What's your Fairy Godfather want to know all those things for, Barnaby? . . . Mrs. Krump's Kiddie Kamp is only for kids. . . . They won't let HIM in. . .
Nonsense!
Obviously this child has no real knowledge of the place, Barnaby. . . I'll fly up there for an enlightening chat with Mrs. Krump herself. . .
CROCKETT JOHNSON

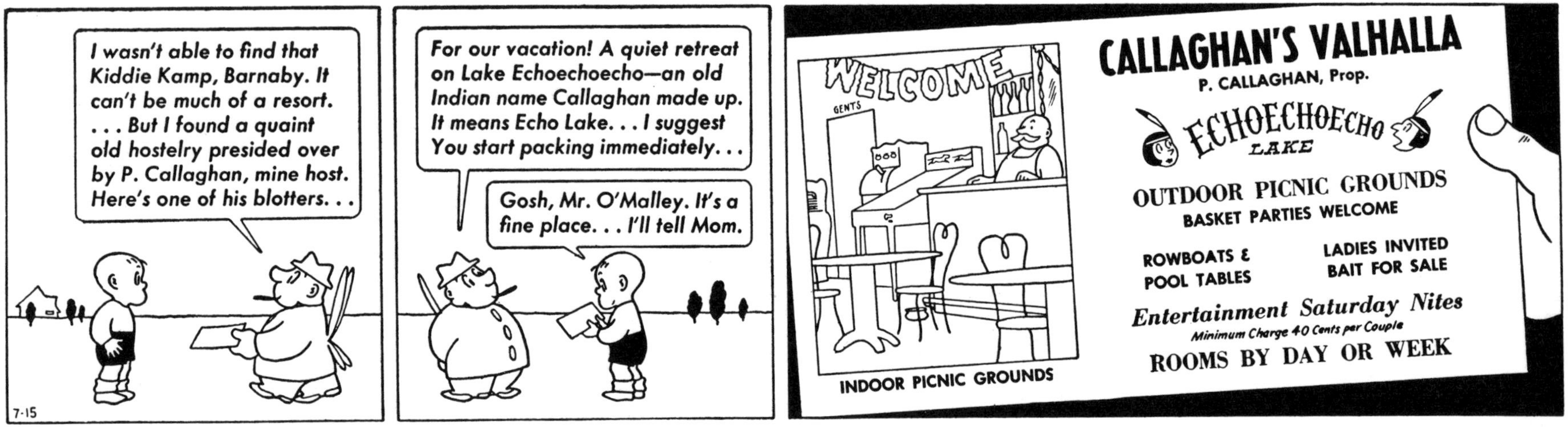
I wasn't able to find that Kiddie Kamp, Barnaby. It can't be much of a resort. . . . But I found a quaint old hostelry presided over by P. Callaghan, mine host. Here's one of his blotters. . .
7-15
For our vacation! A quiet retreat on Lake Echoechoecho—an old Indian name Callaghan made up. It means Echo Lake. . . I suggest You start packing immediately. . .
Gosh, Mr. O'Malley. It's a fine place. . . I'll tell Mom.
WELCOME
GENTS
INDOOR PICNIC GROUNDS
CALLAGHAN'S VALHALLA
P. CALLAGHAN, Prop.
ECHOECHOECHO LAKE
OUTDOOR PICNIC GROUNDS
BASKET PARTIES WELCOME
ROWBOATS & POOL TABLES
LADIES INVITED BAIT FOR SALE
Entertainment Saturday Nites
Minimum Charge 40 Cents per Couple
ROOMS BY DAY OR WEEK

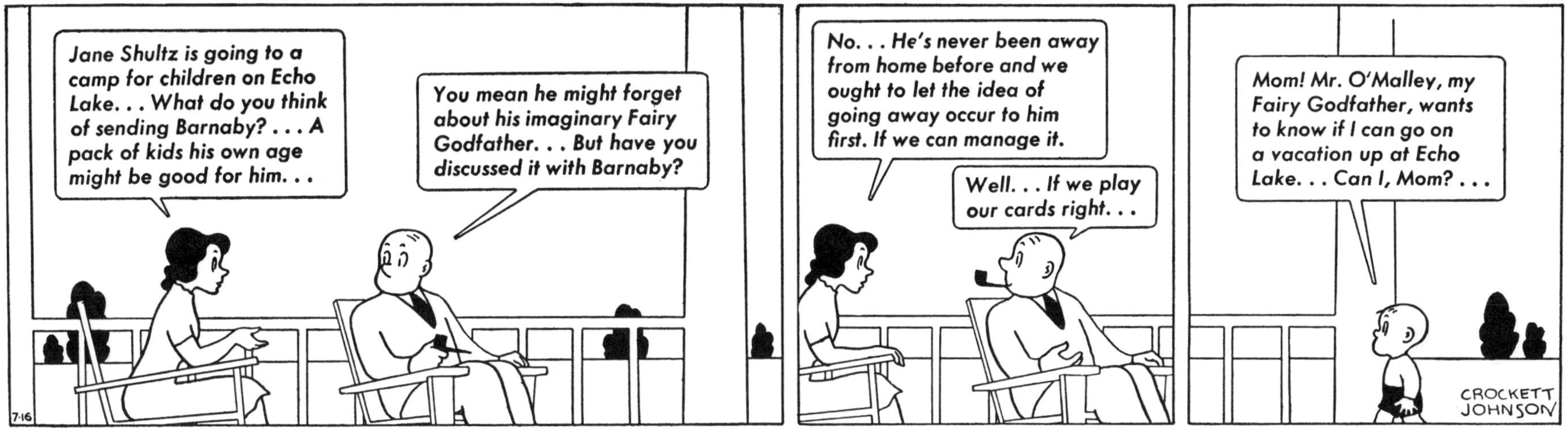
7-16
Jane Shultz is going to a camp for children on Echo Lake. . . What do you think of sending Barnaby? . . . A pack of kids his own age might be good for him. . .
You mean he might forget about his imaginary Fairy Godfather. . . But have you discussed it with Barnaby?
No. . . He's never been away from home before and we ought to let the idea of going away occur to him first. If we can manage it.
Well. . . If we play our cards right. . .
Mom! Mr. O'Malley, my Fairy Godfather, wants to know if I can go on a vacation up at Echo Lake. . . Can I, Mom? . . .
CROCKETT JOHNSON

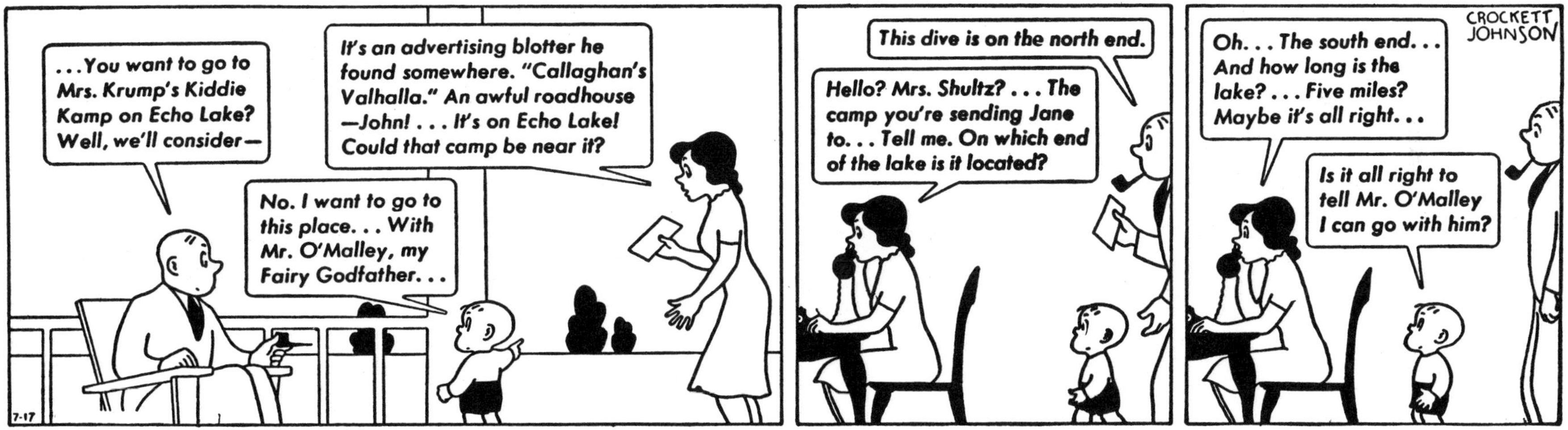
7-17
. . .You want to go to Mrs. Krump's Kiddie Kamp on Echo Lake? Well, we'll consider—
No. I want to go to this place. . . With Mr. O'Malley, my Fairy Godfather. . .
It's an advertising blotter he found somewhere. "Callaghan's Valhalla." An awful roadhouse —John! . . . It's on Echo Lake! Could that camp be near it?
This dive is on the north end.
Hello? Mrs. Shultz? . . . The camp you're sending Jane to. . . Tell me. On which end of the lake is it located?
CROCKETT JOHNSON
Oh. . . The south end. . . And how long is the lake? . . . Five miles? Maybe it's all right. . .
Is it all right to tell Mr. O'Malley I can go with him?

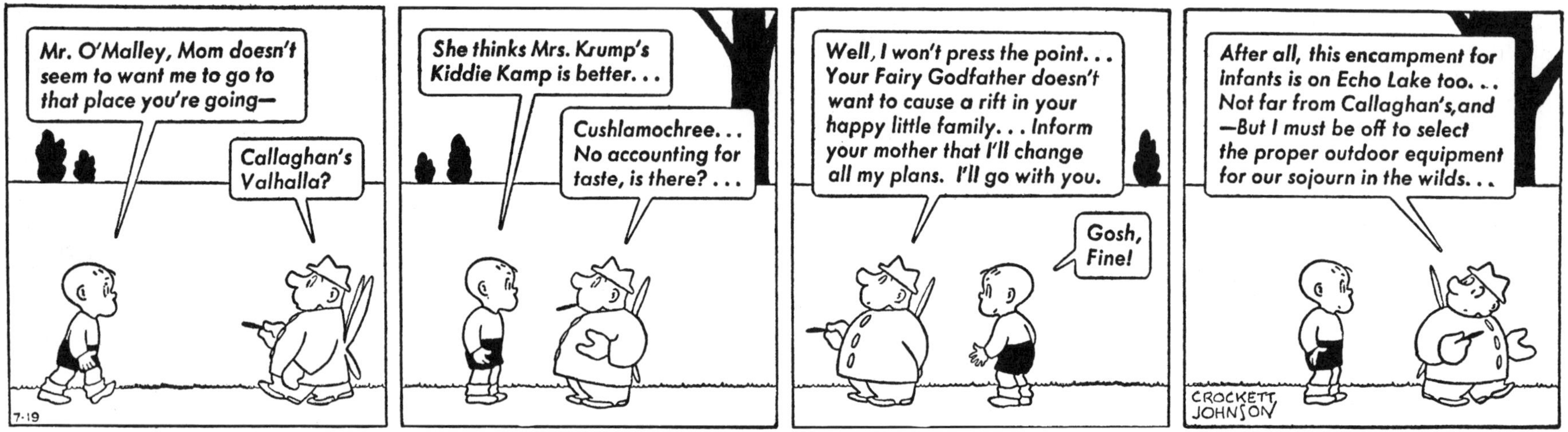
Mr. O'Malley, Mom doesn't seem to want me to go to that place you're going—
Callaghan's Valhalla?
She thinks Mrs. Krump's Kiddie Kamp is better. . .
Cushlamochree. . . No accounting for taste, is there? . . .
Well, I won't press the point. . . Your Fairy Godfather doesn't want to cause a rift in your happy little family. . . Inform your mother that I'll change all my plans. I'll go with you.
Gosh, Fine!
After all, this encampment for infants is on Echo Lake too. . . Not far from Callaghan's, and —But I must be off to select the proper outdoor equipment for our sojourn in the wilds. . .
CROCKETT JOHNSON
7-19

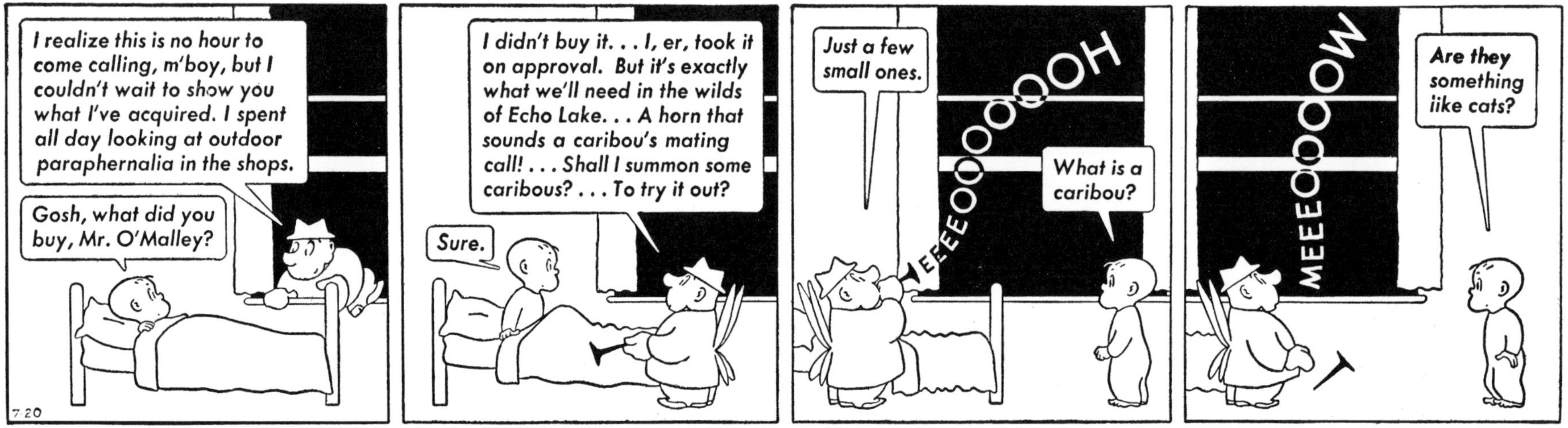
I realize this is no hour to come calling, m'boy, but I couldn't wait to show you what I've acquired. I spent all day looking at outdoor paraphernalia in the shops.
Gosh, what did you buy, Mr. O'Malley?
I didn't buy it. . . I, er, took it on approval. But it's exactly what we'll need in the wilds of Echo Lake. . . A horn that sounds a caribou's mating call! . . . Shall I summon some caribous? . . . To try it out?
Sure.
Just a few small ones.
EEEOOOOOOOH
What is a caribou?
MEEEOOOOOW
Are they something like cats?
7-20

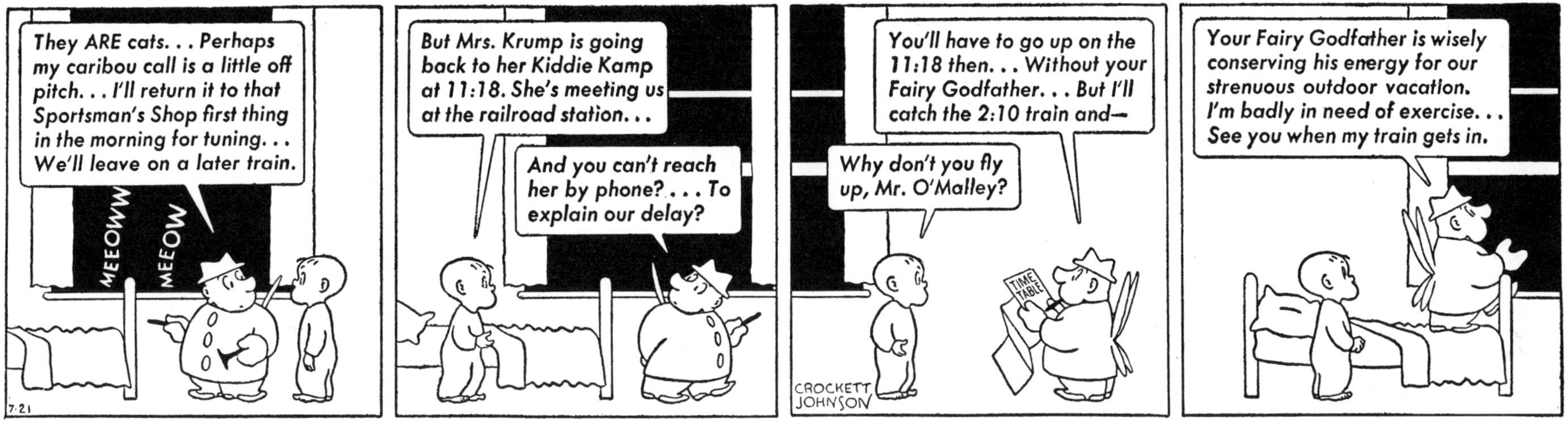
7-21
They ARE cats. . . Perhaps my caribou call is a little off pitch. . . I'll return it to that Sportsman's Shop first thing in the morning for tuning. . . We'll leave on a later train.
MEEOWW
MEEOW
But Mrs. Krump is going back to her Kiddie Kamp at 11:18. She's meeting us at the railroad station. . .
And you can't reach her by phone?. . . To explain our delay?
You'll have to go up on the 11:18 then. . . Without your Fairy Godfather. . . But I'll catch the 2:10 train and—
Why don't you fly up, Mr. O'Malley?
TIME TABLE
CROCKETT JOHNSON
Your Fairy Godfather is wisely conserving his energy for our strenuous outdoor vacation. I'm badly in need of exercise. . . See you when my train gets in.

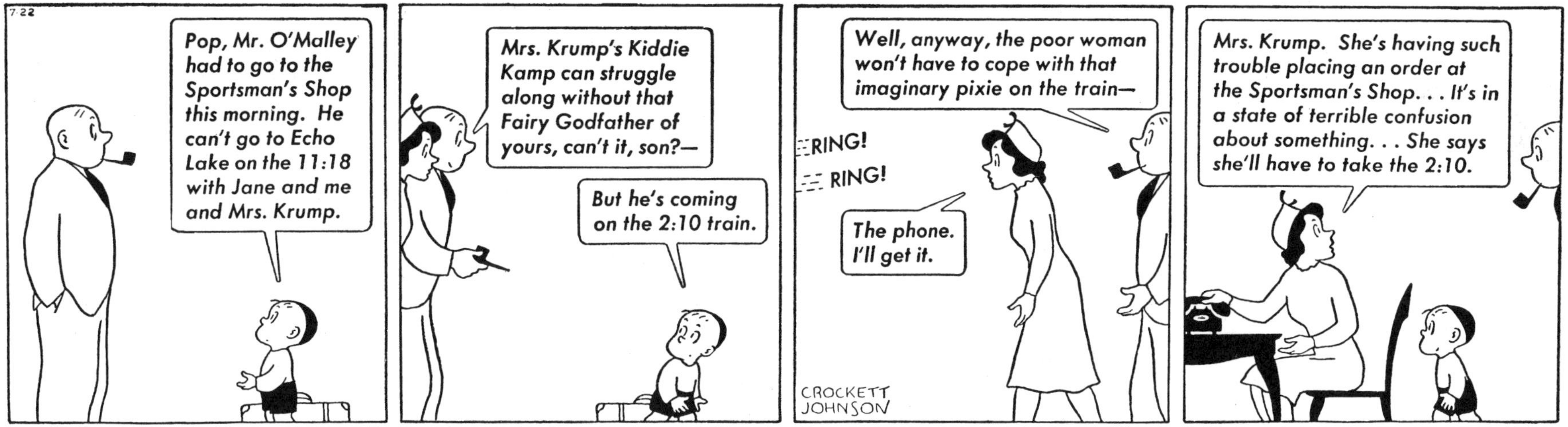
7-22
Pop, Mr. O'Malley had to go to the Sportsman's Shop this morning. He can't go to Echo Lake on the 11:18 with Jane and me and Mrs. Krump.
Mrs. Krump's Kiddie Kamp can struggle along without that Fairy Godfather of yours, can't it, son?—
But he's coming on the 2:10 train.
Well, anyway, the poor woman won't have to cope with that imaginary pixie on the train—
RING!
RING!
The phone. I'll get it.
CROCKETT JOHNSON
Mrs. Krump. She's having such trouble placing an order at the Sportsman's Shop. . . It's in a state of terrible confusion about something. . . She says she'll have to take the 2:10.

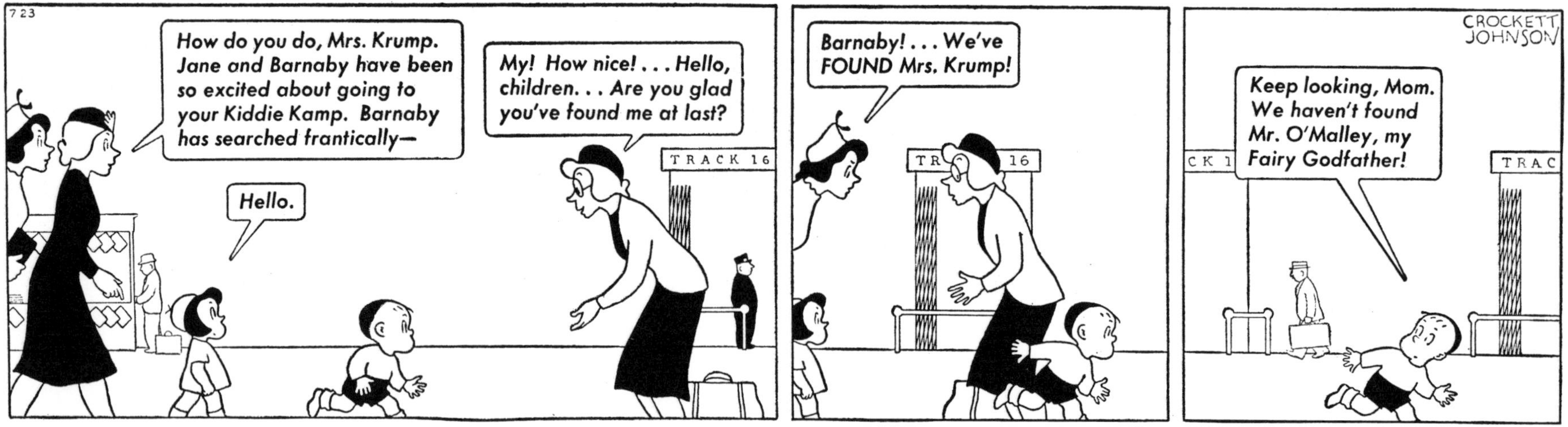
7 23
How do you do, Mrs. Krump. Jane and Barnaby have been so excited about going to your Kiddie Kamp. Barnaby has searched frantically—
Hello.
My! How nice! . . . Hello, children. . . Are you glad you've found me at last?
TRACK 16
Barnaby! . . . We've FOUND Mrs. Krump!
TR 16
CROCKETT JOHNSON
Keep looking, Mom. We haven't found Mr. O'Malley, my Fairy Godfather!
CK 1
TRAC

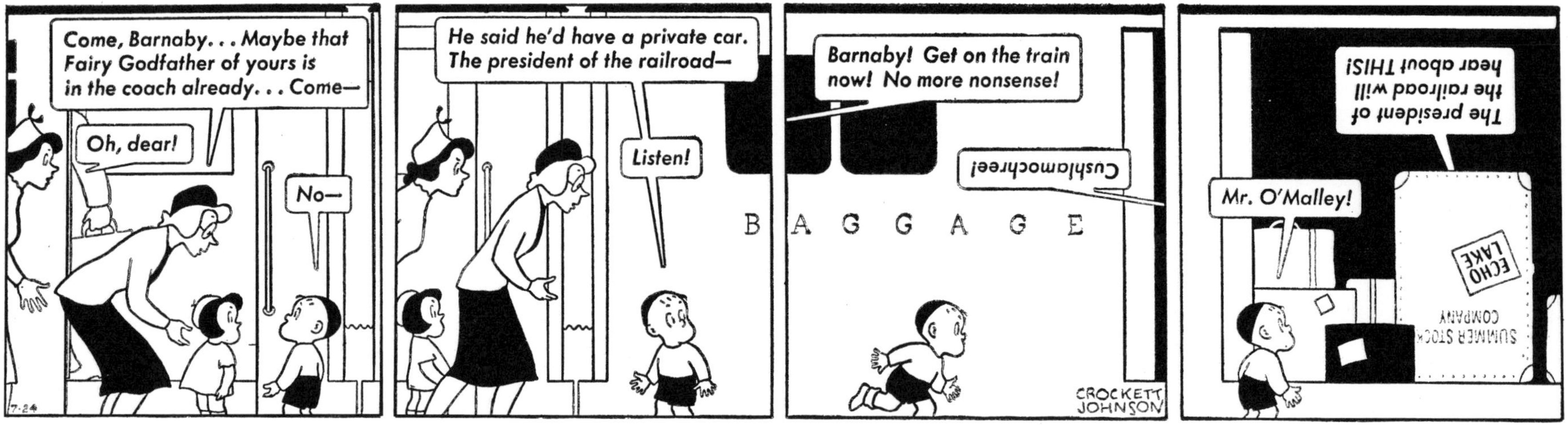
Come, Barnaby. . . Maybe that Fairy Godfather of yours is in the coach already. . . Come—
Oh, dear!
No—
7-24
He said he'd have a private car. The president of the railroad—
Listen!
Barnaby! Get on the train now! No more nonsense!
Cushlamochree!
BAGGAGE
CROCKETT JOHNSON
The president of the railroad will hear about THIS!
Mr. O'Malley!
ECHO LAKE
SUMMER STOCK COMPANY

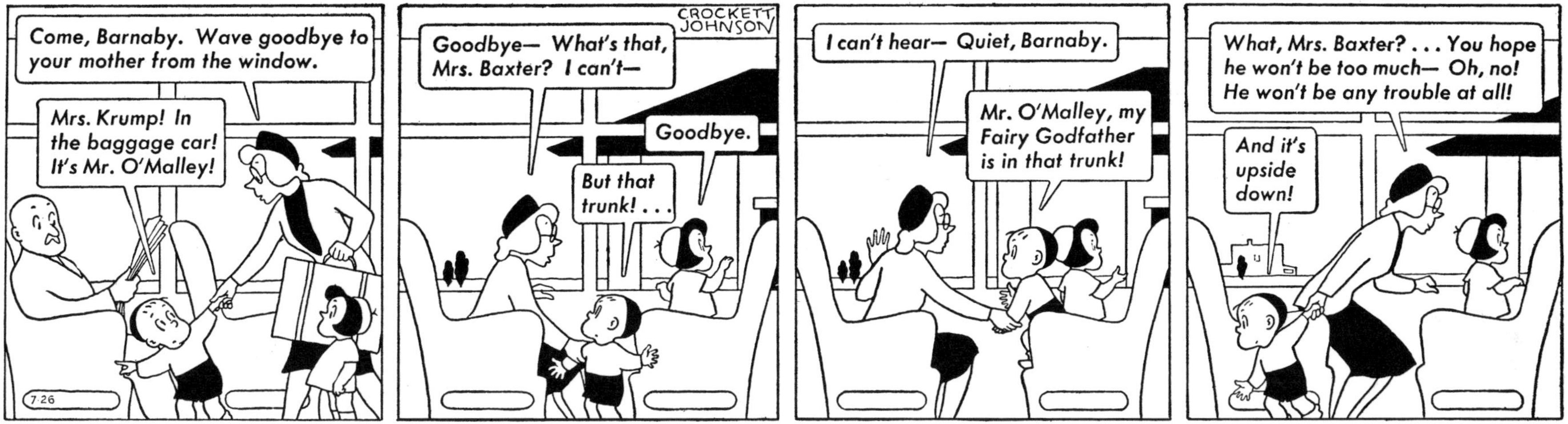
Come, Barnaby. Wave goodbye to your mother from the window.
Mrs. Krump! In the baggage car! It's Mr. O'Malley!
7·26
CROCKETT JOHNSON
Goodbye— What's that, Mrs. Baxter? I can't—
Goodbye.
But that trunk! . . .
I can't hear— Quiet, Barnaby.
Mr. O'Malley, my Fairy Godfather is in that trunk!
What, Mrs. Baxter? . . . You hope he won't be too much— Oh, no! He won't be any trouble at all!
And it's upside down!

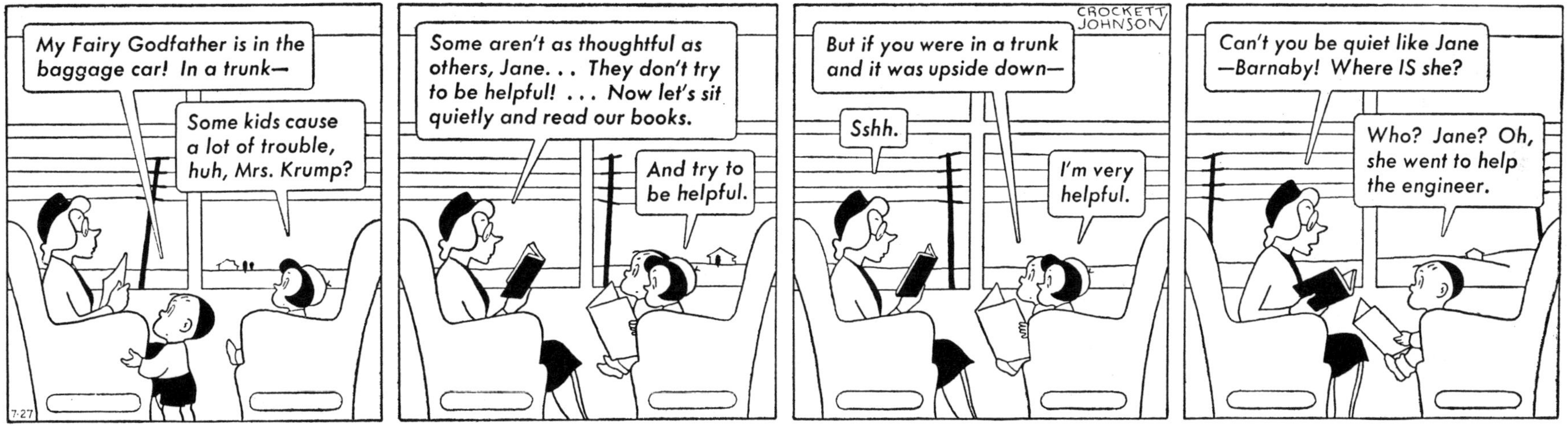
My Fairy Godfather is in the baggage car! In a trunk—
Some kids cause a lot of trouble, huh, Mrs. Krump?
7·27
Some aren't as thoughtful as others, Jane. . . They don't try to be helpful! . . . Now let's sit quietly and read our books.
And try to be helpful.
CROCKETT JOHNSON
But if you were in a trunk and it was upside down—
Sshh.
I'm very helpful.
Can't you be quiet like Jane —Barnaby! Where IS she?
Who? Jane? Oh, she went to help the engineer.

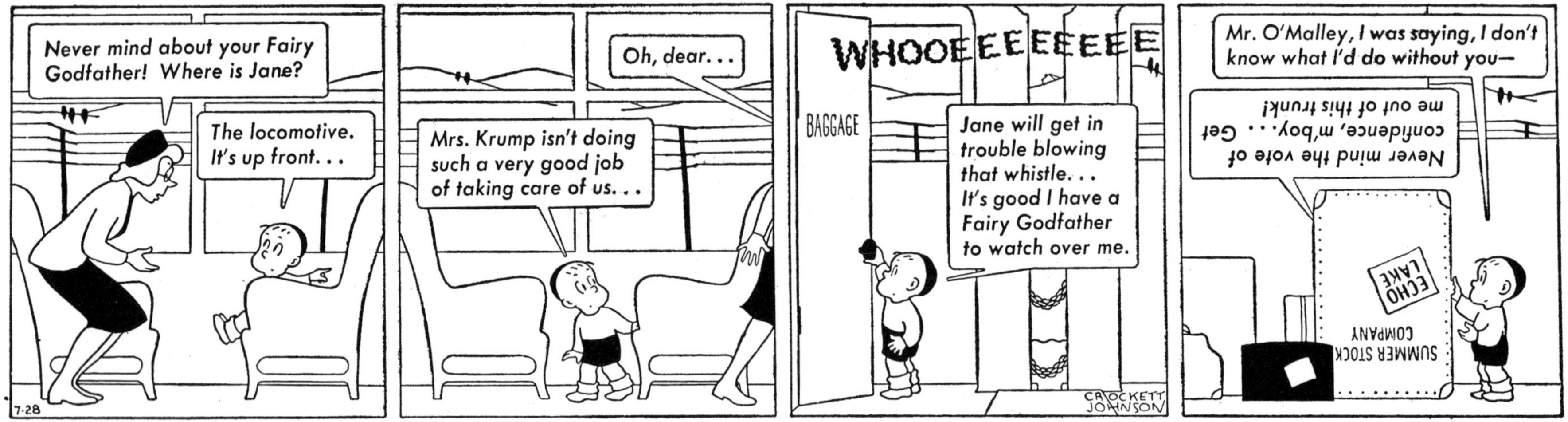
Never mind about your Fairy Godfather! Where is Jane?
The locomotive. It's up front...
7-28
Mrs. Krump isn't doing such a very good job of taking care of us...
Oh, dear...
WHOOEEEEEEEE
BAGGAGE
Jane will get in trouble blowing that whistle... It's good I have a Fairy Godfather to watch over me.
CROCKETT JOHNSON
Mr. O'Malley, I was saying, I don't know what I'd do without you—
Never mind the vote of confidence, m'boy... Get me out of this trunk!
ECHO LAKE
SUMMER STOCK COMPANY

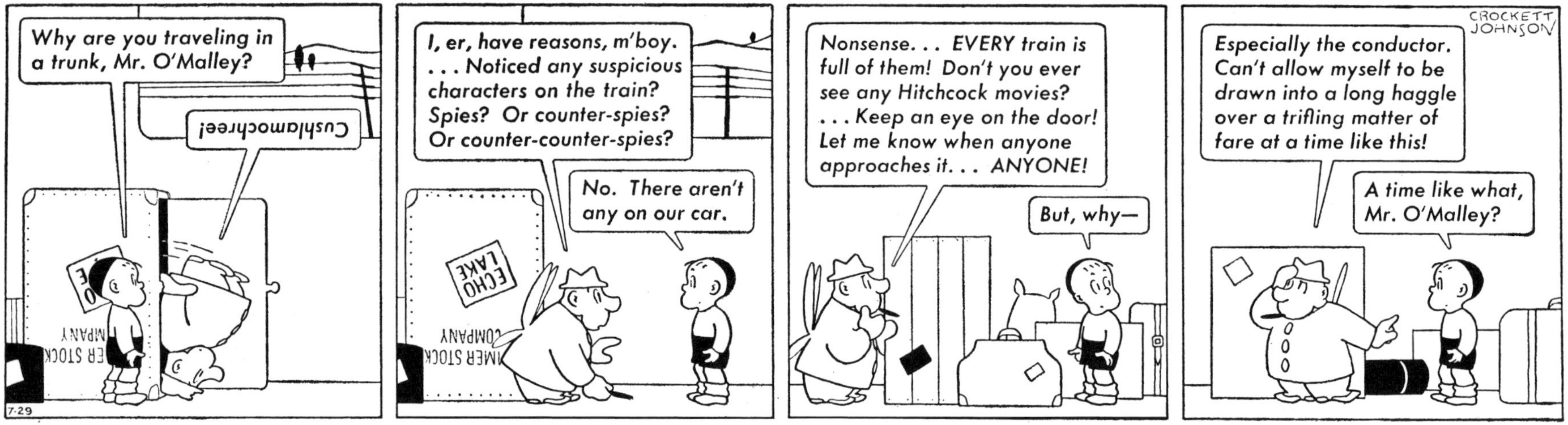
Why are you traveling in a trunk, Mr. O'Malley?
Cushlamochree!
7-29
I, er, have reasons, m'boy. ... Noticed any suspicious characters on the train? Spies? Or counter-spies? Or counter-counter-spies?
No. There aren't any on our car.
Nonsense... EVERY train is full of them! Don't you ever see any Hitchcock movies? ... Keep an eye on the door! Let me know when anyone approaches it... ANYONE!
But, why—
CROCKETT JOHNSON
Especially the conductor. Can't allow myself to be drawn into a long haggle over a trifling matter of fare at a time like this!
A time like what, Mr. O'Malley?

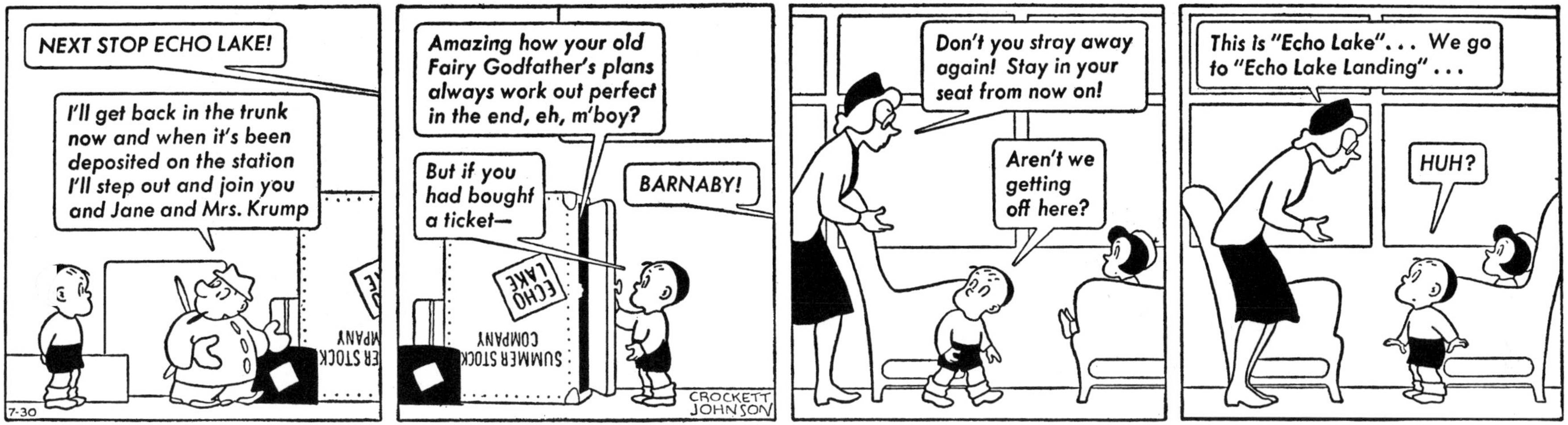
NEXT STOP ECHO LAKE!
I'll get back in the trunk now and when it's been deposited on the station I'll step out and join you and Jane and Mrs. Krump
7-30
Amazing how your old Fairy Godfather's plans always work out perfect in the end, eh, m'boy?
But if you had bought a ticket—
BARNABY!
CROCKETT JOHNSON
Don't you stray away again! Stay in your seat from now on!
Aren't we getting off here?
This is "Echo Lake"... We go to "Echo Lake Landing"...
HUH?

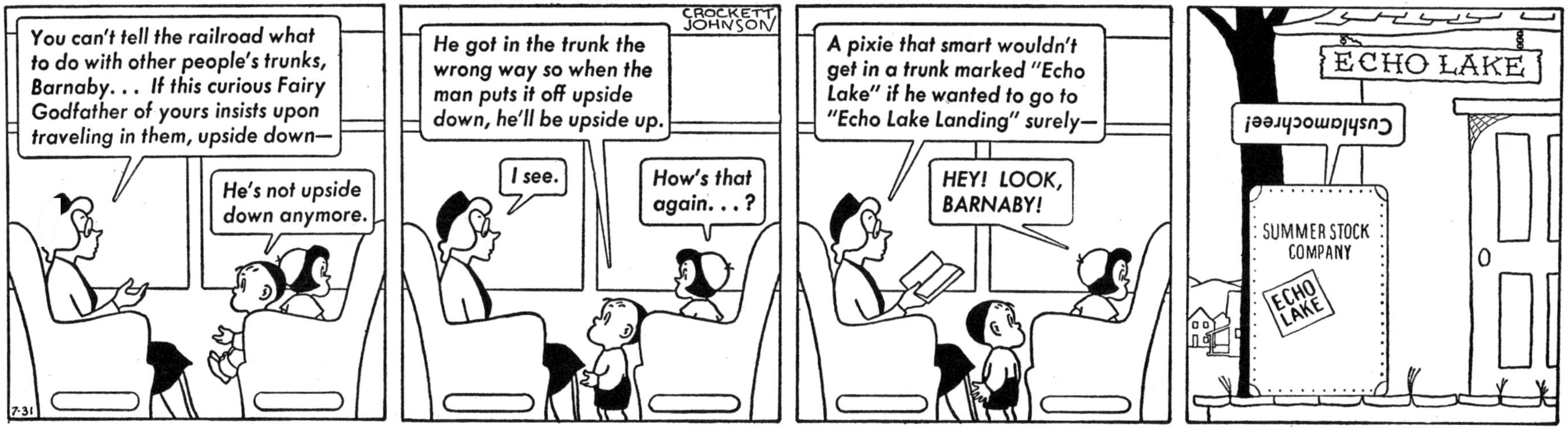
You can't tell the railroad what to do with other people's trunks, Barnaby... If this curious Fairy Godfather of yours insists upon traveling in them, upside down—
He's not upside down anymore.
7-31
CROCKETT JOHNSON
He got in the trunk the wrong way so when the man puts it off upside down, he'll be upside up.
I see.
How's that again...?
A pixie that smart wouldn't get in a trunk marked "Echo Lake" if he wanted to go to "Echo Lake Landing" surely—
HEY! LOOK, BARNABY!
ECHO LAKE
Cushlamochree!
SUMMER STOCK COMPANY
ECHO LAKE

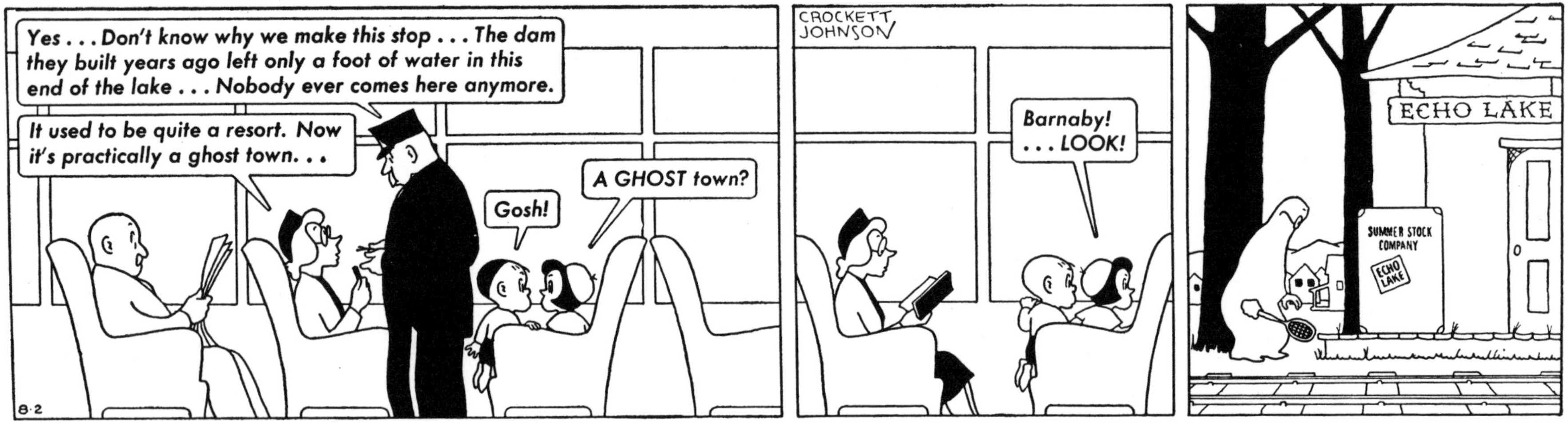
Yes . . . Don't know why we make this stop . . . The dam they built years ago left only a foot of water in this end of the lake . . . Nobody ever comes here anymore.
It used to be quite a resort. Now it's practically a ghost town. . .
Gosh!
A GHOST town?
8·2
CROCKETT JOHNSON
Barnaby! . . . LOOK!
ECHO LAKE
SUMMER STOCK COMPANY
ECHO LAKE

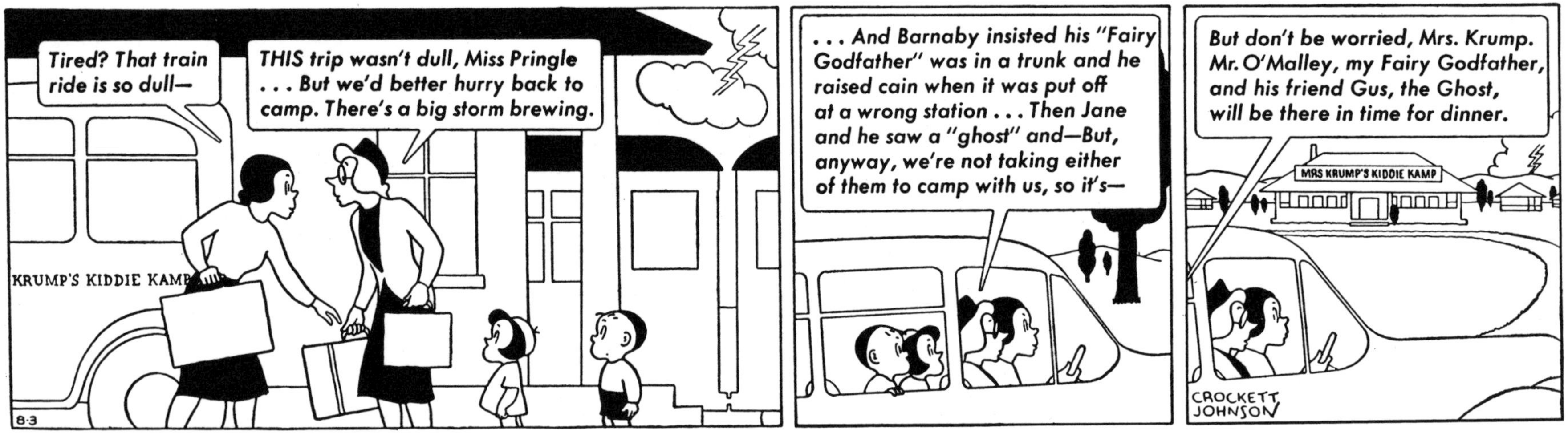
Tired? That train ride is so dull—
THIS trip wasn't dull, Miss Pringle . . . But we'd better hurry back to camp. There's a big storm brewing.
KRUMP'S KIDDIE KAMP
8·3
. . . And Barnaby insisted his "Fairy Godfather" was in a trunk and he raised cain when it was put off at a wrong station . . . Then Jane and he saw a "ghost" and—But, anyway, we're not taking either of them to camp with us, so it's—
But don't be worried, Mrs. Krump. Mr. O'Malley, my Fairy Godfather, and his friend Gus, the Ghost, will be there in time for dinner.
MRS KRUMP'S KIDDIE KAMP
CROCKETT JOHNSON

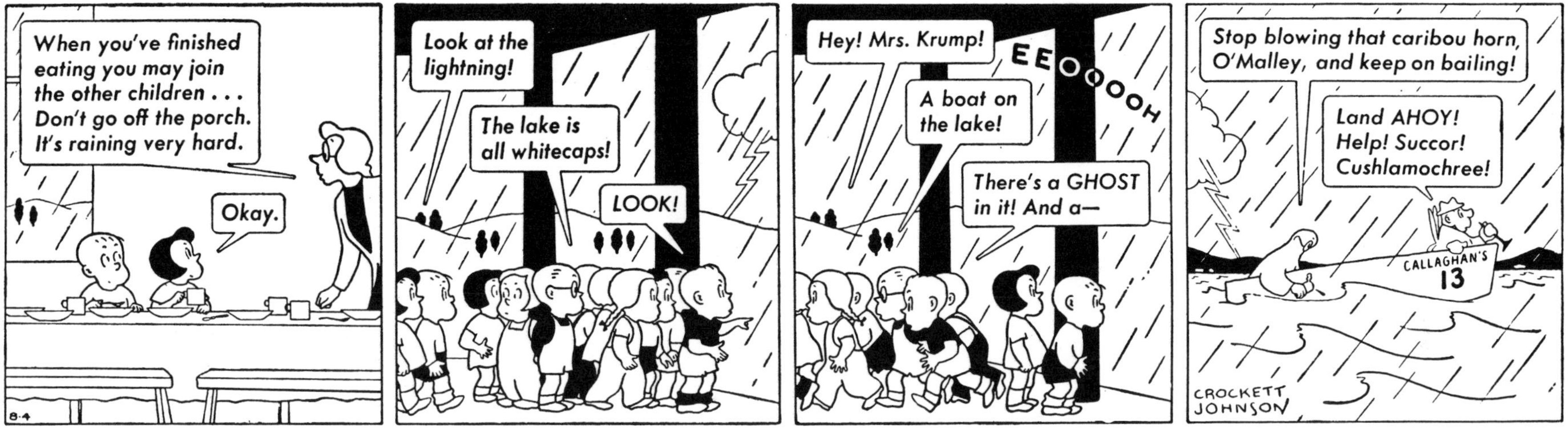
8·4
When you've finished eating you may join the other children . . . Don't go off the porch. It's raining very hard.
Okay.
Look at the lightning!
The lake is all whitecaps!
LOOK!
Hey! Mrs. Krump!
EEOOOOOH
A boat on the lake!
There's a GHOST in it! And a—
Stop blowing that caribou horn, O'Malley, and keep on bailing!
Land AHOY! Help! Succor! Cushlamochree!
CALLAGHAN'S
13
CROCKETT JOHNSON

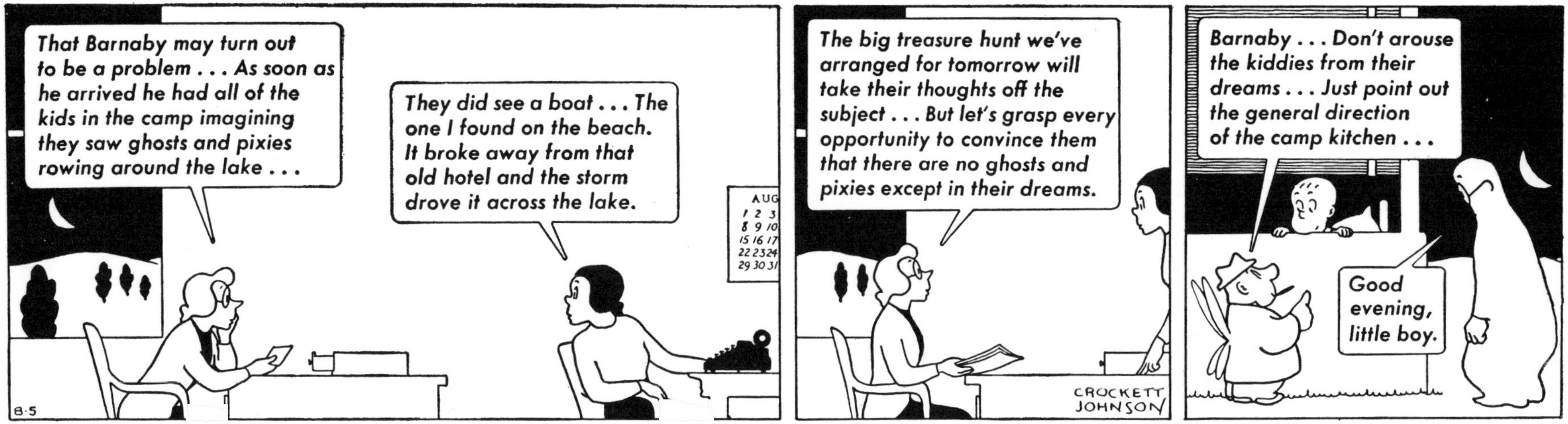
8·5
That Barnaby may turn out to be a problem . . . As soon as he arrived he had all of the kids in the camp imagining they saw ghosts and pixies rowing around the lake . . .
They did see a boat . . . The one I found on the beach. It broke away from that old hotel and the storm drove it across the lake.
The big treasure hunt we've arranged for tomorrow will take their thoughts off the subject . . . But let's grasp every opportunity to convince them that there are no ghosts and pixies except in their dreams.
CROCKETT JOHNSON
Barnaby . . . Don't arouse the kiddies from their dreams . . . Just point out the general direction of the camp kitchen . . .
Good evening, little boy.

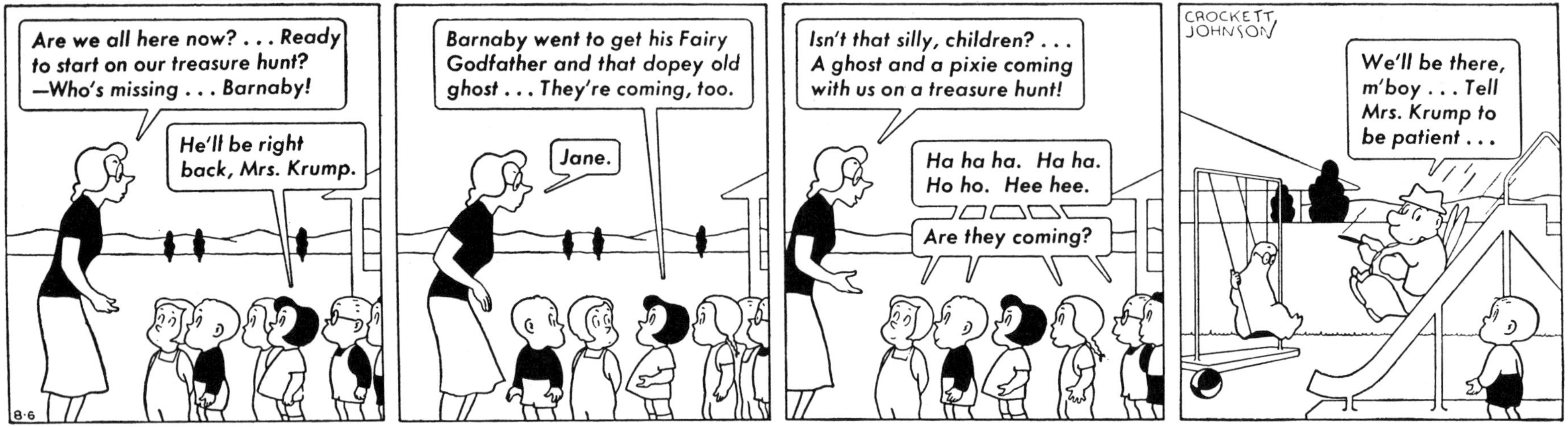
Are we all here now? . . . Ready to start on our treasure hunt? —Who's missing . . . Barnaby!
He'll be right back, Mrs. Krump.
8·6
Barnaby went to get his Fairy Godfather and that dopey old ghost . . . They're coming, too.
Jane.
Isn't that silly, children? . . . A ghost and a pixie coming with us on a treasure hunt!
Ha ha ha. Ha ha. Ho ho. Hee hee.
Are they coming?
CROCKETT JOHNSON
We'll be there, m'boy . . . Tell Mrs. Krump to be patient . . .

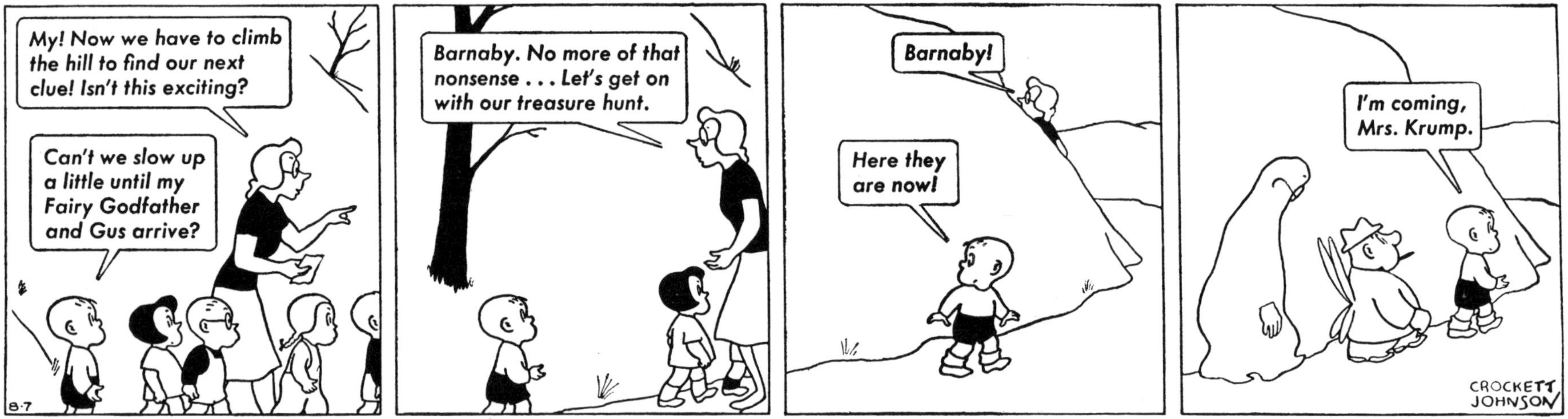
My! Now we have to climb the hill to find our next clue! Isn't this exciting?
Can't we slow up a little until my Fairy Godfather and Gus arrive?
8·7
Barnaby. No more of that nonsense . . . Let's get on with our treasure hunt.
Barnaby!
Here they are now!
I'm coming, Mrs. Krump.
CROCKETT JOHNSON

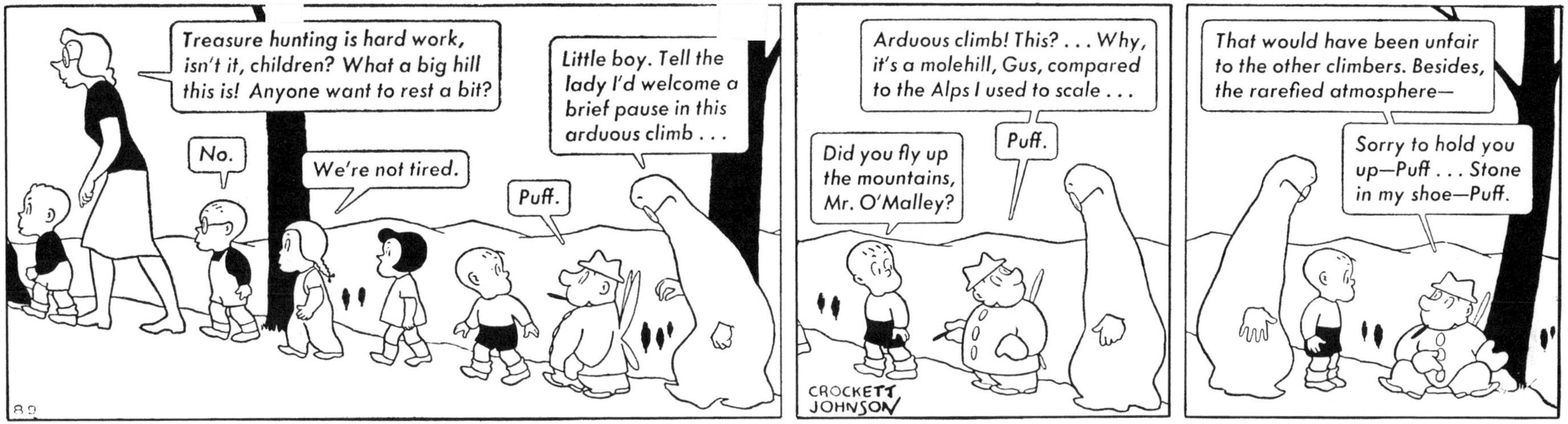
Treasure hunting is hard work, isn't it, children? What a big hill this is! Anyone want to rest a bit?
No.
We're not tired.
Puff.
Little boy. Tell the lady I'd welcome a brief pause in this arduous climb . . .
8.9
Arduous climb! This? . . . Why, it's a molehill, Gus, compared to the Alps I used to scale . . .
Did you fly up the mountains, Mr. O'Malley?
Puff.
CROCKETT JOHNSON
That would have been unfair to the other climbers. Besides, the rarefied atmosphere—
Sorry to hold you up—Puff . . . Stone in my shoe—Puff.

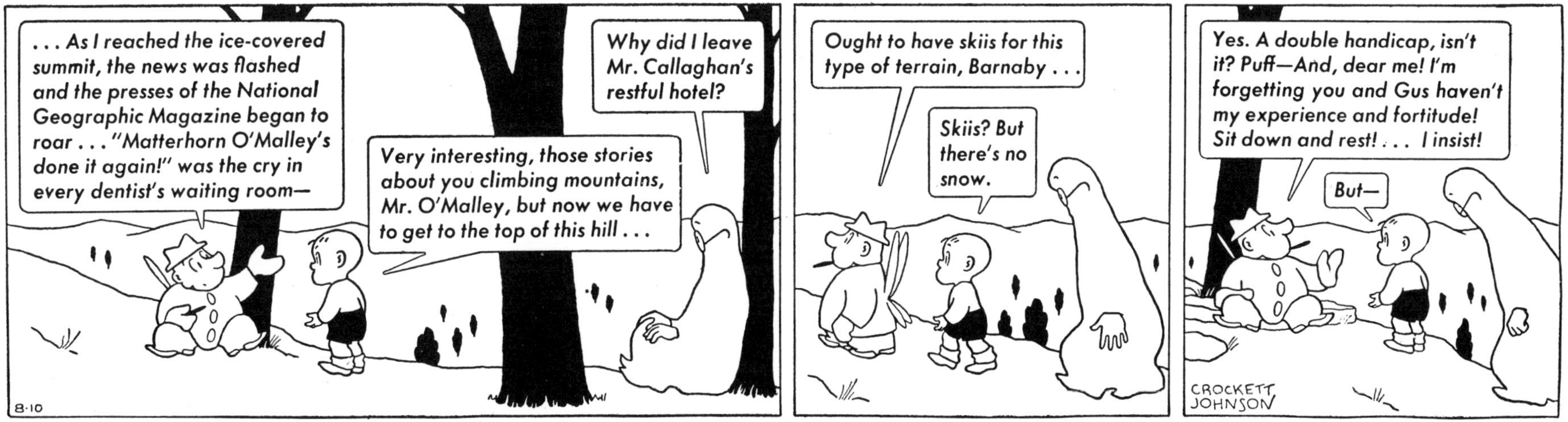
. . . As I reached the ice-covered summit, the news was flashed and the presses of the National Geographic Magazine began to roar . . . "Matterhorn O'Malley's done it again!" was the cry in every dentist's waiting room—
Very interesting, those stories about you climbing mountains, Mr. O'Malley, but now we have to get to the top of this hill . . .
Why did I leave Mr. Callaghan's restful hotel?
8·10
Ought to have skiis for this type of terrain, Barnaby . . .
Skiis? But there's no snow.
Yes. A double handicap, isn't it? Puff—And, dear me! I'm forgetting you and Gus haven't my experience and fortitude! Sit down and rest! . . . I insist!
But—
CROCKETT JOHNSON

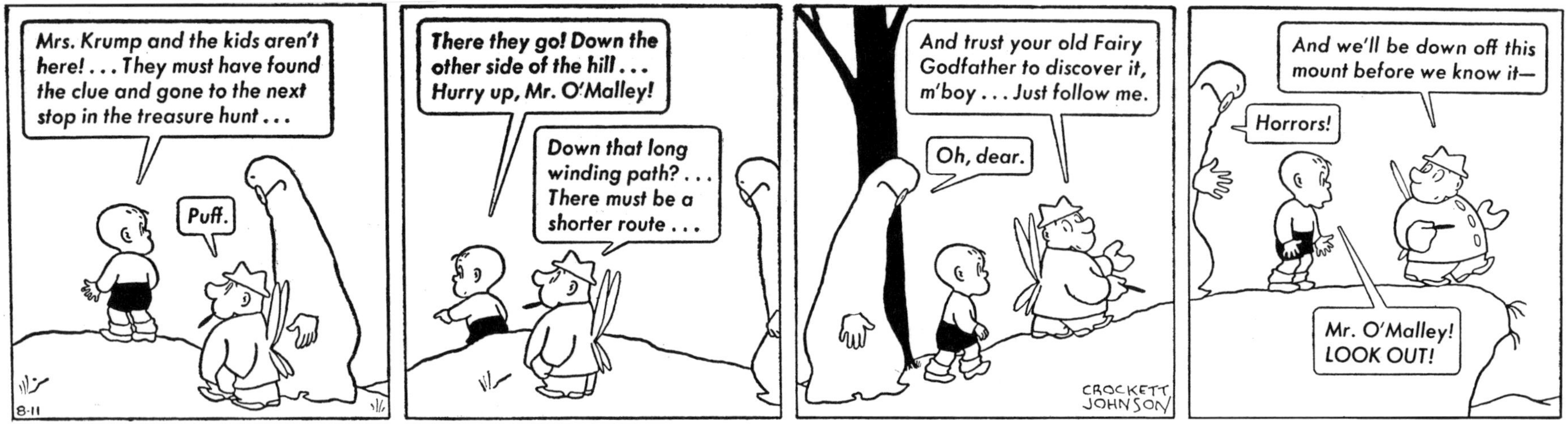
Mrs. Krump and the kids aren't here! . . . They must have found the clue and gone to the next stop in the treasure hunt . . .
Puff.
8-11
There they go! Down the other side of the hill . . . Hurry up, Mr. O'Malley!
Down that long winding path? . . . There must be a shorter route . . .
And trust your old Fairy Godfather to discover it, m'boy . . . Just follow me.
Oh, dear.
CROCKETT JOHNSON
And we'll be down off this mount before we know it—
Horrors!
Mr. O'Malley! LOOK OUT!

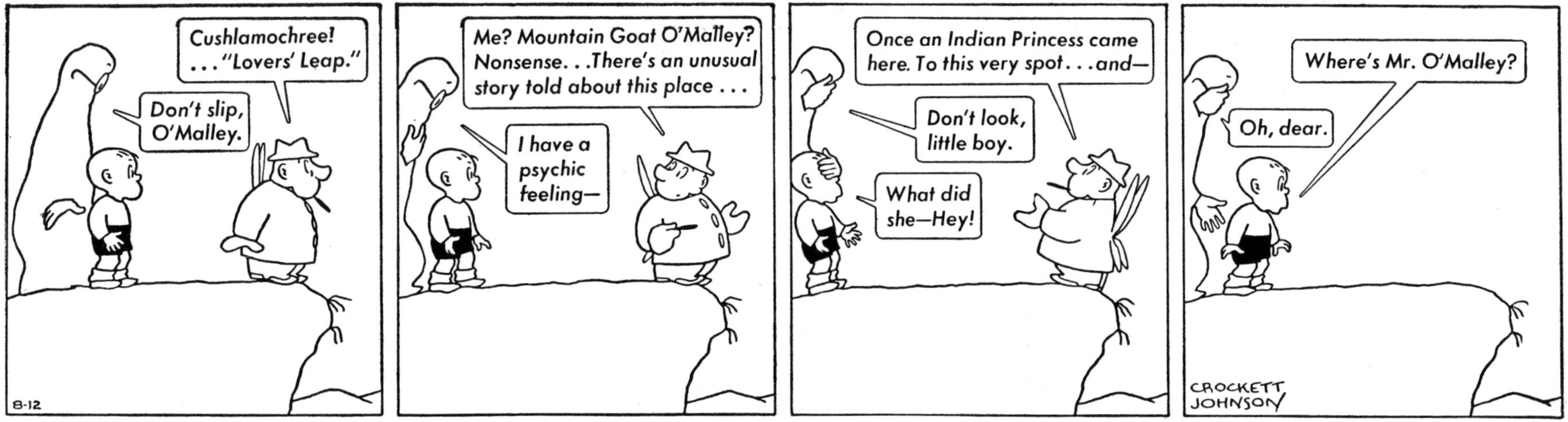
Cushlamochree! . . . "Lovers' Leap."
Don't slip, O'Malley.
8-12
Me? Mountain Goat O'Malley? Nonsense. . .There's an unusual story told about this place . . .
I have a psychic feeling—
Once an Indian Princess came here. To this very spot. . .and—
Don't look, little boy.
What did she—Hey!
Where's Mr. O'Malley?
Oh, dear.
CROCKETT JOHNSON

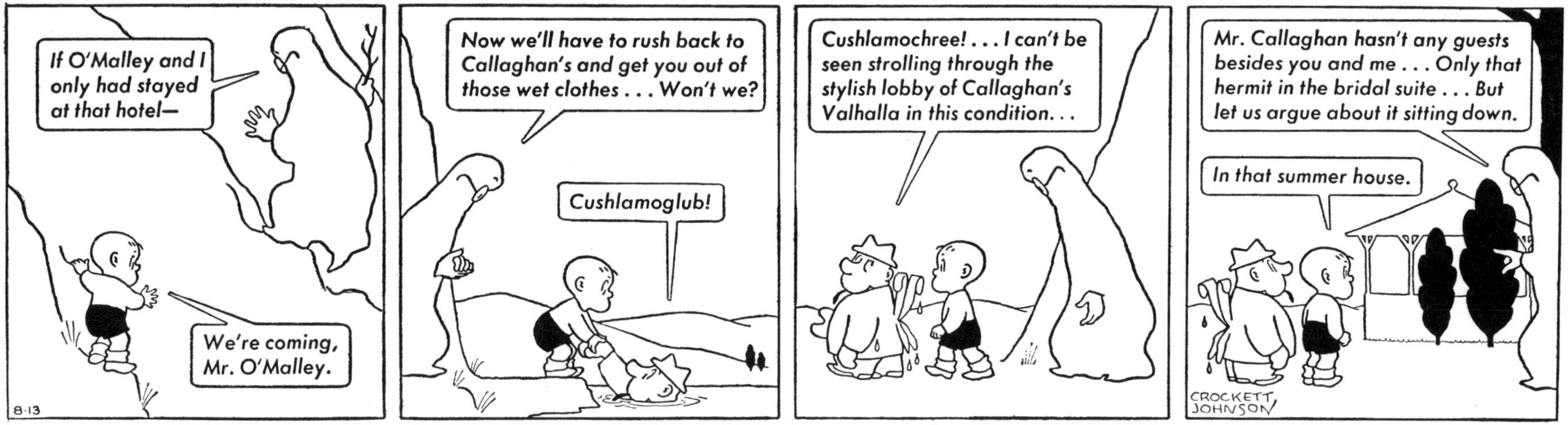
If O'Malley and I only had stayed at that hotel—
We're coming, Mr. O'Malley.
8-13
Now we'll have to rush back to Callaghan's and get you out of those wet clothes . . . Won't we?
Cushlamoglub!
Cushlamochree! . . . I can't be seen strolling through the stylish lobby of Callaghan's Valhalla in this condition. . .
Mr. Callaghan hasn't any guests besides you and me . . . Only that hermit in the bridal suite . . . But let us argue about it sitting down.
In that summer house.
CROCKETT JOHNSON

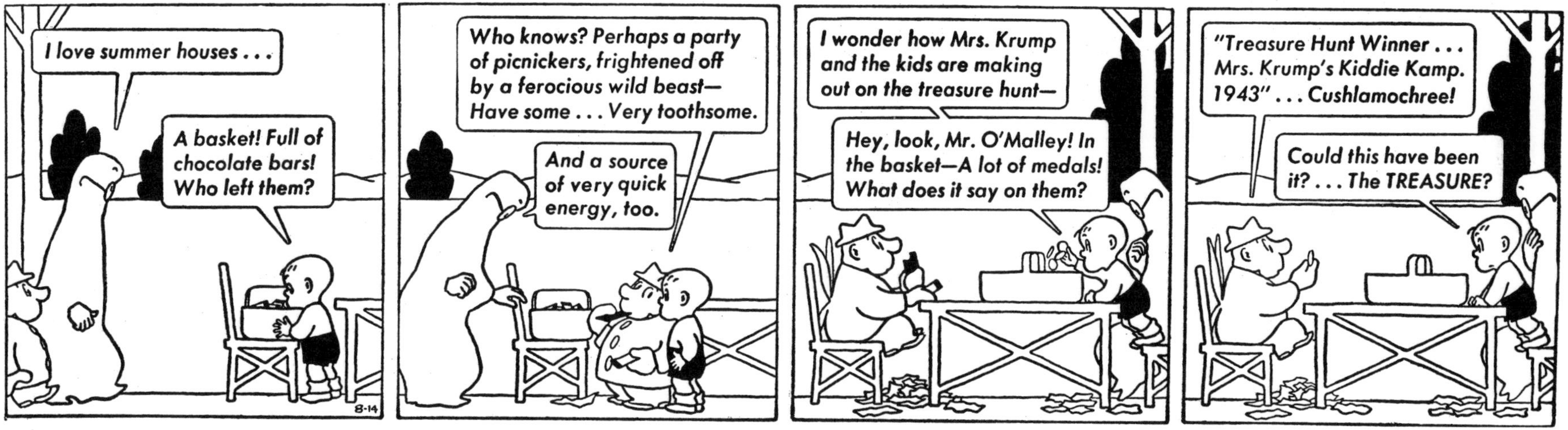
I love summer houses . . .
A basket! Full of chocolate bars! Who left them?
8-14
Who knows? Perhaps a party of picnickers, frightened off by a ferocious wild beast— Have some . . . Very toothsome.
And a source of very quick energy, too.
I wonder how Mrs. Krump and the kids are making out on the treasure hunt—
Hey, look, Mr. O'Malley! In the basket—A lot of medals! What does it say on them?
"Treasure Hunt Winner . . . Mrs. Krump's Kiddie Kamp. 1943" . . . Cushlamochree!
Could this have been it? . . . The TREASURE?

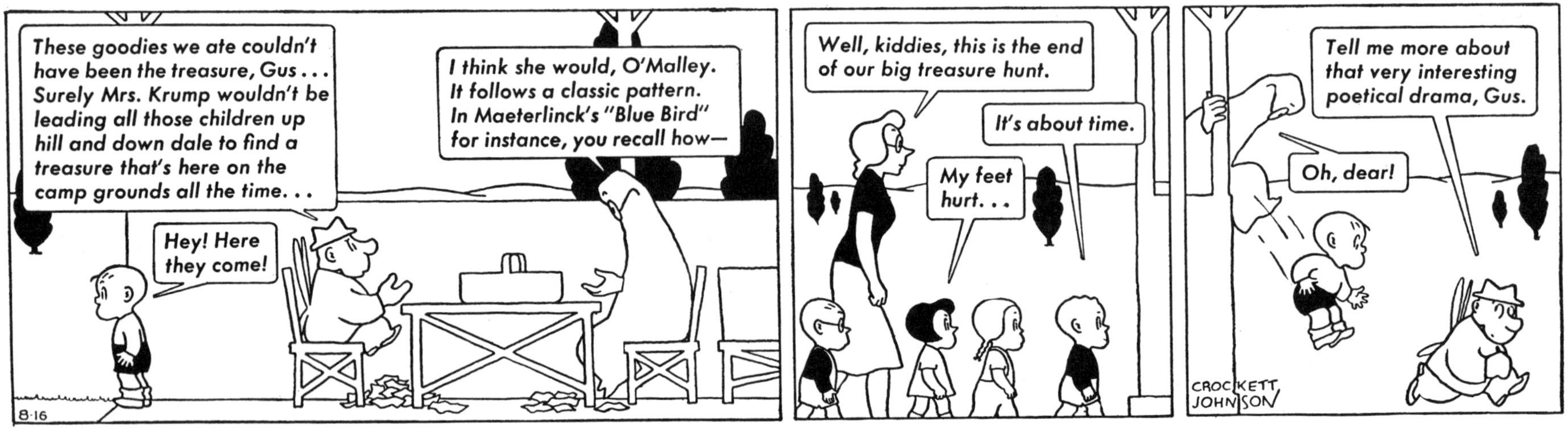
These goodies we ate couldn't have been the treasure, Gus . . . Surely Mrs. Krump wouldn't be leading all those children up hill and down dale to find a treasure that's here on the camp grounds all the time. . .
Hey! Here they come!
I think she would, O'Malley. It follows a classic pattern. In Maeterlinck's "Blue Bird" for instance, you recall how—
8·16
Well, kiddies, this is the end of our big treasure hunt.
It's about time.
My feet hurt. . .
Tell me more about that very interesting poetical drama, Gus.
Oh, dear!
CROCKETT JOHNSON

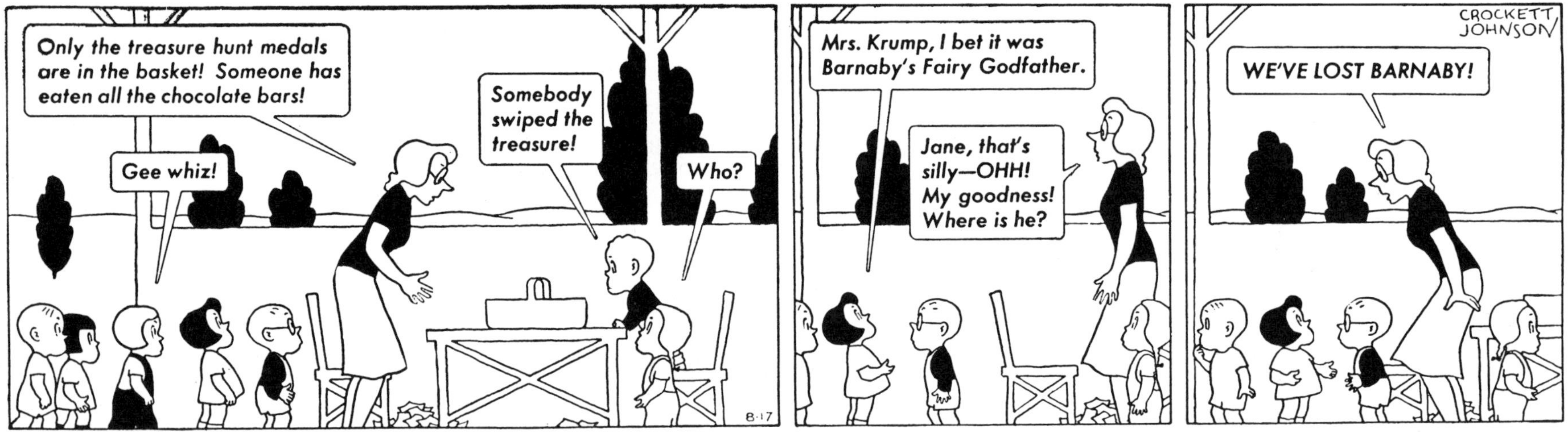
Only the treasure hunt medals are in the basket! Someone has eaten all the chocolate bars!
Gee whiz!
Somebody swiped the treasure!
Who?
8·17
Mrs. Krump, I bet it was Barnaby's Fairy Godfather.
Jane, that's silly—OHH! My goodness! Where is he?
CROCKETT JOHNSON
WE'VE LOST BARNABY!

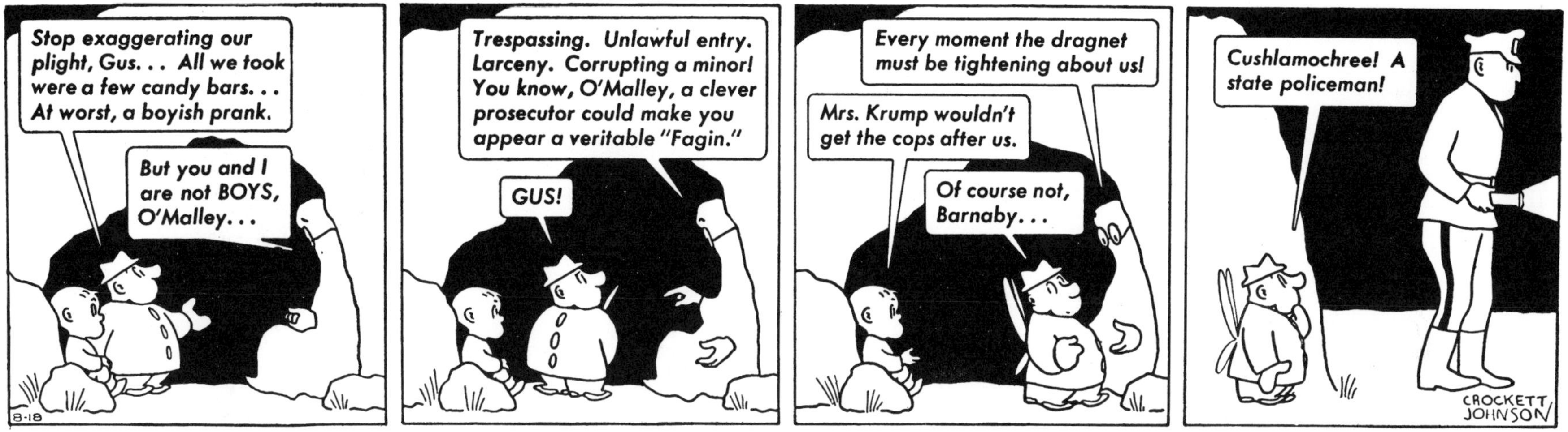
Stop exaggerating our plight, Gus. . . All we took were a few candy bars. . . At worst, a boyish prank.
But you and I are not BOYS, O'Malley. . .
Trespassing. Unlawful entry. Larceny. Corrupting a minor! You know, O'Malley, a clever prosecutor could make you appear a veritable "Fagin."
GUS!
Every moment the dragnet must be tightening about us!
Mrs. Krump wouldn't get the cops after us.
Of course not, Barnaby. . .
Cushlamochree! A state policeman!
CROCKETT JOHNSON
8-18

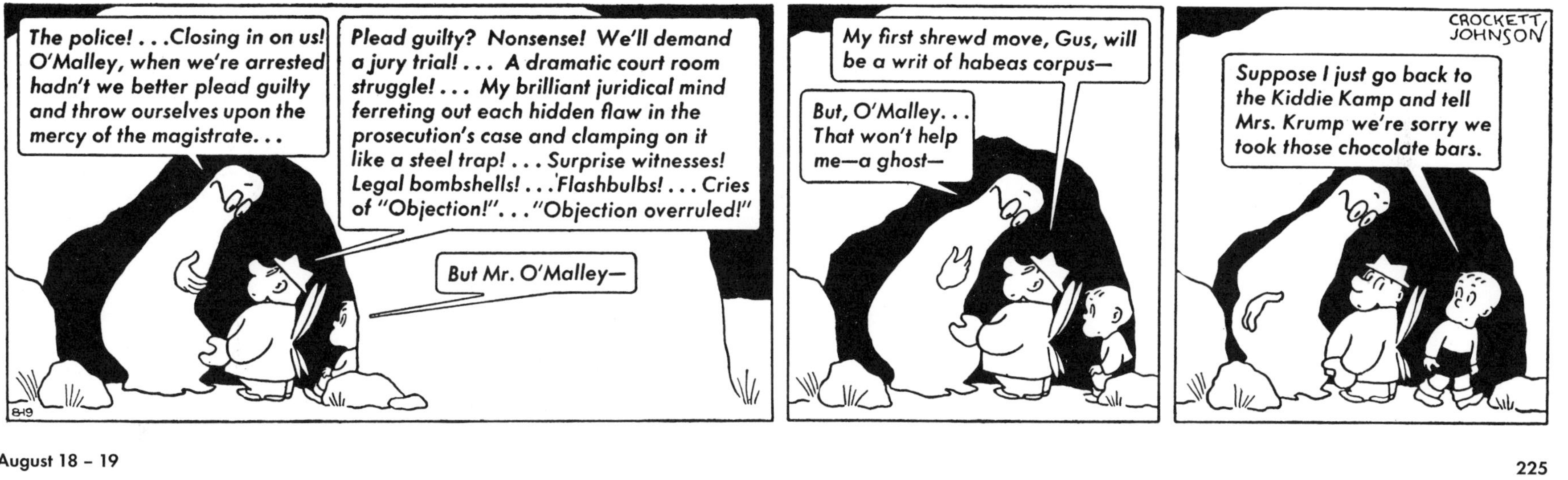
The police! . . .Closing in on us! O'Malley, when we're arrested hadn't we better plead guilty and throw ourselves upon the mercy of the magistrate. . .
Plead guilty? Nonsense! We'll demand a jury trial! . . . A dramatic court room struggle! . . . My brilliant juridical mind ferreting out each hidden flaw in the prosecution's case and clamping on it like a steel trap! . . . Surprise witnesses! Legal bombshells! . . . Flashbulbs! . . . Cries of "Objection!". . . "Objection overruled!"
But Mr. O'Malley—
My first shrewd move, Gus, will be a writ of habeas corpus—
But, O'Malley. . . That won't help me—a ghost—
CROCKETT JOHNSON
Suppose I just go back to the Kiddie Kamp and tell Mrs. Krump we're sorry we took those chocolate bars.
8-19

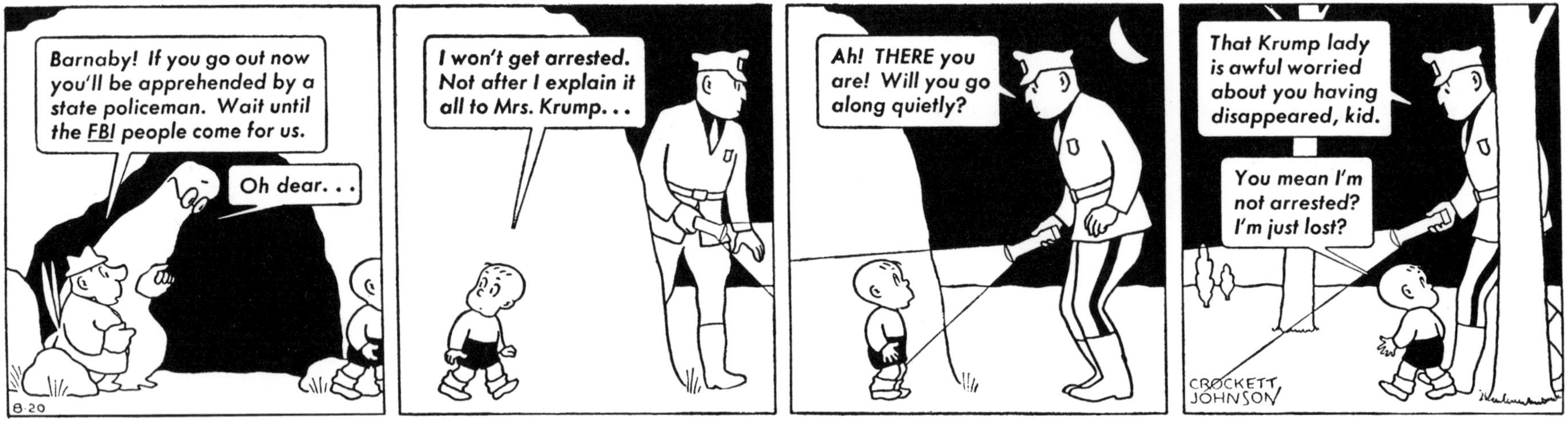
Barnaby! If you go out now you'll be apprehended by a state policeman. Wait until the FBI people come for us.
Oh dear. . .
8·20
I won't get arrested. Not after I explain it all to Mrs. Krump. . .
Ah! THERE you are! Will you go along quietly?
That Krump lady is awful worried about you having disappeared, kid.
You mean I'm not arrested? I'm just lost?
CROCKETT JOHNSON

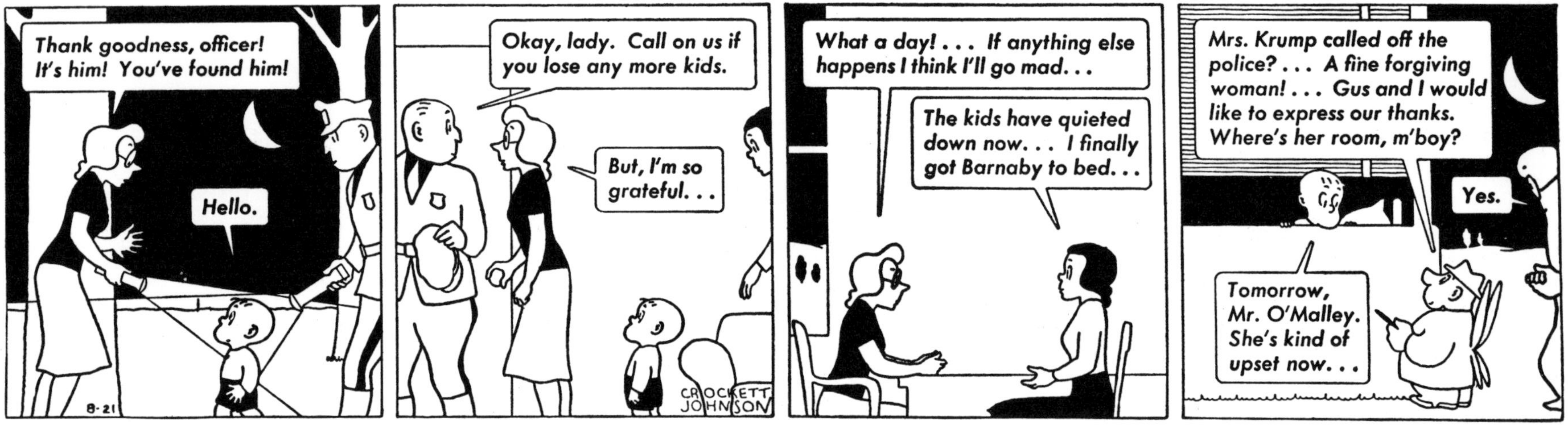
Thank goodness, officer! It's him! You've found him!
Hello.
8·21
Okay, lady. Call on us if you lose any more kids.
But, I'm so grateful. . .
CROCKETT JOHNSON
What a day! . . . If anything else happens I think I'll go mad. . .
The kids have quieted down now. . . I finally got Barnaby to bed. . .
Mrs. Krump called off the police? . . . A fine forgiving woman! . . . Gus and I would like to express our thanks. Where's her room, m'boy?
Yes.
Tomorrow, Mr. O'Malley. She's kind of upset now. . .

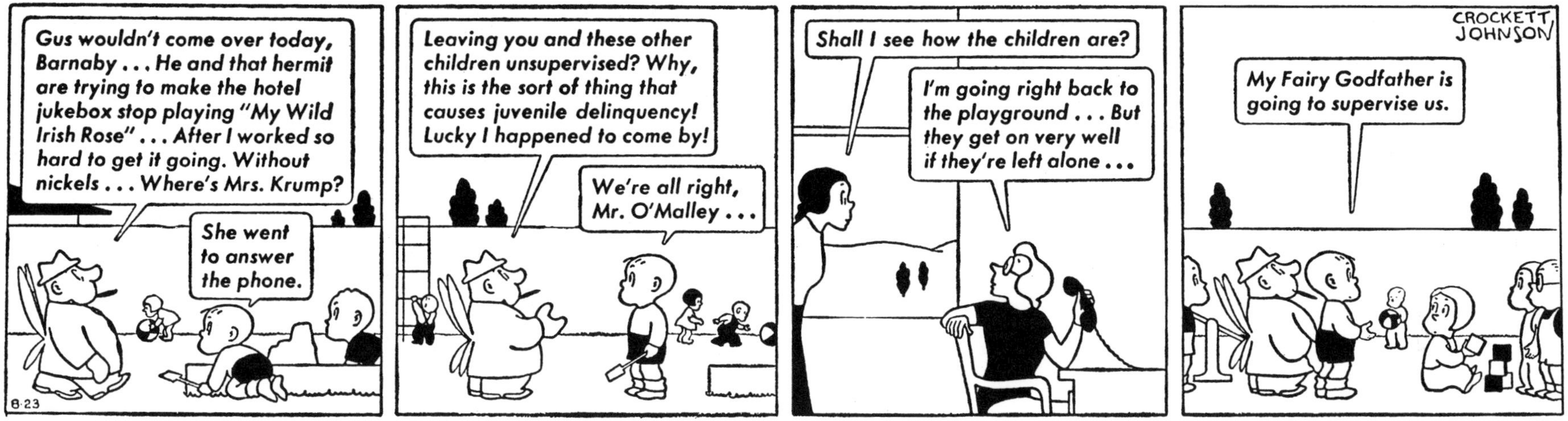
Gus wouldn't come over today, Barnaby . . . He and that hermit are trying to make the hotel jukebox stop playing "My Wild Irish Rose" . . . After I worked so hard to get it going. Without nickels . . . Where's Mrs. Krump?
She went to answer the phone.
8·23
Leaving you and these other children unsupervised? Why, this is the sort of thing that causes juvenile delinquency! Lucky I happened to come by!
We're all right, Mr. O'Malley . . .
Shall I see how the children are?
I'm going right back to the playground . . . But they get on very well if they're left alone . . .
CROCKETT JOHNSON
My Fairy Godfather is going to supervise us.

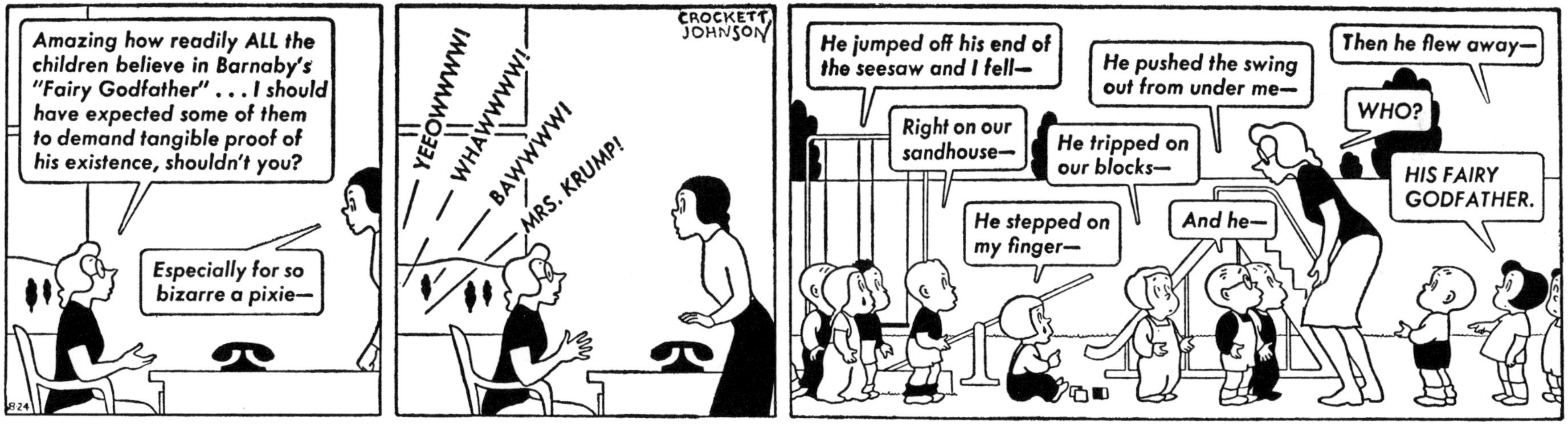
Amazing how readily ALL the children believe in Barnaby's "Fairy Godfather" . . . I should have expected some of them to demand tangible proof of his existence, shouldn't you?
Especially for so bizarre a pixie—
8·24
CROCKETT JOHNSON
YEEOWWWW!
WHAWWWW!
BAWWWW!
MRS. KRUMP!
He jumped off his end of the seesaw and I fell—
Right on our sandhouse—
He pushed the swing out from under me—
He tripped on our blocks—
He stepped on my finger—
And he—
Then he flew away—
WHO?
HIS FAIRY GODFATHER.

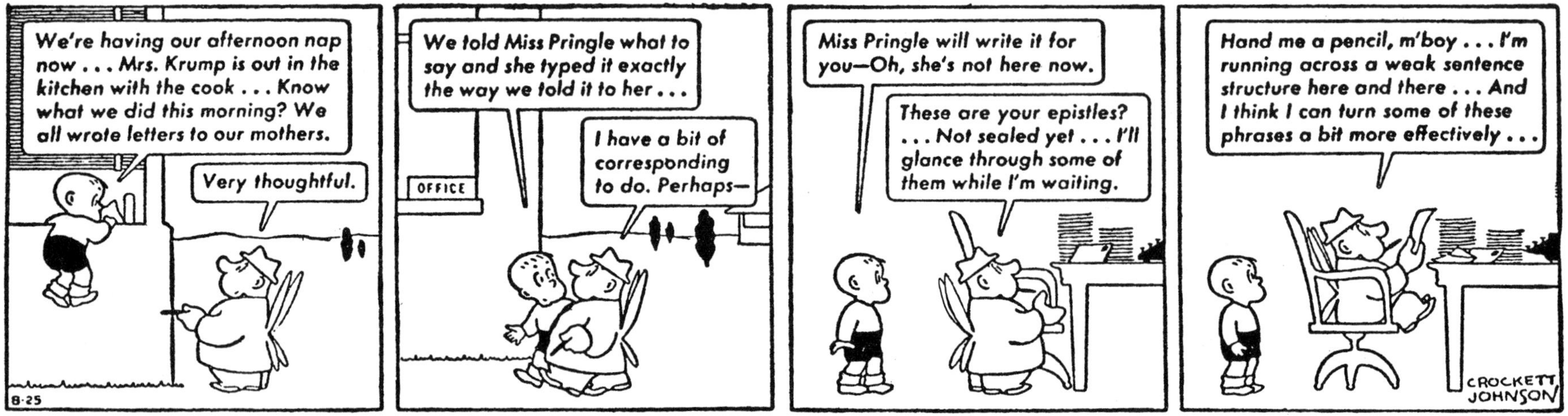
We're having our afternoon nap now . . . Mrs. Krump is out in the kitchen with the cook . . . Know what we did this morning? We all wrote letters to our mothers.
Very thoughtful.
8·25
We told Miss Pringle what to say and she typed it exactly the way we told it to her . . .
OFFICE
I have a bit of corresponding to do. Perhaps—
Miss Pringle will write it for you—Oh, she's not here now.
These are your epistles? . . . Not sealed yet . . . I'll glance through some of them while I'm waiting.
Hand me a pencil, m'boy . . . I'm running across a weak sentence structure here and there . . . And I think I can turn some of these phrases a bit more effectively . . .
CROCKETT JOHNSON

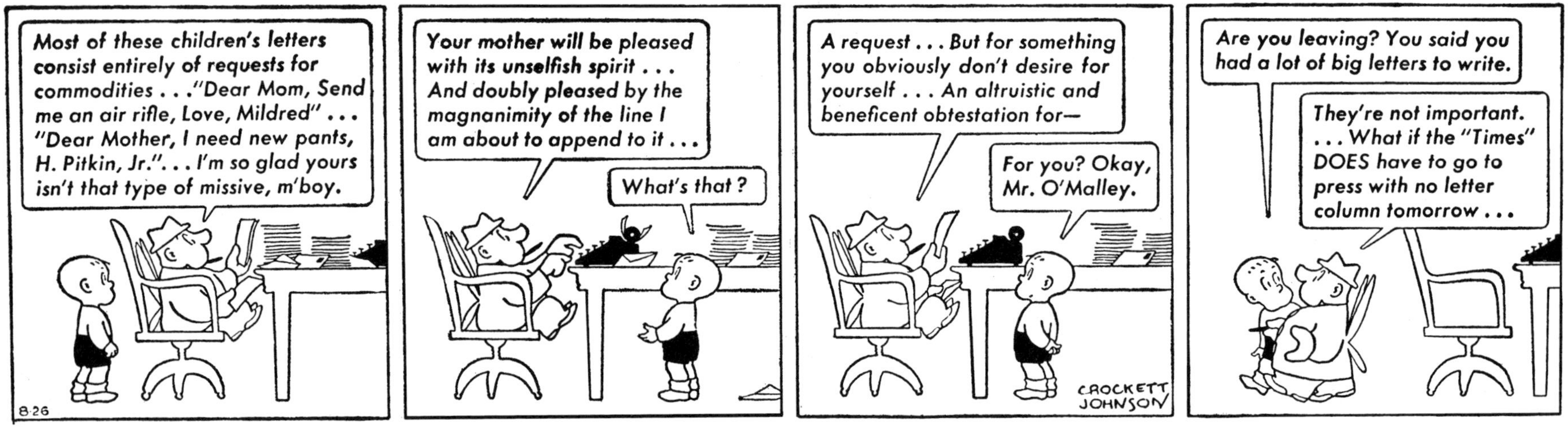
Most of these children's letters consist entirely of requests for commodities . . . "Dear Mom, Send me an air rifle, Love, Mildred" . . . "Dear Mother, I need new pants, H. Pitkin, Jr." . . . I'm so glad yours isn't that type of missive, m'boy.
8·26
Your mother will be pleased with its unselfish spirit . . . And doubly pleased by the magnanimity of the line I am about to append to it . . .
What's that?
A request . . . But for something you obviously don't desire for yourself . . . An altruistic and beneficent obtestation for—
For you? Okay, Mr. O'Malley.
CROCKETT JOHNSON
Are you leaving? You said you had a lot of big letters to write.
They're not important. . . . What if the "Times" DOES have to go to press with no letter column tomorrow . . .

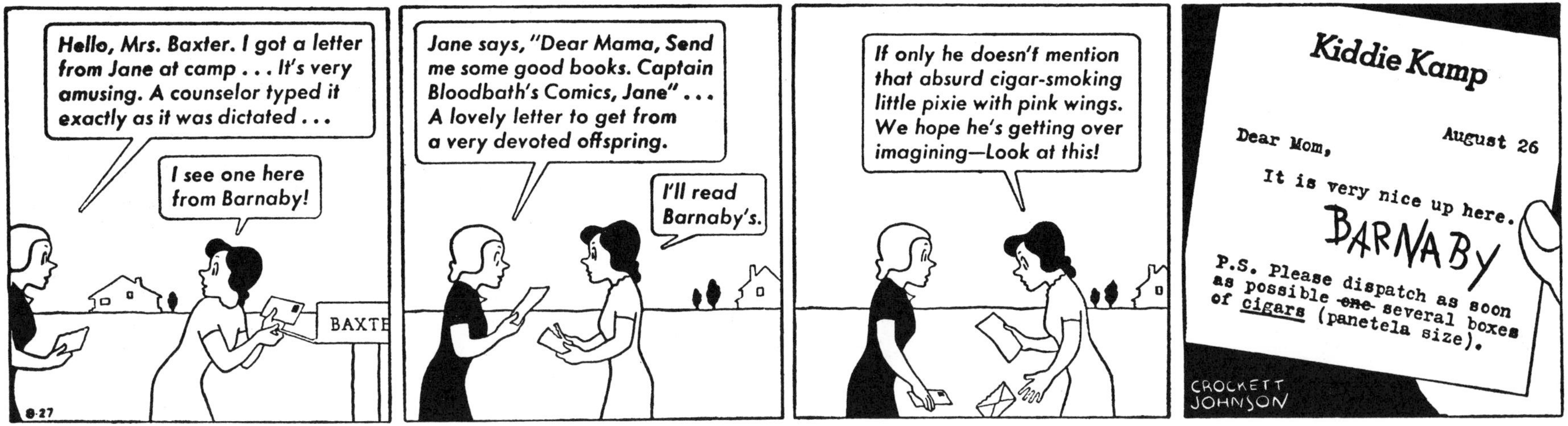
Hello, Mrs. Baxter. I got a letter from Jane at camp . . . It's very amusing. A counselor typed it exactly as it was dictated . . .
I see one here from Barnaby!
BAXTE
8-27
Jane says, "Dear Mama, Send me some good books. Captain Bloodbath's Comics, Jane" . . . A lovely letter to get from a very devoted offspring.
I'll read Barnaby's.
If only he doesn't mention that absurd cigar-smoking little pixie with pink wings. We hope he's getting over imagining—Look at this!
Kiddie Kamp
Dear Mom, August 26
It is very nice up here.
BARNABY
P.S. Please dispatch as soon as possible ~~one~~ several boxes of cigars (panetela size).
CROCKETT JOHNSON

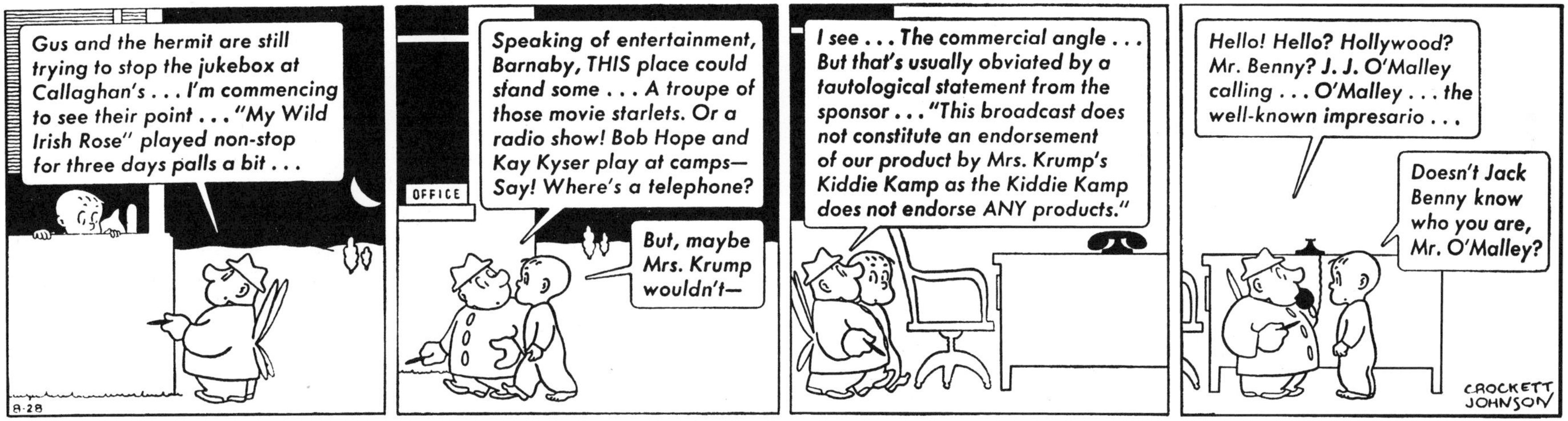
Gus and the hermit are still trying to stop the jukebox at Callaghan's . . . I'm commencing to see their point . . . "My Wild Irish Rose" played non-stop for three days palls a bit . . .
8-28
OFFICE
Speaking of entertainment, Barnaby, THIS place could stand some . . . A troupe of those movie starlets. Or a radio show! Bob Hope and Kay Kyser play at camps— Say! Where's a telephone?
But, maybe Mrs. Krump wouldn't—
I see . . . The commercial angle . . . But that's usually obviated by a tautological statement from the sponsor . . . "This broadcast does not constitute an endorsement of our product by Mrs. Krump's Kiddie Kamp as the Kiddie Kamp does not endorse ANY products."
Hello! Hello? Hollywood? Mr. Benny? J. J. O'Malley calling . . . O'Malley . . . the well-known impresario . . .
Doesn't Jack Benny know who you are, Mr. O'Malley?
CROCKETT JOHNSON

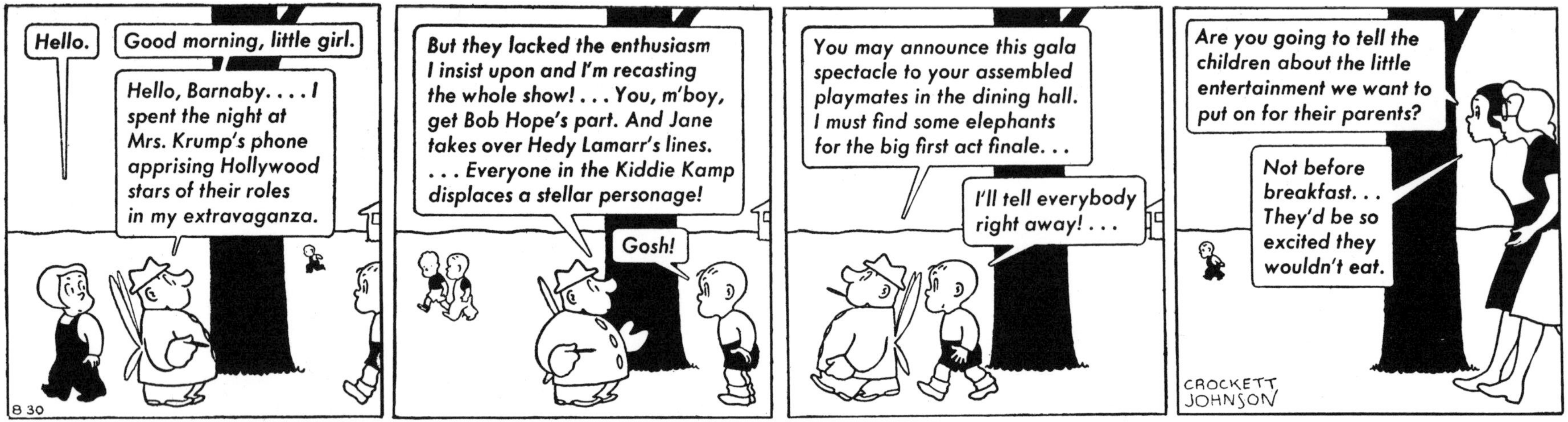
Hello.
Good morning, little girl.
Hello, Barnaby. . . . I spent the night at Mrs. Krump's phone apprising Hollywood stars of their roles in my extravaganza.
8 30
But they lacked the enthusiasm I insist upon and I'm recasting the whole show! . . . You, m'boy, get Bob Hope's part. And Jane takes over Hedy Lamarr's lines. . . . Everyone in the Kiddie Kamp displaces a stellar personage!
Gosh!
You may announce this gala spectacle to your assembled playmates in the dining hall. I must find some elephants for the big first act finale. . .
I'll tell everybody right away! . . .
Are you going to tell the children about the little entertainment we want to put on for their parents?
Not before breakfast. . . They'd be so excited they wouldn't eat.
CROCKETT JOHNSON

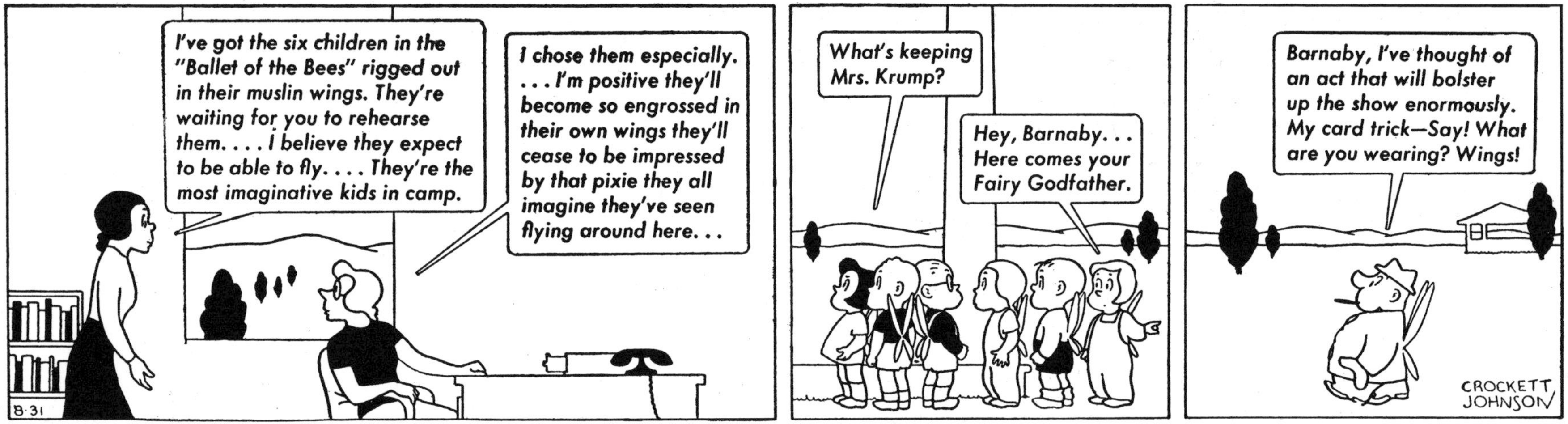
I've got the six children in the "Ballet of the Bees" rigged out in their muslin wings. They're waiting for you to rehearse them. . . . I believe they expect to be able to fly. . . . They're the most imaginative kids in camp.
I chose them especially. . . . I'm positive they'll become so engrossed in their own wings they'll cease to be impressed by that pixie they all imagine they've seen flying around here. . .
8·31
What's keeping Mrs. Krump?
Hey, Barnaby. . . Here comes your Fairy Godfather.
Barnaby, I've thought of an act that will bolster up the show enormously. My card trick—Say! What are you wearing? Wings!
CROCKETT JOHNSON

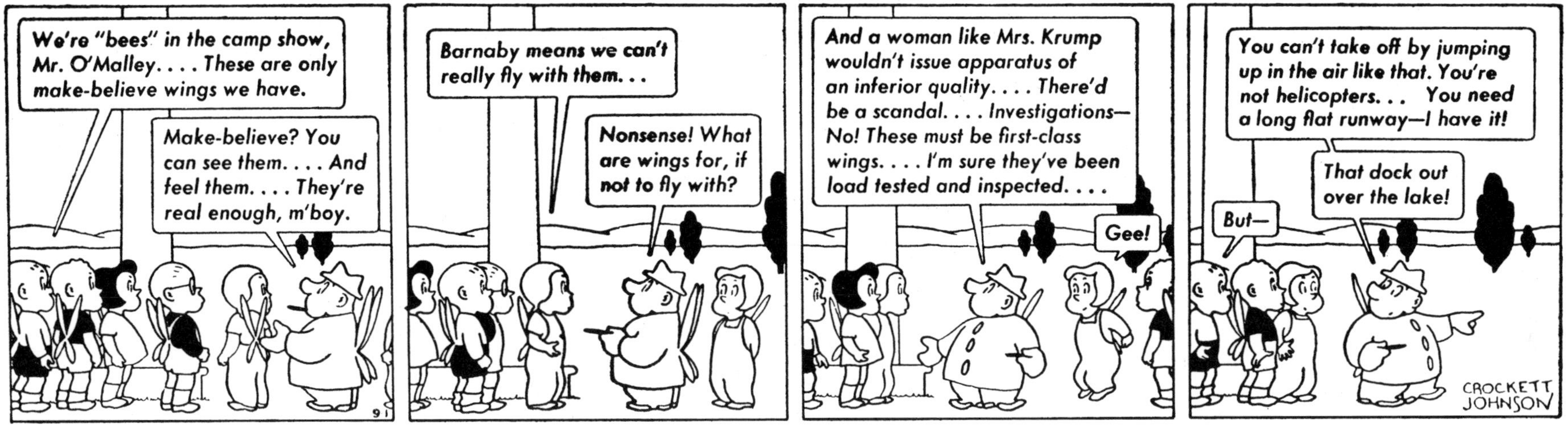
We're "bees" in the camp show, Mr. O'Malley. . . . These are only make-believe wings we have.
Make-believe? You can see them. . . . And feel them. . . . They're real enough, m'boy.
91
Barnaby means we can't really fly with them. . .
Nonsense! What are wings for, if not to fly with?
And a woman like Mrs. Krump wouldn't issue apparatus of an inferior quality. . . . There'd be a scandal. . . . Investigations— No! These must be first-class wings. . . . I'm sure they've been load tested and inspected. . . .
Gee!
You can't take off by jumping up in the air like that. You're not helicopters. . . You need a long flat runway—I have it!
But—
That dock out over the lake!
CROCKETT JOHNSON

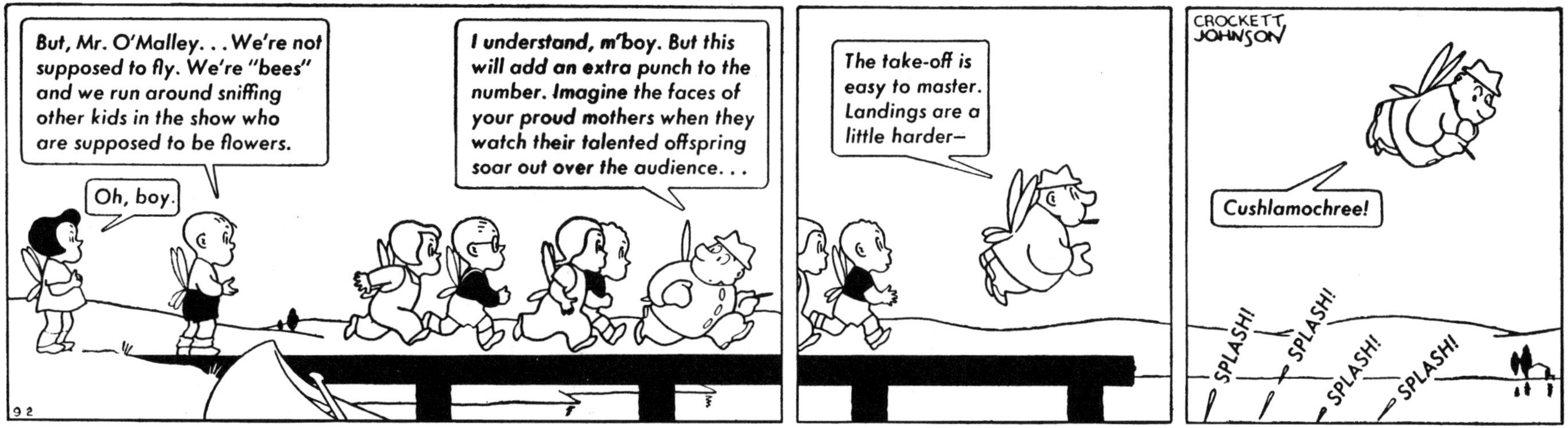
But, Mr. O'Malley. . . We're not supposed to fly. We're "bees" and we run around sniffing other kids in the show who are supposed to be flowers.
Oh, boy.
I understand, m'boy. But this will add an extra punch to the number. Imagine the faces of your proud mothers when they watch their talented offspring soar out over the audience. . .
92
The take-off is easy to master. Landings are a little harder—
CROCKETT JOHNSON
Cushlamochree!
SPLASH!
SPLASH!
SPLASH!
SPLASH!

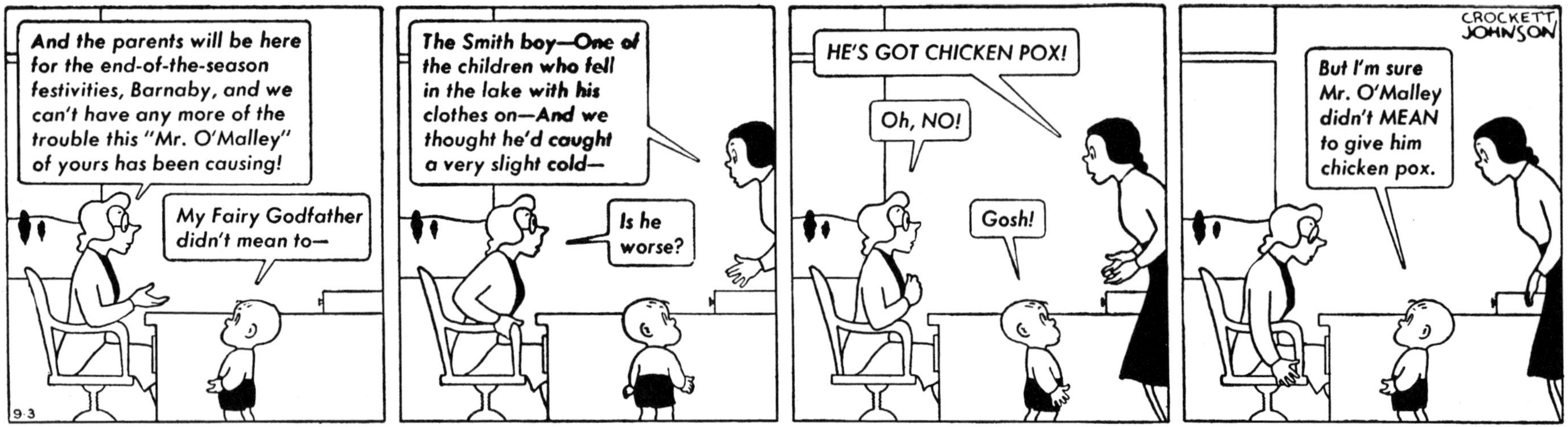
CROCKETT JOHNSON
And the parents will be here for the end-of-the-season festivities, Barnaby, and we can't have any more of the trouble this "Mr. O'Malley" of yours has been causing!
My Fairy Godfather didn't mean to—
9-3
The Smith boy—One of the children who fell in the lake with his clothes on—And we thought he'd caught a very slight cold—
Is he worse?
HE'S GOT CHICKEN POX!
Oh, NO!
Gosh!
But I'm sure Mr. O'Malley didn't MEAN to give him chicken pox.

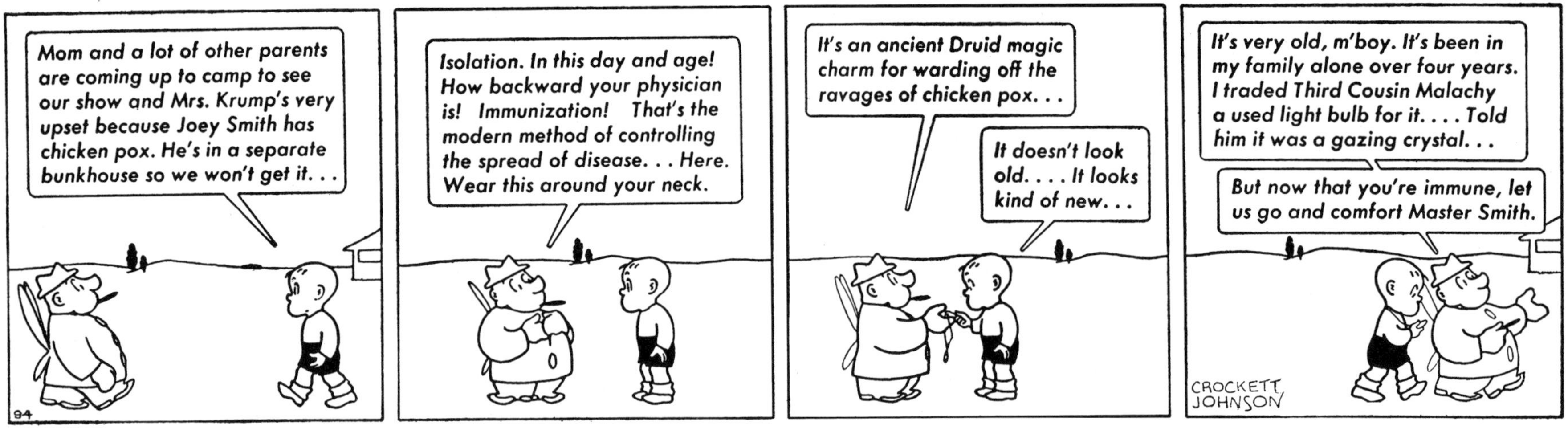
Mom and a lot of other parents are coming up to camp to see our show and Mrs. Krump's very upset because Joey Smith has chicken pox. He's in a separate bunkhouse so we won't get it. . .
9-4
Isolation. In this day and age! How backward your physician is! Immunization! That's the modern method of controlling the spread of disease. . . Here. Wear this around your neck.
It's an ancient Druid magic charm for warding off the ravages of chicken pox. . .
It doesn't look old. . . . It looks kind of new. . .
It's very old, m'boy. It's been in my family alone over four years. I traded Third Cousin Malachy a used light bulb for it. . . . Told him it was a gazing crystal. . .
But now that you're immune, let us go and comfort Master Smith.
CROCKETT JOHNSON

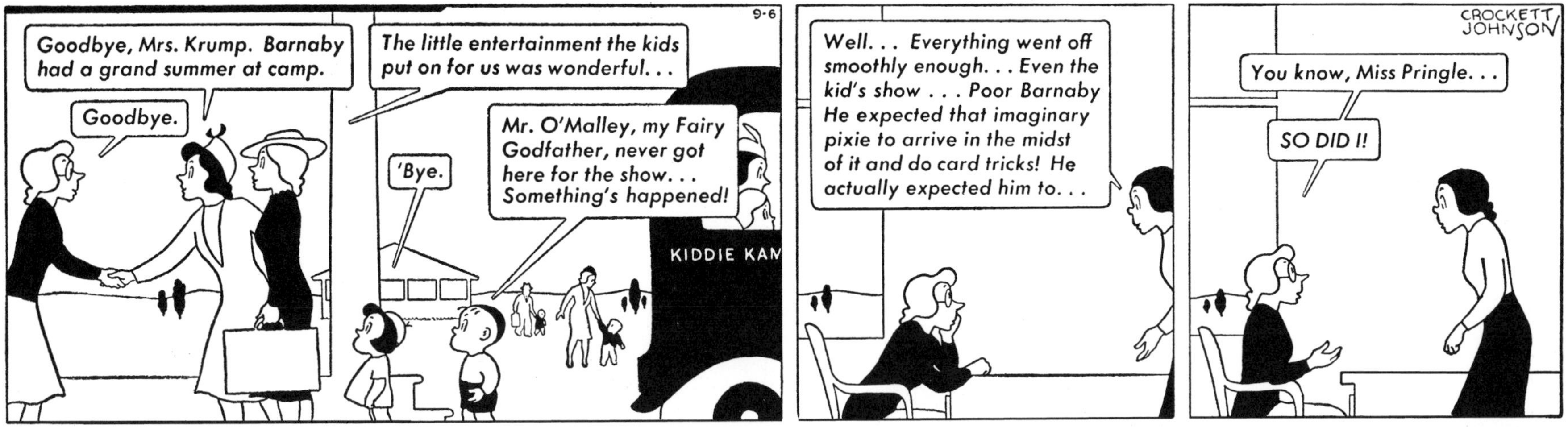
9-6
Goodbye, Mrs. Krump. Barnaby had a grand summer at camp.
Goodbye.
The little entertainment the kids put on for us was wonderful. . .
'Bye.
Mr. O'Malley, my Fairy Godfather, never got here for the show. . . Something's happened!
KIDDIE KAM
Well. . . Everything went off smoothly enough. . . Even the kid's show . . . Poor Barnaby He expected that imaginary pixie to arrive in the midst of it and do card tricks! He actually expected him to. . .
CROCKETT JOHNSON
You know, Miss Pringle. . .
SO DID I!

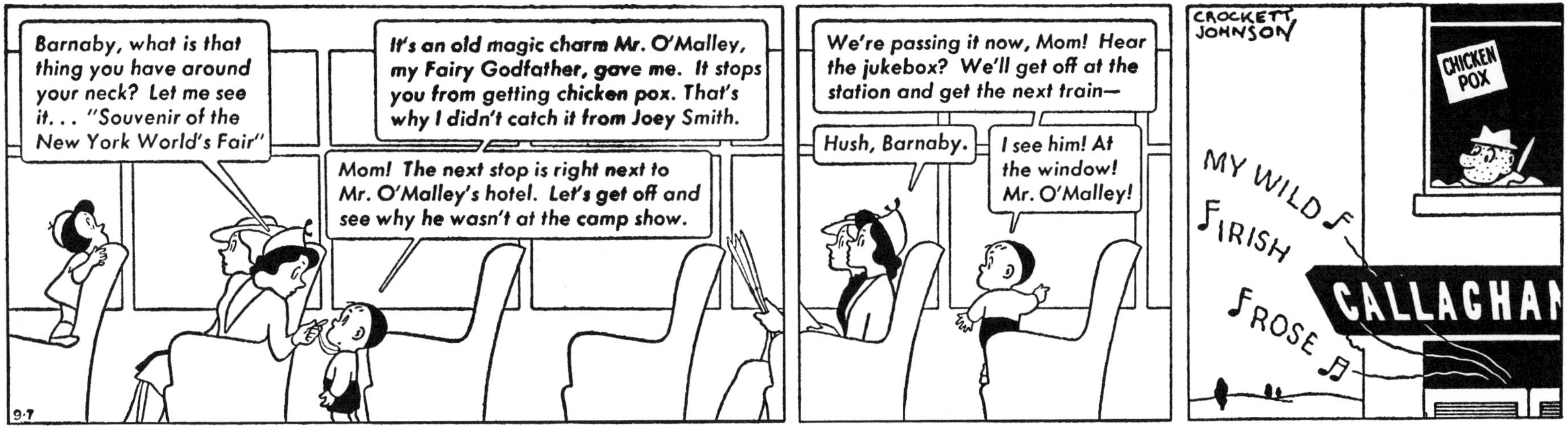
Barnaby, what is that thing you have around your neck? Let me see it. . . "Souvenir of the New York World's Fair"
It's an old magic charm Mr. O'Malley, my Fairy Godfather, gave me. It stops you from getting chicken pox. That's why I didn't catch it from Joey Smith.
Mom! The next stop is right next to Mr. O'Malley's hotel. Let's get off and see why he wasn't at the camp show.
9-7
We're passing it now, Mom! Hear the jukebox? We'll get off at the station and get the next train—
Hush, Barnaby.
I see him! At the window! Mr. O'Malley!
CROCKETT JOHNSON
CHICKEN POX
MY WILD IRISH ROSE
CALLAGHAN

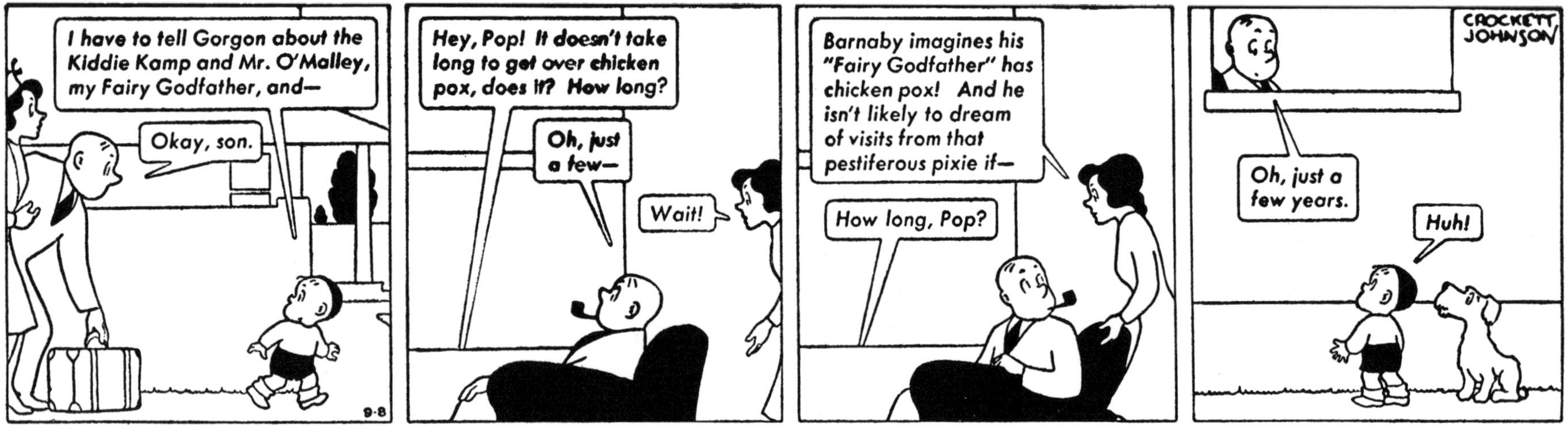
I have to tell Gorgon about the Kiddie Kamp and Mr. O'Malley, my Fairy Godfather, and—
Okay, son.
9-8
Hey, Pop! It doesn't take long to get over chicken pox, does it? How long?
Oh, just a few—
Wait!
Barnaby imagines his "Fairy Godfather" has chicken pox! And he isn't likely to dream of visits from that pestiferous pixie if—
How long, Pop?
CROCKETT JOHNSON
Oh, just a few years.
Huh!

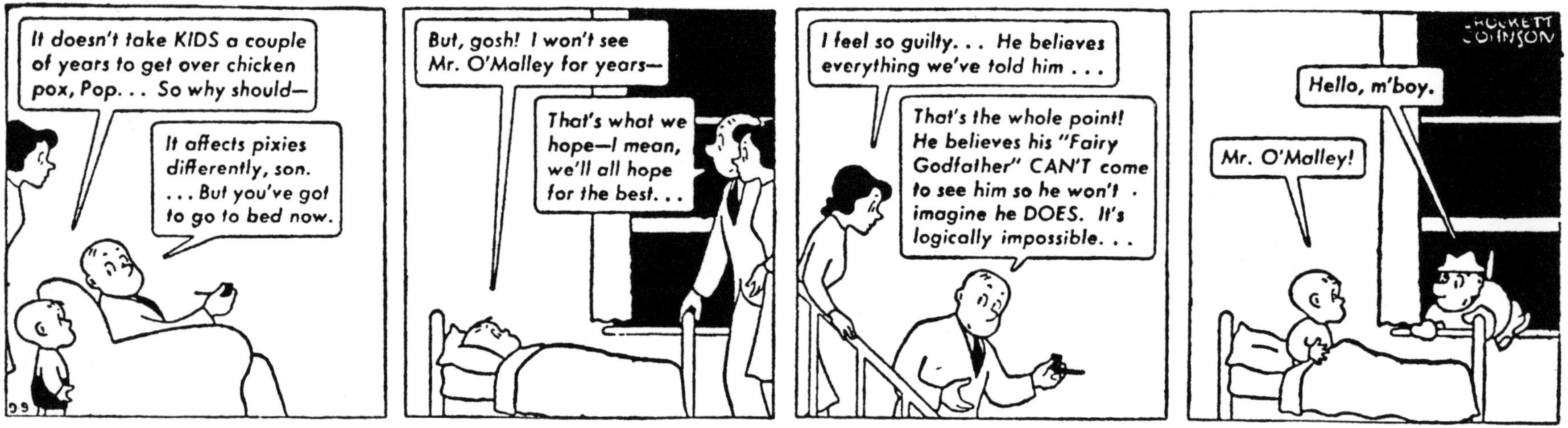
It doesn't take KIDS a couple of years to get over chicken pox, Pop... So why should—
It affects pixies differently, son. ... But you've got to go to bed now.
9-9
But, gosh! I won't see Mr. O'Malley for years—
That's what we hope—I mean, we'll all hope for the best...
I feel so guilty... He believes everything we've told him ...
That's the whole point! He believes his "Fairy Godfather" CAN'T come to see him so he won't imagine he DOES. It's logically impossible...
CROCKETT JOHNSON
Hello, m'boy.
Mr. O'Malley!

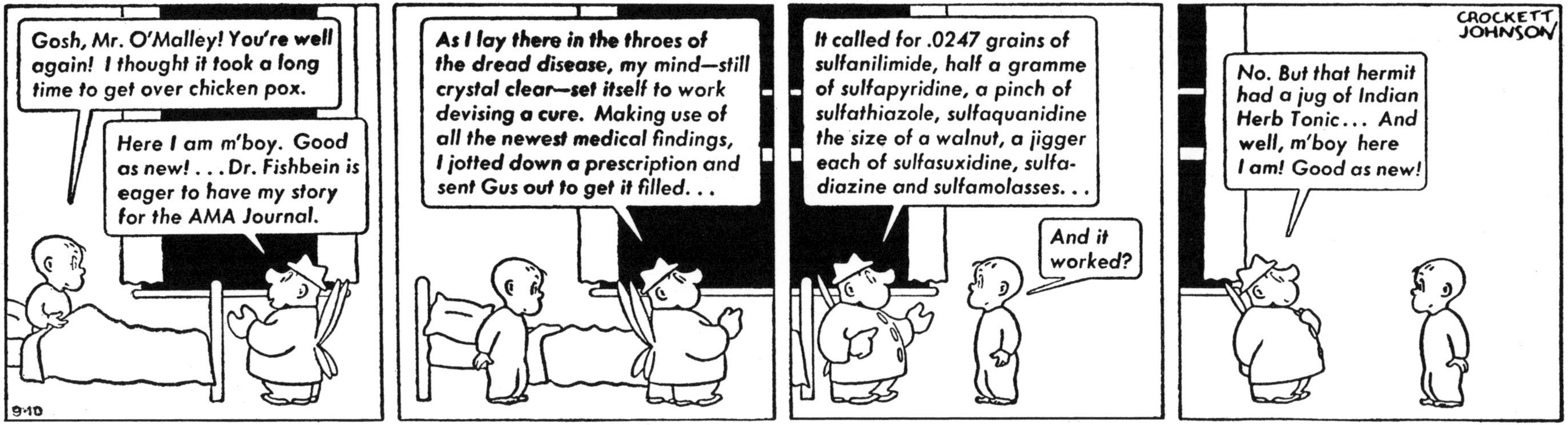
CROCKETT JOHNSON
9·10
Gosh, Mr. O'Malley! You're well again! I thought it took a long time to get over chicken pox.
Here I am m'boy. Good as new! . . . Dr. Fishbein is eager to have my story for the AMA Journal.
As I lay there in the throes of the dread disease, my mind—still crystal clear—set itself to work devising a cure. Making use of all the newest medical findings, I jotted down a prescription and sent Gus out to get it filled. . .
It called for .0247 grains of sulfanilimide, half a gramme of sulfapyridine, a pinch of sulfathiazole, sulfaquanidine the size of a walnut, a jigger each of sulfasuxidine, sulfadiazine and sulfamolasses. . .
And it worked?
No. But that hermit had a jug of Indian Herb Tonic. . . And well, m'boy here I am! Good as new!

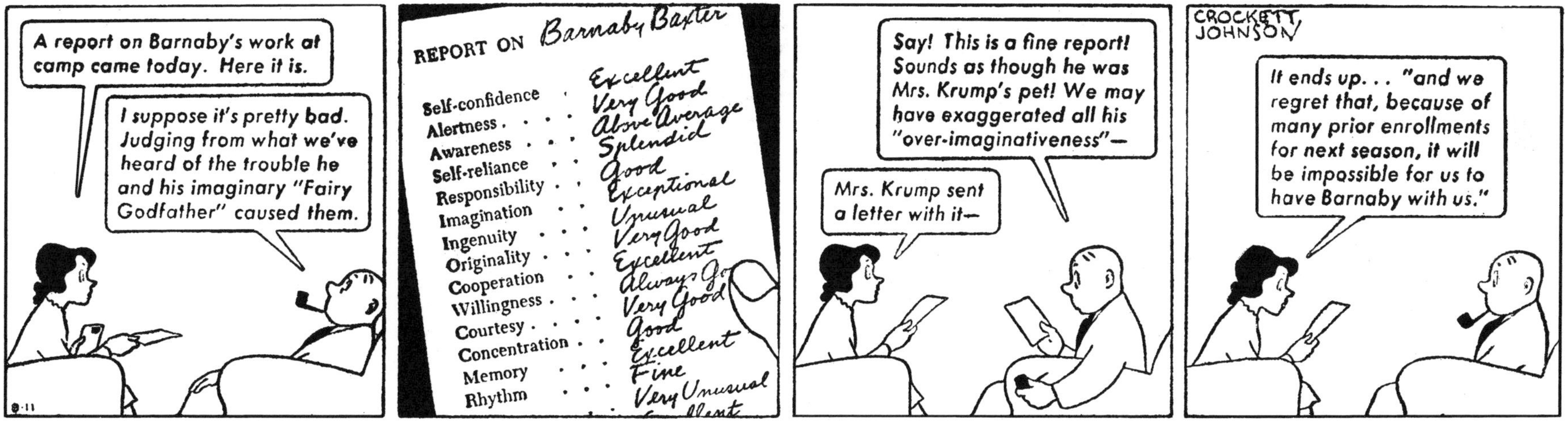
CROCKETT JOHNSON
9·11
A report on Barnaby's work at camp came today. Here it is.
I suppose it's pretty bad. Judging from what we've heard of the trouble he and his imaginary "Fairy Godfather" caused them.
REPORT ON Barnaby Baxter
Self-confidence
Alertness
Awareness
Self-reliance
Responsibility
Imagination
Ingenuity
Originality
Cooperation
Willingness
Courtesy
Concentration
Memory
Rhythm
Excellent
Very Good
Above Average
Splendid
Good
Exceptional
Unusual
Very Good
Excellent
Very Good
Good
Excellent
Fine
Very Unusual
Say! This is a fine report! Sounds as though he was Mrs. Krump's pet! We may have exaggerated all his "over-imaginativeness"—
Mrs. Krump sent a letter with it—
It ends up. . . "and we regret that, because of many prior enrollments for next season, it will be impossible for us to have Barnaby with us."

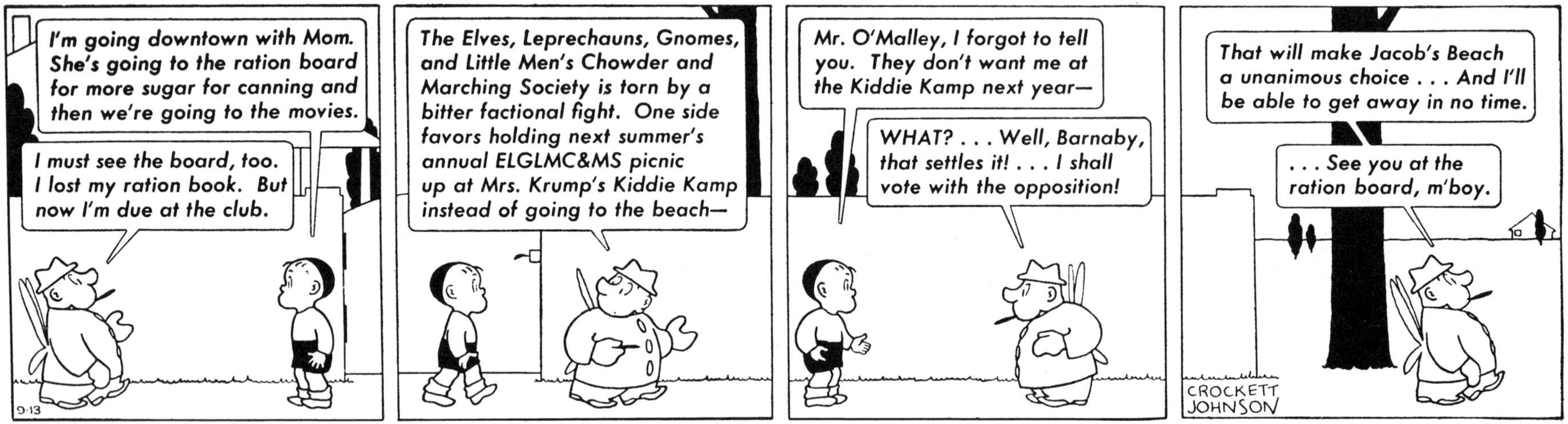
I'm going downtown with Mom. She's going to the ration board for more sugar for canning and then we're going to the movies.
I must see the board, too. I lost my ration book. But now I'm due at the club.
9-13
The Elves, Leprechauns, Gnomes, and Little Men's Chowder and Marching Society is torn by a bitter factional fight. One side favors holding next summer's annual ELGLMC&MS picnic up at Mrs. Krump's Kiddie Kamp instead of going to the beach—
Mr. O'Malley, I forgot to tell you. They don't want me at the Kiddie Kamp next year—
WHAT? . . . Well, Barnaby, that settles it! . . . I shall vote with the opposition!
That will make Jacob's Beach a unanimous choice . . . And I'll be able to get away in no time.
. . . See you at the ration board, m'boy.
CROCKETT JOHNSON

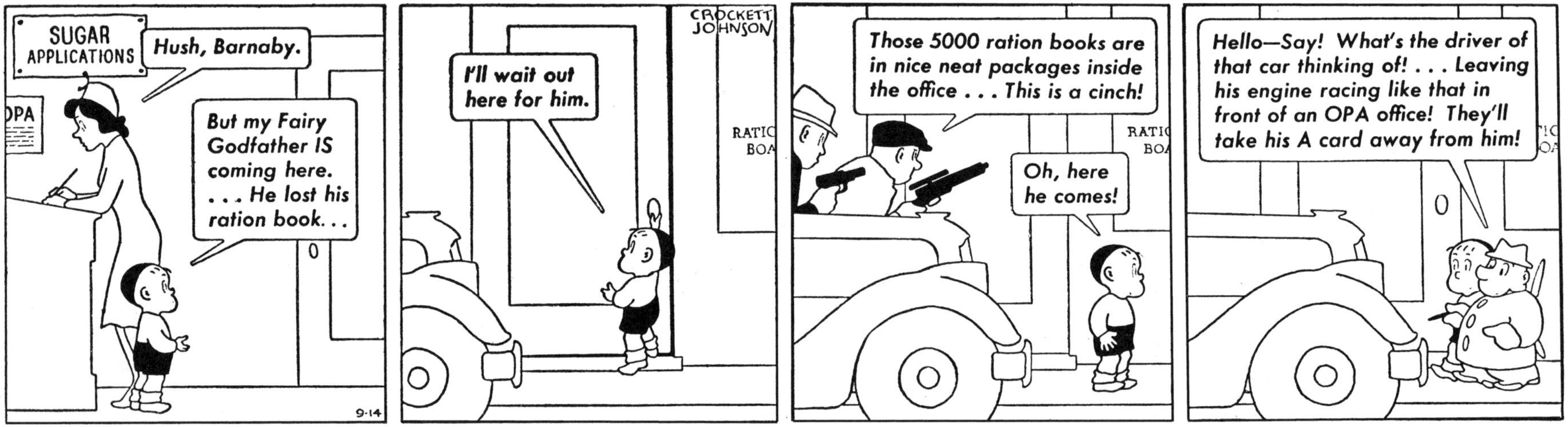
SUGAR APPLICATIONS
Hush, Barnaby.
OPA
But my Fairy Godfather IS coming here. . . . He lost his ration book. . .
9-14
CROCKETT JOHNSON
I'll wait out here for him.
Those 5000 ration books are in nice neat packages inside the office . . . This is a cinch!
Oh, here he comes!
Hello—Say! What's the driver of that car thinking of! . . . Leaving his engine racing like that in front of an OPA office! They'll take his A card away from him!

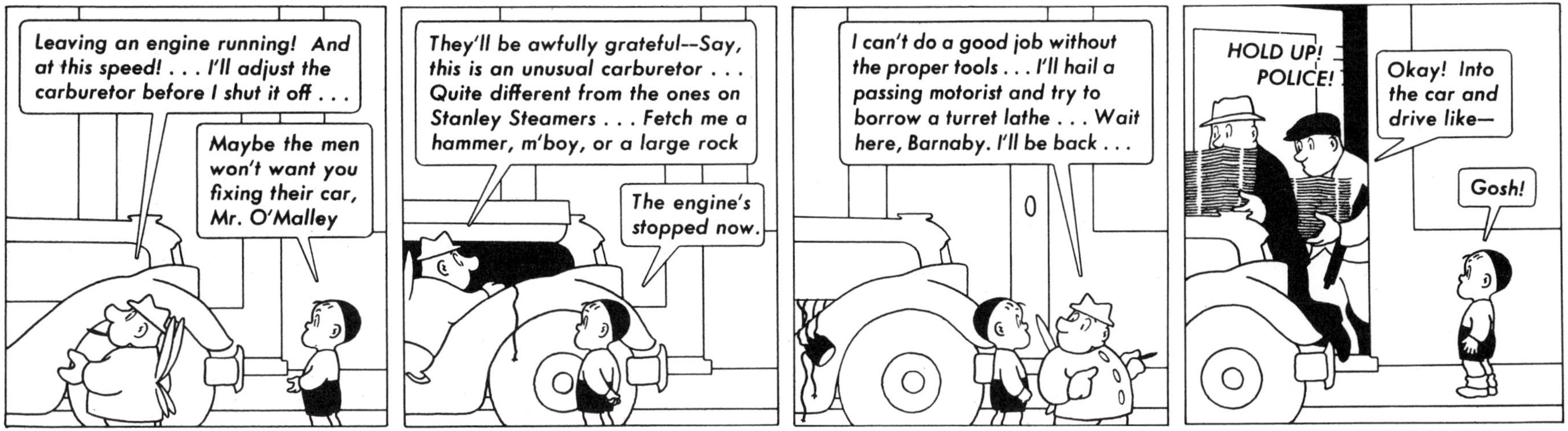
Leaving an engine running! And at this speed! . . . I'll adjust the carburetor before I shut it off . . .
Maybe the men won't want you fixing their car, Mr. O'Malley
They'll be awfully grateful--Say, this is an unusual carburetor . . . Quite different from the ones on Stanley Steamers . . . Fetch me a hammer, m'boy, or a large rock
The engine's stopped now.
I can't do a good job without the proper tools . . . I'll hail a passing motorist and try to borrow a turret lathe . . . Wait here, Barnaby. I'll be back . . .
HOLD UP!
POLICE!
Okay! Into the car and drive like—
Gosh!

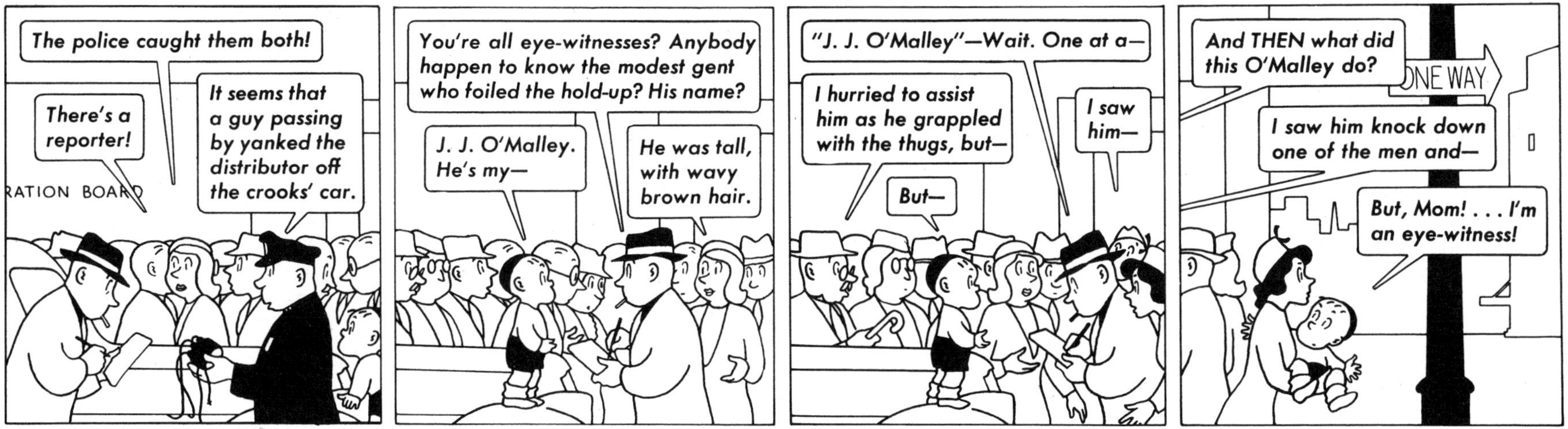
The police caught them both!
There's a reporter!
It seems that a guy passing by yanked the distributor off the crooks' car.
RATION BOARD
You're all eye-witnesses? Anybody happen to know the modest gent who foiled the hold-up? His name?
J. J. O'Malley. He's my—
He was tall, with wavy brown hair.
"J. J. O'Malley"—Wait. One at a—
I hurried to assist him as he grappled with the thugs, but—
I saw him—
But—
And THEN what did this O'Malley do?
ONE WAY
I saw him knock down one of the men and—
But, Mom! . . . I'm an eye-witness!

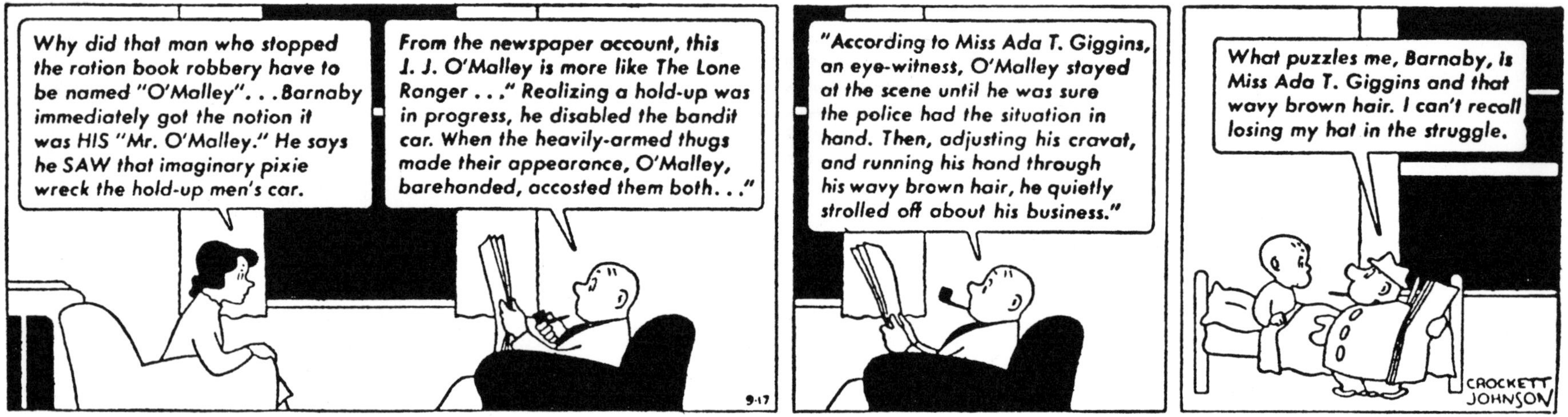
Why did that man who stopped the ration book robbery have to be named "O'Malley". . .Barnaby immediately got the notion it was HIS "Mr. O'Malley." He says he SAW that imaginary pixie wreck the hold-up men's car.
From the newspaper account, this J. J. O'Malley is more like The Lone Ranger . . ." Realizing a hold-up was in progress, he disabled the bandit car. When the heavily-armed thugs made their appearance, O'Malley, barehanded, accosted them both. . ."
"According to Miss Ada T. Giggins, an eye-witness, O'Malley stayed at the scene until he was sure the police had the situation in hand. Then, adjusting his cravat, and running his hand through his wavy brown hair, he quietly strolled off about his business."
What puzzles me, Barnaby, is Miss Ada T. Giggins and that wavy brown hair. I can't recall losing my hat in the struggle.
9-17
CROCKETT JOHNSON

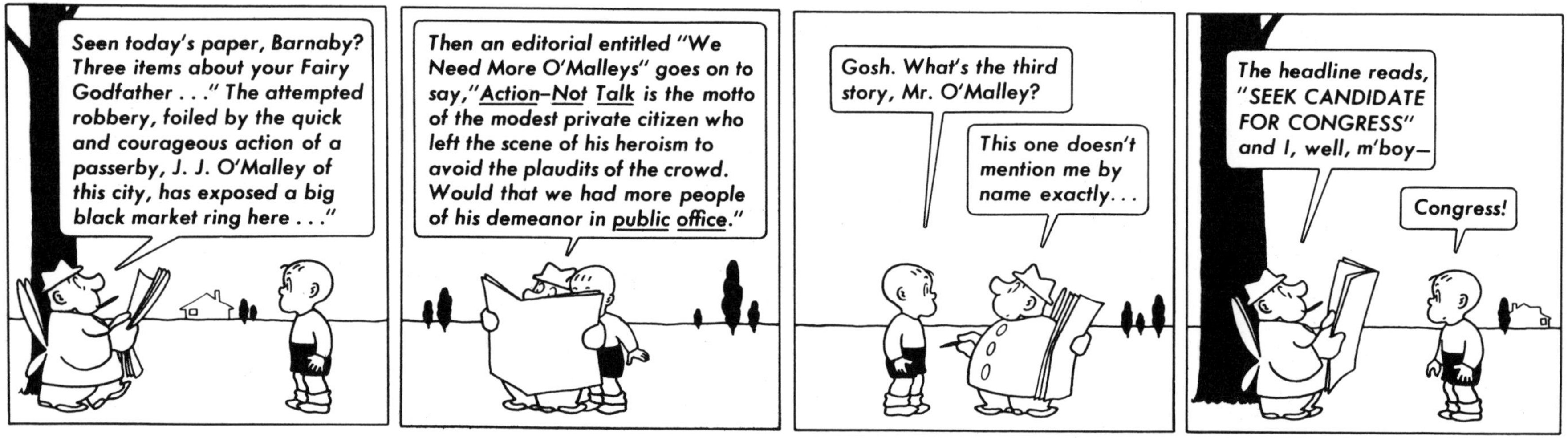
Seen today's paper, Barnaby? Three items about your Fairy Godfather . . ." The attempted robbery, foiled by the quick and courageous action of a passerby, J. J. O'Malley of this city, has exposed a big black market ring here . . ."
Then an editorial entitled "We Need More O'Malleys" goes on to say,"Action–Not Talk is the motto of the modest private citizen who left the scene of his heroism to avoid the plaudits of the crowd. Would that we had more people of his demeanor in public office."
Gosh. What's the third story, Mr. O'Malley?
This one doesn't mention me by name exactly. . .
The headline reads, "SEEK CANDIDATE FOR CONGRESS" and I, well, m'boy—
Congress!

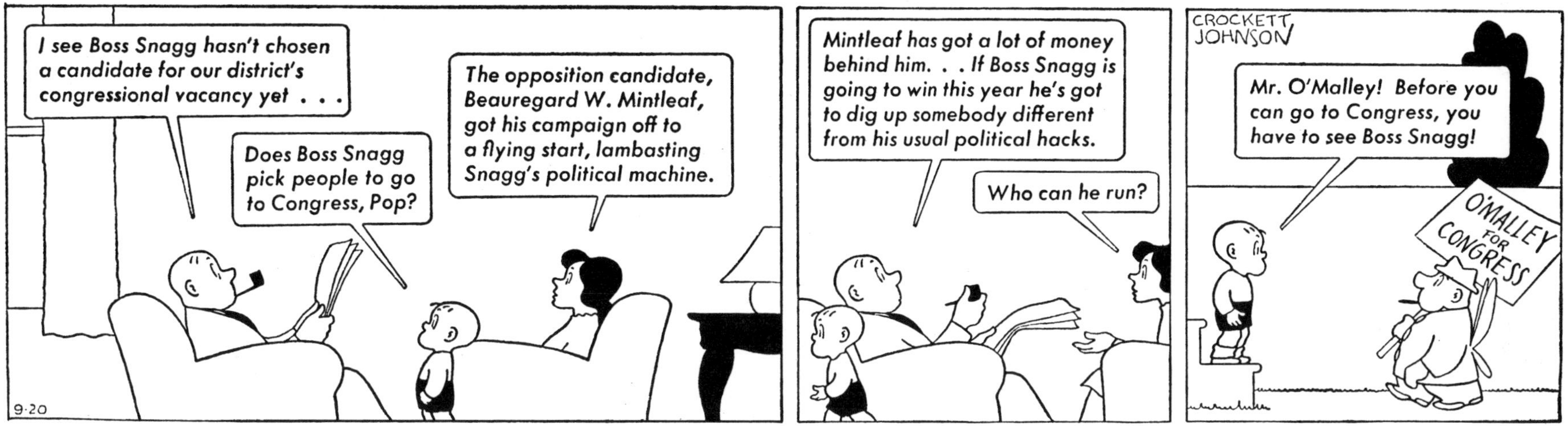
I see Boss Snagg hasn't chosen a candidate for our district's congressional vacancy yet . . .
Does Boss Snagg pick people to go to Congress, Pop?
The opposition candidate, Beauregard W. Mintleaf, got his campaign off to a flying start, lambasting Snagg's political machine.
9·20
Mintleaf has got a lot of money behind him. . . If Boss Snagg is going to win this year he's got to dig up somebody different from his usual political hacks.
Who can he run?
CROCKETT JOHNSON
Mr. O'Malley! Before you can go to Congress, you have to see Boss Snagg!
O'MALLEY FOR CONGRESS

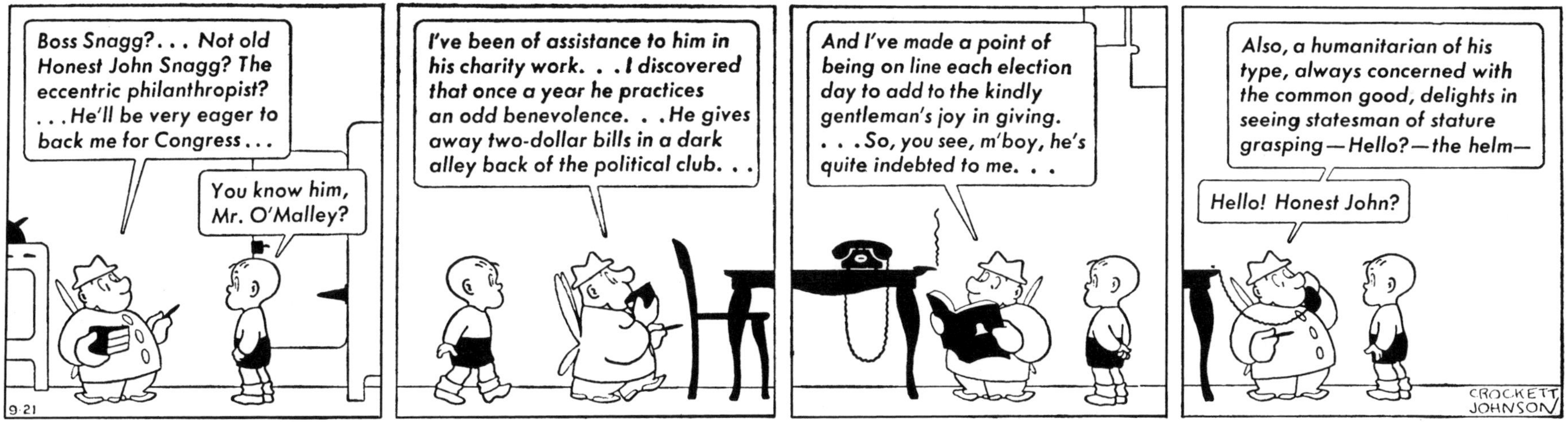
Boss Snagg?... Not old Honest John Snagg? The eccentric philanthropist? ...He'll be very eager to back me for Congress...
You know him, Mr. O'Malley?
9·21
I've been of assistance to him in his charity work. . . I discovered that once a year he practices an odd benevolence. . . He gives away two-dollar bills in a dark alley back of the political club. . .
And I've made a point of being on line each election day to add to the kindly gentleman's joy in giving. . . . So, you see, m'boy, he's quite indebted to me. . .
Also, a humanitarian of his type, always concerned with the common good, delights in seeing statesman of stature grasping—Hello?—the helm—
Hello! Honest John?
CROCKETT JOHNSON

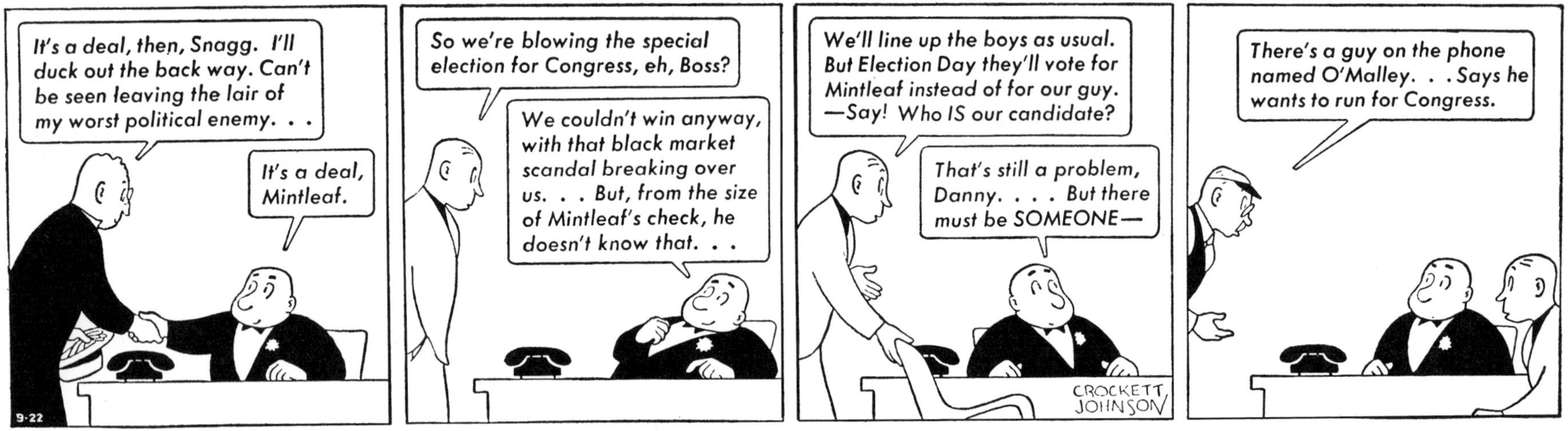
It's a deal, then, Snagg. I'll duck out the back way. Can't be seen leaving the lair of my worst political enemy. . .
It's a deal, Mintleaf.
So we're blowing the special election for Congress, eh, Boss?
We couldn't win anyway, with that black market scandal breaking over us. . . But, from the size of Mintleaf's check, he doesn't know that. . .
We'll line up the boys as usual. But Election Day they'll vote for Mintleaf instead of for our guy. —Say! Who IS our candidate?
That's still a problem, Danny. . . . But there must be SOMEONE—
CROCKETT JOHNSON
There's a guy on the phone named O'Malley. . . Says he wants to run for Congress.
9·22

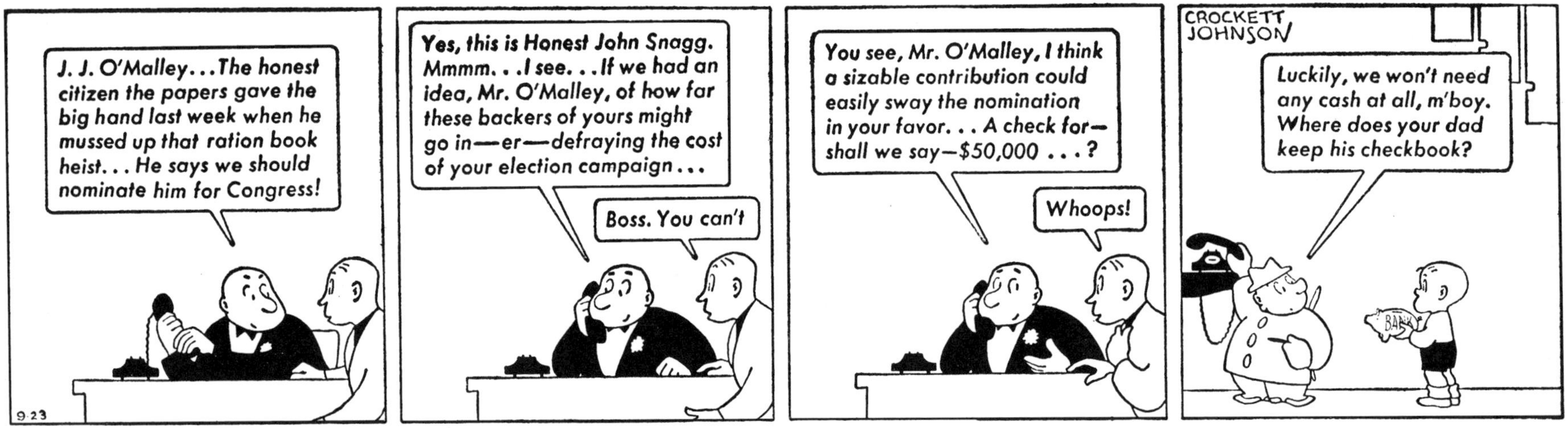
J. J. O'Malley. . . The honest citizen the papers gave the big hand last week when he mussed up that ration book heist. . . He says we should nominate him for Congress!
Yes, this is Honest John Snagg. Mmmm. . . I see. . . If we had an idea, Mr. O'Malley, of how far these backers of yours might go in—er—defraying the cost of your election campaign . . .
Boss. You can't
You see, Mr. O'Malley, I think a sizable contribution could easily sway the nomination in your favor. . . A check for— shall we say—$50,000 . . . ?
Whoops!
CROCKETT JOHNSON
Luckily, we won't need any cash at all, m'boy. Where does your dad keep his checkbook?
9·23

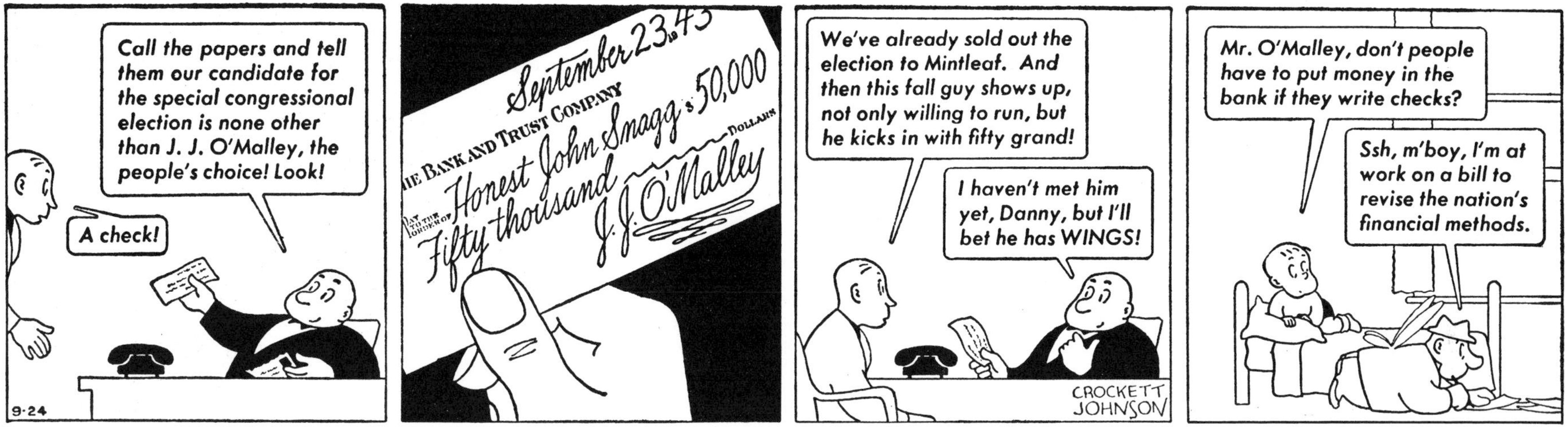
Call the papers and tell them our candidate for the special congressional election is none other than J. J. O'Malley, the people's choice! Look!
A check!
September 23, 43
BANK AND TRUST COMPANY
Honest John Snagg
$50,000
Fifty thousand
DOLLARS
J. J. O'Malley
We've already sold out the election to Mintleaf. And then this fall guy shows up, not only willing to run, but he kicks in with fifty grand!
I haven't met him yet, Danny, but I'll bet he has WINGS!
Mr. O'Malley, don't people have to put money in the bank if they write checks?
Ssh, m'boy, I'm at work on a bill to revise the nation's financial methods.
9·24
CROCKETT JOHNSON

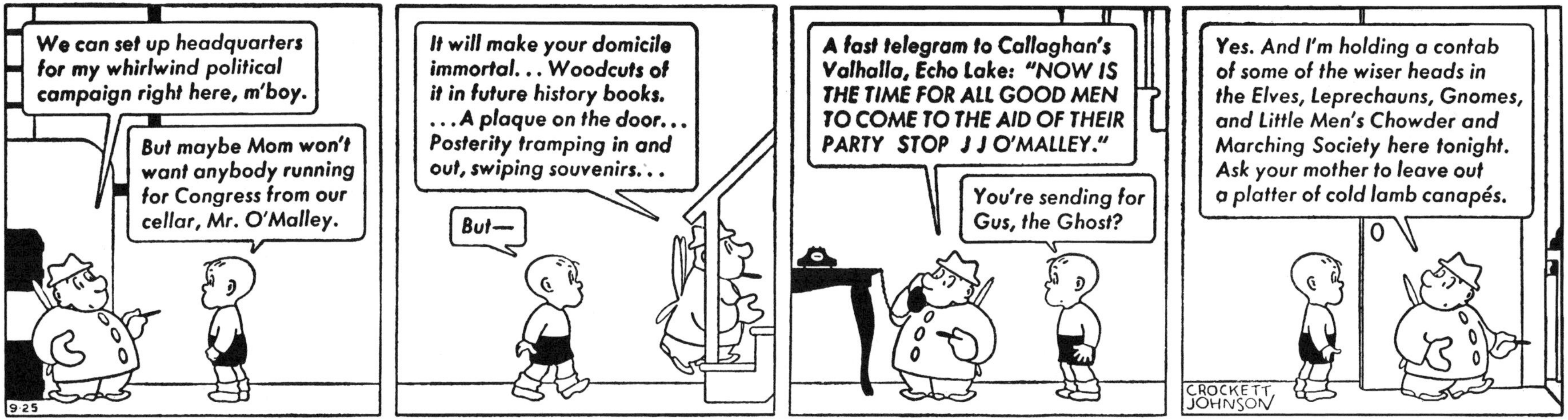
We can set up headquarters for my whirlwind political campaign right here, m'boy.
But maybe Mom won't want anybody running for Congress from our cellar, Mr. O'Malley.
It will make your domicile immortal... Woodcuts of it in future history books. ...A plaque on the door... Posterity tramping in and out, swiping souvenirs...
But—
A fast telegram to Callaghan's Valhalla, Echo Lake: "NOW IS THE TIME FOR ALL GOOD MEN TO COME TO THE AID OF THEIR PARTY STOP J J O'MALLEY."
You're sending for Gus, the Ghost?
Yes. And I'm holding a contab of some of the wiser heads in the Elves, Leprechauns, Gnomes, and Little Men's Chowder and Marching Society here tonight. Ask your mother to leave out a platter of cold lamb canapés.
9·25
CROCKETT JOHNSON

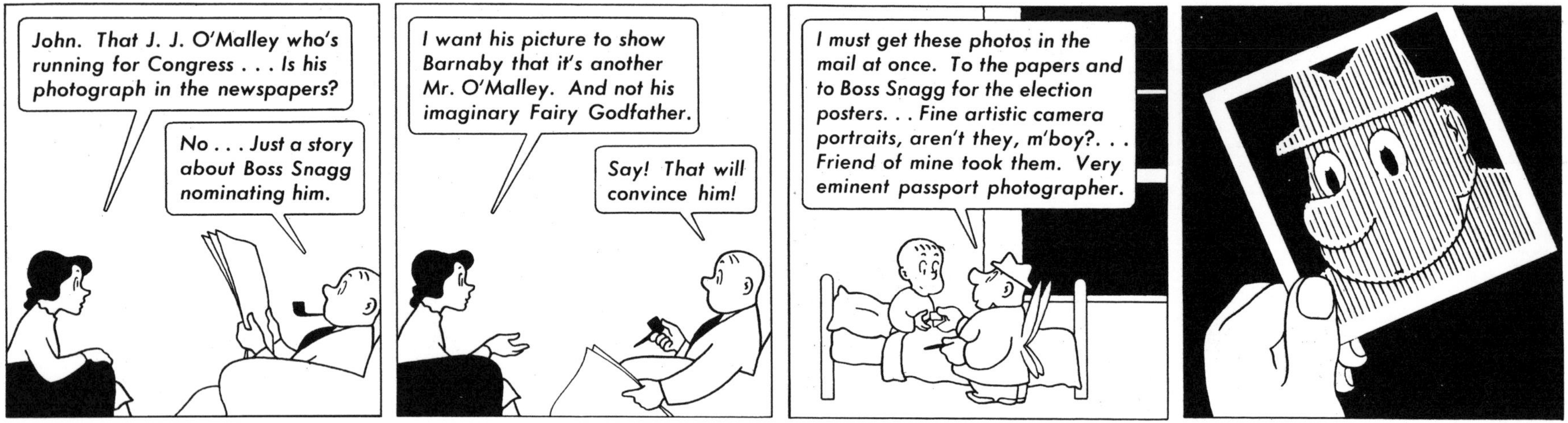
John. That J. J. O'Malley who's running for Congress . . . Is his photograph in the newspapers?
No . . . Just a story about Boss Snagg nominating him.
I want his picture to show Barnaby that it's another Mr. O'Malley. And not his imaginary Fairy Godfather.
Say! That will convince him!
I must get these photos in the mail at once. To the papers and to Boss Snagg for the election posters. . . Fine artistic camera portraits, aren't they, m'boy?. . . Friend of mine took them. Very eminent passport photographer.

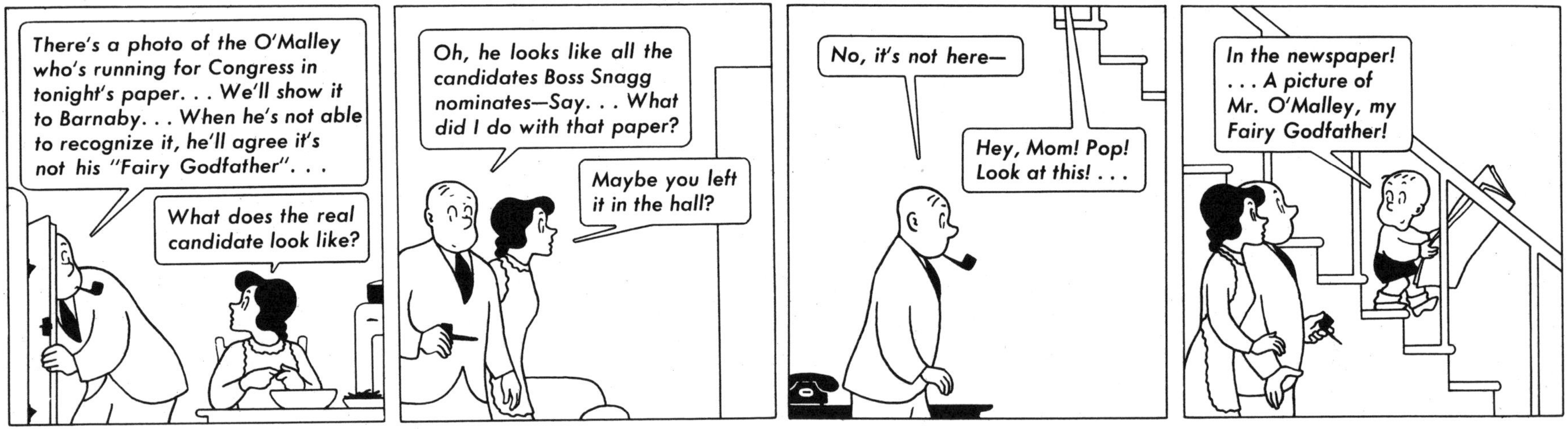
There's a photo of the O'Malley who's running for Congress in tonight's paper. . . We'll show it to Barnaby. . . When he's not able to recognize it, he'll agree it's not his "Fairy Godfather". . .
What does the real candidate look like?
Oh, he looks like all the candidates Boss Snagg nominates—Say. . . What did I do with that paper?
Maybe you left it in the hall?
No, it's not here—
Hey, Mom! Pop! Look at this! . . .
In the newspaper! . . . A picture of Mr. O'Malley, my Fairy Godfather!

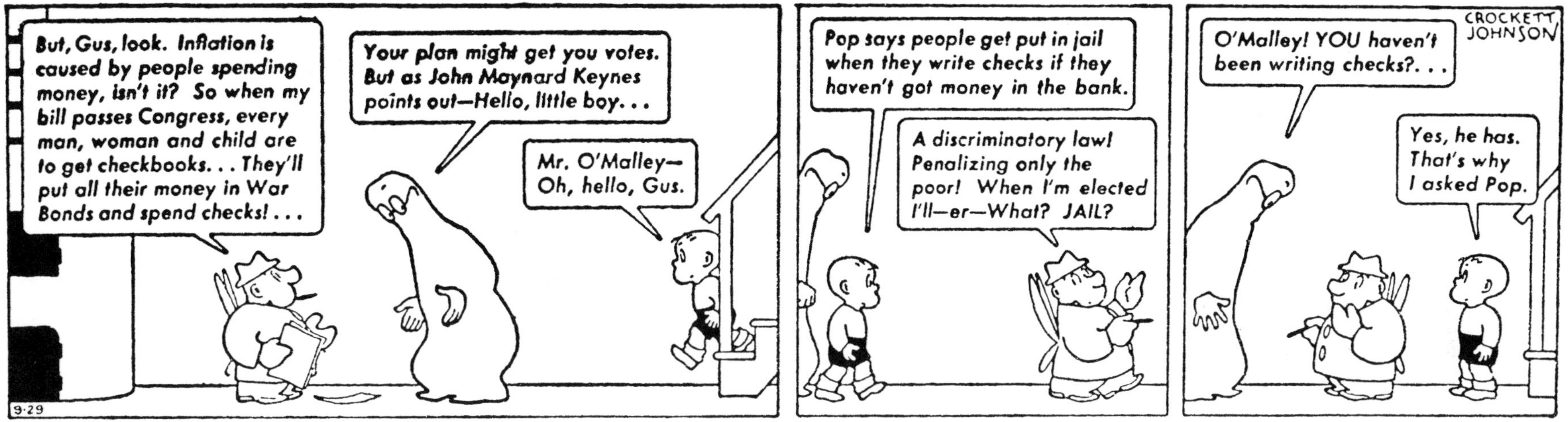
But, Gus, look. Inflation is caused by people spending money, isn't it? So when my bill passes Congress, every man, woman and child are to get checkbooks. . . They'll put all their money in War Bonds and spend checks! . . .
Your plan might get you votes. But as John Maynard Keynes points out—Hello, little boy. . .
Mr. O'Malley—Oh, hello, Gus.
9·29
Pop says people get put in jail when they write checks if they haven't got money in the bank.
A discriminatory law! Penalizing only the poor! When I'm elected I'll—er—What? JAIL?
CROCKETT JOHNSON
O'Malley! YOU haven't been writing checks?. . .
Yes, he has. That's why I asked Pop.

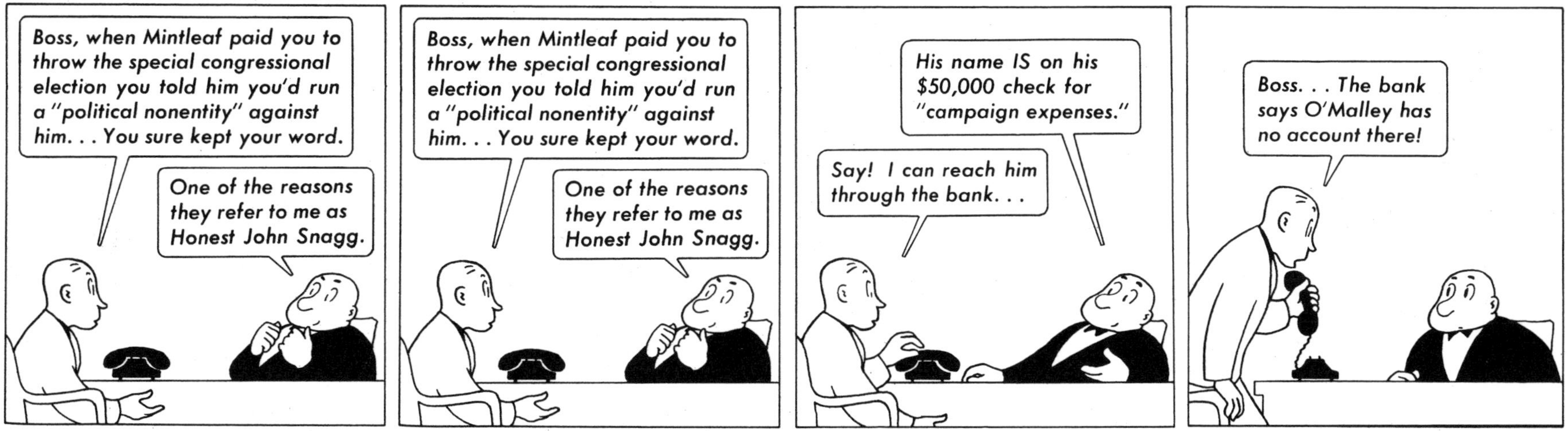
Boss, when Mintleaf paid you to throw the special congressional election you told him you'd run a "political nonentity" against him. . . You sure kept your word.
One of the reasons they refer to me as Honest John Snagg.
Boss, when Mintleaf paid you to throw the special congressional election you told him you'd run a "political nonentity" against him. . . You sure kept your word.
One of the reasons they refer to me as Honest John Snagg.
His name IS on his $50,000 check for "campaign expenses."
Say! I can reach him through the bank. . .
Boss. . . The bank says O'Malley has no account there!

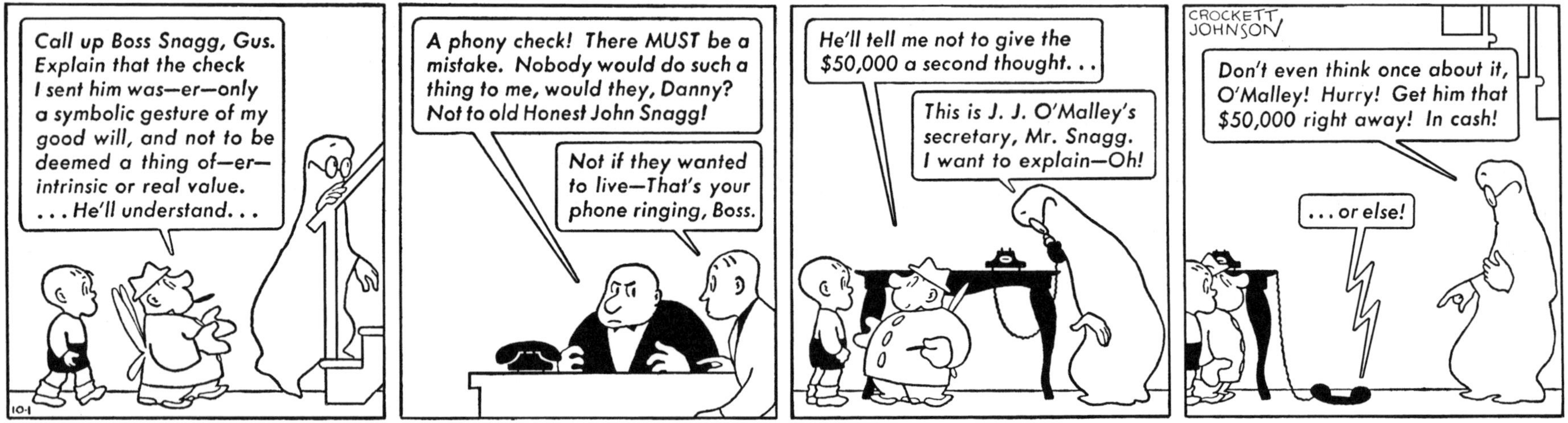
Call up Boss Snagg, Gus. Explain that the check I sent him was—er—only a symbolic gesture of my good will, and not to be deemed a thing of—er—intrinsic or real value. . . . He'll understand. . .
10-1
A phony check! There MUST be a mistake. Nobody would do such a thing to me, would they, Danny? Not to old Honest John Snagg!
Not if they wanted to live—That's your phone ringing, Boss.
He'll tell me not to give the $50,000 a second thought. . .
This is J. J. O'Malley's secretary, Mr. Snagg. I want to explain—Oh!
CROCKETT JOHNSON
Don't even think once about it, O'Malley! Hurry! Get him that $50,000 right away! In cash!
. . . or else!

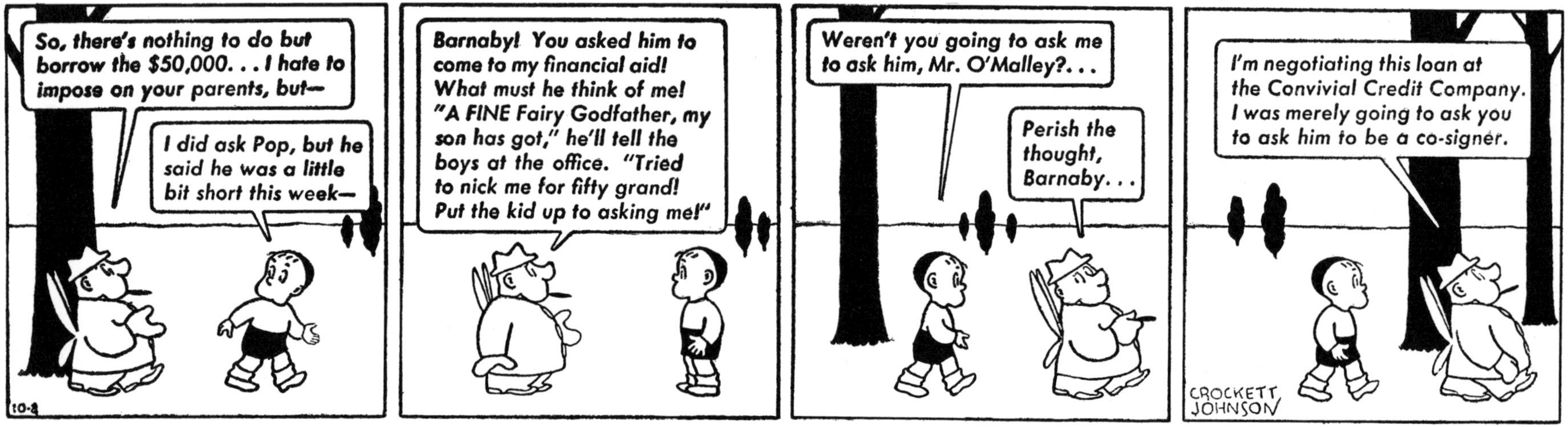
So, there's nothing to do but borrow the $50,000. . . I hate to impose on your parents, but—
I did ask Pop, but he said he was a little bit short this week—
Barnaby! You asked him to come to my financial aid! What must he think of me! "A FINE Fairy Godfather, my son has got," he'll tell the boys at the office. "Tried to nick me for fifty grand! Put the kid up to asking me!"
Weren't you going to ask me to ask him, Mr. O'Malley?. . .
Perish the thought, Barnaby. . .
I'm negotiating this loan at the Convivial Credit Company. I was merely going to ask you to ask him to be a co-signer.
CROCKETT JOHNSON

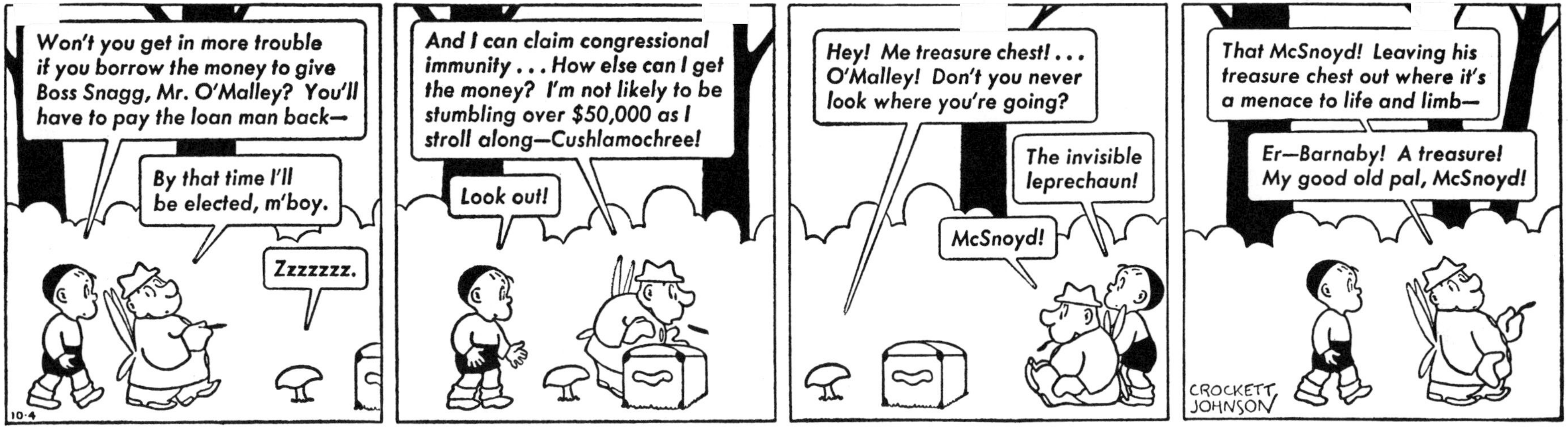
Won't you get in more trouble if you borrow the money to give Boss Snagg, Mr. O'Malley? You'll have to pay the loan man back—
By that time I'll be elected, m'boy.
Zzzzzzz.
10·4
And I can claim congressional immunity . . . How else can I get the money? I'm not likely to be stumbling over $50,000 as I stroll along—Cushlamochree!
Look out!
Hey! Me treasure chest! . . . O'Malley! Don't you never look where you're going?
The invisible leprechaun!
McSnoyd!
That McSnoyd! Leaving his treasure chest out where it's a menace to life and limb—
Er—Barnaby! A treasure! My good old pal, McSnoyd!
CROCKETT JOHNSON

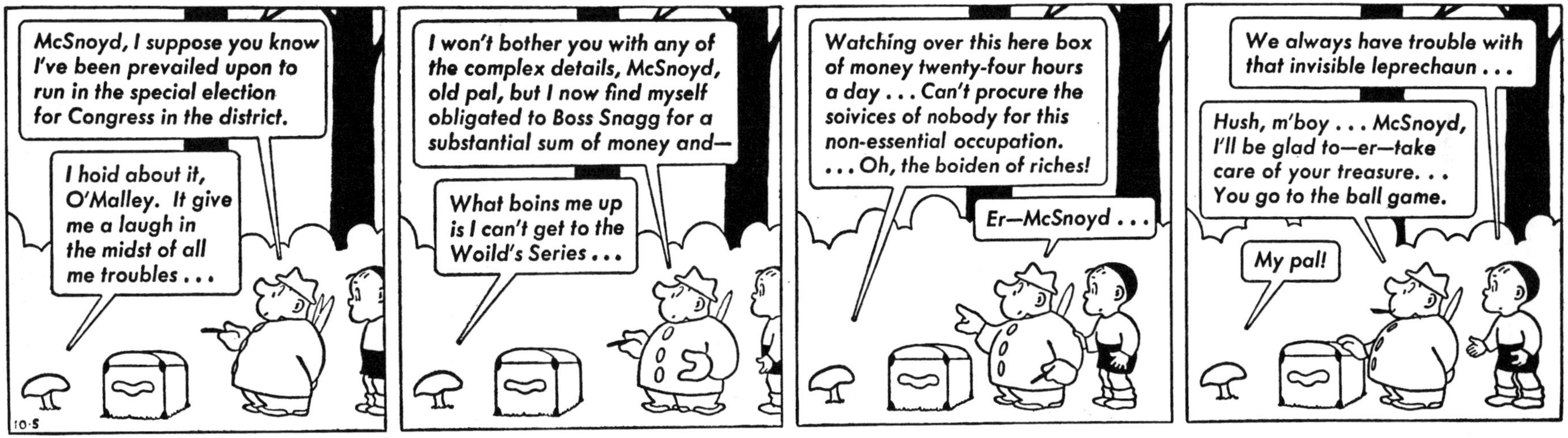
McSnoyd, I suppose you know I've been prevailed upon to run in the special election for Congress in the district.
I hoid about it, O'Malley. It give me a laugh in the midst of all me troubles . . .
10·5
I won't bother you with any of the complex details, McSnoyd, old pal, but I now find myself obligated to Boss Snagg for a substantial sum of money and—
What boins me up is I can't get to the Woild's Series . . .
Watching over this here box of money twenty-four hours a day . . . Can't procure the soivices of nobody for this non-essential occupation. . . . Oh, the boiden of riches!
Er—McSnoyd . . .
We always have trouble with that invisible leprechaun . . .
Hush, m'boy . . . McSnoyd, I'll be glad to—er—take care of your treasure. . . You go to the ball game.
My pal!

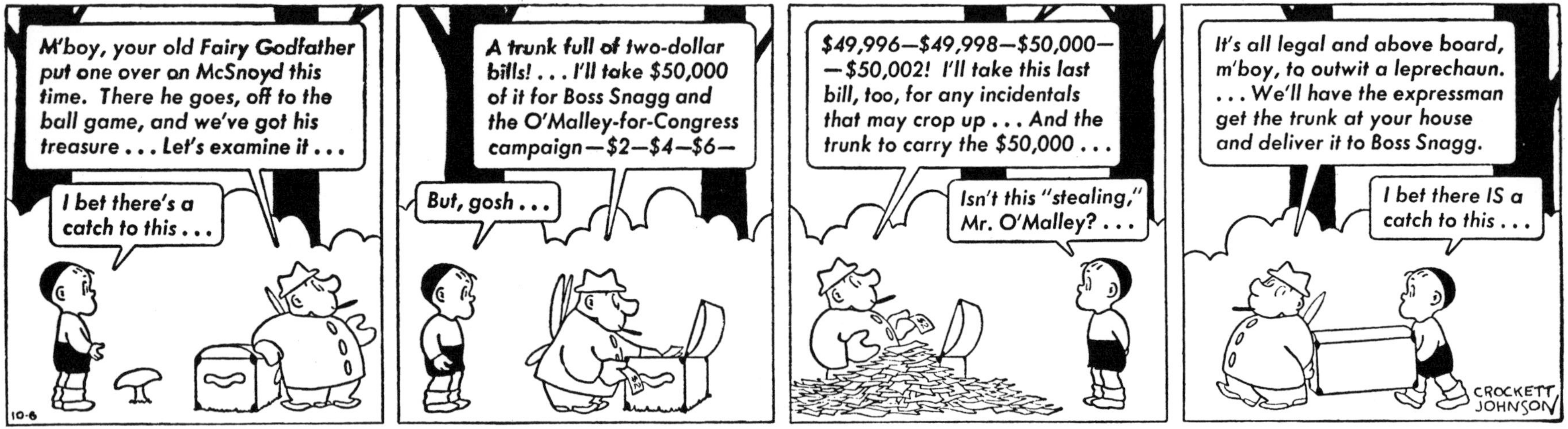

10-6
M'boy, your old Fairy Godfather put one over on McSnoyd this time. There he goes, off to the ball game, and we've got his treasure . . . Let's examine it . . .
I bet there's a catch to this . . .
A trunk full of two-dollar bills! . . . I'll take $50,000 of it for Boss Snagg and the O'Malley-for-Congress campaign—$2—$4—$6—
But, gosh . . .
$49,996—$49,998—$50,000——$50,002! I'll take this last bill, too, for any incidentals that may crop up . . . And the trunk to carry the $50,000 . . .
Isn't this "stealing," Mr. O'Malley? . . .
It's all legal and above board, m'boy, to outwit a leprechaun. . . . We'll have the expressman get the trunk at your house and deliver it to Boss Snagg.
I bet there IS a catch to this . . .
CROCKETT JOHNSON

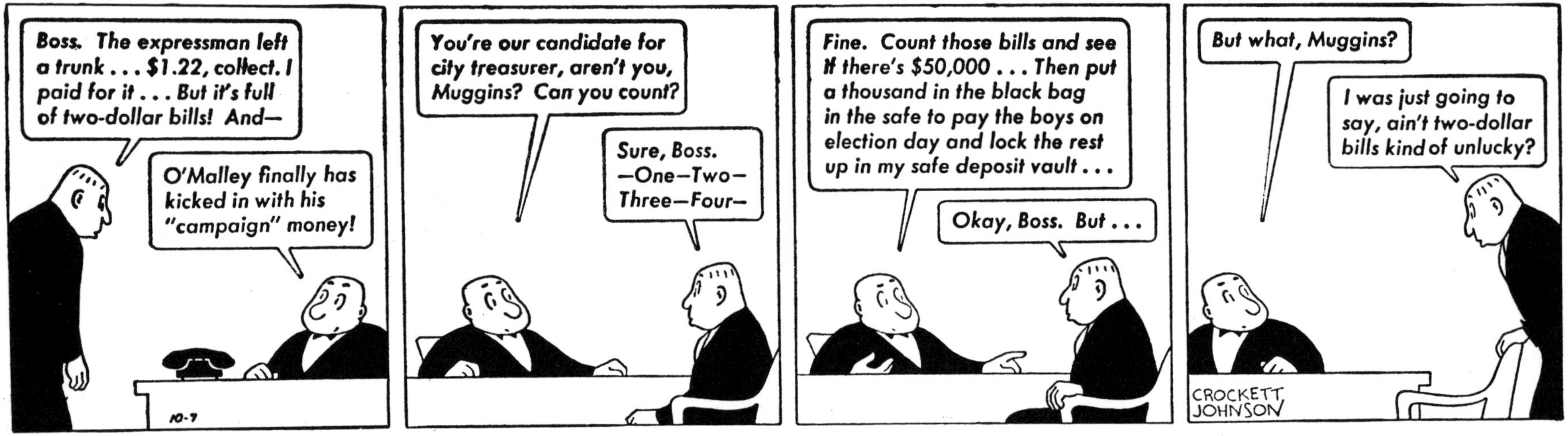

Boss. The expressman left a trunk . . . $1.22, collect. I paid for it . . . But it's full of two-dollar bills! And—
O'Malley finally has kicked in with his "campaign" money!
10-7
You're our candidate for city treasurer, aren't you, Muggins? Can you count?
Sure, Boss. —One—Two—Three—Four—
Fine. Count those bills and see if there's $50,000 . . . Then put a thousand in the black bag in the safe to pay the boys on election day and lock the rest up in my safe deposit vault . . .
Okay, Boss. But . . .
But what, Muggins?
I was just going to say, ain't two-dollar bills kind of unlucky?
CROCKETT JOHNSON

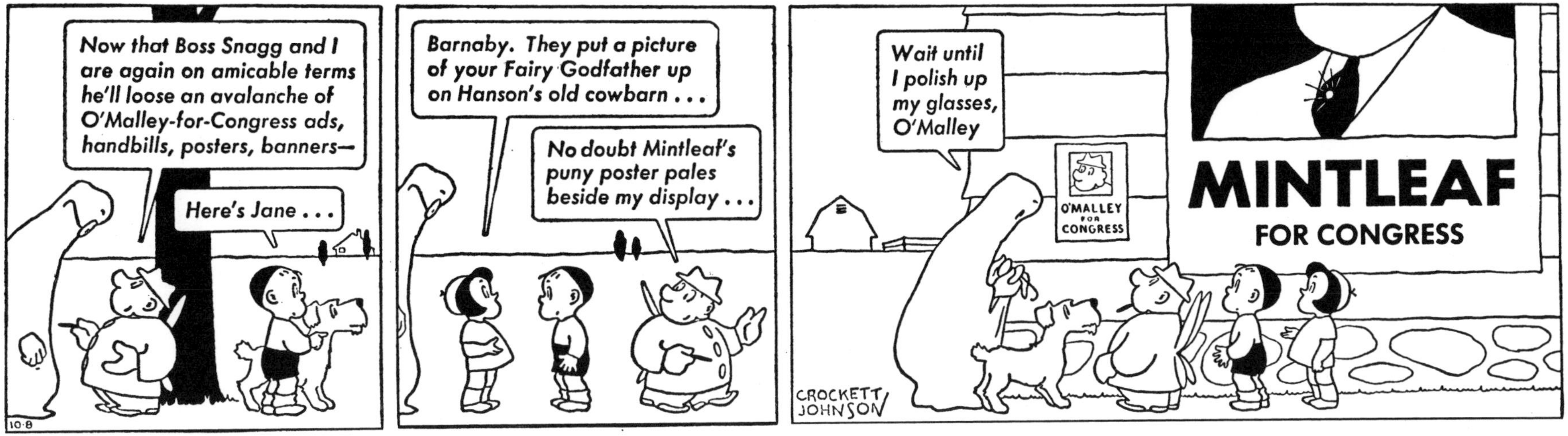

Now that Boss Snagg and I are again on amicable terms he'll loose an avalanche of O'Malley-for-Congress ads, handbills, posters, banners—
Here's Jane . . .
Barnaby. They put a picture of your Fairy Godfather up on Hanson's old cowbarn . . .
No doubt Mintleaf's puny poster pales beside my display . . .
Wait until I polish up my glasses, O'Malley
O'MALLEY FOR CONGRESS
MINTLEAF
FOR CONGRESS
CROCKETT JOHNSON
10·8

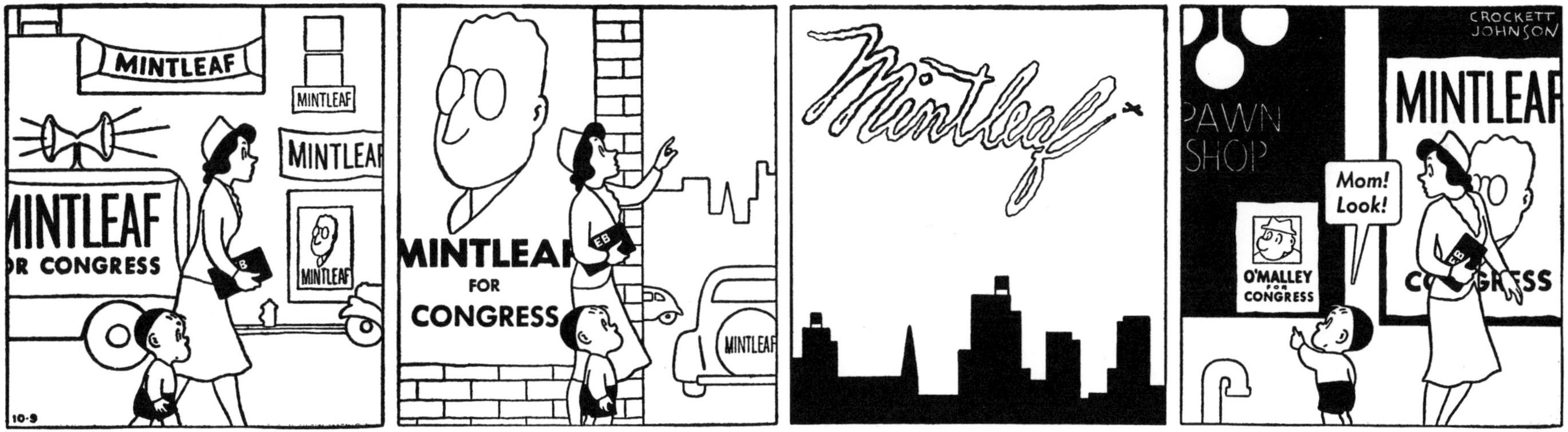

MINTLEAF
MINTLEAF
MINTLEAF
MINTLEAF
FOR CONGRESS
CONGRESS
Mintleaf
PAWN SHOP
O'MALLEY FOR CONGRESS
Mom! Look!
CROCKETT JOHNSON
10·9

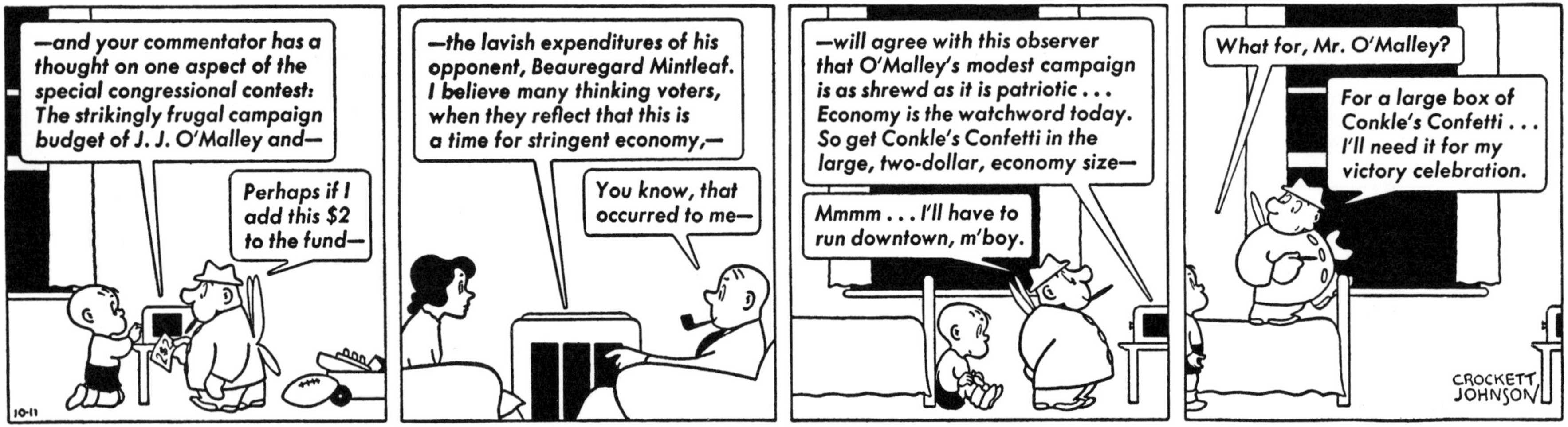
—and your commentator has a thought on one aspect of the special congressional contest: The strikingly frugal campaign budget of J. J. O'Malley and—
Perhaps if I add this $2 to the fund—
10-11
—the lavish expenditures of his opponent, Beauregard Mintleaf. I believe many thinking voters, when they reflect that this is a time for stringent economy,—
You know, that occurred to me—
—will agree with this observer that O'Malley's modest campaign is as shrewd as it is patriotic . . . Economy is the watchword today. So get Conkle's Confetti in the large, two-dollar, economy size—
Mmmm . . . I'll have to run downtown, m'boy.
What for, Mr. O'Malley?
For a large box of Conkle's Confetti . . . I'll need it for my victory celebration.
CROCKETT JOHNSON

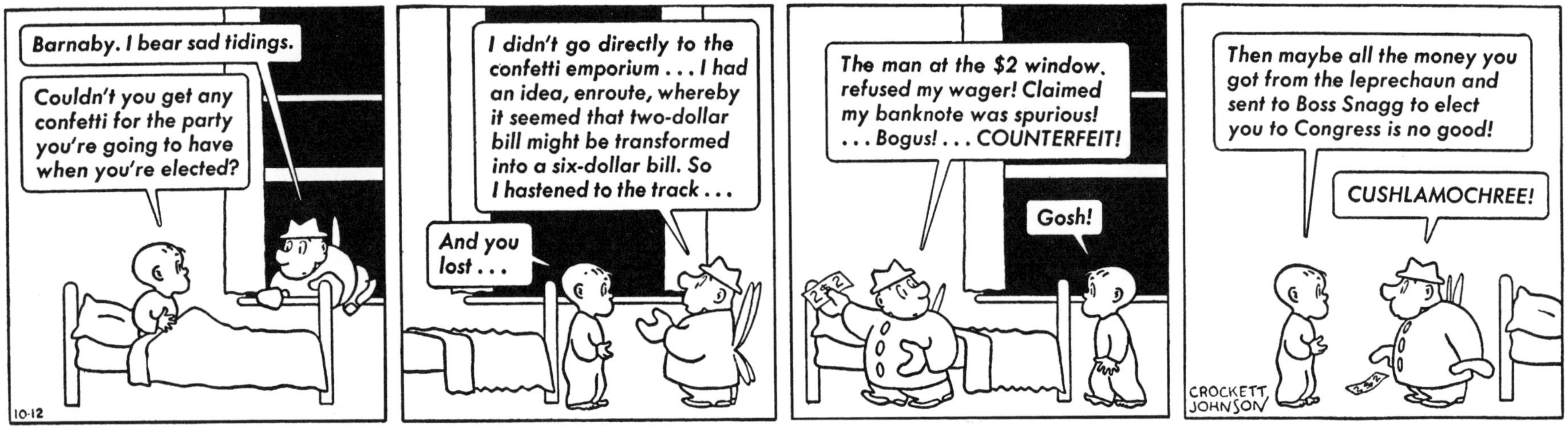
Barnaby. I bear sad tidings.
Couldn't you get any confetti for the party you're going to have when you're elected?
10-12
I didn't go directly to the confetti emporium . . . I had an idea, enroute, whereby it seemed that two-dollar bill might be transformed into a six-dollar bill. So I hastened to the track . . .
And you lost . . .
The man at the $2 window. refused my wager! Claimed my banknote was spurious! . . . Bogus! . . . COUNTERFEIT!
Gosh!
Then maybe all the money you got from the leprechaun and sent to Boss Snagg to elect you to Congress is no good!
CUSHLAMOCHREE!
CROCKETT JOHNSON

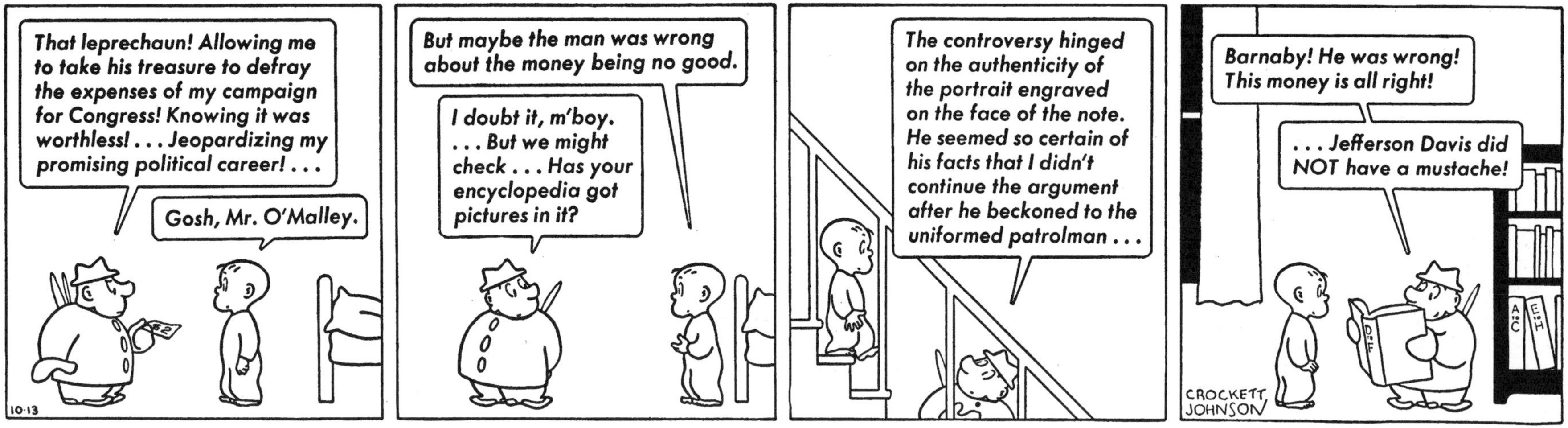

That leprechaun! Allowing me to take his treasure to defray the expenses of my campaign for Congress! Knowing it was worthless! . . . Jeopardizing my promising political career! . . .
Gosh, Mr. O'Malley.
10·13
But maybe the man was wrong about the money being no good.
I doubt it, m'boy. . . . But we might check . . . Has your encyclopedia got pictures in it?
The controversy hinged on the authenticity of the portrait engraved on the face of the note. He seemed so certain of his facts that I didn't continue the argument after he beckoned to the uniformed patrolman . . .
Barnaby! He was wrong! This money is all right!
. . . Jefferson Davis did NOT have a mustache!
CROCKETT JOHNSON

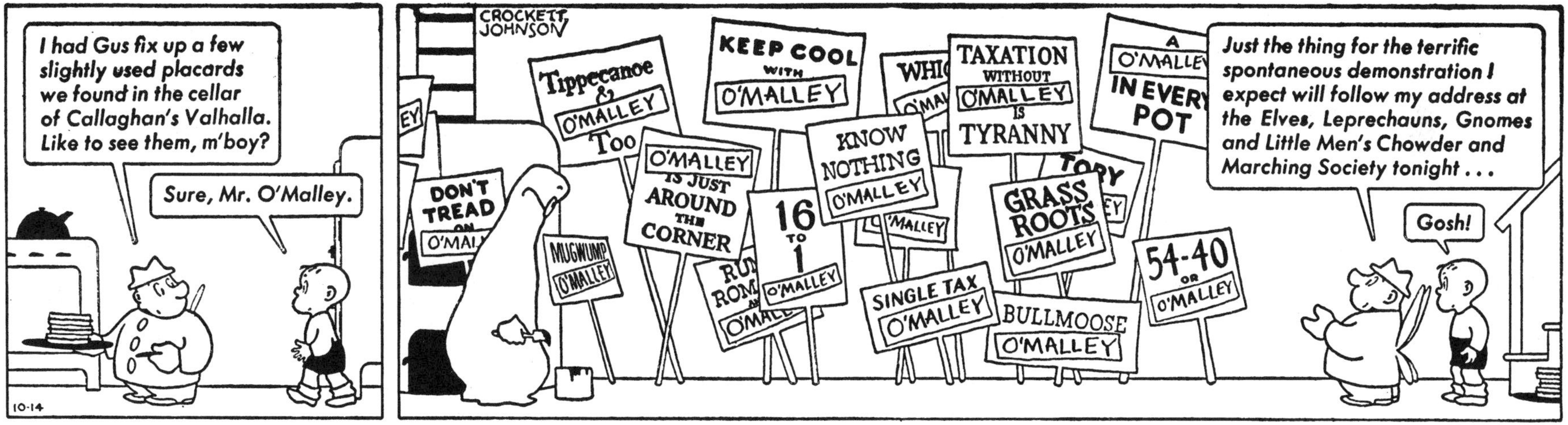

I had Gus fix up a few slightly used placards we found in the cellar of Callaghan's Valhalla. Like to see them, m'boy?
Sure, Mr. O'Malley.
10·14
CROCKETT JOHNSON
Tippecanoe & O'MALLEY Too
KEEP COOL WITH O'MALLEY
TAXATION WITHOUT O'MALLEY IS TYRANNY
O'MALLEY IS JUST AROUND THE CORNER
KNOW NOTHING O'MALLEY
MUGWUMP O'MALLEY
16 TO 1 O'MALLEY
GRASS ROOTS O'MALLEY
SINGLE TAX O'MALLEY
BULLMOOSE O'MALLEY
54-40 OR O'MALLEY
Just the thing for the terrific spontaneous demonstration I expect will follow my address at the Elves, Leprechauns, Gnomes and Little Men's Chowder and Marching Society tonight . . .
Gosh!

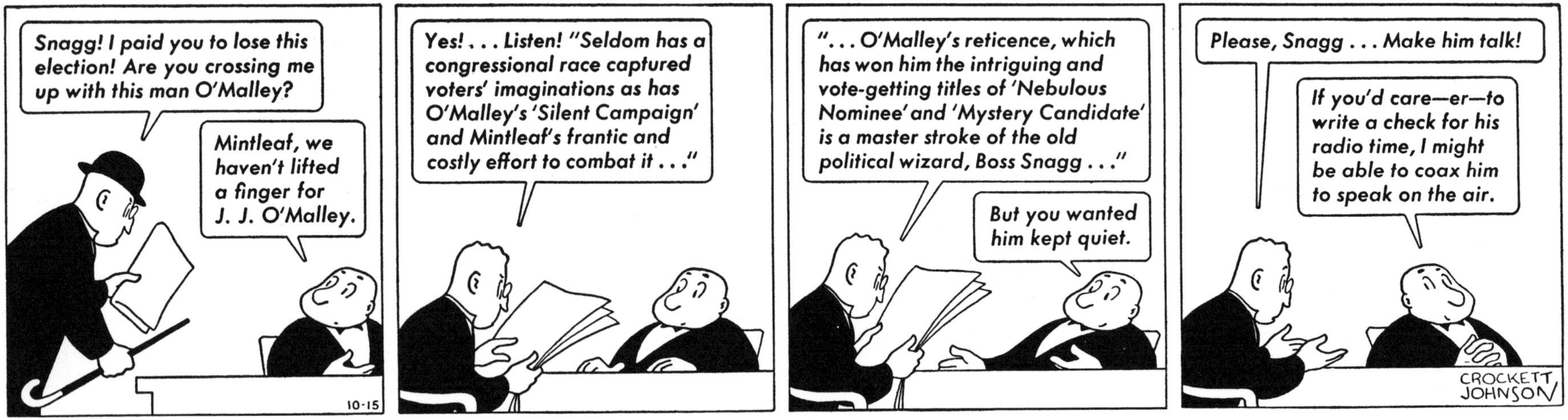
Snagg! I paid you to lose this election! Are you crossing me up with this man O'Malley?
Mintleaf, we haven't lifted a finger for J. J. O'Malley.
10-15
Yes! . . . Listen! "Seldom has a congressional race captured voters' imaginations as has O'Malley's 'Silent Campaign' and Mintleaf's frantic and costly effort to combat it . . ."
". . . O'Malley's reticence, which has won him the intriguing and vote-getting titles of 'Nebulous Nominee' and 'Mystery Candidate' is a master stroke of the old political wizard, Boss Snagg . . ."
But you wanted him kept quiet.
Please, Snagg . . . Make him talk!
If you'd care—er—to write a check for his radio time, I might be able to coax him to speak on the air.
CROCKETT JOHNSON

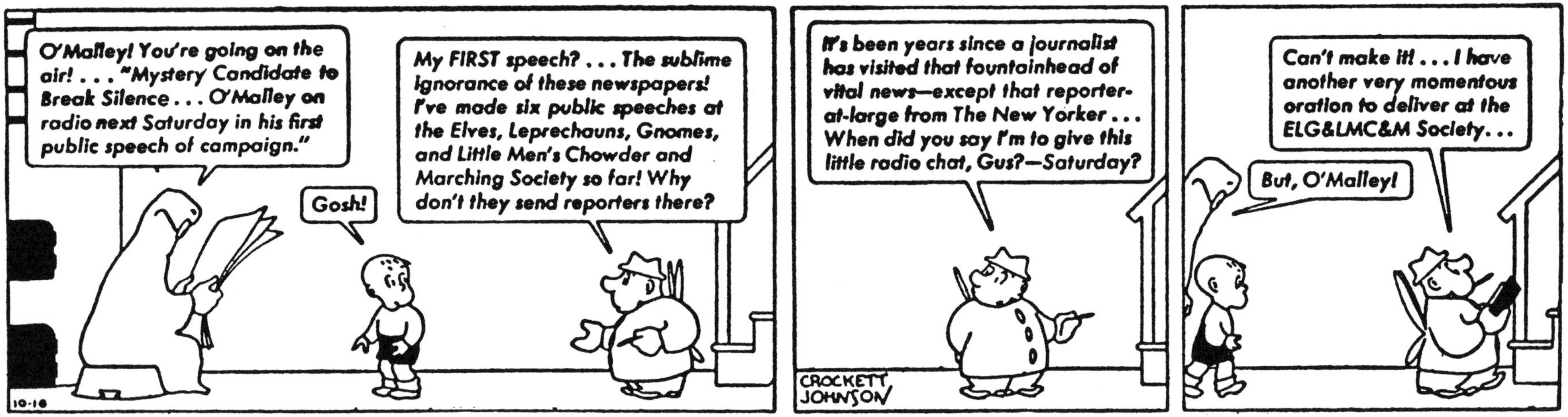
O'Malley! You're going on the air! . . . "Mystery Candidate to Break Silence . . . O'Malley on radio next Saturday in his first public speech of campaign."
Gosh!
My FIRST speech? . . . The sublime ignorance of these newspapers! I've made six public speeches at the Elves, Leprechauns, Gnomes, and Little Men's Chowder and Marching Society so far! Why don't they send reporters there?
10-16
It's been years since a journalist has visited that fountainhead of vital news—except that reporter-at-large from The New Yorker . . . When did you say I'm to give this little radio chat, Gus?—Saturday?
CROCKETT JOHNSON
Can't make it! . . . I have another very momentous oration to deliver at the ELG&LMC&M Society . . .
But, O'Malley!

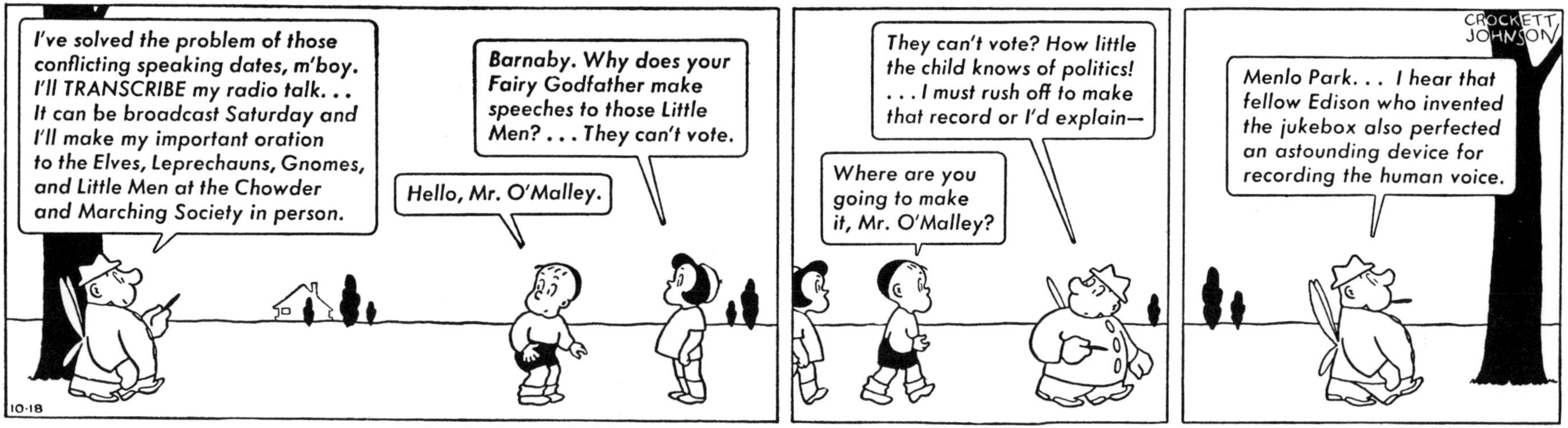

10-18
I've solved the problem of those conflicting speaking dates, m'boy. I'll TRANSCRIBE my radio talk. . . It can be broadcast Saturday and I'll make my important oration to the Elves, Leprechauns, Gnomes, and Little Men at the Chowder and Marching Society in person.
Hello, Mr. O'Malley.
Barnaby. Why does your Fairy Godfather make speeches to those Little Men? . . . They can't vote.
They can't vote? How little the child knows of politics! . . . I must rush off to make that record or I'd explain—
Where are you going to make it, Mr. O'Malley?
Menlo Park. . . I hear that fellow Edison who invented the jukebox also perfected an astounding device for recording the human voice.
CROCKETT JOHNSON

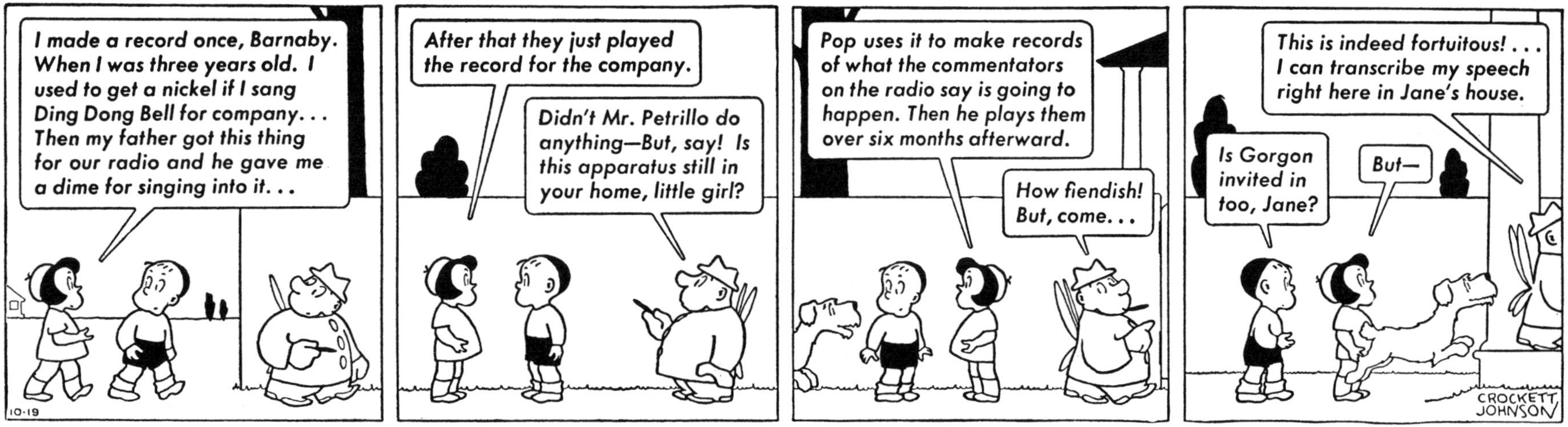

10-19
I made a record once, Barnaby. When I was three years old. I used to get a nickel if I sang Ding Dong Bell for company. . . Then my father got this thing for our radio and he gave me a dime for singing into it. . .
After that they just played the record for the company.
Didn't Mr. Petrillo do anything—But, say! Is this apparatus still in your home, little girl?
Pop uses it to make records of what the commentators on the radio say is going to happen. Then he plays them over six months afterward.
How fiendish! But, come. . .
This is indeed fortuitous! . . . I can transcribe my speech right here in Jane's house.
Is Gorgon invited in too, Jane?
But—
CROCKETT JOHNSON

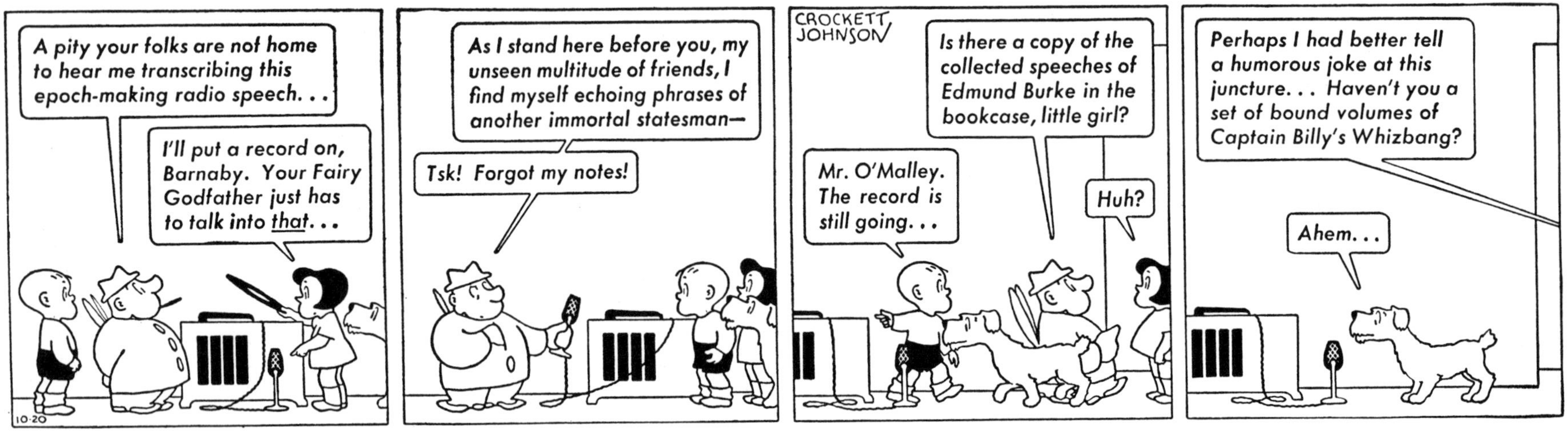
A pity your folks are not home to hear me transcribing this epoch-making radio speech. . .
I'll put a record on, Barnaby. Your Fairy Godfather just has to talk into that. . .
As I stand here before you, my unseen multitude of friends, I find myself echoing phrases of another immortal statesman—
Tsk! Forgot my notes!
CROCKETT JOHNSON
Is there a copy of the collected speeches of Edmund Burke in the bookcase, little girl?
Mr. O'Malley. The record is still going. . .
Huh?
Perhaps I had better tell a humorous joke at this juncture. . . Haven't you a set of bound volumes of Captain Billy's Whizbang?
Ahem. . .
10-20

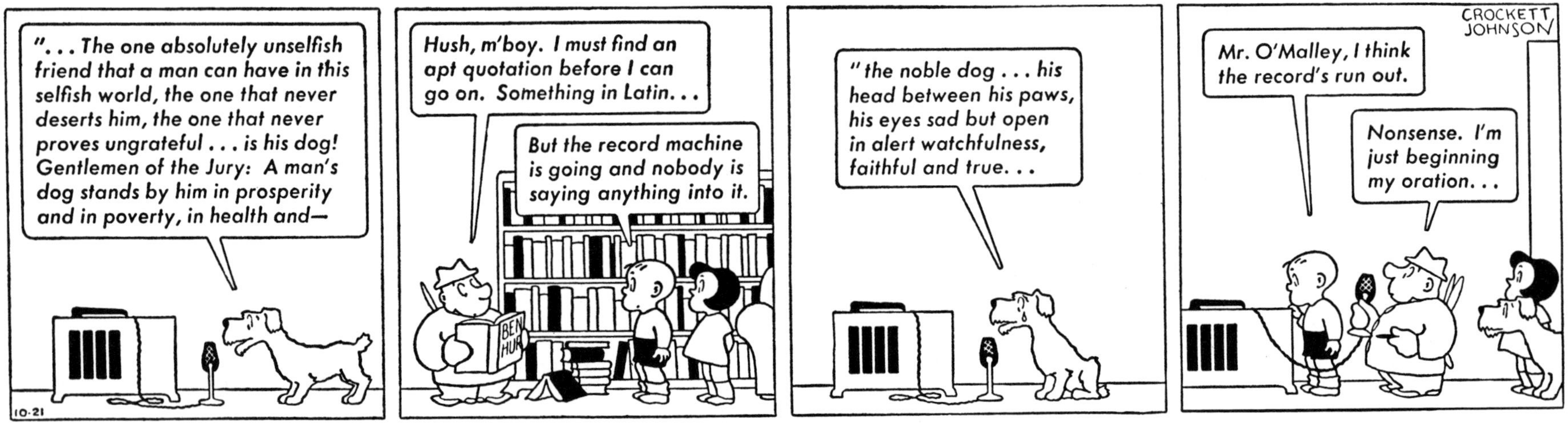
". . . The one absolutely unselfish friend that a man can have in this selfish world, the one that never deserts him, the one that never proves ungrateful . . . is his dog! Gentlemen of the Jury: A man's dog stands by him in prosperity and in poverty, in health and—
10-21
Hush, m'boy. I must find an apt quotation before I can go on. Something in Latin. . .
But the record machine is going and nobody is saying anything into it.
BEN HUR
" the noble dog . . . his head between his paws, his eyes sad but open in alert watchfulness, faithful and true. . .
CROCKETT JOHNSON
Mr. O'Malley, I think the record's run out.
Nonsense. I'm just beginning my oration. . .

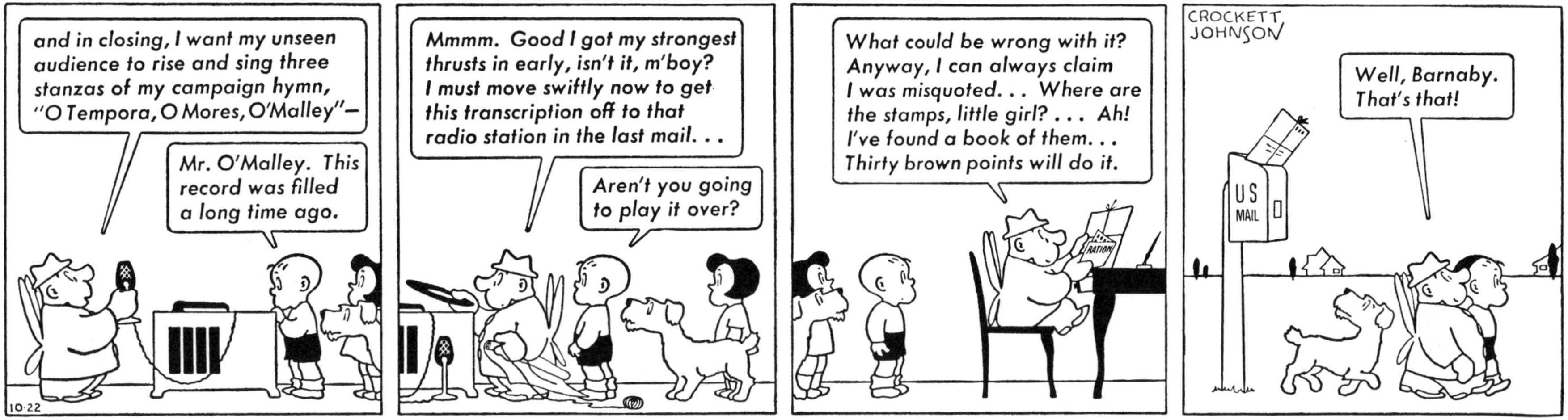
and in closing, I want my unseen audience to rise and sing three stanzas of my campaign hymn, "O Tempora, O Mores, O'Malley"—
Mr. O'Malley. This record was filled a long time ago.
10·22
Mmmm. Good I got my strongest thrusts in early, isn't it, m'boy? I must move swiftly now to get this transcription off to that radio station in the last mail. . .
Aren't you going to play it over?
What could be wrong with it? Anyway, I can always claim I was misquoted. . . Where are the stamps, little girl? . . . Ah! I've found a book of them. . . Thirty brown points will do it.
RATION
CROCKETT JOHNSON
US MAIL
Well, Barnaby. That's that!

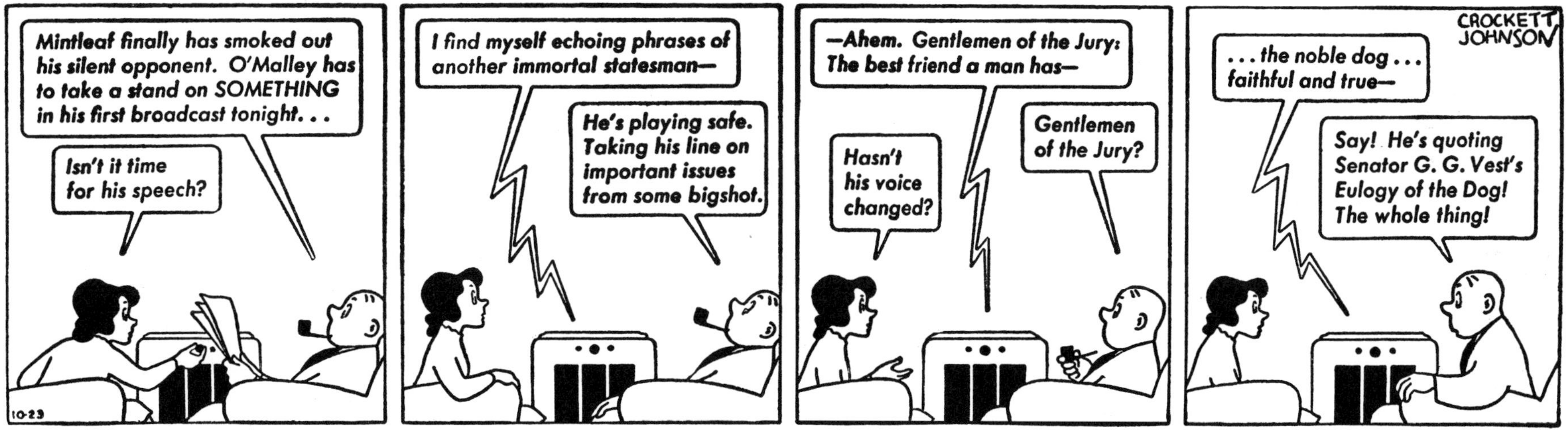
Mintleaf finally has smoked out his silent opponent. O'Malley has to take a stand on SOMETHING in his first broadcast tonight. . .
Isn't it time for his speech?
10·23
I find myself echoing phrases of another immortal statesman—
He's playing safe. Taking his line on important issues from some bigshot.
—Ahem. Gentlemen of the Jury: The best friend a man has—
Hasn't his voice changed?
Gentlemen of the Jury?
CROCKETT JOHNSON
. . . the noble dog . . . faithful and true—
Say! He's quoting Senator G. G. Vest's Eulogy of the Dog! The whole thing!

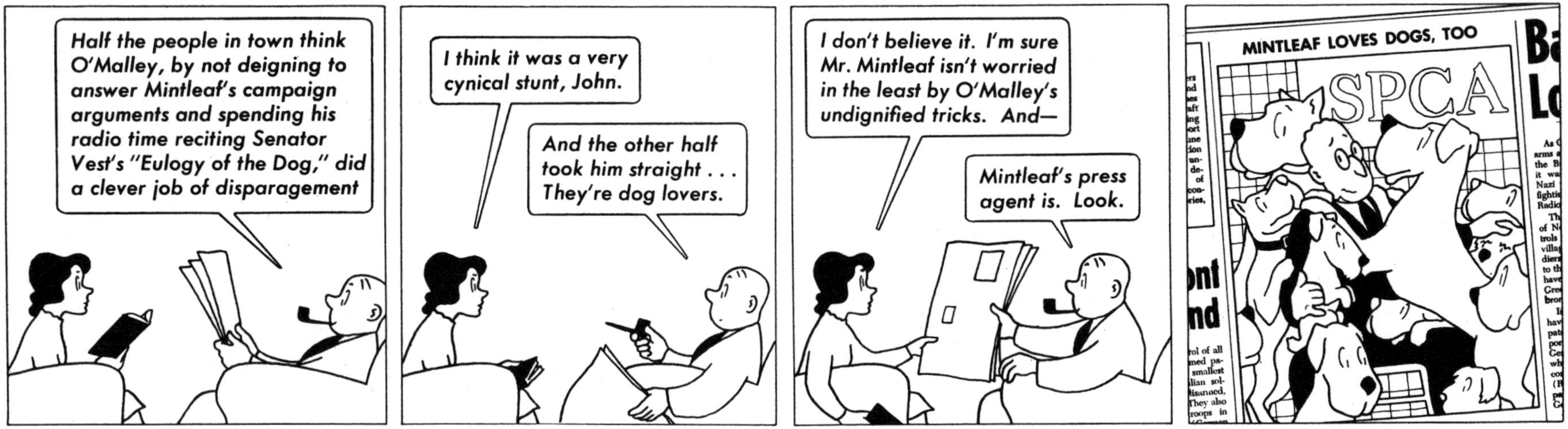
Half the people in town think O'Malley, by not deigning to answer Mintleaf's campaign arguments and spending his radio time reciting Senator Vest's "Eulogy of the Dog," did a clever job of disparagement
I think it was a very cynical stunt, John.
And the other half took him straight . . . They're dog lovers.
I don't believe it. I'm sure Mr. Mintleaf isn't worried in the least by O'Malley's undignified tricks. And—
Mintleaf's press agent is. Look.
MINTLEAF LOVES DOGS, TOO
SPCA

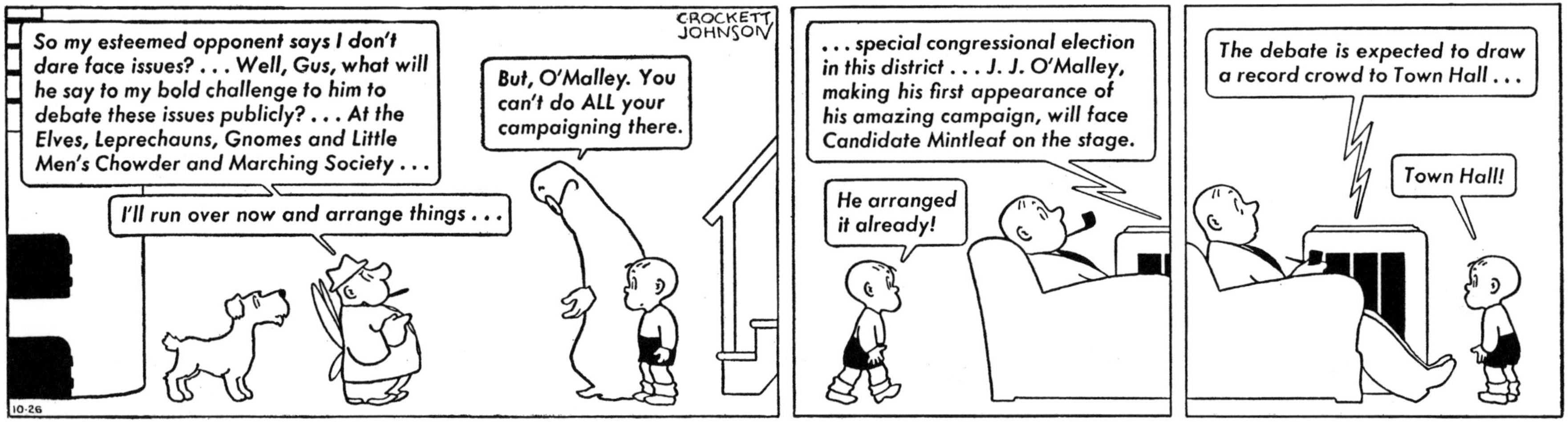
CROCKETT JOHNSON
So my esteemed opponent says I don't dare face issues? . . . Well, Gus, what will he say to my bold challenge to him to debate these issues publicly? . . . At the Elves, Leprechauns, Gnomes and Little Men's Chowder and Marching Society . . .
I'll run over now and arrange things . . .
But, O'Malley. You can't do ALL your campaigning there.
10-26
. . . special congressional election in this district . . . J. J. O'Malley, making his first appearance of his amazing campaign, will face Candidate Mintleaf on the stage.
He arranged it already!
The debate is expected to draw a record crowd to Town Hall . . .
Town Hall!

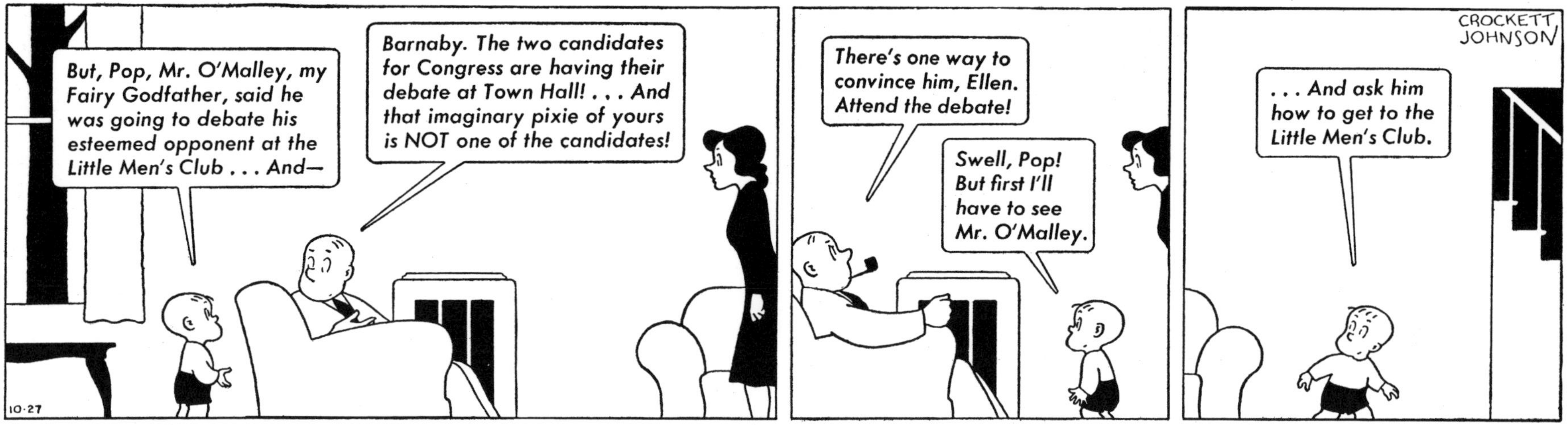
CROCKETT JOHNSON
10·27
But, Pop, Mr. O'Malley, my Fairy Godfather, said he was going to debate his esteemed opponent at the Little Men's Club . . . And—
Barnaby. The two candidates for Congress are having their debate at Town Hall! . . . And that imaginary pixie of yours is NOT one of the candidates!
There's one way to convince him, Ellen. Attend the debate!
Swell, Pop! But first I'll have to see Mr. O'Malley.
. . . And ask him how to get to the Little Men's Club.

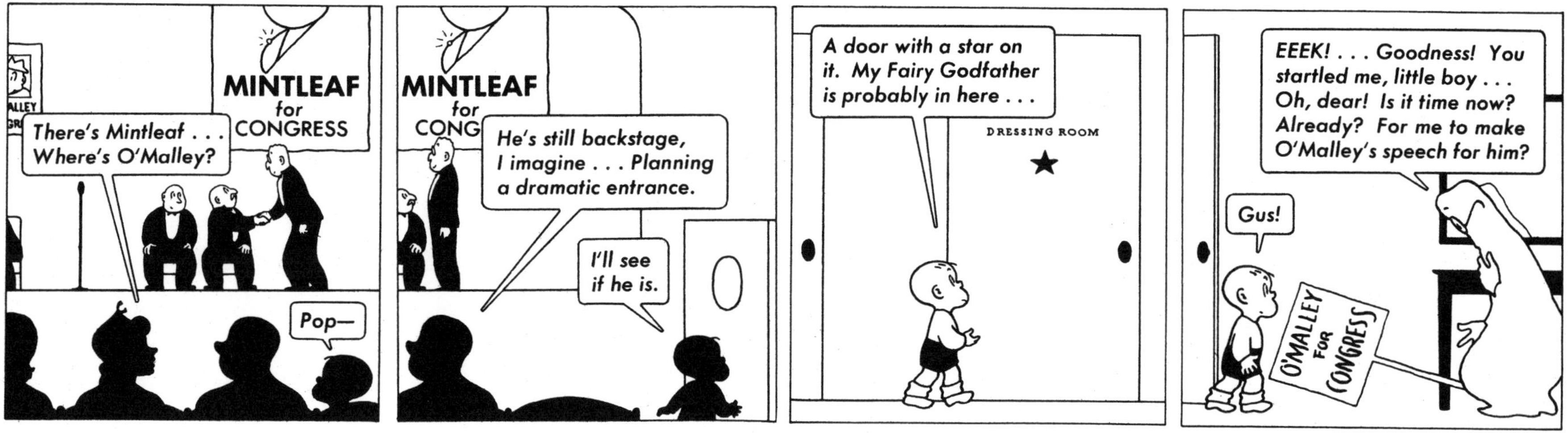
MINTLEAF for CONGRESS
There's Mintleaf . . . Where's O'Malley?
Pop—
MINTLEAF for
He's still backstage, I imagine . . . Planning a dramatic entrance.
I'll see if he is.
A door with a star on it. My Fairy Godfather is probably in here . . .
DRESSING ROOM
EEEK! . . . Goodness! You startled me, little boy . . . Oh, dear! Is it time now? Already? For me to make O'Malley's speech for him?
Gus!
O'MALLEY FOR CONGRESS

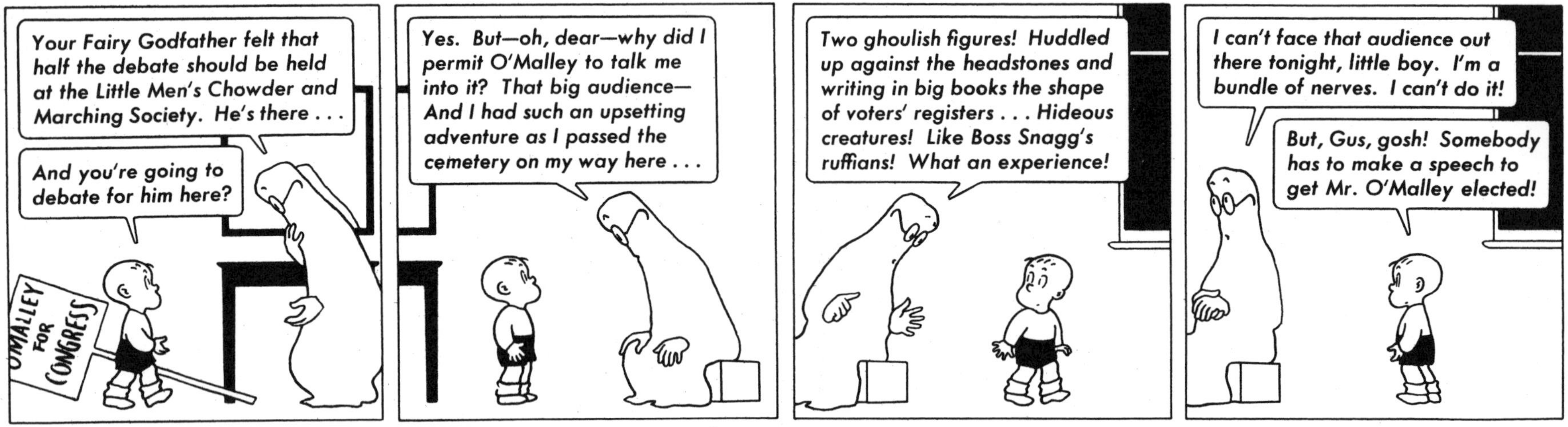
Your Fairy Godfather felt that half the debate should be held at the Little Men's Chowder and Marching Society. He's there . . .
And you're going to debate for him here?
'MALLEY FOR CONGRESS
Yes. But—oh, dear—why did I permit O'Malley to talk me into it? That big audience—And I had such an upsetting adventure as I passed the cemetery on my way here . . .
Two ghoulish figures! Huddled up against the headstones and writing in big books the shape of voters' registers . . . Hideous creatures! Like Boss Snagg's ruffians! What an experience!
I can't face that audience out there tonight, little boy. I'm a bundle of nerves. I can't do it!
But, Gus, gosh! Somebody has to make a speech to get Mr. O'Malley elected!

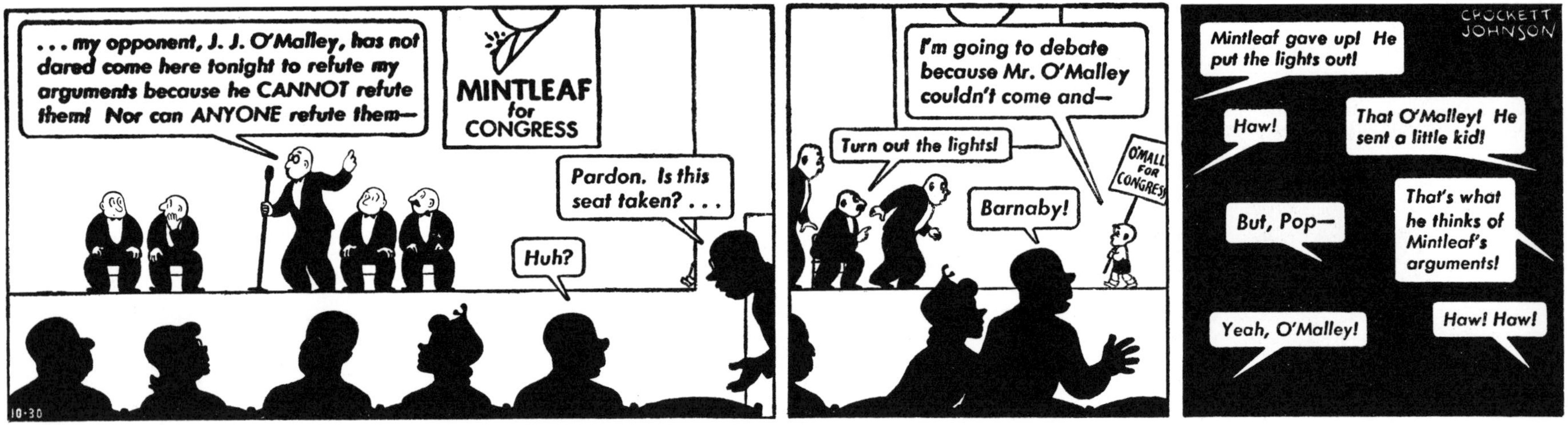
. . . my opponent, J. J. O'Malley, has not dared come here tonight to refute my arguments because he CANNOT refute them! Nor can ANYONE refute them—
MINTLEAF for CONGRESS
Pardon. Is this seat taken? . . .
Huh?
10-30
I'm going to debate because Mr. O'Malley couldn't come and—
Turn out the lights!
Barnaby!
Mintleaf gave up! He put the lights out!
CROCKETT JOHNSON
Haw!
That O'Malley! He sent a little kid!
But, Pop—
That's what he thinks of Mintleaf's arguments!
Yeah, O'Malley!
Haw! Haw!

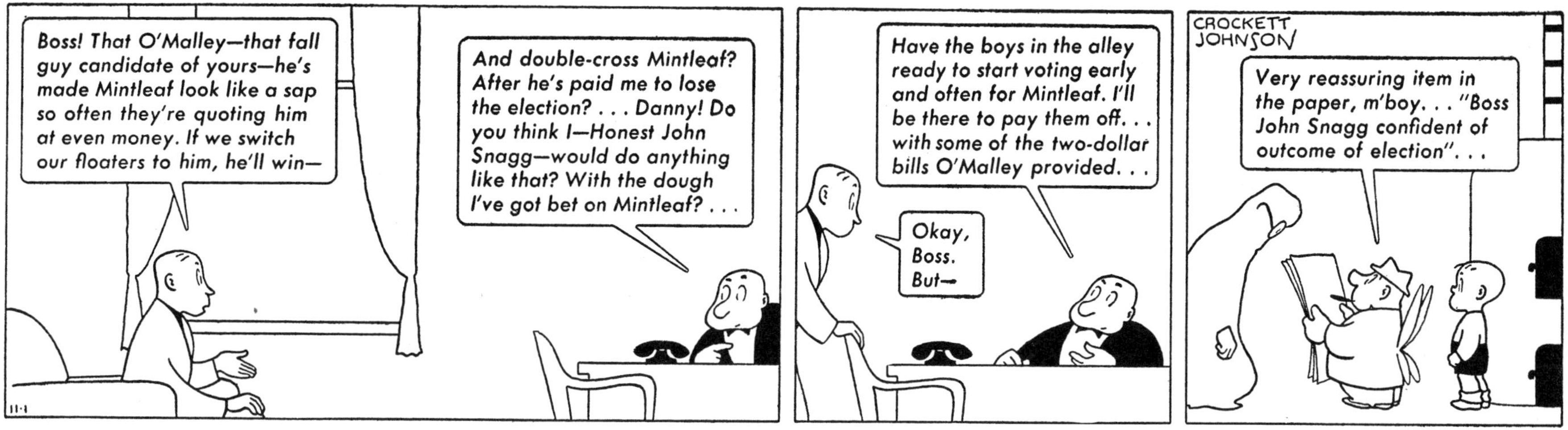
Boss! That O'Malley—that fall guy candidate of yours—he's made Mintleaf look like a sap so often they're quoting him at even money. If we switch our floaters to him, he'll win—
And double-cross Mintleaf? After he's paid me to lose the election? . . . Danny! Do you think I—Honest John Snagg—would do anything like that? With the dough I've got bet on Mintleaf? . . .
11·1
Have the boys in the alley ready to start voting early and often for Mintleaf. I'll be there to pay them off. . . with some of the two-dollar bills O'Malley provided. . .
Okay, Boss. But—
CROCKETT JOHNSON
Very reassuring item in the paper, m'boy. . . "Boss John Snagg confident of outcome of election". . .

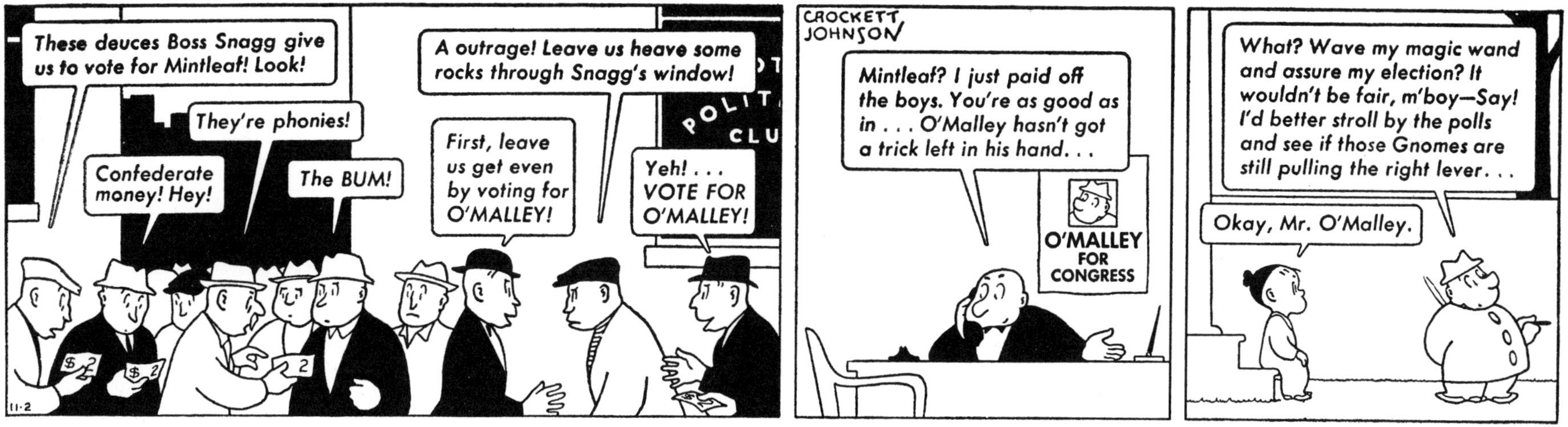
These deuces Boss Snagg give us to vote for Mintleaf! Look!
Confederate money! Hey!
They're phonies!
The BUM!
A outrage! Leave us heave some rocks through Snagg's window!
First, leave us get even by voting for O'MALLEY!
Yeh! . . . VOTE FOR O'MALLEY!
11·2
CROCKETT JOHNSON
Mintleaf? I just paid off the boys. You're as good as in . . . O'Malley hasn't got a trick left in his hand. . .
O'MALLEY FOR CONGRESS
What? Wave my magic wand and assure my election? It wouldn't be fair, m'boy—Say! I'd better stroll by the polls and see if those Gnomes are still pulling the right lever. . .
Okay, Mr. O'Malley.

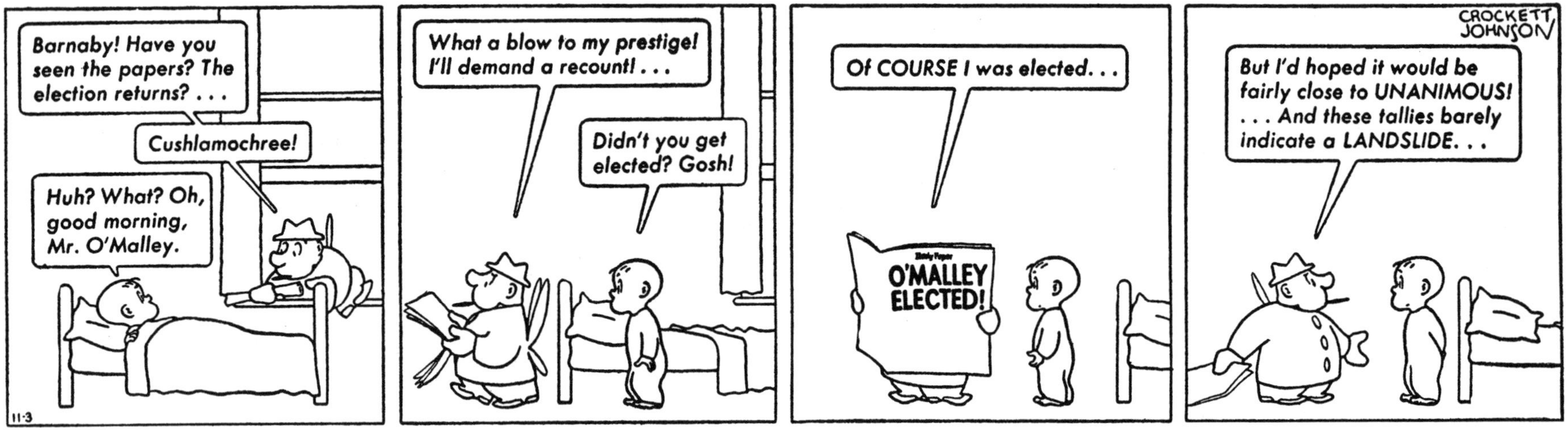
CROCKETT JOHNSON
11-3
Barnaby! Have you seen the papers? The election returns? . . .
Cushlamochree!
Huh? What? Oh, good morning, Mr. O'Malley.
What a blow to my prestige! I'll demand a recount! . . .
Didn't you get elected? Gosh!
Of COURSE I was elected. . .
O'MALLEY ELECTED!
But I'd hoped it would be fairly close to UNANIMOUS! . . . And these tallies barely indicate a LANDSLIDE. . .

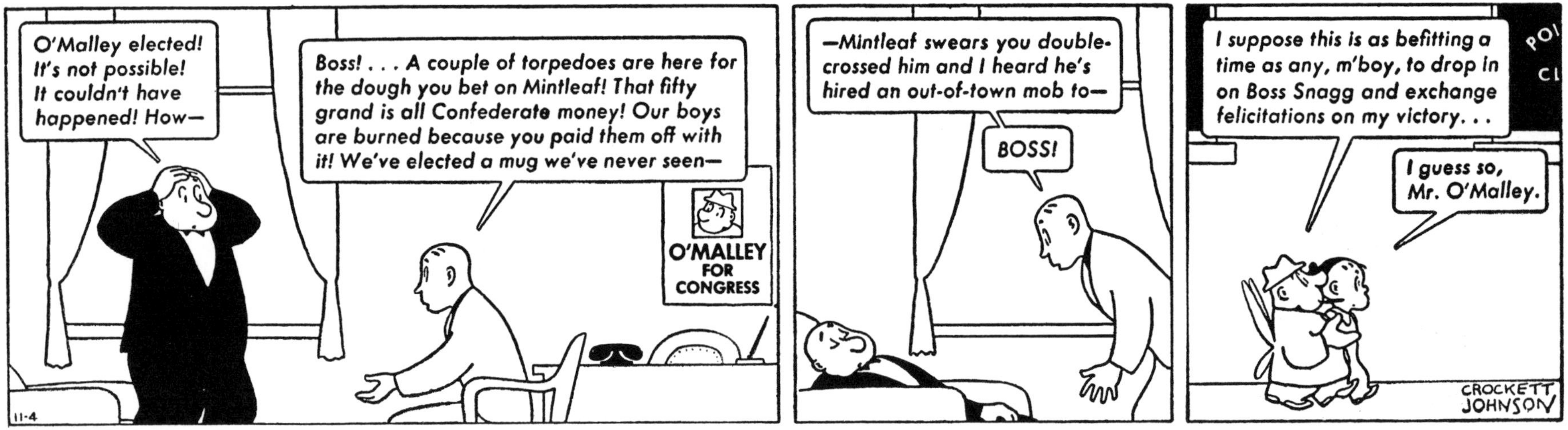
11-4
O'Malley elected! It's not possible! It couldn't have happened! How—
Boss! . . . A couple of torpedoes are here for the dough you bet on Mintleaf! That fifty grand is all Confederate money! Our boys are burned because you paid them off with it! We've elected a mug we've never seen—
O'MALLEY FOR CONGRESS
—Mintleaf swears you double-crossed him and I heard he's hired an out-of-town mob to—
BOSS!
I suppose this is as befitting a time as any, m'boy, to drop in on Boss Snagg and exchange felicitations on my victory. . .
I guess so, Mr. O'Malley.
CROCKETT JOHNSON

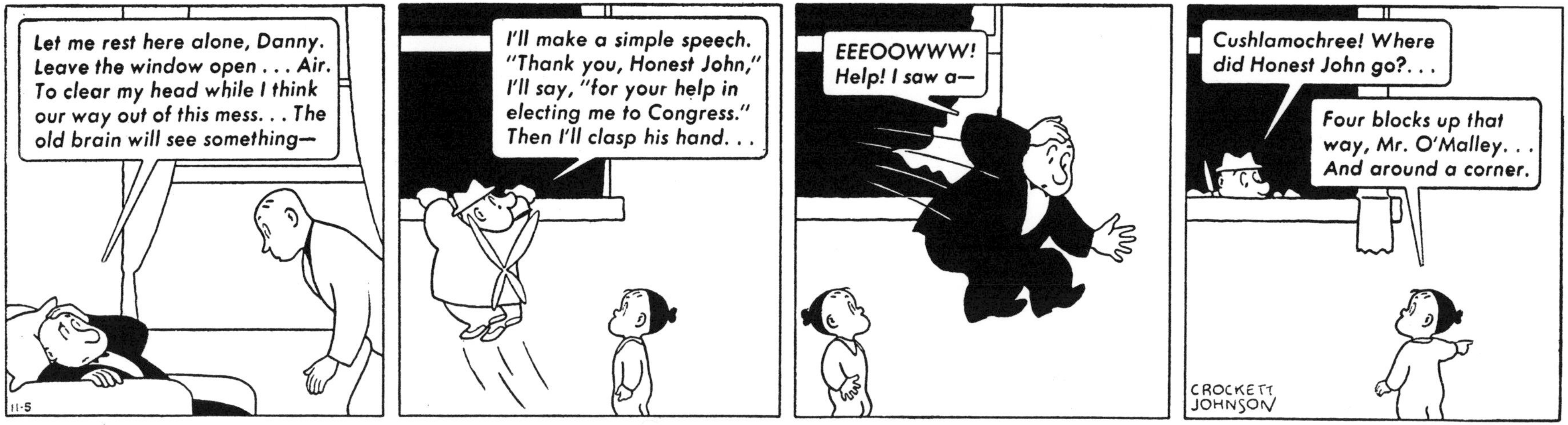

Let me rest here alone, Danny. Leave the window open . . . Air. To clear my head while I think our way out of this mess. . . The old brain will see something—
11-5
I'll make a simple speech. "Thank you, Honest John," I'll say, "for your help in electing me to Congress." Then I'll clasp his hand. . .
EEEOOWWW! Help! I saw a—
Cushlamochree! Where did Honest John go?. . .
Four blocks up that way, Mr. O'Malley. . . And around a corner.
CROCKETT JOHNSON

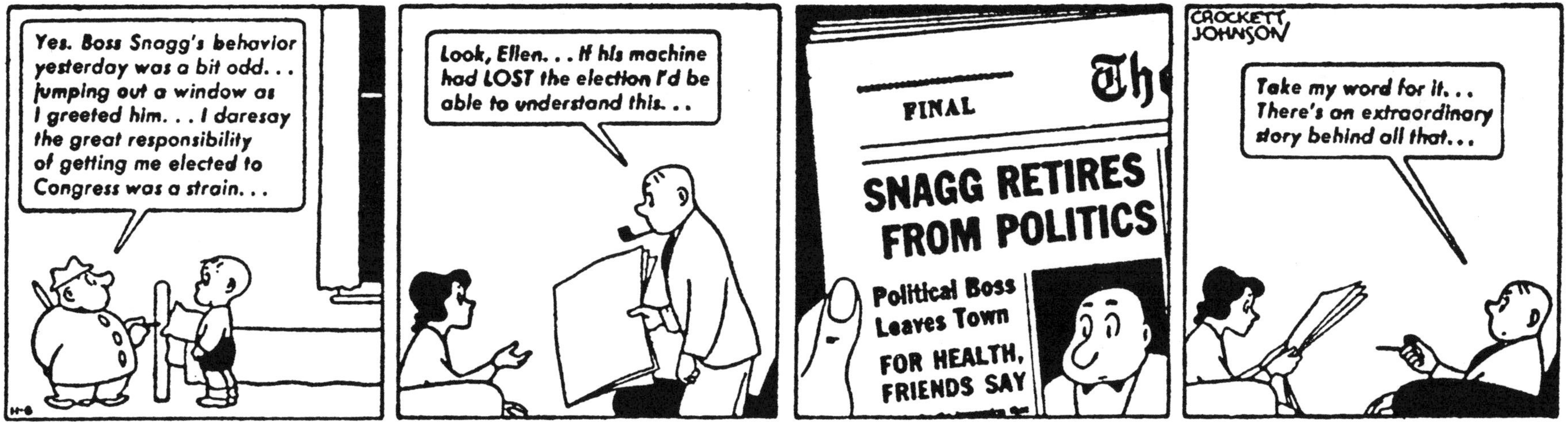

Yes. Boss Snagg's behavior yesterday was a bit odd. . . jumping out a window as I greeted him. . . I daresay the great responsibility of getting me elected to Congress was a strain. . .
11-6
Look, Ellen. . . If his machine had LOST the election I'd be able to understand this. . .
FINAL
SNAGG RETIRES FROM POLITICS
Political Boss Leaves Town
FOR HEALTH, FRIENDS SAY
CROCKETT JOHNSON
Take my word for it. . . There's an extraordinary story behind all that. . .

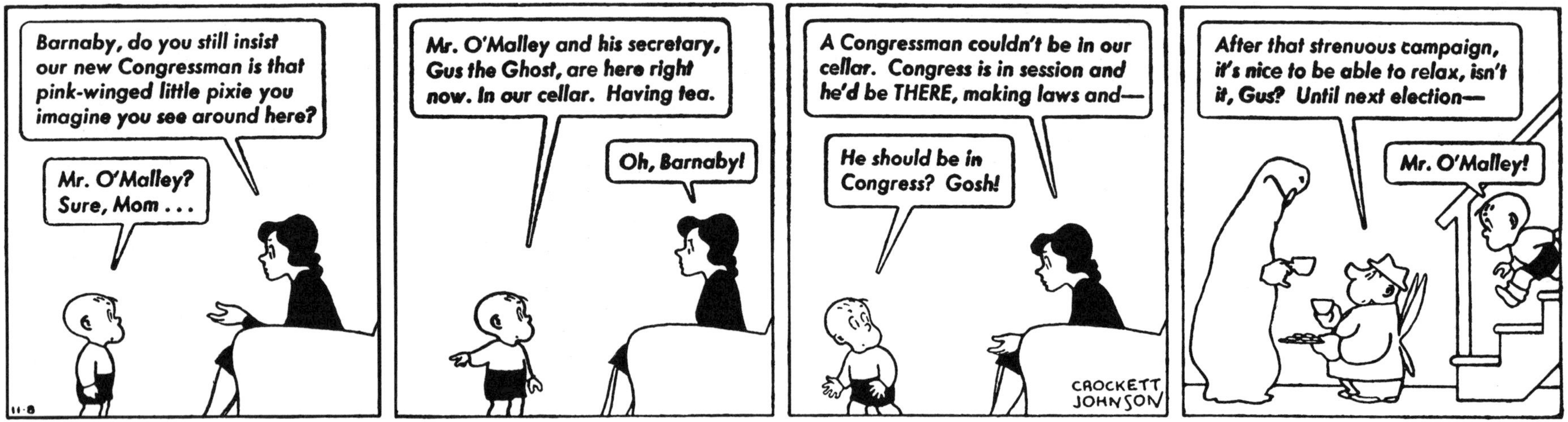
Barnaby, do you still insist our new Congressman is that pink-winged little pixie you imagine you see around here?
Mr. O'Malley? Sure, Mom . . .
11-8
Mr. O'Malley and his secretary, Gus the Ghost, are here right now. In our cellar. Having tea.
Oh, Barnaby!
A Congressman couldn't be in our cellar. Congress is in session and he'd be THERE, making laws and—
He should be in Congress? Gosh!
CROCKETT JOHNSON
After that strenuous campaign, it's nice to be able to relax, isn't it, Gus? Until next election—
Mr. O'Malley!

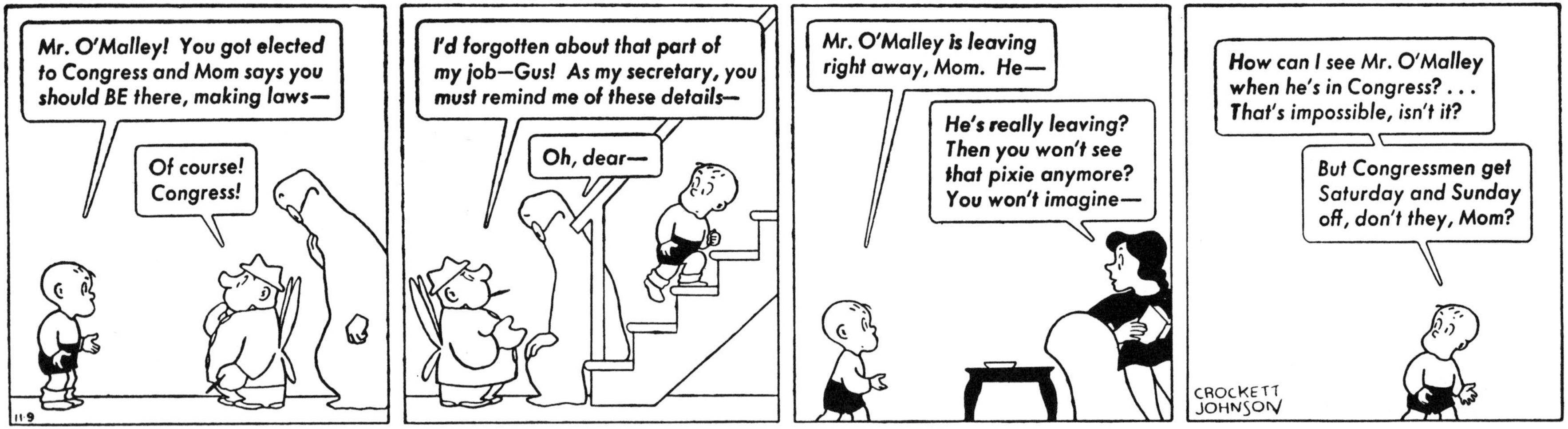
Mr. O'Malley! You got elected to Congress and Mom says you should BE there, making laws—
Of course! Congress!
11-9
I'd forgotten about that part of my job—Gus! As my secretary, you must remind me of these details—
Oh, dear—
Mr. O'Malley is leaving right away, Mom. He—
He's really leaving? Then you won't see that pixie anymore? You won't imagine—
How can I see Mr. O'Malley when he's in Congress? . . . That's impossible, isn't it?
But Congressmen get Saturday and Sunday off, don't they, Mom?
CROCKETT JOHNSON

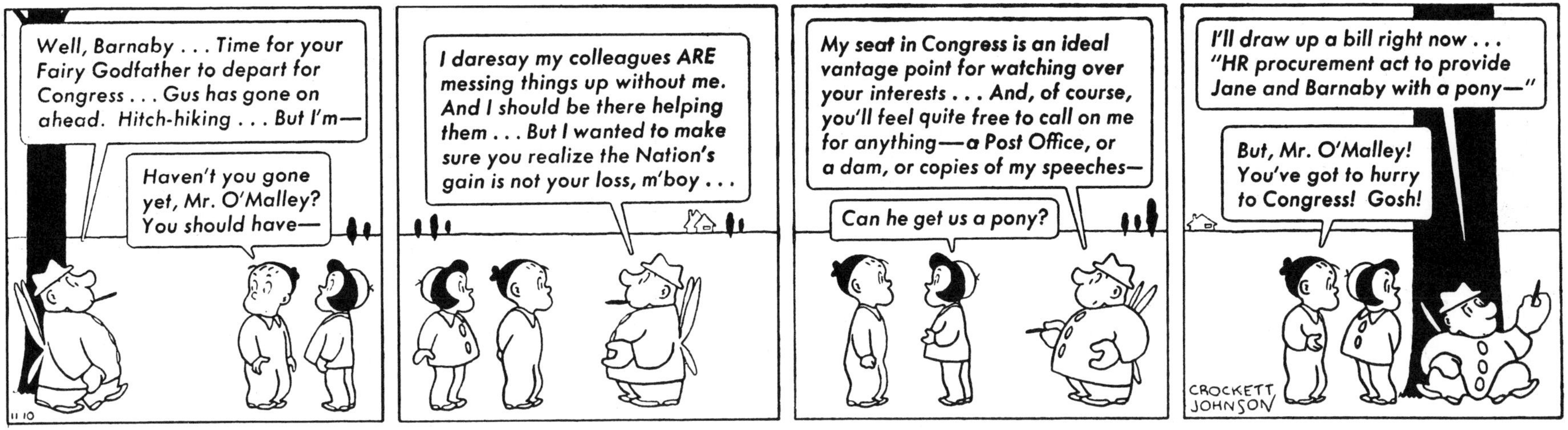
11-10
Well, Barnaby . . . Time for your Fairy Godfather to depart for Congress . . . Gus has gone on ahead. Hitch-hiking . . . But I'm—
Haven't you gone yet, Mr. O'Malley? You should have—
I daresay my colleagues ARE messing things up without me. And I should be there helping them . . . But I wanted to make sure you realize the Nation's gain is not your loss, m'boy . . .
My seat in Congress is an ideal vantage point for watching over your interests . . . And, of course, you'll feel quite free to call on me for anything—a Post Office, or a dam, or copies of my speeches—
Can he get us a pony?
I'll draw up a bill right now . . . "HR procurement act to provide Jane and Barnaby with a pony—"
But, Mr. O'Malley! You've got to hurry to Congress! Gosh!
CROCKETT JOHNSON

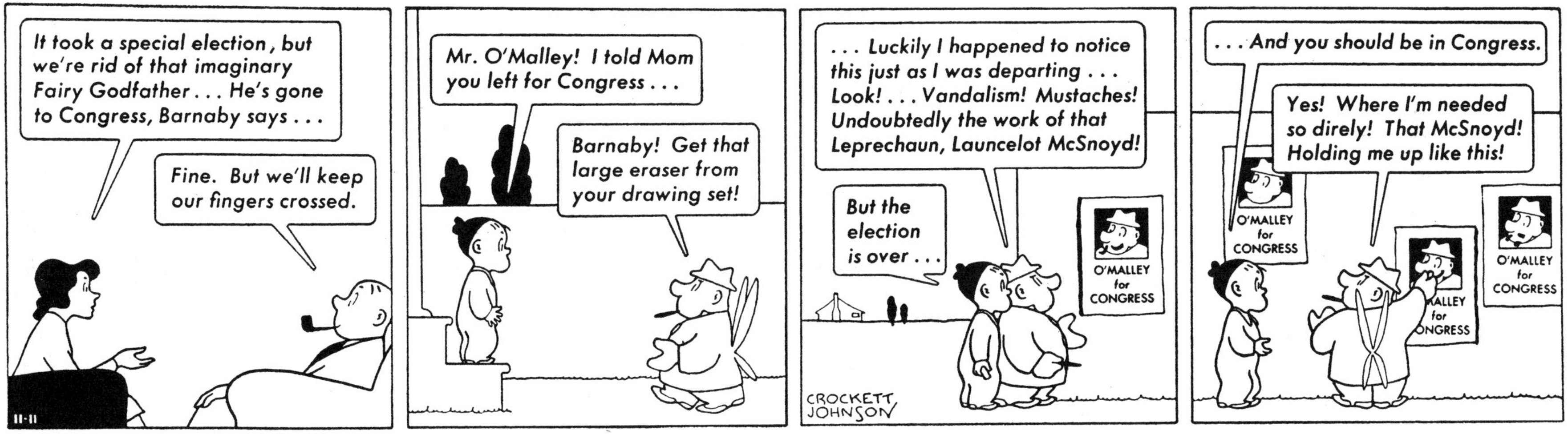
11-11
It took a special election, but we're rid of that imaginary Fairy Godfather . . . He's gone to Congress, Barnaby says . . .
Fine. But we'll keep our fingers crossed.
Mr. O'Malley! I told Mom you left for Congress . . .
Barnaby! Get that large eraser from your drawing set!
. . . Luckily I happened to notice this just as I was departing . . . Look! . . . Vandalism! Mustaches! Undoubtedly the work of that Leprechaun, Launcelot McSnoyd!
But the election is over . . .
O'MALLEY for CONGRESS
CROCKETT JOHNSON
. . . And you should be in Congress.
Yes! Where I'm needed so direly! That McSnoyd! Holding me up like this!
O'MALLEY for CONGRESS
O'MALLEY for CONGRESS

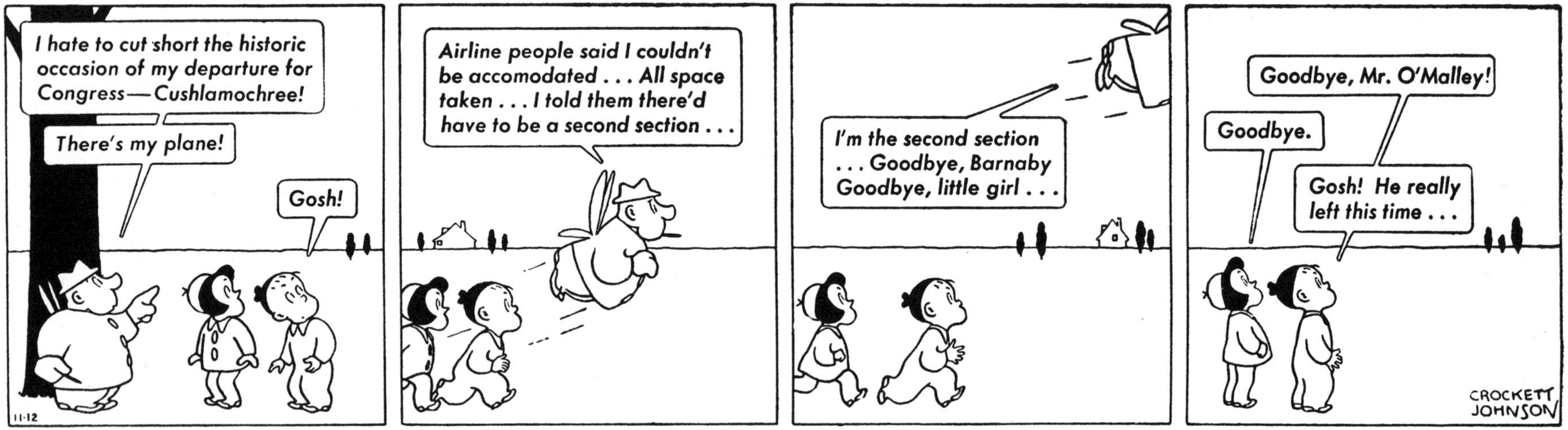
I hate to cut short the historic occasion of my departure for Congress—Cushlamochree!
There's my plane!
Gosh!
11-12
Airline people said I couldn't be accomodated . . . All space taken . . . I told them there'd have to be a second section . . .
I'm the second section . . . Goodbye, Barnaby Goodbye, little girl . . .
Goodbye, Mr. O'Malley!
Goodbye.
Gosh! He really left this time . . .
CROCKETT JOHNSON

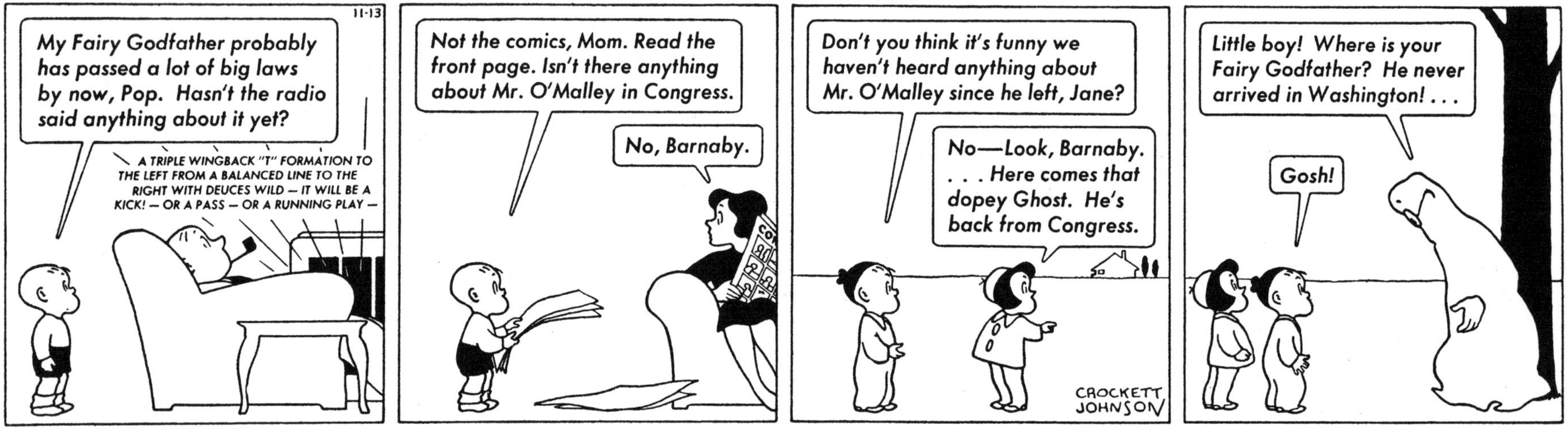
11-13
My Fairy Godfather probably has passed a lot of big laws by now, Pop. Hasn't the radio said anything about it yet?
A TRIPLE WINGBACK "T" FORMATION TO THE LEFT FROM A BALANCED LINE TO THE RIGHT WITH DEUCES WILD — IT WILL BE A KICK! — OR A PASS — OR A RUNNING PLAY —
Not the comics, Mom. Read the front page. Isn't there anything about Mr. O'Malley in Congress.
No, Barnaby.
Don't you think it's funny we haven't heard anything about Mr. O'Malley since he left, Jane?
No—Look, Barnaby. . . . Here comes that dopey Ghost. He's back from Congress.
CROCKETT JOHNSON
Little boy! Where is your Fairy Godfather? He never arrived in Washington! . . .
Gosh!

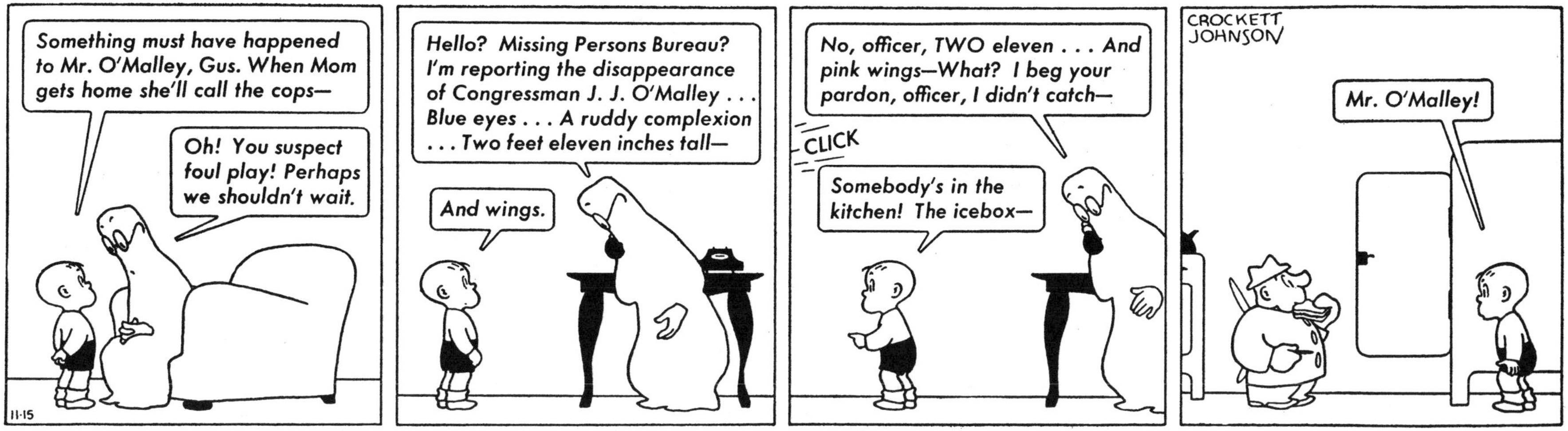
Something must have happened to Mr. O'Malley, Gus. When Mom gets home she'll call the cops—
Oh! You suspect foul play! Perhaps we shouldn't wait.
11-15
Hello? Missing Persons Bureau? I'm reporting the disappearance of Congressman J. J. O'Malley . . . Blue eyes . . . A ruddy complexion . . . Two feet eleven inches tall—
And wings.
No, officer, TWO eleven . . . And pink wings—What? I beg your pardon, officer, I didn't catch—
CLICK
Somebody's in the kitchen! The icebox—
CROCKETT JOHNSON
Mr. O'Malley!

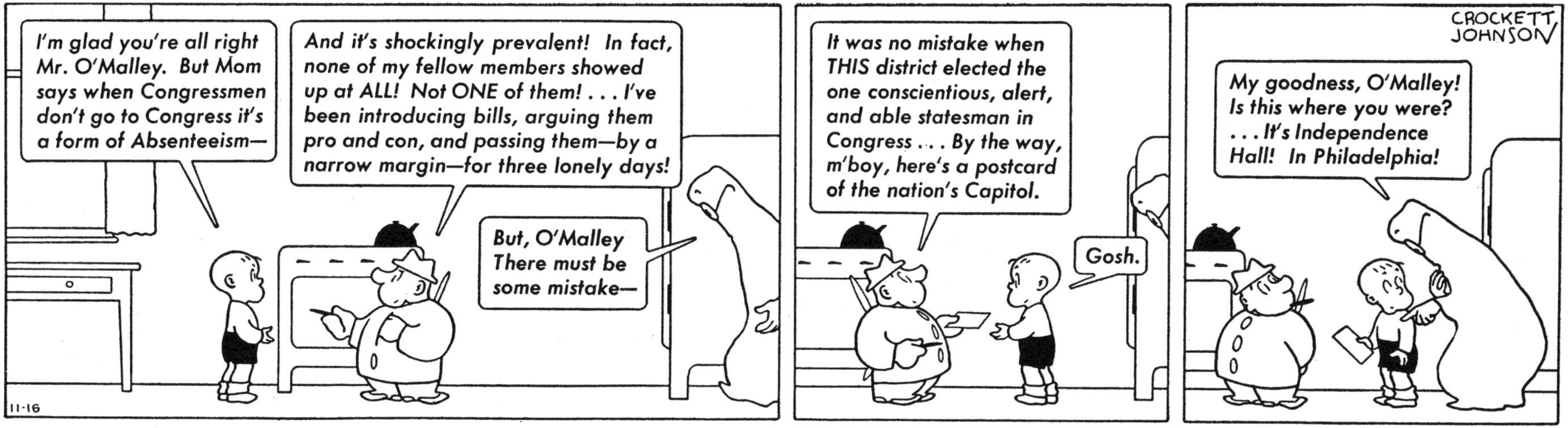
I'm glad you're all right Mr. O'Malley. But Mom says when Congressmen don't go to Congress it's a form of Absenteeism—
And it's shockingly prevalent! In fact, none of my fellow members showed up at ALL! Not ONE of them! . . . I've been introducing bills, arguing them pro and con, and passing them—by a narrow margin—for three lonely days!
But, O'Malley There must be some mistake—
11-16
It was no mistake when THIS district elected the one conscientious, alert, and able statesman in Congress . . . By the way, m'boy, here's a postcard of the nation's Capitol.
Gosh.
CROCKETT JOHNSON
My goodness, O'Malley! Is this where you were? . . . It's Independence Hall! In Philadelphia!

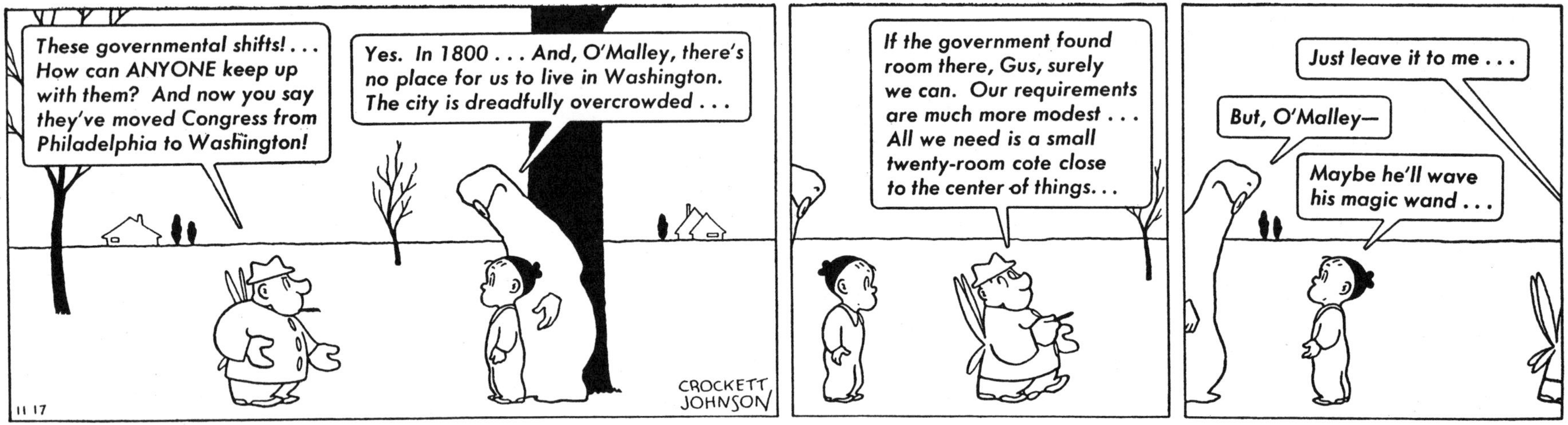
These governmental shifts! . . . How can ANYONE keep up with them? And now you say they've moved Congress from Philadelphia to Washington!
Yes. In 1800 . . . And, O'Malley, there's no place for us to live in Washington. The city is dreadfully overcrowded . . .
CROCKETT JOHNSON
11 17
If the government found room there, Gus, surely we can. Our requirements are much more modest . . . All we need is a small twenty-room cote close to the center of things. . .
Just leave it to me . . .
But, O'Malley—
Maybe he'll wave his magic wand . . .

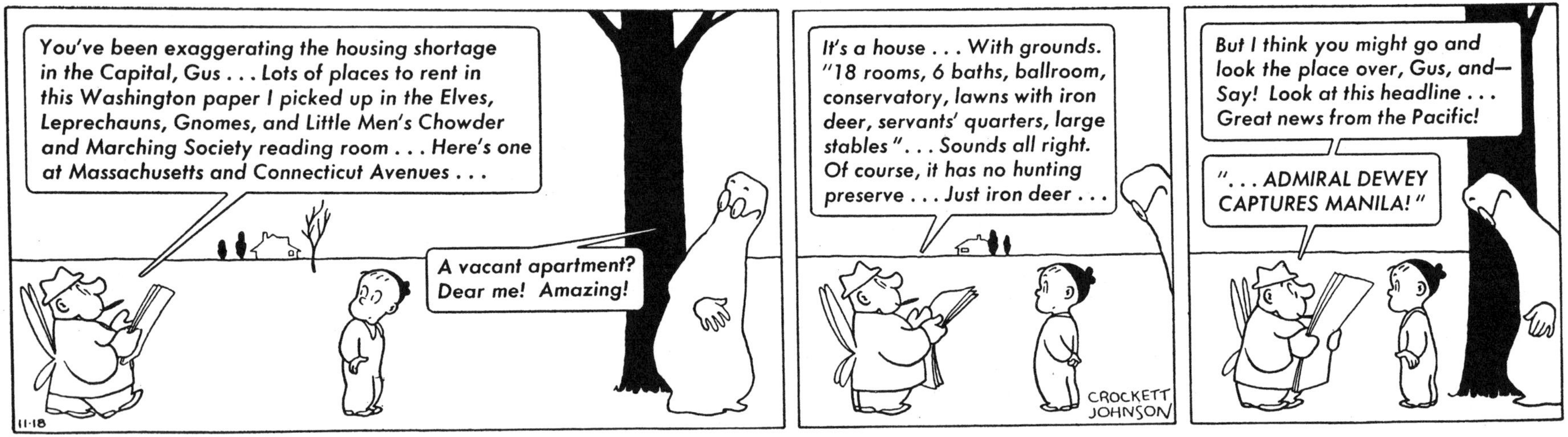
You've been exaggerating the housing shortage in the Capital, Gus . . . Lots of places to rent in this Washington paper I picked up in the Elves, Leprechauns, Gnomes, and Little Men's Chowder and Marching Society reading room . . . Here's one at Massachusetts and Connecticut Avenues . . .
A vacant apartment? Dear me! Amazing!
11·18
It's a house . . . With grounds. "18 rooms, 6 baths, ballroom, conservatory, lawns with iron deer, servants' quarters, large stables" . . . Sounds all right. Of course, it has no hunting preserve . . . Just iron deer . . .
CROCKETT JOHNSON
But I think you might go and look the place over, Gus, and— Say! Look at this headline . . . Great news from the Pacific!
". . . ADMIRAL DEWEY CAPTURES MANILA!"

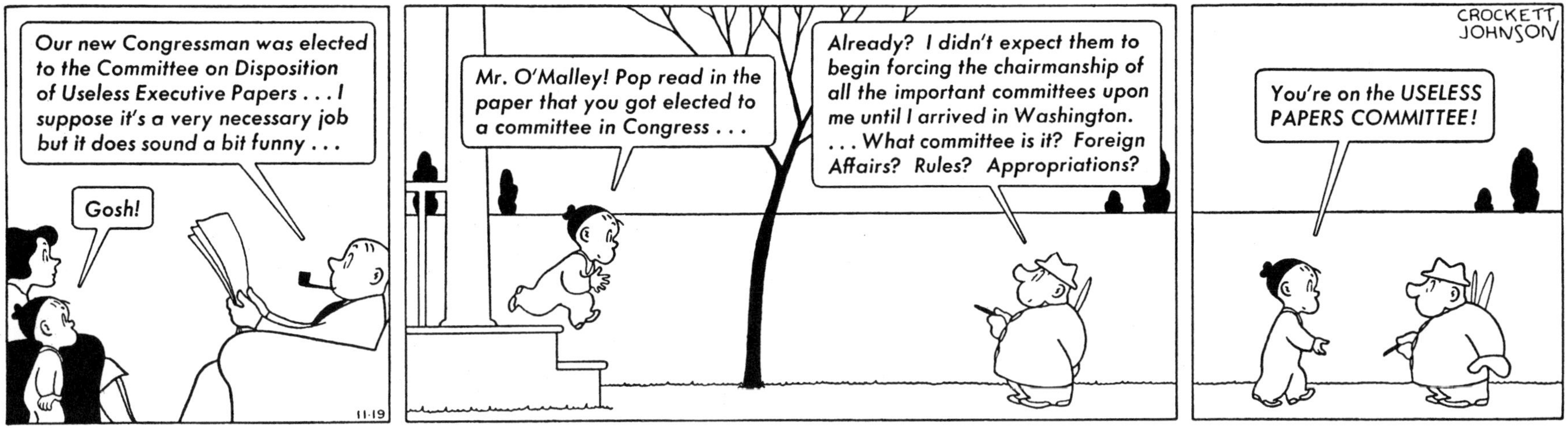
CROCKETT JOHNSON
Our new Congressman was elected to the Committee on Disposition of Useless Executive Papers . . . I suppose it's a very necessary job but it does sound a bit funny . . .
Gosh!
11-19
Mr. O'Malley! Pop read in the paper that you got elected to a committee in Congress . . .
Already? I didn't expect them to begin forcing the chairmanship of all the important committees upon me until I arrived in Washington. . . . What committee is it? Foreign Affairs? Rules? Appropriations?
You're on the USELESS PAPERS COMMITTEE!

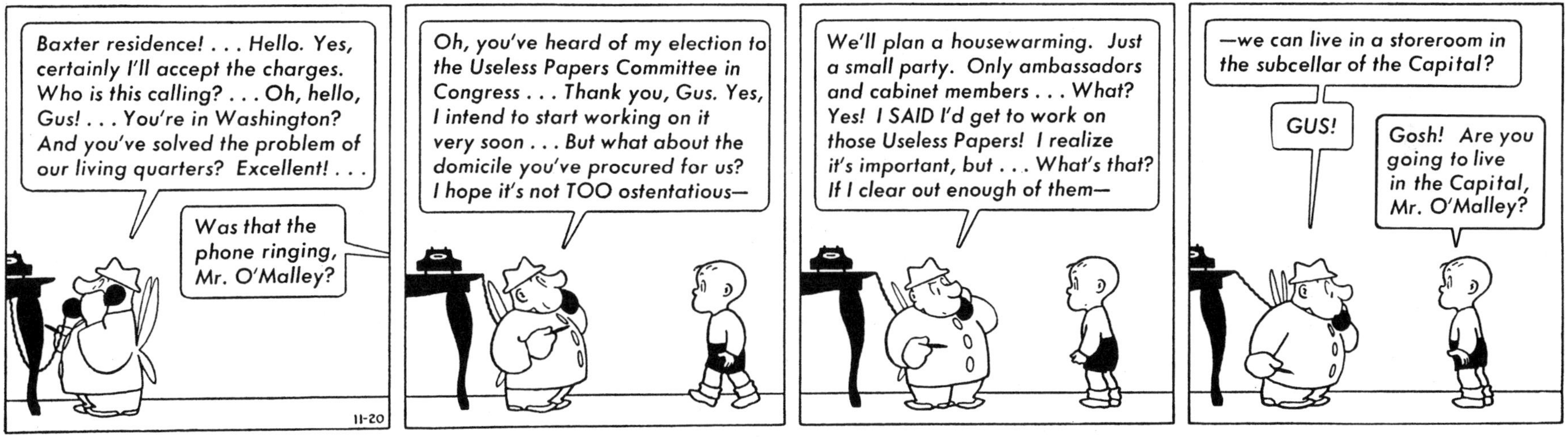
Baxter residence! . . . Hello. Yes, certainly I'll accept the charges. Who is this calling? . . . Oh, hello, Gus! . . . You're in Washington? And you've solved the problem of our living quarters? Excellent! . . .
Was that the phone ringing, Mr. O'Malley?
11-20
Oh, you've heard of my election to the Useless Papers Committee in Congress . . . Thank you, Gus. Yes, I intend to start working on it very soon . . . But what about the domicile you've procured for us? I hope it's not TOO ostentatious—
We'll plan a housewarming. Just a small party. Only ambassadors and cabinet members . . . What? Yes! I SAID I'd get to work on those Useless Papers! I realize it's important, but . . . What's that? If I clear out enough of them—
—we can live in a storeroom in the subcellar of the Capital?
GUS!
Gosh! Are you going to live in the Capital, Mr. O'Malley?

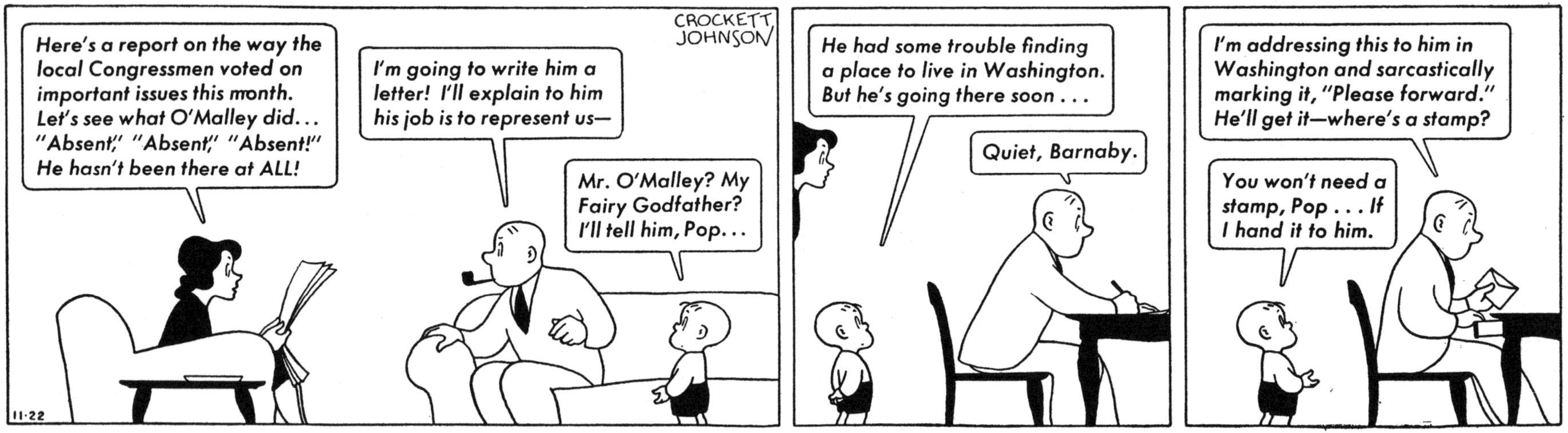
CROCKETT JOHNSON
Here's a report on the way the local Congressmen voted on important issues this month. Let's see what O'Malley did... "Absent," "Absent," "Absent!" He hasn't been there at ALL!
I'm going to write him a letter! I'll explain to him his job is to represent us—
Mr. O'Malley? My Fairy Godfather? I'll tell him, Pop...
11·22
He had some trouble finding a place to live in Washington. But he's going there soon . . .
Quiet, Barnaby.
I'm addressing this to him in Washington and sarcastically marking it, "Please forward." He'll get it—where's a stamp?
You won't need a stamp, Pop . . . If I hand it to him.

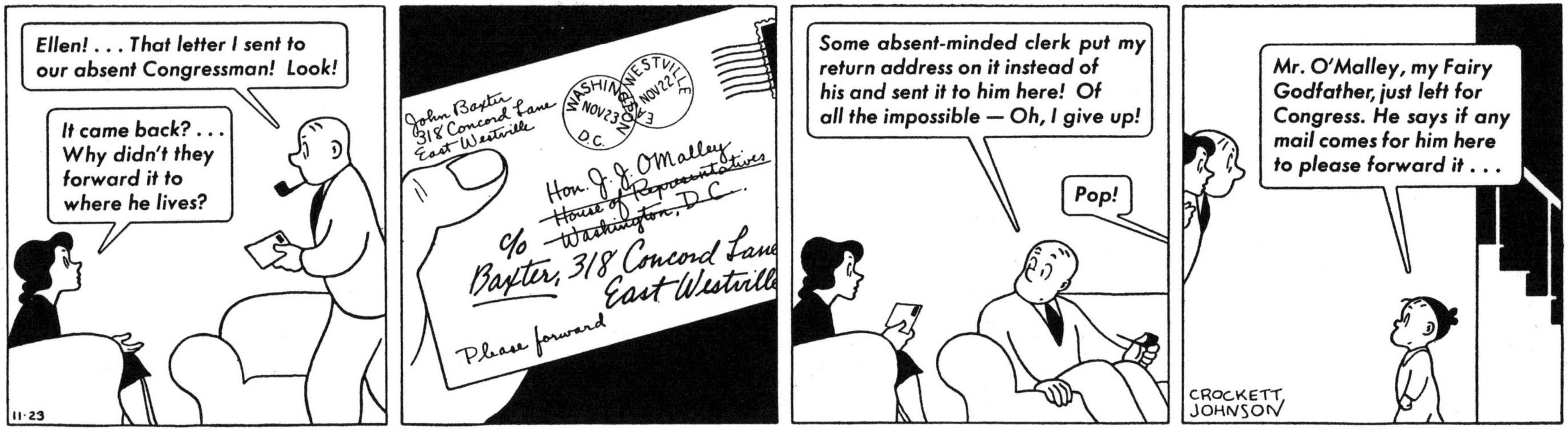
Ellen! . . . That letter I sent to our absent Congressman! Look!
It came back? . . . Why didn't they forward it to where he lives?
11·23
John Baxter
318 Concord Lane
East Westville
Hon. J. J. O'Malley
House of Representatives
Washington, D.C.
c/o
Baxter, 318 Concord Lane
East Westville
Please forward
Some absent-minded clerk put my return address on it instead of his and sent it to him here! Of all the impossible — Oh, I give up!
Pop!
Mr. O'Malley, my Fairy Godfather, just left for Congress. He says if any mail comes for him here to please forward it . . .
CROCKETT JOHNSON

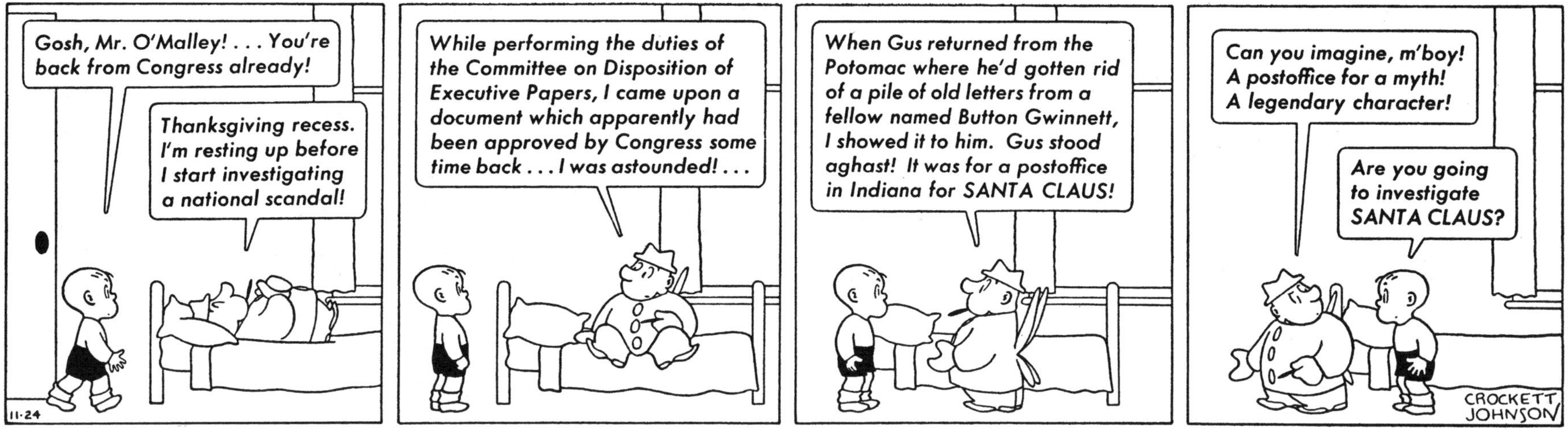

Gosh, Mr. O'Malley! . . . You're back from Congress already!
Thanksgiving recess. I'm resting up before I start investigating a national scandal!
While performing the duties of the Committee on Disposition of Executive Papers, I came upon a document which apparently had been approved by Congress some time back . . . I was astounded! . . .
When Gus returned from the Potomac where he'd gotten rid of a pile of old letters from a fellow named Button Gwinnett, I showed it to him. Gus stood aghast! It was for a postoffice in Indiana for SANTA CLAUS!
Can you imagine, m'boy! A postoffice for a myth! A legendary character!
Are you going to investigate SANTA CLAUS?
11·24
CROCKETT JOHNSON

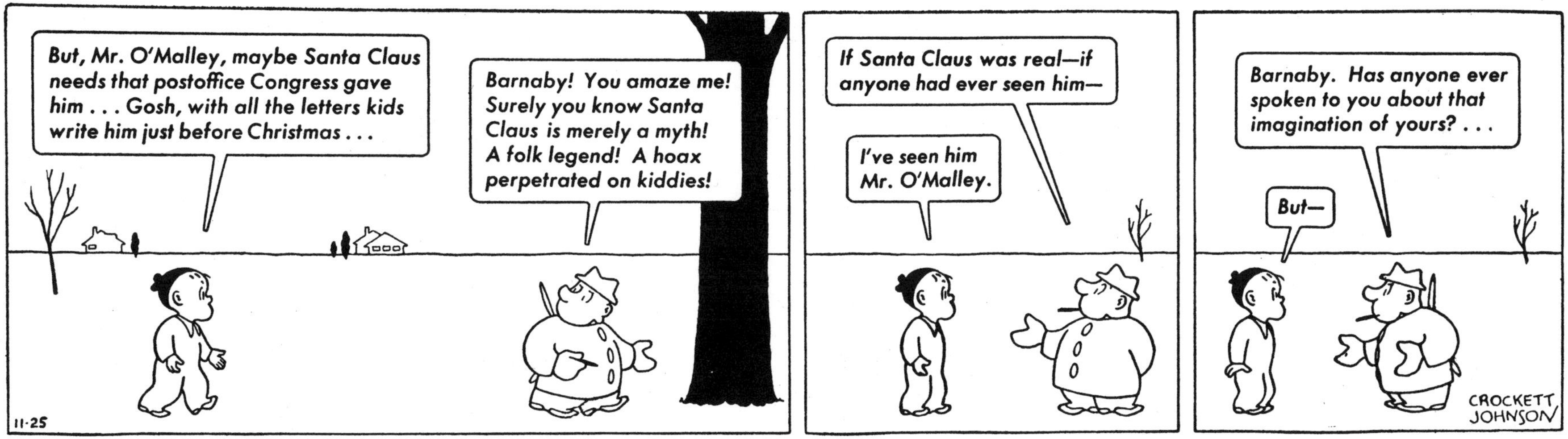

But, Mr. O'Malley, maybe Santa Claus needs that postoffice Congress gave him . . . Gosh, with all the letters kids write him just before Christmas . . .
Barnaby! You amaze me! Surely you know Santa Claus is merely a myth! A folk legend! A hoax perpetrated on kiddies!
If Santa Claus was real—if anyone had ever seen him—
I've seen him Mr. O'Malley.
Barnaby. Has anyone ever spoken to you about that imagination of yours? . . .
But—
11·25
CROCKETT JOHNSON

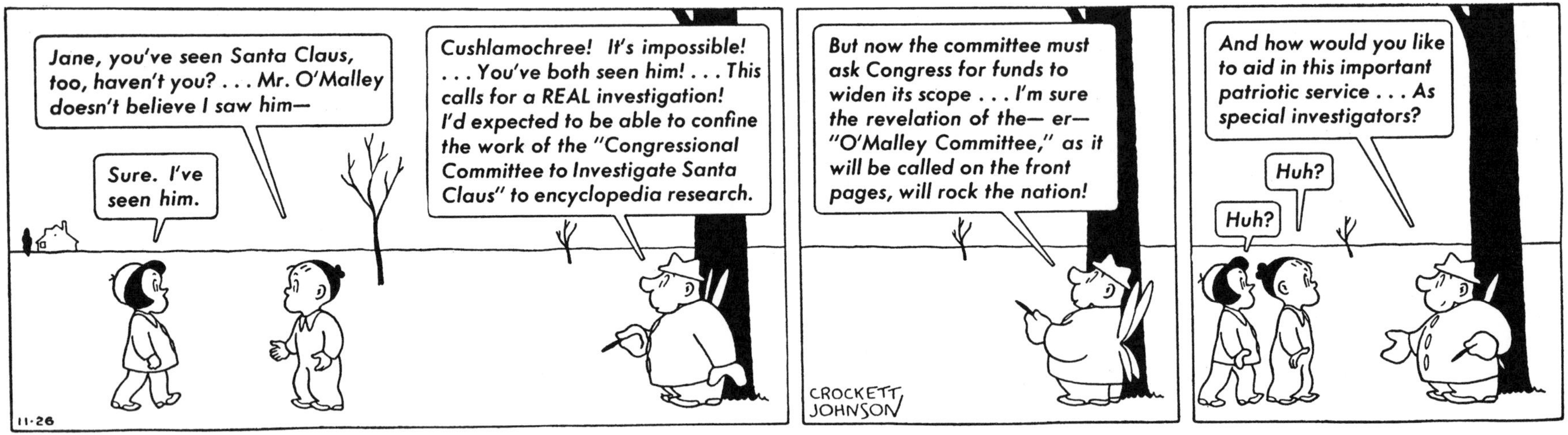
Jane, you've seen Santa Claus, too, haven't you? . . . Mr. O'Malley doesn't believe I saw him—
Sure. I've seen him.
11·26
Cushlamochree! It's impossible! . . . You've both seen him! . . . This calls for a REAL investigation! I'd expected to be able to confine the work of the "Congressional Committee to Investigate Santa Claus" to encyclopedia research.
But now the committee must ask Congress for funds to widen its scope . . . I'm sure the revelation of the— er— "O'Malley Committee," as it will be called on the front pages, will rock the nation!
CROCKETT JOHNSON
And how would you like to aid in this important patriotic service . . . As special investigators?
Huh?
Huh?

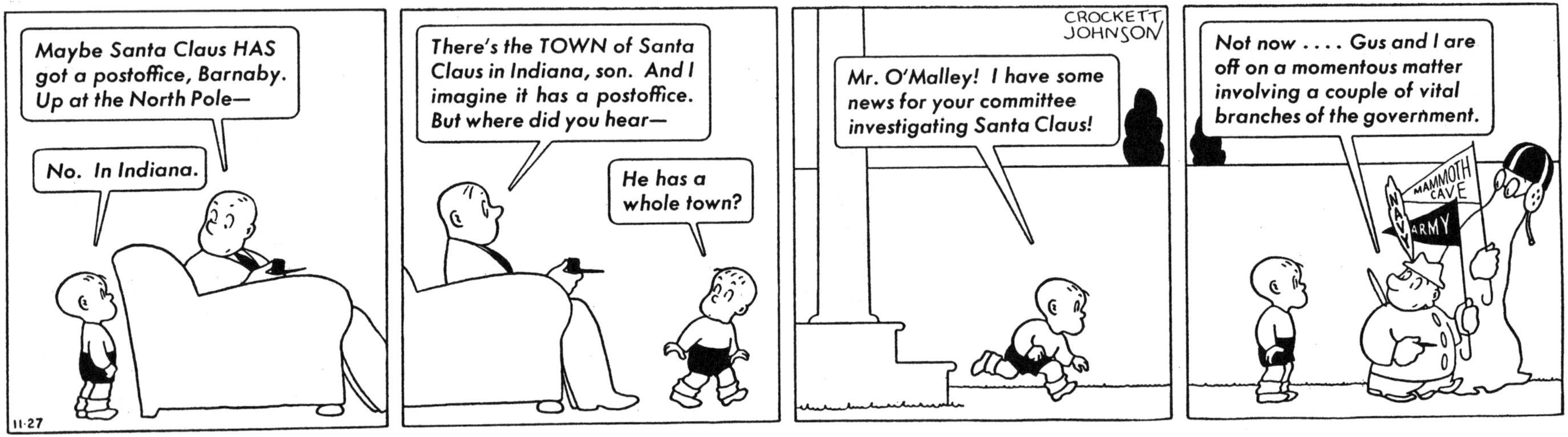
Maybe Santa Claus HAS got a postoffice, Barnaby. Up at the North Pole—
No. In Indiana.
11·27
There's the TOWN of Santa Claus in Indiana, son. And I imagine it has a postoffice. But where did you hear—
He has a whole town?
CROCKETT JOHNSON
Mr. O'Malley! I have some news for your committee investigating Santa Claus!
Not now . . . . Gus and I are off on a momentous matter involving a couple of vital branches of the government.
NAVY
MAMMOTH CAVE
ARMY

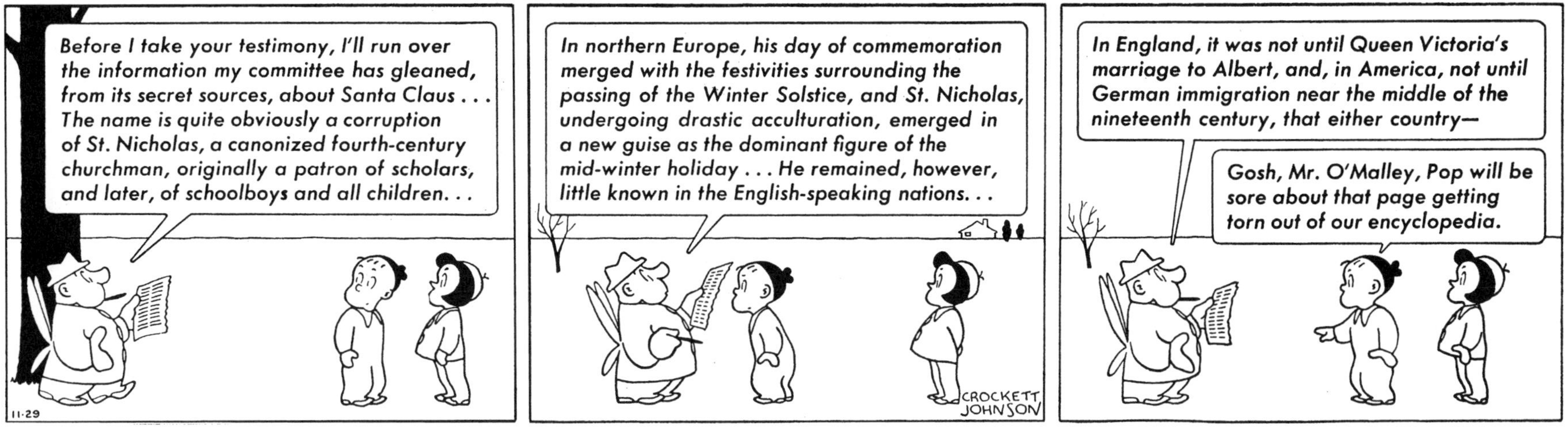
Before I take your testimony, I'll run over the information my committee has gleaned, from its secret sources, about Santa Claus . . . The name is quite obviously a corruption of St. Nicholas, a canonized fourth-century churchman, originally a patron of scholars, and later, of schoolboys and all children. . .
11·29
In northern Europe, his day of commemoration merged with the festivities surrounding the passing of the Winter Solstice, and St. Nicholas, undergoing drastic acculturation, emerged in a new guise as the dominant figure of the mid-winter holiday . . . He remained, however, little known in the English-speaking nations. . .
CROCKETT JOHNSON
In England, it was not until Queen Victoria's marriage to Albert, and, in America, not until German immigration near the middle of the nineteenth century, that either country—
Gosh, Mr. O'Malley, Pop will be sore about that page getting torn out of our encyclopedia.

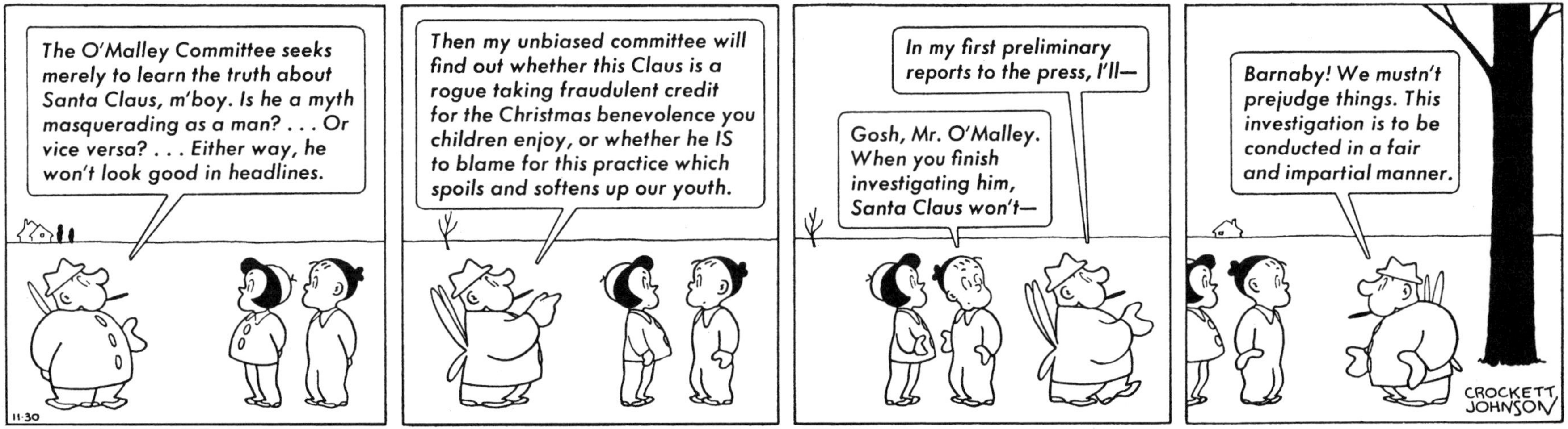
The O'Malley Committee seeks merely to learn the truth about Santa Claus, m'boy. Is he a myth masquerading as a man? . . . Or vice versa? . . . Either way, he won't look good in headlines.
11·30
Then my unbiased committee will find out whether this Claus is a rogue taking fraudulent credit for the Christmas benevolence you children enjoy, or whether he IS to blame for this practice which spoils and softens up our youth.
In my first preliminary reports to the press, I'll—
Gosh, Mr. O'Malley. When you finish investigating him, Santa Claus won't—
Barnaby! We mustn't prejudge things. This investigation is to be conducted in a fair and impartial manner.
CROCKETT JOHNSON

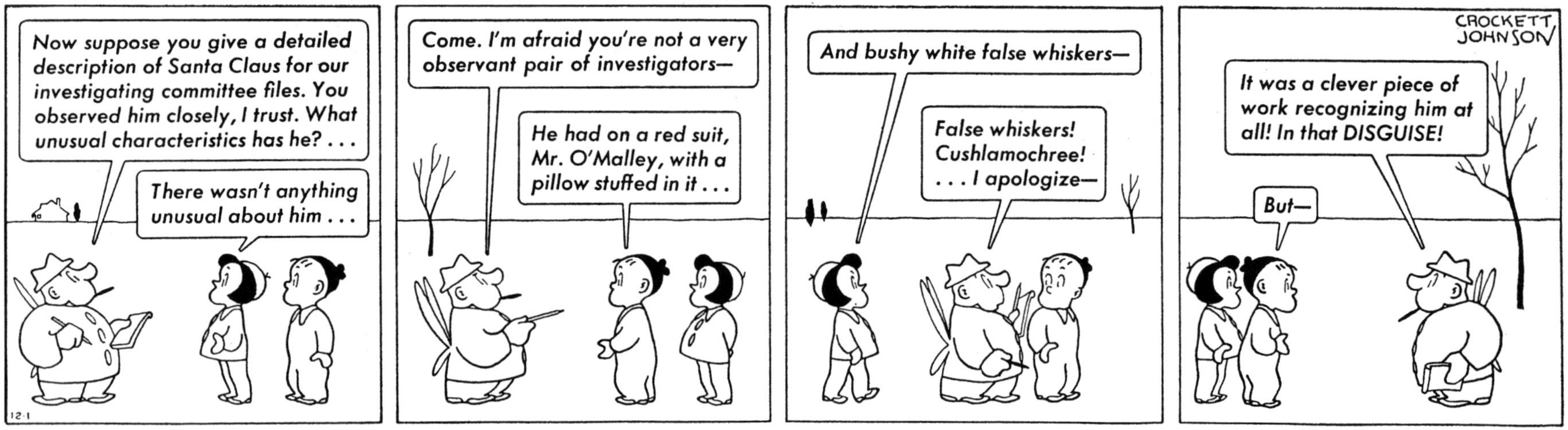
CROCKETT JOHNSON
Now suppose you give a detailed description of Santa Claus for our investigating committee files. You observed him closely, I trust. What unusual characteristics has he? . . .
There wasn't anything unusual about him . . .
Come. I'm afraid you're not a very observant pair of investigators—
He had on a red suit, Mr. O'Malley, with a pillow stuffed in it . . .
And bushy white false whiskers—
False whiskers! Cushlamochree! . . . I apologize—
It was a clever piece of work recognizing him at all! In that DISGUISE!
But—
12·1

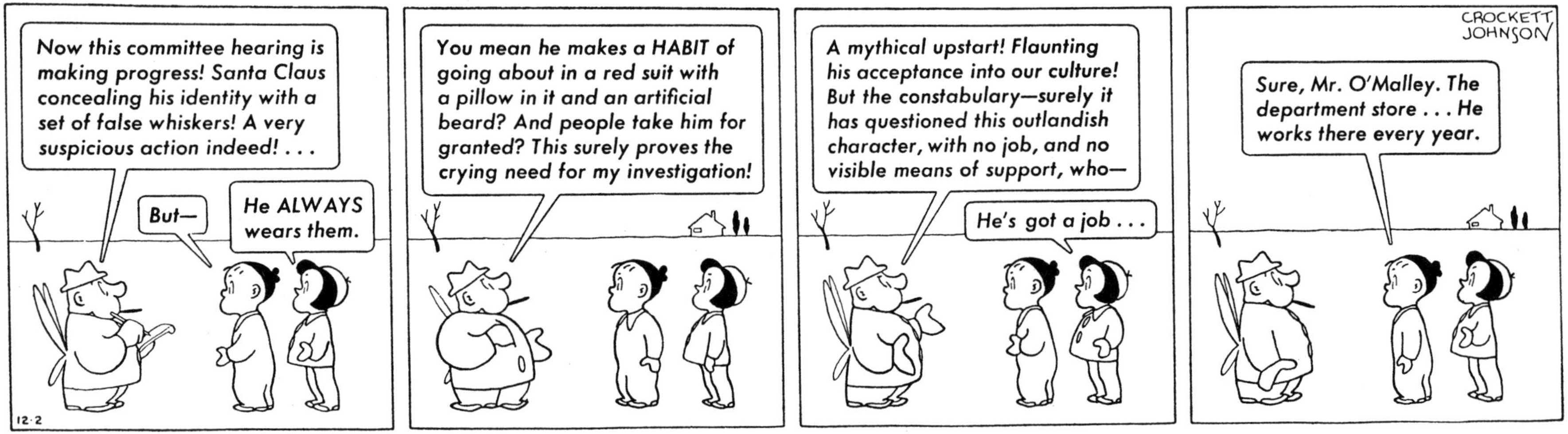
CROCKETT JOHNSON
Now this committee hearing is making progress! Santa Claus concealing his identity with a set of false whiskers! A very suspicious action indeed! . . .
But—
He ALWAYS wears them.
You mean he makes a HABIT of going about in a red suit with a pillow in it and an artificial beard? And people take him for granted? This surely proves the crying need for my investigation!
A mythical upstart! Flaunting his acceptance into our culture! But the constabulary—surely it has questioned this outlandish character, with no job, and no visible means of support, who—
He's got a job . . .
Sure, Mr. O'Malley. The department store . . . He works there every year.
12·2

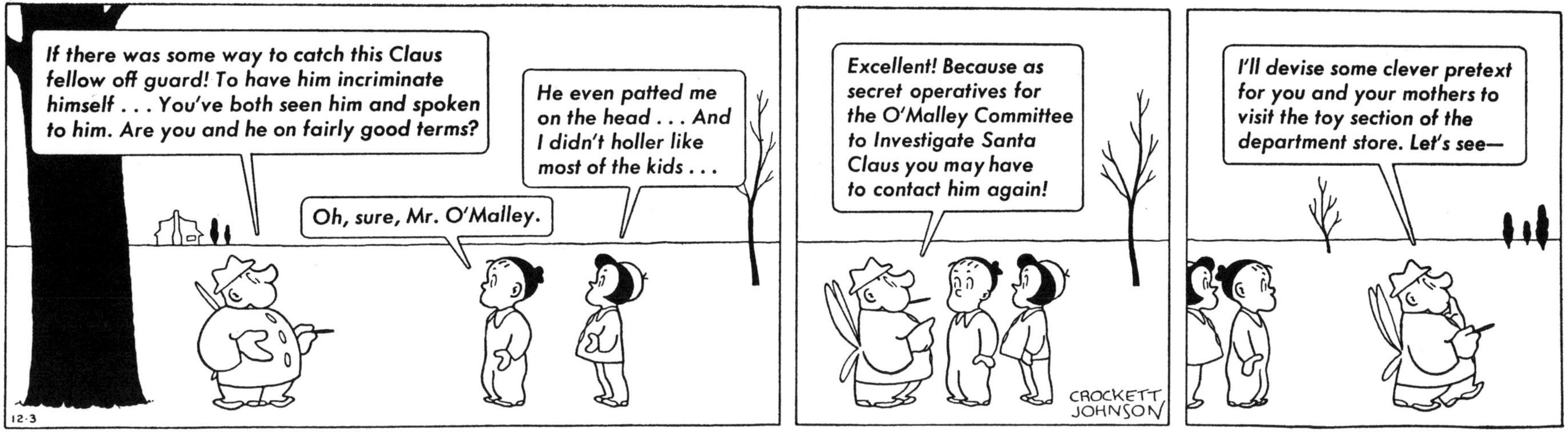
If there was some way to catch this Claus fellow off guard! To have him incriminate himself . . . You've both seen him and spoken to him. Are you and he on fairly good terms?
Oh, sure, Mr. O'Malley.
He even patted me on the head . . . And I didn't holler like most of the kids . . .
Excellent! Because as secret operatives for the O'Malley Committee to Investigate Santa Claus you may have to contact him again!
I'll devise some clever pretext for you and your mothers to visit the toy section of the department store. Let's see—
12-3
CROCKETT JOHNSON

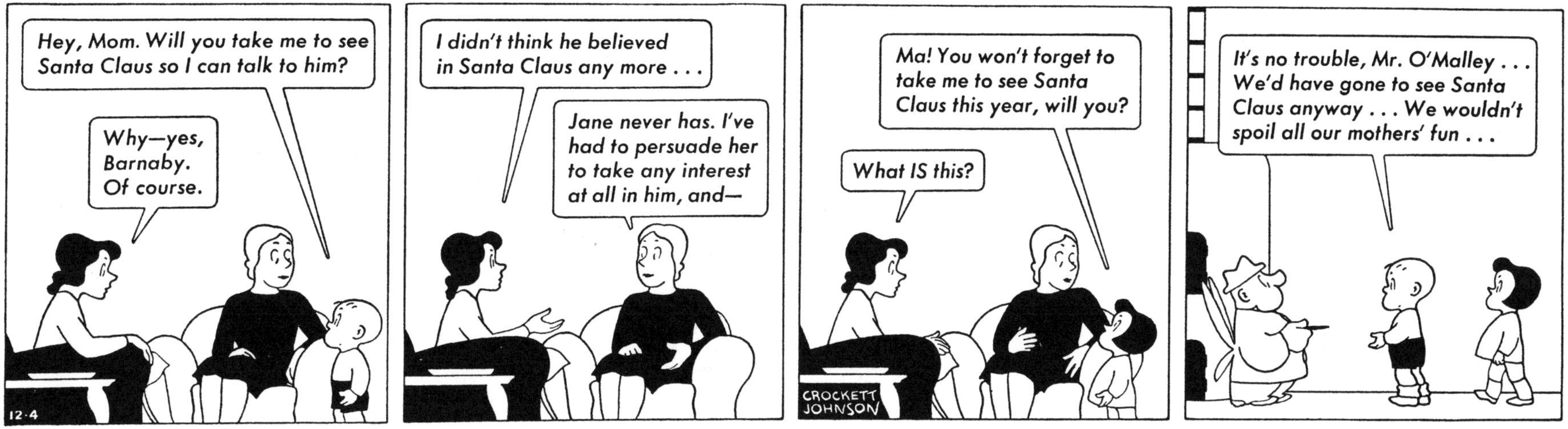
Hey, Mom. Will you take me to see Santa Claus so I can talk to him?
Why—yes, Barnaby. Of course.
I didn't think he believed in Santa Claus any more . . .
Jane never has. I've had to persuade her to take any interest at all in him, and—
Ma! You won't forget to take me to see Santa Claus this year, will you?
What IS this?
It's no trouble, Mr. O'Malley . . . We'd have gone to see Santa Claus anyway . . . We wouldn't spoil all our mothers' fun . . .
12-4
CROCKETT JOHNSON

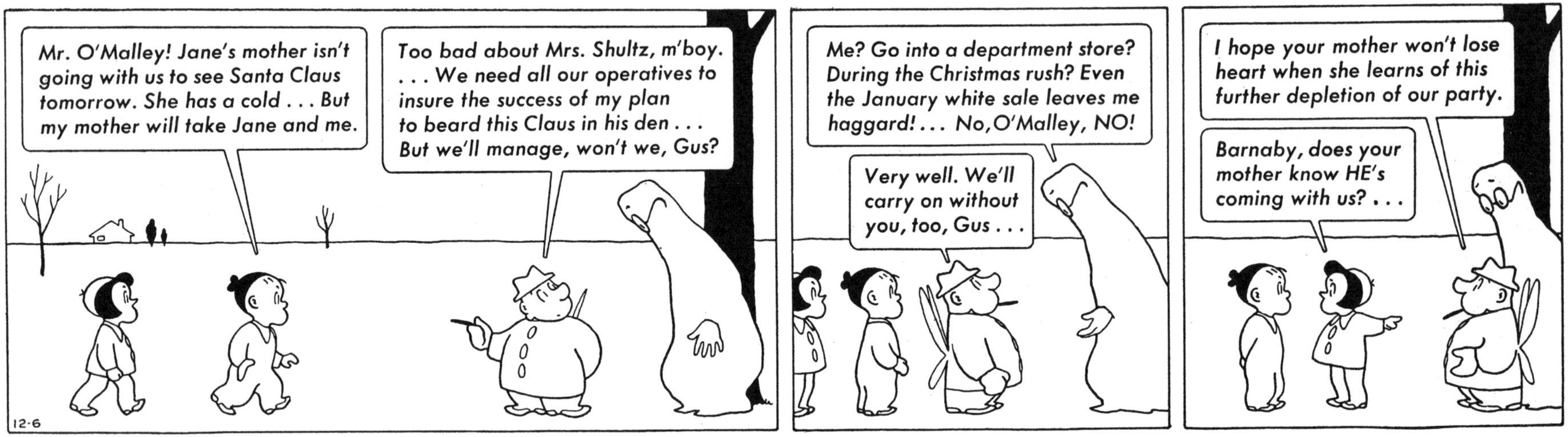
Mr. O'Malley! Jane's mother isn't going with us to see Santa Claus tomorrow. She has a cold . . . But my mother will take Jane and me.
Too bad about Mrs. Shultz, m'boy. . . . We need all our operatives to insure the success of my plan to beard this Claus in his den . . . But we'll manage, won't we, Gus?
Me? Go into a department store? During the Christmas rush? Even the January white sale leaves me haggard! . . . No, O'Malley, NO!
Very well. We'll carry on without you, too, Gus . . .
I hope your mother won't lose heart when she learns of this further depletion of our party.
Barnaby, does your mother know HE's coming with us? . . .
12-6

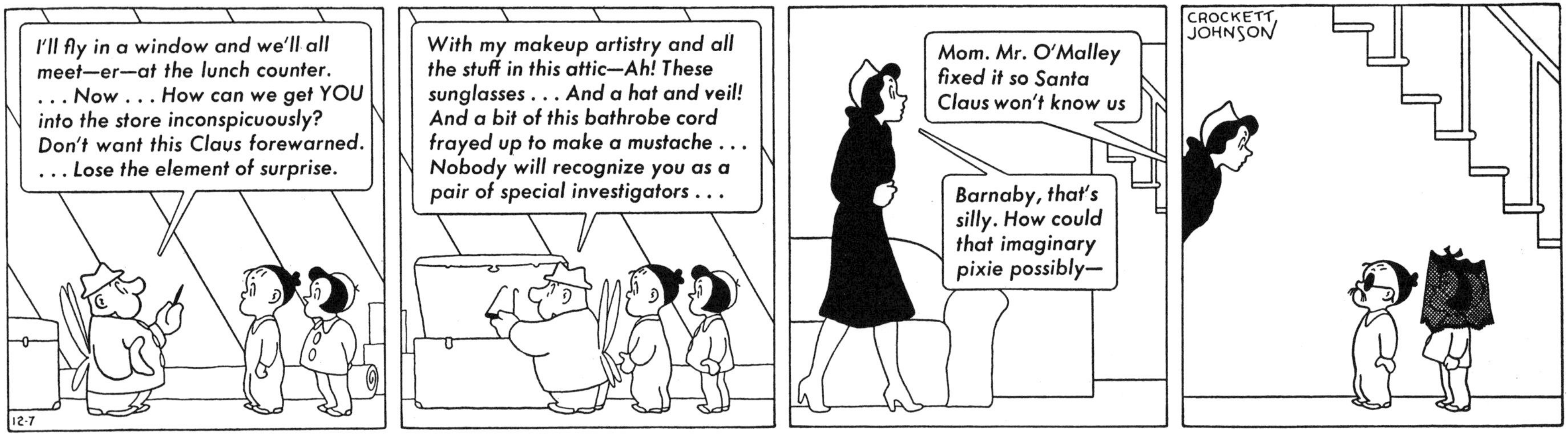
I'll fly in a window and we'll all meet—er—at the lunch counter. . . . Now . . . How can we get YOU into the store inconspicuously? Don't want this Claus forewarned. . . . Lose the element of surprise.
With my makeup artistry and all the stuff in this attic—Ah! These sunglasses . . . And a hat and veil! And a bit of this bathrobe cord frayed up to make a mustache . . . Nobody will recognize you as a pair of special investigators . . .
Mom. Mr. O'Malley fixed it so Santa Claus won't know us
Barnaby, that's silly. How could that imaginary pixie possibly—
CROCKETT JOHNSON
12-7

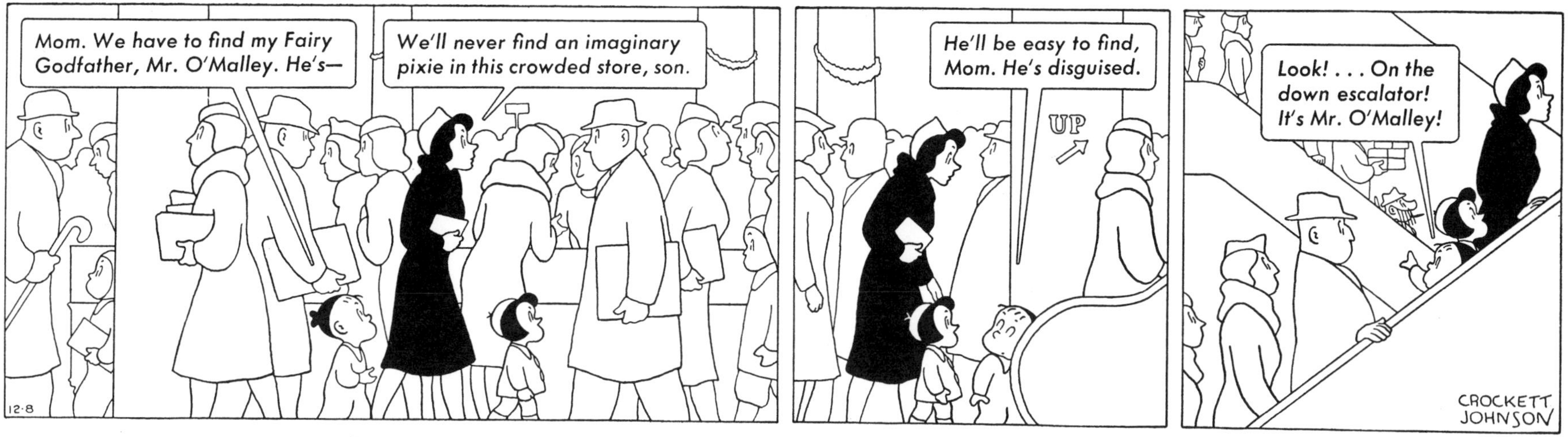
Mom. We have to find my Fairy Godfather, Mr. O'Malley. He's—
We'll never find an imaginary pixie in this crowded store, son.
He'll be easy to find, Mom. He's disguised.
UP
Look! . . . On the down escalator! It's Mr. O'Malley!
CROCKETT JOHNSON
12·8

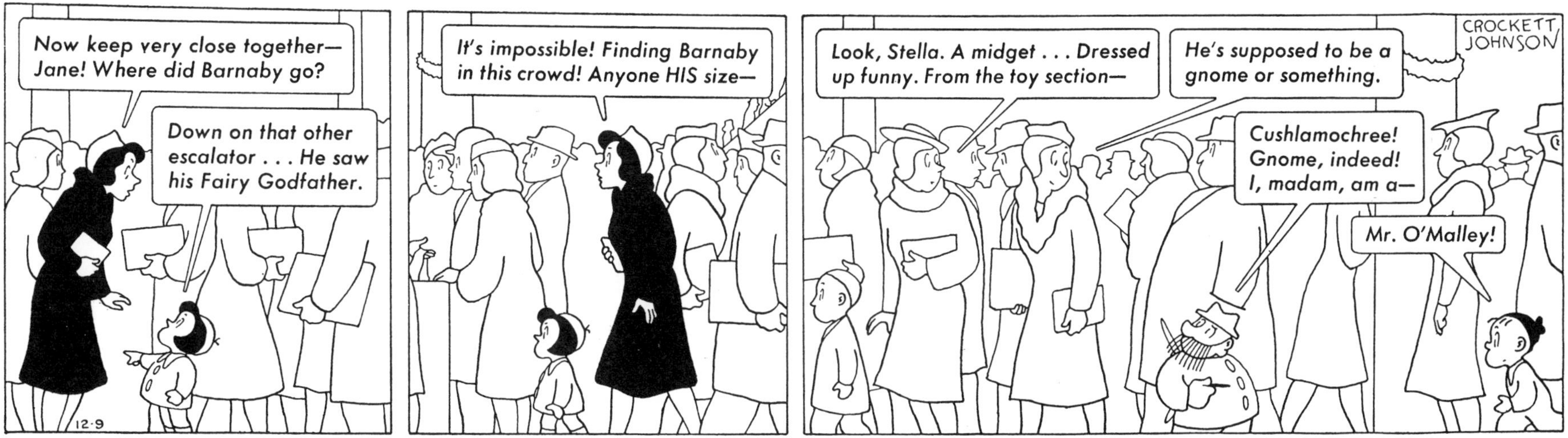
Now keep very close together— Jane! Where did Barnaby go?
Down on that other escalator . . . He saw his Fairy Godfather.
It's impossible! Finding Barnaby in this crowd! Anyone HIS size—
Look, Stella. A midget . . . Dressed up funny. From the toy section—
He's supposed to be a gnome or something.
Cushlamochree! Gnome, indeed! I, madam, am a—
Mr. O'Malley!
CROCKETT JOHNSON
12·9

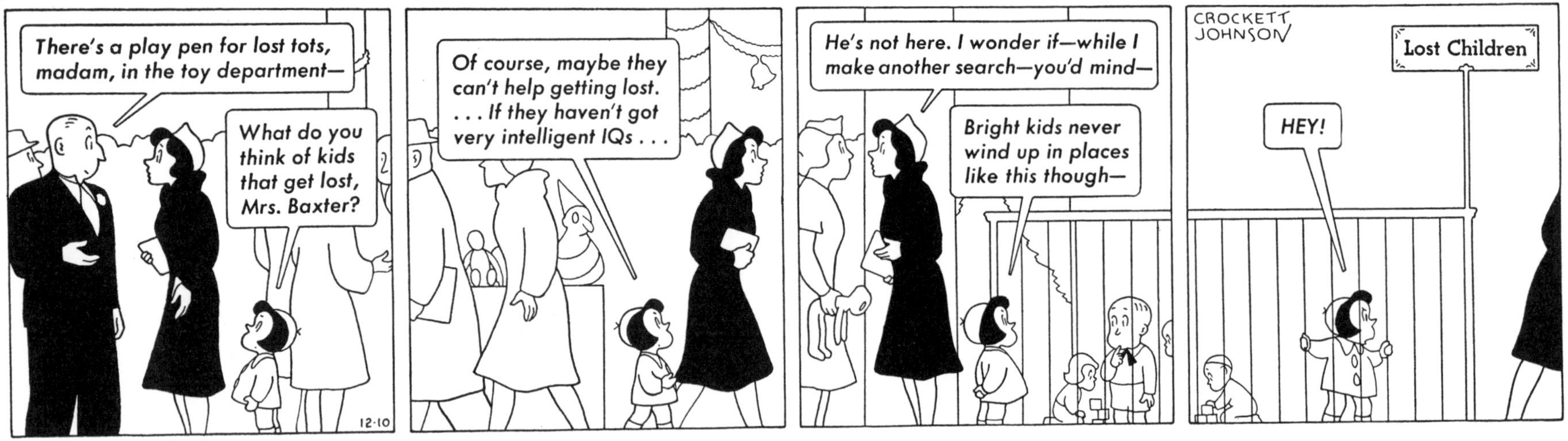
There's a play pen for lost tots, madam, in the toy department—
What do you think of kids that get lost, Mrs. Baxter?
12-10
Of course, maybe they can't help getting lost. . . . If they haven't got very intelligent IQs . . .
He's not here. I wonder if—while I make another search—you'd mind—
Bright kids never wind up in places like this though—
CROCKETT JOHNSON
Lost Children
HEY!

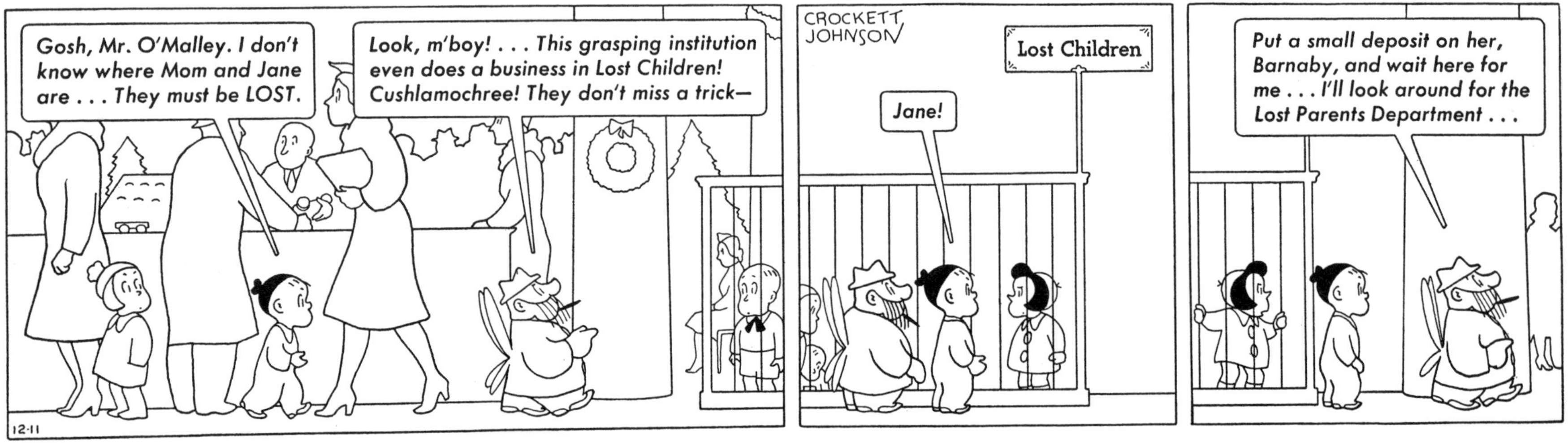
Gosh, Mr. O'Malley. I don't know where Mom and Jane are . . . They must be LOST.
Look, m'boy! . . . This grasping institution even does a business in Lost Children! Cushlamochree! They don't miss a trick—
12-11
CROCKETT JOHNSON
Lost Children
Jane!
Put a small deposit on her, Barnaby, and wait here for me . . . I'll look around for the Lost Parents Department . . .

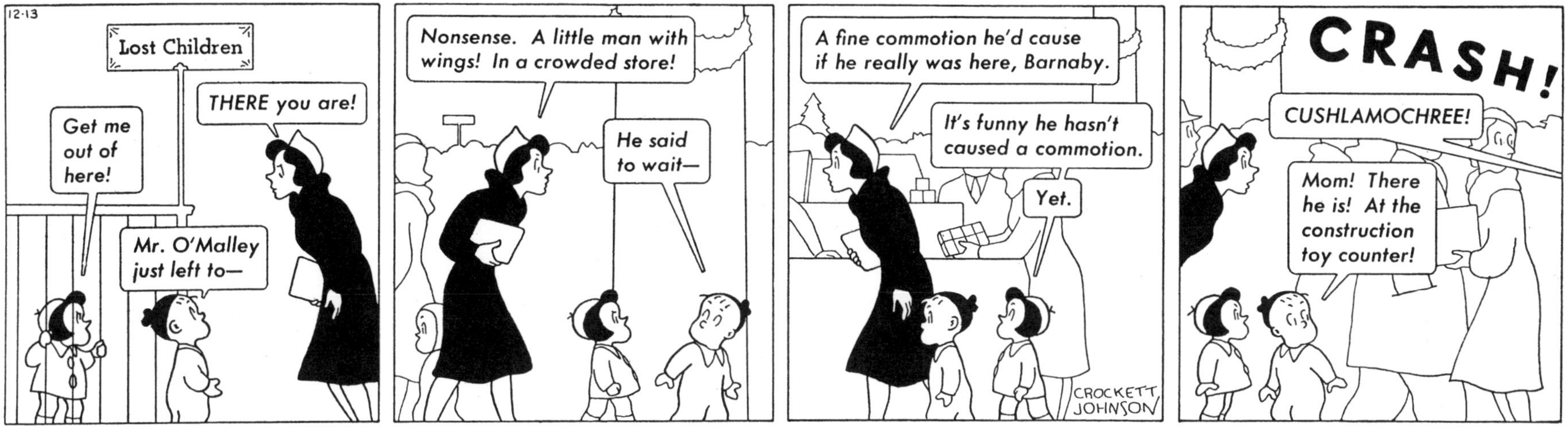
12-13
Lost Children
Get me out of here!
THERE you are!
Mr. O'Malley just left to—
Nonsense. A little man with wings! In a crowded store!
He said to wait—
A fine commotion he'd cause if he really was here, Barnaby.
It's funny he hasn't caused a commotion.
Yet.
CROCKETT JOHNSON
CRASH!
CUSHLAMOCHREE!
Mom! There he is! At the construction toy counter!

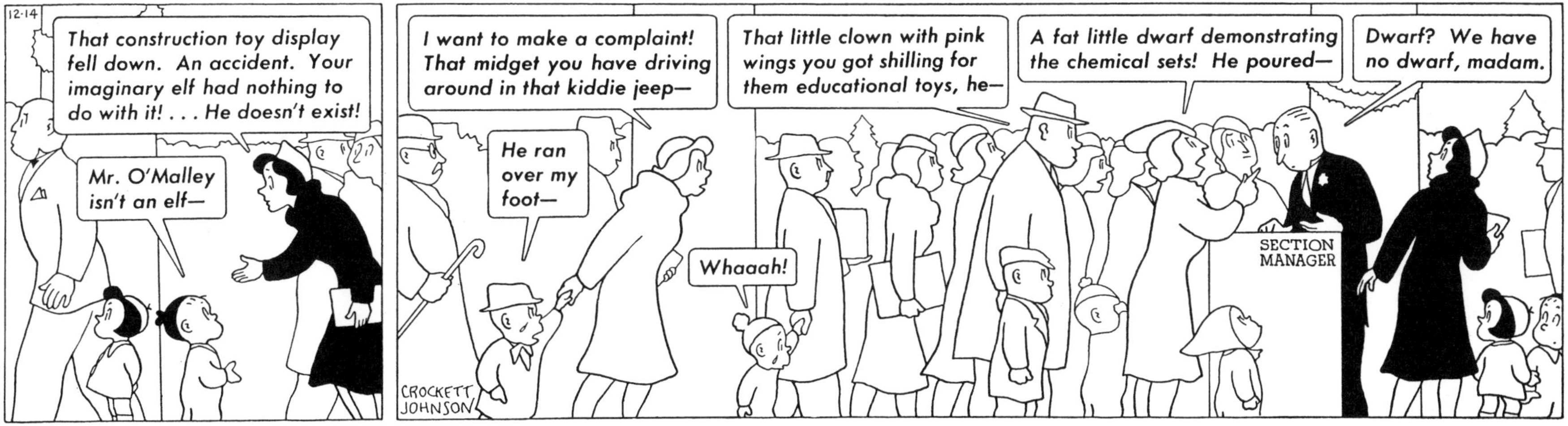
12-14
That construction toy display fell down. An accident. Your imaginary elf had nothing to do with it! . . . He doesn't exist!
Mr. O'Malley isn't an elf—
I want to make a complaint! That midget you have driving around in that kiddie jeep—
He ran over my foot—
That little clown with pink wings you got shilling for them educational toys, he—
Whaaah!
A fat little dwarf demonstrating the chemical sets! He poured—
Dwarf? We have no dwarf, madam.
SECTION MANAGER
CROCKETT JOHNSON

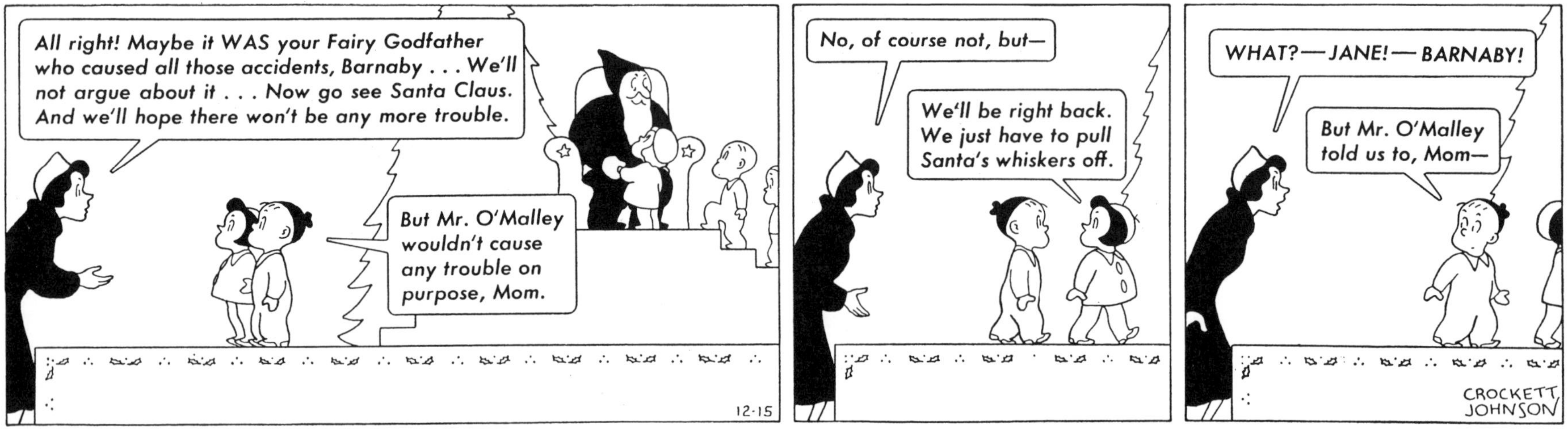
All right! Maybe it WAS your Fairy Godfather who caused all those accidents, Barnaby . . . We'll not argue about it . . . Now go see Santa Claus. And we'll hope there won't be any more trouble.
But Mr. O'Malley wouldn't cause any trouble on purpose, Mom.
12-15
No, of course not, but—
We'll be right back. We just have to pull Santa's whiskers off.
WHAT?—JANE!—BARNABY!
But Mr. O'Malley told us to, Mom—
CROCKETT JOHNSON

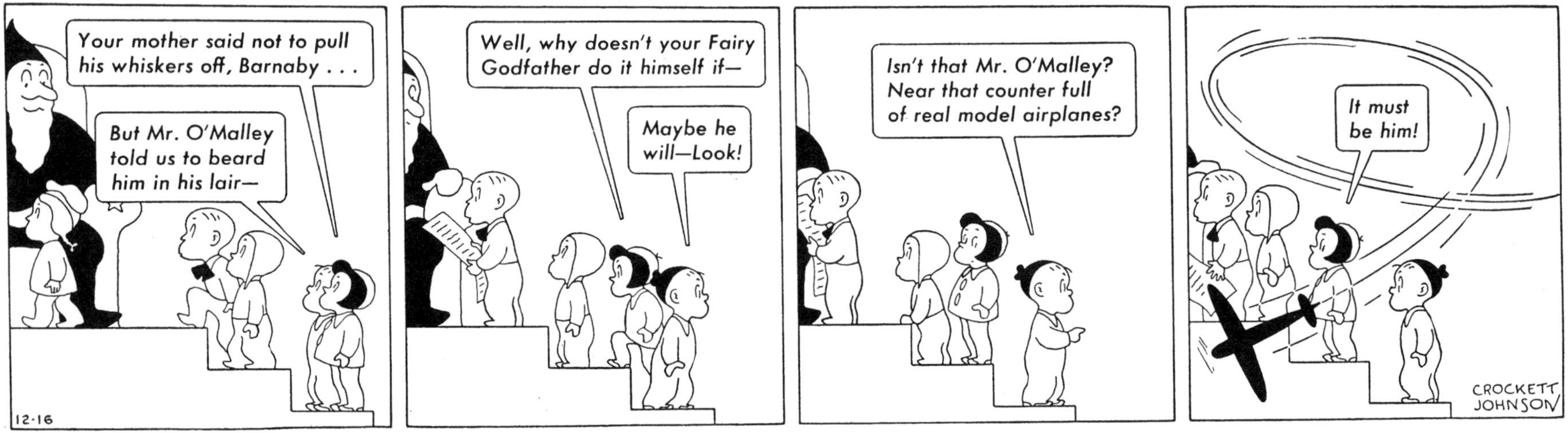
Your mother said not to pull his whiskers off, Barnaby . . .
But Mr. O'Malley told us to beard him in his lair—
12-16
Well, why doesn't your Fairy Godfather do it himself if—
Maybe he will—Look!
Isn't that Mr. O'Malley? Near that counter full of real model airplanes?
It must be him!
CROCKETT JOHNSON

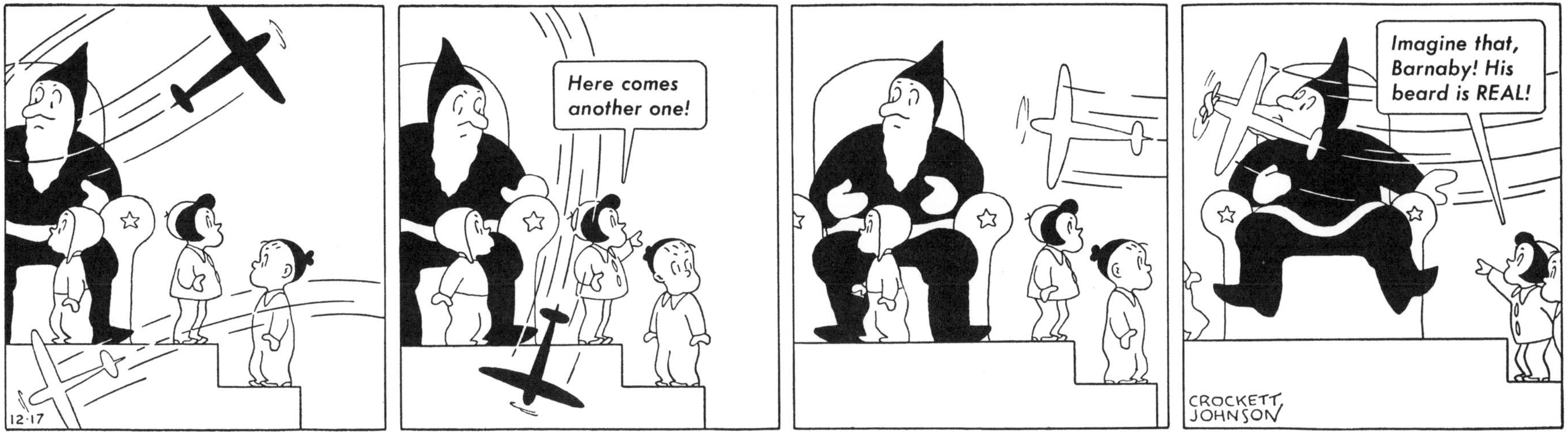
Here comes another one!
Imagine that, Barnaby! His beard is REAL!
CROCKETT JOHNSON
12-17

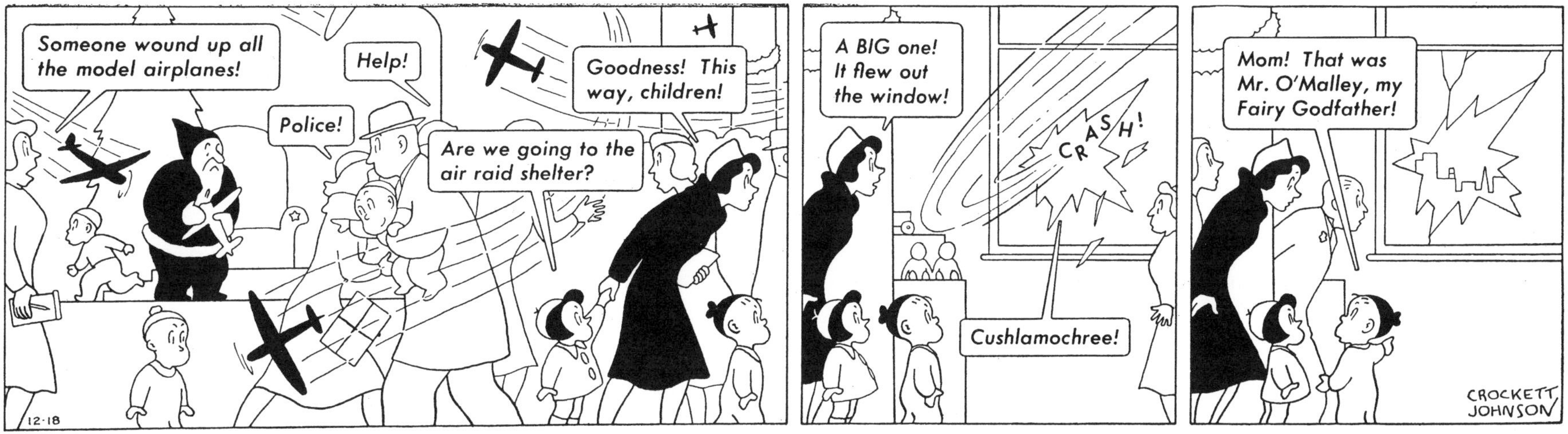
Someone wound up all the model airplanes!
Help!
Police!
Goodness! This way, children!
Are we going to the air raid shelter?
A BIG one! It flew out the window!
CRASH!
Cushlamochree!
Mom! That was Mr. O'Malley, my Fairy Godfather!
CROCKETT JOHNSON
12-18

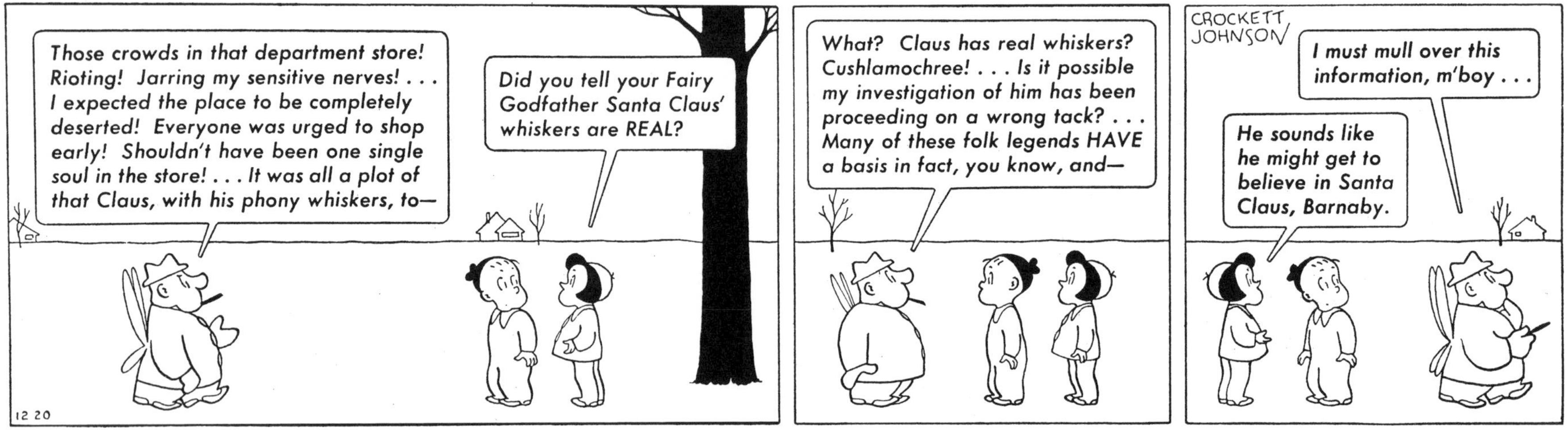
Those crowds in that department store! Rioting! Jarring my sensitive nerves! . . . I expected the place to be completely deserted! Everyone was urged to shop early! Shouldn't have been one single soul in the store! . . . It was all a plot of that Claus, with his phony whiskers, to—
Did you tell your Fairy Godfather Santa Claus' whiskers are REAL?
What? Claus has real whiskers? Cushlamochree! . . . Is it possible my investigation of him has been proceeding on a wrong tack? . . . Many of these folk legends HAVE a basis in fact, you know, and—
CROCKETT JOHNSON
I must mull over this information, m'boy . . .
He sounds like he might get to believe in Santa Claus, Barnaby.
12 20

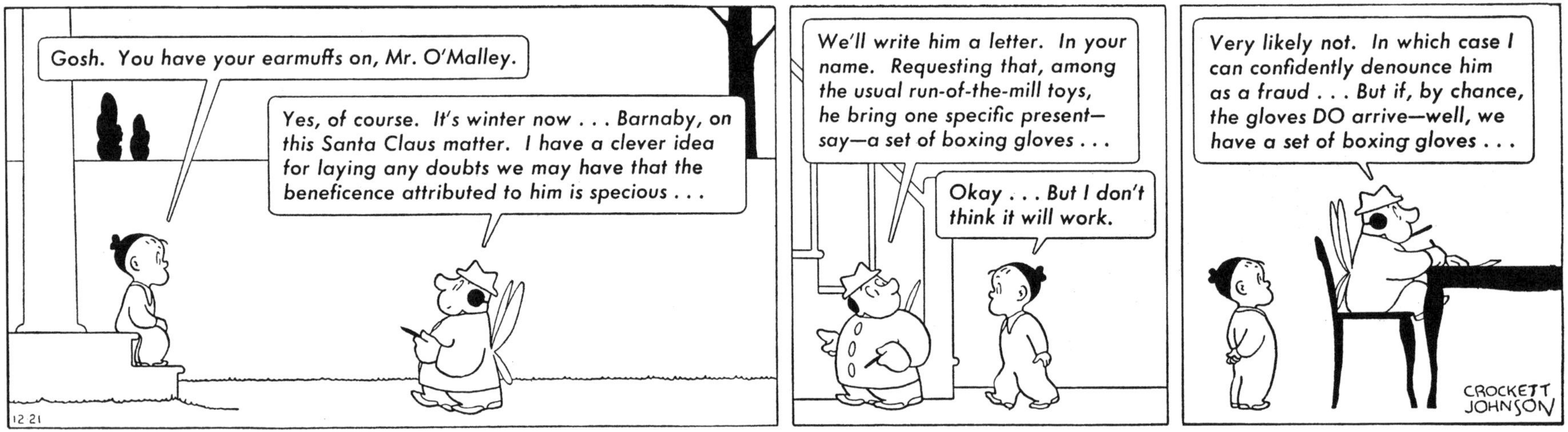
Gosh. You have your earmuffs on, Mr. O'Malley.
Yes, of course. It's winter now . . . Barnaby, on this Santa Claus matter. I have a clever idea for laying any doubts we may have that the beneficence attributed to him is specious . . .
We'll write him a letter. In your name. Requesting that, among the usual run-of-the-mill toys, he bring one specific present— say—a set of boxing gloves . . .
Okay . . . But I don't think it will work.
Very likely not. In which case I can confidently denounce him as a fraud . . . But if, by chance, the gloves DO arrive—well, we have a set of boxing gloves . . .
CROCKETT JOHNSON
12 21

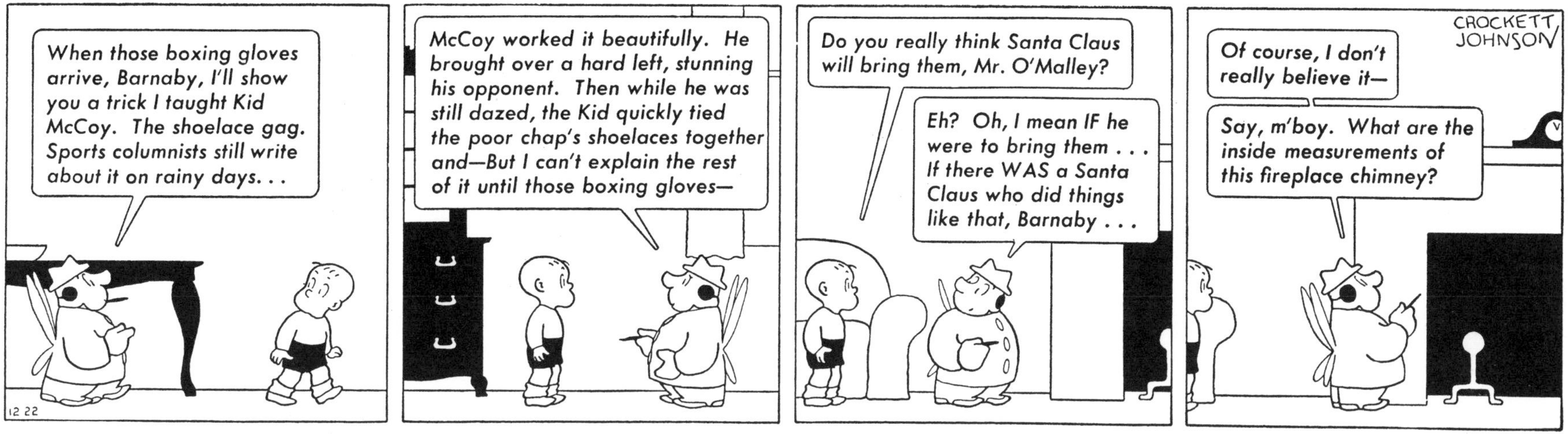
When those boxing gloves arrive, Barnaby, I'll show you a trick I taught Kid McCoy. The shoelace gag. Sports columnists still write about it on rainy days. . .
12 22
McCoy worked it beautifully. He brought over a hard left, stunning his opponent. Then while he was still dazed, the Kid quickly tied the poor chap's shoelaces together and—But I can't explain the rest of it until those boxing gloves—
Do you really think Santa Claus will bring them, Mr. O'Malley?
Eh? Oh, I mean IF he were to bring them . . . If there WAS a Santa Claus who did things like that, Barnaby . . .
CROCKETT JOHNSON
Of course, I don't really believe it—
Say, m'boy. What are the inside measurements of this fireplace chimney?

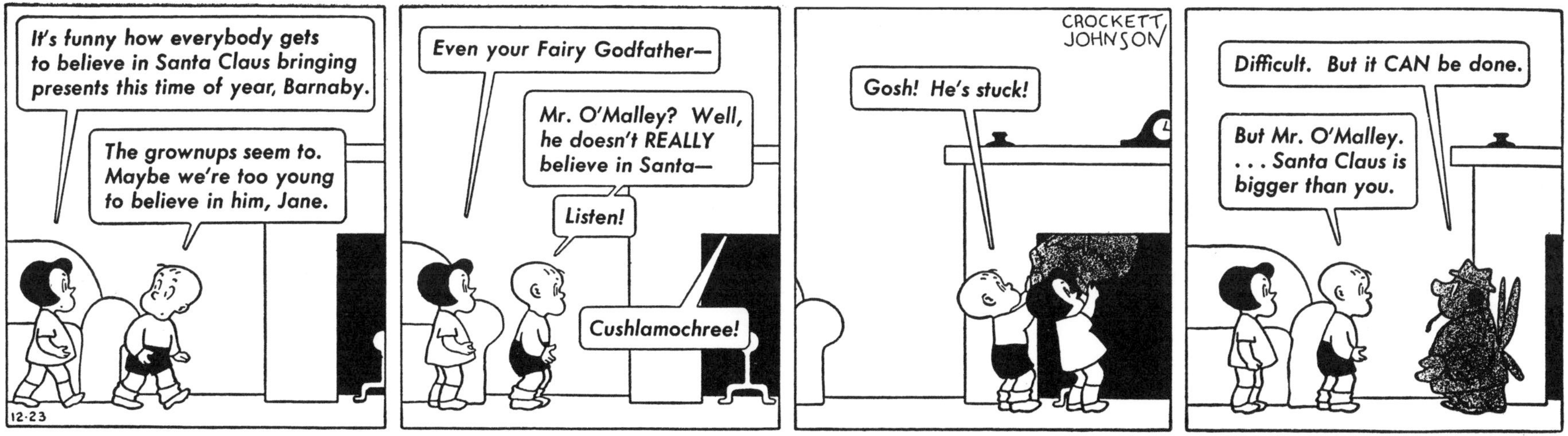
It's funny how everybody gets to believe in Santa Claus bringing presents this time of year, Barnaby.
The grownups seem to. Maybe we're too young to believe in him, Jane.
12·23
Even your Fairy Godfather—
Mr. O'Malley? Well, he doesn't REALLY believe in Santa—
Listen!
Cushlamochree!
CROCKETT JOHNSON
Gosh! He's stuck!
Difficult. But it CAN be done.
But Mr. O'Malley. . . . Santa Claus is bigger than you.

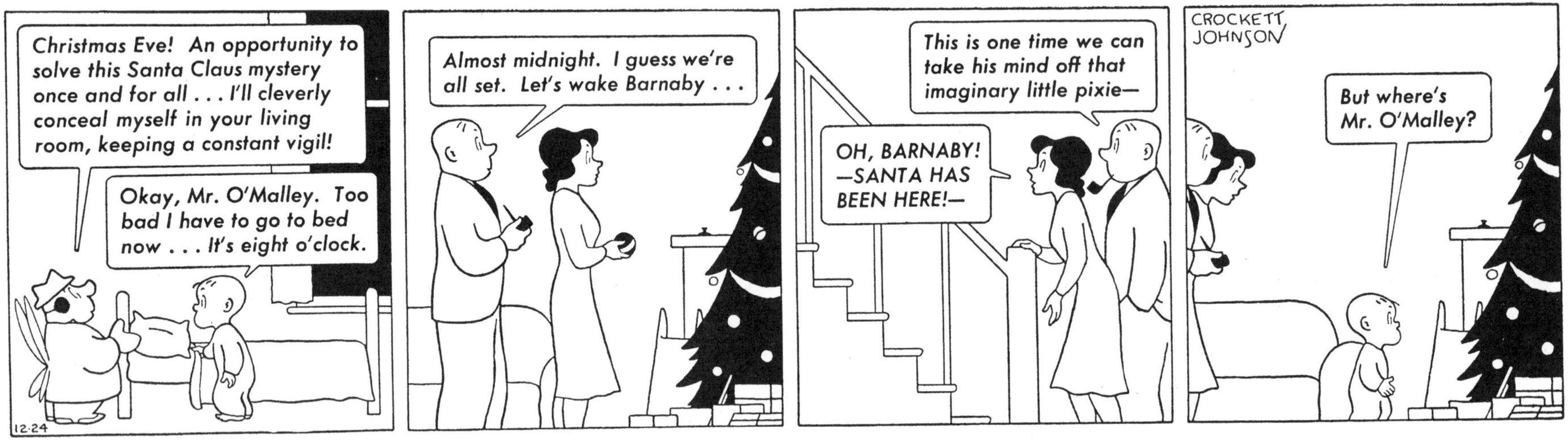
Christmas Eve! An opportunity to solve this Santa Claus mystery once and for all . . . I'll cleverly conceal myself in your living room, keeping a constant vigil!
Okay, Mr. O'Malley. Too bad I have to go to bed now . . . It's eight o'clock.
12·24
Almost midnight. I guess we're all set. Let's wake Barnaby . . .
This is one time we can take his mind off that imaginary little pixie—
OH, BARNABY! —SANTA HAS BEEN HERE!—
CROCKETT JOHNSON
But where's Mr. O'Malley?

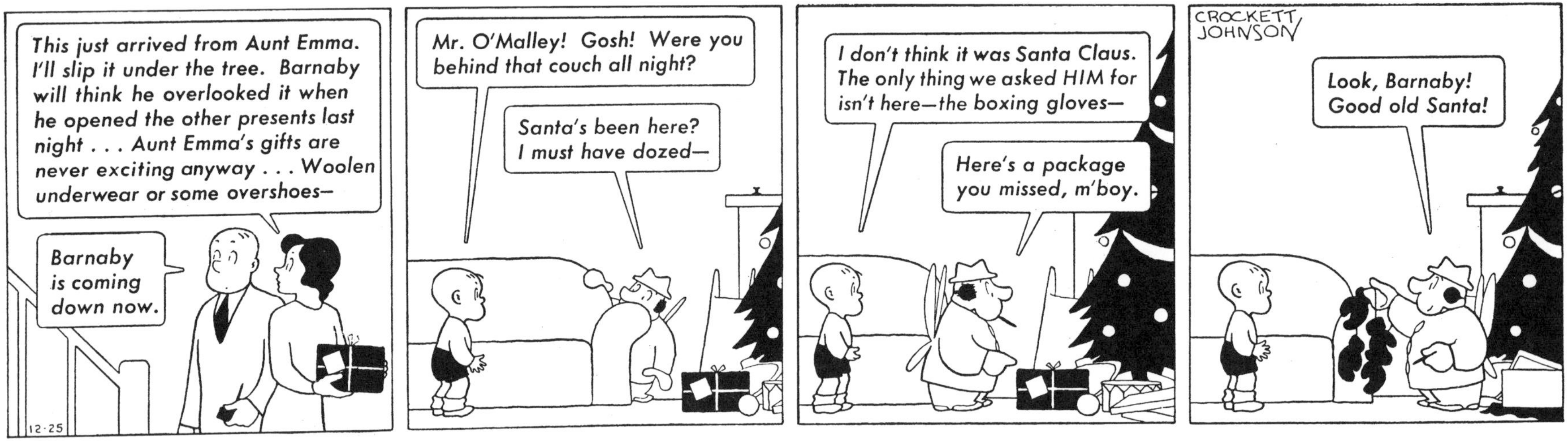
This just arrived from Aunt Emma. I'll slip it under the tree. Barnaby will think he overlooked it when he opened the other presents last night . . . Aunt Emma's gifts are never exciting anyway . . . Woolen underwear or some overshoes—
Barnaby is coming down now.
12·25
Mr. O'Malley! Gosh! Were you behind that couch all night?
Santa's been here? I must have dozed—
I don't think it was Santa Claus. The only thing we asked HIM for isn't here—the boxing gloves—
Here's a package you missed, m'boy.
CROCKETT JOHNSON
Look, Barnaby! Good old Santa!

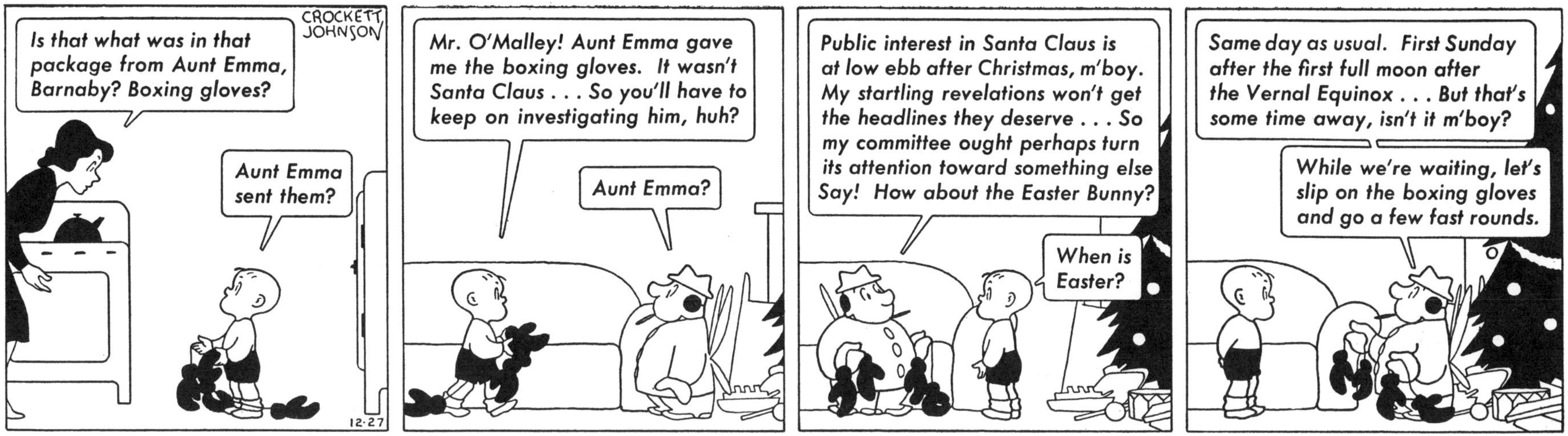
CROCKETT JOHNSON
Is that what was in that package from Aunt Emma, Barnaby? Boxing gloves?
Aunt Emma sent them?
12-27
Mr. O'Malley! Aunt Emma gave me the boxing gloves. It wasn't Santa Claus . . . So you'll have to keep on investigating him, huh?
Aunt Emma?
Public interest in Santa Claus is at low ebb after Christmas, m'boy. My startling revelations won't get the headlines they deserve . . . So my committee ought perhaps turn its attention toward something else Say! How about the Easter Bunny?
When is Easter?
Same day as usual. First Sunday after the first full moon after the Vernal Equinox . . . But that's some time away, isn't it m'boy?
While we're waiting, let's slip on the boxing gloves and go a few fast rounds.

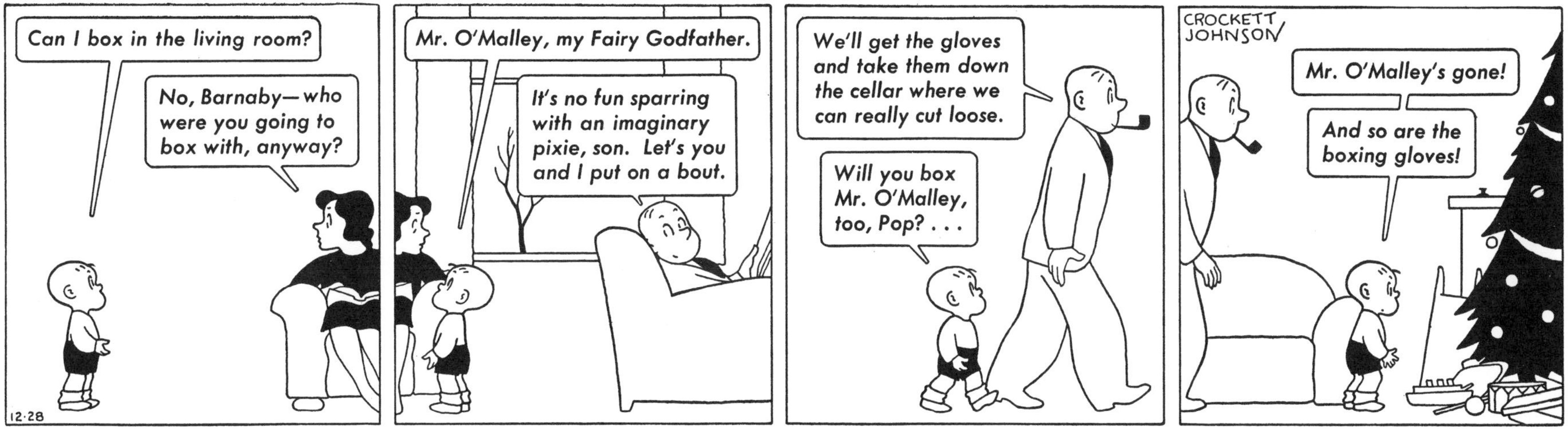
Can I box in the living room?
No, Barnaby—who were you going to box with, anyway?
12-28
Mr. O'Malley, my Fairy Godfather.
It's no fun sparring with an imaginary pixie, son. Let's you and I put on a bout.
We'll get the gloves and take them down the cellar where we can really cut loose.
Will you box Mr. O'Malley, too, Pop? . . .
CROCKETT JOHNSON
Mr. O'Malley's gone!
And so are the boxing gloves!

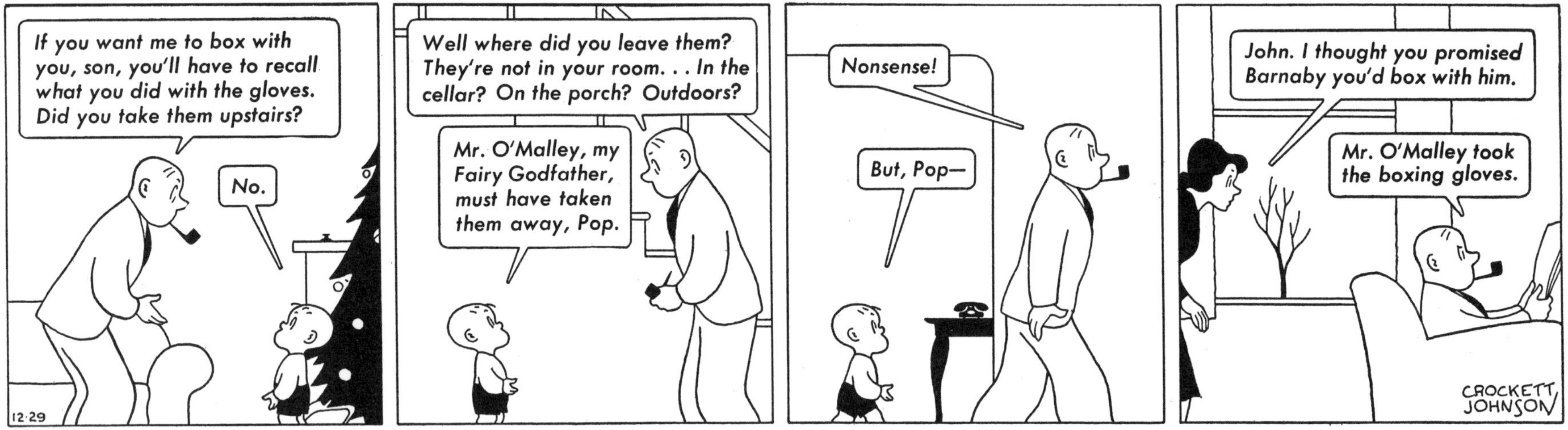
If you want me to box with you, son, you'll have to recall what you did with the gloves. Did you take them upstairs?
No.
Well where did you leave them? They're not in your room. . . In the cellar? On the porch? Outdoors?
Mr. O'Malley, my Fairy Godfather, must have taken them away, Pop.
Nonsense!
But, Pop—
John. I thought you promised Barnaby you'd box with him.
Mr. O'Malley took the boxing gloves.
12·29
CROCKETT JOHNSON

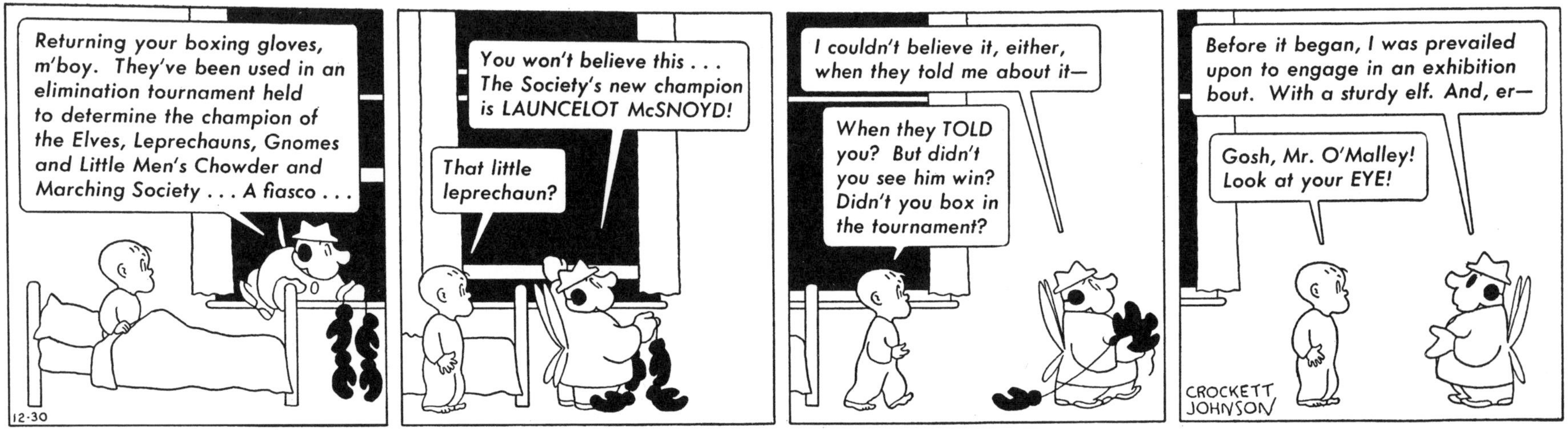
Returning your boxing gloves, m'boy. They've been used in an elimination tournament held to determine the champion of the Elves, Leprechauns, Gnomes and Little Men's Chowder and Marching Society . . . A fiasco . . .
You won't believe this . . . The Society's new champion is LAUNCELOT McSNOYD!
That little leprechaun?
I couldn't believe it, either, when they told me about it—
When they TOLD you? But didn't you see him win? Didn't you box in the tournament?
Before it began, I was prevailed upon to engage in an exhibition bout. With a sturdy elf. And, er—
Gosh, Mr. O'Malley! Look at your EYE!
12·30
CROCKETT JOHNSON

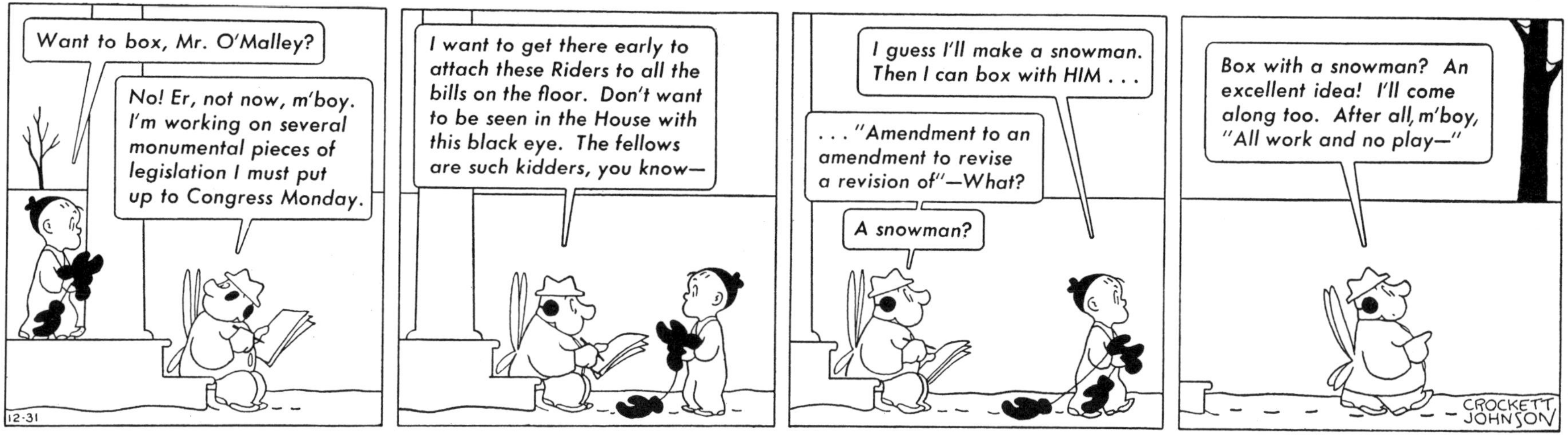
Want to box, Mr. O'Malley?
No! Er, not now, m'boy. I'm working on several monumental pieces of legislation I must put up to Congress Monday.
12-31
I want to get there early to attach these Riders to all the bills on the floor. Don't want to be seen in the House with this black eye. The fellows are such kidders, you know—
I guess I'll make a snowman. Then I can box with HIM . . .
. . . "Amendment to an amendment to revise a revision of"—What?
A snowman?
Box with a snowman? An excellent idea! I'll come along too. After all, m'boy, "All work and no play—"
CROCKETT JOHNSON

. . . continued in Volume 2

Cushlamochree! Broke my magic wand!
You wished for a Godparent who could grant wishes?
Lucky boy! Your wish is granted!

— **Mr. O'Malley, 21 April 1942**

AFTERWORD:
Crockett Johnson and the Invention of *Barnaby*

By Philip Nel

A boy named Barnaby wishes for a fairy godmother. Instead, he gets a Fairy Godfather who uses a cigar for a magic wand. Bumbling, loquacious, but endearing, Mr. O'Malley rarely gets his magic to work — even when he consults his *Fairy Godfather's Handy Pocket Guide*. The true magic of *Barnaby* resides in its canny mix of fantasy and satire, amplified by the understated elegance of Crockett Johnson's clean, spare art. Using typeset dialogue (*Barnaby* was the first daily comic strip to do so regularly) allowed Johnson to include — by his estimation — some 60% more words, giving O'Malley more room to develop a rhetorical style that, as one critic put it, combines the "style of a medicine-show huckster with that of Dickens's Mr. Micawber." In its combination of Johnson's sly wit and O'Malley's amiable windbaggery, a child's feeling of wonder and an adult's wariness, highly literate jokes and a keen eye for the ridiculous, *Barnaby* expanded our sense of what comics can do.

Though one of the classic comic strips, *Barnaby* was never a popular hit — at its height, it was syndicated in only 52 papers. By contrast, Chic Young's *Blondie*, a strip with perhaps the largest circulation, was appearing in as many as 850 papers at that time. As Coulton Waugh noted in his landmark *The Comics*

(1947), *Barnaby*'s audience may not "compare, numerically, with that of the top, mass-appeal strips. But it is a very discriminating audience, which includes a number of strip artists themselves, and so this strip stands a good chance of remaining to influence the course of American humor for many years to come." He was right.

Barnaby's fans have included *Peanuts* creator Charles Schulz, *Family Circus* creator Bil Keane, and graphic novelists Daniel Clowes, Art Spiegelman and Chris Ware. It had many fans beyond the world of comics, too. Composers Duke Ellington and Michael Kamen were both admirers. Dorothy Parker compared *Barnaby* to Mark Twain's *Huckleberry Finn*, and said: "I think, and I am trying to talk calmly, that Barnaby and his friends and oppressors are the most important additions to American arts and letters in Lord knows how many years. I know that they are the most important additions to my heart."

It had a smaller following than other strips, but its admirers were both more influential and more devoted. As Johnson wryly observed in late 1942, "If *Dick Tracy* were dropped from the *News*, 300,000 readers would say, 'Oh dear!' But if *Barnaby* went from [the newspaper] *PM*, his 300 readers would write indignant letters." Though he didn't say so, even reaching those 300 readers was an uphill struggle. If not for a chance meeting with an art editor, Crockett Johnson's graphic masterpiece might never have been published at all.

> **Barnaby. Has anyone ever spoken to you about that imagination of yours? . . .**
>
> — Mr. O'Malley, 25 Nov. 1943

In 1939, Crockett Johnson turned 33, fell in love and began considering a career as a syndicated cartoonist. He'd spent most of his career as an art editor — in 1927, for *Aviation* magazine, and then, in 1929, for a half-dozen McGraw-Hill trade publications. In 1934, he began contributing cartoons to *New Masses*, becoming in 1936 its art editor, a job that paid only $20-$25 per week.

He wasn't working at the Communist weekly for the money. He was there because he believed in its message. His *New Masses* cartoons attack fascists, mock fat-cat capitalists, express doubt that Roosevelt can solve the economic crisis, and argue for international socialism. Still, he thought, perhaps a daily comic strip would provide him with a better source of income. Maybe it was time for a change.

Johnson was then facing other big decisions. After a half-dozen years together, he and his wife Charlotte had decided to divorce. In the fall of 1939, at a party either in Greenwich Village or on Fire Island (sources differ), the soft-spoken, taciturn Johnson met the outgoing, adventurous Ruth Krauss. Recently divorced herself, she was a slender five-feet-four. He was nearly six feet tall, with the build of an ex-football player. Her exuberance drew him out of his natural reticence, and into conversation. Complementary opposites, they felt an immediate attraction to one another. Within a year, she moved into his West Village apartment, he left *New Masses*, and invented a strip that would become a minor classic.

Popularly known as *The Little Man with the Eyes*, Johnson's first comic strip was nearly wordless. Reminiscent of Otto Soglow's *The Little King* in both its spare, clean line and its gentle humor, *The Little Man* made its debut in *Collier's* weekly in March 1940. Using only the caption and the movement of the central character's eyes, the strip offered comic observations on life's daily absurdities. During its nearly-three-year run, it became popular enough to inspire an advertising campaign for Ford later in the decade.

The Little Man was largely apolitical. Johnson, however, was very political. In April of 1940, he donated original artwork to help raise money for the financially-strapped *New Masses*. In May, he contributed his final cartoon to the magazine. "A Liberal at the Crossroads" made clear that there was no time for dithering; war was coming, and America had better get prepared. When, in September, President Roosevelt began the first peacetime conscription in U.S. history, Johnson registered — even though, at age 33, he was not required to do so. (The Selective Training and Service Act required men between 21 and 30 to register.) The military recorded that he was five-feet-eleven inches tall, 215 pounds, with blue eyes and blond hair that is "thin in front" — a feature he comically exaggerated in a self-caricature he did that November.

Seeking a strip with a wider scope than *The Little Man*, by late 1940 he had the idea of building a daily comic around a precocious five-year-old boy living in a proper suburban home. He realized that he had always been thinking of the boy as "Barnaby," and so that became the title character's name. After drawing a few episodes, he realized that Barnaby wasn't enough to sustain the strip. So, as he said, "I fumbled around, just like O'Malley, and O'Malley came in by himself."

With the introduction of Barnaby's cigar-champing con artist of a Fairy Godfather, Johnson's strip found its source of narrative conflict, satire and possibility. Though O'Malley made the strip work, Johnson couldn't interest a syndicate in *Barnaby*. In the middle of 1941, he and a couple of friends formed Colored

1
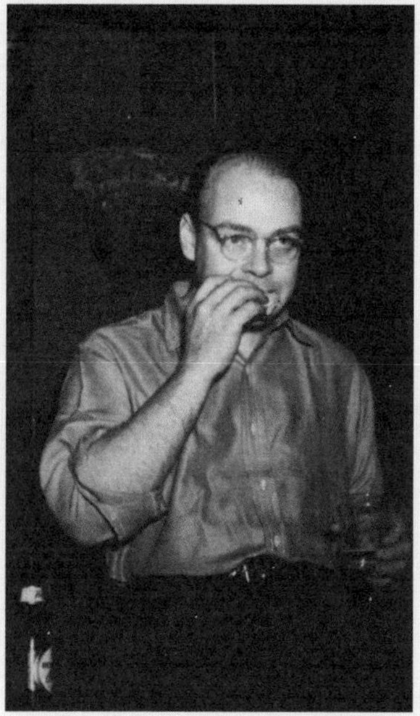

2
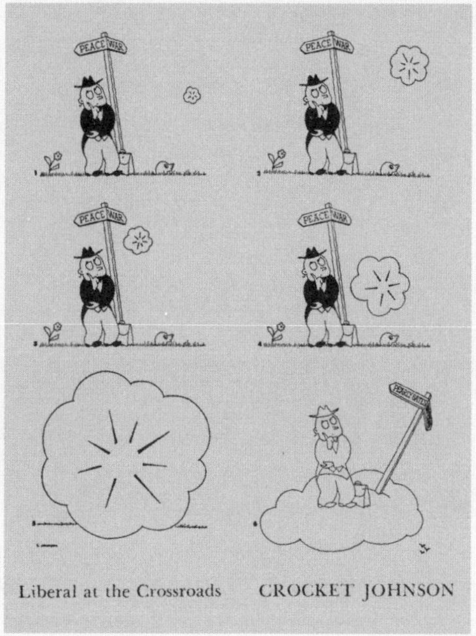
PEACE
WAR
Liberal at the Crossroads
CROCKET JOHNSON

3
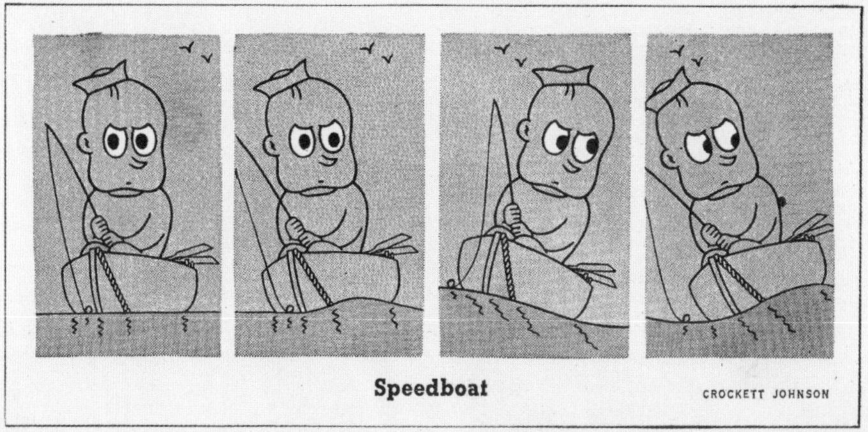
Speedboat
CROCKETT JOHNSON

4
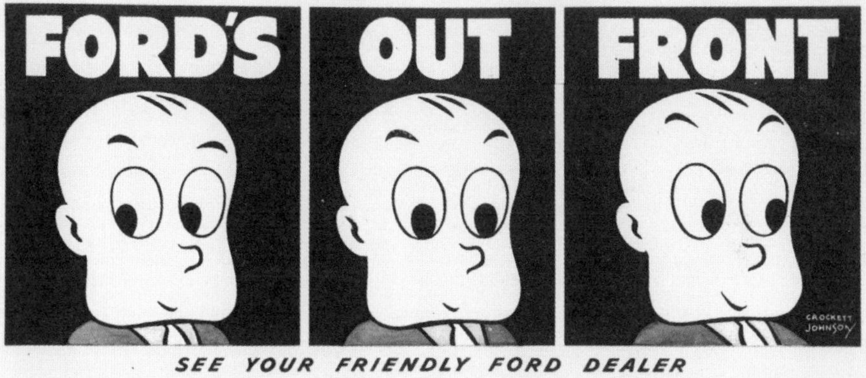
FORD'S
OUT
FRONT
CROCKETT JOHNSON
SEE YOUR FRIENDLY FORD DEALER

1. *Crockett Johnson, c. late 1930s. Image courtesy of the Smithsonian Institution.*
2. *Crockett Johnson, "Liberal at the Crossroads."* New Masses, *14 May 1940, reprinted in Joseph* North's New Masses: An Anthology of the Rebel Thirties.
3. *Crockett Johnson,* The Little Man with the Eyes, Collier's, *6 April 1940.*
4. *Crockett Johnson, "Ford's Out Front." Advertisement produced for the J. Walter Thompson Company, 1947.*

5

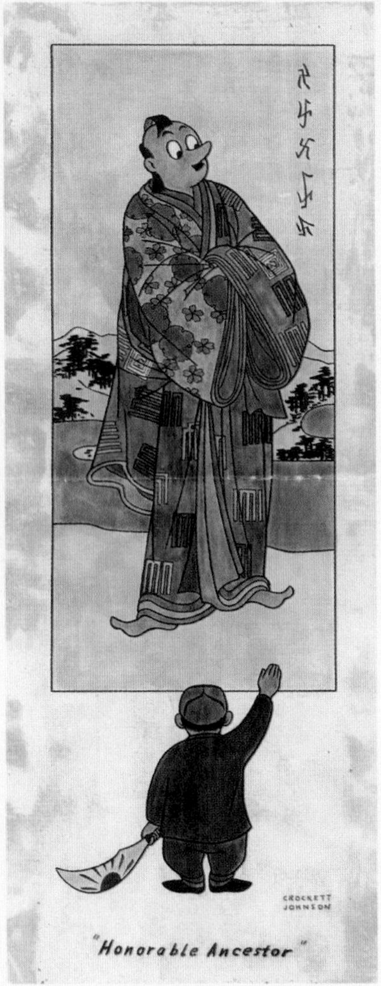
CROCKETT JOHNSON
"Honorable Ancestor"

Continuities, thinking that they could syndicate their comics through their own agency. That plan failed.

In addition to writing *The Little Man,* Johnson was busy. When the Japanese attack on Pearl Harbor drew America into World War II, he was not called to serve. Instead, in January of 1942, he co-founded the American Society of Magazine Cartoonists' Committee on War Cartoons. The following month at the Art Students League, the Committee's *Artists Against the Axis* exhibition made its debut. Charles Addams, Peter Arno, Maurice Becker, William Gropper, Syd Hoff, Charles Martin, Garret Price, Gardner Rea, Ad Reinhardt, Carl Rose, Saul Steinberg, Arthur Szyk, Barney Tobey and of course Crockett Johnson all contributed work. The show would go on to tour the country, raising money for the Allied war effort.

Also in early 1942, Johnson and Krauss moved to the country – Darien, Connecticut. Now living on the coast of Long Island Sound, he could easily step out to go sailing in his boat. Only an hour's train ride to New York City, their new home was also easy commuting distance. He could attend to business in the city, and she could continue going to anthropology classes at Columbia. Away from the bustle of Manhattan, Johnson worked on *The Little Man* – and that strip might have been his best-known creation, but for a visit from his friend Charles Martin.

6

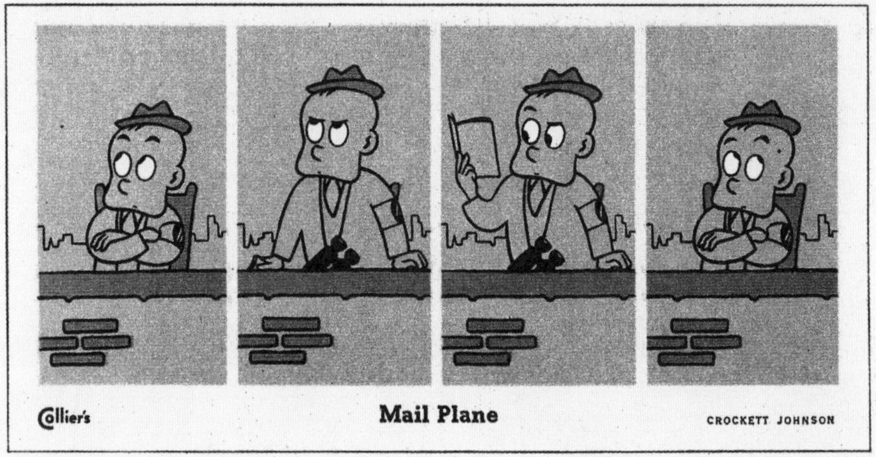
Collier's
Mail Plane
CROCKETT JOHNSON

Martin, whose work was included in the *Artists Against the Axis* show, had recently become Art Editor of the Popular Front newspaper *PM*. Founded in 1940, the newspaper originally included no comics, but by early 1942 it was carrying two strips – Dante Quinterno's *Patoruzu*, and the anti-Fascist adventure strip *Vic Jordan* by Paine (the pseudonym of Kermit Jaediker and Charles Zerner).

5. *Artists Against the Axis, February 1942. Image courtesy of the Terry-D'Alessio Collection, Museum of Comic and Cartoon Art.*
6. *Crockett Johnson,* The Little Man with the Eyes, Collier's, *3 Oct. 1942.*
7. *Crockett Johnson at home in Darien, Connecticut, 1942. Image courtesy of the Smithsonian Institution. Photo by Mary Morris for PM.*
8. *Crockett Johnson, advertisement for* Barnaby, *14 April 1942.*

7

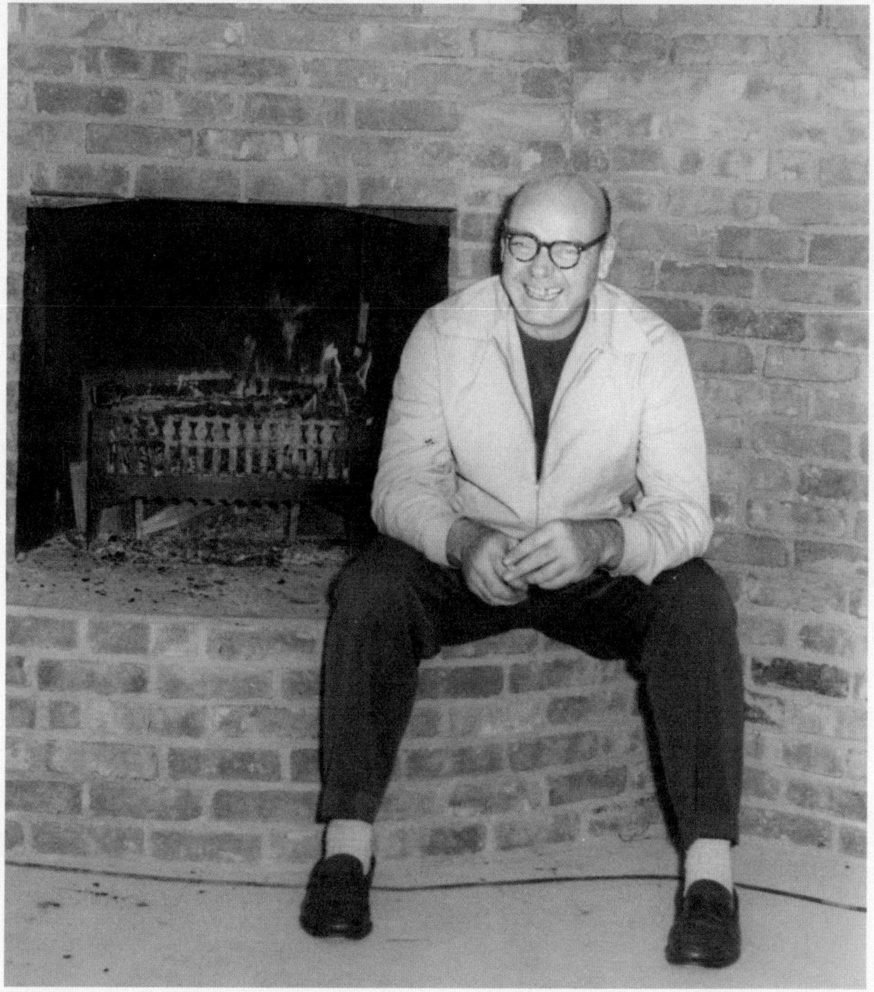

8

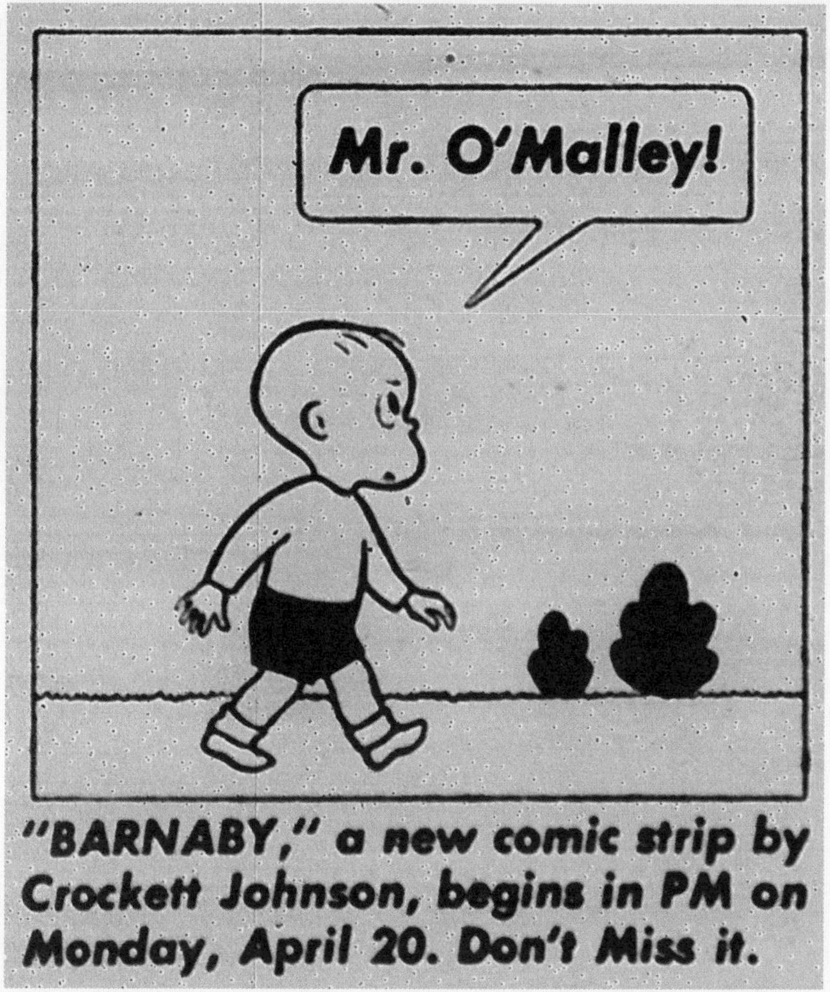
Mr. O'Malley!
"BARNABY," a new comic strip by Crockett Johnson, begins in PM on Monday, April 20. Don't Miss it.

9

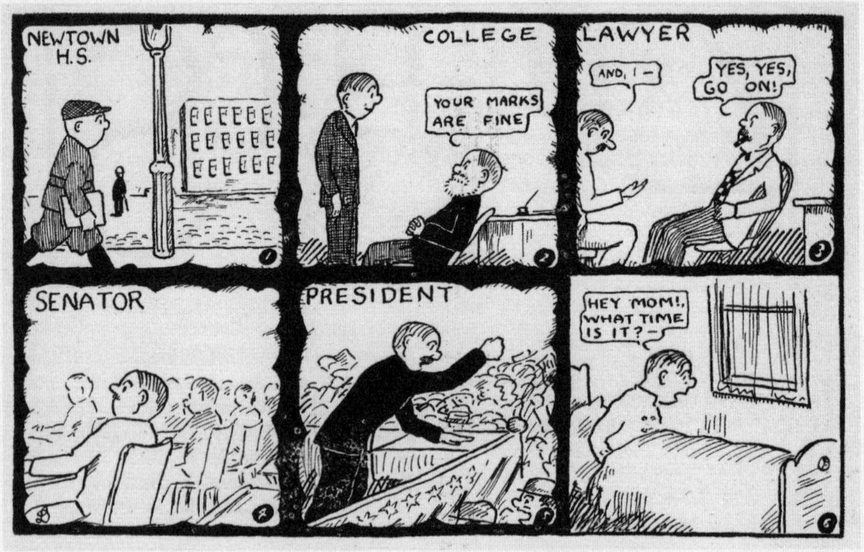
NEWTOWN H.S.
COLLEGE
YOUR MARKS ARE FINE
LAWYER
AND, I —
YES, YES, GO ON!
SENATOR
PRESIDENT
HEY MOM!, WHAT TIME IS IT? —

When Martin saw a half-page color Sunday *Barnaby* strip, he liked it and asked if he could bring it back to the city. Grateful for Martin's interest, Johnson said sure. Back in New York, Martin showed the strip to King Features. They didn't like it. He showed it to *PM*'s new Comics Editor Hannah Baker, and she loved it.

Thanks to her encouragement, on April 14th, 1942, *PM*'s readers got their first glimpse of Barnaby — he is walking, looking skyward, and calling "Mr. O'Malley!" This was the first of several ads announcing *Barnaby*'s debut the following week.

Though Johnson usually claimed that there was no one particular inspiration for Barnaby's fairy godfather, he did admit that "O'Malley is at least a hundred different people. A lot of people think he's W.C. Fields, but he isn't. Still you couldn't live in America and not put some of Fields into O'Malley. O'Malley is partly [New York] Mayor La Guardia and his cigar and eyes are occasionally borrowed from Jimmy Savo," the vaudeville comic and singer.

Likewise, Barnaby was also based on no particular children. "I don't get anything much from kids," he told the *Philadelphia Record*'s Charles Fisher. "How can you? They are all different. And I don't draw or write Barnaby for children. People who write for children usually write down to them. I don't believe in that." Told that children also like Barnaby, Johnson smiled and said, "I'm glad when I hear they do. You see ... well, when it comes to knowing about children, it's a terribly old thing to say, but everyone was once a child himself." In other words, Barnaby comes from the childhood of Crockett Johnson.

I'll just give you the bare facts of my story, Gus ... Ready, now? Ahem ... I was born in —

— Mr. O'Malley, 6 Mar. 1943

Born David Johnson Leisk in Manhattan on October 20, 1906, Crockett Johnson grew up in Corona, Queens — which was then much more like the suburban neighborhood where Barnaby lives. When the Leisk family moved there in around 1912, Queens was a new borough of New York, with plenty of undeveloped spaces for Dave and his younger sister Else to explore. A block west of their home were the Leverich Woods, where they could wander, finding new animals to adopt. They loved animals, and their father indulged them. In the *Barnaby* strip of December 30, 1942, Johnson has Mrs. Baxter compare the dog Gorgon's arrival to popular narrative clichés "of movies, comic strips, and radio sketches," in which parents insist they won't keep the dog, but "dog spots softest parent ... Turns on charm ...

9. *David Johnson Leisk, cartoon in* Newtown H.S. Lantern, *May 1921.*

10. *David Johnson Leisk, cover for* Newtown H.S. Lantern, *May 1922.*

Looks wistful, lovable, sad, friendly, sweet, good, winsome," and parent agrees to let the child have the pet. Johnson isn't only offering a bit of meta-commentary here; he's also remembering his father. Barnaby's dad lets Barnaby keep Gorgon, just as Johnson's dad let him and his sister keep the animals they found.

Johnson's fondness for exploring outside may have led him to a comic strip about frontiersman Davy Crockett. He was not the only "Dave" in the neighborhood, but he could become the only "Crockett." In the 1930s, he used this childhood nickname for the first half of his pen-name, "Crockett Johnson." But he otherwise did not use the name as an adult. Friends knew him as "Dave Johnson."

It's tempting to see in Johnson's invented name a parallel to Mr. O'Malley, also known as Jackeen J. O'Malley, Congressman O'Malley, C.E.O. of O'Malley Enterprises, and filmmaker J. Darryl O'Malley. As a character of possibility, O'Malley would hold a great appeal for a man of diverse interests. Even early in life, Johnson was curious about many different subjects, but did not know where his curiosity might lead — a predicament dramatized in a cartoon he drew for the May 1921 issue of his high school's literary magazine.

However, it's equally likely that autobiographical inspiration for O'Malley derives from Johnson's father, David Leisk. He shared with Barnaby's fairy godfather a creative mind, a taste for stories, a sense of possibility, and the fact that both men are foreigners. Born in the Shetland Islands, the elder David Leisk loved literature, wrote poetry, liked to sing, was a skilled carpenter, enjoyed his weekly pinochle game, and had worked as a journalist before becoming a bookkeeper at New York's Johnson Lumber Company — the source for his son's middle name.

Like Barnaby, young Crockett Johnson was an active child who enjoyed the outdoors — an experience which became harder to come by as Corona grew more developed and more polluted. His father built a sailboat in the backyard, and took Johnson and his sister sailing and swimming on Long Island Sound. However, Flushing's sewage emptied into the Sound and, by the time Johnson turned nine, the Board of Health advised against swimming there. Traces of the polluted outdoors

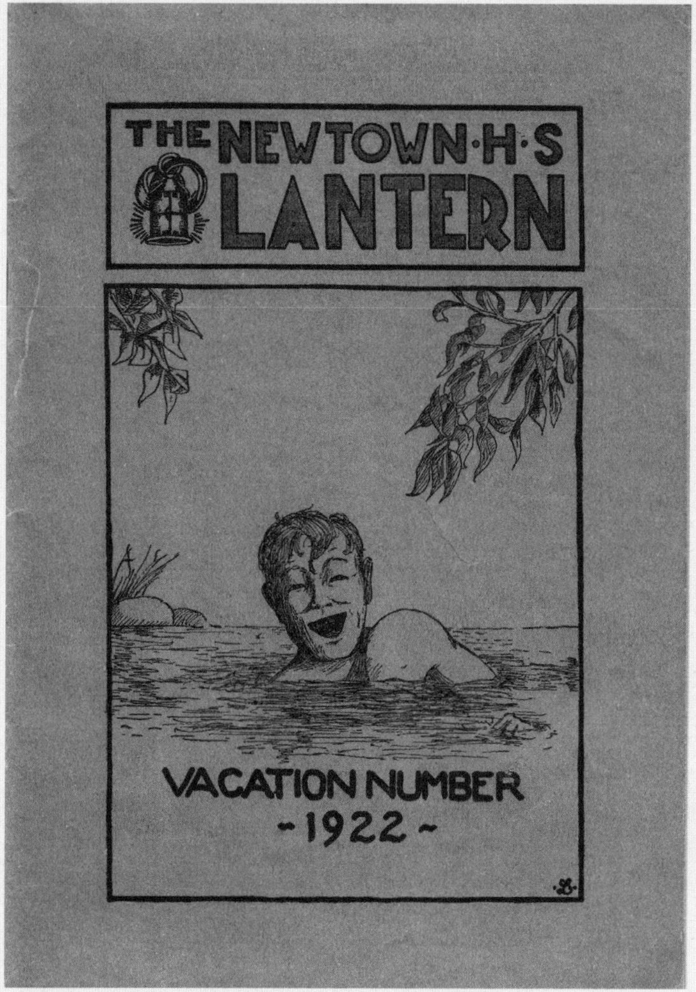
THE NEWTOWN·H·S
LANTERN
VACATION NUMBER
-1922-

10

emerge in Barnaby's world, such as the tire chain, egg beater and abandoned steamroller the five-year-old finds in November 1942.

That the steamroller is named Trilby highlights Crockett Johnson's fascination with odd facts. In addition to being the name of a hat worn by a character in the stage adaptation of George du Maurier's novel, *Trilby*, it's also the name of a U.S. Navy boat used in World War I and of a town in Florida. In calling the rusted steamroller Trilby, Johnson alludes to the absurdity of naming so many unlikely items after the novel's heroine. The best example of Johnson's interest in lesser-explored corners of knowledge is Mr. O'Malley's favorite expression, "Cushlamochree!" It's pronounced "Kush lah m' kree" – "Kush" as in "push," "lah" like the "la" in "umbrella," and "m' kree" as if it were written "McKree" or "Muh Kree," in which "Kree" rhymes with "tree." The primary accent falls on the first syllable, and the secondary accent on the last. What does it mean? Happily, Johnson himself answered that question, responding to a letter from a *Barnaby* fan in Cleveland.

His etymology reads as if he were writing it while sitting next to the *Compact Oxford English Dictionary*, open to the entry for "acushla." And it's highly likely that he was doing exactly that. Johnson enjoyed reference works, collecting peculiar facts – the very sort of information that O'Malley likes to cite, creatively mangling it in support of his latest scheme.

If Trilby and Cushlamochree are slightly obscure, many of his allusions would have been accessible to the educated reader. In the strip of 19 December 1942, O'Malley recalls his "Yukon days" and "a friend named McGrew – poor fellow," an allusion to Robert W. Service's "The Shooting of Dan McGrew," in which a mysterious stranger kills Dangerous Dan McGrew. That was a popular poem, and would have been known to Johnson's audience. Similarly, contemporary

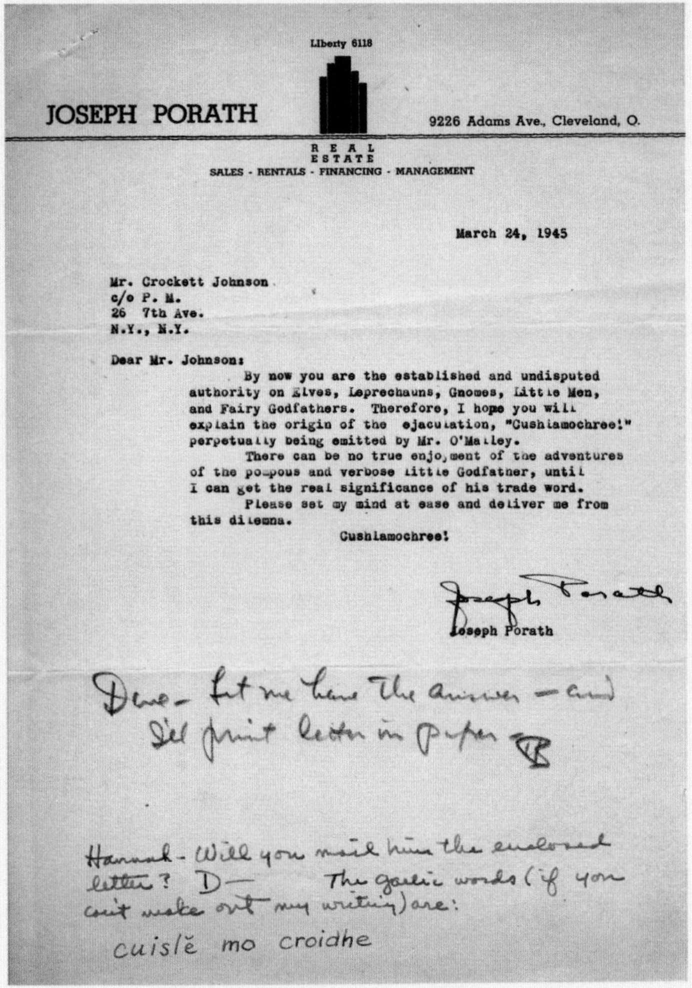

Liberty 6118

JOSEPH PORATH

9226 Adams Ave., Cleveland, O.

REAL ESTATE

SALES - RENTALS - FINANCING - MANAGEMENT

March 24, 1945

Mr. Crockett Johnson
c/o P. M.
26 7th Ave.
N.Y., N.Y.

Dear Mr. Johnson:

By now you are the established and undisputed authority on Elves, Leprechauns, Gnomes, Little Men, and Fairy Godfathers. Therefore, I hope you will explain the origin of the ejaculation, "Cushlamochree!" perpetually being emitted by Mr. O'Malley.

There can be no true enjoyment of the adventures of the pompous and verbose little Godfather, until I can get the real significance of his trade word.

Please set my mind at ease and deliver me from this dilemma.

Cushlamochree!

Joseph Porath

Joseph Porath

Dave- let me have the answer – and I'll print letter in paper

Hannah - Will you mail him the enclosed letter? D— The gaelic words (if you can't make out my writing) are:

cuislě mo croidhe

11

11. *Letter from Joseph Porath. Image courtesy of the Smithsonian Institution.*

12. *Reply from Crockett Johnson. Image courtesy of the Smithsonian Institution.*

12

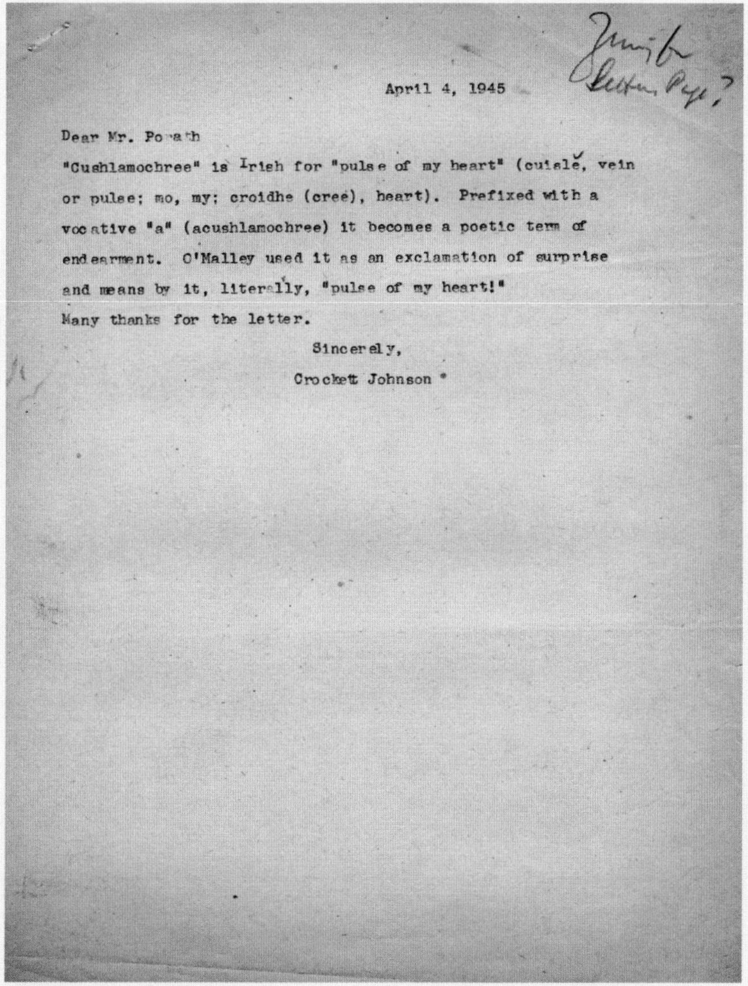
April 4, 1945

Dear Mr. Porath

"Cushlamochree" is Irish for "pulse of my heart" (cuisle, vein or pulse; mo, my; croidhe (cree), heart). Prefixed with a vocative "a" (acushlamochree) it becomes a poetic term of endearment. O'Malley used it as an exclamation of surprise and means by it, literally, "pulse of my heart!"

Many thanks for the letter.

Sincerely,

Crockett Johnson

readers would recognize the "celebrated canine" (22 December 1942) as Lad, Albert Payson Terhune's dog. The bestseller, *Lad: A Dog* (1919), collected Terhune's stories about his dog, Lad.

Johnson's affection for dogs makes his portrayal of Gorgon so resonant to anyone who's ever owned or known a dog. Gorgon is partially based on a dog Johnson had when he began writing *Barnaby*. He liked the dog to be able to roam free, true to its doggy nature. But the dog's desire to chase cars made roaming a bit dangerous. To teach him to roam only *within* the yard, Johnson put the dog on a rope, tied to a stake in the yard. Now, when a car approached, the dog dashed out to chase it, but the rope brought him up short. After a sufficient number of rope-frustrated attempts, Johnson decided the dog had been broken of its habit, and so took off the rope. A car drove by. The dog ran after it at top speed. Smiling, Johnson said, "Well, the dog learned something: not to chase cars when he's tied up." As Dorothy Parker wrote of the *Barnaby* sequence in which Gorgon's ability to talk turns out to be dull, "You have to love dogs before you can go on to the step of taking them down, understandingly. I think Mr. Johnson must love dogs."

Johnson's dog got his name from another of his master's passions – true crime stories and detective fiction. Though Johnson spelled it *Gonsul*, the term – usually spelled *gunsel* – denotes a naïve youth or informer. This volume of *Barnaby* offers many references to the mystery/detective genre, including fictional detectives Ellery Queen, Sherlock Holmes, Auguste Dupin, Hercule Poirot, Doctor Thorndyke, Nero Wolfe and Philo Vance. Some of *Barnaby*'s plots are also mysteries, such as the case of the Nazi ogre (13 July – 29 October 1942), and the case of the coffee fiends (18 January – 1 March 1943).

Another of Johnson's interests appears in the character of Atlas, the Mental Giant who uses mathematical formulae as a mnemonic device. In the Atlas strips Johnson redrew for *Barnaby and Mr. O'Malley* (1944), the formulae are not just gibberish. If solved, they actually do spell words. In the daily strips

included here, though, the equations Atlas uses are not necessarily meaningful. Though fascinated by math (and especially by geometry), Johnson had no formal training in the subject. After high school, he won a scholarship to attend Cooper Union, but, during his freshman year, his father died. To support his mother and sister, Johnson left school to get a job.

After a brief stint working in the Macy's advertising department (a job he thoroughly disliked), Johnson found his way into magazine layout and design, and then into the medium that would bring him acclaim — cartoons.

> *Lucky, isn't it, that your Fairy Godfather is such a discerning reader?*
>
> — Mr. O'Malley, 13 July 1943

Barnaby was an immediate hit with the smart set, reaching them initially through the Popular Front newspaper *PM*. Founded in 1940 by former *Time* editor Ralph Ingersoll, *PM* was proudly pro-Roosevelt, anti-Fascist, and anti-Poll Tax — all political positions that Johnson supported. Whether "PM" stood for the time of day (it was an afternoon paper with its first editions published in late morning) or for Picture Magazine, no one knows. Its innovations, however, made it a pioneer. *PM* used color long before any other paper, employed the latest technology to print photographs with far greater clarity than its competitors, was a consumer advocate when no other newspapers were, and accepted no advertising during its first

13.   *Crockett Johnson and Gonsul, c. 1944. Image courtesy of the Smithsonian Institution.*

14.   *Crockett Johnson, The Little Man with the Eyes, Collier's, 14 September 1940.*

15.   *Advertisement for Barnaby on side of Chicago Sun delivery truck. Image courtesy of the Smithsonian Institution.*

14

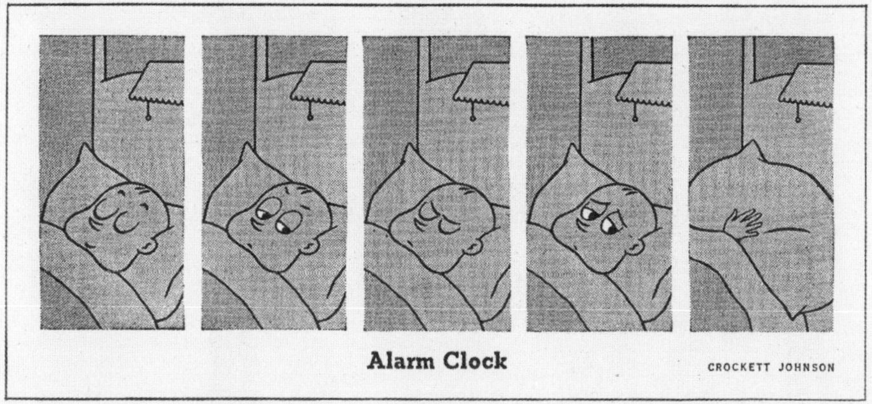
Alarm Clock
CROCKETT JOHNSON

15

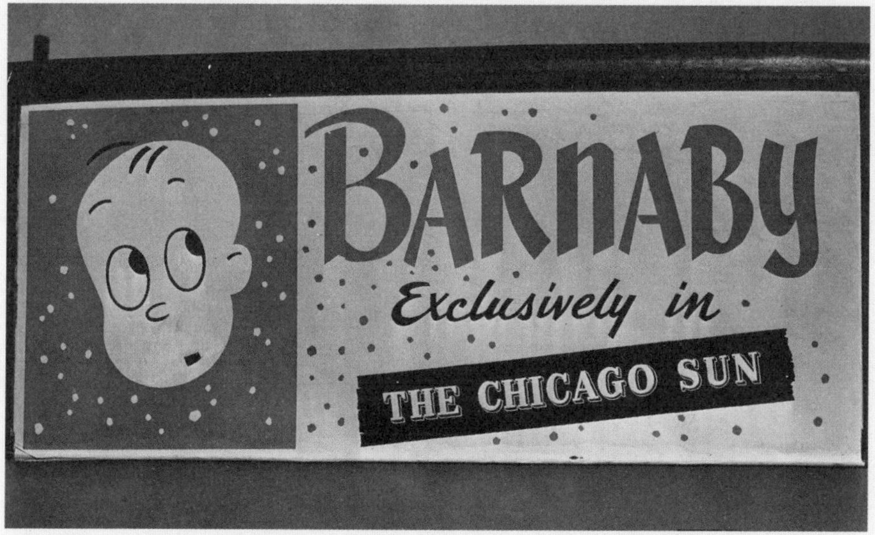
BARNABY
Exclusively in
THE CHICAGO SUN

six-and-a-half years. The paper attracted influential people: The President, Mrs. Roosevelt, Vice President Henry Wallace, bandleader Duke Ellington and writer Dorothy Parker all read it. They enjoyed the prose of future Speaker of the House "Tip" O'Neill, novelists Ernest Hemingway and Erskine Caldwell, the photographs of Margaret Bourke-White and "Weegee" (Arthur Fellig), and the cartoons of Carl Rose, Don Freeman, Ad Reinhardt and Theodor "Ted" Geisel (Dr. Seuss).

Though the cartoons of Crockett Johnson and Dr. Seuss were both running in *PM* between April of 1942 and January of 1943, I can find no evidence that they knew each other. Both worked out of their homes – Johnson in his Darien Connecticut house, and Geisel in his New York apartment (except for summers, when he lived in La Jolla, mailing his cartoons to *PM*). Both came in to *PM*'s offices from time to time, to deliver their work or to meet with their editor Hannah Baker. It is tempting to imagine these future titans of children's literature meeting at *PM*. The door to Ms. Baker's office opens, Geisel steps out, and sees Johnson. They exchange a few words about art or politics, and then Johnson enters her office to discuss *Barnaby*. Yet, while they knew each other's work and may have met socially, they were not friends. The strongest link between Johnson and Geisel is the newspaper that published their work.

Johnson was nocturnal, typically writing *Barnaby* between 11 p.m. and 5 a.m. Generally, he spent the first two nights writing the script, and the next two drawing the art. Next, *PM*'s type shop set Johnson's dialogue in italicized Futura medium, and sent it back to Johnson. He cut out these thin strips of words and pasted them into each panel. Finally done, he would either have to bring the strips into New York himself, or, if he was running late, rely on his neighbor Bob McNell to drop them off at *PM*'s offices on his way to his ad agency job. Sometimes, Johnson was running so late that he would bring them over to McNell at 6 a.m., the glue still drying.

During the first year of *Barnaby*, Johnson hones his sense of what the characters look like, and how the "fairy world" works. Initially, O'Malley is wider, dumpier and has a smaller head. Over the first six months, his features change gradually, until November of 1942, when he settles into the plump figure of mischief we recognize. The most unusual feature of these early strips is the character of Bilharzia Ogre/Mr. Jones, who is unique among *Barnaby* characters: he has a full life in both the "fairy world" and the "real world," interacting regularly with people from either realm. He is also unique in being the only truly menacing villain of the *Barnaby* series – an ogre and Nazi spy who radios Germany, trying to undermine the Allied war effort. By the end of its first year, the darkness of that early narrative has left, replaced by a subtle but sharp satire. And Johnson had established *Barnaby*'s main cast. In addition to the Baxters and O'Malley, he introduced Launcelot McSnoyd (the invisible leprechaun) in October of '42, Jane (the girl next door) and Gorgon in December, Gus (the timid ghost) in January of '43, and Atlas (the mental giant) in May.

By January of '43, Johnson had to give up *The Little Man* – its last strip appeared on the 9th. In addition to writing six *Barnaby* comics each week (a Sunday strip, drawn by others, would be introduced in 1946), he was also revising his favorite episodes from *Barnaby*'s first 10 months, for publication in book form in the fall of '43. Most cartoonists would simply reprint the strips in the same format they appeared in the newspaper. But Johnson was a perfectionist. The books had to be better than the daily strip.

By the fall of 1943, the strip was in *PM*, the *Chicago Sun*, Philadelphia *Record*, St. Louis *Star-Times*, Harrisburg *Telegraph*, St. Petersburg *Times* and Troy (N.Y.) *Record*. In terms of circulation, *Barnaby* was no *Blondie* or *Dick Tracy*, but it was already earning Johnson a $5,000 annual salary – which, in today's dollars, would be about $65,000. And it had prospects. As soon as he could find a sponsor, Johnson was planning on a *Barnaby* radio show. There was talk, that spring, of

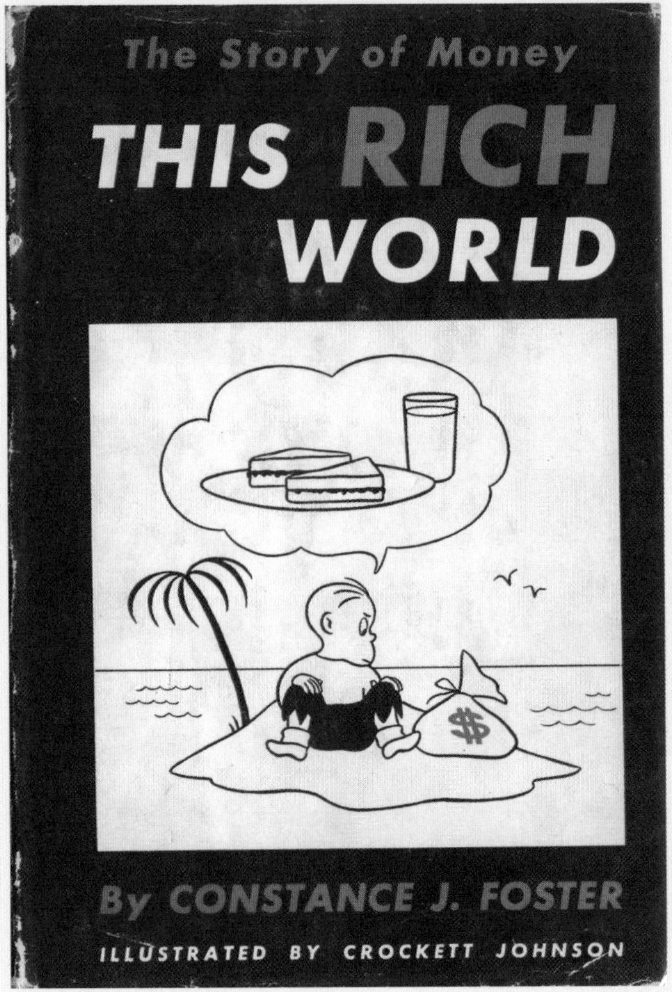

The Story of Money
THIS RICH WORLD
$
By CONSTANCE J. FOSTER
ILLUSTRATED BY CROCKETT JOHNSON

16

16. *Crockett Johnson, cover for Constance J. Foster's* This Rich World *(1943)*

17. *Advertisement for* Barnaby *(1943). Image courtesy of the Smithsonian Institution.*

17

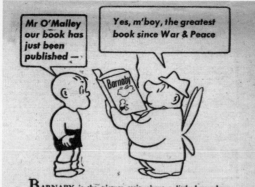

Mr O'Malley our book has just been published —
Yes, m'boy, the greatest book since War & Peace
Barnaby
BARNABY is the picture strip about a little boy who wanted a fairy godmother and wished on a star. What he got was a fairy godfather, with pink wings and a paunch, named Mr. O'Malley. Here is the reaction of some BARNABY devotees to the appearance of Barnaby and Mr. O'Malley in a book, complete with chapters and everything.
LOUIS UNTERMEYER: "The funniest high comedy since Aristophanes and Thurber. I won't be completely happy until I see W. C. Fields in the role of Mr. O'Malley."
ROCKWELL KENT: "I yield to no one in my 'blathering admiration' of BARNABY."
WILLIAM ROSE BENET: "No American home should be without a copy of BARNABY . . . a classic of humor."
PAUL DE KRUIF: "Congratulations on this quietly uproarious book."
GARDNER REA: "Delighted to see that Mr. O'Malley will now be able to drive the majority of us to insanity in a permanent form."
NOMAN CORWIN: "I have been after radio to make a program of BARNABY and after the movies to make a picture and after the Postmaster General to make a BARNABY stamp, so naturally I am glad to see that you have taken the initiative and made a BARNABY book."
RUTH McKENNEY: "BARNABY is: colossal, magnificent, terrific, marvelous, wonderful, witty, funny . . . take your pick!"
Barnaby
by CROCKETT JOHNSON
$2.00, HENRY HOLT AND COMPANY
HENRY HOLT AND COMPANY · HENRY HOLT AND COMPANY

creating a musical comedy based on *Barnaby*. He and Ted and Matilda Ferro, script writers for the radio serial *Lorenzo Jones*, would write the book and lyrics. For the music, they recruited Harold Rome, who had written music and lyrics for *Pins and Needles* (1937-1940), a successful, pro-labor Broadway musical about the garment industry. Also that spring, Johnson made his debut as a children's-book illustrator with the publication of Constance J. Foster's *This Rich World: The Story of Money*.

Amidst this busy schedule, Krauss was working on her first children's book, *A Good Man and His Good Wife*, and was about to become a wife for the second time. After living together for over two years, she and Johnson formalized what most of their neighbors assumed they had already done. In June 1943, they got married.

In October, Krauss signed the contract for *A Good Man and His Good Wife*, and Henry Holt published Johnson's *Barnaby*. It sold its first printing of 10,000 copies in its first week, and would sell 40,000 before the end of the year. The reviews were ecstatic. Rockwell Kent praised "Crockett Johnson's profound understanding of the psychology of the child, of grown-ups and of fairy godfathers." Pulitzer Prize-winning poet William Rose Benét called *Barnaby* "a classic of humor" and declared Mr. O'Malley "a character to live with the Mad Hatter, the White Rabbit, Ferdinand, and all great creatures of fantasy." Poet and anthologist Louis Untermeyer wrote, "Barnaby and his attendant sprites are the funniest high comedy characters since Aristophanes and Thurber." Ruth McKenney, whose *My Sister Eileen* had become an Oscar-nominated film earlier that year, delighted in "that evil intentioned, vain, pompous, wonderful little man with the wings." As she put it, "I suppose Mr. O'Malley has fewer morals than any other character in literature which is, of course, what makes him so fascinating." Dorothy Parker began her "A Mash Note to Crockett Johnson" by confessing that she could not write a review because, despite her efforts, "it never comes out a book review. It is always a valentine for Mr. Johnson." The *New York Times*' Isabelle Mallet called it "a series of comic strips which, laid end to end, reach from here to wherever

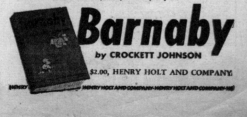

19

Books

It seems doubtful that Crockett Johnson's book, *Barnaby*, will be awarded the Pulitzer prize for creative literature. After all, it's only a collection of comic strips. Nevertheless, for what it's worth—which is precisely nothing—I'm sending in my nomination of *Barnaby* to the Pulitzer Committee. I think the writing in the balloons of this comic strip, currently running in *PM*, is the best American creative writing of this year, and Mr. O'Malley the most brilliantly conceived character in many a year.

Now that Crockett Johnson has given us Mr. O'Malley, that scamp, that rogue, that pink-winged bluff, that wretched and lovable fraud, that passer of bum checks, that stealer of pickings from the icebox, that puller-of-legs of dogs and little children, we suddenly feel that we have come upon a green oasis in the arid desert of good, respectable, competent, dull contemporary American fiction. Mr. O'Malley is, in fact, the great American antidote, the sodium bicarbonate of the great American flatulence. One good O'Malley belch a day and you feel better already. And don't let Mr. Dies tell you that Mr. O'Malley is un-American. He's as American as Micawber is British.

You will have noted, too, how Barnaby's good, liberal-minded, progressive-school-minded parents fade into imbecility in the light of Mr. O'Malley's fantastic commonplaceness. Thanks to Mr. O'Malley, Barnaby will probably grow up to be quite a boy, instead of a miniature blueprint of his unimaginative, reliable parents. Lucky kid, Barnaby! It's not every American kid can have a rascal like Mr. O'Malley for a fairy godfather.

* * *

20

ORIGINAL DRAWINGS OF
Barnaby
(PM'S Famous Comic Strip)
By CROCKETT JOHNSON
NOVEMBER 9TH - DECEMBER 6TH
Meet Crockett Johnson who will autograph copies of the BARNABY book at preview NOV. 9th from 5 to 7 p. m.
59 WEST 56th ST. NEW YORK, N. Y.
NORLYST GALLERY
OPEN FROM 11 A. M. to 6 P. M.

21

22

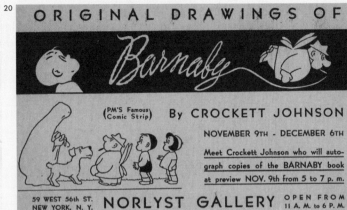

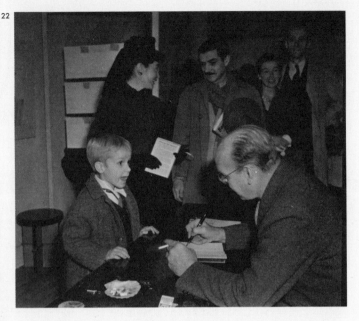

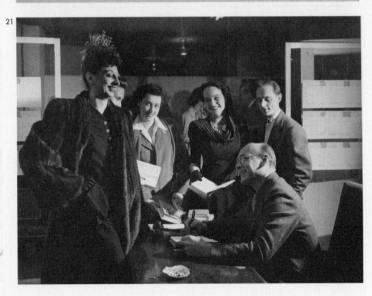

19. *Edwin Seaver, column in* Direction*, 1943. Image courtesy of the Smithsonian Institution.*
20. *Invitation to Norlyst Gallery, November 1943. Image courtesy of the Smithsonian Institution.*
21. *Paula Laurence and Crockett Johnson, Norlyst Gallery, 9 November 1943. Image courtesy of the Smithsonian Institution.*
22. *Unidentified boy and Crockett Johnson, Norlyst Gallery, 9 November 1943. Image courtesy of the Smithsonian Institution.*

you want to go before you die." Lauding the book as "the best American creative writing of this year" and O'Malley as "the most brilliantly conceived character in many a year," novelist and Book-of-the-Month Club publicity director Edwin Seaver nominated *Barnaby* for a Pulitzer.

On November 9, dressed in a coat and tie, Johnson arrived at the Norlyst Gallery to launch its four-week exhibition of original *Barnaby* strips, and to sign copies of his acclaimed *Barnaby* book. Photos show Broadway actress Paula Laurence, Jimmy Ernst (artist, son of Surrealist painter Max), and an unnamed small boy who bears a striking resemblance to Barnaby.

At the age of 37, Crockett Johnson suddenly had fans. *Life* and *Newsweek* had both run features on *Barnaby*. His work was on display — as art — in a gallery. Critics loved his book. However, adulation both pleased him and bemused him. It was great to be a success, but he also enjoyed *not* being the center of attention. And success seemed to bring more work, which took time he might otherwise have spent sleeping, reading, sailing ... or having a lamb sandwich.

He had not only to turn out six *Barnaby* strips per week, but also to make each strip meet his standards. "I never feel that I can let down," he told a journalist in November 1943. "If I did, the stuff wouldn't get to be just mediocre; it would be terrible." While Johnson felt that "There's nothing worse than the obligation to be funny," he also considered *Barnaby* "a pretty good racket." It was, after all, the first of his creative ventures that was making him a comfortable living. Sometimes, he despaired that he would never again have a day off from *Barnaby*, but in the same moment would say with pleasure that his second *Barnaby* collection, due in the spring of 1944, would be better than the first. Success was a mixed blessing. He was doing well. But for how long could he keep this up?

Adapted and expanded from Philip Nel's Crockett Johnson and Ruth Krauss: How an Unlikely Couple Found Love, Dodged the FBI, and Transformed Children's Literature *(University Press of Mississippi, 2012).*

16 PM'S DAILY PICTURE MAGAZINE SUNDAY, OCTOBER 3, 1943

Dorothy Parker Writes

A Mash Note to Crockett Johnson

A Constant Reader of Comics Falls in Love With Our Barnaby

CROCKETT JOHNSON
Mrs. Parker is a woman of rare discrimination, m'boy.

Dorothy Parker

Crockett Johnson

—DOROTHY PARKER

Barnaby appears today in PM's Picture News.

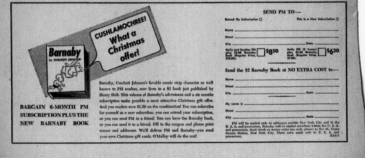

A MASH NOTE TO

By Dorothy Parker

I CANNOT WRITE A REVIEW of Crockett Johnson's book of *Barnaby*. I have tried and tried, but it never comes out a book review. It is always a valentine for Mr. Johnson.

For a bulky segment of a century, I have been an avid follower of comic strips — all comic strips; this is a statement made with approximately the same amount of pride with which one would say, "I've been shooting cocaine into my arm for the past 25 years." I cannot remember how the habit started, and I am presently unable to explain why it persists. I know only that I'm hooked, by now, that's all. I can't stop. I even take a certain unspeakable tabloid for its strips, though, when I am caught with it on my doorstep, I still have shame enough left to try to laugh matters off by explaining that you really ought to know what your enemies are up to. When I tell that you that I am in daily touch with the horrible, sightless, Orphan Annie — who, I am convinced, is Westbrook Pegler's adopted child — that I keep up with the particular nasty experiences of Dick Tracy, that even, for heaven's sake, I was the one who strung along with Deathless Deer until her mercy

CROCKETT JOHNSON

killing, you will know that Mother is a gone pigeon. When cornered, I try to make rather doggy excuses. I say that comic strips are important pieces of Americana. But it doesn't hold, you know. You cannot class the relationship between Flash Gordon and Dale as something peculiarly American. I flatly do not know why I do as I do. For I do not enjoy the strips. I read them solemnly and sourly, and there is no delight in me because of them.

That is, I had no delight and no enjoyment and no love until *Barnaby* came. I suppose you must do it this way; I suppose you must file Barnaby under comic strips, because his biography runs along in strip form in a newspaper. I bow to convention in the matter. But, privately, if the adventures of Barnaby constitute a comic strip, then so do those of Huckleberry Finn.

I think, and I am trying to talk calmly, that Barnaby and his friends and oppressors are the most important additions to American arts and letters in Lord knows how many years. I know that they are the most important additions to my heart. I love Barnaby, I love little Jane, I love Gus, the Ghost, I hate and admire and envy Mr. O'Malley, above all I love Gorgon, the dog.

I think the conception of a dog who talks — "Didn't know I could do it; never tried it before, I guess" — and then turns out to be such a crashing bore that they have to lock him away so they won't be obliged to listen to him, is — well, it's only glorious, that's all. You have to love dogs before you can go on to the step of taking them down, understandingly. I think Mr. Johnson must love dogs. I think Mr. Johnson must love people. I know darned well I must love Mr. Johnson.

Barnaby is fine to have in book form — you can't go on, you know, cutting strips out of *PM* and meaning to paste them in an album the next rainy day. The book will be invaluable to those who must read aloud a while every evening. I am told, by those fortunates who own them, that children love Barnaby; which information has appreciably raised my estimation of children. While for adults — I can only say *Barnaby*, the book, costs $2. If you have $5, save out three for the landlord and spend the remainder to feed your soul.

Well. I told you I couldn't write anything but a valentine, didn't I?

The average person's ignorance and misinformation about Leprechauns, Barnaby, is shocking . . . Of course, very little dependable data of any sort exists and no scientific field work has been done among them.

— Mr. O'Malley, 19 Oct. 1942

The Elves, Leprechauns, Gnomes, and Little Men's Chowder and Marching Society: A Handy Pocket Guide

By Philip Nel

Crockett Johnson's strip alludes to many events, persons and cultural phenomena that may be unfamiliar to contemporary readers. Indeed, many of Johnson's allusions would have gone over the heads of his contemporaries. So, if you're confused by a reference, this glossary should help. The section titles come from *Barnaby* (1943) and *Barnaby and Mr. O'Malley* (1944), except in cases where Johnson chose to omit the narrative sequence from those volumes (Mr. O'Malley Takes Flight, Mr. O'Malley's Mishaps, O'Malley vs. Ogre, The Ghostwriter Moves In, Mrs. Krump's Kiddie Kamp, Congressman O'Malley). In *Barnaby and Mr. O'Malley*, the narrative order is also different: the Man of the Hour story directly follows Gorgon's Father, and incorporates parts of The Ghostwriter Moves In.

MR. O'MALLEY ARRIVES • 20 – 29 APRIL 1942

Cushlamochree! (21 April). See *Afterword*, page 292-293.

AIR RAID WARDEN (29 April, 5 Oct.). During World War II, concern that Nazi planes might bomb the East Coast (or Japanese planes the West Coast) prompted the U.S. Office of Civilian Defense (OCD) to organize blackout drills and appoint neighborhood air raid wardens. The wardens' job was to check that everyone had turned out their lights during the drill. The idea was that enemy bombers couldn't bomb what they couldn't see — if the lights were out, then, from above, they would see only darkness (Zebrowski).

MR. O'MALLEY TAKES FLIGHT • 30 APRIL – 14 MAY 1942

ARP (2 May, 6 May). Air Raid Precautions.

OCD (4 May). Office of Civilian Defense.

MR. O'MALLEY'S MISHAPS • 15 – 28 MAY 1942

Me, who can tear off forty winks in a cowslip's bell without disturbing a dewdrop! (15 May 1942). O'Malley here alludes to the beginning of Act II, Scene 1 in William Shakespeare's *A Midsummer Night's Dream* (1595-96), when a Fairy says: "I must go seek some dewdrops here, / And hang a pearl in every cowslip's ear" (lines 14-15). Cowslips are a yellow English flower, and the fairies in Shakespeare's play are unseen by the mortals. As a student at Newtown High School, Johnson learned Oberon's speech from the *end* of this scene, which appeared his *Newtown High School Handbook*. In addition to school rules and programs of study, the pocket-sized book reprinted 26 literary extracts for students to memorize. (There were three from William Wordsworth, two each from Shakespeare and Robert Louis Stevenson and one from each of the rest). Perhaps, as a high school student, Johnson also read the entire scene or play — or committed more of it to memory.

Victory Garden (20 May 1942, 3 – 17 April 1943, 19 – 24 May 1943). To cope with food rationing during the war, the U.S. government encouraged people to grow their own food. Crockett Johnson was among the 20 million Americans who did. He enjoyed gardening, though — as the April and May *Barnaby* sequences reflect — often found his efforts failing to bear fruit (or beans, as the case may be).

O'MALLEY VS. OGRE • 29 MAY – 31 OCTOBER 1942

Mr. Hoover (17 June). J. Edgar Hoover (1895-1972) was Director of the Federal Bureau of Investigation from 1924 to 1972.

P-38 (19 June). Built by Lockheed and renowned for its speed, the P-38 Lightning was a new fighter plane (the U.S. Army began using it in 1942). The P-38J model had a top speed of 420 mph ("Lockheed P-38 Lightning — USA").

HE'S TRYING TO COVER US WITH LEAVES! (8 July). In the poem "Babes in the Wood" (collected in *English Fairy Tales* by Flora Annie Steel, 1918), two children, abandoned in a wood, die in one another's arms, and "No burial this pretty pair / From any man receives, / Till Robin Redbreast piously / Did cover them with leaves."

And in another book an ogre got them (9 July). Child-eating ogres are a staple of fairy tales, though the child usually outwits the ogre — Gretel pushing the witch into the oven in the Grimms' "Hansel and Gretel," and Tom Thumb saving his brothers by tricking the Ogre into eating his (the Ogre's) own children.

Bilharzia (14 July). This Nazi ogre takes his name from a disease caused by parasitic worms. According to the Centers for Disease Control, "In terms of impact this disease is second only to malaria as the most devastating parasitic disease" ("Parasites - Schistosomiasis").

Nuremburg Ogres (14 July). Nuremburg, Germany was the site of major Nazi rallies in the 1930s. In addition to serving as a location for the staging of propaganda, Nuremberg also lent its name to the Nuremburg Laws — anti-Semitic laws enacted in 1935. In identifying Bilharzia as coming from Nuremburg, Johnson — whose wife, Ruth Krauss, was Jewish — is unambiguously labeling him as coming from a place of evil.

Laaban, laaban (15 July). In Hebrew, the word "laban" means "white" — so, possibly, Johnson is alluding to Bilharzia's support of Aryan supremacy. Or this may have some other meaning: Laban is also a figure in the Old Testament and Rabbinical literature. I'll leave it to a scholar of Christianity or Judaism (which I am decidedly not) to speculate further on what the term might mean (Hirsch, Seligsohn, Schechter).

FLAHOOLAGH! (15 July). Derivation unknown. May simply be an onomatopoetic expression.

Nabob (23 July). "a wealthy, influential, or powerful landowner or other person, esp. one with an extravagantly luxurious lifestyle," and even more relevant for this *Barnaby* strip, "any wealthy or high-ranking foreigner (*rare*)" (*Oxford English Dictionary*).

Druid's egg (25 July). A Druid is "One of an order of men among the ancient Celts of Gaul and Britain, who, according to Cæsar were priests or religious ministers and teachers, but who figure in native Irish and Welsh legend as magicians, sorcerers, soothsayers, and the like" (*OED*). The Druid's egg is an allegedly magical object said to be carried by members of this order.

Berchtesgaden (30 July), in the German Alps (near the Austrian border) was the location of Hitler's mountain home, and was a favorite vacation spot for senior Nazi leaders. News stories in 1942 frequently associate Hitler with the location, one calling him "the lunatic of Berchtesgaden," and another mocking him as "The Seer of Berchtesgaden" (Hutchens; Anderson).

Schwarzwald (31 July). The Black Forest, located in southwestern Germany.

Ripley ... very skeptical type of fellow (18 August). Robert Ripley (1890-1949), the cartoonist and creator of *Ripley's Believe It or Not!* — which in 1942 had appeared as a single-panel comic, a radio show and a short film subject.

MR. O'MALLEY'S MALADY • 1 – 11 SEPTEMBER 1942

Bramble Bug — Aqueduct — to win — $2 (3 Sept.). Evidence of O'Malley betting at the races: Bramble Bug is a horse, and Aqueduct is a race track in Queens.

THE DOCTOR'S ANALYSIS • 12 – 24 SEPTEMBER 1942

A&P store (17 Sept.). A chain of supermarkets that from the 1920s through 1975 was the largest such retailer in the U.S. (Jackson 502).

POP VS. MR. O'MALLEY • 25 SEPTEMBER – 6 OCTOBER 1942

Cannonball Express (6 Oct.). O'Malley associates himself with a famously fast train that was also famously in a wreck — see note on "Casey" (7 & 8 Oct.).

THE TEST BLACKOUT • 7 – 16 OCTOBER 1942

The "Old 97" (7 Oct.). A fast train that crashed in 1903, inspiring the ballad "The Wreck of the Old 97."

Casey (7 & 8 Oct.). O'Malley alludes to Casey Jones, who on April 30, 1900, was working as engineer of the Cannonball Express, trying to make up time on a run from Memphis, Tennessee to Canton, Mississippi. As the train approached Vaughn, Mississippi, he realized too late that a disabled train was blocking the tracks. He reversed throttle, and applied the brakes, but the resulting crash killed him. No one else was killed, and Casey became the subject of a popular song, "The Ballad of Casey Jones," hence the humor in O'Malley's notion of composing a ballad about the accident (Shaw).

THE INVISIBLE MCSNOYD • 17 – 31 OCTOBER 1942

"The Front Page" (20 Oct.). A newsroom drama by Ben Hecht and Charles MacArthur, adapted for film many times, notably as *The Front Page* (1931, starring Adolphe Menjou), and the classic *His Girl Friday* (1940, starring Cary Grant and Rosalind Russell).

THE POT OF GOLD • 2 – 20 NOVEMBER 1942

I got plenty of nothin' (4 Nov.). "I Got Plenty o' Nuttin" is from *Porgy and Bess* (1935), with music by George Gershwin and lyric by Ira Gershwin and DuBose Heyward. The song suggests that lack of wealth is liberating because there's less to worry about: "Folks with plenty of plenty / They've got a lock on the door / 'fraid somebody's a-goin' to rob 'em / While they're out a-makin' more. / What for?" The album *Selections from George Gershwin's folk opera Porgy and Bess* (Decca, 1942) included this song along with others that have since become standards: "Summertime" and "It Ain't Necessarily So."

scrap metal drive (6 Nov.). To support the war effort, people were encouraged to collect scrap metal that could then be recycled for use in tanks, planes and so on. Iron and steel were especially valuable.

Trilby (13 – 14 Nov.). See Afterword, page 292.

Fred Allen (17 Nov.). Popular comedian and radio star, then hosting the program *Texaco Star Theatre* on CBS.

Charlie McCarthy (20 Nov.). Ventriloquist's dummy and foil to Edgar Bergen. Bergen and McCarthy were stars of stage, screen and radio — hence their inclusion here.

That's not your imaginary Fairy Godfather! It's the MAYOR! (24 Nov.).
The inside joke is that Barnaby is confusing Mr. O'Malley with a real-life inspiration for him — Mayor Fiorello LaGuardia.

Duke Ellington (25 Nov.). The musician, bandleader and composer ("Mood Indigo," "Solitude," "It Don't Mean a Thing If It Ain't Got That Swing"). Ellington read *PM*, saw this strip, and sent in the following letter, published 1 December 1942:

Dear Editor:
Please tell Crockett Johnson to thank Mr. O'Malley on my behalf for coming out as an Ellington fan. That makes the admiration mutual.
I hope my music isn't responsible for getting Barnaby into more trouble — which, judging from today's (Nov. 25) strip, seems dangerously likely. Anyway, if it will help, you can tell Barnaby that I believe in Mr. O'Malley — solidly.
New York   DUKE ELLINGTON

There are fairies at the bottom of my gar-den (27 Nov.). "There Are Fairies at the Bottom of Our Garden" (words by Rose Fyleman, music by Liza Lehmann, 1917) was the signature song of Beatrice Lillie (1894-1989), who is quite possibly the "lady singer" to whom Barnaby refers. These are the lyrics:

There are fairies at the bottom of our garden,
It's not so very, very far away,
You pass the gard'ner's shed
and you just keep straight ahead,
I do so hope they've really come to stay,

There's a little wood with moss in it and beetles,
And a little stream that quietly runs though,
You wouldn't think they'd dare to come merry-making there,
Well, they do, yes, they do!

There are fairies at the bottom of our garden,
They often have a dance on summer nights,
The butterflies and bees make a lovely little breeze,
And the rabbits stand about and hold the lights,
Did you know that they could sit upon the moonbeams,
And snatch a little star to make a fan,
And dance away up there in the middle of the air?
Well they can, yes they can!

Oh those fairies at the bottom of our garden,
You cannot think how beautiful they are,
They all stand up and sing
when the Fairy Queen and King,
Come lightly floating down upon their car.
Oh, the King is very proud and very handsome,
And the Queen, now can you guess who that could be?
She's a little girl all day, but at night she steals away.
Well, it's ME! Yes, it's ME! (Fyleman)

Madam deCibel (28 Nov.). This fictional character's name offers a pun on the volume — or decibel — of the opera singer.

Scarlatti (28 Nov.). Alessandro Scarlatti (1660-1725) and his son Domenico Scarlatti (1685-1757) were Italian composers; the former is known for his operas and cantatas, the latter, for his harpsichord sonatas.

BOOGIE-WOOGIE MAMA (28 Nov.). Possibly a reference to the song "Scrub Me Mama with a Boogie Beat," recorded in 1940 by both the Andrews Sisters and Will Bradley with Ray McKinley. It also inspired the 1941 Walter Lantz cartoon of the same name. This could also simply be a more generic reference to the boogie-woogie piano style, which was then popular.

THE NEW NEIGHBORS • 30 NOVEMBER – 16 DECEMBER 1942

Amos 'n' Andy (29 Nov.). A popular minstrel program, in which two white actors portrayed the two black title characters as racial caricatures. Though they had appeared on film, Johnson likely knew the radio program, which aired each weeknight. Given Johnson's support for civil rights for African-Americans, contemporary readers may wonder at the casual reference to a program that perpetuates racist stereotypes. Some context may be helpful. In the 1950s, the NAACP protested the television version, but in the 1930s and 1940s the NAACP's national office did not protest its radio antecedent (Ely). In one 1930 film, the blackface characters appeared alongside Duke Ellington and His Orchestra. This is to say that in 1942, it would not be incongruent to listen to *Amos 'n' Andy* and to support civil rights.

POP IS GIVEN A DOG • 17 – 30 DECEMBER 1942

McGrew, Malemute Cocktail Lounge (19 Dec.). See *Afterword*, page 292.

Gremlins (19 Dec.). A reference to Roald Dahl's first children's story, published in *Cosmopolitan* in December 1942. A former RAF pilot then stationed in Washington, Dahl wrote of these gremlins, a "tribute of funny little people" who seek revenge on humans who have cut down their forests to build airstrips on them. As retribution, the gremlins — in Dahl biographer Donald Sturrock's words — "turn on their tormentors, the airmen, and their 'big tin birds,' causing innumerable inexplicable air accidents, even going so far as to move entire mountains to deceive RAF pilots and make their planes crash" (174).

Man o' War (22 Dec.). Another reference to O'Malley's fondness for horse racing. Man o' War was an extremely successful racehorse, winning 20 out of 21 races in his 16-month career (1919-1920) (Peters).

Albert Payson Terhune (22 Dec.). See *Afterword*, page 293.

THE DOG CAN TALK • 31 DECEMBER 1942 – 17 JANUARY 1943

MAJOR BOWES (3 Jan.). Edward Bowes (1874-1946) was the host of the hit radio show, *Major Bowes Amateur Hour*.

Shaggy Dog Stories (14 Jan.). A term of relatively recent coinage (the first example the *OED* locates is 1937), a shaggy dog story is "a lengthy tediously detailed story of an inconsequential series of events, more amusing to the teller than to his audience, or amusing only by its pointlessness" (*OED*).

GUS, THE GHOST • 18 JANUARY – 4 FEBRUARY 1943

Lindy's old place on Broadway (22 Jan.). A deli at the northwest corner of Broadway and 51st Street (and thus near many theatres), Lindy's had many famous patrons. Some were gangsters, and many were from the theatre world — notably Al Jolson, Jack Benny and Eddie Cantor. Damon Runyon, a favorite writer of Crockett Johnson's, was a regular and wrote about the restaurant in his stories, fictionalizing it as "Mindy's." Gus says "Lindy's old place" because, after a disagreement with his business partner, Leo Lindenmann (aka "Lindy") in 1930 opened up a second Lindy's across the street from the original one (which opened in 1921). The first Lindy's closed in 1957, and the second in 1969 (Bloom 299-301).

Lucia Sextette (29 Jan.). In *Scarface* (1932), hitman Tony Camonte (played by Paul Muni) whistles the sextet from Act 2 of Gaetano Donizetti's opera *Lucia de Lammermoor* (1835) (Scott). O'Malley's whistling of this piece, then, indicates his familiarity not with the opera, but with the gangster film.

THE HOT COFFEE RING • 5 – 27 FEBRUARY 1943

Auguste Dupin, Hercule Poirot, Doctor Thorndyke, Nero Wolfe, Philo Vance (8 Feb.). All fictional detectives, created (respectively) by Edgar Allan Poe, Agatha Christie, R. Austin Freeman, Rex Stout and S. S. Van Dine.

Professor Moriarity (10 Feb.). Created by Arthur Conan Doyle, Moriarty (misspelled by Johnson) is the nemesis of Sherlock Holmes.

Ellery Queen (11 Feb.). Fictional detective created by *and* pseudonym for cousins Frederic Dannay and Manfred Bennington Lee, Ellery Queen appeared in novels, in his own magazine and on a popular radio show.

THE GHOSTWRITER MOVES IN • 1 – 11 MARCH 1943

Dutch Treat Club (5 Mar.). An organization of artists and writers based in New York, and founded in 1906, the Dutch Treat Club counted among its members Don Marquis (creator of *Archy and Mehitabel*), critic George Jean Nathan, artist James Montgomery Flagg, and cartoonists Otto Soglow and Rea Irwin (Lawson and Lawson 78; "History of the Dutch Treat Club").

my friend Ike on the old feature desk, when he was a princess fleeing over the Russian steppes and I led the major leagues in homers (6 Mar.). Beyond the comic incongruity of O'Malley's typical hyperbole, I'm not sure whether there's any other significance — that is, I don't know whether these are specific allusions or not.

Boswell (6 Mar.). James Boswell (1740-1795), lawyer and diarist famous for his detailed biography of Samuel Johnson (*The Life of Johnson*).

Horatio Alger (6 Mar.). Alger (1832-1899) was the author of popular rags-to-riches stories, in which poor young boys — through hard work, persistence and good morals — gain wealth and station. The tales promote the false notion of capitalism as a meritocracy, the enduring myth that underwrites the American dream. The allegation that all of Alger's stories are versions of O'Malley's life story is another example of his combination of naïveté, a healthy ego and indifference to facts.

how I was born in a log cabin, Gus? … And how I got out of a cradle one night to play a cadenza for my most recent concerto on the grand piano in our music room? … And the time I was showing a kid on our block by the name of Paul Bunyan a few tricks with my hatchet and I chopped down that cherry tree? … And then how I toddled up to the pater and said, "Oh, Father, dear Father, come home with me now … " We'll want at least a passing reference to the time I held my finger in the dike … While I stood on the burning deck … (8 Mar.). O'Malley here "borrows" from other famous biographies, both accurate and invented. The log cabin is from Abraham Lincoln's, and the cadenza-playing infant may be an embellished version from the life of a child prodigy like Mozart. In American folklore, Paul Bunyan is a giant lumberjack who, with Babe the Blue Ox, is responsible for many features of the landscape. Thanks to Mason Weems' popular *Life of George Washington* (1808), many assume the myth (created by Weems) of the cherry tree to be true. But there's no evidence that young Washington ever destroyed such a tree or confessed to doing so. Henry Clay Work's "Come Home, Father" (1864) is a melodramatic temperance song, in which the child speaker pleads with her father to come home to help her mother take care of her dying brother. The final two references, both about heroic children, are to (1) the 19th-century story of the little boy who held his finger in the dike (popularized in Mary Mapes Dodge's *Hans Brinker; or, the Silver Skates* [1865]), and (2) Felicia Hemans' poem "Casabianca" (1826), about a noble boy who goes down with the (burning) ship.

THE TESTIMONIAL DINNER • 12 MARCH – 2 APRIL 1943

Pat Rooney, Chauncey Olcott, McCormack (15 Mar.). Rooney (1880-1962) was a vaudeville song-and-dance man who also appeared in Broadway musicals. Olcott (1858-1932) was a minstrel performer and singer who co-wrote (and sang) several popular songs, including "My Wild Irish Rose," "When Irish Eyes Are Smiling" and "Mother Machree" — the last of these was also a favorite of Johnson's father. John McCormack (1884-1945) was a famous Irish tenor.

"The Fox Has Left His Lair" (17 - 18 & 22 Mar.). With music by Peggy Connor and lyrics by Douglas Furber, "The Fox Has Left His Lair" was a popular music-hall novelty song.

BARNABY'S GARDEN • 3 – 16 APRIL 1943

Victory Garden (3 - 17 April 1943, 19 - 24 May 1943). See 20 May 1942.

Luther Burbank (9 April). Luther Burbank (1849-1926) was a botanist who developed many varieties of plants. Like Carver (below), he was famous and would have been known to Johnson's readership.

Doctor Carver (9 April). George Washington Carver (1864-1943), the African-American botanist, scientist and inventor, noted for promoting crop rotation and discovering many uses for peanuts, among many other accomplishments. Indicative of his fame and range of abilities, the 24 May 1941 issue of *Time* called him the "Black Leonardo," comparing him to the original Renaissance man, Leonardo da Vinci ("Art: Black Leonardo").

Johnstown Flood (14 April). Catastrophic flood in southwestern Pennsylvania, May 31, 1889. Exacerbated by heavy rain, a dam broke, creating a vast wave of water and debris that wiped out several towns, killing over 2,000 people.

that 1938 hurricane (14 April). On 21 Sept. 1938, a devastating hurricane struck New Jersey, New York, Connecticut, Rhode Island and Massachusetts. According to R. A. Scotti, author of *Sudden Sea: The Great Hurricane of 1938* (2003), "The 1938 hurricane was the most-destructive national disaster that had ever struck the U.S. — worse than the San Francisco Earthquake, the Chicago Fire, or any Mississippi flood. ... It claimed almost 700 lives and cost an estimated 4.7 billion in today's dollars (only five percent of the losses were covered by insurance).

Coming as it did between the Depression and World War II, it stands as a benchmark in the history of New England. A way of life was lost. As the Associated Press said, 'The day of the biggest wind has just passed, and a great part of the most picturesque America, as old as the Pilgrims, has gone beyond recall or replacement'" (qtd. in Lopez).

O'MALLEY AND THE LION • 17 APRIL – 17 MAY 1943

Phineas Taylor Barnum (21 April). Better known as P.T. Barnum (1810-1891), the showman and entrepreneur whose name adorns the Barnum & Bailey Circus.

Pogey O'Brien (22 April). John V. "Pogey" O'Brien (1836-1889) was a famously unscrupulous circus promoter.

Androcles (29 April). In Aesop's fable, "Androcles and the Lion," the escaped slave Androcles removes a thorn from the paw of a lion. After the two are both captured, Androcles is thrown to the lion (as punishment). However, when the lion sees his friend, he behaves more like a tame dog, licking Androcles' hands. Androcles gets pardoned, and the lion is freed. The story's moral is "Gratitude is the sign of noble souls" (Jacobs 61).

Signor Bambini (17 May). As far as I know, Bambini (which, in Italian, means "Children") is a purely fictional circus performer.

ATLAS, THE GIANT • 18 MAY – 3 JUNE 1943

Atlas (25 May 1943 – 3 June 1943, 19 June 1943). Named for the figure in Greek mythology who carried the globe on his shoulders.

More treaties and confabs than you can shake a fist at, Versailles, Geneva, Munich — (31 May). O'Malley here invokes two treaties and one international organization, all of which were regarded as failures. Versailles ended the First World War, but also imposed costly reparations on Germany, creating some of the resentment that fed the Nazi Party's rise to power, and thus the Second World War. After concluding negotiations for the Munich

Agreement in September 1938, British Prime Minister Neville Chamberlain pronounced it "peace for our time." Less than a year later, Germany invaded Poland, starting World War II. Geneva is a reference to the home of the League of Nations, founded after the First World War in the hope that it could prevent a Second World War, which (obviously) it failed to do. So, for O'Malley to claim that he "had a hand" betrays his happy ignorance of their failures.

GORGON'S FATHER • 4 JUNE – 10 JULY 1943

Baskerville (11 June). A reference to Arthur Conan Doyle's Sherlock Holmes novel *The Hound of the Baskervilles* (1902) — and, possibly, to the many film adaptations of same.

a "Tom" show (14 June). A stage adaptation of Harriet Beecher Stowe's *Uncle Tom's Cabin*, which were popular from the mid-19th century to the early 20th century. "Tom" shows were rare by 1943, and so the reference here is to an outdated form of popular entertainment.

4-F (19 June). Not fit for military service. Johnson registered for the draft, but received the 4-F classification himself. He was not called to serve.

I once got a fire under control in Chicago so neatly and with such dispatch that some of the outlying districts were scarcely scorched ... it was the evening I'd had such a trying time attempting to extract some milk for an eggnog from a cow owned by a Mrs. O'Leary (2 July). Johnson suggests that O'Malley caused the Great Chicago Fire of 1871, alleged to have started when Mr. O'Leary's cow kicked over a lantern — though the fire's actual cause is unknown.

The magazine "Smart Set" ... Mencken's editorials (8 July). Literary critic for *The Smart Set* (1908-1924) and journalist/columnist for the *Baltimore Sun* (1899-1948), H.L. Mencken (1880-1956) was known for his skepticism, gift for turning a phrase, acid wit and iconoclasm (Winokur 22-24). Johnson would

have admired these qualities, though he disagreed with Mencken politically — Johnson supported the New Deal, and Mencken did not.

MRS. KRUMP'S KIDDIE KAMP • 12 JULY – 13 SEPTEMBER 1943

A tour of the Orient! ... "Visit Manila, Batavia, Singapore, Hongkong, Shanghai, Tokyo —" (13 July). All of these places were under the control of the Japanese in July 1943.

Pismo Beach (14 July). Pismo Beach is in southern California. Traveling there would be a long and costly trip for the Baxters.

Echo Lake (15 July). There are many Echo Lakes in North America. The nearest ones to the Baxters are in New York's Catskill Mountains, in Acadia National Park (Maine), in Charleston Vermont, north of Milford Massachusetts, and two in New Hampshire: one west of North Conway, and the other in Franconia Notch.

EVERY train is full of them! Don't you ever see any Hitchcock movies? ... Keep an eye on the door! (29 July). Likely an allusion to Alfred Hitchcock's *The Lady Vanishes* (1938).

Maeterlinck's "Blue Bird" (16 Aug.). *The Blue Bird* (1908) is the most popular play by Maurice Maeterlinck (1862-1949). It's about a brother and sister who seek the Blue Bird (of happiness) for the fairy Berylune — at the end, it turns out that the bird has been there all along, and they need not have gone on their quest. That treasure, too, had been "here on the camp grounds all the time" (to borrow O'Malley's words).

"Fagin" (18 Aug.). Introduced in Chapter 8 of Charles Dickens' *Oliver Twist* (1838-39), Fagin is a corruptor of minors (hence Gus' claim). He leads a gang of child-thieves and, in the novel's penultimate chapter, is hanged for his crimes.

"My Wild Irish Rose" (23 & 28 Aug., 7 Sept.). A popular and sentimental song written by Chauncey Olcott (see 15 Mar. 1943). The flower reminds the singer of the woman who gave it to him: "'Twas given to me by a girl that I know, / Since we've met, faith, I've known no repose, / She is dearer by far than the world's brightest star, / And I call her my wild Irish Rose" (qtd. in Studwell and Schueneman 67-70).

Captain Bloodbath Comics (27 Aug.). Johnson alludes to the sometimes violent content of comic books, a subject that within a few years would become headline news. In 1948, Fredric Wertham argued that violent, immoral comics were leading children toward delinquency. The issue received national attention from then into the 1950s, culminating in 1954, with the publication of Wertham's *The Seduction of the Innocent* and Senate hearings on comic books. Unlike Wertham, Johnson is more amused by the children's affection for violent comics.

Kay Kyser (28 Aug.). Kyser (1905-1985) — bandleader, vocalist and radio personality — created and hosted his own radio show, *Kay Kyser's Kollege of Musical Knowledge*. He and his band also appeared (as themselves) in several films in the 1940s.

Jack Benny (28 Aug.). Benny (1894-1974) was a popular comedian who hosted his own weekly radio show from 1932 to 1955. In the 1940s, he also starred in several films, including *To Be or Not to Be* (1942), *George Washington Slept Here* (1942) and *The Meanest Man in the World* (1943)

Hedy Lamarr (30 Aug.) After gaining notoriety by performing nude in the 1933 Czech film *Ecstacy* (which was banned in the U.S.), the Austrian-born actress moved to the U.S. in the late 1930s and became a contract star at MGM. Part of the humor in this strip is the notion of five-year-old Jane delivering lines intended to be performed by a beautiful actress known for her sexual allure ("The Ecstasy Girl Wins Cheers from Hollywood").

"Souvenir of the New York World's Fair" (7 Sept.). The 1939 New York World's Fair was held in what would become Flushing Meadows-Corona Park, four blocks east of the house in which Crockett Johnson grew up: 104

-11 39th Avenue. The Leisk family lived at that address (which was then 2 Ferguson Street) from c. 1912 until 1924.

Dr. Fishbein (10 Sept.). Dr. Morris Fishbein, editor of the *Journal of the American Medical Association* from 1924 to 1950. As his *New York Times* obituary notes, in his early years, "he waged war on medical quackery and championed the public's right to basic medical education" (Thomas) — and thus his reported eagerness for O'Malley's story would derive not from medical insights gained from the Fairy Godfather's swift recovery, but rather from the quackery that allegedly cured him (the "jug of Indian Herb Tonic").

MAN OF THE HOUR • *14 – 18 SEPTEMBER 1943*

OPA office (14 Sept.). During World War II, the U.S. Office of Price Administration rationed vital commodities (such as meat, sugar, coffee, gasoline) and limited the availability of things (bicycles, cars, rubber tires). People kept ration books, keeping track of the amount these commodities they were allowed to buy. The idea behind the program was to stabilize pricing and prevent hoarding; while this was one effect of rationing, the other was a black market.

Stanley Steamers (15 Sept.). These were the steam-powered antecedents to the modern automobile — by the 1940s, an antiquated technology.

O'MALLEY FOR CONGRESS! • *20 SEPTEMBER – 8 OCTOBER 1943*

John Maynard Keynes (29 Sept.). Keynes (1883-1946) was a British economist who was then proposing a single world currency for the post-war world, but this allusion here seems to be to his *The Economic Consequences of the Peace* (1920), in which he argued that inflation would "debauch the currency": "As the inflation proceeds and the real value of the currency fluctuates wildly from month to month, all permanent relations between debtors and creditors, which form the ultimate foundation of capitalism, become so utterly disordered as to be almost meaningless; and the process of wealth-getting degenerates into a gamble and a lottery" (220). He argued that governments should intervene to prevent inflation. If a government "refrains from regulation and allows matters to take their course," he wrote, then "essential commodities soon attain a level of price out of the reach of all but the rich, the worthlessness of the money becomes apparent, and the fraud upon the public can be concealed no longer" (225). At the time of the book's publication, these theories made him internationally famous but were out of step with established economic thought (Holroyd 464). However, by the 1940s, his analysis had been vindicated (his book seemed to predict what happened to post-war Germany) and was well-regarded as an economic thinker.

THE ELECTION • 9 OCTOBER – 12 NOVEMBER 1943

Jefferson Davis (13 Oct.). The President of the Confederate States of America (1861-1865), whose face was *not* on the Confederacy's $2 bill. (Judah P. Benjamin's face was.) *Thomas* Jefferson's face is (and was) on the U.S. $2 bill. So, McSnoyd's $2 bills are not and never were legal currency — they're counterfeit Confederate money.

KNOW NOTHING O'MALLEY, TAXATION WITHOUT O'MALLEY IS TYRANNY, A O'MALLEY IN EVERY POT, GRASS ROOTS O'MALLEY, SINGLE TAX O'MALLEY, BULLMOOSE O'MALLEY, 54-40 OR O'MALLEY (14 Oct.). These "used placards" are all famous slogans for earlier and ideologically disparate American political campaigns. The Know-Nothings were an anti-immigrant party active in the 1850s. "Taxation Without Representation" dates to the 1760s and Colonial America's protests against the Stamp Act and other British laws. The Republican Party used the phrase "a chicken in every pot" to support the 1928 presidential campaign of Herbert Hoover. "Grass Roots" dates to U.S. politicians in the early 20th-century proclaiming affiliation with the common people rather than the elite. A "Single Tax" platform has cropped up at various times in U.S. history, but it began with Henry George in 1887 (Young 110-111). The Bull Moose Party was the nickname for was Teddy Roosevelt's Progressive Party, founded in 1912 after the former president split with the Republican Party. "54-40 or Fight!" was the battle cry of those Americans who, in the 1840s, wanted the disputed northern boundary of Oregon to be established at 54º40' north instead of at the 49th parallel (which ultimately became the boundary).

Menlo Park. . . I hear that fellow Edison who invented the jukebox also perfected an astounding device for recording the human voice (18 Oct.). O'Malley gets his chronology backwards. Thomas Edison (1847-1931), whose laboratory was in Menlo Park, New Jersey, invented the phonograph in 1877 (Welch et al 6). Its invention made possible the jukebox, later in the century — though the term "jukebox" dates only to the late 1930s (*OED*).

Mr. Petrillo (19 Oct.). James C. Petrillo, head of the American Federation of Musicians. As president of this union, he imposed a recording ban from 1942 to 1944, in order to win better royalties from recording companies and broadcasters (Sterling and Kittross 257).

Edmund Burke (20 Oct.). Burke (1727-1797), an Irishman and Whig politician, is best remembered for his *Reflections on the Revolution in France* (1789-1790). According to scholar J.G.A. Pocock, in the House of Commons, Burke "was a noted though not a popular orator — his long-windedness and Irish intonation caused him to empty the floor" (x). In having Barnaby's Fairy Godfather seek Burke's speeches, Johnson is inviting a chuckle at O'Malley's fondness for long-windedness.

Captain Billy's Whizbang (20 Oct.). That O'Malley seeks a "humorous joke" from this publication indicates both that the material is dated (the publication was most popular in the 1920s) and that he has a lowbrow sense of humor. *Capt. Billy's Whiz Bang* contained bawdy puns, jokes about censorship and

Prohibition, and many examples of humor that would today be considered sexist or racist (Coyle). Today, the publication is remembered (if at all) because of a line in Meredith Willson's *The Music Man* (Broadway musical, 1957; film, 1962), when Professor Harold Hill invokes it as a corruptor of youth. In the song, "Ya Got Trouble," Hill says: "Mothers of River City, heed that warning before it's too late. Watch for the telltale signs of corruption. The minute your son leaves the house, does he rebuckle his knickerbockers below the knee? Is there a nicotine stain on his index finger? A dime novel hidden in the corn crib? Is he starting to memorize jokes from *Capt. Billy's Whiz Bang?*"

Senator G. G. Vest's Eulogy of the Dog (23-24 Oct.). In 1870, George Graham Vest (1830-1904) — who had been a Senator in the Confederacy (1862-1865), and would later be a U.S. Senator from Missouri (1879-1903) — delivered this speech in defense of Old Drum, a dog shot for allegedly killing sheep. Old Drum's owner filed suit against the farmer who killed the dog, seeking $50 in damages. Vest, representing the dog's owner, said the following in his summation to the jury:

Gentlemen of the jury. The best friend a man has in the world may turn against him and become his enemy. His son or daughter whom he has reared with loving care may prove ungrateful. Those who are nearest and dearest to us, those whom we trust with our happiness and our good name, may become traitors to their faith. The money that a man has he may lose. It flies away from him perhaps when he needs it most. A man's reputation may be sacrificed in a moment of ill-considered action. The people who are prone to fall on their knees to do us honor when success is with us may be the first to throw the stone of malice when failure settles its cloud upon our heads. The one absolutely unselfish friend that a man can have in this selfish world, the one that never deserts him, the one that never proves ungrateful or treacherous, is the dog.

Gentlemen of the jury, a man's dog stands by him in prosperity and poverty, in health and in sickness. He will sleep on the cold ground when the wintry winds blow and the snow drives fiercely, if only he can be near his master's side. He will kiss the hand that has no food to offer, he will lick the wounds and sores that come in encounter with the roughness of the world. He guards the sleep of his pauper master as if he were a prince.

When all other friends depart, he remains. When riches take wings and reputation falls to pieces, he is as constant in his love as the sun is in its journey through the heavens. If fortune rives the master forth an outcast into the world, friendless and homeless, the faithful dog asks no higher privilege than that of accompanying him, to guard him against danger, to fight against his enemies, And when the last scene of all comes, and death takes his master in its embrace and his body is laid in the cold ground, no matter if all other friends pursue their way, there by his graveside will the noble dog be found, his head between his paws and his eyes sad but open, in alert watchfulness, faithful and true, even unto death.

In addition to helping win the case, the speech became a classic piece of (somewhat purple) oratory, reprinted in many anthologies (Byrd).

CONGRESSMAN O'MALLEY • 13 – 23 NOVEMBER 1943

"ADMIRAL DEWEY CAPTURES MANILA!" (18 Nov.). Another dated source for O'Malley: This was a decisive battle during the Spanish-American War. American forces, led by Commodore George Dewey (1837-1917), captured Manila in May 1898.

Button Gwinnett (24 Nov.). Gwinnett (1735-1777) was one of Georgia's representatives to the Continental Congress, and a signer of the Declaration of Independence.

The O'Malley Committee (28 Nov.). Johnson's mockery of the Dies Committee. Martin Dies (1900-1972), Democratic Congressman from Texas (1931-45, 1953-59) established and chaired the House Un-American Activities Committee, known as the Dies Committee during the congressman's tenure. It investigated real and imagined threats to U.S. national security. In the summer of 1943, for example, it hounded John Bovingdon, a Harvard-educated economist, resulting in his firing from the Office of Economic Warfare — a story that was front-page news in the *New York Times* on August 5th. Though one might think that Bovingdon's ability to speak French, German, Japanese, Russian, and Spanish would be useful, his linguistic ability, coupled with his hobby of "rhythmic gymnastics," led Dies to brand the economist as a security risk. Though Bovingdon was not a ballet dancer, Dies proclaimed, "this is no time for the appointment of ballet dancers to fill positions which require the best brains and ability from our people." If Congress can investigate and fire a Harvard-trained economist, then why not Santa Claus? (Nel, "Never overlook..." 151).

Kid McCoy (22 Dec.). Charles Kid McCoy (1872-1940) was a successful boxer who "mastered every trick in the book to gain an advantage in a fight." Despite (and because of) his trickery, he was also a skilled boxer, who gained the nickname "The Real McCoy" (Bearden).

WORKS CITED

In addition to the works cited below, I also made frequent use of the *Internet Movie Database* <http://www.imdb.com> and the *Internet Broadway Database* <http://www.ibdb.com/>.

"Art: Black Leonardo." *Time* 24 May 1941.

Anderson, Isaac. "Notes on Books and Authors." *New York Times Book Review* 21 Jun. 1942: 10

Bearden, B. R. "Time Tunnel: The Real McCoy." *East Side Boxing.* <http://www.eastsideboxing.com/timetunnel3.html>. 25 Nov. 2011.

Bloom, Ken. *Broadway: Its History, Its People, Its Places. An Encyclopedia.* New York: Routledge, 2004.

Byrd, Robert C. *The Senate, 1789-1989: Classic Speeches, 1830-1993.* Washington, D.C.: Government Printing Office, 1994. <http://www.senate.gov/artandhistory/history/common/generic/Speeches_Vest_Dog.htm>

Coyle, William. "From Scatology to Social History: *Captain Billy's Whiz Bang.*" *Studies in American Humor* 3.3 (1977): 135-41.

"The Ecstasy Girl Wins Cheers from Hollywood." *Life* 25 Jul. 1938: 27-29.

Ely, Melvin Patrick. *The Adventures of Amos 'n' Andy: A Social History of an American Phenomenon.* Tenth Anniversary Edition. Charlottesville and London: University of Virginia, 2001.

Fyleman, Rose. "There Are Fairies at the Bottom of Our Garden." Music by Liza Lehmann. Chappell Music Co., 1917. *Ball State University Digital Media Repository.* <http://libx.bsu.edu/u?/ShtMus,1000>. 26 Nov. 2011.

"History of the Dutch Treat Club." *Dutch Treat Club.* <http://dwp.bigplanet.com/dutchtreat/history/> 27 Nov. 2011.

Hirsch, Emil G., M. Seligsohn, Solomon Schechter, "Laban." *Jewish Encyclopedia: The unedited full-text of the 1906 Jewish Encyclopedia.* <http://www.jewishencyclopedia.com/articles/9568-laban>. 25 Nov. 2011.

Holroyd, Michael. *Lytton Strachey: The New Biography.* New York: Farrar, Straus and Giroux, 1995.

Hutchens, John K. "'Dear Adolf —': Mr. Benet Writes a Series of Letters to Herr S. That Are Really Letters to Us." 5 July 1942: 8.

Jackson, Kenneth, ed. *The Encyclopedia of New York City.* New Haven: Yale UP, 1995.

Jacobs, Joseph, translator. *The Fables of Aesop: Selected, Told Anew, and Their History Traced by Joseph Jacobs.* London & New York: MacMillan & Co, 1894.

Keynes, John Maynard. *The Economic Consequences of the Peace.* 1919. London: Macmillan and Co., 1920.

Lawson, Benjamin S., and Anita. *Irvin S. Cobb.* Bowling Green University Popular Press, 1984.

Lopez, Kathryn Jean. "Storms of Two Centuries." *National Review Online* 18 Sept. 2003.

<http://old.nationalreview.com/interrogatory/interrogatory091803.asp>. 27 Nov. 2011.

"Lockheed P-38 Lightning — USA" *Aviation History Museum.* 14 Mar. 2010 <http://www.aviation-history.com/lockheed/p38.html>. 24 Nov. 2011.

Nel, Philip. "'Never overlook the art of the seemingly simple': Crockett Johnson and the Politics of the Purple Crayon." *Children's Literature* 29 (2001): 142-74.

"Parasites - Schistosomiasis" Centers for Disease Control. 2 Nov. 2010. <http://www.cdc.gov/parasites/schistosomiasis/>. 25 Nov. 2011.

Peters, Anne. "Man o' War." *Thoroughbred Heritage.* <http://www.tbheritage.com/Portraits/ManOWar.html>.

Pocock, J.G.A. "Introduction" to Edmund Burke's *Reflections on the Revolution in France.* Indianapolis/Cambridge: Hackett Publishing Company, 1987. vii-xlvii.

Scott, Bruce. "A Romantic Sensation: 'Lucia Di Lammermoor.'" *World of Opera.* National Public Radio. 11 Sept. 2011. <http://www.npr.org/2011/09/09/140333090/a-romantic-sensation-lucia-di-lammermoor>. 27 Nov. 2011.

Shaw, T. Clark. "The Legend of Casey Jones." *Casey Jones Home & Railroad Museum.* <http://www.caseyjones.com/caseyjones/legend.htm>. 26 Nov. 2011.

Steel, Flora Annie. *English Fairy Tales.* MacMillan & Co., 1918. Project Gutenberg eBook #17034. Release date: Nov. 9, 2005.

Sterling, Christopher H., and John M. Kittross. *Stay Tuned: A History of American Broadcasting.* Third Edition. 2002. Taylor & Francis e-Library, 2009.

Studwell, William Emmett and Bruce R. Schueneman. *Barbershops, Bullets, and Ballads: an Annotated Anthology of Underappreciated American Musical Jewels, 1865-1918.* Binghamton, NY: Haworth Press, 1999.

Sturrock, Donald. *Storyteller: The Authorized Biography of Roald Dahl.* New York: Simon & Schuster, 2010.

Thomas, Robert McG. Jr., "Dr. Morris Fishbien Dead at 87; Former Editor of A.M.A. Journal." *New York Times* 28 Sept 1976: 40.

Young, Arthur Nichols. *The single tax movement in the United States.* Princeton: Princeton University Press, 1916.

Welch, Walter Leslie, Leah Brodbeck Stenzel Burt, and Oliver Read. *From tinfoil to stereo: the acoustic years of the recording industry, 1877-1929.*

Winokur, Jon. *The Portable Curmudgeon.* New York: New American Library, 1987.

Zebrowski, Carl. "Busy with the Blitz-Proofing." *America in WWII: The Magazine of a People at War.* Oct. 2005. <http://www.americainwwii.com/stories/busywiththeblitzproofing.html>. 25 Nov. 2011.

Gosh, Mr. O'Malley, how the news of our book is getting around! . . .
Yes, m'boy, your Fairy Godfather has set the literary world agog. Every ten years a great hero sweeps the public off its feet . . . Anthony Adverse . . . Rhett Butler . . . MR. O'MALLEY! Imagine the cheers and bravos which now greet me at the Elves, Leprechauns, Gnomes and Little Men's Chowder & Marching Society. I'll have to begin giving some thought to movie and radio rights . . . magazine serialization . . . even comic strips . . .
Barnaby

Mr. O'Malley, LIFE magazine reprinted a whole chapter of our book...
Yes, m'boy, and a revolting characterization of your Fairy Godfather they set before their paltry 3,722,870 readers . . . "A man of considerable magical powers, he is nevertheless as inept and bumbling as a pocket-size W. C. Fields" . . . Inept and bumbling indeed . . . This is a sordid and obvious attempt to increase circulation by hitching their wagon to a meteoric new star.

Gee, Mr. O'Malley, our publishers have had to print 30,000 copies in an awful hurry . . .

The inexorable workings of the law of supply and demand, m'boy. Somehow word got around that I am appearing in a book called BARNABY, though think how much better it would have been had they called it "O'Malley." I trust that the ill-effects of this shortsighted policy will be rectified by a gigantic advertising campaign . . . skywriting . . . car cards . . . sandwich men from coast to coast.

Quiet, Mr. O'Malley

and let the critics get a word in edgewise . . .

DOROTHY PARKER: "If the adventures of Barnaby constitute a comic strip, then so do those of Huckleberry Finn. *Barnaby* is the most important addition to American arts and letters in Lord knows how many years." — *from a review in* PM.

LOS ANGELES TIMES: "What a comic! Something utterly original, devastating in its humor . . . as right as the perfect nonsense of a Lewis Carroll or a James Stephens. If you don't like *Barnaby*, better have an alienist examine your dome."

LOUIS UNTERMEYER: "The funniest high comedy since Aristophanes and Thurber. I won't be completely happy until I see W. C. Fields in the role of Mr. O'Malley."

ROCKWELL KENT: "I yield to no one in my 'blathering admiration' of BARNABY."

WILLIAM ROSE BENET: "No American home should be without a copy of BARNABY . . . a classic of humor."

PAUL DE KRUIF: "Congratulations on this quietly uproarious book."

NORMAN CORWIN: "I have been after radio to make a program of BARNABY, and after the movies to make a picture, and after the Postmaster-General to make a BARNABY stamp, so naturally I am glad to see that you have taken the initiative and made a BARNABY book."

RUTH McKENNEY: "BARNABY is: colossal, magnificent, terrific, marvelous, wonderful, witty, funny . . . take your pick!".

CREDITS

Barnaby strips reproduced courtesy of the Oolong Blue Collection of Charles D. Cohen and the Whole Seuss; newspaper *PM*, KJ 785, Widener Library, Harvard University; Crockett Johnson Papers, Mathematics Documentation, Division of Medicine & Science, National Museum of American History, Smithsonian Institution; and Rosebud Archives.

Additional images courtesy of Crockett Johnson Papers, Mathematics Documentation, Division of Medicine & Science, National Museum of American History, Smithsonian Institution: photo of Crockett Johnson, c. late 1930s; photo Crockett Johnson at home in Darien, Connecticut, 1942; letter from Joseph Porath, 24 Mar. 1945; reply from Crockett Johnson, 4 Apr. 1945; photo of Crockett Johnson and Gonsul, c. 1944; photo of advertisement for *Barnaby* on side of Chicago *Sun* delivery truck; advertisement for *Barnaby* (1943); Dorothy Parker's review and Crockett Johnson's cartoon, *PM*, 3 October 1943, page 16; Edwin Seaver, column in *Direction*, 1943; invitation to Norlyst Gallery, November 1943; photo of Paula Laurence and Crockett Johnson, Norlyst Gallery, 9 November 1943; unidentified boy and Crockett Johnson, Norlyst Gallery, 9 November 1943.

Fantagraphics Books wishes to thank the National Association for the Advancement of Colored People for authorizing the use of Dorothy Parker's work; the Harry Ransom Center at the University of Texas at Austin for use of Eliot Elisofon's photo of Crockett Johnson that appears on the back cover; the Smithsonian Institution for providing both that photo and the original Barnaby strips used on the endpapers.

THANK YOU

A great big "Cushlamochree!"-sized thanks to: Charles Cohen, Maggie Hale (Widener Library, Harvard University), Stewart Edelstein and Monte Frank (Cohen & Wolf), Peggy Kidwell (Division of Medicine & Science, National Museum of American History, Smithsonian Institution), Kay Peterson (Archives Center, Smithsonian Institution), George Nicholson and Erica Silverman (Sterling Lord), Richard Marschall and Jonathan Barli (Rosebud Archives), Patricia Adams (Gordon Feinblatt LLC), Jason Hill, Chris Ware and Jeet Heer.

Additional thanks to Kurt Busiek, Colin Myers, Mark Newgarden, Art Spiegelman, Alison M. Scott, Ben Schwartz, Maggie Thompson, Kent Worcester, Ted Geier, James Babcock and the late Toby Holtzman.

ABOUT THE AUTHOR

Crockett Johnson was the pen name of cartoonist and children's book illustrator David Johnson Leisk (October 20, 1906 – July 11, 1975). He is best known for the comic strip *Barnaby* (1942–1952) and the *Harold* series of books begun with *Harold and the Purple Crayon* (1955). Born in New York City, Johnson grew up in Corona, Queens, studying art at Cooper Union in 1924. On his choice of pseudonym, Johnson explained: "Crockett is my childhood nickname. My real name is David Johnson Leisk. Leisk was too hard to pronounce — so — I am now Crockett Johnson!" Johnson also collaborated on four children's books with his wife, the writer Ruth Krauss, including *The Carrot Seed* (1945).

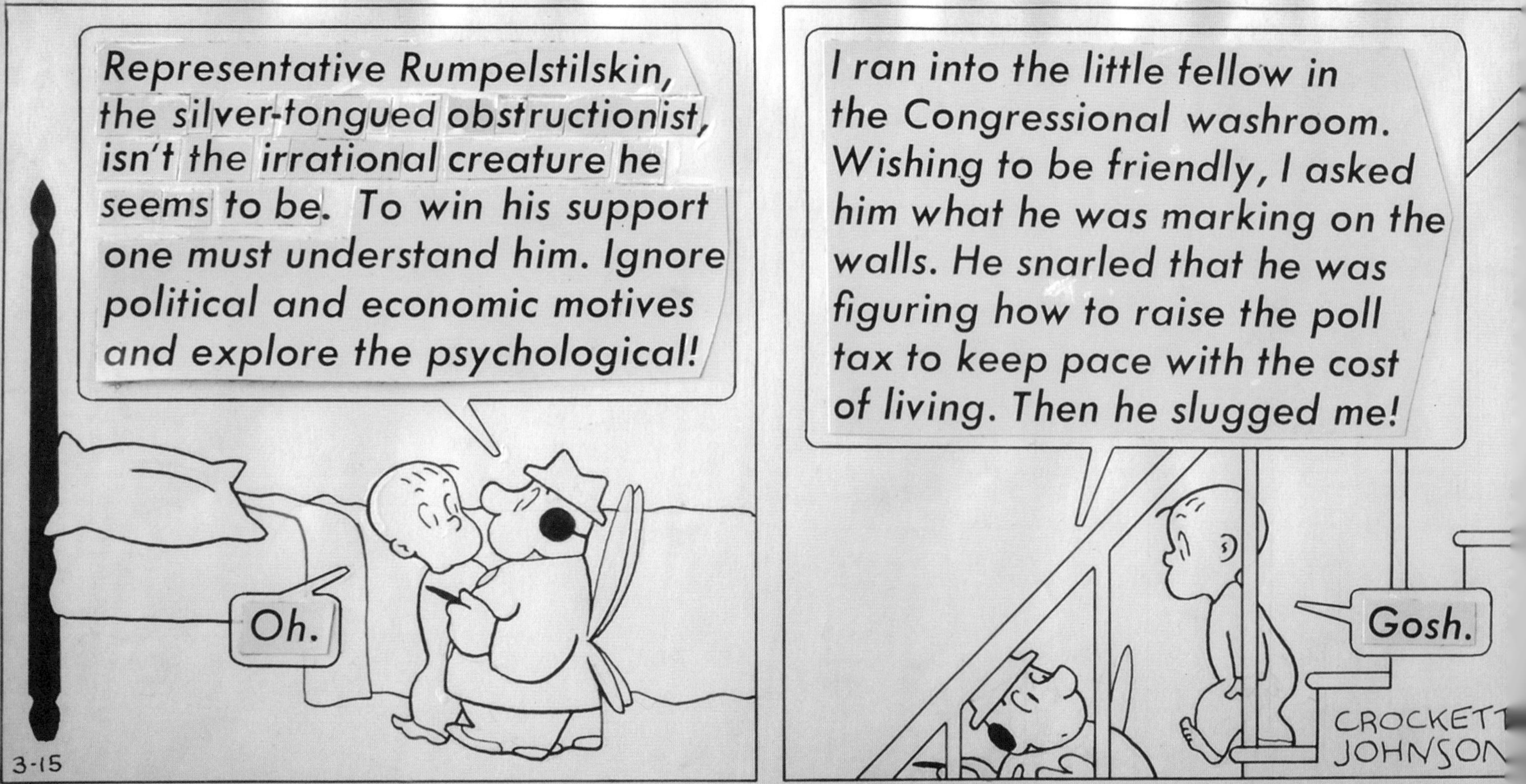
Representative Rumpelstilskin, the silver-tongued obstructionist, isn't the irrational creature he seems to be. To win his support one must understand him. Ignore political and economic motives and explore the psychological!
Oh.
I ran into the little fellow in the Congressional washroom. Wishing to be friendly, I asked him what he was marking on the walls. He snarled that he was figuring how to raise the poll tax to keep pace with the cost of living. Then he slugged me!
Gosh.
CROCKETT JOHNSON
3-15